Communications
in Computer and Information Science   1315

More information about this series at http://www.springer.com/series/7899

Jeffrey Nichols · Becky Verastegui ·
Arthur 'Barney' Maccabe ·
Oscar Hernandez · Suzanne Parete-Koon ·
Theresa Ahearn (Eds.)

Driving Scientific and Engineering Discoveries Through the Convergence of HPC, Big Data and AI

17th Smoky Mountains Computational Sciences
and Engineering Conference, SMC 2020
Oak Ridge, TN, USA, August 26–28, 2020
Revised Selected Papers

 Springer

Editors
Jeffrey Nichols 🅾
Oak Ridge National Laboratory
Oak Ridge, TN, USA

Becky Verastegui 🅾
Oak Ridge National Laboratory
Oak Ridge, TN, USA

Arthur 'Barney' Maccabe 🅾
Oak Ridge National Laboratory
Oak Ridge, TN, USA

Oscar Hernandez 🅾
Oak Ridge National Laboratory
Oak Ridge, TN, USA

Suzanne Parete-Koon 🅾
Oak Ridge National Laboratory
Oak Ridge, TN, USA

Theresa Ahearn 🅾
Oak Ridge National Laboratory
Oak Ridge, TN, USA

ISSN 1865-0929   ISSN 1865-0937 (electronic)
Communications in Computer and Information Science
ISBN 978-3-030-63392-9   ISBN 978-3-030-63393-6 (eBook)
https://doi.org/10.1007/978-3-030-63393-6

This Springer imprint is published by the registered company Springer Nature Switzerland AG
The registered company address is: Gewerbestrasse 11, 6330 Cham, Switzerland

Preface

The Smoky Mountains Computational Sciences and Engineering Conference (SMC 2020) was held in Oak Ridge, Tennessee, USA, during August 26–28, 2020. This year, we had a new virtual venue due to the COVID-19 pandemic and a new theme: the convergence of high-performance computing (HPC) and artificial intelligence (AI) for driving future science and engineering discoveries through the integration of experiment, big data, and modeling and simulation.

Throughout the past year, the U.S. Department of Energy's National Laboratories, in collaboration with other institutions, completed a series of town hall meetings to gather insights about the opportunities and challenges facing the scientific community as HPC and AI technologies converge. This convergence will integrate large-scale simulation, advanced data analysis, data-driven predictive modeling, theory, and high-throughput experiments. SMC 2020 marks the 5th year our conference has covered these topics, and our outcomes have played a significant role in framing the landscape for HPC-AI convergence. At Oak Ridge National Laboratory (ORNL), our Summit supercomputer (currently the second most powerful in the world) is hosting a wide range of projects to solve some of science's most daunting challenges, and the system's revolutionary architecture is ideal for making discoveries in line with our conference theme.

We have already begun preparing for the post-Summit world with Frontier, a Cray system expected to debut in 2021 as the world's most powerful supercomputer with a performance of more than 1.5 exaflops. As a second-generation AI system, Frontier will provide new capabilities for machine learning, deep learning, and data analytics that will inform manufacturing, human health, and many other applications. Because of the rapid innovations in HPC and AI, SMC 2020 organizers decided this year's conference needed to gather new ideas with fresh perspectives to make a larger impact in the scientific community.

To reach this goal, we issued a call for papers (CFP), enabling scientists to share research breakthroughs at our conference, discuss ideas and experiences, and contribute to our program via peer-reviewed papers. SMC 2020's Program Committee consisted of 70 leading experts who helped advertise the CFP, then reviewed papers for the main program and our scientific data challenge competition. The accepted papers, which are compiled in the SMC 2020 conference proceedings, describe the most important directions for research, development, and production, as well as elucidate experiences and advocate for investment in areas related to the conference theme. These important areas were defined by the following sessions:

Session 1. Computational Applications: Converged HPC and Artificial Intelligence. This session addressed applications that embrace data-driven and first-principle methods, and participants focused on converging AI methods and approaches with high-performance modeling and simulation applications. Topics included experiences, algorithms, and numerical methods that will play an important role in this area. Papers and invited talks explained how simulation can be used to train and integrate AI models to work with simulation applications while quantifying errors.

Session 2. System Software: Data Infrastructure and Life Cycle. In this session, participants discussed the scientific data life cycle from collection to archive, including all the aspects in between and the infrastructure needed to support it. The session covered techniques and system designs needed to securely publish, curate, stage, store, reduce, and compress data. The session also covered techniques for annotating data with metadata and automatically extracting information from massive data sets.

Session 3. Experimental/Observational Applications: Use Cases That Drive Requirements for AI and HPC Convergence. Participants discussed ways to use multiple federated scientific instruments with data sets and large-scale compute capabilities, including sensors, actuators, instruments for HPC systems, data stores, and other network-connected devices. The session explored some of the AI and HPC workloads that are being pushed to the edge (closer to the instruments) while large-scale simulations are scheduled on HPC systems with large capacities. This session focused on use cases that require multiple scientific instruments and emphasized examples that combine AI and HPC with edge computing.

Session 4. Deploying Computation: On the Road to a Converged Ecosystem. Topics included industry experiences and plans for deploying the hardware and software infrastructure needed to support applications used for AI methodologies and simulation to deploy next-generation HPC and data science systems. Participants discussed how emerging technologies can be co-designed to support compute and data workflows at scale.

The Smoky Mountain Poster Session. For this session, SMC 2020 organizers highlighted accepted papers that provided novel contributions to the main themes of the conference proceedings, including new benchmarks for HPC and AI, advances in data science and AI software stacks, and visualization as a service to smart homes.

The Smoky Mountain Data Challenge. Scientific data sponsors developed challenges based on eminent ORNL data sets from scientific simulations and instruments in physical and chemical sciences, electron microscopy, bioinformatics, neutron sources, urban development, and other areas for the SMC Data Challenge (SMCDC 2020) competition. Students and data analytics experts submitted papers describing their strategies and solutions to a series of increasingly difficult challenge questions. Overall, 52 teams registered for the competition and 23 teams completed the challenges. A peer-review process selected nine finalists and eight honorable mentions, all of whom presented lightning talks at SMC 2020. An online audience poll selected the best lightning talk.

SMC 2020 had an excellent lineup of speakers eager to engage with our attendees. Conference organizers accepted 37 high-quality papers from 94 submissions for a competitive acceptance rate of 39%. The accepted papers came from more than 40 international institutions, including universities, national laboratories, HPC centers, and vendors. Of these papers, 18 were presented during session talks, 10 were presented in the poster session, and 9 were presented in the data challenge competition. All papers were peer-reviewed by at least three experts, and the majority had four reviewers. The conference also included three invited talks to cover important topics not addressed by the papers. SMC 2020 began with a keynote panel made up of prominent researchers and visionaries who shared their perspectives in a session called "The Future of HPC Systems in the Presence of AI."

SMC 2020 would not have been possible without our attendees, who once again came together in our shared mission to discuss solutions to the most complex problems in energy science and computing.

August 2020

Jeffrey Nichols
Becky Verastegui
Arthur 'Barney' Maccabe
Oscar Hernandez
Suzanne Parete-Koon
Theresa Ahearn

Organization

General Chair

Jeffrey Nichols   Oak Ridge National Laboratory, USA

Conference Organizers

Theresa Ahearn   Oak Ridge National Laboratory, USA
Becky Verastegui   Oak Ridge National Laboratory, USA

Media and Communications

Scott Jones   Oak Ridge National Laboratory, USA
Elizabeth Rosenthal   Oak Ridge National Laboratory, USA

Program Committee Chairs

Oscar Hernandez   Oak Ridge National Laboratory, USA
Arthur 'Barney' Maccabe   Oak Ridge National Laboratory, USA

Data Challenge Chair

Suzanne Parete-Koon   Oak Ridge National Laboratory, USA

Steering Committee

Mathew Baker   Oak Ridge National Laboratory, USA
Jim Hack   Oak Ridge National Laboratory, USA
Jeffrey Nichols   Oak Ridge National Laboratory, USA
Gina Tourassi   Oak Ridge National Laboratory, USA
Becky Verastegui   Oak Ridge National Laboratory, USA
David Womble   Oak Ridge National Laboratory, USA

Session Chairs

Kate Evans   Oak Ridge National Laboratory, USA
Bronson Messer   Oak Ridge National Laboratory, USA
Steven Hamilton   Oak Ridge National Laboratory, USA
Vincent Paquit   Oak Ridge National Laboratory, USA
Amy Rose   Oak Ridge National Laboratory, USA
Arjun Shankar   Oak Ridge National Laboratory, USA

Sudharshan Vazhkudai   Oak Ridge National Laboratory, USA
Verónica Vergara   Oak Ridge National Laboratory, USA

Program Committee

Sadaf Alam   Swiss National Supercomputing Centre, Switzerland
Vassil Alexandrov   Hartree, UK
Jim Ang   Pacific Northwest National Laboratory, USA
Manuel Arenaz   University of Coruña and Appentra, Spain
Scott Atchley   Oak Ridge National Laboratory, USA
Matthew Baker   Oak Ridge National Laboratory, USA
Jonathan Beard   ARM, USA
Anne Berres   Oak Ridge National Laboratory, USA
Patrick Bridges   The University of New Mexico, USA
David Brown   Lawrence Berkeley National Laboratory, USA
Barbara Chapman   Stony Brook University, USA
Norbert Eicker   Jülich Supercomputing Centre, Germany
Kate Evans   Oak Ridge National Laboratory, USA
Marta Garcia   Barcelona Supercomputing Center, Spain
Aric Hagberg   Los Alamos National Laboratory, USA
Stephen Hamilton   Oak Ridge National Laboratory, USA
Victor Hazlewood   The University of Tennessee, Knoxville, USA
Andreas Herten   Jülich Supercomputing Centre, Germany
Jeff Hittinger   Lawrence Livermore National Laboratory, USA
Shantenu Jha   Brookhaven National Laboratory, USA
Travis Johnston   Oak Ridge National Laboratory, USA
Guido Juckeland   Helmholtz-Zentrum Dresden Rossendorf, Germany
Olivera Kotevska   Oak Ridge National Laboratory, USA
Kody Law   The University of Manchester, UK
Bernd Mohr   Jülich Supercomputing Centre, Germany
C. J. Newburn   NVIDIA, USA
Vincent Paquit   Oak Ridge National Laboratory, USA
Suzanne Parete-Koon   Oak Ridge National Laboratory, USA
Greg Peterson   The University of Tennessee, Knoxville, USA
Dirk Pleiter   Jülich Supercomputing Centre, Germany
Swaroop Pophale   Oak Ridge National Laboratory, USA
Laura Pullum   Oak Ridge National Laboratory, USA
Roxana Rositoru   ARM, UK
Amy Rose   Oak Ridge National Laboratory, USA
Jibo Sanyal   Oak Ridge National Laboratory, USA
Mitsuhisa Sato   RIKEN, Japan
Thomas Schulthess   ETH Zurich and CSCS, Switzerland
Jim Sexton   IBM, USA
Stuart Slattery   Oak Ridge National Laboratory, USA
Jim Stewart   Sandia National Laboratories, USA
Arjun Shankar   Oak Ridge National Laboratory, USA

Tjerk Straatsma	Oak Ridge National Laboratory, USA
Valerie Taylor	Argonne National Laboratory, USA
Christian Terboven	RWTH Aachen University, Germany
Stan Tomov	The University of Tennessee, Knoxville, USA
Sudharshan Vazhkudai	Oak Ridge National Laboratory, USA
Rio Yokota	Tokyo Institute of Technology, Japan

Data Challenge Program Committee

Sadaf Alam	Swiss National Supercomputing Centre, Switzerland
Folami Alamudun	Oak Ridge National Laboratory, USA
Anne Berres	Oak Ridge National Laboratory, USA
Stuart Campbell	Brookhaven National Laboratory, USA
Ioana Danciu	Oak Ridge National Laboratory, USA
Pravallika Devineni	Oak Ridge National Laboratory, USA
Melissa Dumas	Oak Ridge National Laboratory, USA
Shang Gao	Oak Ridge National Laboratory, USA
Tirthankar Ghosal	Indian Institute of Technology Patna, India
Garrett Granroth	Oak Ridge National Laboratory, USA
Max Grossman	BP Numerical Algorithms Group, USA
Dasha Herrmannova	Oak Ridge National Laboratory, USA
Jacob Hinkle	Oak Ridge National Laboratory, USA
Monica Ihli	The University of Tennessee, Knoxville, USA
Travis Johnston	Oak Ridge National Laboratory, USA
Guido Juckeland	Helmholtz-Zentrum Dresden Rossendorf, Germany
Martin Klein	Los Alamos National Laboratory, USA
Olivera Kotevska	Oak Ridge National Laboratory, USA
Kuldeep Kurte	Oak Ridge National Laboratory, USA
Ketan Maheshwari	Oak Ridge National Laboratory, USA
Esteban Meneses	Costa Rica Institute of Technology, Costa Rica
Peter Peterson	Oak Ridge National Laboratory, USA
Dirk Pleiter	Jülich Supercomputing Centre, Germany
Zahra Ronaghi	NVIDIA, USA
Roxana Rusitoru	ARM, UK
Angelo Salatino	The Open University, UK
Jibonananda Sanyal	Oak Ridge National Laboratory, USA
Shervin Sammak	University of Pittsburgh, USA
Xukai Shen	British Petroleum, USA
Tjerk Straatsma	Oak Ridge National Laboratory, USA
Wojtek Sylwestrzak	ICM University of Warsaw, Poland
Madhav Vyas	British Petroleum, USA
Ryan Warnick	BP Numerical Algorithms Group, USA
Junqi Yin	Oak Ridge National Laboratory, USA

Contents

Experimental/Observational Applications: Use Cases That Drive Requirements for AI and HPC Convergence

Deploying Computation: On the Road to a Converged Ecosystem

Scientific Data Challenges

Computational Applications: Converged HPC and Artificial Intelligence

Improving Seismic Wave Simulation and Inversion Using Deep Learning

Lei Huang[✉], Edward Clee, and Nishath Ranasinghe

Department of Computer Science, Prairie View A&M University,
Prairie View, TX 77446, USA
{lhuang,niranasinghe}@pvamu.edu, T_Clee@acm.org

Abstract. Accurate simulation of wave motion for the modeling and inversion of seismic wave propagation is a classical high-performance computing (HPC) application using the finite difference, the finite element methods and spectral element methods to solve the wave equations numerically. The paper presents a new method to improve the performance of the seismic wave simulation and inversion by integrating the deep learning software platform and deep learning models with the HPC application. The paper has three contributions: 1) Instead of using traditional HPC software, the authors implement the numerical solutions for the wave equation employing recently developed tensor processing capabilities widely used in the deep learning software platform of PyTorch. By using PyTorch, the classical HPC application is reformulated as a deep learning recurrent neural network (RNN) framework; 2) The authors customize the automatic differentiation of PyTorch to integrate the adjoint state method for an efficient gradient calculation; 3) The authors build a deep learning model to reduce the physical model dimensions to improve the accuracy and performance of seismic inversion. The authors use the automatic differentiation functionality and a variety of optimizers provided by PyTorch to enhance the performance of the classical HPC application. Additionally, methods developed in the paper can be extended into other physics-based scientific computing applications such as computational fluid dynamics, medical imaging, nondestructive testing, as well as the propagation of electromagnetic waves in the earth.

Keywords: Machine learning · Inverse problem · Wave propagation

1 Introduction

Physical simulation and inversion are classical scientific computing applications to discover the physical phenomenon and reveal the underlying properties. The simulation solves the partial differential equations (PDE) that governs the physical phenomenon using numerical approximation methods, while the inversion applies the gradient-based optimizations to find the underlying properties by minimizing the observed data and the simulated results. The entire process takes

© Springer Nature Switzerland AG 2020
J. Nichols et al. (Eds.): SMC 2020, CCIS 1315, pp. 3–19, 2020.
https://doi.org/10.1007/978-3-030-63393-6_1

significant computing resources to achieve the satisfied accuracy. However, the inverse problem is naturally challenging since it is ill-posed and nonlinear for most cases.

Recent advances in high-performance tensor processing hardware and software are providing new opportunities for accelerated linear algebra calculations as used in machine learning, especially for deep learning neural networks, that contributes significantly to the success of data science. Such calculations are also at the heart of many simulations of physical systems such as wave propagation. The use of tensor processing in neural networks, with its need for backpropagation through multi-layered networks, has led to capabilities for automatic differentiation [1] for gradient calculations in deep learning software.

Motivations: The motivations of the work have twofold. The first one is to understand the new deep learning software package such as PyTorch and TensorFlow, and their capacity of solving a scientific computational problem. Especially, we are interested in how to model the traditional partial differential equations (PDEs) used in the scientific computational problem with a deep learning model. The other is to study how to integrate the machine learning models that are data-driven into the scientific computational model that are physics-driven. The differentiable programming has the potential to smoothly integrate them together with a global optimization. The authors believe the study will lead to more interesting research findings in the topic of Scientific Machine Learning (SciML) and to find an efficient way to combine the power of these two different methods to facilitate scientific discovery.

In this paper, we study how to use the tensor-based machine learning software to formulate the physical simulation and to compute the gradients for optimizations to solve the inverse problem. We use the seismic wave propagation simulation and the Full Wave Inversion (FWI) as the physical case study. We have adapted the techniques of others in this area of wave propagation [2, 3] to demonstrate how direct finite difference integration can be implemented via a deep learning software platform, allowing the gradients calculated by automatic differentiation to be used for the FWI of seismic reflection survey data as an augmentation to the well-known PySIT [4] seismic research platform.

We summarize the paper's contributions in the following:

 i) We formulate the PDE solver in the seismic forward model using the Recurrent Neural Network (RNN) implemented with the deep learning software package PyTorch, which allows us to take advantages of the tensor processing software and its accelerator implementation.
 ii) We apply the automatic differentiation implemented in PyTorch to solve the seismic inverse problem to uncover the earth's interior physical properties.
iii) We improve the automatic differentiation efficiency by creating a hybrid back propagation method with the adjoint-state method to calculate the gradients.
iv) We implement an AutoEncoder network to reduce the dimensions of the inverted parameters to argument the convergence process and get more accurate results for the ill-posed problem.

2 Wave Equations and RNN

2.1 Wave Equations

The wave motion is governed by physical rules that can be expressed in the following partial differential equation (PDE) (1) and the boundary conditions (2) and (3). We use the 1D scalar wave equation for simplicity purpose in this paper:

$$\frac{1}{c^2(x)}\frac{\partial^2 u(x,t)}{\partial t^2} - \frac{\partial^2 u(x,t)}{\partial x^2} = f(x,t) \tag{1}$$

$$\frac{1}{c(0)}\frac{\partial u(0,t)}{\partial t} - \frac{\partial u(0,t)}{\partial x} = 0 \tag{2}$$

$$\frac{1}{c(1)}\frac{\partial u(1,t)}{\partial t} - \frac{\partial u(1,t)}{\partial x} = 0 \tag{3}$$

where $c(x)$ is the spatial velocity distribution, $u(x,t)$ is the wave field distribution in space and time, and $f(x,t)$ is the energy source distribution in space and time.

The Eq. (1) can be solved numerically using a finite difference approximation:

$$\begin{aligned}
f(x,t) = &-\frac{u(x-\Delta x,t) - 2u(x,t), +u(x+\Delta x,t)}{\Delta x^2} \\
&+\frac{1}{c^2}\frac{u(x,t-\Delta t) - 2u(x,t) + u(x,t+\Delta t)}{\Delta t^2}.
\end{aligned} \tag{4}$$

After factoring, the Eq. (4) can be expressed as

$$\begin{aligned}
u(x,t+\Delta t) = &f(x,t)c^2\Delta t^2 + (2u(x,t) - u(x,t-\Delta t)) \\
&+c^2\frac{\Delta t^2}{\Delta x^2}(u(x-\Delta x,t) - 2u(x,t) + u(x+\Delta x,t))
\end{aligned} \tag{5}$$

which shows that the next wave field in time $u(x,t+\Delta t)$ can be calculated based on the current and prior wave fields, as well as spatial neighbors in the current wave field. The wave motion simulation follows the time sequence to produce the next state based on the prior ones, which is similar to the Recurrent Neural Network (RNN) in deep learning to model a time sequence function.

2.2 Recurrent Neural Network

Recurrent Neural Network (RNN) is used to model the pattern in a sequence of data, mostly in time sequence. In recent years, RNN and its variants have been applied successfully to problems such as speech recognition, machine translation, and text-to-speech rendering. It has an internal cell that repeatedly processes an input, carries a hidden state, and produces an output at each step. The RNN cell can be designed to be simple or complex to model a problem with a forgettable memory mechanism (Long Short-Term Memory (LSTM) [5]) or/and a gating mechanism (Gated Recurrent Unit (GRU) [6]).

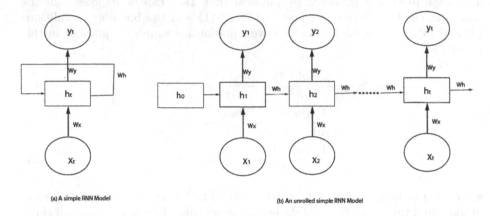

(a) A simple RNN Model   (b) An unrolled simple RNN Model

Fig. 1. A Simple RNN Model (a) with feedback loop, and (b) with loop unfolded

Figure 1(a) shows a typical RNN structure that repeatedly takes an input, updates its hidden state, and produces an output at every step. The RNN model can be unfolded as shown in Fig. 1(b) that learns the recurrence relationship from a sequence of data. The hidden state h_i remembers the prior state of the process and is updated at each step. The hidden state enables RNN to learn the temporal relationships among the inputs since most of the time sequence data do contain temporal patterns. LSTM allows RNN to forget long-term relationships built up in the hidden state and emphasizes the short-term relationships, which can be useful for many cases.

A simple RNN can be expressed in the Eq. (6):

$$h_t = \sigma_h(W_h x_t + W_h h_{t-1} + b_h)$$
$$y_h = \sigma_y(W_y h_t + b_y)$$
(6)

where x_t is the input, h_t is the hidden state, W is the weights, b is the bias, and σ is the activation function.

Looking back to the Eq. (5), there are two hidden states $u(x,t)$ and $u(x, t - \Delta t)$ if we can restructure the finite difference method using an RNN. There is also a spatial stencil relationship of neighboring velocity distribution. We define a new function F with input of $f(x,t)$, two hidden states $u(x,t)$ and $u(x, t-1)$, and the constant velocity distribution c:

$$F(f(x,t), u(x,t), u(x,t-1), c)$$
$$= f(x,t)c^2 \Delta t^2 + (2u(x,t) - u(x,t-1))$$
$$+ c^2 \frac{\Delta t^2}{\Delta x^2}(u(x-1,t) - 2u(x,t) + u(x+1,t)). \tag{7}$$

Then, the Eq. (5) can be restructured as an RNN format:

$$h_{t+1} = \sigma(F(f(t), h(t), h(t-1), c))$$
$$y_{t+1} = P(h_{t+1}) \tag{8}$$

where P is the projection function to get the sample of a trace from a receiver. The Eq. (8) is then a non-learnable, deterministic physical solution represented as the deep learning RNN model. Figure 2 shows the RNN model we designed that solves the wave equation with four inputs $f(x,t)$, $h(t)$, $h(t-1)$, and c, the velocity distribution which is constant in the equation. The output y_t is the trace sample of a receiver at each time step.

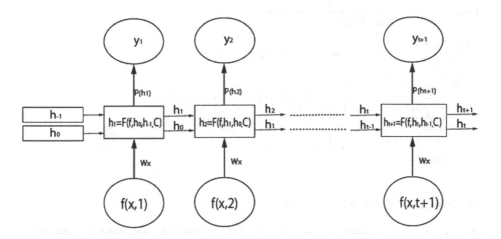

Fig. 2. A RNN model for wave equation

2.3 PyTorch RNN Implementation

The wave equation RNN model we designed in Fig. 2 enables us to utilize the deep learning software platform to solve the wave equations. The benefits of using a deep learning model to represent an HPC application include: (1) we will be able to leverage the HPC implementation of the deep learning model exploiting the advantages of GPUs/multicores and vectorization for better performance; (2) have an automatic gradients calculation using the built-in automatic differentiation package in deep learning; (3) utilize the variety of built-in optimizers to apply the gradients to find the global/local optimums; (4) use the data- and model- parallelism framework implemented in deep learning package to run the application on a HPC cluster.

The following shows a code snippet of our RNN-similar implementation of wave equation using PyTorch. There are two classes derived from torch.nn.Module for RNN cell and RNN driver respectively. We called them Wave_PGNNcell and Wave_Propagator in our code. The Wave_PGNNcell implemented a cell function in RNN that computes the wavefield at a time step. The Wave_Propagator iterates over all time steps and takes the Ricker source waveform sample as the input at each time step. The hidden state (self.H) contains the next and current wavefields, which are fed into the cell for the next iteration. The trace is collected by projecting the current wavefield based on the receiver location. The program returns the simulated wavefield and sampled trace at the end.

```
class Wave_PGNNcell(torch.nn.Module):
    def forward(self, H, src ):
        uC,uP = [ H[0], H[1] ]
        ...
        return [uN,uC]

class Wave_Propagator(torch.nn.Module):
    self.cell = Wave_PGNNcell(C, config)

    def forward(self):
        us = []        # list of output wavefields
        traces = []
        rcv = self.rcvrs
        for it in range(self.nt):
            self.H = self.cell.forward(self.H, self.ws[it])
            us.append( self.H[0].detach().numpy() )
            # Extract wavefield sample at each receiver
            samps = rcv.sample( self.H[0].clone() )
            traces.append( samps )
        trc = torch.stack(traces,dim=1)
        return us, trc
```

2.4   Seismic Wave Simulation

For seismic wave simulation, we use our RNN model to simulate the acoustic wave propagation for the scalar wave equation. We create a "true" synthetic model and an initial model, which can be a smoothed version of the true model or some other separately chosen function. We use the Ricker wavelet as a waveform for one or more energy sources (shots) and create an array of receivers for collecting traces. We assume the constant density in these models.

As we stated earlier, one benefit of using deep learning software is to take advantage of its multiple CPUs and GPUs implementation. We only need to specify which devices the code will operate on and define tensors to these devices. All remaining device-specific implementation and optimizations are done internally by PyTorch. We do not need to use CUDA or OpenACC to port the code to these devices.

Another benefit is to use the data-parallelism implemented in PyTorch. We can parallelize the code by the number of the sources/shots to run the code on multiple GPUs and distributed clusters.

In our implementation, we use PyTorch[1] 1.5 to build the RNN model. PyTorch is an open source machine learning framework developed by Facebook by merging Torch and Caffe2, which supports a variety of hardware platforms including multiple CPUs, GPUs, distributed systems, and mobile devices. Besides the machine learning and deep learning functions, one unique feature of PyTorch is that it contains a just-in-time compiler to optimize the code if it complies with TorchScript, which is a subset of Python. It has a built-in automatic differentiation package for calculating derivatives, as well as a distributed training module to train a model on a HPC cluster. PyTorch has both Python and C++ frontends.

Figure 3 shows a 1D seismic Velocity Inversion case applying our physics-ruled RNN implementation. The Fig. 3(a) shows a true synthetic velocity model and an initial model; Fig. 3(b) shows the inverted model comparing with the true model (up) and a slightly smoothed final inverted model (down); Fig. 3(c) shows the comparison of the true traces and the inverted traces; and Fig. 3(d) shows the wavefield on how the seismic wave propagates with respect to space and time.

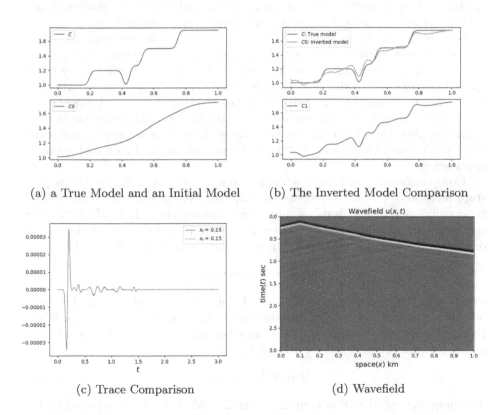

(a) a True Model and an Initial Model   (b) The Inverted Model Comparison

(c) Trace Comparison   (d) Wavefield

Fig. 3. Applying RNN for 1D seismic velocity inversion

---

[1] https://pytorch.org/.

The 1D inversion experiment finds a close-to the true model solution after 100 iterations. We use Adam optimizer [7] with L2 regularization. We are currently working on 2D cases by revising PySIT package. We continue performing more testing cases to evaluate the performance with both data and model parallelism provided by PyTorch on a CPU cluster and multiple GPUs.

3   Differentiable Programming

3.1   Automatic Differentiation and Adjoint-State Method

The automatic differentiation (AD) is also called algorithmic differentiation that calculates the derivatives of any arbitrary differentiable program. Unlike using the numerical differentiation of the adjoint state method that is an approximation to calculate the derivatives, the automatic differentiation returns the exact answer of the derivatives, though subject to the intrinsic rounding error. Machine learning software such as TensorFlow and Pytorch all have the built-in implementation of AD as the core functionality of backpropagation to optimize machine learning models. Accurate gradients are critical to the gradient-based optimizations used in both scientific computing and machine learning.

In order to calculate the derivatives of any differentiable programs, AD needs to store all operations on the execution path along with the intermediate results. It then propagates derivatives backward from the final output for every single operation connected with the chain rule. For large scale application, AD faces the challenge of meeting the demands of fast-growing storage in proportion to the executed operations. Furthermore, the individual derivative function for each operation also slows down the computation with intrinsic sequential execution. More work needs to be done if AD can be directly applied to a real scientific application.

Computationally expensive scientific applications typically use the adjoint state method to calculate the gradient of a function with much better computation efficiency, although it is a numerical approximation. In FWI, the adjoint state method calculates the derivative of a forward function $J(m)$ that depends on $u(m)$. The forward function J can be defined using h, as following [8]:

$$J(m) = h(u(m), m) \tag{9}$$

where m is the model parameter, which belongs to the model parameter space $\mathbf{M}$ and u belongs to the state variable space, $\mathbf{U}$. The state variables, u follow the state equations outlined with the mapping function, F, which is also known as the forward problem or forward equation [8]:

$$F(u(m), m) = 0. \tag{10}$$

The mapping function F is mapping from $\mathbf{U} * \mathbf{M}$ to $\mathbf{U}$ and is satisfied by the state variable u. If the condition $F(u, m) = 0$ is satisfied, the state variable u becomes a physical realization. Then, the adjoint state equation can be given as following, where λ is the adjoint state variable and $\tilde{u}$ is any element of $\mathbf{U}$ [8]:

$$[\frac{\delta F(u, m)}{\delta \tilde{u}}]^* \lambda = \frac{\delta h(u, m)}{\delta \tilde{u}}. \tag{11}$$

This adjoint-state gradient calculation involves computing the reverse-time propagated residual wavefield, combining with the saved forward-propagated wavefield snapshots at specified time intervals to provide adjustments to the medium properties (the gradient) at each spatial mesh point. In summary, the forward propagation computes data observations representing the response of the model, and the residual between the model response and actual observed data is backward propagated and combined with the forward model response to compute adjustments to the current model estimate.

Intervening in the calculation of the gradient in this manner allows for management of the required computational resources by saving the forward wavefields only as often as numerically required, explicitly managing data resources through staging to disk or check-pointing as needed, implementing shot-level parallelism, and other specially tailored techniques.

3.2   Extended Automatic Differentiation

A difficulty with the auto-differentiation (AD) procedure is that memory requirements for the back-propagation graph can become excessive, as noted by Richardson [2]. Applying chain-rule differentiation on elemental network nodes over thousands of RNN time steps for a large mesh of physical parameter values is a reasonably-sized task for 1D problems, but the graph quickly becomes intractable for 2D and 3D models. This issue renders impractical the use of pure AD for such model inversion problems.

In order to solve the problem, we extended the AD backward process using PyTorch AD workflow to integrate the adjoint-state method for the more efficient gradient calculation. In PyTorch, we can customize the AD workflow by providing a backward function to calculate the gradients of any function. We need to pass the required parameters of the forward function, the model parameters and loss function to allow the backward function to pick up these parameters for the adjoint-state calculation.

Control over this auto-differentiation process is available through use of a PyTorch extension to the Autograd feature pictured conceptually in Fig. 4, wherein the RNN layer of the network can be replaced by a forward propagation loop and corresponding adjoint back-propagation loop for an equivalent gradient calculation provided by the user. This alternative gradient calculation can take advantage of well-known techniques in seismic inversion processing, enabling existing performance enhancements to be applied using the extended PyTorch capability for specially designed back-propagation.

In the present case, the physical medium properties to be optimized are provided to the "forward" wave propagation problem implemented using the publicly available PySIT seismic inversion toolkit [4], creating a simulated seismic response. The corresponding "backward" propagation consists in using the residual wavefield represented by the difference between the simulated data and the

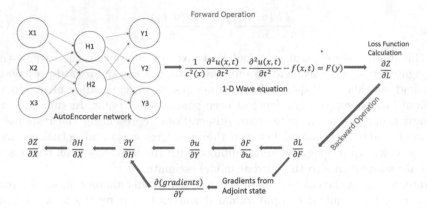

Fig. 4. Adjoint gradient: Automatic differentiation vs. Adjoint gradient calculation. Differentiation respect to model parameters are replaced by gradients from adjoint state in the backward automatic differentiation.

observed seismic trace data from the corresponding actual field data recording (or recordings from a "true" model in our synthetic studies), and implementing the "adjoint-state" solution to provide the required gradient of the model parameters. Other implementations of wave propagation solutions may also be used in this framework, such as spectral-element methods [9] for 2D, 3D and spherical 3D wave propagation.

The beneficial end result is that traditional adjoint-state solution methods are incorporated into the AD workflow, so that seismic inversion calculations can be integrated within the broader deep learning process with efficient calculation.

4   Seismic Inversion

4.1   Seismic Inversion

Seismic Inversion [10] is the method to reconstruct the earth subsurface image by inverting seismic data observed via the multiple distributed sensors on the surface. It is typically implemented using the adjoint state method [8] to calculate the gradients. As described in Sect. 2 and Sect. 3, by reconstructing the forward problem using deep learning software, the seismic inversion problem can be solved by the automatic differentiation package, a variety of optimizers provided by PyTorch, and a customized loss function. The automatic differentiation package in PyTorch implements the methodology of automatic differentiation by recording all the forward operations in sequence and performing backward derivative computation based on the chain rule.

Figure 5 shows the workflow of seismic inversion. The initial model $M0$ is a guess of the true model M that needs to be inverted. In these early experiments using several shots of a synthetic seismic reflection survey over a small 2D Earth model, we used for convenience an initial model guess that is a smoothed version

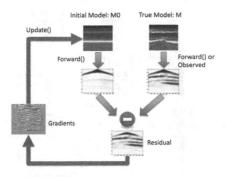

Fig. 5. The full waveform inversion workflow

of the true model. The seismic traces are either observed via distributed sensors on top of the earth surface in the real-world application or are simulated using the seismic wave forward function in this paper. The residual is obtained by comparing the synthetic data and observed data. The gradient $\frac{\partial u}{\partial M}$ is calculated based on the residual with respect to the initial model. The gradients are used by a gradient-based optimizer to update the initial model to get a step close to the real model. The entire process ends when the initial model and the true model are converged or exceeded the specified number of iterations.

4.2 AutoEncoder for Dimensionality Reduction

The seismic inversion process needs to uncover the physical properties at every point represented in the geological space, which quickly leads to a large number of model parameters to optimize in the traditional FWI process. The nature of the nonlinear and ill-posed inverse problem often falls into the local minimum traps. It is a sound solution to apply the dimensionality-reduction technique to reduce the optimization parameters to improve the optimization accuracy by engaging with machine learning models.

Since we have customized the automatic differentiation workflow by integrating the adjoint state method for the FWI gradients (described in Sect. 3), it is now feasible to integrate the machine learning models into the FWI workflow and keep the program differentiable. Since the AutoEncoder $A(x)$ is differentiable and the forward model $F(x)$ is differentiable, the composition of the $F(A(x))$ is differentiable. We choose the AutoEncoder as the dimensionality-reduction method and apply it before the forward model as shown in Fig. 6.

The AutoEncoder contains 743,938 parameters as shown in Fig. 7a and b. The AutoEncoder is an unsupervised learning model that compresses the information representation of the input data to a sparse latent variable with less dimensions at the middle of the encoded layer. It then reconstructs the data from the encoded latent variable to the original or enhanced data. The compression process is called encoder and the reconstruction is called decoder. The encoder learns how to compress the input data and describes it with the latent variable, while the decoder learns how to reconstruct the data from the latent variable.

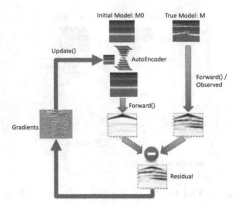

Fig. 6. The full waveform inversion workflow

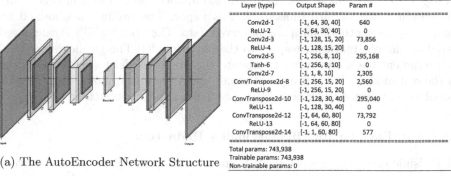

Layer (type)	Output Shape	Param #
Conv2d-1	[-1, 64, 30, 40]	640
ReLU-2	[-1, 64, 30, 40]	0
Conv2d-3	[-1, 128, 15, 20]	73,856
ReLU-4	[-1, 128, 15, 20]	0
Conv2d-5	[-1, 256, 8, 10]	295,168
Tanh-6	[-1, 256, 8, 10]	0
Conv2d-7	[-1, 1, 8, 10]	2,305
ConvTranspose2d-8	[-1, 256, 15, 20]	2,560
ReLU-9	[-1, 256, 15, 20]	0
ConvTranspose2d-10	[-1, 128, 30, 40]	295,040
ReLU-11	[-1, 128, 30, 40]	0
ConvTranspose2d-12	[-1, 64, 60, 80]	73,792
ReLU-13	[-1, 64, 60, 80]	0
ConvTranspose2d-14	[-1, 1, 60, 80]	577

Total params: 743,938
Trainable params: 743,938
Non-trainable params: 0

(a) The AutoEncoder Network Structure

(b) The AutoEncoder Model Parameters

Fig. 7. Traditional seismic velocity inversion

We start the AutoEncoder training by generating a large number of random seismic velocity models. In this work, we are using some simple and flat velocity layers representing the velocities of different earth interiors including water and rocks. Specifically, these models contain one or more low velocity layers in the middle or bottom of these layers that is challenging for the low velocity inversion. All of these models have the fixed dimensions of 60×80. As indicated in Fig. 7a, the AutoEncoder has two components: a encoder and a decoder. The encoder compresses the input model with dimension of 60×80 to an encoded latent variable with dimension of 8×10, which is 1/60 of the original dimension. The latent variable is then decompressed by the decoder to restore to its original dimension.

The loss function we used to train the AutoEncoder is the mean-square-error (MSE) loss and the optimizer is Adam with learning rate of 0.001. The batch size used is 128. The loss values during the training process is shown in Fig. 8.

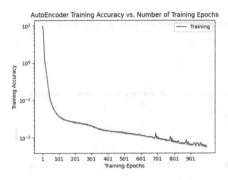

Fig. 8. The autoEncoder training loss

Figure 6 shows the AutoEncoder enhanced FWI process, where the AutoEncoder is inserted before the forward function simulation starts. Note that the encoder is only applied to the first iteration to get the encoded latent variable. For the rest of optimization iterations, the decoder is applied to decompress the encoded latent variable to get a new velocity model with the original dimension. During the gradient-based optimization process, the gradients are calculated with respected to the encoded latent variable, instead of the original model, which reduced the dimensionality of the optimization search space to 1/60. We use the MSE loss and Adam optimizer during the process.

4.3   Results

PyTorch has a list of optimizers including Adam [7], RMSprop [11], stochastic gradient descent (SGD), Adadelta [12], Adagrad [13], LBFGS, and their variants. The learning rate, scheduler and regularizations can be specified to fit different optimization problems. There are also multiple regression and classification loss functions implemented in PyTorch. All of these packages provide a rich environment to solve inverse problems.

In our implementation, we have demonstrated how to invoke the extended automatic gradient calculation for the velocity model. We choose the Adam optimizer and the MSE loss function to compare the misfit of the simulated traces and observed traces after each iteration of the forward model. The partial derivative (the gradient) of the loss function with respect to the initial model and the encoded latent variable is calculated by the automatic differentiation process, which is applied by the optimizer to minimize the misfit. These iterations gradually find an approximation of the true velocity distribution.

Figure 9 and Fig. 10 show the differences of the traditional FWI and the AutoEncoder enhanced FWI results. Fig. 9(a) shows the initial model, the true model, and the inverted model; the loss graph Fig. 9(b) shows the loss values (at different scales) after each optimization iteration, and Fig. 9(c) shows the difference between the inverted model and the initial model (top), as well as the difference between the inverted model and the true model. It appears that

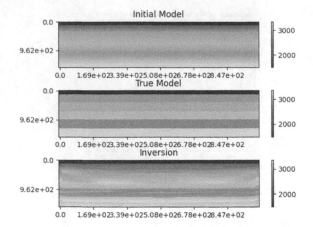

(a) The Initial, True and Inverted Model Comparison

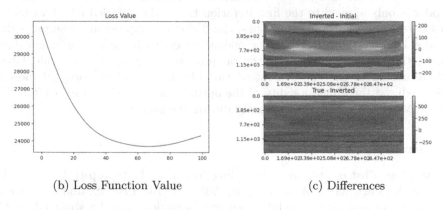

(b) Loss Function Value   (c) Differences

Fig. 9. Traditional seismic velocity inversion

the traditional FWI does not optimize well in the low velocity layer case after 40 iterations ended with a high loss value, which falls into a local trap. The AutoEncoder-enhanced FWI discovers the low velocity layer very well and continues to optimize the misfit for all 100 iterations. The difference graphs also confirm that the AutoEncoder case identifies all layers well showing less structured misfits. Noticeably, there are also less artifacts introduced in the AutoEncoder enhanced FWI compared with the traditional FWI.

As described in Sect. 3, the automatic differentiation provided by the PyTorch software does not provide sufficient efficiency to solve the FWI 2D problem. The gradients calculated for the whole program takes too long and too much space to store them. We use the hybrid method describe in Sect. 3.2 to overcome the problem by incorporating the adjoint state method. As the result, the gradient calculation using the hybrid approach achieves both accuracy and efficiency,

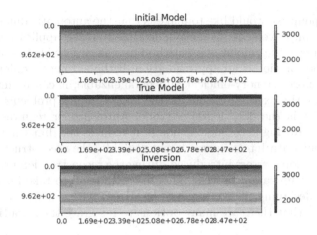

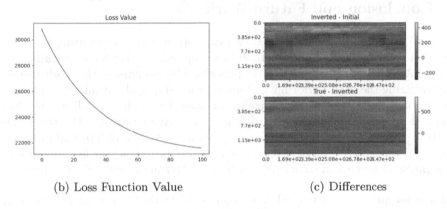

(a) The Initial, True and Inverted Model Comparison

(b) Loss Function Value   (c) Differences

Fig. 10. The AutoEncoder enhanced seismic velocity inversion

which is feasible to be used for a large scale scientific computation problem integrating with machine learning models.

5   Discussion

There are a few of points that worth noting for the work. The first is that the automatic differentiation is key for differentiable programming, which can bridge the physics-based scientific computing with the machine learning (ML)/artificial intelligence (AI) technologies. ML/AI methods do not have physics principles built in that may create an infeasible solution given the fact that most of the scientific inverse problems may be ill-posed. In our prior work [14], the convergence of ML with a scientific application without differentiable programming may not find a generalized solution since optimizations of the two different methods are disconnected.

The second point we would like to make is that the automatic differentiation needs additional improvements to make it feasible to other applications. In our method, we integrate the adjoint-state method to make it feasible to solve a large case, however the solution is an approximation. If the automatic differentiation method can be more memory-efficient and parallelizable, it can be much more useful to compute the exact gradients for the large complex problems.

The last point is the deep learning model AutoEncoder requires a revisit to reduce the loss during decoding. Although it reduces the dimension by compressing the input data into a sparse latent variable, the reconstruction is not lossless. There are some errors introduced during the reconstruction process that may hinder the optimization process. There is a trade-off to take into the consideration when designing the convergence of ML/AI with scientific computing. The good news is that there are many options to integrate them waiting for us to explore.

6   Conclusion and Future Work

We have successfully demonstrated two case studies of restructuring the wave equation using finite difference method in a deep learning RNN model framework and an AutoEncoder enhanced FWI process. The benefits of the work include fully utilizing the high-performance tensor processing and optimization capabilities implemented in the deep learning package PyTorch, as well as the deep integration of machine learning models with the inverse problem. By integrating an HPC application with a deep learning framework with differential programming, we can explore a large number of combinations of machine learning models with physical numerical solutions to achieve better accuracy and efficiency.

Acknowledgment. This research work is supported by the US National Science Foundation (NSF) awards ##1649788, #1832034 and by the Office of the Assistant Secretary of Defense for Research and Engineering (OASD(R&E)) under agreement number FA8750-15-2-0119. The U.S. Government is authorized to reproduce and distribute reprints for Governmental purposes notwithstanding any copyright notation thereon. The views and conclusions contained herein are those of the authors and should not be interpreted as necessarily representing the official policies or endorsements, either expressed or implied, of the US NSF, or the Office of the Assistant Secretary of Defense for Research and Engineering (OASD(R&E)) or the U.S. Government. The authors would also like to thank the XSEDE for providing the computing resources.

References

1. Baydin, A.G., Pearlmutter, B.A., Radul, A.A., Siskind, J.M.: Automatic differentiation in machine learning: a survey. J. Mach. Learn. Res. **18**(1), 5595–5637 (2017)
2. Richardson, A.: Seismic full-waveform inversion using deep learning tools and techniques (2018). https://arxiv.org/pdf/1801.07232v2.pdf

3. Hughes, T.W., Williamson, I.A.D., Minkov, M., Fan, S.: Wave physics as an analog recurrent neural network (2019). https://arxiv.org/pdf/1904.12831v1.pdf
4. Hewett, R.J., Demanet, L., The PySIT Team: PySIT: Python seismic imaging toolbox (January 2020). https://doi.org/10.5281/zenodo.3603367
5. Hochreiter, S., Schmidhuber, J.: Long short-term memory. Neural Comput. **9**(8), 1735–1780 (1997). https://doi.org/10.1162/neco.1997.9.8.1735
6. Chung, J., Gulcehre, C., Cho, K., Bengio, Y.: Empirical evaluation of gated recurrent neural networks on sequence modeling (2014)
7. Kingma, D.P., Ba, J.: Adam: a method for stochastic optimization (2014)
8. Plessix, R.-E.: A review of the adjoint-state method for computing the gradient of a functional with geophysical applications. Geophys. J. Int. **167**(2), 495–503 (2006). https://doi.org/10.1111/j.1365-246X.2006.02978.x
9. Tromp, J., Komatitsch, D., Liu, Q.: Spectral-element and adjoint methods in seismology. Commun. Comput. Phys. **3**(1), 1–32 (2008)
10. Schuster, G.: Seismic Inversion. Society of Exploration Geophysicists (2017). https://library.seg.org/doi/abs/10.1190/1.9781560803423
11. Ruder, S.: An overview of gradient descent optimization algorithms (2016)
12. Zeiler, M.D.: ADADELTA: an adaptive learning rate method (2012)
13. Duchi, J., Hazan, E., Singer, Y.: Adaptive subgradient methods for online learning and stochastic optimization. J. Mach. Learn. Res. **12**, 2121–2159 (2011)
14. Huang, L., Polanco, M., Clee, T.E.: Initial experiments on improving seismic data inversion with deep learning. In: 2018 New York Scientific Data Summit (NYSDS), August 2018, pp. 1–3 (2018)

Large-Scale Neural Solvers for Partial Differential Equations

Patrick Stiller[1,2(✉)], Friedrich Bethke[1,2], Maximilian Böhme[3],
Richard Pausch[1], Sunna Torge[2], Alexander Debus[1], Jan Vorberger[1],
Michael Bussmann[1,3], and Nico Hoffmann[1]

[1] Helmholtz-Zentrum Dresden-Rossendorf, Dresden, Germany
p.stiller@hzdr.de
[2] Technische Universität Dresden, Dresden, Germany
[3] Center for Advanced Systems Understanding (CASUS), Görlitz, Germany

Abstract. Solving partial differential equations (PDE) is an indispensable part of many branches of science as many processes can be modelled in terms of PDEs. However, recent numerical solvers require manual discretization of the underlying equation as well as sophisticated, tailored code for distributed computing. Scanning the parameters of the underlying model significantly increases the runtime as the simulations have to be cold-started for each parameter configuration. Machine Learning based surrogate models denote promising ways for learning complex relationship among input, parameter and solution. However, recent generative neural networks require lots of training data, i.e. full simulation runs making them costly. In contrast, we examine the applicability of continuous, mesh-free neural solvers for partial differential equations, physics-informed neural networks (PINNs) solely requiring initial/boundary values and validation points for training but no simulation data. The induced curse of dimensionality is approached by learning a domain decomposition that steers the number of neurons per unit volume and significantly improves runtime. Distributed training on large-scale cluster systems also promises great utilization of large quantities of GPUs which we assess by a comprehensive evaluation study. Finally, we discuss the accuracy of GatedPINN with respect to analytical solutions-as well as state-of-the-art numerical solvers, such as spectral solvers.

1 Introduction

Scientific neural networks accelerate scientific computing by data-driven methods such as physics-informed neural networks. One such prominent application is surrogate modelling which is e.g. used in particle physics at CERN [1]. Enhancing neural networks by prior knowledge about the system makes the prediction more robust by regularizing either the predictions or the training of neural networks. One such prominent approach is a physics-informed neural network (PINN) which makes use of either learning [2] or encoding the governing equations of a physical system into the loss function [3] of the training procedure.

© Springer Nature Switzerland AG 2020
J. Nichols et al. (Eds.): SMC 2020, CCIS 1315, pp. 20–34, 2020.
https://doi.org/10.1007/978-3-030-63393-6_2

Surrogate models based on PINN can be seen as a *neural solvers* as the trained PINN predicts the time-dependent solution of that system at any point in space and time. Encoding the governing equations into the training relies on automatic differentiation (AD) as it is an easy computing scheme for accessing all partial derivatives of the system. However, AD also constrains the neural network architecture to use C^{k+1} differentiable activation functions provided the highest order of derivatives in the governing system is k. Furthermore, the computational cost increases with the size of the neural network as the whole computational graph has to be evaluated for computing a certain partial derivative. The main contribution of this paper is three-fold. First, we introduce a novel 2D benchmark dataset for surrogate models allowing precise performance assessment due to analytical solutions and derivatives. Second, we improve the training time by incorporating and learning domain decompositions into PINN. Finally, we conduct a comprehensive analysis of accuracy, power draw and scalability on the well known example of the 2D quantum harmonic oscillator.

2   Related Works

Accelerated simulations by surrogate modelling techniques are carried out in two main directions. Supervised learning methods require full simulation data in order to train some neural network architecture, e.g. generative adversarial networks [1] or autoencoders [4], to reproduce numerical simulations and might benefit from interpolation between similar configurations. The latter basically introduces a speedup with respect to numerical simulations, however generalization errors might challenge this approach in general. In contrast, self-supervised methods either embed neural networks within numerical procedures for solving PDE [5], or incorporate knowledge about the governing equations into the loss of neural networks, so called physics-informed neural networks (PINN) [3]. The latter is can be seen as variational method for solving PDE. Finally, [2] demonstrated joint discovery of a system (supervised learning) and adapting to unknown regimes (semi-supervised learning). Recently, [6] proved convergence of PINN-based solvers for parabolic and hyperbolic PDEs. Parareal physics-informed neural networks approach domain decomposition by splitting the computational domain into temporal slices and training a PINN for each slice [7]. We are going to generalize that idea by introducing conditional computing [8] into the physics-informed neural networks framework, hereby enabling an arbitrary decomposition of the computational domain which is adaptively tuned during training of the PINN.

3   Methods

The governing equations of a dynamic system can be modeled in terms of non-linear partial differential equations

$$u_t + \mathcal{N}(u; \lambda) = 0 \ ,$$

with $u_t = \frac{\partial u}{\partial t}$ being the temporal derivative of the solution u of our system while $\mathcal{N}$ denotes a non-linear operator that incorporates the (non-)linear effects of our system. One example of such a system is the quantum harmonic oscillator,

$$i\frac{\partial \psi(\mathbf{r}, t)}{\partial t} - \hat{H}\psi(\mathbf{r}, t) = 0 \ ,$$

where $\psi(\mathbf{r}, t)$ denotes the so-called state of the system in the spatial base and $\hat{H}$ is the Hamilton-operator of the system. The systems state absolute square $|\psi(\mathbf{r}, t)|^2$ is interpreted as the probability density of measuring a particle at a certain point $\mathbf{r}$ in a volume $\mathcal{V}$. Thus, $|\psi(\mathbf{r}, t)|^2$ has to fulfill the normalization constraint of a probability density

$$\int_{\mathcal{V}} d^3r \, |\psi(\mathbf{r}, t)|^2 = 1.$$

The Hamilton operator of a particle in an external potential is of the form

$$\hat{H} = -\frac{1}{2}\Delta + V(\mathbf{r}, t),$$

where Δ is the Laplace operator and $V(\mathbf{r}, t)$ is a scalar potential. The first term is the kinetic energy operator of the system and $V(\mathbf{r}, t)$ its potential energy. In this work, we use the atomic unit system meaning that $\hbar = m_e = 1$. $\hat{H}$ is a Hermitian operator acting on a Hilbertspace $\mathcal{H}$. In this work we are focusing on the 2D quantum harmonic oscillator (QHO), which is described by the Hamiltonian

$$\hat{H} = -\frac{1}{2}\left(\frac{\partial^2}{\partial x^2} + \frac{\partial^2}{\partial y^2}\right) + \frac{\omega_0^2}{2}(x^2 + y^2) = \hat{H}_x + \hat{H}_y.$$

where $x \in \mathbb{R}$ and $y \in \mathbb{R}$ denote spatial coordinates. The solution of the QHO can be determined analytically and is the basis for complicated systems like the density function theory (DFT). Therefore the QHO is very well suited as a test system which allows a precise evaluation of the predicted results. In addition, the QHO can also be used as a test system for evaluating the results. Furthermore, the QHO is classified as linear parabolic PDE, which guarantees the functionality of the chosen PINN approach according to Shin et al. [6]. Figure 1 shows the analytic solution of the quantum harmonic oscillator over time.

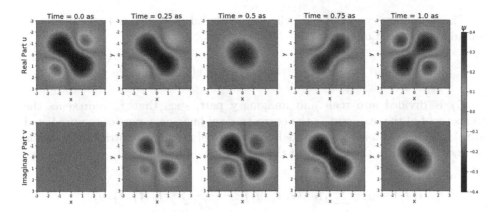

Fig. 1. Analytic solution of the quantum harmonic oscillator

3.1 Physics-Informed Quantum Harmonic Oscillator

The solution $\psi(x, y, t)$ of our quantum harmonic oscillator at some position x, y and time t is approximated by a neural network $f : \mathbb{R}^3 \to \mathbb{C}$, i.e.

$$\widehat{\psi}(x, y, t) = f(x, y, t) \ .$$

In this work, we model f by a simple multilayer perceptron (MLP) of $1 \leq l \leq m$ layers, a predetermined number of neurons per layer k_l and respective weight matrices $W^l \in \mathbb{R}^{k_l \times k_l}$

$$y^l = g(W^l y^{l-1}) \ ,$$

with $y^0 = (x, y, t)$ and $y^m = \widehat{\psi}(x, y, t)$. The training of Physics-informed neural networks relies on automatic differentiation which imposes some constraints on the architecture. In our case, the network has to be 3 times differentiable due to the second-order partial derivatives in our QHO (Eq. 3). This is achieved by choosing at least one activation function g which fulfills that property (e.g. tanh). The training of the neural network is realized by minimizing the combined loss $\mathcal{L}$ defined in Eq. (2). The three terms of $\mathcal{L}$ relate to the error of representing the initial condition L_0, the fulfillment of the partial differential equation L_f as well as boundary condition L_b.

$$\mathcal{L} = \alpha L_0(\mathcal{T}_0) + L_f(\mathcal{T}_f) + L_b(\mathcal{T}_b) \tag{1}$$

$\mathcal{L}_0$ is the summed error of predicted real- $u = real(\psi)$ and imaginary- $v = imag(\psi)$ of the initial state with respect to groundtruth real- u^i and imaginary part v^i at points $\mathcal{T}_f$. We introduce a weighting term α into $\mathcal{L}$ allowing us to emphasize the contribution of the initial state.

$$L_0(\mathcal{T}_0) = \frac{1}{|\mathcal{T}_0|} \sum_{i=1}^{|\mathcal{T}_0|} \left| u\left(t_0^i, x_0^i, y_0^i\right) - u^i \right|^2 + \frac{1}{|\mathcal{T}_0|} \sum_{i=1}^{|\mathcal{T}_0|} \left| v\left(t_0^i, x_0^i, y_0^i\right) - v^i \right|^2$$

The boundary conditions (Eq. 3) are modelled in terms of L_b at predetermined spatial positions T_b at time t.

$$L_b\left(T_b, t\right) = 1 - \left(\iint_{T_b} \left(u(t,x,y)^2 + v(t,x,y)^2\right) dx dy\right)^2$$

$\mathcal{L}_f$ is divided into real- and imaginary part, such that f_u represents the correctness of the real- and f_v the correctness of imaginary part of the predicted solution. This loss term is computed on a set T_f of randomly distributed *residual points* that enforce the validity of the PDE at residual points T_f.

$$L_f(T_f) = \frac{1}{|T_f|}\sum_{i=1}^{|T_f|}\left|f_u\left(t_f^i, x_f^i, y_f^i\right)\right|^2 + \frac{1}{|T_f|}\sum_{i=1}^{|T_f|}\left|f_v\left(t_f^i, x_f^i, y_f^i\right)\right|^2$$

$$f_u = -u_t - \frac{1}{2}v_{xx} - \frac{1}{2}v_{yy} + \frac{1}{2}x^2 v + \frac{1}{2}y^2 v$$

$$f_v = -v_t + \frac{1}{2}u_{xx} + \frac{1}{2}u_{yy} - \frac{1}{2}x^2 u - \frac{1}{2}y^2 u$$

3.2   GatedPINN

Numerical simulations typically require some sort of domain decomposition in order to share the load among the workers. physics-informed neural networks basically consist of a single multilayer perceptron network f which approximates the solution of a PDE for any input (x, y, t). However, this also implies that the capacity of the network per unit volume of our compute domain increases with the size of the compute domain. This also implies that the computational graph of the neural network increases respectively meaning that the time and storage requirements for computing partial derivatives via automatic differentiation increases, too. This limits the capacity of recent physics-informed neural network.

We will be tackling these challenges by introducing conditional computing into the framework of physics-informed neural networks. Conditional Computing denotes an approach that activate only some units of a neural network depending on the network input [9]. A more intelligent way to use the degree of freedom of neural networks allows to increase the network capacity (degree of freedom) without an immense blow up of the computational time [8]. [7] introduced a manual decomposition of the compute domain and found that the capacity of the neural network per unit volume and thus the training costs are reduced. However, this approach requires another coarse-grained PDE solver to correct predictions. A decomposition of the compute domain can be learned by utilizing the mixture of expert approach [8] based on a predetermined number of so-called experts (neural networks). A subset k of all N experts are active for any point in space and time while the activation is determined by gating network which introduces an adaptive domain decomposition. The combination of mixture of experts and physics-informed neural networks leads to a new architecture called *GatedPINN*.

Architecture. The architecture comprises of a gating network $G(x, y, t)$ that decides which expert $E_i(x, y, t)$ to use for any input (x, y, t) in space and time (see Fig. 2). Experts E_i with $1 \leq i \leq N$ are modelled by a simple MLP consisting of linear layers and tanh activation functions. The predicted solution $\widehat{\psi}$ of our quantum harmonic oscillator (QHO) becomes a weighted sum of expert predictions E_i

$$\widehat{\psi}(x, y, t) = \sum_{i=1}^{N} G(x, y, t)_i \cdot E_i(x, y, t) .$$

GatedPINN promise several advantages compared to the baseline PINN: First, the computation of partial derivatives by auto differentiation requires propagating information through a fraction k/N of the total capacity of all experts. That allows to either increase the computational domain and/or increase the overall capacity of the neural network without a blow up in computational complexity.

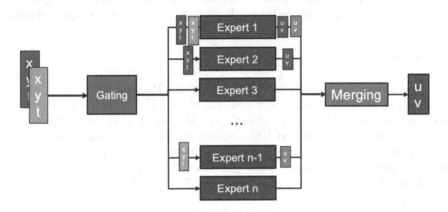

Fig. 2. Visualization of the Gated-PINN architecture

Similarly to [8], an importance loss $L_I = w_\text{I} \cdot CV(I(x, y, t))^2$ penalizes uneven distribution of workload among all N experts:

$$L(\mathcal{T}, \theta) = L_0(\mathcal{T}_0, \theta) + L_f(\mathcal{T}_f, \theta) + L_b(\mathcal{T}_b, \theta) + \sum_{(x,y,t) \in T} L_I(X) , \qquad (2)$$

given $T = T_0 \cup T_b \cup T_f$. The importance loss $L_I(X)$ requires the computation of an importance measure $I(X) = \sum_{x \in X} G(x, y, t)$. The coefficient of variation $CV(z) = \sigma(z)/\mu(z)$ provided $I(X)$ quantifies the sparsity of the gates and thus the utilization of the experts. Finally, coefficient w_I allows us to weight the contribution of our importance loss with respect to the PDE loss. The importance loss is defined as follows:

$$L_I(X) = w_I \cdot CV(\mathrm{I}(X))^2 .$$

Adaptive Domain Decomposition. A trainable gating network G allows us to combine the predictions of k simple neural networks for approximating the solution of our QHO at any point in space x, y and time t. Hereby, we restrict the size of the computational graph to k-times the size of each individual neural network E^i with $0 \leq i \leq k$.

$$G(x, y, t) = \mathrm{Softmax}(\mathrm{KeepTopK}(H(x, y, t, \omega)))$$

and basically yields a N dimensional weight vector with k non-zero elements [8]. The actual decomposition is learnt by the function H:

$$H(x, y, t) = ([x, y, t] \cdot W_g) + \mathrm{StandardNormal}() \cdot \mathrm{Softplus}(([x, y, t]^T \cdot W_{noise})) \, .$$

The noise term improves load balancing and is deactivated when using the model. Obviously, this gating results in a decomposition into linear subspaces due to W_g. Non-linear domain decomposition can now be realized by replacing the weight matrix W_g by a simple MLP NN_g, i.e. $([x, y, t] \cdot W_g)$ becomes $NN_g(x, y, t)$. This allows for more general and smooth decomposition of our compute domain.

4   Results

All neural networks were trained on the Taurus HPC system of the Technical University of Dresden. Each node consists of two IBM Power9 CPUs and is equipped with six Nvidia Tesla V-100 GPUs. We parallelized the training of the neural networks using Horovod [10] running on MPI communication backend. Training of the Physics-informed neural network, i.e. solving our QHO, was done on batches consisting of 8.500 points of the initial condition (i.e. $|T_0|$), 2.500 points for the boundary condition (i.e. $|T_b|$) and 2 million residual points (i.e. $|T_f|$).

4.1   Approximation Quality

Training of physics-informed neural networks can be seen as solving partial differential equations in terms of a variational method. State-of-the-art solvers for our benchmarking case, the quantum harmonic oscillator, make us of domain knowledge about the equation by solving in Fourier domain or using Hermite polynomials. We will be comparing both, state-of-the-art spectral method [11] as well as physics-informed neural networks, to the analytic solution of our QHO. This enables a fair comparison of both methods and allows us to quantify the approximation error.

For reasons of comparison, we use neural networks with similar capacity. The baseline model consists of 700 neurons at 8 hidden layer. The GatedPINN with linear and nonlinear gating consists of $N = 10$ experts while the input is processed by one expert ($k = 1$). The experts of the GatedPINN are small MLP with 300 neurons at 5 hidden layers. Furthermore, the gating network for the nonlinear gating is also a MLP. It consists of a single hidden layer with 20 neurons and the ReLu activation function.

The approximation error is quantified in terms of the infinity norm:

$$err_\infty = ||\widehat{\psi} - \psi||_\infty \, , \tag{3}$$

which allow us to judge the maximum error while not being prone to sparseness in the solution. The relative norm is used for quantifying the satisfaction of the boundary conditions. The relative norm is defined with the approximated surface integral and the sampling points from dataset T_b as follows

$$err_{rel} = ||1 - \iint_{T_b} \psi \; dxdy|| \cdot 100\% \, . \tag{4}$$

Table 1. Real part statistics of the infinity norm

Approach	err_∞	Min	Max
Spectral solver	**0.01562** $\pm$ 0.0023	5.3455e$-$7	0.0223
PINN	0.0159 $\pm$ 0.0060	0.0074	0.0265
Linear GatedPINN	0.0180 $\pm$ 0.0058	0.0094	0.0275
Nonlinear GatedPINN	0.0197 $\pm$ 0.0057	0.0098	0.0286

Table 2. Imaginary part statistics of the infinity norm

Approach	err_∞	Min	Max
Spectral solver	0.01456 $\pm$ 0.0038	0.0000	0.0247
PINN	**0.0144** $\pm$ 0.0064	0.0034	0.0269
Linear GatedPINN	0.0164 $\pm$ 0.0069	0.0043	0.0296
Nonlinear GatedPINN	0.0167 $\pm$ 0.0066	0.0046	0.0291

Physics-informed neural networks as well as GatedPINN are competitive in quality to the spectral solver for the quantum harmonic oscillator in the chosen computational domain as can be seen in Fig. 3. The periodic development in the infinity norm relates to the rotation of the harmonic oscillator which manifests in the real as well as imaginary at different points in time (see Fig. 1).

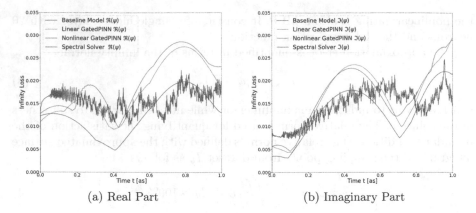

(a) Real Part   (b) Imaginary Part

Fig. 3. Quality of the real part and imaginary part predictions over time in comparison to the spectral solver in reference to the analytically solution

Figure 4 and Fig. 5 show the time evolution of the PINN predictions. The prediction of the baseline model and the GatedPINN models show the same temporal evolution as in Fig. 1.

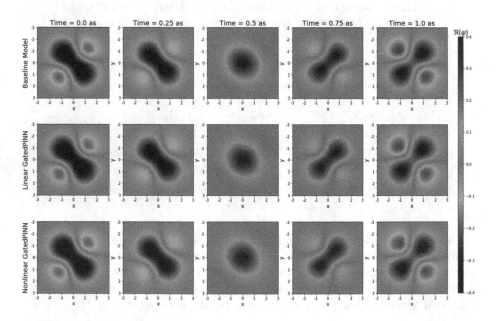

Fig. 4. Real Part predictions of the Baseline and the GatedPINN models

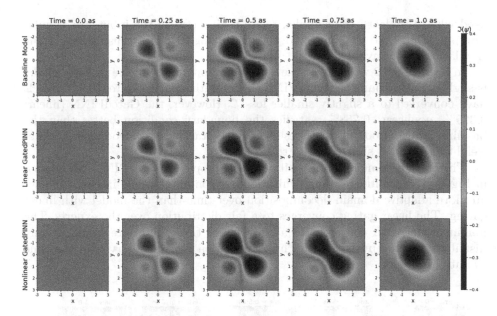

Fig. 5. Imaginary Part predictions of the Baseline and the GatedPINN models

4.2 Domain Decomposition

Table 3. Training time of physics-informed neural networks is significantly reduced by incorporating a domain decomposition into the PINN framework.

Model	Parameters	$\mathcal{L}$	Training time
PINN	**3,438,402**	2.51e−4	29 h 19 min
Linear GatedPINN	3,627,050	**2.115e−4**	**17 h 42 min**
Nonlinear GatedPINN	3,627,290	2.270e−4	18 h 08 min

Table 3 shows the convergence of the PINN-Loss of the baseline, the GatedPINN with linear and nonlinear gating. The Baseline model and the GatedPINN models are trained with 2 million residual points and with the same training setup in terms of batch size, learning rate. Both, the GatedPINN with linear and nonlinear gating have converged to a slightly lower PINN-Loss as the baseline model. However, the training times of the Gated PINN are significantly shorter although the GatedPINN models have more parameters than the baseline model. These results show the efficient usage of the model capacity and automatic differentiation of the GatedPINN architecture. However, both the training time of the PINN and the GatedPINN approach is not competitive to the solution time of the spectral solver (1 min 15 sec). The full potential of PINN can only be used when they learn the complex relationship between the input, the simulation parameters and the solution of the underlying PDE and thus restarts of the simulation can be avoided.

In Table 1 and 2 we see that the approximation quality of the baseline model is slightly better than the GatedPINN models although the GatedPINN models have converged to a slightly smaller loss $\mathcal{L}$. However, the GatedPINN (linear: 0.329%, nonlinear: 0.268%) satisfies the boundary condition better than the baseline model (1.007%). This result could be tackled by introducing another weighting constant similarly to α to Eq. 2.

The learned domain decomposition of the proposed GatedPINN can be seen in Fig. 6. The nonlinear gating, which is more computationally intensive, shows an more adaptive domain decomposition over time than the model with linear gating. The linear gating converges to a fair distribution over the experts. The nonlinear approach converges to a state where the experts are symmetrically distributed in the initial state. This distribution is not conserved in the time evolution.

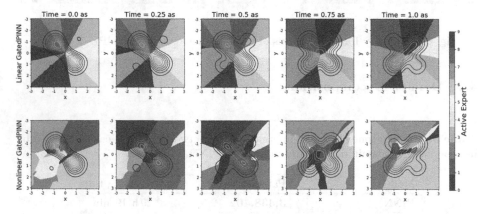

Fig. 6. Learned domain decomposition by the GatedPINN with linear and non-linear gating. The squared norm of the solution ψ is visualized as a contour plot

4.3 Scalability and Power Draw

Training of neural solvers basically relies on unsupervised learning by validating the predicted solution ψ on any residual point (Eq. 2). This means that we only need to compute residual points but do not have to share any solution data. We utilize the distributed deep learning framework Horovod [10]. The scalability analysis was done during the first 100 epochs on using 240 batches consisting of 35000 residual points each and 20 epochs for pretraining. The baseline network is a 8-layer MLP with 200 neurons per layer. Performance measurements were done by forking one benchmark process per compute node.

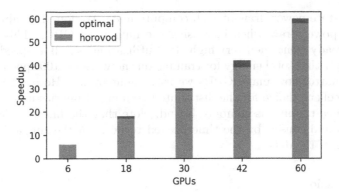

Fig. 7. Speedup comparison

Figure 7 compares the optimal with the actual speedup. The speedup $S(k)$ for k-GPUs was computed by

$$S(k) = t_k/t_1 \ ,$$

provided the runtime for 100 epochs of a single GPU t_1 compared to the runtime of k GPUs: t_k. We found almost linear speedup, though the difference to the optimum is probably due to the latency of the communication between the GPUs and the distribution of residual points and gradient updates. The training achieved an average GPU utilization of $95\% \pm 0.69\%$ almost fully utilizing each GPU. Memory utilization stays relatively low at an average of $65\% \pm 0.48\%$ while most of the utilization relates to duplicates of the computational graph due to automatic differentiation.

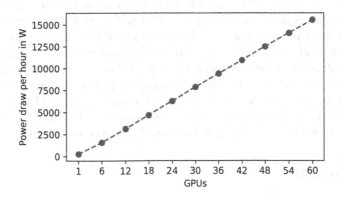

Fig. 8. Power draw comparison

We also quantified the power draw relating to the training in terms of the average hourly draw of all GPUs (See Fig. 8). Note that this rough measure omits the resting-state power draw of each compute node. We found an almost linear increase in power draw when increasing the number of GPUs. This correlates with the already mentioned very high GPU utilization as well as speedup. These findings imply that total energy for training our network for 100 epochs stays the same - no matter how many GPUs we use. Summarizing, Horovod has proven to be an excellent choice for the distributed training of physics-informed neural networks since training is compute bound. Note that the linear scalability has an upper bound caused by the time needed to perform the ring-allreduce and the splitting of the data.

4.4   Discussion

The experimental results of this paper agree with theoretical results on convergence of PINNs for parabolic and elliptic partial differential equations [6] even for large two-dimensional problems such as the quantum harmonic oscillator. This benchmark dataset[1] provides all means for a comprehensive assessment of approximation error as well as scalability due to the availability of an analytic solution while the smoothness of the solution can be altered by frequency ω of the QHO. The approximated solution of Physics-informed neural networks approached the quality of state-of-the-art spectral solvers for the QHO [11]. The training time of PINN or GatedPINN is not competitive to the runtime of spectral solvers for *one* 2D simulation. However, PINN enable warm-starting simulations by transfer learning techniques, integrating parameters (e.g. ω in our case) or Physics-informed solutions to inverse problems [12] making that approach more flexible than traditional solvers. The former two approaches might tackle that challenge by learning complex relationships among parameters [13] or adapting a simulation to a new configuration at faster training time than learning it from scratch while the latter might pave the way for future experimental usage. The GatedPINN architecture finally allows us to approach higher dimensional data when training physics-informed neural networks by training k sub-PINN each representing a certain fraction of the computational domain at $1/k$ of the total PINN capacity. GatedPINN preserve the accuracy of PINN while the training time was reduced by 40% (Table 3). This effect will become even more evident for 3D or higher dimensional problems. Limiting the computational blowup of PINN and retaining linear speedup (see Fig. 7) are crucial steps towards the applications of physics-informed neural networks on e.g. three-dimensional or complex and coupled partial differential equations.

5   Conclusion

Physics-informed neural networks denote a recent general purpose vehicle for machine learning assisted solving of partial differential equations. These neural

---

[1] The PyTorch implementations of the benchmarking dataset as well as the neural solvers for 1D and 2D Schrodinger equation and pretrained models are available online: https://github.com/ComputationalRadiationPhysics/NeuralSolvers.

solvers are solely trained on initial conditions while the time-dependent solution is recovered by solving an optimization problem. However, a major bottleneck of neural solvers is the high demand in capacity for representing the solution which relates to the size, dimension and complexity of the compute domain. In this work, we approach that issue by learning a domain decomposition and utilizing multiple tiny neural networks. GatedPINNs basically reduce the number of parameters per unit volume of our compute domain which reduces the training time while almost retaining the accuracy of the baseline neural solver. We find these results on a novel benchmark based on the 2D quantum harmonic oscillator. Additionally, GatedPINN estimate high-quality solutions of the physical system while the speedup is almost linear even for a large amount of GPUs.

Acknowledgement. This work was partially funded by the Center of Advanced Systems Understanding (CASUS) which is financed by Germany's Federal Ministry of Education and Research (BMBF) and by the Saxon Ministry for Science, Culture and Tourism (SMWK) with tax funds on the basis of the budget approved by the Saxon State Parliament. The authors gratefully acknowledge the GWK support for funding this project by providing computing time through the Center for Information Services and HPC (ZIH) at TU Dresden on the HPC-DA.

References

1. Vallecorsa, S.: Generative models for fast simulation. J. Phys. Conf. Ser. **1085**(2), 022005 (2018)
2. Raissi, M.: Deep hidden physics models: deep learning of nonlinear partial differential equations. J. Mach. Learn. Res. **19**, 1–24 (2018)
3. Raissi, M., Perdikaris, P., Karniadakis, G.E.: Physics Informed Deep Learning (Part I): Data-driven Solutions of Nonlinear Partial Differential Equations (Part I), pp. 1–22 (2017)
4. Kim, B., Azevedo, V.C., Thuerey, N., Kim, T., Gross, M., Solenthaler, B.: Deep fluids a generative network for parameterized fluid simulations. Comput. Graph. Forum (Proc. Eurograph.) **38**(2), 59–70 (2019)
5. Tompson, J., Schlachter, K., Sprechmann, P., Perlin, K.: Accelerating Eulerian fluid simulation with convolutional networks. In: Proceedings of the 34th International Conference on Machine Learning (2017)
6. Shin, Y., Darbon, J., Karniadakis, G.E.: On the Convergence and generalization of Physics Informed Neural Networks, vol. 02912, pp. 1–29 (2020)
7. Meng, X., Li, Z., Zhang, D., Karniadakis, G.E.: PPINN: Parareal physics-informed neural network for time-dependent PDEs (2019)
8. Shazeer, N., et al.: The sparsely-gated mixture-of-experts layer, Outrageously large neural networks (2017)
9. Bengio, E., Bacon, P.L., Pineau, J., Precup, D.: Conditional computation in neural networks for faster models (2015)
10. Sergeev, A., Del Balso, M.: Horovod: fast and easy distributed deep learning in TensorFlow (2018)
11. Feit, M.D., Fleck Jr., J.A., Steiger, A.: Solution of the schrödinger equation by a spectral method. J. Comput. Phys. **47**(3), 412–433 (1982)

12. Chen, Y., Lu, L., Karniadakis, G.E., Negro, L.D.: Physics-informed neural networks for inverse problems in nano-optics and metamaterials. Opt. Exp. **28**(8), 11618 (2020)
13. Michoski, C., Milosavljevic, M., Oliver, T., Hatch, D.: Solving irregular and data-enriched differential equations using deep neural networks. CoRR **78712**, 1–22 (2019)

Integrating Deep Learning in Domain Sciences at Exascale

Rick Archibald[1], Edmond Chow[2], Eduardo D'Azevedo[1], Jack Dongarra[1,3],
Markus Eisenbach[1], Rocco Febbo[3], Florent Lopez[3], Daniel Nichols[3],
Stanimire Tomov[3(✉)], Kwai Wong[3], and Junqi Yin[1]

[1] Oak Ridge National Laboratory, Oak Ridge, USA
{archbaldrk,dazevedoef,eisenbackm,yinj}@ornl.gov
[2] Georgia Institute of Technology, Atlanta, USA
echow@cc.gatech.edu
[3] University of Tennessee, Knoxville, USA
{dongarra,flopez,tomov}@icl.utk.edu, {rfebbo,dnicho22}@vols.utk.edu,
kwong@utk.edu

Abstract. This paper presents some of the current challenges in designing deep learning artificial intelligence (AI) and integrating it with traditional high-performance computing (HPC) simulations. We evaluate existing packages for their ability to run deep learning models and applications on large-scale HPC systems efficiently, identify challenges, and propose new asynchronous parallelization and optimization techniques for current large-scale heterogeneous systems and upcoming exascale systems. These developments, along with existing HPC AI software capabilities, have been integrated into MagmaDNN, an open-source HPC deep learning framework. Many deep learning frameworks are targeted at data scientists and fall short in providing quality integration into existing HPC workflows. This paper discusses the necessities of an HPC deep learning framework and how those needs can be provided (e.g., in MagmaDNN) through a deep integration with existing HPC libraries, such as MAGMA and its modular memory management, MPI, CuBLAS, CuDNN, MKL, and HIP. Advancements are also illustrated through the use of algorithmic enhancements in reduced- and mixed-precision, as well as asynchronous optimization methods. Finally, we present illustrations and potential solutions for enhancing traditional compute- and data-intensive applications at ORNL and UTK with AI. The approaches and future challenges are illustrated in materials science, imaging, and climate applications.

This manuscript has been authored by UT-Battelle, LLC., under contract DE-AC05-00OR22725 with the US Department of Energy (DOE). The US government retains and the publisher, by accepting the article for publication, acknowledges that the US government retains a nonexclusive, paid-up, irrevocable, worldwide license to publish or reproduce the published form of this manuscript, or allow others to do so, for US government purposes. DOE will provide public access to these results of federally sponsored research in accordance with the DOE Public Access Plan (http://energy.gov/downloads/doe-public-access-plan).

J. Nichols et al. (Eds.): SMC 2020, CCIS 1315, pp. 35–50, 2020.
https://doi.org/10.1007/978-3-030-63393-6_3

1 Background

Deep learning (DL) has become one of the most prevalent technologies today. Applications extend from image recognition to natural language processing. While its commercial applications have garnered the efforts of major technology companies, DL has proven vital to works in numerous scientific domains.

Some of these domain problems are vital to solving many of today's global issues—for instance, in solving modern, data-dense problems in climate science. This field has seen several advancements with the recent integration of deep neural networks (DNNs). Ise et al. [1] propose a modern approach towards utilizing neural networks to predict global temperature data. They further conclude that the accuracy of their model increases with the number of input images used. Thus, the model's accuracy and utility grow with the amount of compute power available. Wang et al. [2] provide further uses for DNNs in weather forecasting, which compete with the current state-of-the-art, physically based simulations. The neural networks can also reduce the computations necessary, as they possess the ability to extend one trained network to similar environments, or train once, and predict frequently.

Additionally, DL has proven useful in materials science, even leading the field of materials informatics [3]. Feng et al. [4] were able to utilize deep networks to predict material defects with an accuracy above 98%, even for small data sets. However, these great accuracies require deep and/or pre-trained networks. As with climate modelling, deep learning can be used to replace current physically based simulations, which are expensive and/or do not scale well [5].

Providing high performance hardware and software stacks to facilitate deep learning has become a focus in the high-performance computing (HPC) field. An overview of the parallel algorithms and their challenges for distributed, deep neural networks can be found in Ben-Nun and Toefler [6]. Large-scale modern systems, such as the US DOE's Summit, are fully loaded with high-performance GPUs to support the compute-intensive nature of deep learning. Additionally, some HPC distributed file systems under-perform in providing I/O for data-hungry DL training [7]. Even in terms of sheer performance, many state-of-the-art deep learning models and libraries fail to utilize a significant portion of the maximum floating-point operations (FLOPs) rate of current top systems [8]. There is significant research in the area of accelerating DL on cloud and other commercial systems, but these methods may not integrate well with varying HPC technologies and modern scientific workflows.

One major area in which HPC can innovate deep learning is model parallelism. In many domain applications, networks can become large, leading to growth beyond the memory of a single GPU. By utilizing existing HPC communication standards, a robust model-parallel training standard needs to be developed in addition to efficient implementations. Currently, several libraries attempt to integrate model parallelism [9], but this requires extensive knowledge of the code base, model, and hardware. There is an active research push into further developing model parallel approaches [10–13].

R. Stevens presented a vision of the landscape of machine learning as DOE moves towards the exascale era [14], stressing the importance of machine learning as an integral part of DOE exascale applications. The new paradigm of "HPC + AI" on exascale computing leads towards an "Integrated Sim, Data, Learn Stack." There has been a long history of application code development for compute-intensive applications in the areas of climate, materials, medical, high energy, and urban sciences applications. In light of these needs, we will highlight developments and discuss the necessity of a set of tools and methods particularly relevant to deploying AI on HPC systems.

Realizing the paradigm of "HPC + AI" requires three major components: (1) the HPC system and investments in scaling application-driven capabilities; (2) the AI software achieving the potential performance; and (3) the "+", innovative algorithms and implementations/tools that combine the components of compute- and data-driven applications seamlessly on exascale machines.

2   Deep Learning Software on Modern HPC Systems

There are countless deep learning frameworks in existence today: TensorFlow [15], PyTorch [16], MxNet [17], and many others. Each framework has its own advantages and each falls short in some areas. One advantage of each of these frameworks is their strong corporate backings. Companies pour significant amounts of money into making production-ready libraries, which support various hardware. However, when using these frameworks in an HPC setting, this can cause issues. Much of the research and advancements by the library designers are production focused and target cloud environments. Some of these advancements translate well onto HPC systems, such as the use of hardware accelerators and mixed precision. However, many communication paradigms and implementations differ dramatically between the two. For example, the parameter server method in TensorFlow is more suited for heterogeneous cloud environments, although it is more bandwidth efficient than allreduce; and the socket-based GLOO communication backend built into PyTorch cannot efficiently utilize high-performance interconnects on HPC systems, although it is more flexible.

2.1   Towards a Deep Learning Framework for HPC

We evaluated a number of existing packages for their readiness to efficiently run deep learning models and applications on large-scale HPC systems. As pointed out previously, we found various limitations. Our vision of what is important and needed in deep leaning AI packages for HPC is incorporated into the design of the MagmaDNN open source framework [18,19] (see Fig. 1) with current release MagmaDNN v1.2 [20], which we discuss briefly in what follows.

Firstly, MagmaDNN targets HPC systems, rather than cloud systems. It is written in C++ and is open source (available at bitbucket.org/icl/magmadnn).

Many of the core components of MagmaDNN are the same as other frameworks: operations are represented in a compute graph, data is passed around via tensors, gradients are computed using backpropagation, etc. However, each of these was designed with an HPC environment in mind.

MagmaDNN is centered around existing high-performance software packages, enabling easy integration into existing environments and Exascale Computing Project (ECP) software products. First and foremost, MagmaDNN uses the Matrix Algebra on GPU and Multicore Architectures (MAGMA) [21] package for heterogeneous linear algebra, since deep learning is heavily dependent on linear algebra routines. For strictly CPU computations, the package allows the use of any Basic Linear Algebra Subprograms (BLAS)/LAPACK packages such as Intel MKL, OpenBLAS, ATLAS, etc.

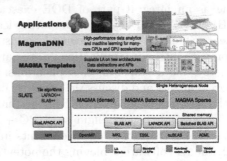

Fig. 1. MagmaDNN software stack.

To better operate with hardware accelerators, MagmaDNN uses CUDA packages to harness GPU acceleration. Custom CUDA kernels, along with CUDNN's routines for GPU-accelerated deep learning, allows the package to get maximal performance on GPU-enabled systems.

For distributed computing, MagmaDNN relies on existing HPC tools such as the Message Passing Interface (MPI) for its communication. Most systems have an MPI distribution tuned to that hardware, while some even have custom distributions. Relying on MPI for inter-node communication allows the framework to utilize existing optimized implementations while providing simpler integration with existing scientific codes.

This integration of existing HPC frameworks allows MagmaDNN to compile and link with the fastest libraries for particular hardware. Utilizing existing optimized packages is a consistent design pattern within HPC libraries, and MagmaDNN uses interfaces that are commonly installed on HPC clusters. In terms of integrating with existing systems and scientific codes, this approach offers the package a significant advantage over other frameworks and workflows.

Not only does MagmaDNN integrate with current HPC frameworks, it provides modularity in its design and linking so that users have flexibility in use. Conforming to standard APIs allows linking with any choice of framework; any BLAS/LAPACK/MPI choice implementations can be used. However, it is not just libraries with which MagmaDNN is modular. By utilizing computation graphs and extendable C++ classes, the package allows users to fully customize their neural networks. For instance, to utilize a unique network interface for distributed training, one can define a custom node on the computation graph which handles the transfer of data on that network component. This can be further utilized to define any desired data movement or computational elements. By providing modular components, MagmaDNN provides a structure onto which domain scientists can easily implement desired custom functionality.

Much of this customizability is fully supported through MagmaDNN's interfaces. For instance, working with GPU and distributed memory is abstracted away in the `MemoryManager` class. Thus, library users do not need to worry about where memory is stored and how it is transferred. The package identifies the memory type, and whenever a memory operation is used (e.g., copy, put, get, etc.), and the MagmaDNN implementation handles the low-level specifics. Likewise, communication operations between devices or nodes are abstracted into the library as well. However, users can define their own operations, meaning they can redefine those in existing code. This makes it easy, for example, to try out different convolution algorithms and determine which one performs optimally. Another common example is to determine which distribution strategy is optimal for a specific machine. The same training code will run on any machine, and only the communication code might need to be altered.

Looking towards next-generation hardware and exascale systems, MagmaDNN aims to incorporate more technology stacks such as AMD's HIP (e.g., hipMAGMA is already available) and Intel's OneAPI. Support for more technologies will allow researchers at various labs and institutions to focus on domain research—and not on how to integrate their code with HPC stacks. We also hope to provide streamlined and optimal support for model parallelism. As the size of models grows, so does the necessary memory requirements on devices. Soon many cutting-edge networks, which can provide state-of-the-art accuracy in classification, will require model parallelism. Supporting fast, scalable model parallelism on HPC systems is crucial to facilitating next-generation research, and MagmaDNN is moving towards this goal.

2.2   Workflow Software for Modern HPC Systems

Another major component in the integration of AI and HPC is the availability of workflow software: which is critical, for example, in launching, collecting results from, and analyzing various simulations in hyperparameter tuning, DL networks discoveries, etc. Exascale applications largely have their own set of workflow procedures and tools to launch their simulations. Integrating traditional applications seamlessly with existing AI software—either TensorFlow, PyTorch, or MagmaDNN—takes on a new level of challenges. Most workflow frameworks available today focus on cloud deployment, yet a workflow framework tailored to scale on HPC systems is critical to the success to "Automate and Accelerate" the task of "Sim, Data, and Learn Stack". SWIFT-T [22] is a tool that offers the choice to run on large-scale HPC systems. At The University of Tennessee, Knoxville (UTK), we have developed a parallel workflow framework called openDIEL that aims to give researchers and users of HPC machines an efficient way to coordinate, organize, and interconnect many disparate modules of computation in order to effectively utilize and allocate HPC resources [23,24]. It provides users an adaptive avenue to run compute-intensive and data science jobs concurrently, allowing specification of DNN architectures, data processing, and hyperparameter tuning. Existing ML tools can be readily used in openDIEL, allowing for easy experimentation with various models and approaches. Most importantly, openDIEL provides a platform to run existing ECP applications in their own workflow procedures. When conducting multi-discipline simulations, it is often required to use a large variety of software, and serial or parallel codes, to answer a research question. Utilizing disparate modules of computation requires the careful coordination of dependencies, communication, and synchronization between them, and there is not always a clear path. This problem is solved by openDIEL: it enables researchers to define complex dependencies between modules and schedule communication between them. OpenDIEL consists of three primary components: the workflow control file, the communication library (COMMLIB), and the Executive, shown in Fig. 2. Workflow is defined by users via the control file, which consists of two parts, the definition of functional modules and the interactions and sequence of execution of modules. OpenDIEL provides two communication libraries, one for direct point-to-point data transfer between two modules, and a store-and-move tuple space library for collective and asynchronous data transfers. The Executive is a lightweight manager designed to run and scale on heterogeneous HPC platforms.

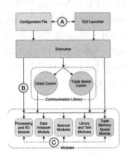

Fig. 2. OpenDIEL structure.

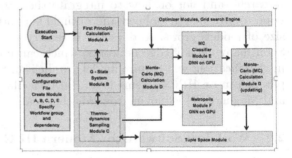

Fig. 3. Workflow in materials sciences.

OpenDIEL specifically focuses on unifying modules into a single executable that uses MPI for communication. Climate and materials sciences simulations, with typical workflow shown in Fig. 3, are two of the applications that are incorporating deep learning into their simulations.

3   Algorithmic Improvements for DNN AI in HPC

In this section, we select and highlight the development of two technologies that we believe are critical for the scalability and efficient use of HPC systems. The first (Sect. 3.1) addresses scalability of DL training, stressing the benefits and need for asynchronous methods on today's highly parallel and heterogeneous systems, featuring powerful nodes and relatively slow interconnects. The second (Sect. 3.2) addresses hardware changes motivated by DL—in particular powerful hardware acceleration for low-precision arithmetic—and techniques for harnessing this in scientific HPC applications.

3.1   Asynchronous Methods

In a multi-core or many-core shared-memory environment, the speed at which the parameters can be updated by different threads may be a limiting factor for stochastic gradient descent (SGD) performance. This is because threads must lock the parameter vector while they are updating it, preventing other threads from reading or updating the parameters, so that they must wait. Asynchronous versions of SGD may relax the data dependencies and order of operations compared to the classical SGD algorithm, allowing the algorithm to update parameters more rapidly—but also making the asynchronous algorithm mathematically different and non-deterministic in its execution [25].

In a distributed-memory environment, a common implementation option for SGD is for each compute node to store a copy of the model parameters [26]. When each compute node has computed a gradient for its mini batch of data, all the gradients must be summed and then shared among the compute nodes so that they can update their copies of the model parameters. This leads to a potential bottleneck in the global all-reduce computation at every step of SGD. In addition, nodes that compute their gradients faster than others must wait for the other nodes (sometimes called "stragglers"). This can be a very high synchronization overhead that may be difficult to reduce by load balancing on heterogeneous architectures. An asynchronous approach can address these high overheads, as we demonstrate below.

Another common implementation option for distributed-memory computers is the parameter server approach [27]. Here, one or more compute nodes are dedicated to storing and updating the model parameters. The worker nodes compute gradients for their partition of the data and send these gradients to the parameter server. The parameter server then sends back the updated values of the model parameters. The parameter server model can be used to run SGD synchronously—with the same issues of stragglers slowing down the iteration for all nodes—but it has the advantage that it can also be run asynchronously (i.e., the worker nodes do not have to send gradients at the same time). Workers, however, may be working with different sets of values for the parameters at any instant. This makes the computation asynchronous. In distributed memory implementations, the gradients are typically updated by the parameter server using atomic memory operations, which differs from the shared memory case.

Asynchronous parameter server implementations were proposed around 2012 or earlier, but it was Hogwild! [25], with inconsistent reads and writes of the parameter vector in shared memory, that popularized the asynchronous approach. In particular, Hogwild! showed that, at least in cases of convex problems and gradient sparsity, asynchrony with inconsistent reads and writes does not have to harm convergence asymptotically. Hogwild! was extended in many directions, such as HogBatch [28], designed for efficiently running on multi-core CPU architectures, and Buckwild [29] which exploits low-precision arithmetic to accelerate the training. Improvements on the analysis of Hogwild! showed that convergence can be maintained for the non-convex and non-sparse case [30]. In MagmaDNN, we designed a parallel asynchronous variant of SGD that is similar to a parameter server approach, but on multi-core CPU and GPU architectures [31].

In practice, the accuracy of machine learning models can be dramatically improved by increasing the number of model parameters as well as the sizes of the training sets. As a result, the memory footprint needed for model training often exceeds the memory storage available on a single node. In such cases, models must be trained on large-scale machines where the dataset, and possibly the model as well, are distributed among the compute nodes. From a performance perspective, it is crucial to efficiently parallelize the training in this setup—and this means overcoming the communication costs. It has been shown that when targeting large-scale platforms, asynchronous algorithms can outperform the synchronous ones as in the shared-memory case. In Google's DistBelief framework [27], for example, the Downpour SGD algorithm uses a centralized parameter server for storing the model, and distributes the dataset to other participating nodes. Asynchrony enables communications to overlap with computations, thus improving resource usage. In addition, the algorithm is particularly well adapted to heterogeneous computing environments where resources may have different processing and communication speeds.

In MagmaDNN, we take a different approach, exploiting remote memory access (RMA) using MPI one-sided communication capabilities for implementing asynchronous SGD in order to maximize the scalability of parallel training. This approach has already been proven efficient in implementing several asynchronous numerical algorithms such as the Jacobi [32] or optimized Schwarz [33] methods for solving sparse systems of linear equations.

3.2 Reduced and Mixed Precision

Deep neural networks can be efficiently trained using low-precision floating-point arithmetic, such as single (fp32) or lower precision, improving the training times on modern hardware [34]. Popular floating-point formats include the 16-bit IEEE half-precision format (fp16) and the 16-bit bfloat16 [35] format. With fewer bits in the mantissa compared to fp16, the bfloat16 format offers less precision but has the advantage of having the same range as fp32—thereby removing the risk of overflow and underflow when converting from fp32 data.

Motivated by the success of low-precision arithmetic in machine learning applications, many specialized hardware accelerators have been designed with reduced- or mixed-precision arithmetic capabilities. For example, the NVIDIA Tensor Cores introduced in the Volta GPU can issue 4×4 matrix multiplication $D = C + A * B$ in one clock cycle, where the input matrices A and B are fp16, whereas D and C can be either fp16 or fp32. The theoretical performance peak on Volta GPU is 125 teraFLOP/s, which is 8 times the performance peak for fp32; and, although the accuracy of tensor core operations is lower than fp32, the ability to accumulate the result of matrix multiplication in fp32 rather than fp16 yields a considerable gain with respect to accuracy over fp16 [36]. In [37], authors use Tensor Cores for computing a reduced-precision LU factorization of a dense linear system, initially generated in double precision (fp64), and use these factors as a preconditioner for a Krylov solver in order to retrieve an fp64 solution. By doing this, they manage to reduce the time to solution up to 4× fp64 arithmetic for the factorization.

Tensor Cores can also be used in performing FFTs [38]. Note that a matrix in fp32 can be well approximated as the scaled sum of two fp16 matrices

$$A_{32} \approx a1_{32} * A1_{16} + a2_{32} * A2_{16} \tag{1}$$

where $a1_{32}$ and $a2_{32}$ are in fp32. Scaling by $a1_{32}(a2_{32})$ ensures $A1_{16}(A2_{16})$ is within the limited dynamic range of fp16. Conceptually, $A1_{16}$ roughly captures the 3 most significant decimal digits, and $A2_{16}$ the next 3 lower significant decimal digits. If A_{32} is already well scaled, then one can expect $a1_{32} = 1$ and $a2_{32} = 2^{-11} * a1_{32}$. Matrix multiplication of two fp32 matrices can be approximated by 3 matrix multiplications of fp16 matrices on Tensor Cores, which may give a theoretical speedup of 8/3× on Volta GPU. For another perspective, Eq. (1) suggests the form of operations in DNN are theoretically able to well approximate operations of fp32 using mixed-precision operations in fp16.

4   Applications

4.1   Materials Science and Microscopy

There are multiple opportunities to exploit machine learning techniques in materials science. While many applications have concentrated on materials discovery—as exemplified by the use of ML in conjunction with databases such as The Materials Project [39], AFLOW [40], or OQMD [41]—a tightly coupled integration of traditional simulation techniques has great promise for bridging the accuracy and computational cost divide between first principles calculations and effective models. One promising combination for a tight coupling is for first principles statistical mechanics of materials to calculate the temperature dependence of materials. This requires the calculations of many possible atomic configurations within these materials using a Monte Carlo approach, where the probability of the individual states would be evaluated using an expensive density functional theory calculation [42]. Thus, we will utilize ML to construct surrogate models as an intermediate step to link the first principles calculations to the Monte Carlo simulation. Here, the calculation of ordering phase transitions in alloys might serve as an example [43]. In a solid solution alloy, different chemical species can occupy the sites of an underlying lattice structure (note that the total number of states grows exponentially with the number of atoms in the system). Each of these possible configurations has a different energy that determines the probability of the system being found in this state at a given temperature. To build a model for these interactions, density functional calculations for representative configurations O(1,000–10,000) will be performed to train a surrogate model that can replace the expensive (in the order of multiple node hours per data point) first principles calculation within the Monte Carlo sampling of possible configurations. While this approach can be conducted in a linear workflow, DFT → ML → MC, we envision a tighter coupled workflow, which augments the original training set with new points from important regions of the phase space discovered during the MC simulation, and retrains the model to improve the quantitative predictive power of this approach.

A long-standing inverse problem in atomic imaging is the loss of phase information during measurement (a.k.a., the phase problem). Given the sparse data collection of scanning transmission electron microscopic (STEM) images on different types of materials, a comprehensive database is needed for the community to study the subject. State-of-the-art electron microscopes produce focused electron beams with atomic dimensions and capture of convergent beam electron diffraction (CBED) patterns. In this dataset [44], we use newly developed electron scattering simulation codes to generate CBED patterns from over 60,000 materials (solid-state materials) from a material project database, representing nearly every known crystal structure. A data sample from this data set is given by a 3D array formed by stacking 3 CBED patterns simulated from the same material at 3 distinct material projections (i.e., crystallographic orientations). Associated with each data sample in the data set is a host of material attributes or properties which are, in principle, retrievable via analysis of this CBED stack. These consists of the crystal space group to which the material belongs, atomic lattice constants and angles, and chemical composition, to name but a few. Of note is the crystal space group attribute (or label).

This dataset could be augmented with experimental data in the future. The generated dataset, based on simulations, will emphasize the scalability aspect of the model with the use of very large images ($\sim$10 GB per image).

4.2   Super-Resolution for HPC Simulations

Image compression is a very active field of study, with new methods being constantly generated [45]. The need for improvements in image compression quality is growing in the field of HPC simulations because of the exponential trend in data generation. There exists an untapped potential in this situation due to the nature of simulated data that is not currently exploited. Simulation data from numerical systems of partial differential equations exist on a solution manifold [46]. Thus, the manifold hypothesis in machine learning—which states that real-world, high-dimensional data lie on low-dimensional manifolds embedded within the high-dimensional space—is concrete for simulation data. We can therefore expect that identifying this map to the low-dimensional manifold will provide ideal compression for HPC Simulations. In the next paragraph we describe the basic setup that allows researchers to test in situ machine learning for climate simulations.

The shallow water equations on a sphere is a well-known model used in climate science to simulate basic dynamics of the Earth's atmosphere. There exist many test case scenarios for this model [47–50], and in this paper we use the challenging test known as the barotropic instability test [50], which involves perturbing the atmospheric flow with a localized bump to the balanced height field. We simulate the shallow water equations on the sphere by using a fourth-order Runge-Kutta method [51] for time-stepping and a discontinuous Galerkin (DG) spatial discretization with a Legendre basis on a cubed-sphere mesh [52,53].

The data structure for this simulation consists of a time series of images for each of the six faces of the cube, which for analysis can be converted to a single series lat-lon gridded images. Arguably, the most commonly used form of lossy compression is the discrete cosine transform (DCT) method [54]. ECP has two projects on the development of FFTs and related transformations, one of which is heFFTe [55], already integrated in the ECP software stack, delivering high-performance (close to 90% of the theoretical roofline peak), and very good weak and strong scaling on systems like Summit at ORNL. This common compression method fills out the setup of the in situ machine learning super resolution method. At each time step of the barotropic instability simulation, in situ machine learning methods are exposed to both the compressed image data and the original image. As the simulation progresses, only the compressed image data is stored to disk, and the machine learning method adaptively learns correct super-resolution transformation of the compressed data. Final stored data contain all compressed image data with the trained machine learning method. It has been demonstrated in [56] that, using this setup, it is possible to train in situ networks to reduce the error in lossy compression—obtaining multiple orders of improvement. Going forward, it will be necessary to further improve in situ compression and analysis in order to maximize discovery with HPC simulations.

5   Meeting Exascale

Exascale systems will appear in 2021. These machines incorporate accelerators from NVIDIA, AMD, and Intel. Efforts in preparing the software stack for exascale systems have been a major focus in the DOE ECP program [57]. We believe a native DNN framework such as MagmaDNN will pave a unique path to meet the challenges of exascale platforms. Assisted by the openDIEL parallel workflow engine, which admits a diverse spectrum of applications as functional modules, we will be able to exploit the full capabilities of exascale machines. In-situ data augmentation will be incorporated with compute-intensive simulations, leading to discovery in multi- and inter-disciplinary, systems-wide, real-time recommendation systems. From instrumentation calibration, experimental and observable results, theoretical simulations, to validation and analysis—exascale computing will be brought to bear on health, transportation, environment, and social sciences. For example, climate and weather recommendation systems will be able to integrate models in storms prediction, rainfall, vegetation, farm growth, pollution, power usage, traffic flow, etc. [58–62]. As inputs and outputs from many sensor devices become ubiquitous, the importance of a scalable AI framework and an extensible workflow tool will grow.

Challenges will rise from algorithmic approaches as HPC systems continue to expand and evolve. Multiple-precision implementation will be unavoidable. Setting the basis and preparing for product diversity from different vendors will be an important consideration of an AI framework, as well. One challenge in performance is to reduce the impact of communication while maintaining good convergence of the algorithm, such as SGD, in the DNN framework. In the Horovod framework [26], for example, the solution is to distribute the training of neural network on large machines using an efficient gradient reduction strategy referred to as ring-allreduce. Notably, in the 2018 Gordon-Bell award winning paper [63], Horovod was used in the context of TensorFlow to train two DNN models on large systems, including the Summit machine, to detect extreme weather patterns from climate data. Similarly, Horovod was used in [64] to train a large DNN model for tackling inverse problems in imaging. Algorithmic improvements towards individual or combined synchronous, asynchronous, and pipeline approaches are essential to improve resource usage as well as convergence.

There is a trend in increasingly larg model sizes (especially in NLP—the latest model [65] has 17 Billion parameters), and a need in scientific applications (e.g., geospatial imaging) to process larger-dimension inputs. Although there exist exascale deep learning applications [63,66] on pre-exascale system such as Summit thanks to the Tensor Core technology, those use cases push the limit on large-batch training for data parallelism and are not generally applicable to exascale learning challenges. Early efforts [9,67] on model parallelism have made progress, but are not yet mature or generic. An AI framework that can efficiently exploit various level of parallelisms (data parallel, model parallel, hyperparameter search, etc.) will be in demand.

6   Conclusion

Exascale systems are an important investment in the US. With exascale, we envision a stronger economy and improved quality of life. It will also lead to important scientific discovery and resolution of complex issues related to national security. Development in AI software and tools that scale well on these systems is important, and even more critical for AI frameworks that also work well across the existing spectrum of exascale applications. Although many challenges exist, a primary roadblock is the lack of direct collaborative effort, and a software platform that values performance as the foremost priority. In this paper, we present a unique set of AI tools and algorithms, as well as efforts between collegiate and ORNL researchers, demonstrating that there is a pathway to integrate and deploy machine learning to those ends—with emphasis on two major applications on exascale systems.

Acknowledgments. This material is based upon work supported in part by the Laboratory Directed Research and Development program at the Oak Ridge National Laboratory, which is operated by UT-Battelle, LLC., for the U.S. Department of Energy under Contract DE-AC05-00OR22725. The work was partly supported by the Scientific Discovery through Advanced Computing (SciDAC) program funded by U.S. Department of Energy, Office of Science, Advanced Scientific Computing Research, with specific thanks to the FASTMath Institutes.

This work was conducted at the Joint Institute for Computational Sciences (JICS) and the Innovative Computing Laboratory (ICL), sponsored by the National Science Foundation (NSF), through NSF REU Award #1659502 and NSF Award #1709069. This work used hardware donations from NVIDIA as well as the Extreme Science and Engineering Discovery Environment (XSEDE), which is supported by NSF grant number ACI-1548562. Computational Resources are available through a XSEDE education allocation award TG-ASC170031.

References

1. Ise, T., Oba, Y.: Forecasting climatic trends using neural networks: an experimental study using global historical data. Front. Robot. AI **6**, 32 (2019)
2. Wang, J., Balaprakash, P., Kotamarthi, R.: Fast domain-aware neural network emulation of a planetary boundary layer parameterization in a numerical weather forecast model. Geosci. Model Dev. **12**(10), 4261–4274 (2019)
3. Agrawal, A., Choudhary, A.: Deep materials informatics: applications of deep learning in materials science. MRS Commun. **9**(3), 779–792 (2019)
4. Feng, S., Zhou, H., Dong, H.: Using deep neural network with small dataset to predict material defects. Mater. Des. **162**, 300–310 (2019). Citation Key: FENG2019300
5. Ye, W., Chen, C., Wang, Z., Chu, I.-H., Ong, S.P.: Deep neural networks for accurate predictions of crystal stability. Nat. Commun. **9**, 3800 (2018)
6. Ben-Nun, T., Hoefler, T.: Demystifying parallel and distributed deep learning: an indepth concurrency analysis. ACM Comput. Surv. **1**, 1–37 (2019)
7. Han, J., Xu, L., Rafique, M.M., Butt, A.R., Lim, S.: A quantitative study of deep learning training on heterogeneous supercomputers. In: 2019 IEEE International Conference on Cluster Computing (CLUSTER), pp. 1–12 (2019)
8. You, Y., Zhang, Z., Hsieh, C.-J., Demmel, J., Keutzer, K.: ImageNet training in minutes. In: Proceedings of the 47th International Conference on Parallel Processing, ICPP 2018. NY, USA. Association for Computing Machinery, New York (2018)
9. Shazeer, N., et al.: Mesh-TensorFlow: deep learning for supercomputers. In: Bengio, S., Wallach, H., Larochelle, H., Grauman, K., Cesa-Bianchi, N., Garnett, R. (eds.) Advances in Neural Information Processing Systems, vol. 31, pp. 10414–10423, Curran Associates Inc. (2018)
10. Geng, J., Li, D., Wang, S.: ElasticPipe: an efficient and dynamic model-parallel solution to DNN training. In: Proceedings of the 10th Workshop on Scientific Cloud Computing, ScienceCloud 2019, New York, USA, pp. 5–9. Association for Computing Machinery (2019)
11. Huang, Y.: GPipe: efficient training of giant neural networks using pipeline parallelism. In: Advances in Neural Information Processing Systems, vol. 32, pp. 103–112. Curran Associates Inc. (2019)
12. Gholami, A., Azad, A., Jin, P., Keutzer, K., Buluc, A.: Integrated model, batch, and domain parallelism in training neural networks. In: Proceedings of the 30th on Symposium on Parallelism in Algorithms and Architectures, SPAA 2018, New York, USA, pp. 77–86. Association for Computing Machinery (2018)
13. Chen, C.-C., Yang, C.-L., Cheng, H.-Y.: Efficient and robust parallel DNN training through model parallelism on multi-GPU platform. arXiv abs/1809.02839 (2018)

14. Stevens, R.: Exascale computing: the coming integration of simulation, data and machine learning. In: European Technology Platform for High-Performance Computing (ETP4HPC) ISC'18 Workshop (2018)
15. Abadi, M., et al.: Tensorflow: large-scale machine learning on heterogeneous distributed systems. CoRR, vol. abs/1603.04467 (2016)
16. Paszke, A., et al.: PyTorch: an imperative style, high-performance deep learning library. In: Advances in Neural Information Processing Systems, vol. 32, pp. 8026–8037. Curran Associates Inc. (2019). Citation Key: NIPS2019_9015
17. Chen, T., et al.: MXNet: a flexible and efficient machine learning library for heterogeneous distributed systems. CoRR, vol. abs/1512.01274 (2015)
18. Nichols, D., Wong, K., Tomov, S., Ng, L., Chen, S., Gessinger, A.: MagmaDNN: accelerated deep learning using MAGMA. In: Proceedings of the Practice and Experience in Advanced Research Computing on Rise of the Machines (Learning), PEARC 2019. NY, USA. Association for Computing Machinery, New York (2019)
19. Nichols, D., Tomov, N.-S., Betancourt, F., Tomov, S., Wong, K., Dongarra, J.: MagmaDNN: towards high-performance data analytics and machine learning for data-driven scientific computing. In: Weiland, M., Juckeland, G., Alam, S., Jagode, H. (eds.) ISC High Performance 2019. LNCS, vol. 11887, pp. 490–503. Springer, Cham (2019). https://doi.org/10.1007/978-3-030-34356-9_37
20. Nichols, D., Febbo, R., Lopez, F., Wong, K., Tomov, S., Dongarra, J.: MagmaDNN (Version 1.2), July 2020. https://doi.org/10.5281/zenodo.3972406
21. Tomov, S., Dongarra, J., Baboulin, M.: Towards dense linear algebra for hybrid GPU accelerated manycore systems. Parallel Comput. **36**, 232–240 (2010)
22. Ozik, J., Collier, N., Wozniak, J., Spagnuolo, C.: From desktop to large-scale model exploration with Swift/T. In: Proceedings of the 2016 Winter Simulation Conference (2016)
23. Wong, K., Trzil, Z.: Tuple space implementation in a parallel workflow engine, OpenDIEL. In: Student Paper, PEARC 2018 (2018)
24. Betancourt, F., Wong, K., Asemota, E., Marshall, Q., Nichols, D., Tomov, S.: openDIEL: a parallel workflow engine and data analytics framework. In: Proceedings of the Practice and Experience in Advanced Research Computing on Rise of the Machines Learning, Student Paper, PEARC 2019, NY, USA. Association for Computing Machinery, New York (2019)
25. Niu, F., Recht, B., Re, C., Wright, S.J.: HOGWILD! A lock-free approach to parallelizing stochastic gradient descent. In: Proceedings of the 24th International Conference on Neural Information Processing Systems, NIPS 2011, Red Hook, NY, USA, pp. 693–701. Curran Associates Inc. (2011)
26. Sergeev, A., Balso, M.D.: Horovod: fast and easy distributed deep learning in TensorFlow. arXiv preprint arXiv:1802.05799 (2018)
27. Dean, J., et al.: Large scale distributed deep networks. In: Advances in Neural Information Processing Systems, vol. 25, pp. 1223–1231. Curran Associates Inc. (2012)
28. Sallinen, S., Satish, N., Smelyanskiy, M., Sury, S.S., Ré, C.: High performance parallel stochastic gradient descent in shared memory. In: IPDPS, pp. 873–882. IEEE Computer Society (2016)
29. Sa, C.D., Zhang, C., Olukotun, K., Ré, C.: Taming the wild: a unified analysis of HOG WILD! -style algorithms. In: Proceedings of the 28th International Conference on Neural Information Processing Systems, NIPS 2015, Cambridge, MA, USA, vol. 2, pp. 2674–2682. MIT Press (2015)

30. Lian, X., Huang, Y., Li, Y., Liu, J.: Asynchronous parallel stochastic gradient for nonconvex optimization. In: Cortes, C., Lawrence, N.D., Lee, D.D., Sugiyama, M., Garnett, R. (eds.) Advances in Neural Information Processing Systems, vol. 28, pp. 2737–2745. Curran Associates Inc. (2015)

31. Lopez, F., Chow, E., Tomov, S., Dongarra, J.: Asynchronous SGD for DNN training on shared-memory parallel architectures. Technical report, ICL-UT-20-04. Innovative Computing Laboratory, University of Tennessee (March 2020). (To appear in IPDPSW'20 proceedings)

32. Wolfson-Pou, J., Chow, E.: Modeling the asynchronous Jacobi method without communication delays. J. Parallel Distrib. Comput. **128**, 6 (2019)

33. Yamazaki, I., Chow, E., Bouteiller, A., Dongarra, J.: Performance of asynchronous optimized Schwarz with one-sided communication. Parallel Comput. **86**, 66–81 (2019)

34. Courbariaux, M., Bengio, Y., David, J.-P.: Training deep neural networks with low precision multiplications (2014)

35. Intel Corporation: BFLOAT16–Hardware Numerics Definition. White paper. Document number 338302–001US, November 2018

36. Blanchard, P., Higham, N.J., Lopez, F., Mary, T., Pranesh, S.: Mixed precision block fused multiply-add: error analysis and application to GPU tensor cores. SIAM J. Sci. Comput. **42**(3), C124–C141 (2020)

37. Haidar, A., Tomov, S., Dongarra, J., Higham, N.J.: Harnessing GPU tensor cores for fast FP16 arithmetic to speed up mixed-precision iterative refinement solvers. In: Proceedings of the International Conference for High Performance Computing, Networking, Storage, and Analysis, pp. 1–11 (2018)

38. Sorna, A., Cheng, X., D'Azevedo, E., Wong, K., Tomov, S.: Optimizing the Fast Fourier Transform using mixed precision on tensor core hardware. In: 2018 IEEE 25th International Conference on High Performance Computing Workshops (HiPCW), pp. 3–7 (2018)

39. Jain, A., et al.: Commentary: the materials project: a materials genome approach to accelerating materials innovation. APL Mater. **1**(1), 011002 (2013)

40. Gossett, E., et al.: AFLOW-ML: a RESTful API for machine-learning predictions of materials properties. Comput. Mater. Sci. **152**, 134–145 (2018)

41. Kirklin, S., et al.: The Open Quantum Materials Database (OQMD): assessing the accuracy of DFT formation energies. npj Comput. Mater. **1**, 15010 (2015)

42. Eisenbach, M., Zhou, C.-G., Nicholson, D.M., Brown, G., Larkin, J., Schulthess, T.C.: A scalable method for Ab Initio computation of free energies in nanoscale systems. In: Proceedings of the Conference on High Performance Computing Networking, Storage and Analysis, SC 2009, New York, NY, USA, pp. 64:1–64:8. ACM (2009)

43. Eisenbach, M., Pei, Z., Liu, X.: First-principles study of order-disorder transitions in multicomponent solid-solution alloys. J. Phys. Condens. Matter **31**, 273002 (2019)

44. Laanait, N., Borisevich, A., Yin, J.: A Database of Convergent Beam Electron Diffraction Patterns for Machine Learning of the Structural Properties of Materials (May 2019). https://doi.org/10.13139/OLCF/1510313

45. Sayood, K.: Introduction to Data Compression. The Morgan Kaufmann Series in Multimedia Information and Systems. Elsevier Science (2017)

46. Rheinboldt, W.C.: On the computation of multi-dimensional solution manifolds of parametrized equations. Numer. Math. **53**(1), 165–181 (1988)

47. Williamson, D., Drake, J., Hack, J., Jakob, R., Swarztrauber, P.: A standard test set for numerical approximations to the shallow water equations in spherical geometry. J. Comput. Phys. **102**, 211–224 (1992)
48. Nair, R.D., Jablonowski, C.: Moving vortices on the sphere: a test case for horizontal advection problems. Mon. Weather Rev. **136**(2), 699–711 (2008)
49. Mcdonald, A., Bates, J.R., McDonald and Bates: Semi-Lagrangian integration of a shallow water model on the sphere. Mon. Weather Rev. **117**, 130 (1989)
50. Galewsky, J., Scott, R., Polvani, L.: An initial-value problem for testing numerical models of the global shallow-water equations. Tellus **56A**, 429–440 (2004)
51. Abramowitz, M., Stegun, I. (eds.): Handbook of Mathematical Functions, chap. 9. Dover Publications (1972)
52. Sadourny, R.: Conservative finite-difference approximations of the primitive equations on quasi-uniform spherical grids. Mon. Weather Rev. **100**(2), 136–144 (1972)
53. Nair, R., Thomas, S., Loft, R.: A discontinuous Galerkin global shallow water model. Mon. Weather Rev. **133**(4), 876–888 (2005)
54. Ahmed, N., Natarajan, T., Rao, K.R.: Discrete Cosine transform. IEEE Trans. Comput. **C−23**(1), 90–93 (1974)
55. Tomov, S., Ayala, A., Haidar, A., Dongarra, J.: FFT-ECP API and high-performance library prototype for 2-D and 3-D FFTs on large-scale heterogeneous systems with GPUs. ECP WBS 2.3.3.13 Milestone Report FFT-ECP STML13-27. Innovative Computing Laboratory, University of Tennessee (2020)
56. Lee, S., et al.: Improving scalability of parallel CNN training by adjusting mini-batch size at run-time. In: 2019 IEEE International Conference on Big Data (Big Data), pp. 830–839 (2019)
57. Exascale Computing Project. https://www.exascaleproject.org
58. Zhou, K., Zheng, Y., Li, B., Dong, W., Zhang, X.: Forecasting different types of convective weather: a deep learning approach. J. Meteorol. Res **33**(5), 797–809 (2019). https://doi.org/10.1007/s13351-019-8162-6
59. Samsi, S., Mattioli, C., Mark, V.: Distributed deep learning for precipitation nowcasting. In: 2019 IEEE High Performance Extreme Computing Conference (HPEC) (2019)
60. Keaney, M., Neal, T.: Comparing Deep Neural Network and Econometric Approaches to Predicting the Impact of Climate Change on Agricultural Yield. UNSW Economics Working Paper (2020)
61. Yi, X.X., Zhang, J., Wang, Z., Li, T., Zheng, Y.: Deep distributed fusion network for air quality prediction. In: Proceedings of KDD 2018, London, United Kingdom (2018)
62. Chen, K., Chen, K., Wang, Q., He, Z., Hu, J., He, J.: Short-term load forecasting with deep residual networks. arXiv abs/1805.11956v1 (2018)
63. Kurth, T., et al.: Exascale deep learning for climate analytics. In: Proceedings of the International Conference for High Performance Computing, Networking, Storage, and Analysis, SC 2018. IEEE Press (2018)
64. Laanait, N., et al.: Exascale deep learning for scientific inverse problems (2019)
65. Rajbhandari, S., Rasley, J., Ruwase, O., He, Y.: ZeRO: memory optimization towards training a trillion parameter models. arXiv abs/1910.02054 (2019)
66. Laanait, N., et al.: Exascale deep learning for scientific inverse problems. arXiv. abs/1909.11150 (2019)
67. Huang, Y., et al.: GPipe: efficient training of giant neural networks using pipeline parallelism. arXiv abs/1811.06965 (2018)

Improving the Performance of the GMRES Method Using Mixed-Precision Techniques

Neil Lindquist[1]([⊠]) [iD], Piotr Luszczek[1], and Jack Dongarra[1,2,3] [iD]

[1] University of Tennessee, Knoxville, TN, USA
{nlindqu1,luszczek,dongarra}@icl.utk.edu
[2] Oak Ridge National Laboratory, Oak Ridge, TN, USA
[3] University of Manchester, Manchester, UK

Abstract. The GMRES method is used to solve sparse, non-symmetric systems of linear equations arising from many scientific applications. The solver performance within a single node is memory bound, due to the low arithmetic intensity of its computational kernels. To reduce the amount of data movement, and thus, to improve performance, we investigated the effect of using a mix of single and double precision while retaining double-precision accuracy. Previous efforts have explored reduced precision in the preconditioner, but the use of reduced precision in the solver itself has received limited attention. We found that GMRES only needs double precision in computing the residual and updating the approximate solution to achieve double-precision accuracy, although it must restart after each improvement of single-precision accuracy. This finding holds for the tested orthogonalization schemes: Modified Gram-Schmidt (MGS) and Classical Gram-Schmidt with Re-orthogonalization (CGSR). Furthermore, our mixed-precision GMRES, when restarted at least once, performed 19% and 24% faster on average than double-precision GMRES for MGS and CGSR, respectively. Our implementation uses generic programming techniques to ease the burden of coding implementations for different data types. Our use of the Kokkos library allowed us to exploit parallelism and optimize data management. Additionally, KokkosKernels was used when producing performance results. In conclusion, using a mix of single and double precision in GMRES can improve performance while retaining double-precision accuracy.

Keywords: Krylov subspace methods · Mixed precision · Linear algebra · Kokkos

1 Introduction

The GMRES method [22] is used for solving sparse, non-symmetric systems of linear equations arising from many applications [21, p. 193]. It is an iterative, Krylov subspace method that constructs an orthogonal basis by Arnoldi's procedure [2] then finds the solution vector in that subspace such that the resulting

© Springer Nature Switzerland AG 2020
J. Nichols et al. (Eds.): SMC 2020, CCIS 1315, pp. 51–66, 2020.
https://doi.org/10.1007/978-3-030-63393-6_4

residual is minimized. One important extension of GMRES is the introduction of restarting, whereby, after some number of iterations, GMRES computes the solution vector, then starts over with an empty Krylov subspace and the newly computed solution vector as the new initial guess. This limits the number of basis vectors required for the Krylov subspace thus reducing storage and the computation needed to orthogonalize each new vector. On a single node system, performance of GMRES is bound by the main memory bandwidth due to the low arithmetic intensity of its computational kernels. We investigated the use of a mix of single and double floating-point precision to reduce the amount of data that needs to be moved across the cache hierarchy, and thus improve the performance, while trying to retain the accuracy that may be achieved by a double-precision implementation of GMRES. We utilized the iterative nature of GMRES, particularly when restarted, to overcome the increased round-off errors introduced by reducing precision for some computations.

The use of mixed precision in solving linear systems has long been established in the form of iterative refinement for dense linear systems [24], which is an effective tool for increasing performance [6]. However, research to improve the performance of GMRES in this way has had limited scope. One similar work implemented iterative refinement with single-precision Krylov solvers, including GMRES, to compute the error corrections [1]. However, that work did not explore the configuration of GMRES and tested only a limited set of matrices. Recent work by Gratton et al. provides detailed theoretical results for mixed-precision GMRES [12]; although, they focus on non-restarting GMRES and understanding the requirements on precision for each inner-iteration to converge as if done in uniform, high precision. Another approach is to use reduced precision only for the preconditioner [10]. One interesting variant of reduced-precision preconditioners is to use a single-precision GMRES to precondition a double-precision GMRES [3].

In this paper, we focus on restarted GMRES with left preconditioning and with one of two orthogonalization schemes: Modified Gram-Schmidt (MGS) or Classical Gram-Schmidt with Reorthogonalization (CGSR), as shown in Algorithm 1. The algorithm contains the specifics of the GMRES formulation that we used. MGS is the usual choice for orthogonalization in GMRES due to its lower computational cost compared to other schemes [20]. CGSR is used less often in practice but differs in interesting ways from MGS. First, it retains good orthogonality relative to round-off error [11], which raises the question of whether this improved orthogonality can be used to circumvent some loss of precision. Second, it can be implemented as matrix-vector multiplies, instead of a series of dot-products used by MGS. Consequently, CGSR requires fewer global reductions and may be a better candidate when considering expanding the work to a distributed memory setting. Restarting is used to limit the storage and computation requirements of the Krylov basis generated by GMRES [4,5].

Algorithm 1. Restarted GMRES with left preconditioning [21]

1: $A \in \mathbb{R}^{n \times n}$, $x_0, b \in \mathbb{R}^n$, $M^{-1} \approx A^{-1}$
2: **for** $k = 1, 2, \ldots$ **do**
3:      $z_k \leftarrow b - Ax_k$ ▷ compute residual
4:      If $\|z_k\|_2$ is small enough, stop
5:      $r_k \leftarrow M^{-1} z_k$
6:      $\beta \leftarrow \|r_k\|_2$, $s_0 \leftarrow \beta$, $v_1 \leftarrow r_k/\beta$, $V_1 \leftarrow [v_1]$
7:      $j \leftarrow 0$
8:      **loop** until the restart condition is met
9:          $j \leftarrow j + 1$
10:         $w \leftarrow M^{-1} A v_j$
11:         $w, h_{1,j}, \ldots, h_{j,j} \leftarrow \text{orthogonalize}(w, V_j)$ ▷ MGS or CGSR
12:         $h_{j+1,j} \leftarrow \|w\|_2$
13:         $v_{j+1} \leftarrow w/h_{j+1,j}$
14:         $V_{j+1} \leftarrow [V_j, v_{j+1}]$
15:         **for** $i = 1, \ldots, j - 1$ **do**
16:             $\begin{bmatrix} h_{i,j} \\ h_{i+1,j} \end{bmatrix} \leftarrow \begin{bmatrix} \alpha_i & \beta_i \\ -\beta_i & \alpha_i \end{bmatrix} \times \begin{bmatrix} h_{i,j} \\ h_{i+1,j} \end{bmatrix}$ ▷ apply Givens rotation
17:         **end for**
18:         $\begin{bmatrix} \alpha_j \\ \beta_j \end{bmatrix} \leftarrow \text{rotation\_matrix}\left(\begin{bmatrix} h_{j,j} \\ h_{j+1,j} \end{bmatrix} \right)$ ▷ form j-th Givens rotation
19:         $\begin{bmatrix} s_j \\ s_{j+1} \end{bmatrix} \leftarrow \begin{bmatrix} \alpha_j & \beta_j \\ -\beta_j & \alpha_j \end{bmatrix} \times \begin{bmatrix} s_j \\ 0 \end{bmatrix}$
20:         $\begin{bmatrix} h_{j,j} \\ h_{j+1,j} \end{bmatrix} \leftarrow \begin{bmatrix} \alpha_j & \beta_j \\ -\beta_j & \alpha_j \end{bmatrix} \times \begin{bmatrix} h_{j,j} \\ h_{j+1,j} \end{bmatrix}$
21:     **end loop**
22:     $H \leftarrow \{h_{i,\ell}\}_{1 \leq i,\ell \leq j}$, $s \leftarrow [s_1, \ldots s_j]^T$
23:     $u_k \leftarrow V_j H^{-1} s$ ▷ compute correction
24:     $x_{k+1} \leftarrow x_k + u_k$ ▷ apply correction
25: **end for**

26: **procedure** MGS(w, V_j)
27:     $[v_1, \ldots, v_j] \leftarrow V_j$
28:     **for** $i = 1, 2, \ldots, j$ **do**
29:         $h_{i,j} \leftarrow w \cdot v_i$
30:         $w \leftarrow w - h_{i,j} v_i$
31:     **end for**
32:     **return** $w, h_{1,j}, \ldots, h_{j,j}$
33: **end procedure**

34: **procedure** CGSR(w, V_j)
35:     $h \leftarrow V_j^T w$
36:     $w \leftarrow w - V_j h$
37:     $[h_{0,j}, \ldots, h_{j,j}]^T \leftarrow h$
38:     **return** $w, h_{1,j}, \ldots, h_{j,j}$
39: **end procedure**

---

2   Numerics of Mixed Precision GMRES

To use mixed precision for improving the performance of GMRES, it is important to understand how the precision of different parts of the solver affects the final achievable accuracy. First, for the system of linear equations $Ax = b$; A, b, and x all must be stored in full precision because changes to these values change the problem being solved and directly affect the backward and forward error bounds. Next, note that restarted GMRES is equivalent to iterative refinement where the error correction is computed by non-restarted GMRES. Hence, adding the error correction to the current solution must be done in full precision to prevent x from suffering round-off to reduced precision. Additionally, full precision is critical for the computation of residual $r = Ax - b$ because it is used to compute the error correction and is computed by subtracting quantities of similar value. Were the residual computed in reduced precision, the maximum error that could be corrected is limited by the accuracy used for computing the residual vector [7].

Next, consider the effects of reducing precision in the computation of the error correction. Note that for stationary iterative refinement algorithms, it has long been known that reduced precision can be used in this way while still achieving full accuracy [24], which, to some extent, can be carried over to the non-stationary correction of GMRES. The converge property derives from the fact that if each restart $i = 1, \ldots, k$ computes an update, u_i, fulfilling $\|r_i\| = \|r_{i-1} - Au_i\| \leq \delta \|r_{i-1}\|$ for some error reduction $\delta < 1$, then after k steps we get $\|r_k\| \leq \delta^k \|r_0\|$ [1]. Thus, reducing the accuracy of the error-correction to single precision does not limit the maximum achievable accuracy. Furthermore, under certain restrictions on the round-off errors of the performed operations, non-restarted GMRES behaves as if the arithmetic was done exactly [12]. Therefore, when restarted frequently enough, we hypothesize that mixed-precision GMRES should behave like the double-precision implementation.

3   Restart Strategies

Restart strategies are important to the convergence. In cases when limitations of the memory use require a GMRES restart before the accuracy in working precision is reached, the restart strategy needs no further consideration. However, if mixed-precision GMRES may reach the reduced precision's accuracy before the iteration limit, it is important to have a strategy to restart early. But restarting too often will reduce the rate of convergence because improvement is related to the Arnoldi process's approximation of the eigenvalues of A, which are discarded when GMRES restarts [23]. As a countermeasure, we propose four possible approaches for robust convergence monitoring and restart initiation.

There are two points to note before discussing specific restart strategies. First, the choice of orthogonalization scheme is important to consider, because some Krylov basis vectors usually become linearly dependent when GMRES reaches the working precision accuracy, e.g., MGS [20], while other methods remain nearly orthogonal, e.g., CGSR [11]. Second, the norm of the Arnoldi residual, the residual for GMRES's least-squares problem, approximates the norm of the residual of the original preconditioned linear system of equations and is computed every iteration when using Givens rotations to solve the least-squares problem (s_{j+1} in Algorithm 1) [21, Proposition 6.9]. However, this approximation only monitors the least-squares problem and is not guaranteed to be accurate after reaching working precision [13]. The explanation is unknown, but it has been noted that the Arnoldi residual typically decreases past the true residual if and only if independent vectors continue to be added to the Krylov basis. Hence, the choice of orthogonalization scheme must be considered when using restarts based on the Arnoldi residual norm.

Our first restart strategy derives from the observation that the number of iterations before the convergence stalls appears to be roughly constant after each restart. See Sect. 4.1 for numerical examples. While this does not alleviate the issue determining the appropriate point for the first restart, this can be used for subsequent restarts either to trigger the restart directly or as a heuristic for when to start monitoring other, possibly expensive, metrics.

The second restart strategy is to monitor the approximate preconditioned residual norm until it drops below a given threshold, commonly related to the value after the prior restart. The simplest threshold is a fixed, scalar value. Note that if the approximated norm stops decreasing, such as for MGS, this criterion will not be met until GMRES is restarted. Thus, the scalar thresholds must be carefully chosen when using MGS. More advanced threshold selection may be effective, but we have not explored any yet.

Inspired by the problematic case of the second strategy, the third strategy is to detect when the Arnoldi residual norm stops improving. Obviously, this approach is only valid if the norm stops decreasing when GMRES has stalled. Additionally, GMRES can stagnate during normal operation, resulting in iterations of little or no improvement, which may cause premature restarts.

The final strategy is to detect when the orthogonalized basis becomes linearly dependent. This relates to the third strategy but uses a different approach. For the basis matrix V_k computed in the kth inner iteration, let $S_k = (I + U_k)^{-1}U_k$, where U_k is the strictly upper part of $V_k^H V_k$ [18]. Then, the basis is linearly dependent if and only if $\|S_k\|_2 = 1$. It has been conjectured that MGS-GMRES converges to machine precision when the Krylov basis loses linear independence [19,20]. This matrix can be computed incrementally, appending one column per inner iteration, requiring $2nk + 2k^2$ FLOP per iteration. Estimating the 2-norm for a GMRES-iteration with i iterations of the power method requires an additional $i(2k^2 + 3k)$ FLOP by utilizing the strictly upper structure of the matrix.

4   Experimental Results

First, Sect. 4.1 shows accuracy and rate of convergence results to verify the results in Sect. 2 and to better understand the strategies proposed in Sect. 3. Next, Sect. 4.2 compares the performance of our mixed-precision approach and double-precision GMRES. Based on the results in Sect. 2, we focused on computing the residual and updating x in double-precision and computing everything else in single-precision. This choice of precisions has the advantage that it can be implemented using uniform-precision kernels and only casting the residual to single-precision and the error-correction back to double precision. Note that in this approach, the matrix is stored twice, once in single-precision and once in double-precision; this storage requirement may be able to be improved by storing the high-order and low-order bytes of the double-precision matrix in separate arrays [14].

Matrices were stored in Compressed Sparse Row format and preconditioned with incomplete LU without fill in. So, the baseline, double-precision solver requires $24n_{nz} + 8nm + 28n + 8m^2 + O(m)$ bytes while the mixed-precision solver requires $24n_{nz} + 4nm + 32n + 4m^2 + O(m)$ where n_{nz} is the number of matrix nonzero elements, n is the number of matrix rows, and m is the maximum number of inner iterations per restart. All of the tested matrices came from the SuiteSparse collection [8] and entries of the solution vectors were independently drawn from a uniform distribution between 0 and 1.

We used two implementations of GMRES: a configurable one for exploring the effect various factors have on the rate of convergence, and an optimized one for testing a limited set of factors for performance. Both implementations are based on version 2.9.00 of the Kokkos performance portability library [9]. The OpenMP backend was used for all tests. Furthermore, for performance results we used the KokkosKernels library, with Intel's MKL where supported, to ensure that improvements are compared against a state-of-the-art baseline. The rate of convergence tests were implemented using a set of custom, mixed-precision kernels for ease of experimentation.

All experiments were run on a single node with two sockets, each containing a ten-core Haswell processor, for a total of twenty-cores and 25 MiB of combined Level 3 cache. Performance tests were run with Intel C++ Compiler version 2018.1, Intel MKL version 2019.3.199, and Intel Parallel Studio Cluster Edition version 2019.3. The environment variables controlling OpenMP were set to: `OMP_NUM_THREADS=20`, `OMP_PROC_BIND=spread`, and `OMP_PROC_BIND=places`.

4.1   Measurement of the Rate of Convergence

To verify the analysis of Sect. 2, we first demonstrate that each variable behaves as predicted when stored in single-precision, while the rest of the solver components remain in double-precision. Figure 1 shows the normwise backward error after each inner iteration as if the solver had terminated, for GMRES solving a linear system for the `airfoil_2d` matrix. This matrix has 14 214 rows, 259 688 nonzeros, and a condition of 1.8×10^6. In the figure, the "Refinement Variables" include the matrix when used for the residual, the right-hand side, the solution, and the vector used to compute the non-preconditioned residual; the "Correction Variables" include the matrix when used to compute the next Krylov vector, the non-preconditioned residual, the Krylov vector being orthogonalized, the orthogonal basis, the upper triangular matrix from the orthogonalization process, and the vectors to solve the least-squares problems with Givens rotations.

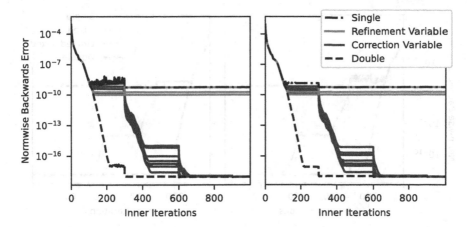

Fig. 1. Rate of convergence results for the `airfoil_2d` matrix when restarting every 300 iterations for MGS (left) and CGSR (right) orthogonalization schemes

The convergence when storing the preconditioner in single-precision was visually indistinguishable from the double-precision baseline and omitted from the figure for the sake of clarity. Each solver was restarted after 300 iterations. All of the solvers behaved very similarly until single-precision accuracy was reached, where all of the solvers, except double-precision, stopped improving. After restarting, the solvers with reduced precision inside the error correction started improving again and eventually reached double-precision accuracy; however, the solvers with reduced precision in computing the residual or applying the error correction were unable to improve past single-precision accuracy.

The convergence test was repeated with two mixed-precision solvers that use reduced precision for multiple variables. The first used double precision only for computing the residual and error correction, i.e., using single precision for lines 4–23 of Algorithm 1. The second was more limited, using single precision only to store A for computing the next Krylov vector, the preconditioner M^{-1}, and the Krylov basis V_j from Algorithm 1; these three variables make up most of the data that can be stored in reduced precision. Figure 2 shows the normwise backward error after each inner iteration for single, double, and mixed precisions solving a linear system for the `airfoil_2d` matrix. After restarting, both mixed-precision GMRES implementations were able to resume improvement and achieve double-precision accuracy. This ability to converge while using reduced precision occurred for all of the matrices tested, as can be seen in Sect. 4.2. Note that while limiting the use of mixed precision can increase the amount of improvement achieved before stalling, this improvement is limited and does not reduce the importance of appropriately restarting. Additionally, the limited mixed-precision implementation requires several mixed-precision kernels, while the fully mixed-precision implementation can be implemented using uniform-precision kernels by copying the residual to single-precision and copying the error-correction back to double-precision.

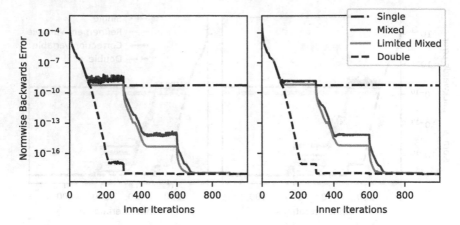

Fig. 2. Rate of convergence results for the `airfoil_2d` matrix when restarting every 300 iterations for MGS (left) and CGSR (right) orthogonalization schemes

Table 1. Number of iterations before the improvement stalls in mixed-precision MGS-MRES

Matrix	Iterations per Restart	Iterations for 1st Stall	Iterations for 2nd Stall	Iterations for 3rd Stall
`airfoil_2d`	300	137	141	142
`big`	500	360	352	360
`cage11`	20	7	7	8
`Goodwin_040`	1250	929	951	924
`language`	75	23	21	21
`torso2`	50	28	27	25

One interesting observation was that the number of iterations before improvement stalled was approximately the same after each restart. Table 1 displays the number of iterations before stalling after the first three restarts in the mixed-precision MGS-GMRES. Stalling was defined here to be the Arnoldi residual norm improving by less than a factor of 1.001 on the subsequent 5% of inner iterations per restart. This behavior appears to hold for CGSR too but was not quantified because stalled improvement cannot be detected in the Arnoldi residual for CGSR.

Next, restart strategies based on the Arnoldi residual norm were tested. First, Fig. 3 shows the convergence when restarted after a fixed improvement. Note that for MGS, when the threshold is too ambitious, mixed-precision GMRES will stall because of roundoff error before reaching the threshold, at which point the approximated norm stops decreasing. However, the choice of restart threshold becomes problematic when considering multiple matrices. Figure 4 shows the same test applied to the `big` matrix, which has 13 209 rows,

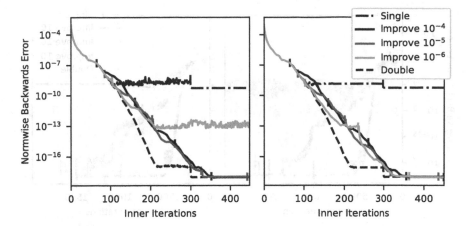

Fig. 3. Rate of convergence results for the `airfoil_2d` matrix when restarting mixed-precision GMRES after a fixed improvement in the Arnoldi residual norm for MGS (left) and CGSR (right) orthogonalization schemes, with vertical ticks to indicate when restarts occurred

91 465 nonzeros, and an L2 norm of 4.4×10^7. Note that the successful threshold with the most improvement per restart is two orders of magnitude less improvement per restart than that of `airfoil_2d`. Next, Fig. 5 uses the first restart's iteration count as the iteration limit for the subsequent restarts when solving the `airfoil_2d` system. Because only the choice of the first restart is important, a more ambitious threshold was chosen than for Fig. 3. Note that, except for when the first restart was not triggered, this two-staged approach generally performed a bit better than the simple threshold. Figure 6 shows the mixed restart strategy for the `big` matrix. Note how the same thresholds were used for the `big` test as the `airfoil_2d` test but were still able to converge and outperform the matrix-specific, scalar threshold. This two-part strategy appears to behave more consistently than the simple threshold.

Finally, we tested restarts based on the loss of orthogonality in the basis. Because CGSR retains a high degree of orthogonality, this strategy was only tested with MGS-GMRES. Figure 7 shows the rate of convergence when restarting based on the norm of the S matrix. The spectral norm was computed using 10 iterations of the power method. Additionally, the Frobenius norm was tested as a cheaper alternative to the spectral norm, although it does not provide the same theoretical guarantees. Interestingly, when using the spectral norm, a norm of even 0.5 was not detected until improvement had stalled for a noticeable period. Note that even the Frobenius norm, which is an upper bound on the spectral norm, did not reach 1 until, visually, improvement had stalled for a few dozen iterations. The cause of this deviation from the theoretical results [18] is unknown.

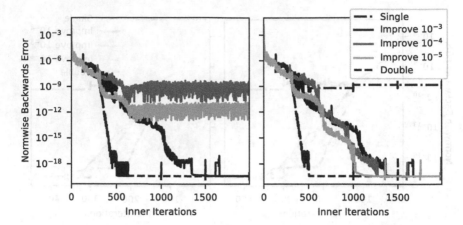

Fig. 4. Rate of convergence results for the `big` matrix when restarting mixed-precision GMRES after a fixed improvement in the Arnoldi residual norm for MGS (left) and CGSR (right) orthogonalization schemes, with vertical ticks to indicate when restarts occurred

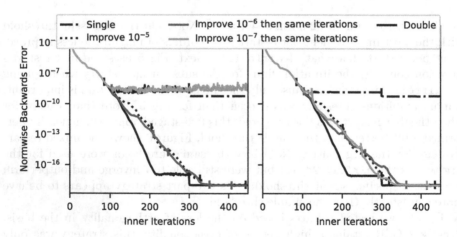

Fig. 5. Rate of convergence results for the `airfoil_2d` matrix when restarting mixed-precision GMRES after a fixed improvement in the Arnoldi residual norm for the first iteration and the same number of iterations thereafter for MGS (left) and CGSR right) orthogonalization schemes, with vertical ticks to indicate when restarts occurred. The rate of convergence using just a fixed improvement threshold of 10^{-5} is added for comparison's sake

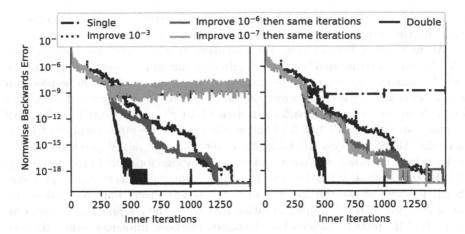

Fig. 6. Rate of convergence results for the `big` matrix when restarting mixed-precision GMRES after a fixed improvement in the Arnoldi residual norm for the first iteration and the same number of iterations thereafter for MGS (left) and CGSR (right) orthogonalization schemes, with vertical ticks to indicate when restarts occurred. The rate of convergence using just a fixed improvement threshold of 10^{-5} is added for comparison's sake

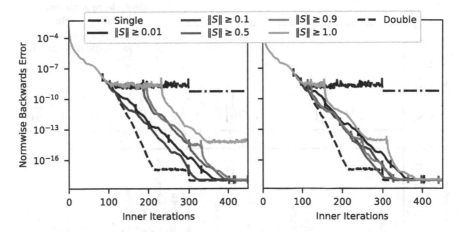

Fig. 7. Rate of convergence results for the `airfoil_2d` matrix when restarting mixed-precision GMRES based on the spectral norm (left) or Frobenius norm (right) of the S matrix, for MGS orthogonalization, with vertical ticks to indicate when restarts occurred

4.2 Performance

Finally, we looked at the effect of reduced precision on performance. Additionally, in testing a variety of matrices, these tests provide further support for some of the conclusions from Sect. 4.1. The runtimes include the time spent constructing the preconditioner and making any copies of the matrix. In addition to comparing

the performance of mixed- and double-precision GMRES, we tested the effect of
reducing the precision of just the ILU preconditioner.

We first tested the performance improvement when other constraints force
GMRES to restart more often than required by mixed precision. For each of the
tested systems, we computed the number of iterations for the double-precision
solver to reach a backward error of 10^{-10}. Then, we measured the runtime
for each solver to reach a backward error of 10^{-10} when restarting after half
as many iterations. All but 3 of the systems took the same number of iterations for MGS; two systems took fewer iterations for mixed precision (ec132
and mc2depi), while one system took more iterations for mixed precision (dc1).
CGSR added one additional system that took more iterations for mixed precision
(big). Figure 8 shows the speedup of the mixed-precision implementation and
the single-precision ILU implementation relative to the baseline implementation
for each of the tested matrices. For the mixed-precision implementation, the geometric mean of the speedup was 19% and 24% for MGS and CGSR, respectively.
For the single-precision ILU implementation, those means were both 2%.

The second set of performance tests show what happens when GMRES is not
forced to restart often enough for mixed precision. All of the matrices from Fig. 8

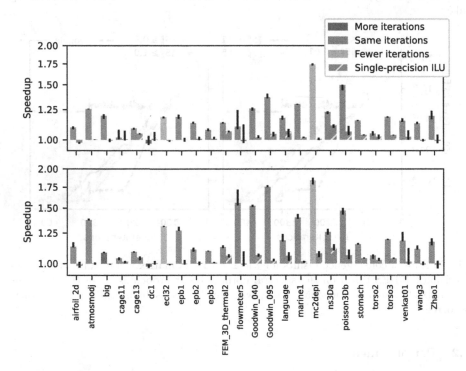

Fig. 8. Speedup of the median runtime out of five tests for mixed-precision versus
double-precision restarted in half the number of iterations needed for double-precision,
for MGS (top) and CGSR (bottom) orthogonalization schemes, with error bars indicating the minimum and maximum speedups

that were restarted after fewer than 50 iterations were tested again, except they were restarted after 50 iterations. For mixed-precision GMRES, the first restart could additionally be triggered by an improvement in the Arnoldi residual by a factor of 10^{-6} and subsequent restarts were triggered by reaching the number of inner-iterations that caused the first restart. To ensure the mixed-precision solver was not given any undue advantage, the other two solvers' performance was taken as the best time from three restart strategies: (1) the same improvement-based restart trigger as mixed-precision GMRES; (2) after 50 iterations, or (3) after an improvement in the Arnoldi residual by a factor of 10^{-8}. Figure 9 shows the new performance results. For the mixed-precision implementation, the geometric mean of the speedup was -4% and 0% for MGS and CGSR, respectively. For the single-precision ILU implementation, those means were 2% and 1% respectively. The matrices for which the mixed-precision implementation performed worse were exactly the matrices that did not require restarting when solved by the double-precision implementation.

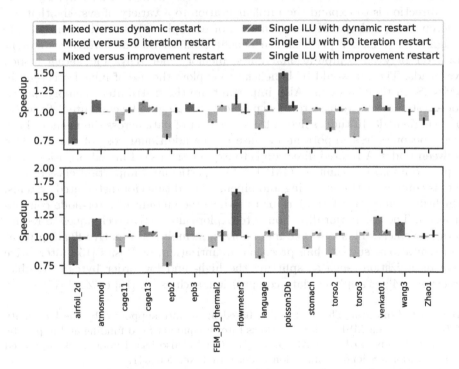

Fig. 9. Speedup of the median runtime out of five tests for mixed-precision versus double-precision restarted after 50 iterations or an improvement in the Arnoldi residual, for MGS (top) and CGSR (bottom) orthogonalization schemes, with error bars indicating the minimum and maximum speedups

5 Conclusion

As a widely used method for solving sparse, non-symmetric systems of linear equations, it is important to explore ways to improve the performance of GMRES. Towards this end, we experimented with the use of mixed-precision techniques to reduce the amount of data moved across the cache hierarchy to improve performance. By viewing GMRES as a variant of iterative refinement, we found that GMRES was still able to achieve the accuracy of a double-precision solver while using our proposed techniques of mixed-precision and restart initiation. Furthermore, we found that the algorithm, with our proposed modifications, delivers improved performance when the baseline implementation already requires restarting for all but one problem, even compared to storing the preconditioner in single precision. However, our approach reduced performance when the baseline did not require restarting, at least for problems that require less than 50 inner iterations.

There are a few directions in which this work can be further extended. The first direction is to expand the implementation to a variety of systems that are different from a single CPU-only node. For example, GPU accelerators provide a significantly higher performance benefit than CPUs but involve a different trade-off between computational units, memory hierarchy, and kernel launch overheads. Thus, it would be beneficial to explore the use of mixed precision in GMRES on these systems. Also important are the distributed memory, multi-node systems that are used to solve problems too large to be computed efficiently on a single node. In these solvers, the movement of data across the memory hierarchy becomes less important because of the additional cost of moving data between nodes. A related direction is to explore the use of mixed-precision techniques to improve variants of GMRES. One particularly important class of variants is communication-avoiding and pipelined renditions for distributed systems, which use alternative formulations to reduce the amount of inter-node communication. The last major direction is to explore alternative techniques to reduce data movement. This can take many forms, including alternative floating-point representations, such as half-precision, quantization, or Posits [15]; alternative data organization, such as splitting the high- and low-order bytes of double-precision [14]; or applying data compression, such as SZ [16] or ZFP [17].

Acknowledgments. This material is based upon work supported by the University of Tennessee grant MSE E01-1315-038 as Interdisciplinary Seed funding and in part by UT Battelle subaward 4000123266. This material is also based upon work supported by the National Science Foundation under Grant No. 2004541.

References

1. Anzt, H., Heuveline, V., Rocker, B.: Mixed precision iterative refinement methods for linear systems: convergence analysis based on Krylov subspace methods. In: Jónasson, K. (ed.) PARA 2010. LNCS, vol. 7134, pp. 237–247. Springer, Heidelberg (2012). https://doi.org/10.1007/978-3-642-28145-7_24

2. Arnoldi, W.E.: The principle of minimized iteration in the solution of the matrix eigenvalue problem. Quart. Appl. Math. **9**, 17–29 (1951). https://doi.org/10.1090/qam/42792
3. Baboulin, M., et al.: Accelerating scientific computations with mixed precision algorithms. CoRR abs/0808.2794 (2008). https://doi.org/10.1016/j.cpc.2008.11.005
4. Baker, A.H.: On improving the performance of the linear solver restarted GMRES, Ph.D. thesis. University of Colorado (2003)
5. Baker, A.H., Jessup, E.R., Manteuffel, T.: A technique for accelerating the convergence of restarted GMRES. SIAM J. Matrix Anal. Appl. **26**(4), 962–984 (2005). https://doi.org/10.1137/S0895479803422014
6. Buttari, A., Dongarra, J., Langou, J., Langou, J., Luszczek, P., Kurzak, J.: Mixed precision iterative refinement techniques for the solution of dense linear systems. Int. J. High Perform. Comput. Appl. **21**(4), 457–466 (2007). https://doi.org/10.1177/1094342007084026
7. Carson, E., Higham, N.J.: A new analysis of iterative refinement and its application to accurate solution of ill-conditioned sparse linear systems. SIAM J. Sci. Comput. **39**(6), A2834–A2856 (2017). https://doi.org/10.1137/17M1122918
8. Davis, T.A., Hu, Y.: The University of Florida sparse matrix collection. ACM Trans. Math. Softw. **38**(1), 25 (2011). https://doi.org/10.1145/2049662.2049663
9. Edwards, H.C., Trott, C.R., Sunderland, D.: Kokkos: enabling manycore performance portability through polymorphic memory access patterns. J. Parallel Distr. Comput. **74**(12), 3202–3216 (2014). https://doi.org/10.1016/j.jpdc.2014.07.003
10. Giraud, L., Haidar, A., Watson, L.T.: Mixed-precision preconditioners in parallel domain decomposition solvers. In: Langer, U., Discacciati, M., Keyes, D.E., Widlund, O.B., Zulehner, W. (eds.) Domain Decomposition Methods in Science and Engineering XVII. LNCSE, vol. 60. Springer, Heidelberg (2008). https://doi.org/10.1007/978-3-540-75199-1_44
11. Giraud, L., Langou, J., Rozloznik, M.: The loss of orthogonality in the Gram-Schmidt orthogonalization process. Comput. Math. Appl. **50**(7), 1069–1075 (2005). https://doi.org/10.1016/j.camwa.2005.08.009
12. Gratton, S., Simon, E., Titley-Peloquin, D., Toint, P.: Exploiting variable precision in GMRES. SIAM J. Sci. Comput. (2020, to appear)
13. Greenbaum, A., Rozložník, M., Strakoš, Z.: Numerical behaviour of the modified Gram-Schmidt GMRES implementation. Bit. Numer. Math. **37**(3), 706–719 (1997). https://doi.org/10.1007/BF02510248
14. Grützmacher, T., Anzt, H.: A modular precision format for decoupling arithmetic format and storage format. In: Revised Selected Papers, Turin, Italy, pp. 434–443 (2018). https://doi.org/10.1007/978-3-030-10549-5_34
15. Gustafson, J.L., Yonemoto, I.T.: Beating floating point at its own game: posit arithmetic. Supercomput. Front. Innov. **4**(2), 71–86 (2017). https://doi.org/10.14529/jsfi170206
16. Liang, X., et al.: Error-controlled lossy compression optimized for high compression ratios of scientific datasets. In: 2018 IEEE International Conference on Big Data (Big Data), pp. 438–447. IEEE (2018). https://doi.org/10.1109/BigData.2018.8622520
17. Lindstrom, P.: Fixed-rate compressed floating-point arrays. IEEE Trans. Vis. Comput. Graph. **20**(12), 2674–2683 (2014). https://doi.org/10.1109/TVCG.2014.2346458
18. Paige, C.C.: A useful form of unitary matrix obtained from any sequence of unit 2-norm n-vectors. SIAM J. Matrix Anal. Appl. **31**(2), 565–583 (2009). https://doi.org/10.1137/080725167

19. Paige, C.C., Rozlozník, M., Strakos, Z.: Modified Gram-Schmidt (MGS), least squares, and backward stability of MGS-GMRES. SIAM J. Matrix Anal. Appl. **28**(1), 264–284 (2006). https://doi.org/10.1137/050630416

20. Paige, C.C., Strakos, Z.: Residual and backward error bounds in minimum residual Krylov subspace methods. SIAM J. Sci. Comput. **23**(6), 1898–1923 (2001). https://doi.org/10.1137/S1064827500381239

21. Saad, Y.: Iterative Methods for Sparse Linear Systems, 2nd edn. SIAM Press, Philadelphia (2003)

22. Saad, Y., Schultz, M.H.: GMRES: a generalized minimal residual algorithm for solving nonsymmetric linear systems. SIAM J. Sci. Stat. Comput. **7**(3), 856–869 (1986). https://doi.org/10.1137/0907058

23. Van der Vorst, H.A., Vuik, C.: The superlinear convergence behaviour of GMRES. J. Comput. Appl. Math. **48**(3), 327–341 (1993). https://doi.org/10.1016/0377-0427(93)90028-A

24. Wilkinson, J.H.: Rounding Errors in Algebraic Processes. Prentice-Hall, Princeton (1963)

On the Use of BLAS Libraries in Modern Scientific Codes at Scale

Harry Waugh[✉] and Simon McIntosh-Smith

High Performance Computing Research Group, University of Bristol, Bristol, UK
{Harry.Waugh,Simon.McIntosh-Smith}@bristol.ac.uk

Abstract. As we approach the Exascale era, computer architectures are evolving ever-greater vector and matrix acceleration units—NVIDIA's Ampere Tensor Cores, Intel's AMX, and Arm's SVE vector instruction set developments are just three recent examples [1,2,10]. To exploit these, it is expected that optimised math libraries such as those for dense and sparse linear algebra, will play an increasing role in achieving optimal performance. It is therefore useful to understand which of these functions dominate an application's runtime, and in particular how this changes with increasing scale. This work aims to provide a contemporary dataset regarding how much dense linear algebra (BLAS) is used in HPC codes at scale. We have analysed several science codes widely used on the UK HPC service, ARCHER (https://www.archer.ac.uk), including CASTEP, CP2K, QuantumESPRESSO, and Nektar++. To capture demands from the AI community, we have additionally traced the training stage of the Convolutional Neural Network (CNN), AlexNet [7]. HPLinpack is also included as a reference, as it exhibits a well-understood BLAS usage pattern. Results from across all the codes show that, unlike HPLinpack, BLAS usage is never more than 25% of the total runtime, even when running at a modest scale (32 nodes of the Arm-based supercomputer, Isambard). This presents limited speedup opportunity when considering Amdahl's law, and suggests that application developers may need to adjust their algorithms to spend more time in optimised BLAS libraries to capitalise on new architectures and accelerators.

1 Introduction

High-performance computing processors are becoming progressively more advanced, with many featuring dedicated execution units or technologies that allow them to accelerate critical workloads. A driving force behind this innovation is the rise in popularity of deep learning, which requires efficient methods for computing vector and matrix operations in order to train and infer from, neural networks. Recent examples of these architectures are the TensorCores found in NVIDIA's Ampere GPUs and the enhanced vector operations in Arm SVE [1,10]. We expect this accelerator trend to continue with more processors adopting specialised linear alebra units in forthcoming years [6].

Exploiting this hardware often requires writing custom code or intrinsics on an individual application basis, and while this could result in high-performance

© Springer Nature Switzerland AG 2020
J. Nichols et al. (Eds.): SMC 2020, CCIS 1315, pp. 67–79, 2020.
https://doi.org/10.1007/978-3-030-63393-6_5

code, this is more labour-intensive and reduces an application's portability. One solution to this, is to encapsulate the complexity within optimized math libraries - such as BLAS and LAPACK allowing applications to freely swap in a machine specific library on different systems. This also allows existing AI and HPC applications to benefit from accelerated linear algebra operations, without code modifications.

To understand how these libraries are affecting application performance, we must collect data on how real science codes are using BLAS today. Furthermore, if this data is to be relevant in the rapidly approaching Exascale era, we must also understand how this usage changes with increasing scale. Given this dataset, we'll be able to understand if our leading applications can take advantage of these architectures, and in the future, design even more effective hardware accelerators.

In this study, we have chosen a representative set of popular BLAS-using applications from the UK's national supercomputing service, ARCHER, to investigate how much linear algebra is used at different node counts. The reason for selecting codes from ARCHER was to ensure that any results are directly relevant to UK HPC users. We have gathered this dataset by intercepting dynamic calls to BLAS, allowing us to capture both the time spent in each function, and the parameters of each call. We have provided a detailed analysis of this data and have extracted key features that will be useful for designing hardware accelerators, and ultimately, improving HPC application performance in the future.

2   Related Work

Recent years have seen a plethora of modern architectures adapted to accelerating deep learning workloads including Google's TPU, Graphcore's IPU, Intel's Nervana, and NVIDIA's Tensor Cores, to name but a few. The heart of these technologies, is their ability to rapidly compute tensor operations with maximal efficiency, for example, NVIDIA's Tensor Cores perform a 4×4 matrix-multiply operation in a single cycle. These tensor operations form a critical part of both the inference and training stages of neural networks [4].

Since the release of these technologies, the HPC community has shown increasing interest in exploiting dedicated-function sillicon to accelerate the linear algebra widespread in HPC applications. Work has already been completed that shows it's possible to achieve a performance benefit in HPC applications, even with the lower precision units found in modern hardware [9]. Interestingly, even this caveat is likely to be now obsolete with the recent announcement of NVIDIA's double precision Ampere Tensor Cores [1].

Given that this new market for accelerators seems to be a perfect fit for HPC applications, one would inuitively believe that there exists a substantial dataset on how much our popular codes are actually using linear algebra. Yet as of June 2020, there is no existing dataset that shows the prevalence of BLAS in scientific codes, even though a large body of literature exists on several other usage aspects of HPC applications, including MPI communication, memory, and I/O [8,12,13].

3   Methodology

To uncover how much BLAS is used across the HPC application spectrum, we examined a usage report from the ARCHER system and decided on a representative set of codes that are commonly run by its users. Table 1 shows the proportion of time that ARCHER spends running each of our chosen applications; the aggregate total of these equates to over 15% of ARCHER's total annual usage.

Table 1. ARCHER usage report, from April 1, 2019 to March 31, 2020.

Application	Code type	ARCHER usage
CASTEP	Quantum materials modelling	4.7%
CP2K	Quantum materials modelling	5.8%
LAMMPS	Classical materials modelling	2.9%
Nektar++	Computational fluid dynamics	0.6%
QuantumESPRESSO	Quantum materials modelling	2.1%

Clearly, this table shows a significant bias towards material modelling codes, but as mentioned by Turner [11], this is to be expected given that both the EPSRC and NERC are heavy users of ARCHER. These material modelling codes have been found to exhibit widely varying BLAS profiles, and thus were included to allow comparison. VASP is a notable exception from this list, and wasn't included because of its licensing model and similarities to CASTEP - the same reasons for its omittance from the ARCHER2 procurement benchmarks [11].

As HPC and AI applications are clearly converging, we have increased the scope of this study by tracing the Convolutional Neural Network (CNN), AlexNet [7], to capture demands from the AI community. Future architectures will want to improve performance for both HPC and AI, and therefore it is interesting to compare each field's linear algebra patterns, in an effort to find architectural features that will accomodate both.

BLAS usage is, of course, highly variable across a set of applications, and is dependent on the benchmark case being run and its corresponding code path. In light of this, we endeavored to select benchmarks according to the following criteria:

- The benchmark can be completed in no more than a few hours on a single node setup, allowing applications to be traced within a reasonable time frame. This allows results to be reproduced more easily, either to check our results, or for future comparison.
- The benchmark is representative of what the community is currently running, allowing users to immediately benefit from this study.
- The benchmark scales well, and represents what users will want to run in the next few years, on the largest supercomputers. The benchmarks of today may

be very different to the benchmarks that are run on future accelerators, and this should be taken into account, where possible.

3.1 Nektar++

Nektar++[1] is a parallel spectral framework used for solving partial differential equations, and is the only computational fluid dynamics code in this study. To find a benchmark that adhered to the criteria we set out, we consulted the developers of Nektar++, who provided a 2D shock wave boundary layer benchmark. This benchmark used the compressible flow solver in Nektar++ and consists of 2400 elements, with $4*4$ modes per element.

Nektar++ 5.0 was built using: the Arm 19.2 compiler, the Arm 19.2 performance libraries, Boost 1.70, Scotch 6.0.8, and HDF5.

3.2 QuantumESPRESSO

QuantumESPRESSO[2], is a periodic electronic structure code which is in the top 15 most heavily used codes on ARCHER. Before selecting benchmarks for this application, we tested several of the QuantumESPRESSO benchmarks that are maintained in the official benchmark repository. Of this set, we then chose the AUSURF112 and GRIR433 benchmarks, which featured radically different proportions of BLAS usage.

QuantumESPRESSO 6.1 was built using with both the Arm 19.2 compiler, the Arm 19.2 performance libraries, and ScaLAPACK 2.0.2. The code was run with the recommended -npools x flag, where x is the number of k-points used in the benchmark case. Note, for node counts of 1 and 2 for the AUSURF112 benchmark, and 1, 2 and 4 for the GRIR443 benchmark, this -npools x value was reduced to allow the program to fit into Isambard's 256 GB of RAM per node.

3.3 CASTEP

CASTEP[3] is a commonly run Fortran code on UK HPC systems, where it is used to calculate material properties including energetics and atomic-level structure using density functional theory (DFT). We used a modified version of the 'al3x3' benchmark, which simulates a 270 atom sapphire surface, with a vacuum gap. We modified this benchmark after consulting the developers of CASTEP, who advised that the pseudopotentials in 'al3×3' were both less accurate and computationally less demanding than modern ones. This modified benchmark can be replicated by updating the 'al3×3' benchmark with cut-off energy, 700 eV, and letting CASTEP generate new pseudopotential files.

CASTEP 19.1 was built using: the Cray 8.6 compiler, the Cray 18.12 Libsci library, and Cray FFTW 3.3.8.

---

[1] https://www.nektar.info.
[2] https://www.quantum-espresso.org.
[3] http://www.castep.org.

3.4 CP2K

CP2K[4] is another Fortran DFT-based software package that can be used to run different atomistic simulations. For this application we used the 'H20–1024' benchmark, which is a version of the well known 'H20–64' benchmark that simulates a larger number of water particles.

CP2K 5.1 was built using: the GCC 8.3 compiler, the Arm 19.2 performance libraries, ScaLAPACK 2.0.2, and Cray FFTW 3.3.8.

3.5 LAMMPS

LAMMPS[5] is a massively parallel molecular dynamics simulation program that mainly focuses on modelling materials. The code is used in a large range of different research fields, and has a correspondingly large number of additional packages that it can be run with. While there is extensive use of linear algebra in these packages, most of them use custom in-house methods for computation and only a select few link to BLAS libraries. The point on using in-house methods and not BLAS library calls is important, as it shows a weakness in our methodology, as our tracing tool can't detect these methods. Of the niche few packages that use BLAS, most use insignificant amounts, or don't scale beyond 1 MPI process. Given these reasons, and the lack of recognised benchmarks in the LAMMPS community, we have included this information here to prevent repeated work, but LAMMPS won't be analyzed further in our results section.

3.6 AlexNet

AlexNet is a Convolutional Neural Network (CNN) developed by Krizhevsky [7]. The network competed in the ImageNet Large Scale Visual Recognition Challenge, and achieved an error rate of 15.3%, which was well above the competition at the time. Unlike the other codes in this study, it is not commonly used on the ARCHER system, but we have included it to capture the linear algebra usage of an AI workload, to see how this differs from HPC applications. In this study, we use a subset of 20 out of the 200 classes in the ImageNet dataset, and train the network for 10 epochs, with a batch size of 32.

AlexNet was run with: TensorFlow 2.2.0, Bazel 2.0.0, MKL-DNN 0.21.3, SciPy 1.4.1, NumPy 1.17, OpenCV 4.4.0, and ArmPL 20.0.

3.7 Library Tracing Tools

We obtained a BLAS trace for each application by adapting the Arm library tracing tool, perf-libs-tools[6]. The tool works by using LD_PRELOAD to intercept dynamic calls to BLAS, LAPACK and FFT libraries, and then recording

---

[4] https://www.cp2k.org.
[5] https://lammps.sandia.gov.
[6] https://github.com/ARM-software/perf-libs-tools.

parameter data and computation time at the end of each intercepted function. Given that the tracer works by intercepting dynamic BLAS calls, it is critical to note that inline linear algebra code cannot be detected by the tracer, as referenced in Subsect. 3.5. The modified version of the tracer[7] was adapted to work with BLAS libraries other than the Arm performance library, and features a low-memory version suitable for use with applications that make a large number of unique BLAS calls, including CASTEP.

4   Results

These results were collected by running each application on the Arm-based supercomputer, Isambard. Each node in this Cray XC50 machine features an Arm-based, dual-socket 32-core Marvell ThunderX2 processor, with 256 GB of DDR4 DRAM.

For all tested HPC applications, we present the percentage of runtime spent computing BLAS, at scales of 1 node up to 32 nodes inclusively. Each code was strong-scaled, with the exception of HPLinpack, which is weakly scaled. Note that QuantumESPRESSO uses different parameters for low node counts due to memory constraints - more detail is included on this in Subsect. 3.2. The proportion of time that each application spends in BLAS, at each scale, can be seen in Fig. 1.

Clearly, there is a negative correlation between the percentage of time spent in BLAS, and the number of nodes. Even at a modest node count of 32 (2048 cores), the maximum amount of time a code spent in BLAS was just 22%. This implies that, even with unlimited BLAS acceleration, each application would only go a maximum of $1.28\times$ faster at this scale [5].

4.1   Interpreting Matrix Distribution Figures Using HPLinpack

HPLinpack is the only application that maintains its proportion of BLAS as we increase the number of nodes. Although this is expected, and arguably trivial, we've included it as a well-known example to demonstrate confidence in our methodology, and to explain how to interpret Figs. 2, 3, 4, 5 and 6. These figures show the A and B matrix size distributions for the dominant general matric multiply (GEMM) call in each application. This note on which GEMM operation an application uses is important, as it will directly affect the amount of elements in a vector instruction or the type of matrix multiplication unit that is required. These GEMM level-3 BLAS calls are responsible for 80–100% of all BLAS usage in our tested applications, which is to be expected, given that these level-3 algorithms are of $O(n^3)$ time complexity. Figure 2 shows the matrix size distribution for the DGEMM calls in HPLinpack's LU decomposition. In these GEMM figures, each data point represents the time that a code spends computing GEMM functions at a given matrix size, of which, the time spent is proportional to the area of each

---

[7] https://github.com/UoB-HPC/perf-libs-tools.

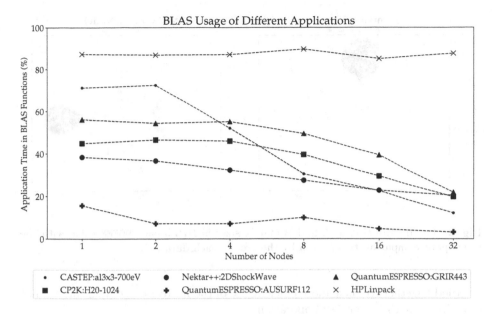

Fig. 1. The proportion of runtime spent computing BLAS operations, and how this changes as we increase the number of nodes.

data point. Darker, denser points on these graphs represent a large number of calls of similar, but not exactly the same, size. This explains the intuitive truth that an equal amount of time is spent computing A and B matrices, and thus the total area on each subplot should also be equal.

4.2 Nektar++

The proportion of time that Nektar++ spends in BLAS, shown in Fig. 1, is the most consistent code as we scale the number of nodes. Using 1 node, 38% of Nektar++'s runtime is in BLAS, which gradually reduces to 20.5% as we scale up to 32 nodes. As given in Table 2, the majority, 82%, of this BLAS usage is made up of double precision matrix multiply (DGEMM) calls, with only 17% being double precision matrix-vector multiply (DGEMV) calls. The distribution of matrix sizes that DGEMM is called with is shown in Fig. 3.

This figure shows that Nektar++ spends a large amount of its time in BLAS computing DGEMM calls on matrix sizes of less than '100 by 100', with a significant number of these being smaller than '10 by 10'. Given these small matrices, its remarkable how high the proportion of time spent in BLAS is when compared with other codes, and highlights the sheer number of calls that Nektar++ is making. Interestingly, Nektar++ only calls DGEMM with a handful of unique matrix sizes compared to other applications in the study. These observations suggest that Nektar++ may be a strong candidate for using batched BLAS operations, as described by Dongarra [3]. These allow lots of smaller GEMM operations to be

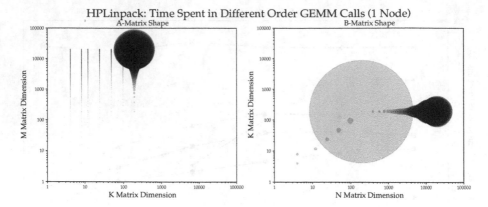

Fig. 2. The distribution of A and B matrix sizes in HPLinpack `DGEMM` calls, with the time spent computing them given by the area of each data point.

bundled together to make more efficient use of the hardware, comparable to that of a single much larger `GEMM` operation.

4.3   QuantumESPRESSO

Figure 1 shows the proportion of time that both the AUSURF112 and GRIR443 benchmarks spend in BLAS. These benchmarks demonstrate that applications can exhibit widely varying BLAS usage, which is highly dependent on the case being run. The proportion of time in BLAS at a scale of 32 nodes is a clear example of this, with AUSURF112 at 3.2% and GRIR443 at 21.9%—the lowest and highest fractions found in this study. Both of these benchmarks spend over

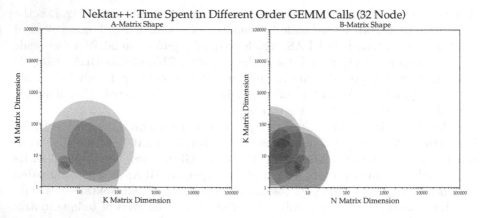

Fig. 3. The distribution of A and B matrix sizes in Nektar++ `DGEMM` calls, and the time spent computing them. These `DGEMM` calls operate on a large number of very small matrices.

90% of their time in BLAS computing double precision complex matrix multiply (ZGEMM) calls; the GRIR443 distribution of ZGEMM matrix sizes is shown in Fig. 4.

This figure shows that the GRIR443 benchmark spends the majority of its time computing roughly square ZGEMM matrices of size '1000 by 1000' up to '10,000 by 10,000'. These matrices are the largest found in the study, and explain the highest proportion of BLAS at 32 nodes in the study.

4.4   CASTEP

The results in Fig. 1 show that the majority of CASTEP's runtime is spent in BLAS for runs using up to 4 nodes, but beyond this, BLAS usage falls to 12.2% when using 32 nodes. Of this usage, 90% of the time CASTEP spends in BLAS operations is taken up by level-3 BLAS, and specifically, ZGEMM calls or complex double-precision matrix multiplications. There is a minority of DGEMM operations used in the 2 k-point 'al3×3' benchmark, although interestingly, when using CASTEP with special cases that have 1 k-point, the majority of CASTEP's BLAS usage becomes DGEMM operations. The distribution of matrix sizes that ZGEMM is called with is shown in Fig. 5.

This figure show that CASTEP spends a significant amount of time computing matrix multiplications with M and N dimensions of 100–1000, but with larger K dimensions of 1,000–10,000. This implies that CASTEP typically multiplies a square A matrix with a rectangular B matrix.

4.5   CP2K

Figure 1 shows that 45% of CP2K's run time is spent in BLAS routines when using 1–4 nodes, with this proportion reducing to 20% as we scale to 32 nodes. This is significantly different from the other periodic electronic structure code, CASTEP, which spends more time in BLAS at low node counts, and less time in higher node counts. Another key difference is shown in Table 2, which notes that 99% of CP2K's BLAS funtions are DGEMM or double-precision matrix multiplications. The distribution of matrix sizes that DGEMM is called with is shown in Fig. 6.

Considering the A matrix size distribution, we can see a distinct bimodal distribution with peaks around (25, 25) and (1000, 1000). This implies that CP2K spends a substantial proportion of time computing matrix multiplications with either very small or moderately sized A matrices. When considering the 'K by N' B matrix, it can be seen that the N dimension is nearly always less than or equal to 100, and the K dimension varies between 10–1000.

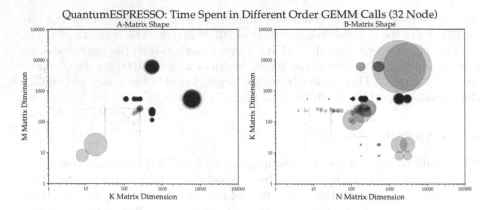

Fig. 4. The distribution of A and B matrix sizes in QuantumESPRESSO GRIR443 `ZGEMM` calls, and the time spent computing them. These `ZGEMM` calls operate on very large square matrices.

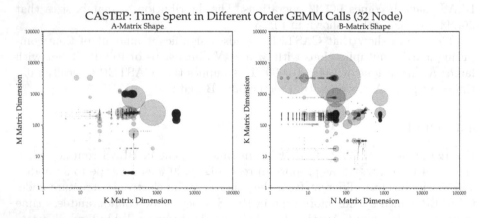

Fig. 5. The distribution of A and B matrix sizes in CASTEP `ZGEMM` calls, and the time spent computing them. The majority of usage is spent computing roughly square A matrices, with rectangular B matrices.

4.6   AlexNet

The BLAS profile we recorded from tracing the training stage of AlexNet shows that 0.1% of the runtime is spent computing BLAS, with all of the routines being `DGEMM` operations that multiply a '3 by 3' A matrix by a '3 by 3' B matrix. This is an unexpected result and leads us to believe that a significant amount of TensorFlow's linear algebra is either inlined or contained within custom BLAS implementations, beyond the reach of the tracing tool—see Subsect. 3.7.

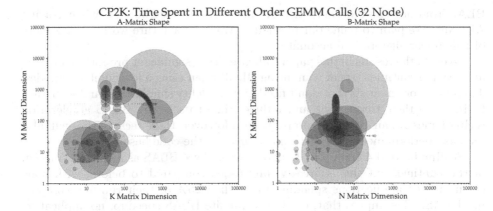

Fig. 6. The distribution of A and B matrix sizes in CP2K `DGEMM` calls, and the time spent computing them. A significant proportion of runtime is spent computing A matrices that are around '25 by 25' and '1000 by 1000' in size.

Table 2. BLAS Characteristics Summary

Application	Benchmark case	BLAS usage - 32 node	Constituent BLAS functions
CASTEP	al3×3–700 eV	12.2%	90% ZGEMM, 6% ZHERK
CP2K	H20–1024	19.8%	99% DGEMM
Nektar++	2DShockWave	20.5%	82% DGEMM, 17% DGEMV
QuantumESPRESSO	GRIR443	21.9%	98% ZGEMM
QuantumESPRESSO	AUSURF112	3.2%	92% ZGEMM. 5% ZGEMV

5 Conclusion

In this study, we have observed a diverse mix of new architectures being rapidly developed to accelerate linear algebra in codes—in direct response to the rise in popularity of deep learning. We have examined a range of the codes from the UK national HPC service, ARCHER, and provided the first dataset on how much each application is using BLAS. We have analysed this BLAS usage, and identified `GEMM` routines as being responsible for the majority of BLAS computation. Examining `GEMM` usage further, we have given a matrix size distribution for each application, which will be useful for chip manufacturers looking to design optimal vector widths and the size of matrix multiplication units.

The method demonstrated in this study is not infallible, and we note two areas in our work that could be improved. The first is highlighted by our trace profiles of the QuantumESPRESSO benchmarks, which show widely varying amounts of BLAS. Clearly, benchmark choice can have a great impact on the amount of BLAS used, although this can be mitigated by choosing a representative benchmark. The second limitation of this study is more subtle, and is a consequence of our chosen tracing tool. This tracer works by intercepting dynamic BLAS library calls, and therefore any inline linear algebra or custom

BLAS routines can't be detected by our tool, as was the case when tracing AlexNet. We plan to refine our method of tracing for future work to take more of this linear algebra into account.

Overall, the results in this paper indicate that a significant proportion of HPC application runtime is spent computing BLAS when using a low number of nodes. Therefore, for scientists that don't need higher fidelity simulations, and who want to increase their throughput and reduce 'time to science', BLAS acceleration technologies are an attractive proposition. Moreover, these technologies will also increase performance today, with no changes to the code base required.

Scaling beyond 4 and up to 32 nodes, we still see BLAS as a definite fraction of the runtime, but this is greatly diminished compared to before, with none of the tested applications spending more than 25% of their runtime computing BLAS. This implies that, even with infinite BLAS speedup, no application would perform more than $1.33\times$ faster. Given this result, one could assume that BLAS acclerator architectures are not significant in the forthcoming Exascale era, however, this is only a reflection on the current state of applications. In fact, these results illustrate an urgent need for adapting our application algorithms to make use of more BLAS, as we develop processors with more powerful and efficient linear algebra units.

Acknowledgment. This work used the Isambard UK National Tier-2 HPC Service, funded by the EPSRC (EP/P020224/1). We would like to thank Chris Goodyer (Arm) for his work on developing the Arm library tracing tool. We would also like to thank Andy Turner (EPCC), Filippo Spiga (NVIDIA), Phil Hasnip (CASTEP), and Spencer Sherman (Imperial College London) for their expertise on choosing benchmarks, and running each application.

References

1. NVIDIA A100 Tensor Core GPU Architecture: Unprecedented Acceleration At Every Scale (2020). https://www.nvidia.com/content/dam/en-zz/Solutions/Data-Center/nvidia-ampere-architecture-whitepaper.pdf
2. The x86 Advanced Matrix Extension (AMX) Brings Matrix Operations; To Debut with Sapphire Rapids (2020). https://fuse.wikichip.org/news/3600/the-x86-advanced-matrix-extension-amx-brings-matrix-operations-to-debut-with-sapphire-rapids/
3. Dongarra, J., Hammarling, S., Higham, N., Relton, S., Valero-Lara, P., Zounon, M.: The design and performance of batched BLAS on modern high-performance computing systems. Proc. Comput. Sci. **108**, 495–504 (2017). https://doi.org/10.1016/j.procs.2017.05.138
4. Goodfellow, I., Bengio, Y., Courville, A.: Deep Learning. MIT Press (2016). http://www.deeplearningbook.org
5. Gustafson, J.L.: Amdahl's Law. In: Padua, D. (ed.) Encyclopedia of Parallel Computing, vol. xx, pp. 53–60. Springer, US, Boston, MA (2011). https://doi.org/10.1007/978-07-09766-4_77
6. Hennessy, J.L., Patterson, D.A.: A new golden age for computer architecture. Commun. ACM **62**(2), 48–60 (2019). https://doi.org/10.1145/3282307

7. Krizhevsky, A., Sutskever, I., Hinton, G.E.: Imagenet classification with deep convolutional neural networks. In: Proceedings of the 25th International Conference on Neural Information Processing Systems, NIPS'12, vol. 1, pp. 1097–1105. Curran Associates Inc., Red Hook, NY, USA (2012)

8. Laguna, I., Marshall, R., Mohror, K., Ruefenacht, M., Skjellum, A., Sultana, N.: A large-scale study of MPI usage in open-source HPC applications. In: Proceedings of the International Conference for High Performance Computing, Networking, Storage and Analysis, SC'19. Association for Computing Machinery, New York, NY, USA (2019). https://doi.org/10.1145/3295500.3356176

9. Markidis, S., Chien, S.W.D., Laure, E., Peng, I.B., Vetter, J.S.: NVIDIA tensor core programmability, performance and precision. In: 2018 IEEE International Parallel and Distributed Processing Symposium Workshops (IPDPSW) (2018). https://doi.org/10.1109/IPDPSW.2018.00091

10. Stephens, N., et al.: The ARM scalable vector extension. IEEE Micro **37**(2), 26–39 (2017). https://doi.org/10.1109/mm.2017.35

11. Turner, A.: UK National HPC Benchmarks. Technical report, EPCC (2016)

12. Turner, A., McIntosh-Smith, S.: A survey of application memory usage on a national supercomputer: an analysis of memory requirements on archer. In: PMBS@SC (2017)

13. Turner, A., Sloan-Murphy, D., Sivalingam, K., Richardson, H., Kunkel, J.M.: Analysis of parallel I/O use on the UK national supercomputing service, ARCHER using Cray LASSi and EPCC SAFE. ArXiv:abs/1906.03891 (2019)

System Software: Data Infrastructure and Life Cycle

A Systemic Approach to Facilitating Reproducibility via Federated, End-to-End Data Management

Dale Stansberry[✉], Suhas Somnath, Gregory Shutt, and Mallikarjun Shankar

Oak Ridge National Laboratory, Oak Ridge, TN 37831, USA
stansberrydv@ornl.gov

Abstract. Advances in computing infrastructure and instrumentation have accelerated scientific discovery in addition to exploding the data volumes. Unfortunately, the unavailability of equally advanced data management infrastructure has led to ad hoc practices that diminish scientific productivity and exacerbate the reproducibility crisis. We discuss a system-wide solution that supports management needs at every stage of the data lifecycle. At the center of this system is DataFed - a general purpose, scientific data management system that addresses these challenges by federating data storage across facilities with central metadata and provenance management - providing simple and uniform data discovery, access, and collaboration capabilities. At the edge is a Data Gateway that captures raw data and context from experiments (even when performed on off-network instruments) into DataFed. DataFed can be integrated into analytics platforms to easily, correctly, and reliably work with datasets to improve reproducibility of such workloads. We believe that this system can significantly alleviate the burden of data management and improve compliance with the Findable Accessible Interoperable, Reusable (FAIR) data principles, thereby improving scientific productivity and rigor.

1 Introduction

Scientific research has been facing a reproducibility crisis [5,6,14]. One important and surmountable factor is the typical absence of sufficient information (data, metadata, provenance, workflow, software, etc.) associated with reports on scientific discoveries that are critically important for reproducing the research [20]. Software containers and modern workflow softwares have proven to be reasonably successful in facilitating reproducibility with respect to the software stack

D. Stansberry et al.—Contributed Equally

This manuscript has been co-authored by UT-Battelle, LLC, under contract DE-AC05-00OR22725 with the US Department of Energy (DOE). The US government retains and the publisher, by accepting the article for publication, acknowledges that the US government retains a nonexclusive, paid-up, irrevocable, worldwide license to publish or reproduce the published form of this manuscript, or allow others to do so, for US government purposes. DOE will provide public access to these results of federally sponsored research in accordance with the DOE Public Access Plan (http://energy.gov/downloads/doe-public-access-plan).

J. Nichols et al. (Eds.): SMC 2020, CCIS 1315, pp. 83–98, 2020.
https://doi.org/10.1007/978-3-030-63393-6_6

[7,8,19,22]. However, readily available, user-friendly, and comprehensive tools to access, search, share, organize, curate, publish, and otherwise manage scientific data remain a long-standing need. This is also an urgent need since the time spent on data management is projected to rise exponentially [11,17] due to the explosion in scientific data [9,15]. Despite the dearth of data management tools, increased globalization of scientific research, and the need to publicly share data [21], facilities and research groups are at best grappling with the data challenges individually/independently or are typically resorting to ad-hoc methods. These ad-hoc practices not only result in loss/poor quality of data and metadata but also a substantial decrease in scientific productivity.

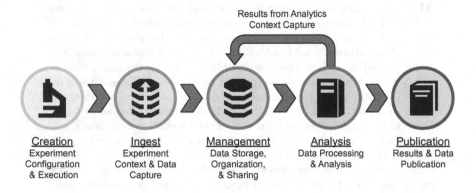

Fig. 1. Data lifecycle for reproducibility

Figure 1 illustrates the lifecycle of scientific data. Traditionally, sub-optimal and ad-hoc data management practices occur throughout the lifecycle. Research investigations start with the design, configuration, and execution of experiments which produce scientific data. Most experiments (simulations/observations, etc.) produce metadata that capture the context of the experiment in addition to the raw data itself. At the *ingest* step - since the context regarding experiments is often not comprehensively captured at the source (instrument, simulation module, etc.), researchers manually capture the remaining context (e.g., sample ID, etc.) in physical or electronic lab notebooks in a non-standardized, ad-hoc, and error-prone manner. However, these metadata are rarely collated and therefore do not support the data when necessary.

Moving on to the *management* step - when data is generated off-network (e.g., some scientific instruments), scientists resort to collecting and transporting measurement data using portable storage drives. The collected data and metadata are often stored in traditional file-systems which only provide primitive data sharing, search, and management capabilities. Since data in file-systems are discoverable largely based on file names and paths, most researchers resort to embedding key metadata into the file paths. Since each user stores and represents data and metadata in unique ways, such information collected by users is often usable only by the user who collected the data thereby exacerbating the reproducibility crisis. Desired data are still exchanged using emails, shared folders, and portable storage drives, each having their own set of limitations. Challenges in sharing and reusing data are further exacerbated by the diversity in the representation (schema and ontology for data and metadata), storage (file formats and data repositories), availability (proprietary/open), dimensionality (1D signals to multidimensional hypercubes) and semantics of scientific data and metadata within and across scientific domains.

At the *analysis* step - results from data processing and analyses are stored back into the file-systems, often without capturing the complete context of the analyses, thereby inheriting many of the aforementioned problems. Finally, at the *publish* step - scientific discoveries are reported/published often without the supporting data. Even when data directly used in the publication are published, data deemed redundant or unimportant for the primary investigation are left untracked, unused, and unpublished despite their latent value [24] leading to the so-called "dark data" [13] problem. When data are published, they are often not discoverable since the scientific metadata associated with the data are not exposed to search engines. As a result of such practices and challenges, it is exceedingly challenging to comply with the Findable Accessible, Interoperable, and Reusable (FAIR) data principles, which were proposed to facilitate open, collaborative, and reproducible scientific research [27].

Improving reproducibility in science through better data practices therefore necessitates the use of comprehensive scientific data management tools that can effectively support scientific data throughout the data lifecycle from *ingest* to *publishing*. Revisiting Fig. 1; using data management tools, researchers will be able to *ingest* - comprehensively capture context/metadata along with raw data from experiments, *manage* - intuitively and easily share, search for, organize, transport data, *analyze* - capture secondary data products from analyses and visualization along with context and provenance between products, and *publish* data for reuse in the broader scientific community. Importantly, other researchers should be able to easily find such published data and use the rich metadata and provenance associated with the data to reproduce the original results. Though there are several tools [3] that address specific data management challenges, there are very few flexible, system-wide solutions that support every stage of the data lifecycle for all scientific domains [1,4,12,18,23,25]. Limitations of existing solutions will be discussed later in appropriate sections.

2   Systemic Approach to Reproducibility

To facilitate reproducibility in science, we are proposing a systemic solution that will emphasize and directly support the critical data lifecycle phases of *ingest, management*, and *analysis*, shown in Fig. 1, that are often overlooked or poorly executed. It is within these data lifecycle phases that full data provenance and rich domain-specific metadata can be captured and utilized to enhance the scientific context needed to ultimately reproduce experimental or computational results. The proposed solution includes components, services, and communication protocols that would be deployed across facilities in order to create a common, FAIR-principled "data federation" - enabling simple, uniform, and

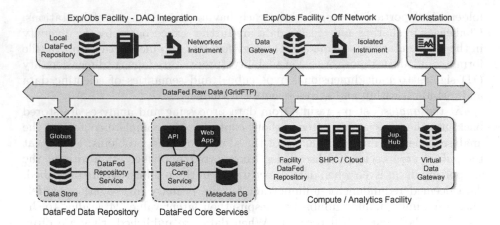

Fig. 2. Proposed data system architecture

performant data access, management, analysis, and collaboration from anywhere within, or across, this federation.

Figure 2 shows a conceptual view of this system where experimental and/or observation facilities are connected to compute and/or analytics resources via the primary component of the system: a distributed scientific data management system (SDMS) called "DataFed" [26]. The key concepts of DataFed are distributed raw data storage, centralized metadata and provenance management, and performant data transfer. DataFed primarily addresses the needs of the *management* component of the data lifecycle phase; however, two additional components, the "Data Gateway" and "JupyterHub" (as an example), address the needs of the *ingest* and *analytics* phases of the data lifecycle respectively.

In addition to metadata and provenance management, the DataFed central, or "core", services, shown in Fig. 2, provide system-wide command and control for raw data access-control and transfer. This is implemented using DataFed-specific application programming interfaces (APIs) and protocols that are used by other system components, such as the Data Gateway, integrated instrument data acquisition (DAQ) systems, or even user compute jobs at high performance computing (HPC) facilities, in order to ingest, locate, access, or share data, on behalf of scientific users. Upon data ingestion, raw data is transferred to DataFed "Data Repositories", which are managed data stores, and, unlike local file systems, these data repositories are connected to the DataFed data network and managed by DataFed core services. DataFed data repositories are not required to be collocated with instruments or facilities, and can be centrally located and/or shared by multiple facilities. An expanded view of a DataFed data repository is shown at the bottom left of Fig. 2.

Experimental and/or observational facilities can be directly integrated with DataFed, such as through modification or extension of existing data acquisition or instrument control systems (top-left of Fig. 2). For network-isolated instruments (top-right of Fig. 2), the "Data Gateway" appliance is available to both provide network buffering as well as easy to use data ingest and context capture services. The Data Gateway can also be deployed virtually, as shown in the "Compute/Analytics Facility" in Fig. 2, to provide general data ingest support for users without access to an DataFed integrated facility.

Data analytics platforms deployed within Compute/Analytics facilities could provide data analytics and visualization capabilities for one or more facilities. We use Jupyter Notebooks [16] and JupyterHub [10] (multi-user) as an example since they capture context regarding analytics for reproducibility. Appropriate DataFed commands could be incorporated within analytics scripts to download/stage data, capture context regarding the analytics, and push results data back to DataFed for management later. By comprehensively capturing the software stack in containers, analytics related context within Jupyter Notebooks, data ingest operations via Data Gateway, and repeatable data operations using DataFed, analysis workloads can be more easily reproduced.

While the described system is intended to address specific aspects of the reproducibility crisis, it is vital that it also be easy for users to learn, adopt, and use. Moreover, use of this system should improve research productivity, not hinder it. The components of this system have been designed with this philosophy in mind - resulting in features and capabilities that directly reduce complexity, improve productivity, and help ensure correctness of data handling when compared to ad-hoc solutions. The individual components of this system are described in detail in Sects. 3, 4 and 5 below. For general use cases as well as examples of how this system would be useful for modeling, simulations, experiments, and data analytics, refer to Sect. 6.

2.1 Development and Deployment

The full system solution described above is currently in the design and prototyping stage of development. However, two of the components of the system, the Data Gateway and DataFed, have been partially implemented and deployed at ORNL within the Center for Nanophase Materials Science (CNMS) and the Compute and Data Environment for Science (CADES) facilities, respectively. DataFed is currently deployed as an alpha-release production service. One instance of the Data Gateway has been deployed for scanning probe microscopes at CNMS as a proof-of-concept and is currently capable of authenticating users at the instruments, capturing metadata and transmitting data and metadata to a remote data repository. A dedicated CNMS DataFed repository has been deployed within CADES, and a data repository within the OLCF is planned. In the future, integration with the SNS, and HFIR is anticipated, and JupyterHub services and a Virtual Data Gateway would be deployed within CADES. Additional funding is being actively pursued in order to complete development and deployment at ORNL.

3   Data Ingest

The need for DataFed to serve the broader scientific community in a domain-agnostic manner necessitates a tool that can ingest data and metadata while accommodating the high heterogeneity in data generation sources and data types across scientific domains, especially from off-network data producers. Some solutions do indeed exist that purport to solve some of the above data infrastructure challenges [4,18,23]. However, these solutions are typically monolithic in nature and ingest data into a built-in SDMS with limited configurability/features with regards to data storage, data analytics/post-processing, and metadata capture and indexing. Furthermore, these capabilities are implemented using technologies that are not scalable to accommodate the needs of highly heterogeneous and large datasets. Importantly, these solutions result in disjoint silos of data that do not and cannot exchange data elsewhere in the world. Therefore, we are developing a "Data Gateway" to facilitate and streamline data ingest and metadata capture into DataFed.

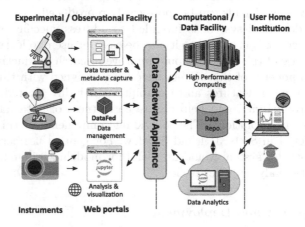

Fig. 3. Overview of the data gateway

Often, instrumentation software are incompatible with the latest security patches or operating system updates. Consequently, such instrumentation computers are often kept off the network to avoid security vulnerabilities. Yet, there is a need to capture data and metadata from such instruments. For such instruments, we would deploy a Data Gateway "appliance", as shown in Fig. 3, that would consist of both a server (physical hardware) and a software stack (deployed within the server) that provides local data ingest services as well as configurable internet routing to expose remote web services such as the DataFed web portal and an analytics service such as JupyterHub. The Data Gateway consists of a suite of web-based data services pre-installed on a server, with local storage, that would be deployed within a given experiment facility and networked with the facility's individual scientific instrument control workstations. This configuration allows the scientific user at each instrument to access the Data Gateway services while maintaining general network isolation of the instruments (which may be required for IT security purposes). Due to this network isolation, scientists operating scientific instruments cannot directly access data stored in DataFed;

therefore, the Data Gateway acts as a data "buffer" between the instrument control workstation and DataFed, providing temporary data storage for both data uploads and downloads. While data upload is essential for the data ingest processes, data downloads may be needed in order to analyze data using proprietary software that may only be available on an instrument control workstation due to licensing or operating system constraints.

The Data Gateway's data services are configurable for both specific instruments and specific experiments and include data upload/download, metadata capture and extraction, and optional data preprocessing. The Data Gateway provides a graphical web-based "companion application" that can be used from an instrument control workstation while conducting an experiment or measurement - allowing users to easily upload resulting data files and capture associated metadata. Metadata can be captured using configurable input forms or by extracting metadata automatically from data files, or using a combination of both approaches. The API supporting the "companion application" could be exposed to allow instruments to push data and metadata from instruments without the need for humans in the loop.

Users may also opt to utilize available data preprocessing methods, such as file format translations or data reduction, prior to the transfer of the data into DataFed. Such data preprocessing code would be encapsulated in containers to simplify isolation, development and maintenance of the core Data Gateway software stack from the data preprocessing code. Additionally, the use of containers would provide freedom to for domain-scientists to write pre-processing codes in the language and using the software stack they are comfortable with. These metadata extraction and data preprocessing codes would be part of a centralized and vetted library of codes that could be shared across multiple physical and "virtual" Data Gateways. We are in the process of defining standards and an API that would be used for the containers to interact with the Data Gateway. Subsequently, we will start to populate and solicit such codes or references to containers in a public repository at https://github.com/ORNL/MD_Extractors. Additionally, we will provide documentation on the best practices for developing such data preprocessing codes that will lower the barrier for researchers to develop and provide their own codes. Domain scientists would need to develop these codes as they integrate new kinds of simulation codes/instruments with the Data Gateway and update codes only when they need to modify the data processing or account for changes in the simulation code/instrumentation.

For fully networked facilities, full automation of data and metadata capture can be achieved through DataFed's application programming interfaces (APIs) through a one-time integration into existing instrument control systems, data acquisition systems, data pipelines, job scripts, and/or workflows. Data preprocessing and metadata extraction codes from the library mentioned above could be reused optionally. Once this integration effort is complete, users need only authenticate prior to running an experiment or utilizing a resource, and data and metadata will be captured and ingested into DataFed with no further user interaction. Optionally, users may use DataFed to install local security

credentials to avoid the need for subsequent authentication. For large user facilities, direct DataFed integration represents the ideal configuration as all relevant scientific context (instrument configuration, experiment/simulation parameters, run information, etc.) will be automatically captured and raw data will be
ingested into DataFed with no additional burden on end-users.

Users outside such facilities that utilize the Data Gateway appliance or direct
DataFed integration, such as those running simulations or analytics within a
compute facility, can also utilize DataFed through one of two options: 1) users
may use the DataFed command-line-interface (CLI) to add DataFed commands
to their job scripts, or 2) a Data Gateway can be installed as a "virtual" service
within a facility to provide generalized, web-based data ingest services to all
users of the facility. Though, much of the software stack developed for the Data
Gateway appliance can be readily deployed for "virtual" Data Gateways, users
would need to develop metadata extraction and data-preprocessing codes specific
to their needs if they are not available in the shared repository of vetted codes.

4   Data Management

A SDMS represents a type of laboratory informatics software for capturing, cataloging, and sharing heterogeneous scientific data. It is common to find products
that combine SDMS features with other processing capabilities such as data
distribution, workflow management, or even instrument interfacing and control.
While there are many available SDMS or SDMS-like products available for use
[12,25], these systems are based on older, non-scalable user authentication technologies and tend to be more applicable to the fixed data distribution needs of
large-scale, domain-specific research efforts. Thus, there is still a need for scalable
and user-friendly data management tools that work across scientific domains and
profoundly empower scientists.

An SDMS suitable for use in open, cross-facility, and domain-agnostic scientific research contexts must be able to scale with the volumes and varieties of data
being generated from research conducted at large scale experiment, compute, and
analytics facilities. It must be able to function across organizational boundaries
and efficiently cope with thousands of users, including both resident staff scientists and visiting researchers. It must be able to function within, and across,
many different operating environments with varying security policies, ranging
from individual scientific instruments to leadership class high-performance computing systems. And, importantly, it must offer simple and uniform interfaces to
minimize the need for training and encourage adoption by non-technical users.

Based on these requirements and a lack of an appropriate existing solution,
the decision was made to design and develop a new SDMS that would better
match the needs of the scientific research community within DOE laboratories.
This system is called "DataFed" with the name being derived from the approach
of federating data management across existing organizations and facilities to
provide flexibility, scalability, and cross-facility data access.

4.1   DataFed Overview

DataFed is a *federated* scientific data management system that differs from existing SDMS products by offering a scalable, cross-facility data management solution with decentralized raw data storage and high performance, secure, and reliable data movement. DataFed is able to scale-out through its ability to incorporate additional organizations/facilities, users, and shared storage resources without the typical burdens and bottlenecks associated with centrally administered systems that rely on virtual organizations (VO) and/or manually deployed user security credentials. Individual users, facilities, or entire organizations may join or leave the DataFed federation at any time without requiring any administrative actions on the part of other federation members. DataFed uses the scalable GridFTP protocol (via Globus [2,3]) for all raw data transfers and supports integration with high performance storage systems and networks. This ensures optimal and reliable handling of very large data files (up to petabyte scale).

DataFed provides a centralized orchestration service that integrates and manages remote raw data storage resources (aka "data repositories") physically housed within member facilities; however, while DataFed manages the raw data files in these repositories, individual facilities own the storage hardware and retain full administrative control over data policies and user/project allocations. DataFed data repositories may be configured to use most types of data storage systems including low-cost commodity disk-backed systems, fast SSD systems, and high-reliability archival storage systems. Facilities may opt to provide more data robustness by implementing periodic back-ups of these storage systems, or by utilizing data replication to prevent data loss from hardware failures. Ideally, facilities would integrate the management of DataFed allocations (assignment, capacity, durability, accounting, etc.) into existing user and project management systems and funding sources. The storage properties and policies of a facility's repositories are visible to users via DataFed, and users can easily migrate data between different facilities, or repositories within a facility, based on availability, locality, reliability, or performance requirements. Because DataFed utilizes Globus federated identity technology for user accounts and fine-grained access control, individual facilities no longer need to manually manage user security credentials or maintain complex and/or constantly changing cross-organizational access control lists.

When data is initially stored in a data repository, DataFed captures and retains any associated metadata and provenance (along with tracking information) in a centralized database. The use of a centralized metadata database does not significantly impact system scalability due to the relatively small storage requirements of metadata (on the order of 10's of kilobytes) when compared to raw data files (ranging from megabytes to terabytes, or more). Access to raw data stored in a DataFed data repository is controlled (managed) by DataFed - not the local storage system. By preventing users or processes from directly accessing or modifying raw files within a repository, DataFed ensures that associated tracking information and metadata remains synchronized with raw data and eliminates potential ambiguity regarding which file should be accessed (a common problem when using unmanaged file sharing technologies for large collections of data). The central DataFed database would be deployed on a reliable and fast storage system (i.e. RAID) and would be regularly backed-up.

The raw data stored in a data repository is private and secure by default - meaning only the owner, or creator, of the data can access it, and data transfers are encrypted. Data owners may choose to share their data with other DataFed users or groups regardless of organizational affiliation through DataFed's own fine-grained access control system. Specific permissions such as read, write, create, or even administrative control can be granted; Moreover, by using DataFed's hierarchical data organization features, these permissions can be easily granted and managed for large collections of data. DataFed also provides a data project feature to facilitate teams of collaborators working with semi-private or collectively owned data. Due to the need for substantial compliance testing for higher-level data security policies, DataFed currently only supports open research.

DataFed creates a central database data record for each raw data file stored in a data repository in order to track and control access to the raw data and to store and index associated metadata and provenance relationships. A variety of built-in metadata fields are supported for data records (such as title, description, and keywords), but, importantly, domain-specific structured metadata may also be stored with a data record. Retaining and indexing all of this information within a central database enables powerful data organization, discovery, and dissemination capabilities that will be discussed later in this paper. DataFed does not support incremental versioning of metadata or raw data, but provenance-based, full-record versioning is supported by adding "deprecation" dependencies between new and old versions of a record.

4.2   FAIR Compliance

DataFed was designed to be as FAIR compliant as reasonably possible within the context of both pre-publication "working" data and "static" data that is published from DataFed. DataFed specifically addresses FAIR principles as follows:

- **Findable** - DataFed assigns persistent system-unique identifiers to every data record. DataFed also captures and indexes rich metadata that can be used to query for matching records.
- **Accessible** - DataFed identifiers can be used to locate and access associated data, and DataFed enforces authentication and authorization for all access. The protocol for access to data within DataFed is open and easily implementable (implementations are provided for Python and C++).
- **Interoperable** - DataFed utilizes a simple JSON representation for metadata with optional schema support; however, external metadata references are not directly supported.
- **Reusable** - DataFed represents domain-specific metadata and provenance in a uniform manner in addition to facilitating keywords and tags which would allow users to discover and reuse data shared by others for similar or other novel applications.

4.3   Data Organization, Sharing, and Dissemination

While FAIR compliance is an important aspect of DataFed, DataFed includes a number of features that extend beyond the scope of FAIR to more actively assist researchers in complex collaborative contexts. For example, DataFed can significantly assist with the challenges of managing and utilizing large volumes of data within the complex environments associated with high performance computing, cross-facility workflows, and data processing pipelines. In these situations, being able to locate a single data record is less important than being able to stage specific collections or subsets of data for processing within a compute environment. In addition, the ability for an upstream researcher (data producer) to automatically and precisely coordinate with and/or notify downstream collaborators (data consumers) is vital.

DataFed provides named data "collections" which provide a basic form of hierarchical data organization that resembles directories in a file system; however, unlike directories, data is only linked within collections rather than being "owned" by the collection. This allows data to be organized in multiple parallel collection hierarchies, if desired, without duplication of data. Both individual data records and collections can be shared by setting fine-grained permissions for specific users or groups of users. Collections can be assigned a topic and made public, which results in such collections being internally "published" as a DataFed catalog where they can be discovered and accessed by all DataFed users.

As an alternative to collections, DataFed also provides dynamic views of data records based on saved queries. The built-in data search capability allows users to search private, shared, and public data records by identifier, alias, keyword, words and phrases, tags, and arbitrary metadata expressions. For example, a view could be created to show only data records that were most recently created or updated by a collaborator, or records that include specific values or ranges in domain-specific metadata, such as sample type, temperature range, or experiment category.

As an aide in maintaining data awareness, users with appropriate access may opt to subscribe to specific data records and collections such that they will receive notifications whenever certain events occur, such as data or metadata updates, record creation, deprecation, and deletion, or changes in provenance information. If issues arise concerning specific shared data records or collections, users may choose to create linked annotations that will notify and convey additional information, warnings, and/or questions to all concerned parties (i.e. data producers and downstream data consumers via subscription or provenance links). These annotations function similarly to typical document review systems and are preferred over external methods (such as email) as they remain linked and visible on the subject record or collection within DataFed.

5   Data Analytics

Jupyter Notebooks have emerged as a popular framework for data processing and analytics workloads [16]. These notebooks not only contain the code to process information but can also contain rich markdown to provide contextual information such as equations, and provide a rich narrative using static or interactive visualizations in-line with code snippets. Users can add a preamble to the notebook to check and install necessary software or encapsulate the notebook, input data (when data is small) and necessary software stack in software containers [19] to facilitate reproducibility of data analytics workloads. A deployment of JupyterHub [10] would facilitate reproducible data analytics for several researchers. DataFed can further improve the reproducibility of analytics workloads through its ability to address specific datasets, stage multiple datasets (potentially located in multiple repositories) at specific file-systems, and capture the context (analytics algorithm parameters) and results (data) of data analytics runs systematically. Users could also share unpublished/private scripts or notebooks via DataFed.

6   Scientific Applications

The many features of the proposed system substantially alleviate data management burdens and improve scientific productivity. Many of the benefits of the system are shared for all modes of scientific discovery and are discussed below. Common use-cases and benefits specific to each modes of scientific discovery are discussed in dedicated subsections below.

DataFed facilitates capture of metadata and provenance, thereby obviating the need for scientists to embed selected metadata into file paths. Using DataFed, users could perform complex searches for data based on the rich domain-specific metadata over multiple repositories that span multiple facilities or organizations. By standardizing metadata representation, DataFed enables users to find and reuse data owned by themselves, others, or available publicly and also facilitates multi-disciplinary and multi-modal scientific (experiments, observations, simulation, analytics) collaborations. However, note that neither the Data Gateway, nor DataFed mandates the use of specific file formats for the raw data or schemas for metadata.

DataFed's use of Globus allows users to transport data quickly and seamlessly between repositories or facilities without concerning themselves about navigating complex security restrictions or the kind of file-system supporting these repositories. DataFed obviates the use portable storage drives. The barriers to publish data (downloading/uploading data, entering metadata again, repeating the process for multiple datasets) is also substantially mitigated since DataFed can integrate with data publishing services and repositories. Users would only need to switch a setting on the individual record or a large collection from private to published. Similarly, users can also accrue citations by publishing otherwise "dark data".

6.1 Modelling and Simulations

Researchers performing modelling or simulations could incorporate DataFed instructions within their scripts for reliable data staging and capture that:

1. Download input file from DataFed
2. Run modeling/simulation codes
3. Capture metadata
4. Put resulting data and metadata into DataFed repository

In step 1, researchers can use DataFed to unambiguously identify input files or other required files and reliably stage such files at the remote file-systems even if the data records are in repositories located in other institutions. In step 3, researchers can extract metadata from their input scripts and/or the results of the simulations by leveraging the repository of vetted codes for data pre-processing. Once the raw data (from the simulation) and metadata are available, researchers can push this information to a DataFed repository in step 4. Via 1–2 simple commands using the DataFed client, the researchers can create a DataFed record, add the metadata, and push the raw data. Optionally, links to related data records such as input files could be added to capture the complete provenance of the experiment. The same methodology would also accommodate common scenarios where several simulations are run as a function of one or more parameters. Once DataFed commands are integrated into the simulation script, the same/similar commands could be reused for a given type of simulation code.

Through consistent, correct, and careful handling of data, DataFed facilitates traceability and reproducibility of experiments. Once information from simulation runs is captured in DataFed, researchers can search for, share, organize, and move their data. Such consistent collection of data with rich metadata can enable scientists to build large collections of data that would be necessary to train surrogate models using machine learning (ML) or deep learning (DL). These surrogate models could replace expensive kernels of simulations, thereby accelerating the exploration of large and multidimensional parameter spaces.

6.2 Observations and Experiments

Unlike modeling and simulation workflows, the data handling processes for observational sciences are handled almost entirely by the Data Gateway. Researchers working on off-network scientific instruments could use the "companion web application" on the Data Gateway appliance to seamlessly capture the raw data and metadata from experiments and add them to a DataFed repository as experiments are being conducted. Scientific instruments used predominantly for conducting automated and long-running (days, weeks, or months) experiments/observations could instead be configured to automatically and periodically push data and metadata to DataFed repositories via the Data Gateway without the need for a human to manually upload data while at the instrument. This would allow researchers to analyze the data stream collecting in a DataFed repository while working away from the instrument. Similarly, future iterations of the Data Gateway could potentially facilitate instrument control. The burden for extracting and standardizing metadata when pushing data into DataFed would also be diminished if researchers use the vetted set of codes for automated data-preprocessing at the Data Gateway.

Researchers could search, organize, share, and manage data with their collaborators via DataFed and use a data analytics platform like JupyterHub to analyze data in DataFed repositories even while operating the off-network instruments using the Data Gateway. Clearly, the proposed system dramatically simplifies the processes of capturing metadata, standardizing data formats, and collecting data in readily accessible and well connected data repositories. In addition, the data management capabilities offered by the proposed system are substantially superior to file explorers on personal computers.

6.3 Data Analytics

As discussed above, the proposed system is a conducive platform for researchers from multiple disciplines and working on disparate modes of scientific discovery to collaboratively assemble large collections of richly annotated datasets that are required for ML/DL applications. Similar to modeling and simulation workflows, data analytics applications could benefit immensely by incorporating a few DataFed commands into the scripts or Jupyter notebooks that:

1. Identify data records or collections of interest
2. Get datasets from DataFed repositories
3. Run data analytics application
4. Capture metadata context from analytics
5. Put resulting data and metadata into DataFed repository
6. Establish provenance

In step 1, researchers could optionally use the DataFed's search capability to identify collections and/or datasets of interest for the data analytics application. In step 2, researchers could stage large collections of datasets, that may potentially be spread over multiple institutions in multiple repositories, with a single 'get' command. After performing data analytics, researchers could capture metadata (analytics software version, algorithm identifier, algorithmic parameters, etc.) that are typically available within the data analytics script or notebook in step 4. In step 5, results such a weights for ML/DL models, model inference results, plots, etc. could all be captured as new data records as necessary and enriched with the collected metadata. Finally, the relationship between the results and the source dataset or collection could be captured via the provenance capability in DataFed in step 6. Thus, DataFed can facilitate traceability and reproducibility even in data analytics workflows through comprehensive and unambiguous data handling and management.

7 Conclusions

We presented a system architecture aimed at significantly alleviating the burden of data management, improving scientific productivity, facilitating compliance with FAIR data principles, lowering the barrier to cross-facility and collaborative research, and improving scientific rigor in general. Each component of the system is specifically designed to support the needs of each state of the data lifecycle past data acquisition. DataFed - a general purpose and domain-agnostic SDMS forms the backbone of this system and it is supported by the Data Gateway to capture raw data and context from experiments into DataFed. Optional components include a data analytics platform, such as a JupyterHub server, or other computational workflow software that can work with DataFed, software containers, and the Data Gateway to facilitate reproducible analytics workloads.

The Data Gateway's modular design allows it to be readily deployed for different scientific domains to comprehensively, swiftly, and seamlessly capture data and metadata, especially from off-network instruments, in a consistent, automated and repeatable manner. DataFed provides users with a logical view of data that abstracts routine nuances of data storage and facilitates capture and enrichment of scientific metadata and provenance associated with the raw data. DataFed users benefit from powerful data organization, search, sharing, and discovery capabilities. DataFed enables users to easily, correctly, repeatably, and reliably work with datasets within appropriate compute or analytic contexts to facilitate reproducible research. We are in the process of deploying the broader data management system described in this paper at select facilities at ORNL. We welcome interested readers to use DataFed at https://datafed.ornl.gov and get in touch with the authors for integrating the proposed system with their group/facility.

Acknowledgments. This research used resources of the Oak Ridge Leadership Computing Facility (OLCF) and of the Compute and Data Environment for Science (CADES) at the Oak Ridge National Laboratory, which is supported by the Office of Science of the U.S. Department of Energy under Contract No. DE-AC05-00OR22725.

References

1. Allan, C., et al.: Omero: flexible, model-driven data management for experimental biology. Nat. Methods **9**(3), 245 (2012)
2. Allcock, W.: GridFTP: protocol extensions to ftp for the grid (2003). http://www.ggf.org/documents/GFD.20.pdf
3. Allcock, W., Bresnahan, J., Kettimuthu, R., Link, M., Dumitrescu, C., Raicu, I., Foster, I.: The globus striped GridFTP framework and server. In: Proceedings of the 2005 ACM/IEEE Conference on Supercomputing, p. 54. IEEE Computer Society (2005)
4. Arkin, A.P., et al.: The DOE systems biology knowledgebase (KBase). BioRxiv, p. 096354 (2016)
5. Baker, M.: 1,500 scientists lift the lid on reproducibility (2016)
6. Baker, M.: Biotech giant posts negative results. Nature **530**(7589), 141–141 (2016)
7. Bartusch, F., Hanussek, M., Krüger, J., Kohlbacher, O.: Reproducible scientific workflows for high performance and cloud computing. In: 2019 19th IEEE/ACM International Symposium on Cluster, Cloud and Grid Computing (CCGRID), pp. 161–164 (2019)

8. Beaulieu-Jones, B.K., Greene, C.S.: Reproducibility of computational workflows is automated using continuous analysis. Nat. Biotechnol. **35**(4), 342–346 (2017)
9. Blair, J., et al. High performance data management and analysis for tomography. In: Developments in X-Ray Tomography IX, vol. 9212, p. 92121G. International Society for Optics and Photonics (2014)
10. Fernández, L., Hagenrud, H., Zupanc, B., Laface, E., Korhonen, T., Andersson, R.: Jupyterhub at the ESS. An interactive python computing environment for scientists and engineers (2016)
11. Furche, T., Gottlob, G., Libkin, L., Orsi, G., Paton, N.W.: Data wrangling for big data: challenges and opportunities. In: EDBT, vol. 16, pp. 473–478 (2016)
12. Garonne, V., et al.: Rucio-the next generation of large scale distributed system for atlas data management. J. Phys: Conf. Ser. **513**, 042021 (2014). IOP Publishing
13. Heidorn, P.B.: Shedding light on the dark data in the long tail of science. Libr. Trends **57**(2), 280–299 (2008)
14. Hutson, M.: Artificial intelligence faces reproducibility crisis (2018)
15. Kalinin, S.V., et al. Big, deep, and smart data in scanning probe microscopy. ACS Nano, pp. 9068–9086 (2016)
16. Kluyver, T., et al.: Jupyter notebooks-a publishing format for reproducible computational workflows. In: ELPUB, pp. 87–90 (2016)
17. Marder, K., Patera, A., Astolfo A., Schneider, M., Weber, B., Stampanoni, M.: Investigating the microvessel architecture of the mouse brain: an approach for measuring, stitching, and analyzing 50 teravoxels of data. In: 12th International Conference on Synchrotron Radiation Instrumentation, p. 73. AIP (2015)
18. Marini, L., et al.: Clowder: open source data management for long tail data. In: Proceedings of the Practice and Experience on Advanced Research Computing, p. 40. ACM (2018)
19. Merkel, D.: Docker: lightweight linux containers for consistent development and deployment. Linux J. **2014**(239), 2 (2014)
20. Miyakawa, T.: No raw data, no science: another possible source of the reproducibility crisis (2020)
21. Nosek, B.A., et al.: Promoting an open research culture. Science **348**(6242), 1422–1425 (2015)
22. Pouchard, L., et al.: Computational reproducibility of scientific workflows at extreme scales. Int. J. High Perform. Comput. Appl. **33**(5), 763–776 (2019)
23. Quintero, C., Tran, K., Szewczak, A.A.: High-throughput quality control of DMSO acoustic dispensing using photometric dye methods. J. Lab. Autom. **18**(4), 296–305 (2013)
24. Raccuglia, P., et al.: Machine-learning-assisted materials discovery using failed experiments. Nature **533**(7601), 73–76 (2016)
25. Rajasekar, A., Moore, R., Vernon, F.: iRODS: a distributed data management cyber infrastructure for observatories. In: AGU Fall Meeting Abstracts (2007)
26. Stansberry, D., Somnath, S., Breet, J., Shutt, G., Shankar, M.: DataFed: towards reproducible research via federated data management. In: 2019 International Conference on Computational Science and Computational Intelligence (CSCI), pp. 1312–1317. IEEE (2019)
27. Wilkinson, M.D., et al.: The FAIR guiding principles for scientific data management and stewardship. Sci. Data **3**, 160018 (2016)

Fulfilling the Promises of Lossy Compression for Scientific Applications

Franck Cappello$^{(\boxtimes)}$, Sheng Di, and Ali Murat Gok

Argonne National Laboratory, Lemont, USA
{cappello,sdi1,agok}@anl.gov

Abstract. Many scientific simulations, machine/deep learning applications and instruments are in need of significant data reduction. Error-bounded lossy compression has been identified as one solution and has been tested for many use-cases: reducing streaming intensity (instruments), reducing storage and memory footprints, accelerating computation and accelerating data access and transfer. Ultimately, users' trust in lossy compression relies on the preservation of science: same conclusions should be drawn from computations or analysis done from lossy compressed data. Experience from scientific simulations, Artificial Intelligence (AI) and instruments reveals several points: (i) there are important gaps in the understanding of the effects of lossy compressed data on computations, AI and analysis, (ii) each use-case, application and user has its own requirements in terms of compression ratio, speed and accuracy, and current generic monolithic compressors are not responding well to this need for specialization. This situation calls for more research and development on the lossy compression technologies. This paper addresses the most pressing research needs regarding the application of lossy compression in the scientific context.

Keywords: Scientific data · Lossy compression

1 Promises of Lossy Compression for Scientific Data

In the past five years with the arrival of the pre-exascale systems, many scientific applications have seen significant increase of the volume and velocity of their produced or consumed data. This trend has numerous implications for users of scientific data. The first implication is the significant increase of the storage need. A concrete example of this implication's impact on users is the storage system cost increase of the simulation platform used at National Center for Atmospheric Research (NCAR). In the precedent platform, the cost of the storage system represented 20% of the total procurement. In the new version of the platform, the storage system represents more than 50% of the total procurement [1]. Another common implication is the increase of the input/output (I/O) time relative to the overall execution time of scientific applications. The I/O time increase is due to the growing difference between the memory size in leadership systems

© UChicago Argonne, LLC 2020
J. Nichols et al. (Eds.): SMC 2020, CCIS 1315, pp. 99–116, 2020.
https://doi.org/10.1007/978-3-030-63393-6_7

and the I/O bandwidth. The increase of I/O time concerns the data produced for analysis and also the checkpoints the applications take periodically [2–6]. The generalization of heterogeneous architectures, the future exascale systems and the upgrade of physics instruments have other implications: (i) accelerators are difficult to saturate because of the time to move data between the accelerators and the node's main memory, (ii) exascale performance will be difficult to achieve for many applications because the memory of the exascale systems will not grow commensurately to the increase in floating point performance compared to current systems, (iii) the increased detector resolution will exceed the communication and storage capacities of updated instrument facilities.

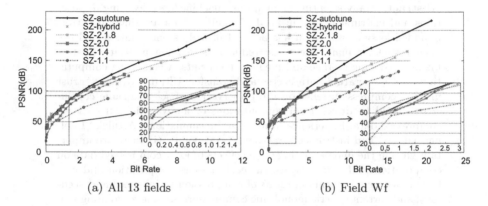

(a) All 13 fields   (b) Field Wf

Fig. 1. Illustration of the progress of lossy compression techniques in the past five years: rate distortion of various versions of SZ (Hurricane simulation: Step 48): SZ 1.1 [7] (2016), SZ 1.4 [8] (2017), SZ 2.0 [9] (2018), SZ 2.1.8 [10] (2019), SZ hybrid [11] (2019), and SZ autotune [12] (2020).

The remarkable increase of scientific data volume and velocity calls for significant data reduction mechanisms. Application-specific techniques or algorithm-specific techniques exist. Users also support generic lossy compression software based on prediction (SZ [13], FPZIP) [14], orthogonal (or not) block transforms (ZFP [15]), wavelet transforms (Vapor [16]), singular value decomposition (Tucker decomposition [17]) and multi-grid approach (MGARD [18–21]) because of several important characteristics:

– Generic lossy compression can achieve effective data reduction. A large body of work [8,9,15,17,18,22–25] has shown excellent performance concerning the data reduction speed (up to 30+GB/s on GPU [26,27]), reduction ratio (from 5:1 for particle simulations to 10:1 or even 100:1 for fluid dynamics simulations[1]), and reduction accuracy that has improved drastically in the past five years. For example, Fig. 1 shows the evolution of the compression quality

---

[1] Lossy compressors can even achieve compression ratios of x100:1 for visualization purpose, if high accuracy is not needed.

(peak signal-to-noise ratio vs. bit-rate[2]) of the SZ lossy compression framework [13] across its successive versions on the Hurricane datasets [28]. Figure 2 through Fig. 5 present the visual quality of the lossy decompressed data with the bestfit version of SZ (either hybrid version [11] or the parameter auto-tuning version [12]) for different applications/datasets from various research domains (such as cosmology, climate and molecular simulations). We zoomed in a small region for each case and plotted the region based on its narrowed value range so it has a clearer palette to highlight the differences. We observed the compression ratio reach up to 100+:1 in some cases (e.g., compressing the velocity-x field in the Nyx cosmology simulation and the V field in Hurricane simulation) or 30:1 (e.g., compressing Miranda simulation data) with identical visualization between original data and decompressed data. In some cases, the compression ratio has to be relatively low (such as 8.8:1) in order to keep an identical visualization between the original raw data and decompressed data, as shown in Fig. 5. These results highlight that lossy compression performance depends on applications and data sets.

- Generic lossy compression is agnostic to the specific ways the data has been produced or will be consumed. This is important for scientific data reuse [29]. For example, the Coupled Model Intercomparison Project [30] compares the predictions of multiple climate models. With respect to data reduction, what matters is preserving the scientifically important characteristics of the data produced by these models, not the specific algorithms or numerical methods that any particular model used to produced them. The same is true for the field data assimilation: the design of data reduction techniques should not be specific to an algorithm that consumes the data at one point in time because different algorithms may reuse the data in a later time.

- Generic lossy compressors are tools used as black boxes that application developers and users do not need to maintain. There are several production quality lossy compression software for scientific data with very similar interfaces[3], which gives users choices, provides long-term support and maintenance and reduces the risk associated with a single source of software products. The main lossy compressors for scientific data are supported by the Exascale Computing Project (ECP), and as such, they must abide by high software quality standard for testing and continuous integration.

All these promises (effectiveness, performance, preservation; application/algorithm agnosticism; third-party support and maintenance) of lossy compression are quite compelling for application developers and users. However, two important gaps limit its broad adoption by the scientific community. First, performance improvement in lossy compression in the past five years mostly came from some form of specialization. However, there is a broad spectrum of solutions between generic and dedicated compression algorithms, and the research

---

[2] Bit-rate is defined as the average number of bits used to represent each data point after compression. That is, the smaller the bit-rate, the higher the compression ratio.

[3] There is even an effort to standardize the application programming interface (API).

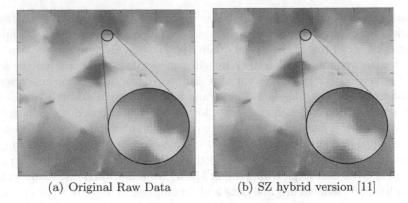

(a) Original Raw Data   (b) SZ hybrid version [11]

Fig. 2. Visualization (The zoomed-in image adopts a smaller value range (thus a different palette) to make it clearer to observe.) of original data vs. SZ decompressed data with compression ratio of 143 on the NYX cosmology simulation data (velocity x, PSNR = 64 dB).

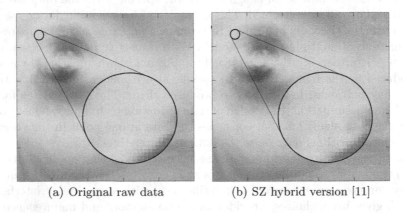

(a) Original raw data   (b) SZ hybrid version [11]

Fig. 3. Visualization (The zoomed-in image adopts a smaller value range (thus a different palette) to make it clearer to observe.) of original data vs. SZ decompressed data with compression ratio of 138 on the Hurricane simulation data (Vf48, PSNR = 53 bB).

toward specialization is still nascent. Second, while agnosticism to the methods/algorithms used for production or consumption of scientific data is a major strength of lossy compressors, it can also be a weakness. Losing the connection to application-specific algorithms/methods means losing the possibility to formally establish a profound mathematical relation between the compression error and the algorithms or numerical methods that produce or consume the data. This ultimately means users need to build trust on lossy compression from empirical experiences. This is why users initially struggle to trust that lossy compression preserves the important information in the produced or consumed data (Fig. 3).

To fulfill the promise of lossy compression for scientific data, the community needs to (Fig. 4):

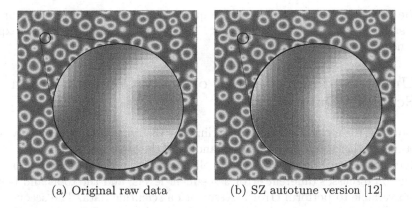

(a) Original raw data   (b) SZ autotune version [12]

Fig. 4. Visualization (The zoomed-in image adopts a smaller value range (thus a different color palette) to make it clearer to observe.) of original data vs. SZ decompressed data with compression ratio of 30 on the Miranda radiation hydrodynamics simulation data (density, PSNR = 96 dB).

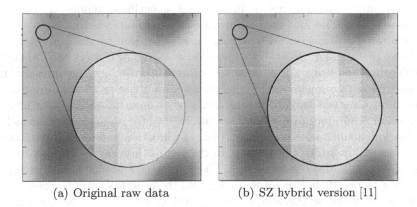

(a) Original raw data   (b) SZ hybrid version [11]

Fig. 5. Visualization[1] of original data vs. SZ decompressed data with compression ratio of 8.8:1 on the QMCPack Quantum Monte Carlo simulation data (PSNR = 120 dB).

- develop a profound understanding of the effects (result distortion, derived quantities distortion, convergence slow down) of lossy compression error on different types of simulations, AI execution and experiments and build new tools and potentially new metrics to quantify lossy compression effects;
- develop sophisticated error controls in lossy compression algorithms to preserve the important information in the data that can be the data itself and its derived quantities;

– design and implement (potentially automatically) customizable compression frameworks that provide further opportunities of performance optimization through specialization without being application specific.

The following sections discuss these questions in detail, present the current progress for several U.S. Department of Energy (DOE) applications and expose gaps and research directions.

2   Understanding the Effect of Lossy Compression on Scientific Data

Indisputably, the most important factor limiting the broad adoption of lossy compression is the lack of profound understanding of the lossy compression error and its effects on scientific data and the applications using them. The first part of this section discusses different error assessment levels, and the tools and benchmarks available to perform error assessment on scientific data. The second part of the section discusses the overall approach used for nine different use-cases to mitigate the errors introduced by lossy compression of scientific data.

2.1   Methodologies, Tools and Benchmarks

Our experience shows users deciding to use lossy compression algorithms for their data only if the data result in the same scientific outcomes as with non-compressed data. The first step to provide this guarantee is to assess the data quality after compression. Such a guarantee is subject to the conditions and knowledge presumed during the compression assessment. If users need to explore new scientific directions not considered beforehand, the lossy compression may have unexpectedly remove the key information for these new explorations.

We have observed three different levels of assessment to evaluate how the compression results are preserving the data fidelity for science: assessment from visualization, quantitative assessment of data distortion and quantitative assessment of derived quantities distortion. In the rest of this section we refer to these levels as level 1, 2 and 3 respectively. These three assessment levels correspond to different trade-offs between the quality and the practicality of the assessment.

The most direct assessment method (level 1) asks human subjects if they would derive the same scientific conclusions from a visual analysis of the lossy decompressed data and a visual analysis of the non-compressed data. This approach has been used by the NCAR climate team to assess lossy compression quality [31]. This method quickly identifies compression defects or appropriate compression levels. It does not provide a quantitative measure of the distortion, and it does not help users understand the nature of compression errors. However, this important work connects compressor developers and domain experts.

The second level of assessment characterizes and quantifies the compression errors. Compression of scientific data originated from the visualization communities. As a consequence, the initial metrics used for quantifying the compression errors were considering visual distortions and signal analysis metrics, such as peak signal-to-noise ratio (PSNR), mean squared error (MSE), and structural similarity index measurement (SSIM). The discussions with application users pointed out the importance of computing error distribution (0 centred or skewed) and the auto-correlation of the compression error. Users often consider the compression error as a type of noise, and they prefer to deal with pure random noise rather than more structured alterations since structures in errors add artifacts in the data that can lead to wrong results or wrong scientific interpretations. The first generic tool providing level 2 assessment of compression errors is Z-checker [32], which is a modular community software computing more than 30 point-wise and statistical metrics [32]. Z-checker is routinely used to help understand the profound nature of the compression errors. Compression error assessment tools are not only helping users gain confidence in a lossy compression software but also helping compression algorithm designers understand the nature of the errors their algorithm produces and compare compression qualities with other compressors. In addition, compression algorithm designers need some common/reference datasets to test and evaluate the performance of their compressors. The Scientific Data Repository Benchmark (SDRBench) [28] has been established to provide the community of developers and users of compression reference datasets representative of applications in different scientific domains. Since the opening of the website in July 2019, the SDRBench datasets have been used by researchers to assess and develop new compression methods. However, SDRBench does not provide the user compression requirements for each scientific dataset. This gap needs to be filled to focus developers on compression techniques relevant to the users.

The level 3 assessment compares the derived quantities computed from the user software analysis (usually non-trivial) or application execution (i.e., in the case of a workflow of multi-physics application) by using the decompressed data with the derived quantities computed from the same analysis or application execution using the non-compressed data. For example, the lossy compression error assessment runs the halo mass distribution and the power spectrum analysis codes for the Hardware/Hybrid Accelerated Cosmology Code (HACC) [33]. These two codes are executed to compare the lossy compressed particles' positions and velocities to the positions and velocities of the non-compressed version of these particles. For this application, guaranteeing a maximum error bound on each data point is not enough. The analysis codes running on these compressed particles should produce halo mass distribution and power spectrum deviations lower than a user specified threshold. VizAly [34] is the first tool offering a level 3 compression error assessment. It integrates user-provided analysis code and generates visualizations to assess the distortions on derived quantities produced by lossy compression. Currently, VizAly only integrates HACC halo mass distribution and power spectrum modules. These comparisons are not always possible to perform online (during the simulation) or even offline because they require significant resources (storage, communication, computation) to store the non-compressed and the compressed versions of the data and to run two instances of the analysis of application execution codes. In such situations, users can still rely on the quantitative assessment of data distortion (level 2).

Research Opportunities. New research and development are needed in (i) the understanding of the profound nature of the error produced by the most effective compressors and compression algorithms, (ii) tools to support level 1, 2 and 3 assessments, (iii) metrics to perform quickly and with limited resources accurate quantitative assessment of lossy compression errors and their impacts, (iv) benchmarks to represent with fidelity and completeness the user communities requirements.

2.2　Understanding and Mitigating Lossy Compression Error Effects on Applications

In a recent article [35], we exposed several of the currently identified use-cases of lossy compression for scientific data. We detailed their diversity, their constraints and the current performance advanced lossy compressors can achieve for these use-cases. The good performance of lossy compression was obtained in these cases after a rigorous, usually long, iterative process of interactions with the application and user teams. Table 1 presents these use-cases, applications examples, the main potential adverse effects of lossy compression, the levels of

Table 1. Lossy compression use-cases, potential adverse effects and their mitigation

Use-cases	Examples	Potential adverse effects	Assessment levels	Mitigation
Visualization	Climate simulation	Visual quality, PSNR and SSIM alteration, creation of artifacts	L1, L2	Compression parameter tuning
Reducing data stream intensity	LCLS/APS[1] X-ray data christalography	No/wrong atom detection	L1, L2, L3	Hybrid lossless/lossy compression algorithm
Reducing footprint on storage	HACC[1]	Alteration of halo mass distribution and power spectrum	L2, L3	Improvement of compression algorithm, compression parameter tuning
Accelerating checkpoint/restart	NWChem	No/slow/wrong convergence	L3	Compression parameter tuning
Reducing footprint in memory	Quantum circuit simulation	Lower simulation accuracy	L2, L3	New compression algorithm
Accelerating execution	GAMESS[1]	Incorrect simulation results	L2, L3	New compression algorithm
AI training accelerating	CANDLE NT3	Classification errors	L3	Compression parameter tuning
Deep learning model reduction	IOT[1]/sensors	Incorrect DNN[6] classification/regression results	L3	Compression parameter tuning

[1] Glossary: LCLS: Linac Coherent Light Source. APS: Advanced Photon Source. HACC: Hardware/Hybrid Accelerated Cosmology Code. CESM: Community Earth Science Model. ATM: Atmospheric Model. GAMESS: General Atomic and Molecular Electronic Structure System. IOT: Internet of Things. DNN: Deep Neural Network

assessment used to understand the effects of the compression error and the mitigation defined with the users to avoid adverse effects or make the compression errors acceptable.

The iterative process followed for each of these use-cases illustrates the need and the difficulty of reaching a profound understanding of the effects of lossy compression on scientific data and their derived quantities. This process involved a series of trials and errors where the application developers, users and compression teams assessed the effects of compression and tuned parameters. If the effects were still unacceptable, the compression teams would try to develop other algorithms and repeat the assessment and tuning steps with the application developers and users. These steps were repeated until a solid mitigation of the compression error was identified, tested and implemented.

These successful experiences still point out the lack of broadly established methodology, techniques and tools to thoroughly understand the effects of lossy compressed data on applications and analysis. Ideally, the most precise assessment of the effect of the compression error on the analysis or application results is formulating mathematically the compression error and propagating it in the numerical algorithms and methods of the analysis or applications using the compressed data. The community has progressed in this direction by formulating the round-off error of compression schemes [36] and, more recently, by developing formal analysis of the impact of lossy compression error on some numerical methods [37,38]. One of the very first works in this domain evaluates the feasibility of using lossy compression in checkpointing partial differential equation simulations by leveraging their numerical properties [3]. However, the mathematical link between the compression error and the application or analysis is not always feasible because of the complexity or requirements of the numerical methods. For example, Agullo et al. [37] formulates the impact of lossy compression error on the flexible generalized minimal residual method (FGMRES) linear algebra algorithms. Yet, formulating the impact of compression errors on GMRES itself (as opposed to FGMRES) seems extremely difficult because lossy compression does not maintain the orthogonal vector space.

Research Opportunities. New research and development are needed in (i) the mathematical formulation of compression error and its propagation in numerical methods for simulation and analysis, (ii) identification of compression algorithms that are friendly to numerical methods, (iii) identification of numerical methods for simulation or analysis that are more tolerant to compression errors.

3   Sophisticated Error Controls to Preserve Derived Quantities and Features

Until recently, lossy compressors for scientific data at best provided point-wise error control. In these compressors, users control the data distortion by setting absolute and relative error bounds [7,8,15,23]. This type of error control provides an important guarantee for users that the data will not be distorted beyond a certain level on each data point. Some users are also interested in statistical error controls. Some compressors added this type of controls. For example, SZ provides fixed PSNR control [39]. In that mode, the user specifies a PSNR in the compressor command (or API), and the compressor reduces the data making sure the lossy compressed data has a PSNR no lower than the one fixed by the users. MGARD [18] can also provide the control of MSE. However, neither point-wise error controls nor statistical error controls can prevent a compressor from introducing undesired artifacts in the compressed datasets that are undesirable for users. For example, artifacts have been reported by climate scientists testing lossy compressors [40]. Moreover, users want to keep important features in their datasets, and the current point-wise and statistical error controls provided by lossy compressors are insufficient for certain applications to preserve this information. For example, some analysis algorithms running on fusion data focus on the number of local maxima, ISO area, ISO volume, and the number of ISO connected components [41]. Ultimately, this raises the question of feature preservation in lossy compression.

Research teams have identified three directions to preserve advanced characteristics of datasets, like features, that we can refer to as white box, grey box and black box. In the white box approach, the features preserved after compression are formalized mathematically and integrated into the error control algorithms of the compressor. Examples of this white box approach are lossy compression algorithms designed to respect critical points in flows [42] or more generally important structures in the dataset through topological data analysis [43]. Another example is the IDEALEM compression algorithm [24] that specifically preserves the distribution of the data by segments in the dataset without preserving the data order. When possible, the white box feature-preserving approach provides excellent compression performance and feature preservation. However, expressing feature mathematically could be too complex for designing a compression scheme integrating a mathematical formulation of the features to preserve. Another important limitation is this approach requires specific compression algorithm designs for each feature to preserve. Moreover, how to preserve a combination of features in a lossy compressor has not been addressed. The grey box approach leverages user-provided feature detection algorithms to assist the lossy compression. The idea is to compress differently (different block sizes, different algorithms, different meshing, etc.) the features and the rest of the data in the dataset, in order to maximize feature preservation. The lossy compression scheme developed for LCLS in the context of the ECP [35] compresses the X-ray detector images using a peak finding stage that separates the peaks of the images from the background. The peaks are kept intact while the background is compressed with high error bounds. This approach is nascent, and more research is needed to understand how to efficiently integrate user-provided feature detection algorithms in compression schemes. The black box direction attempts to use the controls offered by the compression algorithms to preserve the important features. A control loop uses an iterative optimization process searching for the compressor control settings, which will preserve the features important to users and optimize the compression ratios. The control loop automatically compares the results of user-defined feature extraction/detection algorithms from the decompressed data with the ones obtained from the non-compressed data. Depending on the comparison results, the compressor controls are relaxed or tightened to optimize the feature preservation/compression ratio trade-off. The principle of the control loop concept for black box feature preservation has been successfully validated for a very simple feature: final compressed file size [44]. New tests are ongoing to evaluate the capability of the control loop concept to preserve more sophisticated features. However, without adequate controls, the optimization process might not find any good solution.

Research Opportunities. New research and development are needed in (i) white box approach: mathematical formulation of features to preserve and propagate in compression algorithms, (ii) grey box approach: identification of methods and interfaces for the integration of user-defined feature detection algorithms in lossy compression pipelines, (iii) black box approach: identification of new compressor error controls allowing the preservation of different features in scientific datasets while providing effective compression, (iv) black box approach: search and optimization frameworks to select parameters for compression pipelines respecting user-defined derived quantities and features.

4 Customizable Compression Frameworks

One of the key characteristics of compression, in particular of lossless compression, is agnosticism. Most lossless compressors (GZIP, BZIP, BLOSC, Zstd, etc.) have been designed and optimized to compress streams of bytes. Compressing streams of bytes is generally not specific to any application or subject to specific data formats such as int, float, double, etc. Additionally, compressing streams of bytes provides acceptable performance (speed, compression ratio) in many situations. When applications have higher data reduction requirements (e.g., higher compression ratio while keeping decompressed data quality high), specific compression algorithms are needed. This is the case in video (MPEG, AV1), photo (JPEG) and audio (MP3).

In the beginning, compressors for scientific data were designed to address the specific characteristics of scientific data as opposed to consumer application data. Various compression algorithms target applications demanding high levels of compression and data preservation. Various compression algorithms, for instance, are optimized for floating point data (SZ [7,8], FPZIP [14], ZFP [15], FPC [45], etc.), medical image data and genomics data. Most compression algorithms are designed to be generic: a single algorithm, potentially parametrizable, is used for many different types of scientific data (from simulation data to instrument images) and for different use-cases (visualization, storage footprint reduction, I/O acceleration, etc.). However, in practice, lossy compression algorithms perform differently on various datasets. For example, no single algorithm is known to effectively compress 1D arrays of particles or quantum chemistry datasets and 3D arrays of computational fluid dynamics (CFD) datasets. Another example is the Tucker decomposition that performs particularly well at high compression ratios for highly dimensional datasets [17,25]. With the increasing demand in compression performance for exascale platforms and upgrades of scientific instruments, application agnostic compression schemes will become even less relevant. This observation has recently resulted in a body of research focusing on the automatic selection of compression algorithms. These selection methods either estimate the compression performance based on a modeling of the compression algorithms of different compressors or directly compares the performance of different compression algorithms on samples of the data to compress [46,47]. Compression algorithm selection is only effective to a certain extent: if none of the compression schemes have been designed to effectively compress some datasets, such a selection-based compression method will not help.

In order to obtain high compression ratios and performance with acceptable data distortions regarding data features, a potential strategy would be to design, develop and optimize dedicated compression schemes for each application with different needs and requirements. Nonetheless, the diverse use-cases and features that users want to preserve require too much effort to develop and maintain many lossy compressors, making the dedicated compression approach unpractical. Specializable or customizable compressors offer a third direction between generic application agnostic compressors and dedicated compressors. One example of a cutomizable compressor is the SZ lossy compression framework [7–9]. The SZ framework allows various customizations for improving compression quality and performance. Specifically, the SZ framework has three main stages: decorrelation based on prediction, approximation based on quantization and a customized entropy/dictionary encoding. The recent generic version of the SZ compressor [9] combines three predictors and selects the best fit one for each fine-grained block (e.g., $6 \times 6 \times 6$ for 3D dataset) of the dataset based on data sampling during the compression. Moreover, extensions of SZ and ZFP have been proposed to improve their performance in certain situations. For example, several studies have explored adding different preconditioning stages [23,48].

The fundamental multi-stage architecture of lossy compressors combines different algorithms for each stage and naturally leads to the principle of customization of stage combination. This principle has been used for several applications using different customizations of the SZ compression framework. Table 2 illustrates the benefit of customization, by comparing the generic and customized versions of SZ for different applications. The table also shows the implemented customization.

Table 3 and Fig. 6 present another illustration of the benefit of customization. Table 3 shows how the performance of SZ for particle datasets was optimized through successive customization steps. Customization allowed increasing the compression ratio by up to 67% and the compression speed by 9X. HACC is an N-body simulation that can involve trillions of particles at each snapshot, and the particles' positions and velocities are maintained using six 1D arrays (x, y, z, vx, vy, and vz). Figure 6 shows that, at the same time as the compression ratio and speed improved, the compression distortions on positions reduced across SZ versions. In this compression assessment, we targeted a compression ratio

Table 2. SZ customization for different applications

Application	Generic performance	Customization	Customized performance
Cosmology	CR = 3.8 (Velocities)	Log precontionner for relative error bounds	CR = 4.2 [9]
Quantum chemistry	CR = 7	New pattern matching based predictor	CR = 16.8 [49]
Quantum circuit simulation	CR = 16–25	New quantization stage	CR = 33–36 [50]
Light source	CR = 14.5	New preconditioning to adjust compression dimension setting	CR = 18.1 [35]
Molecular dynamics	CR = 4.3	New predictor based on time-dimension	CR = 10.7 [22]
DNN models (AlexNet)	CR = 15.1	Pruning preconditioner	CR = 45.5 [51]

of (∼6:1) for all versions of SZ. To reach this compression ratio, different error bounds were used for the different version of SZ (0.04 for sz 1.1, 0.021 for sz 1.2 and 0.01 for sz 2.1, respectively). With a lower error bound, SZ 2.1 produces much less distortion than previous version for the same compression ratio.

Table 3. Compression ratio & performance of different SZ versions on HACC's dataset (absolute error bound = 0.003 for x, y, z; relative error bound = 1% for vx, vy, vz)

	x		y		z	
Compressor	CR	Throughput	CR	Throughput	CR	Throughput
SZ 1.1	3.51	20.8 MB/s	2.9	23.2 MB/s	2.76	23.6 MB/s
SZ 1.4	4.96	81 MB/s	4.8	74.3 MB/s	4.61	74.5 MB/s
SZ 2.0.2	4.96	104 MB/s	4.8	95 MB/s	4.61	95 MB/s
SZ 2.1.8	4.96	189.6 MB/s	4.8	178 MB/s	4.61	202 MB/s
	vx		vy		vz	
Compressor	CR	Throughput	CR	Throughput	CR	Throughput
SZ 1.1	N/A	N/A	N/A	N/A	N/A	N/A
SZ 1.4	3.74	57.5 MB/s	3.76	58.2 MB/s	3.8	58.5 MB/s
SZ 2.0.2	4.16	66.2 MB/s	4.2	71.1 MB/s	4.24	73.5 MB/s
SZ 2.1.8	4.14	144 MB/s	4.16	142 MB/s	4.22	143 MB/s

Composing a customized compression pipeline for an application is non-trivial because it involves selecting the algorithms and parameters for each stage. This composition is mainly done manually for each application or use-case and

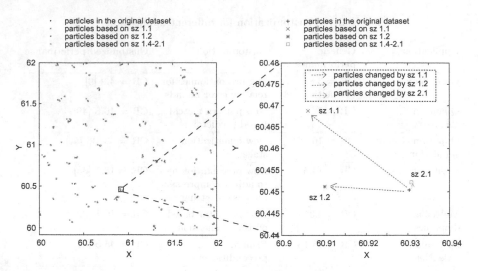

Fig. 6. Particles' positions in the original dataset and with different versions of SZ (HACC) for the same compression ratio.

requires a significant number of trials. A true realization of the compressor customization approach would require an automatic process searching for the compression pipeline (succession of stages and their parametrization) based on user requirements. Ideas along the line of automatic composition or synthesis of compression pipelines have been published for lossless compressors. We refer the readers to [52] for a list of previous works on this domain. Automatic composition of lossy compression pipelines for floating point data would be more complex because for at least three reasons: 1) it requires to consider in the search problem the user requirements with respect to data accuracy. 2) the introduction of AI algorithms notably in the prediction stage [53] adds the AI training process in the search problem, 3) the recent introduction of preconditioning stages increases the size of he compression pipeline and increases the search space.

Research Opportunities. New research and development are needed in (i) understanding and modeling the role of each compression stage in the different aspects of the compression performance, (ii) developing flexible, modular compression frameworks capable of composing compression pipelines, (iii) developing libraries of interchangeable compression stages, (iv) designing automatic techniques to select and compose lossy compression pipelines responding to user needs and requirements.

5   Conclusion

Lossy compression can become a game changer technology for scientific computing by accelerating I/O, communication and computation, and by allowing to store more scientific data in memory or on storage systems and allowing to compute larger problems faster than before. This paper discussed the current situation of the lossy compression for scientific data. In summary, the compression performance (compression ratios and speed) is promising, but the broad adoption of lossy compression for scientific data is limited by the lack of trust that users have in the lossy compressors to keep important scientific information (data and derived quantities) in the compressed version of the dataset. We have presented and discussed the most pressing research needs regarding the application of lossy compression in the scientific context: increase the user trust in lossy compression and improve the performance through customization. We also listed research directions that we believe are important to fulfill the promises of lossy compression for scientific applications.

Acknowledgments. The co-authors wish to thank (in alphabetical order): Mark Ainsworth, Julie Bessac, Jon Calhoun, Ozan Tugluk and Robert Underwood for the fruitfull discussions within the ECP CODAR project. This research was supported by the ECP, Project Number: 17-SC-20-SC, a collaborative effort of two DOE organizations – the Office of Science and the National Nuclear Security Administration, responsible for the planning and preparation of a capable exascale ecosystem, including software, applications, hardware, advanced system engineering and early testbed platforms, to support the nation's exascale computing imperative. The material was based upon work supported by the DOE, Office of Science, under contract DE-AC02-06CH11357, and supported by the National Science Foundation under Grant No. 1763540, Grant No. 1617488 and Grant No. 2003709. We acknowledge the computing resources provided on Bebop, which is operated by the Laboratory Computing Resource Center at Argonne National Laboratory. This research also used computing resources of the Argonne Leadership Computing Facility.

References

1. Hammerling, D.M., Baker, A.H., Pinard, A., Lindstrom, P.: A collaborative effort to improve lossy compression methods for climate data. In: 2019 IEEE/ACM 5th International Workshop on Data Analysis and Reduction for Big Scientific Data (DRBSD-5), pp. 16–22 (2019)
2. Sasaki, N., Sato, K., Endo, T., Matsuoka, S.: Exploration of lossy compression for application-level checkpoint/restart. In: 2015 IEEE International Parallel and Distributed Processing Symposium, pp. 914–922 (2015)
3. Calhoun, J., Cappello, F., Olson, L.N., Snir, M., Gropp, W.D.: Exploring the feasibility of lossy compression for PDE simulations. Int. J. High Perform. Comput. Appl. **33**(2), 397–410 (2019)
4. Tao, D., Di, S., Liang, X., Chen, Z., Cappello, F.: Improving performance of iterative methods by lossy check pointing. In: Proceedings of the 27th International Symposium on High-Performance Parallel and Distributed Computing, HPDC 2018, pp. 52–65, New York, NY, USA. Association for Computing Machinery (2018)
5. Chen, Z., Son, S.W., Hendrix, W., Agrawal, A., Liao, W., Choudhary, A.: Numarck: machine learning algorithm for resiliency and checkpointing. In: SC 2014: Proceedings of the International Conference for High Performance Computing, Networking, Storage and Analysis, pp. 733–744 (2014)

6. Zhang, J., Zhuo, X., Moon, A., Liu, H., Son, S.W.: Efficient encoding and reconstruction of HPC datasets for checkpoint/restart. In: 2019 35th Symposium on Mass Storage Systems and Technologies (MSST), pp. 79–91 (2019)
7. Di, S., Cappello, F.: Fast error-bounded lossy hpc data compression with SZ. In: 2016 IEEE International Parallel and Distributed Processing Symposium, pp. 730–739. IEEE (2016)
8. Tao, D., Di, S., Chen, Z., Cappello, F.: Significantly improving lossy compression for scientific data sets based on multidimensional prediction and error-controlled quantization. In: 2017 IEEE International Parallel and Distributed Processing Symposium, pp. 1129–1139. IEEE (2017)
9. Liang, X., et al.: Error-controlled lossy compression optimized for high compression ratios of scientific datasets. In: 2018 IEEE International Conference on Big Data (Big Data), pp. 438–447. IEEE (2018)
10. Liang, X., et al.: Improving performance of data dumping with lossy compression for scientific simulation. In: 2019 IEEE International Conference on Cluster Computing (CLUSTER), pp. 1–11 (2019)
11. Liang, X., et al.: Significantly improving lossy compression quality based on an optimized hybrid prediction model. In: Proceedings of International Conference for High Performance Computing, Networking, Storage and Analysis, pp. 1–26 (2019)
12. Zhao, K., et al.: Significantly improving lossy compression for HPC datasets with second-order prediction and parameter optimization. In: 29th International Symposium on High-Performance Parallel and Distributed Computing (ACM HPDC20), pp. 1–12 (2020)
13. SZ lossy compressor team. https://github.com/disheng222/sz
14. Lindstrom, P., Isenburg, M.: Fast and efficient compression of floating-point data. IEEE Trans. Visual Comput. Graph. **12**(5), 1245–1250 (2006)
15. Lindstrom, P.: Fixed-rate compressed floating-point arrays. IEEE Trans. Visual Comput. Graph. **20**(12), 2674–2683 (2014)
16. Clyne, J., Mininni, P., Norton, A., Rast, M.: Interactive desktop analysis of high resolution simulations: application to turbulent plume dynamics and current sheet formation. New J. Phys. **9**(8), 301 (2007)
17. Ballard, G., Klinvex, A., Kolda, T.G.: TuckerMPI: a parallel C++/MPI software package for large-scale data compression via the tucker tensor decomposition. ACM Trans. Math. Softw. **46**(2) (2020)
18. Ainsworth, M., Tugluk, O., Whitney, B., Klasky, S.: Multilevel techniques for compression and reduction of scientific data–the univariate case. Comput. Vis. Sci. **19**(5), 65–76 (2018)
19. Ainsworth, M., Tugluk, O., Whitney, B., Klasky, S.: Multilevel techniques for compression and reduction of scientific data–the multivariate case. SIAM J. Sci. Comput. **41**(2), A1278–A1303 (2019)
20. Ainsworth, M., Tugluk, O., Whitney, B., Klasky, S.: Multilevel techniques for compression and reduction of scientific data-quantitative control of accuracy in derived quantities. SIAM J. Sci. Comput. **41**(4), A2146–A2171 (2019)
21. Ainsworth, M., Tugluk, O., Whitney, B., Klasky, S.: Multilevel techniques for compression and reduction of scientific data–the unstructured case. SIAM J. Sci. Comput. **42**(2), A1402–A1427 (2020)
22. Li, S., Di, S., Liang, X., Chen, Z., Cappello, F.: Optimizing lossy compression with adjacent snapshots for n-body simulation. In: 2018 IEEE International Conference on Big Data (Big Data), pp. 428–437. IEEE (2018)

23. Liang, X., Di, S., Tao, D., Chen, Z., Cappello, F.: An efficient transformation scheme for lossy data compression with point-wise relative error bound. In: IEEE International Conference on Cluster Computing (CLUSTER), pp. 179–189, New York, NY, USA. IEEE (2018)

24. Lee, D., Sim, A., Choi, J., Wu, K.: Improving statistical similarity based data reduction for non-stationary data. In: Proceedings of the 29th International Conference on Scientific and Statistical Database Management, SSDBM 2017, New York, NY, USA. Association for Computing Machinery (2017)

25. Ballester-Ripoll, R., Lindstrom, P., Pajarola, R.: TTHRESH: tensor compression for multidimensional visual data. IEEE Trans. Vis. Comput. Graph. 1 (2019)

26. Authors not disclosed (double blind submission). cuSZ: an efficient GPU-based error-boundedlossy compression framework for scientific data (submitted, 2020)

27. Jin, S., et al.: Understanding GPU-based lossy compression for extreme-scale cosmological simulations (2020)

28. Scientific Data Reduction Benchmark (2019). https://sdrbench.github.io/

29. Pasquetto, I.V., Borgman, C.L., Wofford, M.F.: Uses and reuses of scientific data: the data creators' advantage. Harvard Data Sci. Rev. 1(2), 11 (2019). https://hdsr.mitpress.mit.edu/pub/jduhd7og

30. Eyring, V., et al.: Overview of the coupled model intercomparison project phase 6 (CMIP6) experimental design and organization. Geosci. Model Dev. 9(5), 1937–1958 (2016)

31. Kay, J.E., et al.: Evaluating lossy data compression on climate simulation data within a large ensemble. Geosci. Model Dev. 9(12) (2016)

32. Tao, D., Di, S., Guo, H., Chen, Z., Cappello, F.: Z-checker: a framework for assessing lossy compression of scientific data. Int. J. High Perform. Comput. Appl. 33(2), 285–303 (2017)

33. Habib, S., et al.: HACC: extreme scaling and performance across diverse architectures. Commun. ACM 60(1), 97–104 (2016)

34. VisAly-Foresight (2019). https://github.com/lanl/VizAly-Foresight

35. Cappello, F., et al.: Use cases of lossy compression for floating-point data in scientific data sets. Int. J. High Perform. Comput. Appl. 33(6), 1201–1220 (2019)

36. Diffenderfer, J., Fox, A.L., Hittinger, J.A., Sanders, G., Lindstrom, P.G.: Error analysis of ZFP compression for floating-point data. SIAM J. Sci. Comput. 41(3), A1867–A1898 (2019)

37. Agullo, E., et al.: Exploring variable accuracy storage through lossy compression techniques in numerical linear algebra: a first application to flexible GMRES. Res. Report RR-9342, Inria Bordeaux Sud-Ouest (2020)

38. Fox, A., Diffenderfer, J., Hittinger, J., Sanders, G., Lindstrom, P.: Stability analysis of inline ZFP compression for floating-point data in iterative methods. CoRR, ArXiv:abs/2003.02324 (2020)

39. Tao, D., Di, S., Liang, X., Chen, Z., Cappello, F.: Fixed-PSNR lossy compression for scientific data. In: 2018 IEEE International Conference on Cluster Computing (CLUSTER), pp. 314–318 (2018)

40. Hammerling, D.M., Baker, A.H., Pinard, A., Lindstrom, P.: A collaborative effort to improve lossy compression methods for climate data. In: 2019 IEEE/ACM DRBSD-5), pp. 16–22 (2019)

41. Yakushin, I., et al.: Feature-preserving lossy compression for in situ data. In: International Workshop on Performance Modelling, Runtime System and Applications at the Exascale (EXA-PMRA20) (2020)

42. Liang, X., et al.: Toward feature-preserving 2D and 3D vector field compression. In: 2020 IEEE Pacific Visualization Symposium (PacificVis), pp. 81–90 (2020)

43. Soler, M., Plainchault, M., Conche, B., Tierny, J.: Topologically controlled lossy compression. In: IEEE Pacific Visualization Symposium, PacificVis 2018, Japan, 2018. IEEE Computer Society (2018)
44. Underwood, R., Di, S., Calhoun, J.C., Cappello, F.: Fraz: a generic high-fidelity fixed-ratio lossy compression framework for scientific floating-point data. In: Proceedings of the 34th IEEE International Parallel and Distributed Symposium (IEEE IPDPS2020) (2020)
45. Burtscher, M., Ratanaworabhan, P.: FPC: a high-speed compressor for double-precision floating-point data. IEEE Trans. Comput. **58**(1), 18–31 (2009)
46. Lu, T., et al.: Understanding and modeling lossy compression schemes on HPC scientific data. In: 2018 IEEE International Parallel and Distributed Processing Symposium (IPDPS), pp. 348–357 (2018)
47. Tao, D., Di, S., Liang, X., Chen, Z., Cappello, F.: Optimizing lossy compression rate-distortion from automatic online selection between SZ and ZFP. IEEE Trans. Parallel Distrib. Syst. **30**(8), 1857–1871 (2019)
48. Luo, H., et al.: Identifying latent reduced models to precondition lossy compression. In: IEEE International Parallel and Distributed Processing Symposium (IPDPS), 2019, pp. 293–302 (2019)
49. Gok, A.M., et al.: PaSTRI: error-bounded lossy compression for two-electron integrals in quantum chemistry. In 2018 IEEE International Conference on Cluster Computing (CLUSTER), pp. 1–11 (2018)
50. Wu, X.-C., et al.: Full-state quantum circuit simulation by using data compression. In: Proceedings of the International Conference for High Performance Computing, Networking, Storage and Analysis, SC'19, New York, NY, USA. Association for Computing Machinery (2019)
51. Jin, S., Di, S., Liang, X., Tian, J., Tao, D., Cappello, F.: DeepSZ: a novel framework to compress deep neural networks by using error-bounded lossy compression. In: Proceedings of the 28th International Symposium on High-Performance Parallel and Distributed Computing, HPDC 2019, pp. 159–170, New York, NY, USA. Association for Computing Machinery (2019)
52. Burtscher, M., Mukka, H., Yang, A., Hesaaraki, F.: Real-time synthesis of compression algorithms for scientific data. In: Proceedings of the International Conference for High Performance Computing, Networking, Storage and Analysis, SC 2016. IEEE Press (2016)
53. Chandak, S., Tatwawadi, K., Wen, C., Wang, L., Ojea, J.A., Weissman, T.: LFZip: lossy compression of multivariate floating-point time series data via improved prediction. In: Bilgin, A., Marcellin, M.W., Serra-Sagristà, J., Storer, J.A. (eds.) Data Compression Conference, DCC 2020, Snowbird, UT, USA, March 24–27, 2020, pp. 342–351. IEEE (2020)

DataStates: Towards Lightweight Data Models for Deep Learning

Bogdan Nicolae[✉]

Argonne National Laboratory, Lemont, USA
bogdan.nicolae@acm.org

Abstract. A key emerging pattern in deep learning applications is the need to capture intermediate DNN model snapshots and preserve or clone them in explore a large number of alternative training and/or inference paths. However, with increasing model complexity and new training approaches that mix data, model, pipeline and layer-wise parallelism, this pattern is challenging to address in a scalable and efficient manner. To this end, this position paper advocates for rethinking how to represent and manipulate DNN learning models. It relies on a broader notion of data states, a collection of annotated, potentially distributed data sets (tensors in the case of DNN models) that AI applications can capture at key moments during the runtime and revisit/reuse later. Instead explicitly interacting with the storage layer (e.g., write to a file), users can "tag" DNN models at key moments during runtime with metadata that expresses attributes and persistency/movement semantics. A high-performance runtime is the responsible to interpret the metadata and perform the necessary actions in the background, while offering a rich interface to find data states of interest. Using this approach has benefits at several levels: new capabilities, performance portability, high performance and scalability.

Keywords: Deep learning · State preservation · Clone · Model reuse

1 Introduction

Deep learning applications are rapidly gaining traction both in industry and scientific computing. A key driver for this trend has been the unprecedented accumulation of big data, which exposes plentiful learning opportunities thanks to its massive size and variety. Unsurprisingly, there has been significant interest to adopt deep learning at very large scale on supercomputing infrastructures in a wide range of scientific areas: fusion energy science, computational fluid dynamics, lattice quantum chromodynamics, virtual drug response prediction, cancer research, etc.

Initially, scientific applications have gradually adopted deep learning more or less in an ad-hoc fashion: searching for the best deep neural network (DNN) model configuration and hyperparameters through trial-and-error, studying the tolerance to outliers by training with and without certain datasets, etc. Often,

© Springer Nature Switzerland AG 2020
J. Nichols et al. (Eds.): SMC 2020, CCIS 1315, pp. 117–129, 2020.
https://doi.org/10.1007/978-3-030-63393-6_8

the lack of *explainability*, i.e., being able to understand why a DNN model learned certain patterns and what correlations can be made between these patterns and the training datasets was overlooked if the results were satisfactory. However, with increasing complexity of the DNN models and the explosion of the training datasets, such a trend is not sustainable. Scientific applications are particularly affected by this because they are often mission-critical (e.g., a patient misdiagnosis can have severe consequences), unlike many industrial applications (e.g., a misclassification of a picture as a dog instead of a cat is mostly harmless).

In a quest to solve this challenge, systematic approaches are beginning to emerge: guided *model discovery* where the DNN architecture [26] and hyperparameters [3] are automatically identified, *sensitivity analysis* [29], which is used to identify what parts/layers of the DNN model and/or training samples are the most influential the learning process and how robust the DNN model is regarding tolerance to outliers or transfer learning (i.e., ability to reuse the learned patterns to solve related problems), etc.

All these approaches rely on several fundamental data management abilities: (1) *capture* intermediate snapshots of the DNN model in order to study its evolution in time and potentially *reuse* it later; (2) *clone* a DNN model whose training has progressed up to a point into many parallel alternatives where slight variations are introduced; (3) apply the *FAIR* principles [2] (findable, accessible, interoperable, reusable) to the snapshots, to make it easy to navigate through their evolution and/or search for interesting snapshots that can be reused.

However, with increasing complexity and sizes of DNN models and training data, a mix of data parallel, model parallel, pipeline parallel and layer-wise parallel approaches are emerging to speed-up the training process. In this context, a training instance is not a single process anymore, but an entire group of tightly coupled processes that are distributed across many devices and/or compute nodes of large scale HPC infrastructures. Such groups of processes collaboratively work on a shared, distributed DNN model state, exhibiting specific properties and access patterns. In addition, HPC data centers are increasingly equipped with complex heterogeneous storage stacks (multi-level memory hierarchies on compute nodes, distributed caches and burst buffers, key-value stores, parallel file systems, etc.). Under such circumstances, the fundamental data management abilities mentioned above become highly challenging to implement in a scalable and efficient manner.

In this position paper we advocate for *DataStates*, a new data model that addresses the aforementioned challenges by rethinking how to represent and manipulate scientific datasets. At its core is the notion of a *data state*, which is a collection of annotated, potentially distributed data structures that applications can capture at key moments during the runtime and revisit/reuse later. Instead explicitly interacting with the storage layer (e.g., to save the dataset into a file), users define such coupled datasets and "tag" them at key moments during runtime with metadata that expresses attributes and persistency/movement semantics. Tagging triggers asynchronous, high performance I/O strategies that run in the background and capture a consistent snapshot of the datasets and associated metadata into the lineage, a history that records the evolution of the snapshots. Using dedicated primitives, users can easily navigate the lineage to identify and revisit snapshots of interest (based on attributes and/or content) and roll back or evolve the lineage in a different parallel direction.

Using this approach, clone and revisit of DNN model states become lightweight primitives focused on high performance, scalability and FAIR capabilities, which not only accelerates existing approaches for model exploration, sensitivity analysis and explainability, but also encourages new algorithms and techniques that can take advantage of frequent reuse of intermediate DNN models. We summarize our contributions as follows:

- We discuss a series of challenges and opportunities that arise in the context of deep learning, where a mix of data parallel, model parallel, pipeline parallel and layer-wise parallel approaches are increasingly applied to improve the performance and scalability of the training (Sect. 2).
- We introduce an overview of *DataStates*, the data model and runtime we advocate in this paper. We insist both on how the notion of data states can be used as a fundamental abstraction to capture, search for and reuse intermediate datasets, as well as the advantages of such an abstraction (Sect. 3).
- We position *DataStates* in the context of state-of-art, insisting both on the gaps filled by our approach and the complementarity that can be achieved by using DataStates in conjunction in other approaches (Sect. 4).

2   Background

Deep learning approaches have evolved from independent training and inference into complex workflows (Fig. 1): they involve training sample pre-processing and augmentation (e.g., create more training samples by stretching or rotating images), model discovery (both DNN architecture and hyperparameters), training and validation of the inference, sensitivity analysis used to explain the model and/or influence the data pre-processing and model discovery.

In this context, there is a need to explore a large number of alternatives, which applies for each step of the workflow. For example, model discovery strategies based on evolutionary techniques [26] (such as genetic algorithms) need to maintain a large population of promising DNN model individuals, which are combined and/or mutated in the hope of obtaining better individuals. Training a DNN model may also involve alternatives, especially in the case of reinforcement learning [35], where there are multiple variations of environments and alternative actions possible. DNN models with early exits [30] are becoming increasingly popular: in this case, the inference can take alternative shorter (and thus faster) paths through the model layers when they provide sufficient accuracy (e.g., non-ambiguous regions in a classification problem). Sensitivity analysis [29] needs to explore many alternative training paths that include/exclude certain training samples and/or layers in order to understand their impact. For example, CANDLE [32] (Cancer Deep Learning Environment) employs an approach where the input data is split into

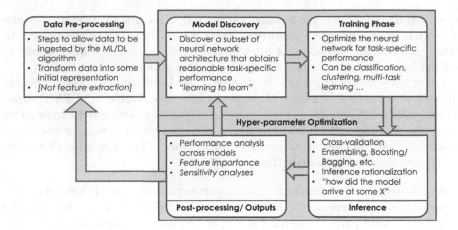

Fig. 1. Structure of a modern deep learning workflow

regions and the training process is forked into alternative directions, each of which excludes one of the regions. This process continues recursively for each excluded region until a desired granularity for the excluded training samples is reached, enabling the study of their impact in the training process.

Such alternatives introduce the need for advanced data management approaches: capture intermediate DNN model/layer snapshots as the training (or inference) progresses and then either preserve them for later study/revisiting, or clone them for the purpose of forking the training (or inference) into different parallel directions. To make these snapshots usable, several capabilities related to the FAIR principles (findable, accessible, interoperable, reusable) are needed: automatically capture the evolution of the snapshots, expose their properties, enable search based on such properties, reshape the snapshots on-the-fly to adapt to a new context where it needs to be used.

However, providing such advanced data management capabilities is challenging, because DNN training approaches are constantly being adapted to take advantage of large-scale infrastructures. In this context, the most widely used technique is *synchronous data-parallel* training. It creates replicas of the DNN model on multiple workers, each of which is placed on a different device and/or compute node. We denote such workers as *ranks*, which is the terminology typically used in high performance computing (HPC). The idea is to train each replica in parallel with a different mini-batch, which can be done in an embarrassingly parallel fashion during the forward pass on all ranks. Then, during back-propagation, the weights are not updated based on the local gradients, but using global average gradients computed across all ranks using all-reduce operations. This effectively results in all ranks learning the same pattern, to which each individual rank has contributed. The process is illustrated in Fig. 2(a).

Model parallelism [11] is another complementary approach (Fig. 3). It works by partitioning the DNN model across multiple ranks, each of which is running

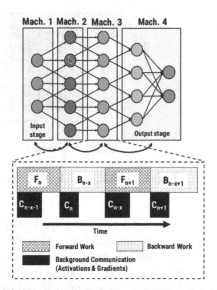

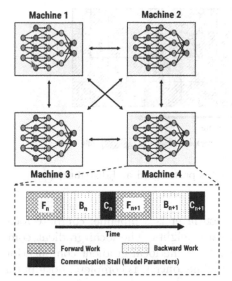

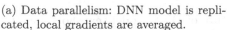

(a) Data parallelism: DNN model is repli- (b) Pipeline parallelism: DNN model
cated, local gradients are averaged.   partitioned and distributed as stages
                                        (full layers).

Fig. 2. Data parallelism vs. pipeline parallelism (adapted from [19])

on a different device and/or compute node. This solves the problem of large DNN models that do not fit in the memory of a rank, but requires data transfers between operations and disallows parallelism within an operation.

Pipeline parallelism [19] combines model parallelism with data parallelism. The idea is to partition the DNN model into stages, each of which is made of one or more layers (and can be replicated like in the case of data-parallelism). Each stage is assigned to a different rank, which effectively form a pipeline (Fig. 2(b)). Unlike data and model parallelism, where only one mini-batch is active at a given moment for the whole duration of the training step, pipeline parallelism injects multiple mini-batches into the stages one after the other: during the forward pass, each stage sends the output activations to the next stage, while simultaneously starting to process another mini-batch. Similarly, after completing the backward-propagation for a mini-batch, each stage sends the gradients to the previous stage and begins to process another mini-batch.

DL algorithms take advantage of multi-core and hybrid architectures (e.g., CPUs + GPUs) to parallelize the gradient computation and weight updates. Specifically, once a rank has finished computing the local gradients for a layer, it immediately proceeds to compute the local gradients of the previous layer. At the same time, it waits for all other ranks to finish computing their local gradients for the same layer, then updates the weights (based on the average gradients obtained using all-reduce in the case of data-parallelism). This is called *layer-wise parallelism*. Another way of reasoning about this process is by means of

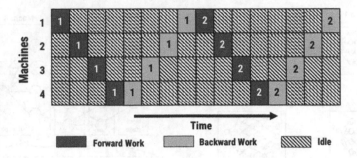

Fig. 3. Model parallelism: DNN model is partitioned and distributed

a DAG (directed acyclic graph), where each layer is a pipeline: compute local gradients, average gradients globally, update weights. The local gradient computation of each layer is a dependency for both the local gradient computation of the previous layer and the rest of the pipeline: once it is complete, both paths in the DAG can be executed in parallel.

As a consequence, the distributed nature of DNN model snapshots and the complex multi-level parallelism considerations make the problem of capturing and preserving/cloning intermediate DNN model snapshots non-trivial. This is further augmented by the need to adopt the FAIR principles and the increasingly complex heterogeneous storage stacks [14] that are deployed in modern HPC data centers. Nevertheless, there are also significant opportunities in this space: according to our previous study [13], the combination of data parallelism and layer-wise parallelism leads to subtle delays that can be exploited to overlap the back-propagation with fine-grain asynchronous data management operations in the background, which can significantly reduce their overhead. We demonstrated the feasibility of this idea both for DNN model checkpointing [23] and DNN model cloning [25], obtaining an overhead reduction of an order of magnitude compared with other state-of-art alternatives.

3   DataStates: An Overview

In this section, we introduce the main ideas and principles behind *DataStates*, the data model we advocate in this paper.

In a nutshell, a data state is a collection of annotated, potentially distributed data structures that applications can capture at key moments during the runtime. For the purpose of this work, we assume such distributed data structures to represent the DNN model state. The application indicates such key moments explicitly (noting that automation of this process opens an interesting research question). More formally, a data state is tuple (C, M_s, M_a) that defines a content C and any associated metadata M_s and M_a. We differentiate between *summary metadata* (denoted M_s), used to label and/or summarize C, and *actionable metadata* (denoted M_a), used to express intents over how C is managed. These intents take the form of hints (e.g., access pattern) and/or properties (e.g., durability, scope, relationship to other data states). Users do not care how the intent is materialized: it is the job of the DataStates runtime to formulate an appropriate plan through a series of actions, which in our case refer to persisting, caching and fetching a data state. This is a general principle: new intents and action plans can be added as needed.

Many distributed ranks (owners) can share the same data state and mutate it collaboratively by updating its content and/or metadata. We assume the owners are directly responsible for concurrency control and consistency, which in our case is transparently handled by the deep learning frameworks. When the owners reach a key moment during runtime (e.g., an epoch of the training has finished), they *tag* the data state. This triggers a transition into a new data state. From the owner's perspective, nothing changed: they can continue working on C as usual. Meanwhile, in the background, the runtime applies the action plan corresponding to M_a for the original data state as it was at the moment of tagging. The runtime guarantees that any side effects due to the action plan are tied to the original data state and do not affect the new data state (which may trigger internal temporary copies during tagging or copy-on-write). A data state that was tagged is *stable* if its action plan completed successfully and *unstable* otherwise. It is illegal to access unstable states, but the runtime offers support to query about their status and wait for them to become stable.

Both the data states and the transitions between them are recorded into the *lineage*, which keeps the evolution of the data states. The lineage exposes primitives to *navigate* (i.e., move to a successor or predecessor) and to *search* (i.e., find data states that satisfy given properties) the lineage. Applications can use such primitives to discover and visit interesting data states. For example, this can be used to follow the evolution of tagged DNN model states during training or to search for previously tagged intermediate DNN models based on their accuracy and/or other attributes. Furthermore, each data state can be part of one or more *scopes*, which are explicitly specified in M_a. To avoid the explosion of storage space utilization, non-critical data states that have gone out of scope (e.g., non-critical or locally relevant intermediate DNN models) and their transitions can be *pruned* from the lineage as needed. Pruning is subject to garbage collection algorithms, but can also be triggered explicitly through a dedicated primitive.

The lineage can be combined with two additional powerful primitives: *fork* and *reshape*. Both of them are similar to tagging (i.e., they trigger a transition to a new data state and the execution of an asynchronous action plan) but with important differences. Fork creates a clone of the data state on an entirely different set of processes and "splits" the lineage into two independent directions that can evolve separately. For example, fork can be used to explore an alternative direction for training a DNN model (e.g., using different hyperparameters and/or training samples). Reshape enables the processes to change the layout and/or distribution of C, by specifying appropriate attributes in M_a. Specifically, this refers to operations such as *migrate* (to different processes) and *shuffle* (i.e., exchange pieces of C between processes, which is a common pattern in distributed training of DNN models). Combined with tagging and search/navigation, these two primitives allow flexible strategies to explore multiple parallel evolutions and revisit/reuse previous data states. Note the versatility of reshape, which can be extended with multiple other patterns. For example, data states could be used to record a lineage for Tensorflow [1] by introducing support for tensor operations: slice, rebalance, stack, etc.

This approach has several advantages. First, it introduces *native constructs* that addresses the FAIR (findable, accessible, inter-operable, reusable) principles [2]: (1) findability is directly enabled by the lineage through navigation and search capabilities; (2) accessibility is enabled in a declarative fashion by specifying the desired intent (thus freeing applications from having to worry where their data is and how to bring it where it is needed); (3) inter-operability hiding the implementation of the I/O strategies from the user (thus eliminating differences in the interpretation of actionable metadata); (4) reusability is naturally facilitated by a single, unified view of all data states and the relationship between them, which can be revisited as desired.

Second, the separation of the intents from the actual implementation of the constraints and desired effects they represent is an important step towards *performance portability*, i.e., avoiding the need to customize the application codes on each machine to account for differences in performance characteristics, custom vendor APIs, etc. Specifically, since data states capture the intent only, action plans can be customized for a dedicated supercomputing infrastructure, potentially taking advantage of differences in architecture, performance characteristics of heterogeneous storage and vendor-specific features in order to introduce specific optimizations.

Third, the design of DataStates is *lightweight and data-centric*. DataStates is focused on the evolution of data and metadata alone, leaving other components to worry about computational and synchronization aspects. The data states are wrapping in-memory user data structures directly and are close to their intended life-cycle, therefore minimizing overheads related to data movements (which is not the case when using external repositories). Furthermore, DataStates masks the data management overhead asynchronously in the background, therefore minimizing the interruption of the application. Combined with clever interleaving of such asynchronous operations at fine-granularity during the back-propagation, this approach becomes crucial in facilitating the goal of achieving high performance and scalability.

4   Related Work and Positioning

Checkpoint-restart is a well researched HPC pattern relevant in the context of clone and revisit. In this regard, *multi-level checkpointing*, as adopted by frameworks such as SCR [18] and FTI [4], is a popular approach that leverages complementary strategies adapted for HPC storage hierarchies. VELOC [24,31] takes this approach further by introducing asynchronous techniques to apply such complementary strategies in the background. When the checkpoints of different processes have similar content, techniques such as [20,21] can be applied to complement multi-level checkpointing. However, redundancy is detected on-the-fly, which can be an unnecessary overhead for clone and revisit (e.g., model replicas are known to be identical for data-parallel training). Dedicated checkpointing techniques for deep learning are rudimentary: TensorFlow checkpoints model to files in its SavedModel format,[1] or in HDF5 files through Keras.[2] These file-based methods, while simple and adapted for single-node training, are becoming a bottleneck when scaling data-parallel training to a large number of compute nodes. Our own previous work [23,25] introduced scalable approaches to address these limitations. Although not flexible enough in the general clone and revisit scenarios, they can be used as a building block for DataStates.

In a quest to achieve scalability and flexibility, HPC storage stacks have become increasingly heterogeneous [14]. In addition to parallel file systems, modern supercomputers feature a variety of additional storage subsystems (e.g., burst buffers [7] or key-value stores such as DAOS [16]) and deep memory hierarchies (HBM, DDRAM, NVM). Such storage subsystems focus on raw I/O performance acceleration by implementing low-level read/write or put/get abstractions. They complement well the rigid POSIX model used by parallel file systems (e.g., lack of efficient support for fine-grained I/O operations and concurrency control). However, this is not enough to implement the high-level capabilities necessary for clone and revisit. Furthermore, the large diversity of services leads to added complexity and limited sharing and reuse potential because of the lack of performance portability.

In the big data community, Spark [28,34] has gained considerable traction as a generic analytics framework. Part of its success lies in the functional data processing model that hides the details of parallelism from the user, enabling ease of use and performance portability through high-level in-memory transformations. Notable in this context is the concept of RDDs [33] (Resilient Distributed Data Sets), which are Spark's abstraction for intermediate data. Despite efforts to leverage heterogeneous storage for RDDs (e.g., Apache Ignite [6]), they are tied to the rigid programming model of Spark, which emphasizes loosely coupled patterns and high-level languages that trade off performance for productivity. Therefore, such abstractions are unsuitable for the HPC ecosystem, which emphasizes high performance and scalability, tightly-coupled patterns and hybrid programming models.

Provenance tracking and reproducibility is another area closely related to DataStates. In the HPC ecosystem, EMPRESS [12] aims to provide an alternative to rudimentary attribute capabilities offered by HDF5 and NetCDF through extensible metadata. This broadens the scope beyond single files or application-specific formats, but does not feature a lineage. In the Spark ecosystem, RDDs feature a computation-centric lineage that records what data transformations were applied. This lineage is hidden from the application and used internally to

---

[1] https://www.tensorflow.org/guide/saved_model.
[2] https://www.tensorflow.org/guide/keras/save_and_serialize.

recompute RDDs (e.g., in case of failures or need to reuse). By contrast, DataStates has the opposite goal: a lineage that records actual data snapshots annotated with metadata (thus avoiding expensive recomputation), which is exposed to the application and used as a tool to revisit previous states. In itself, this is already a powerful introspection mechanism that aids provenance tracking and reproducibility. Of course, there is value in combining both approaches to create a complete picture. Unfortunately, capturing the computational context in the HPC ecosystem is nontrivial, as it involves a large number of libraries and runtimes. Containers are one possible solution and are used by approaches such as Data Pallets [15]. DataStates can complement well such efforts.

Versioning and revision control systems (e.g. SVN [10], GIT [8], Mercurial [5]) are widely used to keep track of changes to source code during software development. They feature native support for data-centric provenance: users can keep track of successive changes and revisit, roll-back, branch, merge, etc. They also feature an entire array of space-efficient techniques to store only incremental differences. However, these optimizations are designed for text data (mostly source code) and are not designed for high-performance and scalability (they assume each user has room to maintain a whole local copy of the repository). Systems were proposed before to address this issue: For example, BlobSeer [22] is a distributed data store for binary large objects that manages intermediate snapshots much like revision control systems. However, it was not designed to handle heterogeneous data and metadata (its abstraction is a blob, i.e., a large sequence of bytes): largely, it behaves like a key-value store with versioning support, therefore missing support to search and navigate the history.

Repositories for VM images [27] and containers (e.g. Docker [17]) are an industry standard to facilitate collaboration and sharing between multiple users for computational environments. In a similar spirit, recent efforts such as DLHub [9] aim to build model repositories for deep learning applications: users publish, discover and share full models, including dependencies (e.g., Python environment), into executable servables (that may include Docker images, Amazon S3 buckets, etc.) through REST APIs. DataStates also focuses on enabling search and reuse semantics, but from a different perspective: it introduces a general data model (useful beyond deep learning), lightweight (HPC-oriented) and data life-cycle oriented (mix ephemeral with persistent data, leverage local storage and in-situ capabilities, data-centric lineage). This is more appropriate for the DNN model clone and revisit scenarios we target, where an external repository can become a bottleneck. On the other hand, DataStates is well complemented by approaches like DLHub, as they can handle security and other aspects needed to enable multi-user sharing beyond a single supercomputer.

5   Conclusions

In this position paper we have introduced *DataStates*, a new data model that exposes high-level primitives to capture, fork, search and reuse of scientific datasets. Such high-level primitives are especially important for an efficient implementation of many deep learning scenarios that involve the need to capture intermediate DNN models and explore a large number of alternative training and/or inference paths.

Despite increasing complexity due to distributed DNN model state, as well as a mix of distributed training approaches (data, model, pipeline, layer-wise parallel), DataStates is well positioned to leverage the opportunity such circumstances present, especially with respect to overlapping the back-propagation phase of training with asynchronous fine-grain operation in the background in order to progress on data management aspects with minimal overhead on an ongoing training. Additionally, DataStates has three other advantages: it brings FAIR (findable, accessible, inter-operable, reusable) semantics to deep learning frameworks, it enables performance portability by separating data management intents (defined by the user) from actions necessary to satisfy them, it enables high performance and scalability by introducing lightweight, in-situ data manipulation semantics that are close to the data life-cycle of DNN models.

Encouraged by promising initial results, especially for the related problem of scalable checkpointing and cloning of DNN models for data-parallel training approaches, we plan to illustrate in future work the benefits of DataStates in the context of deep learning.

Acknowledgments. This material is based upon work supported by the U.S. Department of Energy (DOE), Office of Science, Office of Advanced Scientific Computing Research, under Contract DE-AC02-06CH11357.

References

1. Abadi, M., et al.: TensorFlow: large-scale machine learning on heterogeneous systems (2015). http://tensorflow.org/
2. Wilkinson, M.D., et al.: The fair guiding principles for scientific data management and stewardship. Sci. Data **3**(160018), 1–9 (2016)
3. Balaprakash, P., et al.: Scalable reinforcement-learning-based neural architecture search for cancer deep learning research. In: The 2019 International Conference for High Performance Computing, Networking, Storage and Analysis, SC 2019, pp. 37:1–37:33 (2019)
4. Bautista-Gomez, L., Tsuboi, S., Komatitsch, D., Cappello, F., Maruyama, N., Matsuoka, S.: FTI: High performance fault tolerance interface for hybrid systems. In: The 2011 ACM/IEEE International Conference for High Performance Computing, Networking, Storage and Analysis, SC 2011, Seattle, USA, pp. 32:1–32:32 (2011)
5. Bernard, J.: Mercurial-revision control approximated. Linux J. **2011**, 212 (2011)
6. Bhuiyan, S., Zheludkov, M., Isachenko, T.: High Performance In-memory Computing with Apache Ignite. Lulu Press, Morrisville (2017). https://www.lulu.com/
7. Cao, L., Settlemyer, B.W., Bent, J.: To share or not to share: comparing burst buffer architectures. In: The 25th High Performance Computing Symposium, HPC 2017, Virginia Beach, Virginia, pp. 4:1–4:10 (2017)
8. Chacon, S., Straub, B.: Pro Git, 2nd edn. Apress, Berkely (2014)
9. Chard, R., et al.: Publishing and serving machine learning models with DLHub. In: Practice and Experience in Advanced Research Computing on Rise of the Machines (Learning), PEARC 2019, Chicago, USA (2019)

10. Collins-Sussman, B.: The subversion project: buiding a better CVS. Linux J. **2002**(94) (2002)

11. Dean, J., et al.: Large scale distributed deep networks. In: The 25th International Conference on Neural Information Processing Systems, NIPS 2012, Lake Tahoe, USA, pp. 1223–1231 (2012)

12. Lawson, M., et al.: Empress: extensible metadata provider for extreme-scale scientific simulations. In: The 2nd Joint International Workshop on Parallel Data Storage and Data Intensive Scalable Computing Systems, PDSW-DISCS@SC 2017, pp. 19–24 (2017)

13. Li, J., Nicolae, B., Wozniak, J., Bosilca, G.: Understanding scalability and fine-grain parallelism of synchronous data parallel training. In: 5th Workshop on Machine Learning in HPC Environments (in Conjunction with SC19), MLHPC 2019, Denver, USA, pp. 1–8 (2019)

14. Lockwood, G., et al.: Storage 2020: a vision for the future of HPC storage. Technical Report, Lawrence Berkeley National Laboratory (2017)

15. Lofstead, J., Baker, J., Younge, A.: Data pallets: containerizing storage for reproducibility and traceability. In: 2019 International Conference on High Performance Computing, ISC 2019, pp. 36–45 (2019)

16. Lofstead, J., Jimenez, I., Maltzahn, C., Koziol, Q., Bent, J., Barton, E.: DAOS and friends: a proposal for an exascale storage system. In: The 2016 International Conference for High Performance Computing, Networking, Storage and Analysis, SC 2016, Salt Lake City, Utah, pp. 50:1–50:12 (2016)

17. Merkel, D.: Docker: lightweight Linux containers for consistent development and deployment. Linux J. **2014**(239), 2 (2014)

18. Moody, A., Bronevetsky, G., Mohror, K., Supinski, B.R.D.: Design, modeling, and evaluation of a scalable multi-level checkpointing system. In: The 2010 ACM/IEEE International Conference for High Performance Computing, Networking, Storage and Analysis, SC 2010, New Orleans, USA, pp. 1:1–1:11 (2010)

19. Narayanan, D., et al.: PipeDream: generalized pipeline parallelism for DNN training. In: The 27th ACM Symposium on Operating Systems Principles, SOSP 2019, Huntsville, Canada, pp. 1–15 (2019)

20. Nicolae, B.: Towards scalable checkpoint restart: a collective inline memory contents deduplication proposal. In: The 27th IEEE International Parallel and Distributed Processing Symposium, IPDPS 2013, Boston, USA (2013). http://hal.inria.fr/hal-00781532/en

21. Nicolae, B.: Leveraging naturally distributed data redundancy to reduce collective I/O replication overhead. In: 29th IEEE International Parallel and Distributed Processing Symposium, IPDPS 2015, pp. 1023–1032 (2015)

22. Nicolae, B., Antoniu, G., Bougé, L., Moise, D., Carpen-Amarie, A.: BlobSeer: next-generation data management for large scale infrastructures. J. Parallel Distrib. Comput. **71**, 169–184 (2011)

23. Nicolae, B., Li, J., Wozniak, J., Bosilca, G., Dorier, M., Cappello, F.: DeepFreeze: towards scalable asynchronous checkpointing of deep learning models. In: 20th IEEE/ACM International Symposium on Cluster, Cloud and Internet Computing, CGrid 2020, Melbourne, Australia, pp. 172–181 (2020)

24. Nicolae, B., Moody, A., Gonsiorowski, E., Mohror, K., Cappello, F.: VeloC: towards high performance adaptive asynchronous checkpointing at large scale. In: The 2019 IEEE International Parallel and Distributed Processing Symposium, IPDPS 2019, Rio de Janeiro, Brazil, pp. 911–920 (2019)

25. Nicolae, B., Wozniak, J.M., Dorier, M., Cappello, F.: DeepClone: lightweight state replication of deep learning models for data parallel training. In: The 2020 IEEE International Conference on Cluster Computing, CLUSTER 2020, Kobe, Japan (2020)

26. Real, E., et al.: Large-scale evolution of image classifiers. In: The 34th International Conference on Machine Learning, ICML 2017, Sydney, Australia, pp. 2902–2911 (2017)

27. Saurabh, N., Kimovski, D., Ostermann, S., Prodan, R.: VM image repository and distribution models for federated clouds: state of the art, possible directions and open issues. In: Desprez, F., et al. (eds.) Euro-Par 2016. LNCS, vol. 10104, pp. 260–271. Springer, Cham (2017). https://doi.org/10.1007/978-3-319-58943-5_21

28. Shanahan, J.G., Dai, L.: Large scale distributed data science using apache spark. In: The 21th ACM SIGKDD International Conference on Knowledge Discovery and Data Mining, KDD 2015, Sydney, Australia, pp. 2323–2324 (2015)

29. Shu, H., Zhu, H.: Sensitivity analysis of deep neural networks. In: The 33rd AAAI Conference of Artificial Intelligence, AAAI 2019, pp. 4943–4950 (2019)

30. Teerapittayanon, S., McDanel, B., Kung, H.T.: BranchyNet: fast inference via early exiting from deep neural networks. In: The 23rd International Conference on Pattern Recognition, ICPR 2016, Cancun, Mexico, pp. 2464–2469 (2016)

31. Tseng, S.M., Nicolae, B., Bosilca, G., Jeannot, E., Cappello, F.: Towards portable online prediction of network utilization using MPI-level monitoring. In: 25th International European Conference on Parallel and Distributed Systems, EuroPar 2019, Goettingen, Germany, pp. 1–14 (2019)

32. Wozniak, J., et al.: CANDLE/supervisor: A workflow framework for machine learning applied to cancer research. BMC Bioinform. 19(491), 59–69 (2018)

33. Zaharia, M., et al.: Resilient distributed datasets: a fault-tolerant abstraction for in-memory cluster computing. In: Proceedings of the 9th USENIX Conference on Networked Systems Design and Implementation, NSDI 2012, San Jose, USA, p. 2 (2012)

34. Zaharia, M., Chowdhury, M., Franklin, M.J., Shenker, S., Stoica, I.: Spark: cluster computing with working sets. In: The 2Nd USENIX Conference on Hot Topics in Cloud Computing, HotCloud 2010, Boston, MA, p. 10 (2010)

35. Zhang, S., Boehmer, W., Whiteson, S.: Deep residual reinforcement learning. In: The 19th International Conference on Autonomous Agents and MultiAgent Systems, AAMAS 2020, Auckland, New Zealand, pp. 1611–1619 (2020)

Scalable Data-Intensive Geocomputation: A Design for Real-Time Continental Flood Inundation Mapping

Yan Y. Liu[✉] and Jibonananda Sanyal

Computational Urban Sciences Group, Computational Sciences and Engineering Division, Oak Ridge National Laboratory, Oak Ridge, TN, USA
yanliu@ornl.gov, sanyalj@ornl.gov

Abstract. The convergence of data-intensive and extreme-scale computing behooves an integrated software and data ecosystem for scientific discovery. Developments in this realm will fuel transformative research in data-driven interdisciplinary domains. Geocomputation provides computing paradigms in Geographic Information Systems (GIS) for interactive computing of geographic data, processes, models, and maps. Because GIS is data-driven, the computational scalability of a geocomputation workflow is directly related to the scale of the GIS data layers, their resolution and extent, as well as the velocity of the geo-located data streams to be processed. Geocomputation applications, which have high user interactivity and low end-to-end latency requirements, will dramatically benefit from the convergence of high-end data analytics (HDA) and high-performance computing (HPC). In an application, we must identify and eliminate computational bottlenecks that arise in a geocomputation workflow. Indeed, poor scalability at any of the workflow components is detrimental to the entire end-to-end pipeline. Here, we study a large geocomputation use case in flood inundation mapping that handles multiple national-scale geospatial datasets and targets low end-to-end latency. We discuss the benefits and challenges for harnessing both HDA and HPC for data-intensive geospatial data processing and intensive numerical modeling of geographic processes. We propose an HDA+HPC geocomputation architecture design that couples HDA (e.g., Spark)-based spatial data handling and HPC-based parallel data modeling. Key techniques for coupling HDA and HPC to bridge the two different software stacks are reviewed and discussed.

Y. Y. Liu and J. Sanyal—Contributed Equally.
This manuscript has been co-authored by UT-Battelle, LLC, under contract DE-AC05-00OR22725 with the US Department of Energy (DOE). The US government retains and the publisher, by accepting the article for publication, acknowledges that the US government retains a nonexclusive, paid-up, irrevocable, worldwide license to publish or reproduce the published form of this manuscript, or allow others to do so, for US government purposes. DOE will provide public access to these results of federally sponsored research in accordance with the DOE Public Access Plan (http://energy.gov/downloads/doe-public-access-plan).

J. Nichols et al. (Eds.): SMC 2020, CCIS 1315, pp. 130–144, 2020.
https://doi.org/10.1007/978-3-030-63393-6_9

Keywords: Geocomputation · Data science · High-performance computing

1   Introduction

High-end Data Analytics (HDA) [2] have introduced new infrastructure and tools for data analytics that are now widely adopted in the science community as enabling technologies for rapidly emerging data-intensive science [11]. The convergence of HDA and simulation-oriented high-performance computing (HPC) presents tremendous opportunities for scientific advancement in computing applications and workflows by orchestrating simulations, experiments, data, and learning-based knowledge. However, since HDA and HPC present separate software ecosystems [2], fusing HDA and HPC, at both the application and infrastructure levels, requires the dismantling of the boundaries of computing- and data-intensive paradigms so that an integrated software and data ecosystem can be built.

In Geographic Information Systems (GIS) environments [10], geocomputation [5] provides computing paradigms for interactive computing of geographic data, processes, models, and maps. Geocomputation is data-centric. The computational scalability of a geocomputation workflow is directly related to the scale of the GIS data layers, their resolution and extent, and the velocity of the geolocated data streams to be processed. Scalable geocomputation solutions have evolved from desktop computing to distributed computing paradigms that harness service computing, HDA, or HPC. Because geocomputation is unique in high user interactivity and low end-to-end latency requirements, performance will dramatically improve with the convergence of HDA and HPC. The application level challenge, however, is to identify and eliminate computational bottlenecks that arise along the entire geocomputation workflow. Indeed, poor scalability at any of the workflow components is detrimental to the entire end-to-end pipeline. Similar challenges have arisen in scalable database research [6].

Here, we study the convergence of HDA and HPC in geocomputation by examining a typical large-scale geospatial application—continental flood inundation mapping. We analyze the bottlenecks that arise when scaling the geocomputation workflow from the regional level to the continental level.

2   A Geocomputation Use Case

The continental flood inundation mapping (CFIM) framework is an HPC framework [18] that provides continental-level hydrologic analysis. At the national level, the input datasets include the Digital Elevation Model (DEM) produced by U.S. Geological Survey (USGS) 3DEP (the 3-D Elevation Program), the NHDPlus hydrography dataset produced by USGS and the U.S. Environmental Protection Agency (EPA), and real-time water forecasts from the National Water Model (NWM) at the National Oceanic and Atmospheric Administration (NOAA). With these data, a hydrologic terrain raster, Height Above Nearest

Drainage (HAND) (Fig. 1), and HAND-derived flood inundation measures are computed for 331 river basins in the conterminous U.S. (CONUS) [37]).

Fig. 1. The HAND map 10 m resolution for CONUS, version 0.2.0, produced on March 01, 2020. Deep blue areas are prone to flood inundation. (Color figure online)

The CFIM computation features data-intensive vector and raster operations for water feature querying, clipping, and reprojection, as well as data- and computing-intensive hydrologic analysis of terrain pits, flow direction and accumulation, and stream networks. The entire workflow consists of 20 steps. The input DEM for CONUS 10 m resolution is a 718 GB raster grid of 180 billion cells. When 1 m DEM becomes available, the size of the raster grid will increase 100 fold. The vector input has 2.7 million polygons (watershed boundaries) and lines (flow lines). A higher resolution version would have 30 million vectors. In addition, the NWM water forecast data consists of an hourly data stream for the subsequent 18 h. The hydrologic analyses are parallelized using MPI [18]. In addition, in-situ analytics of HAND and flood inundation, such as flood depth maps, need to be delivered to web browsers and mobile apps. For instance, generating a HAND-sized map layer involves computing 230k map tiles for 8 zoom levels or millions of contour vectors.

Currently, the CFIM HPC workflow is deployed on the Condo cluster at the Compute and Data Environment for Science (CADES) at the Oak Ridge National Laboratory (ORNL). The entire output 10 m resolution, including HAND and derived raster and vector products, is about 3.7 TB. Each version of the dataset [19,20] is registered and published on the Scalable Data Infrastructure for Science (SDIS) [33], housed at the Oak Ridge Leadership Computing Facility (OLCF). Community access is provided via HTTP download as well as the Globus bulk transfer service.

3   Data and Computing Challenges

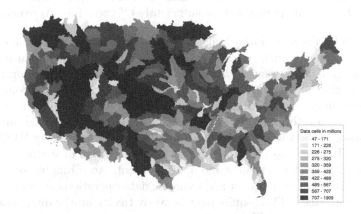

Fig. 2. The computing intensity map for the 331 HUC6 units on CONUS, derived from the number of data cells that are involved in actual computing. This map guides the allocation of HPC resources for the parallel computing of all the HUC6 units.

In the CFIM HPC workflow, a two-level parallelization strategy is applied to systematically scale HAND computation to finer DEM resolutions and flowline scale. The first level of the parallelization strategy spatially decomposes CONUS into contiguous hydrologic units that follow the hierarchical Hydrologic Unit Code (HUC) system. The delineation of the HUC boundary by hydrologists minimizes interference between neighboring HUC units and creates a batch of high-throughput computing jobs at each HUC level, as shown in Fig. 2. For each job, a second-level parallelization via MPI is applied to a series of hydrologic analysis functions that operates on the entire raster grid of each HUC unit.

The most recent HAND data was computed on the CADES Condo cluster using RAM disk and burst buffer. On average, computing an HUC6 unit took half an hour (with a standard deviation of 1,210 s). The MPI parallelization effectively accelerated the performance of several key hydrologic analysis functions so that they were no longer bottlenecks. However, new bottlenecks arose in the serial GIS operations, particularly those that clip DEM and HAND rasters. These two raster clipping functions required 454 s, on average, with a standard deviation of 407 s, which amounted to 25% of the entire computing time.

This geocomputation scenario presents an interesting but challenging case for further acceleration. The workflow does not read and write large geospatial datasets only once, but applies frequent GIS and hydrologic analysis operations on them, generating copious intermediate data at runtime. Furthermore, in order to enable first responders in extreme weather events (e.g., hurricanes), the computing time of HAND and inundation forecast information must be further reduced. For example, to match the pace of real-time water forecasting, the computing time for inundation forecasts must be reduced from hours to minutes. In this quest, HPC alone may not be sufficiently effective for two reasons.

1. First, GIS libraries are often built as a geospatial extension to the common data manipulation, query, and processing capabilities of general database and data management systems. In the literature, HPC-based GIS development are individual efforts. A more systematic approach that manages the complicated interconnectedness of the individual components is needed. Given this base, it is then a daunting task to develop a full-scale reconceptualization of the entire stack of data handling libraries and GIS extensions using HPC.
2. Second, GIS functions often operate on multiple layers of vector and raster data with different resolutions and spatial extent. Accordingly, computing a GIS function requires frequent and dynamic data operations at multiple levels of data granularity. This requirement is overly taxing on the distributed data management model of HPC.

Data-intensive computing software infrastructure, such as Spark [36], provide a desirable solution to the challenges that we have identified, provided that it can be systematically integrated into an HPC workflow. As a scalable data analytic software infrastructure, Spark provides a rich set of data handling features with distributed processing capabilities. Since most of the GIS operations in the CFIM workflow are commutative and associative, it is possible to rewrite them using the *mapreduce* paradigm. With the additional functional programming support through Spark, the dependencies between the steps in the workflow can be represented implicitly in the code. For example, at the infrastructure level, Spark provides distributed data management and associated data parallelism (through the Resilient Distributed Dataset (RDD) abstraction). Spark jobs are executed as Directed Acyclic Graphs (DAG) that optimize the execution plan on managed resources. Accordingly, it is not necessary to consider the task scheduling problem at the infrastructure level. Furthermore, the lazy execution feature in Spark allows a more performant workflow execution by reducing the intermediate data footprints. Spark has been used for vector processing in geocomputation [4,13,14,32,34,35]. Spark connectors to high-dimensional arrays have been developed [16,30]. Spark has also been utilized for large raster-based deep learning inference [21].

4   Data-Driven Geocomputation on HDA+HPC

To harness HDA in a geocomputation workflow, we propose a general HDA+HPC fusion model for geocomputation, shown in Fig. 3, that defines a fusion software architecture to meet the end-to-end performance requirements in data-intensive geospatial computing, such as those in CFIM. To effectively integrate HDA and HPC, an application needs to manage software and data that enables flexible

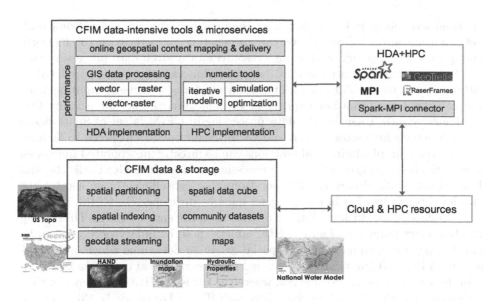

Fig. 3. A geocomputation design for CFIM on integrated HDA and HPC.

construction of computing elements in both HPC in a "move-data-to-code" fashion and HDA in which code is packaged and moved to data nodes for computing (i.e., "move-code-to-data").

In this data-driven model, hydrology and GIS data are imported into a distributed data storage system, which are then spatially partitioned using regular or adaptive 2D domain decomposition mechanism (e.g., adaptive quadtree) into data blocks (e.g., partitioned RDDs in Spark) that are distributed on multiple data nodes or a parallel file system. On a parallel file system, the data parallelism is provided by the parallel IO capability of the system. A spatial index, using the space filling curve, is built to link these partitions. This spatial index then accelerates the spatial selection of the data blocks that participate in the actual computing. The geodata streaming module handles data streams such as the hourly water forecast as well as any data version update by using the spatial data cube as runtime storage. The cube runs in a smaller sized distributed file system (e.g., HDFS) or an in-memory database (e.g., Redis) on RAM disk or burst buffer. The cube also serves the purpose of caching frequently accessed datasets and maps from community users and applications. The use of the cube in the online geospatial content mapping and delivery module provides important and necessary performance for real-time GIS scenarios such as the CFIM application.

Storing and indexing large geospatial datasets into data blocks provides basic computing elements for both HDA and HPC algorithms. Because the data blocks are loaded and processed on multiple computing nodes, we are able to execute GIS operations that do not fit into the memory of a single machine. Spatial knowledge on distributed data blocks can also be effectively leveraged to make runtime scheduling decisions that affect resource management and walltime budget. In the context of Spark, we can use spatial characteristics to efficiently configure CPU, memory, and storage resources for a given data processing job.

Transforming sequential or HPC-based GIS functions into data-parallel algorithms is key to enabling geocomputation on data-intensive computing platforms. This transformation requires algorithmic innovations for existing GIS implementations. To scale GIS data processing in CFIM, a set of Spark-based HDA functions for vector, raster, and vector-raster operations needs to be integrated. For example, individual functions can be directly incorporated from open source Spark-based geospatial data processing tools, such as GeoTrellis [14] and RasterFrames [3]. However, GIS operations that can efficiently implement the two-level parallelization in a single pass must be developed. In CFIM, it is possible to develop an efficient clipping operation on the entire CONUS DEM using the boundary polygons of all the HUC units. These boundary polygons can be checked against each data block's spatial extent to determine which ones intersect with this HUC unit. Multiple clipped raster segments at each data block can then be returned as a key-value list, where the key is the HUC id. They can then be grouped at the reshuffling stage into each HUC's boundary. In this way, the clipping operation for all HUC units can be computed as a Spark job. In CFIM, 70% of the operations can be converted to HDA operations. The chaining of them in the workflow logic is captured in Spark as task DAG. This composition and lazy execution of the DAG in Spark significantly improves a geocomputational workflow in two ways. First, the functional programming pattern in Spark provides a way to dynamically package and send the workflow code to data nodes. Second, the delayed execution of all *transformation* operations on the chain eliminates the need for storing intermediate results at each workflow step. In HPC-based workflow solutions, these intermediate results are usually written to and read from disk for large datasets.

We must also consider that HDA and its *mapreduce* programming paradigm may not be well-suited for iterative processes that involve intensive numerical operations, such as those in iterative modeling, simulation, and optimization. For instance, the pit filling algorithm in CFIM operates on a large elevation raster by flooding the entire terrain first and then iteratively letting water recede until all the pits are filled. Such MPI parallelization does not need to be converted to an HDA function unless a data-driven parallel algorithm is more efficient.

Note that the two-level parallelization strategy employed in the CFIM HPC workflow is still effective in HDA+HPC. For an operation to be applied to all of the HUC units, it can simply be invoked as an independent Spark job. Each job's DAG can then be executed in parallel, managed by Spark. With sufficient resource allocation, the asynchronous *actions* in Spark with the FAIR scheduler setting can be leveraged to process multiple HUC units simultaneously.

At the second level of parallelization where we run the workflow on an HUC unit, we must determine how to invoke an HPC step in the Spark context. In the literature, we evaluate three Spark–MPI connector solutions: Alchemist [8], Spark+MPI [1] (also known as Spark MPI Adapter), and Spark–MPI [23,24].

Table 1. Comparison of three Spark–MPI connectors.

	Alchemist	Spark+MPI	Spark-MPI
MPI coupling	Spark workers contact the Alchemist server, which launches MPI	Spark code runs *mpiexec* as a separate process	Dynamic PMI or MCA OpenRTE launch in Spark
Spark to MPI connection	TCP/IP socket on the Alchemist server	Command line invocation in Python	*mpi4py*
Data exchange	Matrix RDD to/from the *Elemental* format	Node-based HDFS partitions on RAM disk or burst buffer	Python *Pickle* for objects; single-segment buffer for contiguous arrays
Data transfer protocols	TCP/IP between Spark nodes and Alchemist nodes	Distributed file IO	Direct memory access/copy with *mpi4py*

There are two basic requirements to interoperate the two separate software stacks of Spark and MPI. First, we need to launch an MPI executable in the Spark JVM. Second, we must define a message and data exchange protocol between them. Table 1 compares the working mechanisms of these solutions. Alchemist is a broker solution that spawns a set of Alchemist server and worker processes to bridge the communication and data exchange between Spark and MPI. Since it uses a matrix format as a data exchange format between Spark's RDD and MPI's data structure, serializing geospatial raster data in Alchemist is desirable. The data exchange process in Spark–MPI can be efficient here since there is no memory copy when contiguous arrays (such as a raster) are passed from Spark to MPI through *mpi4py*. However, Spark–MPI leverages dynamic process management features in specific MPI implementations. Portability is a potential issue. Spark+MPI uses a file system as a data exchange media, which poses limitations on the IO cost for frequent data exchange.

In general, the proposed geocomputation design captures three aspects of HDA and HPC integration and interoperability. First, the aforementioned Spark–MPI connection is an example of how to launch HPC code in HDA, which is important for compute-intensive functions. Horovod in Spark [12] is another example of machine learning computation using MPI within an HDA context. Second, HDA empowers data gateway functionalities that face end users. In geocomputation, HDA may accelerate geovisualization, spatial analytics, and spatial data and map query, but the computing power on an online gateway may be limited. When large-scale analytics, optimization, and simulation are involved, middleware solutions are needed to launch HDA on HPC. For Spark, Spark connectors are needed to conduct in-situ processing. This can be done in two ways. First, a middleware (e.g., DASK) with application programming interface (API) sends a Spark application to HPC batch schedulers, which then instantiate a dynamic Spark cluster that application drivers connect to. Results are sent back to the gateway using the middleware. Alternatively, a Spark connector can be built in an in-situ service such as ADIOS2 [15,17]). This connector is responsible for connecting a Spark application on gateway to a Spark cluster in HPC and handling the data transfer between them.

At the infrastructure level, the design is based on the assumption that an HPC environment allows the sharing of the data repository between the gateway cloud instance and the backend HPC resources. Otherwise, data transfer cost must be considered. A hybrid infrastructure that supports data center and HPC operations would be desirable for our geocomputation use case.

5   Preliminary Results

GIS operations create heterogeneous computing and data load as a result of graphic and geometric calculations between shapes and geospatial data contained in shapes. As a GIS operation is transformed into data-parallel implementation, it is essential to understand the associated computational performance variants in order to systematically develop algorithmic strategies for data-parallel geocomputation. We conducted computational experiments on a representative vector-raster operation to measure the computational scalability and load balance of a Spark cluster for handling large raster data.

Clipping or subsetting is a common GIS operation for extracting a subset of raster within the boundary of a polygon vector. A serial implementation often creates a rectangle bounding box of the polygon as a clipping window. The polygon is then rasterized to mask the subset of raster cells within the window. The clipped raster is then output with the same spatial extent as the window. The data parallelization of this operation consists of three distributed functions. The *tiling()* function decomposes an input raster into tiles of the same dimensions and registers all the tiles as a binary RDD indexed by their bounding box rectangle. The *clipping()* function applies the clipping on an input tile and supports multi-polygon clipping. The output of the clipping function on a tile is a set of subsets on the tile, indexed by shape id. The clipped tiles of the same shape id are then aggregated into a single raster, which is output by the *save()* function. In this implementation, the tiling and clipping are *map* functions that can be chained for lazy execution. A *groupByKey()* call in Spark shuffles the clipped tiles using unique shape identifiers. Data shuffling is memory- and IO-intensive. The *save()* function is a parallel IO operation for saving multiple clipped rasters simultaneously, each of which is named after their shape id. The clipping algorithm is written using PySpark, the Python library of Spark.

Three test rasters of different sizes, *large*, *medium*, and *small*, are generated from the national elevation dataset produced by the U.S. Geological Survey, as shown in Fig. 4. The default tile size is 10812×10812. A Spark job takes an input of all HUC6 unit shapes, whose boundary is colored in black in Fig. 4, in a test raster and outputs a clipped raster for each of them. A Spark cluster of 8 virtual working nodes is configured on a cloud instance with 128 physical cores (AMD EPYC 7702 2 GHz), 1 TB memory, and 512 GB disk in the private

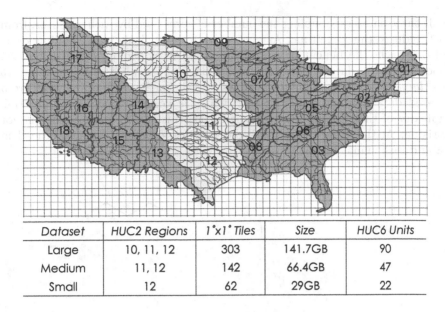

Dataset	HUC2 Regions	1°x1° Tiles	Size	HUC6 Units
Large	10, 11, 12	303	141.7GB	90
Medium	11, 12	142	66.4GB	47
Small	12	62	29GB	22

Fig. 4. Study areas and raster data characteristics.

cloud at the Compute and Data Environment for Science (CADES) at ORNL. The 1 TB memory is split into 512 GB RAMDISK as Spark worker disk cache and 512 GB for the 8 Spark worker nodes. On each node, one Spark executor is launched with 32 GB memory. The number of cores per executor is specified as a runtime parameter. A Jupyter Spark driver connects to the Spark cluster to run each test job.

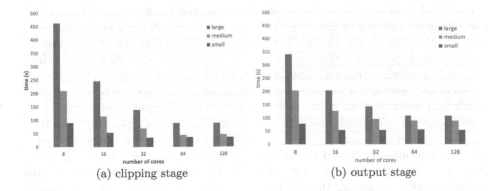

(a) clipping stage   (b) output stage

Fig. 5. Computational performance on the three test datasets.

Figure 5 shows the computational scalability of the *map* stage (Fig. 5a), including the tiling and clipping, and the *reduce* stage of outputting (Fig. 5b).

For all three datasets, doubling the number of cores used by each executor, from 1 to 4, reduced the stage time. As more cores were used, the data shuffling overhead outweighs the benefit of additional cores. Weak scaling can also be seen by looking at the dataset-cores combinations. The (*small–8 cores, medium–16 cores, large–32 cores*) combination shows a sublinear increase of overhead from increased data shuffling cost in Spark, which is normal. Since the computing complexity of the clipping algorithm is linear, this scaling performance is not surprising. At the same time, Spark did not introduce significant overhead in data and task management.

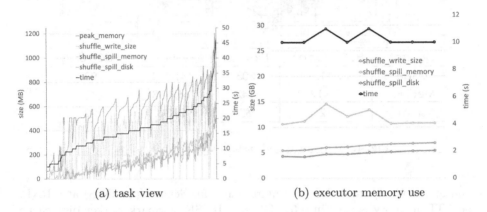

(a) task view   (b) executor memory use

Fig. 6. Memory profile and load balance on the large dataset (303 tasks) using 8 executors, each using 32 GB memory and 8 cores.

Figure 6 shows the computational profile of the *map* stage of a run using 8 executors and 8 cores per executor to clip the 141 GB large dataset, which contains 303 data blocks. Figure 6a depicts the time and memory usage for each of the 303 tasks, ordered by the task time, i.e., the black solid line in the diagram. The clipping time is heterogeneous among tasks, depending on how computing intensive a shape intersection operation can be (tiles out of a shape's bounding box is calculated faster) and how many tile cells are intersected. The memory usage is also heterogeneous. A time-consuming shape intersection operation may result in a small number of data to be extracted, which explains why some tasks took longer but consumed less memory. The four memory profiling measures show the maximum memory usage, the number of clipped tile cells, the average runtime memory and disk cache consumption. Figure 6b, however, shows that the computing and data load of such heterogeneous geocomputation are evenly distributed among the eight executors. The explanation has two components. First, RDD data blocks are evenly sized into tiles and distributed to executors. On aggregation, the memory and cache usage among executors are thus balanced. Second, small variations in time and runtime memory usage, i.e., *shuffle_spill_memory*, are caused by task heterogeneity but smoothed across tasks running on an executor.

Table 2. Turnaround clipping time (in seconds) by different clipping methods using 32 processor cores. The buffered method used a 40 MB memory buffer.

Clipping method	Large dataset	Medium dataset	Small dataset
Buffered	2106	726	247
In-memory	729	389	113
Spark	282	166	89

The turnaround time of the Spark clipping implementation was also compared with embarrassingly parallel processing of sequential clipping functions using the open source GDAL [29] library. The existing clipping in CFIM uses a 40 MB memory buffer. Another configuration that uses only in-memory processing was also tested. The Spark run used 8 executors with 32 GB memory and 4 cores per executor. Each scenario used 32 cores in total. Table 2 shows that the Spark implementation clearly outperformed both batch processing methods on each test dataset, mainly due to the RDD data parallelism and the resulting load balance.

A CONUS clipping test was also conducted to obtain DEMs for each of the 331 HUC6 units on the entire elevation dataset using 32 cores in total. The *map* stage took 7.3 min to tile the input DEM and clip HUC6 shapes, and generated 2829 data blocks, 170 GB in total. The total memory and cache usage was approximately 475 GB. The output stage took 12 min to dump output rasters to a Network File System (NFS) mount due to the limitation of local disk size. The total turnaround time was 19.3 min for all 331 HUC6 units. Compared to the average 4 min of single HUC6 clipping in the existing CFIM workflow, this is a dramatic performance improvement, which can be further optimized by using parallel file system storage.

In summary, these computational experiments demonstrate a desirable computing and data management performance for the Spark environment. Task management, DAG execution, RDD management, and memory/disk spilling at runtime did not introduce obvious overhead and interference with actual computing and data handling.

6   Concluding Discussion

Science communities have been actively employing both data science and scientific computing for science discovery and innovation. The fusion of HDA and HPC becomes a prominent need. Here, we have explored the convergence of HDA and HPC in a geocomputation scenario and studied the software components that require technical innovations to accelerate the end-to-end performance. Spark is a scalable data-intensive computing solution that has comprehensive virtualization, scheduling, and resource allocation strategies. It provides an enabling software infrastructure for HDA in geocomputation. Integrating MPI applications in Spark context is feasible.

Our proposed design is applicable to general geocomputation applications—transforming an HPC workflow into data-driven HDA+HPC hybrid solutions is a promising path for resolving the computational bottlenecks introduced by GIS software limitations and its associated data and computing challenges. Specific spatial characteristics and geospatial workflow patterns may also be leveraged for improving data logistics and resource management on cloud and HPC infrastructure. Raster operations such as local, focal, and zonal map algebra can be effectively transformed into mapreduce functions. Vector operations can also be transformed using distributed graph libraries, such as GraphX in Spark [9], and vector decomposition techniques, such as vector tiles [25]. Sequential implementation can be directly incorporated into the map functions. Development and computation of the reduce functions, however, are non-trivial and require further computational studies. When multiple distributed datasets (RDDs) interoperate, frequent data shuffling may significantly increase computational cost. Specific spatial indexing, caching, and partitioning schemes are needed to address the challenges in runtime data management and task scheduling.

HPC has been a major accelerator for machine learning algorithms. As deep learning turns to self-supervised learning to identify patterns and create knowledge within a dataset itself, large-scale data transformation and augmentation solutions [28] become critical for enabling scalable learning from massive datasets. GeoAI [21,22] is no exception. In general, as data and learning become increasingly important in a scientific computing application, the fusion of HDA and HPC will pave the way to a converged platform and programming interface for domain application development. For instance, to make data interoperable, there have been efforts to make columnized table and distributed datasets [7] standard in data analytics and machine learning libraries for GPU [26,27], data-intensive computing [31,36], and cluster computing to seamlessly share data in different memory hierarchies.

Acknowledgements. Liu's work is partly supported by the Laboratory Directed Research and Development Program of Oak Ridge National Laboratory (ORNL), managed by UT-Battelle, LLC, for the US Department of Energy under contract DE-AC05-00OR22725. This research used resources of the Compute and Data Environment for Science (CADES) at ORNL, which is supported by the Office of Science of the U.S. Department of Energy under Contract No. DE-AC05-00OR22725. The data registration and publishing used the Constellation Data Portal, a feature in the Scalable Data Infrastructure for Science (SDIS) at the Oak Ridge Leadership Computing Facility (OLCF) in ORNL.

References

1. Anderson, M., et al.: Bridging the gap between HPC and big data frameworks. Proc. VLDB Endow. **10**(8), 901–912 (2017)
2. Asch, M., et al.: Big data and extreme-scale computing: pathways to convergence-toward a shaping strategy for a future software and data ecosystem for scientific inquiry. Int. J.High Perform. Comput. Appl. **32**(4), 435–479 (2018)

3. Astraea: RasterFrames (2020). https://rasterframes.io/
4. Baig, F., Mehrotra, M., Vo, H., Wang, F., Saltz, J., Kurc, T.: SparkGIS: Efficient comparison and evaluation of algorithm results in tissue image analysis studies. In: Wang, F., Luo, G., Weng, C., Khan, A., Mitra, P., Yu, C. (eds.) Big-O(Q)/DMAH -2015. LNCS, vol. 9579, pp. 134–146. Springer, Cham (2016). https://doi.org/10. 1007/978-3-319-41576-5_10
5. Bhaduri, B., et al.: High performance geocomputation for assessing human dynamics at planet scale. Technical Report, Oak Ridge National Lab. (ORNL), Oak Ridge, TN (United States) (2019)
6. Boncz, P.A., Zukowski, M., Nes, N.: MonetDB/X100: Hyper-pipelining query execution. In: CIDR, vol. 5, pp. 225–237 (2005)
7. DLPack-RFC: DLPack: Open in memory tensor structure (2020). https://github. com/dmlc/dlpack
8. Gittens, A., et al.: Alchemist: an apache Spark-MPI interface. Concurr. Comput. Pract. Exp. **31**(16), e5026 (2019)
9. Gonzalez, J.E., Xin, R.S., Dave, A., Crankshaw, D., Franklin, M.J., Stoica, I.: GraphX: Graph processing in a distributed dataflow framework. In: 11th {USENIX} Symposium on Operating Systems Design and Implementation, ({OSDI} 14), pp. 599–613 (2014)
10. Goodchild, M.F., Longley, P.A.: The practice of geographic information science (2014)
11. Hey, T., et al.: The Fourth Paradigm: Data-intensive Scientific Discovery, vol. 1. Microsoft Research, Redmond (2009)
12. Horovod: Horovod in spark (2020). https://horovod.readthedocs.io/en/stable/ spark_include.html
13. Hughes, J.N., Annex, A., Eichelberger, C.N., Fox, A., Hulbert, A., Ronquest, M.: Geomesa: a distributed architecture for spatio-temporal fusion. In: Geospatial Informatics, Fusion, and Motion Video Analytics V, vol. 9473, p. 94730F. International Society for Optics and Photonics (2015)
14. Kini, A., Emanuele, R.: GeoTrellis: Adding geospatial capabilities to spark. Spark Summit (2014)
15. Klasky, S., et al.: A view from ORNL: scientific data research opportunities in the big data age. In: 2018 IEEE 38th International Conference on Distributed Computing Systems (ICDCS), pp. 1357–1368. IEEE (2018)
16. Liu, J., Racah, E., Koziol, Q., Canon, R.S., Gittens, A.: H5Spark: bridging the I/O gap between spark and scientific data formats on HPC systems. Cray User Group (2016)
17. Liu, Q., et al.: Hello ADIOS: the challenges and lessons of developing leadership class I/O frameworks. Concurr. Compu. Pract. Exp. **26**(7), 1453–1473 (2014)
18. Liu, Y.Y., Maidment, D.R., Tarboton, D.G., Zheng, X., Wang, S.: A CyberGIS integration and computation framework for high-resolution continental-scale flood inundation mapping. JAWRA J. Am. Water Resour. Assoc. **54**(4), 770–784 (2018)
19. Liu, Y.Y., Tarboton, D.G., Maidment, D.R.: Height above nearest drainage (HAND) and hydraulic property table for CONUS version 0.2.0. (20200301) (2020). https://cfim.ornl.gov/data/
20. Liu, Y.Y., Tarboton, D.G., Maidment, D.R.: Height above nearest drainage (HAND) and hydraulic property table for CONUS version 0.2.1. (20200601) (2020). https://cfim.ornl.gov/data/
21. Lunga, D., Gerrand, J., Yang, L., Layton, C., Stewart, R.: Apache spark accelerated deep learning inference for large scale satellite image analytics. IEEE J. Sel. Top. Appl. Earth Obs. Remote Sens. **13**, 271–283 (2020)

22. Lunga, D.D., Bhaduri, B., Stewart, R.: The trillion pixel GeoAI challenge workshop. Technical Report, Oak Ridge National Lab. (ORNL), Oak Ridge, TN (United States) (2019)
23. Malitsky, N., et al.: Building near-real-time processing pipelines with the Spark-MPI platform. In: 2017 New York Scientific Data Summit (NYSDS), pp. 1–8 (2017)
24. Malitsky, N., Castain, R., Cowan, M.: Spark-MPI: approaching the fifth paradigm of cognitive applications. arXiv preprint arXiv:1806.01110 (2018)
25. Mapbox: Vector tiles reference (2020). https://docs.mapbox.com/vector-tiles/reference/
26. NVIDIA: CUDF - GPU data frames (2020). https://github.com/rapidsai/cudf
27. NVIDIA: GPU data science (2020). https://rapids.ai
28. NVIDIA: The NVIDIA data loading library (DALI) (2020). https://developer.nvidia.com/DALI
29. OSGeo: The geospatial data abstraction library (GDAL) (2020). https://gdal.org
30. Palamuttam, R., et al.: SciSpark: applying in-memory distributed computing to weather event detection and tracking. In: 2015 IEEE International Conference on Big Data (Big Data), pp. 2020–2026. IEEE (2015)
31. Rocklin, M.: DASK: Parallel computation with blocked algorithms and task scheduling. In: Proceedings of the 14th Python in Science Conference, pp. 130–136 (2015)
32. Tang, M., Yu, Y., Malluhi, Q.M., Ouzzani, M., Aref, W.G.: LocationSpark: a distributed in-memory data management system for big spatial data. Proc. VLDB Endow. 9(13), 1565–1568 (2016)
33. Vazhkudai, S.S., et al.: Constellation: a science graph network for scalable data and knowledge discovery in extreme-scale scientific collaborations. In: 2016 IEEE International Conference on Big Data (Big Data), pp. 3052–3061. IEEE (2016)
34. You, S., Zhang, J., Gruenwald, L.: Large-scale spatial join query processing in cloud. In: 2015 31st IEEE International Conference on Data Engineering Workshops, pp. 34–41. IEEE (2015)
35. Yu, J., Wu, J., Sarwat, M.: GeoSpark: a cluster computing framework for processing large-scale spatial data. In: Proceedings of the 23rd SIGSPATIAL International Conference on Advances in Geographic Information Systems, pp. 1–4 (2015)
36. Zaharia, M., et al.: Spark: cluster computing with working sets. HotCloud 10(10), 95 (2010)
37. Zheng, X., Tarboton, D.G., Maidment, D.R., Liu, Y.Y., Passalacqua, P.: River channel geometry and rating curve estimation using height above the nearest drainage. JAWRA J. Am. Water Resour. Assoc. 54(4), 785–806 (2018)

Enabling Scientific Discovery at Next-Generation Light Sources with Advanced AI and HPC

Nicholas Schwarz[1](✉), Stuart Campbell[2], Alexander Hexemer[3],
Apurva Mehta[4], and Jana Thayer[4]

[1] Argonne National Laboratory, Lemont, IL 60439, USA
nschwarz@anl.gov
[2] Brookhaven National Laboratory, Upton, NY 11973, USA
scampbell@bnl.gov
[3] Lawrence Berkeley National Laboratory, Berkeley, CA 94705, USA
ahexemer@lbl.gov
[4] SLAC National Accelerator Laboratory, Menlo Park, CA 94025, USA
{mehta,jana}@slac.stanford.edu

Abstract. The synchrotron and free electron laser light sources, large scientific user facilities, are in the position to help solve some of the most challenging and novel scientific questions facing the world, ranging from the design of new materials to manipulate classical and quantum information with high fidelity and ultra low power consumption, to enabling systems for efficient energy storage, transportation, and conversion that will drive the emerging economy based on renewable energy, to understanding the structure and motion of protein molecules to enable individualized medicine. These scientific opportunities will be addressed by new measurement techniques, technological advances in detectors, multi-modal data utilization, and advances in data analysis algorithms, all of which are being driven to a new level of sophistication. Over the next decade, it is estimated that the US light sources will generate in the exabyte (EB) range of data, require tens to 1,000 PFLOPS of peak on-demand computing resources, and utilize billions of core hours per year. Scientific discovery on this scale will be enabled by data management and workflow tools that integrate user facility instruments with sufficient computing, networking, and storage resources, on-demand utilization of super-computing environments to enable real-time data processing, real-time data analysis capabilities to significantly reduce data volumes and provide feedback during experiments to improve data quality and to drive the direction of ongoing measurements, the application of advanced machine learning algorithms to make crucial experiment decisions, and the integration of simulations and model-based approaches to facilitate automated experiment design and steering of data collection.

Keywords: Scientific user facilities · Experimental/Observational facilities · Machine learning · Real-time · On-demand · Distributed workflows · High-performance computing

© UChicago Argonne, LLC 2020
J. Nichols et al. (Eds.): SMC 2020, CCIS 1315, pp. 145–156, 2020.
https://doi.org/10.1007/978-3-030-63393-6_10

1   Introduction

The synchrotron and free electron laser (FEL) light sources, large scientific user facilities, are in the position to help solve some of the most challenging and novel scientific questions facing the world, ranging from the design of new materials to manipulate classical and quantum information with high fidelity and ultra low power consumption, to enabling systems for efficient energy storage, transportation, and conversion that will drive the emerging economy based on renewable energy, to understanding the structure and motion of protein molecules to enable individualized medicine.

These scientific opportunities will be addressed by new measurement techniques, technological advances in detectors, multi-modal data utilization, and advances in data analysis algorithms, all of which are being driven to a new level of sophistication by existing and new light sources. These problems are complex, requiring multiple techniques; novel and complex data analysis for multi-modal data is needed. Increases in brightness and advances in detector data rates drive the need for real-time analysis, by humans or by advanced machine learning (ML) algorithms, to make crucial experiment decisions.

It is estimated that the US light sources will generate in the exabyte (EB) range of data, require tens to $1,000$ PFLOPS of peak on-demand computing resources, which will only be available at high-end computing facilities, and utilize billions of core hours per year by 2028. Today, the US light sources serve over $11,000$ users per year performing over $10,000$ experiments per year [1]. Unified solutions across the facilities are required in order to leverage efficiencies of scale, and to provide facility users with the ability to easily and transparently manipulate data across multiple facilities. Computing advances are required in four main areas:

Data management and workflow tools that integrate scientific instruments with computing and storage resources, for use during experiments, as well as facile user access for post-experiment analysis.

Real-time data analysis capabilities to significantly reduce data volumes and provide feedback during experiments to improve data quality and to drive the direction of ongoing measurements; the application of advanced machine learning algorithms and the integration of simulations and model-based approaches will allow automated steering of data collection.

On-demand utilization of super-computing environments to enable real-time data processing.

Data storage resources to house the continually increasing volumes of valuable scientific data produced by the light sources.

The light source mission will only truly be realized by coupling the intrinsic capabilities of the facilities with advanced data management and analysis. The consequences of not delivering these developments would result in the following: 1) facilities would be forced to artificially reduce the readout rates of future detectors, constraining the number of experiments that can be performed at each light source and, hence, dramatically limiting the science output of each facility; 2) many experiments requiring high statistics would not be feasible; 3) the ability of users to efficiently acquire, manage and analyze their data would be severely limited, increasing the time to, and limiting the amount of, publication; and 4) experiments requiring complex multi-modal data analysis would not be possible, reducing the scientific impact of the facilities.

2   Scale of the Challenge

The US light sources have performed detailed analysis of their data management and analysis needs. The facilities have worked together to cross-check and review each other's analysis for completeness and soundness. Overall, it is estimated that the US light sources will generate data in the exabyte (EB) range per year within the next decade, requiring tens to 1,000 PFLOPS of peak on-demand computing resources and billions of core hours to process (see Fig. 1 and Table 1). This data will be generated at over 200 planned instruments performing over 15,000 experiments per year across the facilities.

Light source techniques will include ptychography, Bragg coherent diffraction imaging, x-ray photon correlation spectroscopy, and other coherent diffraction imaging modalities, serial crystallography, high-speed tomography, infrared tomography, diffraction tomography, high-speed spectroscopy, high-speed x-ray fluorescence mapping, high-speed 3D micro- and nano-diffraction, high-energy diffraction microscopy, and other scattering mechanisms. The differences in data generation rates across the facilities depend on the number, rate and resolution of the detectors at each instrument which in turn depend on factors like the brightness of the source and the actual requirements of the experimental technique specific to a particular instrument.

Advanced Light Source (ALS) at Lawrence Berkeley National Laboratory. Estimation for the ALS is based on the current and planned beamlines and a 5,000 h per year cycle. Data and compute estimates were based on multiple surveys and discussions with management and beamline staff. Included in the discussions are current and future detectors for beamlines and upgrades in robots and optics. Currently the ALS produces on the order of 2 PB of data a year. The major contributors are currently the tomography and the ptychography beamline. Upgrades in detectors and optics will increase the data rate over the next few years. The ALS Upgrade will have the biggest impact on data rates and compute requirements, increasing the data rate and compute requirements of the facility [2].

Advanced Photon Source (APS) at Argonne National Laboratory. Based on the beamline portfolio planned for the APS over the next decade [3,4], including the planned APS Upgrade feature beamlines and enhancements, and based on today's understanding of the portfolio's data requirements, the APS is able to estimate its data generation rates per year. The APS generated these estimates by conducting a survey of all beamlines and analyzed projected data rates in the future considering technique, detector advances, experiment uptimes and allocations, and the impact of increased flux and coherence from the upgraded APS accelerator and storage ring. Today the facility's managed beamlines generate approximately 4 PB of data annually. This will increase to approximately 7 PB per year before the APS Upgrade storage ring is installed. Once normal operations resume in the APS Upgrade era, the aggregate data volume generated by the facility per year will increase by two orders of magnitude compared to today's rates. In order to cope with this amount of data, by 2021 the APS will require 4 PFLOPS of on-demand computing available, and 50 PFLOPS by 2028.

Linac Coherent Light Source (LCLS) at SLAC National Accelerator Laboratory. In 2021, when the LCLS-II source turns on, the repetition rate will increase 120 Hz to 1 MHz requiring an evolution of the present data system. Based on the set of experiments currently planned for the next decade and based on today's understanding of the computing and data requirements, the computing demand from LCLS-II can be estimated. Once LCLS-II is commissioned, roughly 85% of user experiment time will require up to 1 PFLOPS of computing power (compared to 0.05 PFLOPS today), with a subset requiring up to 60 PFLOPS. This level of real-time computing is required to dynamically process the data and provide on-the-fly analysis that is critical to the execution of the facility's first experiments portfolio. When LCLS-II-HE is commissioned, a conservative estimate is that roughly 85% of experiments will require up to 5 PFLOPS, with peak requirements in the EFLOPS range [5,6]. The actual fraction using large-scale computing is likely to be even higher, as more areas adopt high-end workflows such as coherent imaging.

National Synchrotron Light Source II (NSLS-II) at Brookhaven National Laboratory. The NSLS-II [7,8] generated data production estimates by conducting a survey of all 28 currently operating beamlines. Future projections were made considering current data rates, emerging advances in techniques, detector technologies, experimental uptimes, and anticipated allocations. Given these considerations, the NSLS-II is projected to be ideally collecting approximately 20 PBs of raw data per year by 2021, and up to 80–90 PBs of raw data by 2028. To process this generated data will require on-demand computing power of 2.5 PFLOPS by 2021, and 45 PFLOPS by 2028. Note that these projections do not take into account continued facility build-out, which could significantly increase these already daunting estimates of storage capacity and required compute.

Stanford Synchrotron Radiation Lightsource (SSRL) at SLAC National Accelerator Laboratory. SSRL computing requirements will be significantly less than LCLS, however, they are growing rapidly with commissioning of a new high-brightness scattering beamline, upgrade of the detectors at the macromolecular crystallography beamline, and growth of the full-field imaging activities [9]. SSRL is also increasingly investing software development for rapid extraction of knowledge from raw measurements. To fully meet the growing need SSRL is beginning to explore other resources both for high power computing as well as archival storage of data and data derived products. The SSRL estimates it will collect approximately 1–2 PBs of raw data per year by 2021 requiring up to 1 PFLOPS of on-demand computing resources, and up to 10 PBs of raw data by 2028 requiring up to 10 PFLOPS of on-demand computing resources.

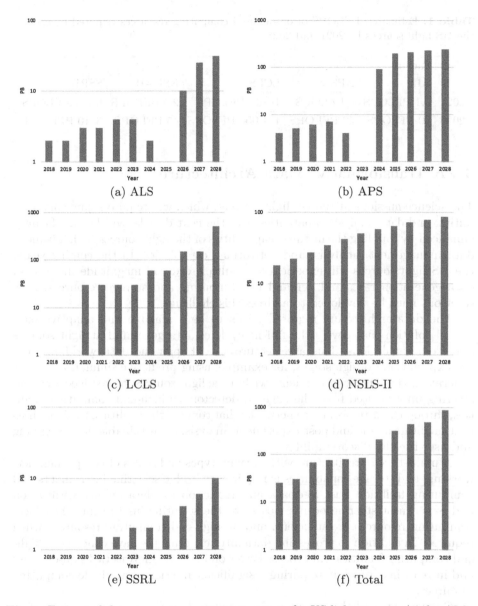

Fig. 1. Estimated data generation rates per year at the US light sources. At the ALS and APS, data generation will stop during 2025 and 2023, respectively, due to installations of new storage rings. Aggregate data generation across the US light sources will approach the exabyte (EB) range per year by 2028.

Table 1. Estimated PFLOPS of on-demand computing resources required by each of the US light sources by 2021 and 2028.

Year	Facility				
	ALS	APS	LCLS	NSLS-II	SSRL
2021	0.1 PFLOPS	4 PFLOPS	1–100 PFLOPS	2.5 PFLOPS	0.1–1 PFLOPS
2028	30 PFLOPS	50 PFLOPS	1–1,000 PFLOPS	45 PFLOPS	5–10 PFLOPS

3   A Transformative Data Architecture

The science missions at the US light sources, which will require significant computing and data analysis capabilities over the next decade, will be significantly enhanced by coupling the intrinsic capabilities of the light sources with advanced data management, analysis, and networking capabilities. In the coming years, the US light sources will experience a multiple order-of-magnitude increase in data generation rates and demand for computing and storage resources. New solutions must be developed to address this challenge.

The data architecture required needs to be a scalable and adaptive end-to-end solution that covers the full lifecycle of data generated at light sources and from simulations. This architecture should span the data workflow from pre-experimental design stages, for example, using predictive simulations, to its generation at scientific instruments within the light sources, to fast feedback and steering implemented from the edge on detectors to high-end computing facilities, through high-performance networks that connect the facilities, to algorithms that facilitate online and post-experiment analysis, to sustainable data archiving and user-friendly discoverability.

A multi-tiered architecture with varying types and scales of computing, networking, and storage capabilities is required to bridge scientific instruments and computing facilities. Fast feedback and reduction for data quality verification and experiment steering occurs closest to the scientific instrument when local computing resources are sufficient, and on high-end computing resources when required. In addition to processing data after experiments have concluded, high-end computing facilities will process larger online data analysis tasks on-demand and in real-time, possibly requiring a significant fraction of available computing resources.

Connecting the light sources and computing facilities requires a robust, feature rich, high-performance network that provides high throughput as well as caching, computation, and traffic engineering services. In order to seamlessly transfer or stream data, facilities need low-latency high-performance networks with bandwidth in the range of multiple terabits per second.

By 2021 the light sources will generate on the order of a few hundred petabytes of data per year; over the next decade this will increase to the exabyte range. Distributed data storage infrastructure is needed to store and archive the wealth of experiment data for publication, dissemination, and future discoverability.

Advanced algorithms, including machine learning, will play a critical role in this architecture. Within the light sources, these algorithms will provide automated setup of the source and sample alignment, intelligent data collection, quality verification, and data reduction. Combining these algorithms with theory, modeling, and simulations will drive experiment design and automated steering.

A broad suite of workflow tools is required so that instrument users and facility scientists can develop and customize data workflows for the over 200 instruments, each utilizing dozens of unique workflows, and over 15,000 experimental starts per year, that will exist at the US light sources in the coming decade. Shared orchestration tools and data transport mechanisms are required to integrate light source instruments with computing and storage resources. These common tools must be designed to enable interoperability between instruments and computing. A uniform authentication and authorization mechanism, as well as a shared allocation system, will be required to enable ease of access to data and analysis across facilities.

A common library of shared, open-source data processing, reduction, analysis, and visualization software should serve the overlapping high-priority needs of the light sources. These tools must scale as needed to operate on current and future high-end computing systems.

An appropriately resourced, diverse, and inclusive workforce is critical to realizing the data architecture described above.

4   The Role of AI/ML

The application and development of advanced artificial intelligence (AI) methodologies is critical to the current and future success of light sources. The light sources require AI developments that will have a transformative impact on the science conducted by its users in support of its mission focusing on autonomous experiments, novel data processing, optimization, and robustness.

Autonomous Experiments to Unlock New Scientific Knowledge. The experimental process targeted at the development and synthesis of new materials, for example, will rely on feedback that must be obtained on timescales too short for humans to react in order to steer ongoing experiments. These experiments require the combination and interpretation of large amounts of experimentally acquired data with knowledge from simulations and models. AI/ML will be key to realizing autonomous experiments.

Novel Data Processing. Data generation rates at the light sources are expected to increase in terms of both its complexity, due to multi-modal data utilization, and in size, by multiple orders-of-magnitude, over the next decade, especially in the coherence diffraction imaging techniques enabled by upgraded sources. This is more data than can be analyzed by conventional processes. AI/ML combined with edge computing will be required to process this anticipated deluge of data.

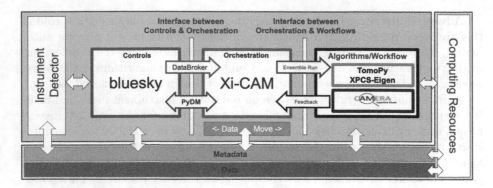

Fig. 2. High-level prototype architecture for common experiment control, data processing and analysis, and visualization tools at the US light sources.

Optimization of Complex Instruments and Accelerators. The optimization of instrumentation and of the facility will become crucial to the productivity of the light sources as complexity increases. Optimization using AI/ML will enable automated beamline alignment, including samples and optics, coupling experimental instrument feedback with accelerator status, and more efficient domain specific data acquisition protocols.

Improve Resilience and Robust Operations of Upgraded Accelerator Complexes. Today, accelerator operation is based on tens of thousands of measurements taken at intervals from seconds to minute. Upgraded facilities will experience a multiple order-of-magnitude increase in the future. AI can enable the prediction of anomalies and failure modes, maintain proper orbit motion, and extend beam lifetime.

5   First Steps

The light sources are beginning to take the first steps toward achieving this overall transformative architecture by developing common data processing tools across facilities following the high-level design in Fig. 2. The Bluesky experiment control system [10,11] serves as the underlying coordination system that interacts with scientific instruments and detectors via low-level control systems, including the Experimental Physics and Industrial Control System (EPICS) [12] and LabView (see Fig. 3). The DataBroker interface in Bluesky facilitates access to data and metadata acquired during data acquisition.

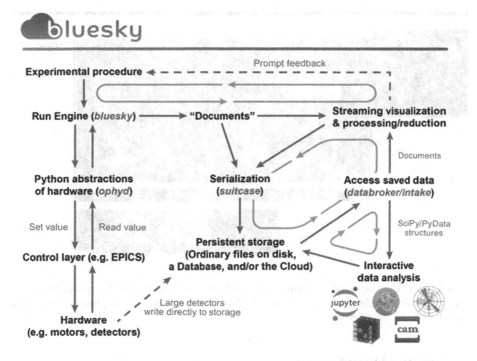

Fig. 3. Diagram to illustrate the software components, interfaces and data flow for an experiment when using Bluesky. The green labels indicate the names of the Python libraries that are part of the Bluesky Project. All communication with hardware occurs through an orchestration engine (Run Engine) that captures readings and metadata and handles any errors safely. Data is organized by Bluesky in "documents" that are dispatched to any number of consumers, such as a database, file writers or live data processing and visualization pipelines. After the experiment, the data may be retrieved either as standard data structures suitable for use with existing scientific Python libraries or suitable for piping back through the same pipelines that were used on the live data.(Color figure online)

Xi-CAM [13] serves as a data visualization and orchestration tool. Custom plug-ins are developed for techniques such as tomography and x-ray photon correlation spectroscopy that provide domain and technique specific views of data (see Fig. 4). Common data processing tools, including TomoPy [14] for tomographic reconstructions and XPCS-Eigen [15] for x-ray photon correlation spectroscopy auto-correlations, interface with Xi-CAM.

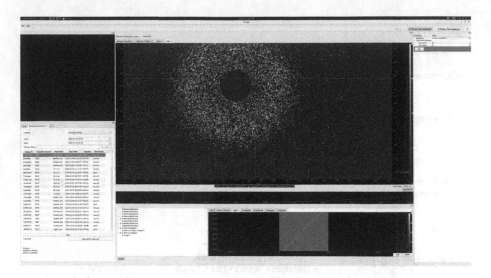

Fig. 4. Xi-CAM graphical user interface and the x-ray photon correlation spectroscopy plug-in displaying data acquired at the APS 8-ID-I instrument using bluesky and processed with XPCS-Eigen.

6   Future Directions

The planned improvements to the sources and instruments at existing and new light source facilities necessitates the development of this transformative data architecture in order to fully realize the light source science mission. Collaborative and consolidated activities are required to begin developing a common end-to-end data management solution that bridges the light sources and computing and networking facilities. To achieve this, the following efforts are needed that will align the path toward a transformative data architecture:

On-Demand, Real-Time Computing Access. A research and development effort to enable scalable, on-demand, and real-time computing access at computing facilities. This effort should include streaming data directly from light source instruments, as well as traditional data transport mechanisms. This capability is crucial to achieve fast feedback and experiment steering. Research and deployment of advanced high-performance network services to support data placement and data streaming are required.

Data Processing Software. A shared suite of user-friendly data processing, reduction, analysis, and visualization software that meets the highest priority needs of the light source user community should be developed. These shared software tools should sufficiently scale to handle the anticipated data rates and computing needs of the light sources and operate on current and future high-end computing systems.

Algorithms and AI/ML. Research and development of data analysis capabilities that utilize advanced algorithms, mathematics, and AI/ML for reduction and processing of data from high-priority light source techniques, such as ptychography, x-ray photon correlation spectroscopy, and serial femtosecond x-ray crystallography, for rare event detection to enable scientific exploration, and instrument optimization and robustness, as new and upgraded light sources come online over the next few years.

Data Storage. A sustainable distributed data storage infrastructure sufficient to store the wealth of valuable scientific data generated at the light sources. To complement this infrastructure a distributed suite of data cataloging, discoverability, and dissemination tools is required, along with appropriate policies.

Policy Implementation. Computing, storage, and networking facilities should calibrate access and allocation policies in order to meet the upcoming computing needs of the light sources and other scientific user facilities and the desired data management architecture, support for on-demand and real-time tasks beyond batch scheduling, an allocation mechanism for data storage, and allocation mechanisms for access that are uniform and portable. A common authentication and authorization mechanism should be developed and implemented across the light sources and computing, storage, and networking facilities.

Workforce. A critical workforce development strategy should be created to ensure the light sources and the computing facilities and research programs have access to necessary skill sets.

Acknowledgements. This research used resources of the Advanced Photon Source, a U.S. Department of Energy (DOE) Office of Science User Facility operated for the DOE Office of Science by Argonne National Laboratory under Contract No. DE-AC02-06CH11357. This research used resources of the Advanced Light Source, a U.S. Department of Energy (DOE) Office of Science User Facility under Contract No. DE-AC02-05CH11231. Use of the Linac Coherent Light Source (LCLS), SLAC National Accelerator Laboratory, is supported by the U.S. Department of Energy (DOE), Office of Science, Office of Basic Energy Sciences under Contract No. DE-AC02-76SF00515. This research used resources of the National Synchrotron Light Source II, a U.S. Department of Energy (DOE) Office of Science User Facility operated for the DOE Office of Science by Brookhaven National Laboratory under Contract No. DE-SC0012704. Use of the Stanford Synchrotron Radiation Lightsource, SLAC National Accelerator Laboratory, is supported by the U.S. Department of Energy (DOE), Office of Science, Office of Basic Energy Sciences under Contract No. DE-AC02-76SF00515.

The authors would like to thank Deborah Bard (National Energy Research Scientific Computing Center, Lawrence Berkeley National Laboratory), Eli Dart (Energy Sciences Network, Lawrence Berkeley National Laboratory), James Sethian (Center for Advanced Mathematics for Energy Research Applications, Lawrence Berkeley National Laboratory), Tom Uram (Argonne Leadership Computing Facility, Argonne National Laboratory), and Sudharshan Vazhkudai (Oak Ridge Leadership Computing Facility, Oak Ridge National Laboratory) for their valued advice and partnerships, and Mike Dunne, John Hill, Steve Kevan, Paul McIntyre, and Stephen Streiffer for their direction and leadership.

References

1. U.S Department of Energy, Office of Science, Basic Energy Sciences, User Facilities. https://science.osti.gov/bes/suf/User-Facilities
2. Soft X-ray Science Opportunities Using Diffraction-Limited Storage Rings. https://als.lbl.gov/wp-content/uploads/2016/09/sxr_workshop_report.pdf
3. The Advanced Photon Source Strategic Plan. https://www.aps.anl.gov/The-Advanced-Photon-Source-Strategic-Plan
4. Early Science at the Upgraded Advanced Photon Source. https://www.aps.anl.gov/files/APS-Uploads/Aps-Upgrade/Beamlines/APS-U%20Early-Science-103015-FINAL.pdf
5. New Science Opportunities Enabled by LCLS-II X-ray Lasers. https://portal.slac.stanford.edu/sites/lcls_public/Documents/LCLS-IIScienceOpportunities_final.pdf
6. Thayer, J., et al.: Data processing at the linac coherent light source. In: IEEE/ACM 1st Annual Workshop on Large-scale Experiment-in-the-Loop Computing (XLOOP), Denver, CO, USA, pp. 32–37 (2019)
7. National Synchrotron Light Source II Strategic Plan. https://www.bnl.gov/ps/docs/pdf/NSLS2-Strategic-Plan.pdf
8. Hill, J., et al.: Future trends in synchrotron science at NSLS-II. J. Phys. Condens. Matter **32**(37), 374008 (2020)
9. Stanford Synchrotron Radiation Lightsource Strategic Plan: 2019–2023. https://www-ssrl.slac.stanford.edu/content/sites/default/files/documents/ssrl_strategic_plan_2019-2023.pdf
10. Allan, D., Caswell, T., Campbell, S., Rakitin, M.: Bluesky's ahead: a multi-facility collaboration for an a la carte software project for data acquisition and management. Synchrotron Radiat. News **32**(3), 19–22 (2019)
11. Bluesky Project website. https://blueskyproject.io
12. Experimental Physics and Industrial Control System. https://epics-controls.org
13. Pandolfi, R.J., et al.: XI-CAM: a versatile interface for data visualization and analysis. J. Synchrotron Radiat. **25**, 1261–1270 (2018)
14. Gursoy, D., De Carlo, F., Xiao, X., Jacobsen, C.: TomoPy: a framework for the analysis of synchrotron tomographic data. J. Synchrotron Radiat. **21**(5), 1188–1193 (2014)
15. Khan, F., Narayanan, S., Sersted, R., Schwarz, N., Sandy, A.: Distributed X-ray photon correlation spectroscopy data reduction using Hadoop MapReduce. J. Synchrotron Radiat. **25**, 1135–1143 (2018)

Visualization as a Service
for Scientific Data

David Pugmire[1]([⊠]), James Kress[1], Jieyang Chen[1], Hank Childs[3], Jong Choi[1], Dmitry Ganyushin[1], Berk Geveci[2], Mark Kim[1], Scott Klasky[1], Xin Liang[1], Jeremy Logan[1], Nicole Marsaglia[3], Kshitij Mehta[1], Norbert Podhorszki[1], Caitlin Ross[2], Eric Suchyta[1], Nick Thompson[1], Steven Walton[3], Lipeng Wan[1], and Matthew Wolf[1]

[1] Oak Ridge National Laboratory, Oak Ridge, TN 37831, USA
`pugmire@ornl.gov`
[2] Kitware, Inc., Clifton Park, NY, USA
[3] University of Oregon, Eugene, OR 97403, USA

Abstract. One of the primary challenges facing scientists is extracting understanding from the large amounts of data produced by simulations, experiments, and observational facilities. The use of data across the entire lifetime ranging from real-time to post-hoc analysis is complex and varied, typically requiring a collaborative effort across multiple teams of scientists. Over time, three sets of tools have emerged: one set for analysis, another for visualization, and a final set for orchestrating the tasks. This trifurcated tool set often results in the manual assembly of analysis and visualization workflows, which are one-off solutions that are often fragile and difficult to generalize. To address these challenges, we propose a serviced-based paradigm and a set of abstractions to guide its design. These abstractions allow for the creation of services that can access and interpret data, and enable interoperability for intelligent scheduling of workflow systems. This work results from a codesign process over analysis, visualization, and workflow tools to provide the flexibility required for production use. Finally, this paper describes a forward-looking research and development plan that centers on the concept of visualization and analysis technology as reusable services, and also describes several real-world use cases that implement these concepts.

Keywords: Scientific visualization · High-performance computing · In situ analysis · Visualization

D. Pugmire et al.—Contributed Equally.
This manuscript has been co-authored by UT-Battelle, LLC, under contract DE-AC05-00OR22725 with the US Department of Energy (DOE). The US government retains and the publisher, by accepting the article for publication, acknowledges that the US government retains a nonexclusive, paid-up, irrevocable, worldwide license to publish or reproduce the published form of this manuscript, or allow others to do so, for US government purposes. DOE will provide public access to these results of federally sponsored research in accordance with the DOE Public Access Plan (http://energy.gov/downloads/doe-public-access-plan).

J. Nichols et al. (Eds.): SMC 2020, CCIS 1315, pp. 157–174, 2020.
https://doi.org/10.1007/978-3-030-63393-6_11

1   Introduction

Gaining insight from large scientific data sets, while challenging, has traditionally been tractable because the process has generally been well understood. This tractability is the result of three key properties: low barrier to entry, collaboration, and standardization. These traditional approaches had a low barrier to entry as the data was written to permanent storage in a standardized way and could easily be shared with others. This in turn enabled rich collaboration among domain, computational and visualization scientists. Once data is stored on disk, each stakeholder can access the data at their convenience, and do so with dedicated visualization and analysis software, custom scripts, etc., which are easily shared. Exploration of data often takes place using GUI-based tools that are well supported and easy to learn. Further, the standardization is helpful on a variety of fronts, not only in how data is stored and represented, but also in how data is accessed and processed. The benefit of standardization is in code reuse, enabling the efforts of a community of software developers to increase their impact. This is particularly needed for visualization and analysis software, since such software often contains a large number of algorithms and data format readers.

The three beneficial properties of low barrier to entry, collaboration, and standardization are rapidly becoming infeasible because of two important trends in high-performance computing: Big Data and hardware complexity. With respect to Big Data, scientific data has been dramatically affected by the three V's—volume, velocity, and variety. With respect to hardware complexity, modern computers increasingly have heterogeneous hardware, deep memory hierarchies, and increased costs for data movement and access. As a result of the volume and velocity components of the Big Data trend, along with the increased costs of data movement and access, saving all data to disk is no longer possible. Instead, data will need to be visualized and analyzed while it is being generated, i.e., in situ processing. But in situ processing presents challenges to the three beneficial properties. In particular, standardization is more difficult since data is being delivered in a variety of ways and locations. Rather than files in known file formats stored to permanent storage, data may come from a computational simulation over a socket, from a remote experimental resource, or it may be located in the memory of a GPU accelerator, just to name a few. Further, the barrier to entry is often substantially higher, requiring highly-experienced, "ninja" programmers to incorporate visualization and analysis algorithms. This limits collaboration, since it is difficult to get visualization and analysis routines applied, leaving the task to only those that can wrangle complex software.

Scientific campaigns have dealt with these challenges by moving toward automated workflows to control the complexities with running simulations. These systems are enabled by middleware systems that provide efficient layers between applications and systems, and by emerging workflow systems that orchestrate executables and the movement of data. That said, visualization and analysis has struggled to adapt to this workflow approach. Despite recent support for in situ processing and heterogeneous architectures, the fundamental "glue" is lacking for bringing together the disparate tools and libraries for a scientific software campaign. Best efforts often are targeted out of necessity at a narrow range of use cases and are often brittle and difficult to reuse at a later date or generalize for usage in other situations. These problems make the practical and widespread use of these tools difficult, further leading to fragmented approaches as every scientific team creates its own customized approach. Finally, while the results to date have been lacking, they have also taken great expertise to achieve. Fundamentally, we feel that this mismatch—great expertise to achieve poor results—indicates a failure in the underlying approach.

In this paper, we advocate for a new model for visualization and analysis of scientific data to address these challenges that is based on following the "aaS" paradigm—as a service. This model is focused on identifying abstractions for points of interaction between visualization, middleware, and workflow systems. The abstractions provide clear interfaces between these three sub-components in a scientific campaign and makes it easier for them to work together. These abstractions will make it much easier to move visualization computation *to the data*, which is a reversal from the previous model, in which it was easier to move the data. This in turn restores the possibility of low barrier to entry, collaboration, and standardization, by making visualization workflows more user-friendly and intuitive and enabling them to become more schedulable, lightweight, and pervasive. Overall, we feel the entire ecosystem will be more cost effective, portable, efficient, and intuitive—a return to the benefits our community has traditionally enjoyed.

An important benefit of an aaS approach is that it enables each participant to focus on their own area of expertise. For application scientists, visualization should be about declarative intentions. For example, isocontours of primary variables are needed in near-real-time (NRT) to track the progress of a simulation, and high-quality renderings of vorticity magnitude and particle traces around regions of interest are needed after the campaign is completed. Visualization experts should focus on algorithms that provide the necessary functionality, perform well on computing platforms, and operate on a variety of data types. Middleware experts should focus on providing efficient I/O and data movement capabilities between data producers and data consumers. Workflow experts should focus on taking scientific intentions and orchestrating the movement of data from producers among all the data consumers to provide the desired results. By providing clear interfaces (i.e., abstractions) between these pieces, it is possible to rethink how analysis and visualization at scale are performed.

The remainder of this paper is organized around the discussion of a set of abstractions (Fig. 3) we have identified that enable Visualization As A Service (VAAS). These abstractions are targeted at addressing the barriers to extracting insight from large scientific data by providing a service based paradigm, and provide a road map for research and development that can take full advantage of the immense power of modern computing systems. At the same time, these abstractions lower the barriers to entry for users giving them the flexibility to build and connect services together in arbitrary ways. In Sect. 2 we provide two motivating examples that helped guide our thinking in the identification of these abstractions, and Sect. 3 discusses related work and complementary efforts towards these goals. Section 4 describes the two tiers of abstractions in detail. The base tier of abstractions provides the foundation necessary for creating visualization services. These abstractions include **data access, data interpretation**, and **service composition/workflow** abstractions. Together, these three abstractions allow for the creation of basic visualization services since there is a way to access the data, a way to interpret the data, and a workflow system that understands how to schedule the visualization services in conjunction with the simulation or experiment. The second tier of abstractions is built on top of the base tier and is concerned with making visualization services more powerful, easier to use and schedule, and more intelligent. Specifically, we identify **portable performance, performance modeling**, and **declarative invocation** as this higher tier. Section 5 discusses how our prior research and experience with application engagements have guided our thinking and the development of these abstractions. We show how these abstractions have proven useful and describe their impact on scientific applications. Finally, Sect. 6 concludes with a discussion on how further research and development in these abstractions can improve the process of analysis and visualization in scientific campaigns.

2 Motivating Workflows

Creating and successfully executing large, complex workflows is a challenging task. These workflows must be extensively vetted before execution to ensure that the necessary results can be captured in a timely manner that efficiently uses computing and/or experimental facilities. This vetting process often requires substantial time from teams of experts, including application scientists, computer scientists, mathematicians, and data analysts. The efforts of these individuals create unique and complicated workflows with a myriad of different analysis and visualization needs [23]. This section describes two different recent visualization and analysis workflows with which our group has been involved and highlights the interesting aspects and complexities of both efforts. The first use case involves work with a simulation, and the second is with an experiment.

2.1 Fusion Simulation Workflow

The simulation use case comes from the high-fidelity whole device modeling (WDM) of magnetically confined fusion plasmas. WDM is among the most computationally demanding and scientifically challenging simulation projects that exists within the US Department of Energy (DOE). The 10 year goal of WDM is to have a complete and comprehensive application that will include all the important physics components required to simulate a full toroidal discharge in a tokamak fusion reactor.

This workflow primarily comprises two different fusion codes, XGC and GENE, which must be coupled together. Coupling these codes enables the simulation to advance further in a shorter amount of time while retaining more accuracy than either code can achieve on its own. XGC is a particle-in-cell code

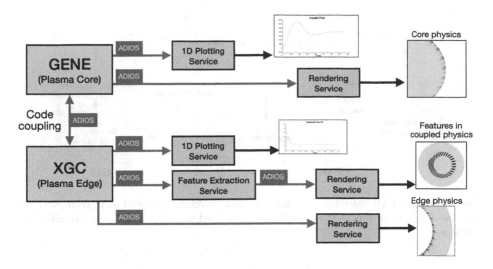

Fig. 1. Workflow for coupled physics simulation. Data from the core and edge coupled physics codes are sent to services to perform analysis and visualization. The resulting images from the rendering services are saved to disk.

optimized for treating the edge plasma, and GENE is a continuum code optimized for the core of the fusion reactor. In the WDM workflow, ADIOS is used to save checkpoint/restart files and offloads variables for in situ analysis and visualization [12]. For in-memory data exchange, ADIOS is used to couple the core and edge simulations [13]. Figure 1 shows the various components of the WDM workflow. The workflow is a complex process that requires sending data to and from multiple separate executables to advance the physics while also visualizing important variables.

2.2   KSTAR

The experiment analysis workflow that comes from fusion experiments is designed to validate and refine simulations that model complex physical processes in the fusion reactor and to test and validate hypotheses. Recent advances in sensors and imaging systems, such as sub-microsecond data acquisition capabilities and extremely fast 2D/3D imaging, allow researchers to capture very large volumes of data at high spatial and temporal resolution for monitoring and diagnostic purposes and post-experiment analyses. Alone, a 2D spatial imaging system, called Electron Cyclotron Emission Imaging, at the Korean Superconducting Tokamak Advanced Research (KSTAR) can capture 10 GB of image data per 10 second shot [51].

A system using ADIOS was developed for KSTAR to support various data challenges by executing remote experimental data processing workflows in fusion science. This system is one of the drivers for the development of the DataMan engine to support science workflows execution over the wide-area network for NRT streaming of experiment data in remote computing resource facilities.

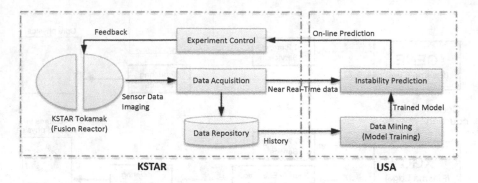

Fig. 2. The KSTAR worfklow showing the data traveling back and forth from KSTAR and the USA. Each box in the workflow is composed of multiple different visualization services.

An example of a KSTAR workflow is shown in Fig. 2. This workflow is a multilevel workflow in that each box comprises one or more sub-workflows. One main goal is to stream online fusion experiment data from KSTAR in Korea to a computing facility in the United States to perform various computationally intensive analyses, such as instability prediction and disruption simulation. Although our previous effort [11] focused on building remote workflows with data indexing, we are currently composing the KSTAR workflow with DataMan. In this workflow, ADIOS provides a remote coupling service to move raw observational data as streams from Korea to the USA. Once data streams arrives in a US computing facility, a set of analysis and visualization workflows will be launched to perform denoising, segmentation, feature detection, and selection to detect any instabilities. Visualization results can then be delivered back to Korea for designing the upcoming shots.

3   On the Shoulders of Giants

The abstractions introduced in Sect. 1 were identified through a careful analysis of our experiences working with application scientists and from the body of published literature. This section describes the systems and concepts that guide our thoughts.

3.1   Tier 1 Related Works

The tier 1 abstractions provide a foundation for data access, data interpretation, and the ability to compose and schedule visualization tasks.

Traditionally, visualization has been performed as a post-processing task, which worked well until the petascale era when it broke down due to the limited I/O bandwith in supercomputers [9,10,49]. In situ processing has been successfully used to avoid this I/O bottleneck, resulting in a rich body of research and production tools. Recent works [4,6] provide surveys of the state-of-the-art in situ visualization. Middleware libraries have been developed to provide scalable I/O. Systems such as ADIOS [31] and HDF5 [47] provide a publish/subscribe model that enables flexible data access abstraction.

In situ processing is a rich space that consists of three predominant forms. In-line in situ is a synchronous method in which the data producer and visualization run concurrently on the same resource. Tools such as VisIt Libsim [48] and ParaView Catalyst [3,17] support this model. In-transit in situ is an asynchronous method in which the data producer and visualization run on separate resources. Tools such as EPIC [16], Freeprocessing [18], and ICARUS [45] support this model. Hybrid in situ methods provide the flexibility of supporting both synchronous and asynchronous processing. Tools such as Damaris/Viz [14] and SENSEI [4] provide interfaces to use VisIt Libsim and ParaView Catalyst to support a hybrid model. Ascent [28] is a lightweight in situ framework that also provides hybrid model support. Both SENSEI and Ascent use the ADIOS [39] middleware library, which provides a publish/subscribe view of data access using several different data transport mechanisms, including files, in-line, and in-transit.

Data interpretation has been largely focused on data models and schemas. Ascent uses the rich capabilities of BluePrint [29], whereas SENSEI, VisIt Lib-Sim, and ParaView Catalyst rely on the Visualization Toolkit (VTK) data model, which is specifically targeted at the needs of visualization. VizSchema [46] provides an interpretation layer on top of ADIOS for streaming and file-based data. The Adaptable Data Interface for Services [2] is a follow-on work to VizSchema that provides more flexibility and better support for streaming data.

Many of the existing production in situ tools are monolithic and difficult to decompose for scheduling by workflow systems. Furthermore, they require instrumentation into application codes (e.g., VisIt Libsim, ParaView Catalyst, Ascent, SENSEI, Damaris, Freeprocessing) or a shared message passing interface communicator (e.g., EPIC), whereas other require coupling with files (e.g., ICARUS).

Using lightweight visualization tasks in addition to production tools has been explored in [21,43], as described in part in Sect. 2.

3.2 Tier 2 Related Works

The tier 2 abstractions are focused on providing flexibility, power, and intelligence in visualization tasks. These build on a substantial body of work by others as well as ourselves; we focus in the following discussion mostly on the connections of the abstractions to our previous work.

The importance of in situ processing highlighted the need for more flexible data models for in-memory layouts and portability across heterogeneous architectures. Early efforts such as the Extreme Scale Analysis and Visualization Library [36], Dax Toolkit [37], and Piston [32] looked at different aspects of these challenges and were combined into a single toolkit, VTK-m [38]. These efforts have demonstrated the benefits of flexible data models [35] and the portable algorithm performance across a wide variety of architectures [44,50].

A declarative view of visualization has been explored through understanding the performance of different algorithm implementations under different workloads, levels of concurrency, and architectures. Particle-tracing algorithms, which are useful methods for understanding flow, can be implemented in several different ways [42], and performance is dependent on factors such as workload, concurrency, and architecture [7,8,20,41]. Similar work was also done to understand the performance of different types of rendering algorithms for in situ settings [27], and the power-performance tradeoffs for visualization [26].

Models for performance and cost prediction can be useful to inform scheduling and placement by workflow systems. Performance and cost models for different in situ visualization methods are described in [24,25,33,34], analysis of costs for in situ analysis algorithms are described in [40], and a model for in situ rendering is provided in [27].

4   Visualization as a Service Abstractions

Moving away from monolithic or aggregated solutions would help address the challenges of visualization in an era of large streaming data and complex computing environments. The ability to break visualization and analysis tasks into pieces that can be deployed, managed, and automated by a workflow system is powerful and aligns well with the principles of service-oriented architectures (SOA) [30].

At a high level, SOA is characterized by a self-contained black box that provides a well-defined set of features for users. SOA takes several forms, including infrastructure as a service (IaaS)[1], software as a service (SaaS)[19], and microservices [15]. Cloud computing is the most common example of IaaS in which costs are controlled by dynamically allocating resources in response to changing user requirements. SaaS is characterized by the delivery of a capability using a thin client or ergonomic application programming interface. Scalability for SaaS is provided by different types of back-end implementations that are appropriately sized. Microservices are small, independently deployable executables with a distinct goal. Groups of microservices can be orchestrated to perform more complex tasks.

We envision that visualization as a service (VaaS) will apply the principles of the SOA paradigm to computational simulations and experiments. Importantly, we think that VaaS should provide a clear separation between the operations that scientists want to apply to data and the implementation details required to perform it. This will allow application scientists to concentrate on understanding their simulations. VaaS draws from several different aspects of SOA implementations.

- Similar to IaaS, visualization and analysis operations must be provisioned on an appropriate amount of resource. Too much or too little of the wrong kind of resource can result in inefficiency.

- Similar to SaaS, abstractions for access to data and execution must be provided so that application scientists can focus on the operations to be performed, and computer scientists can focus on implementation and scalability.
- Similar to microservices, VaaS would support a set of modular analysis and visualization operations that can be chained together to form complex scientific workflows.

4.1 Visualization as a Service Abstractions

Realization of an SOA to visualize large scientific data will require coordination and codesign with application scientists and disciplines within the computer science community. This section describes a set of abstractions that are targeted at guiding the framework design that follows an SOA philosophy. These abstractions serve as guiding principles for the design of visualization frameworks that can function in a service-based way. They have resulted from our work with application scientists to do visualization and from collaborations with other computer scientists in leveraging complimentary technologies.

From the perspective of an application scientist, our vision is that a service-based visualization framework would work as follows. A team of scientists plans a scientific campaign. They specify a set of visualization tasks in a declarative way. For example, isocontours of high vorticity around an inlet are required in NRT (e.g., every minute) to monitor the simulation. Volume renderings of pressure from three different views are necessary after the simulation has completed. These intentions would then be turned into a sequence of analysis and visualization tasks that would be input into an automated workflow system and run as services on the computing resources to provide the results. The abstractions and their relationships are shown in Fig. 3. These abstractions describe the points of interaction between the tasks and their sequencing that are needed to produce the results. The emphasis is on providing interfaces appropriate for the intended users. Declarative intentions separate the action from the particular algorithms selected and the resources used. Data models and schemas provide information to workflow systems about how tasks can be composed and connected. Performance models for algorithms can inform required resources and optimize the placement of tasks onto resources.

The remainder of this section describes the abstractions for VaaS in a bottom-up approach. We begin with a first tier of abstractions that provides a foundation for VaaS. These foundational abstractions address data access across memory hierarchies, service composition for workflow systems, and methods for interpretation of data between services. We then discuss a second tier of abstractions that builds on the first tier and provides improved flexibility, efficiency, and intelligence to services. These tier 2 abstractions help map visualization intentions onto efficiently executing service on the underlying computing resources.

4.2 Tier 1 Abstractions

The foundation required to support visualization requires three basic abstractions. First, a service must be able to access data from a variety of different sources.

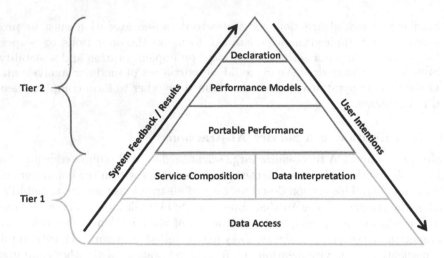

Fig. 3. Chart denoting the two tiers of abstractions that we have identified, their relationships to each other, and proximity to the user.

Second, automated workflow systems must be able to dynamically compose services into sequences and schedule and execute across a variety of resources. Finally, data models, schemas, and ontologies are needed so that workflow systems know how to connect and schedule services and so that services know how to operate on the incoming data.

Work in the first two abstractions has a heavy emphasis on disciplines outside the visualization community. The realization of VaaS will require codesign with these communities so that the pieces work together smoothly. The visualization and analysis community must create and codesign the third abstraction together with the other communities and application scientists so that things work well together. Each of the three abstractions are discussed in more detail in the following sections.

Data Access Abstraction: Visualization services need access to data that come from a variety of sources, including on-node RAM, NVRAM, different nodes in a system, nodes in a different system, and files. Furthermore, the same service might need to consume data from different sources under different circumstances (e.g., from shared memory for an in situ setting, or from disk in a post-processing setting). Supporting all of these data access modes directly in the visualization service is inefficient. Middleware systems such as ADIOS [31] and HDF5 [47] provide a publish/subscribe interface to data that hides the complexity of reading and writing data. The reliance on a data access abstraction allows the visualization community to focus on functionality and performance and the middleware community to focus on providing efficient data access. This also enables greater portability and reuse on different systems and the complex and evolving memory hierarchy.

Service Composition/Workflow Abstraction: Analysis and visualization tasks often consist of a sequence of composed subtasks. For example, rendering an isocontour might involve three steps: (1) recentering a cell-centered variable to the nodes, (2) computing the isocontour, and (3) rendering the geometry. These subtasks might have better performance if the variable recenter and isocontour are performed in situ, and the results are then sent to a set of visualization resources for rendering. In previous work, we have seen the utility of taking these "micro-workflows" and forming integrated in situ visualization libraries (e.g., Catalyst [3], libSim [48]) that can be hard-coded into an application code, as well as interface solutions such as SENSEI [4,5] that allow the workflow mechanics to be embedded into the code while leaving the choice of the in situ visualization or analytics to a run time configuration. However, to fully realize the VaaS design opportunities, we must go further in codesigning the size and scope of the visualization components with high-performance in situ workflow engines. When coupled with the other design abstractions in the VaaS system, this can enable an autonomously adapting visualization environment that can maximize efficiency, latency, or the constraint that is most relevant for that particular scientist's research campaign. One approach we have been exploring is to tie into the extended publish/subscribe semantics for ADIOS, as described in [22], so that VaaS provides context for "editing" and "managing" the data as it is published.

Data Interpretation Abstraction: Data interpretation is required for the workflow system to understand how services can be connected and for individual services to understand the data that is accessed. This information makes it possible for the workflow system to know what must be done and how an intention can be sequenced into a series of services that are chained together and placed onto resources. Data interpretation makes it possible to know which services can be connected together and ensures that inputs are paired with the appropriate outputs; in other literature this is often referred to schemas, data model matching, or ontologies. This includes information about the execution behavior of the service (e.g., the service requires collective communication and so it would run more efficiently on a smaller resource).

Once a service has access to a data stream, ontologies for interpretation and mapping to a data model are needed so that the ontologies can be used by the visualization routines. Ontologies provide the semantics for data, intentions, and operations. These provide information about a service (e.g., a service supports CPU and GPU execution, a service is compute bound or requires collective communication). Ontologies also map the intentions between different data sources (e.g., the variable "pressure" is the same as "press"). Data models include information about the types of meshes in the data (e.g., uniform grid, rectilinear grid, explicit), the fields that exist on the mesh and their associations (e.g., node, cell, edge), and other labels associated with the data. This allows a service to properly process the data. This information also enables the service to perform data conversions where needed or use optimized algorithms when possible (e.g., algorithms for structured data).

4.3   Tier 2 Abstractions

The abstractions in this section build on the aforementioned foundation and provide the ability to optimize functionality and performance and increase flexibility.

Portability Abstraction: Modern computing systems provide rich heterogeneous resources. Furthermore, executables in a workflow can be mapped onto these resources in several ways. A visualization service must be able to run on a variety of different hardware devices. For example, the same visualization service might need to run on all core types in a heterogeneous compute node or be restricted to use only a subset of a particular core type. Visualization services must run on computing systems that have differing architectures and hardware. These complications increase when considering edge computing. This relates to the aforementioned service composition abstraction by providing the workflow system with the flexibility to place services on available resources and across different types of systems. Service portability provides the workflow system with additional options to use for optimizing a scientific campaign.

Performance Models Abstraction: Models that provide performance and cost estimates for algorithms operating on a given type of data and set of resources can provide valuable information to a workflow system. Such models would help the workflow ensure that visualization results are provided in the required time on available resources. These models will inform the selection of cores (e.g., CPU, GPU), task placement on resources, and task dependencies that result from service execution time estimates. The way that a service is executed can have a dramatically different impact on a simulation or experiment. The synchronous in situ processing of expensive services can block the data producer, as can excessive data transfer to additional resources for asynchronous in transit processing.

This abstraction works in conjunction with user intentions, as well as the size and type of data and available resources. The service must be able to provide an estimate on the type and amount of resource required to perform the task or to report that it is impossible so that negotiations can occur with the scientists. For example, an expensive analysis task might be unfeasible to perform in situ for every simulation cycle. However, it might be possible to perform every tenth cycle or, if dedicated visualization resources can be allocated, the user intentions can be satisfied using in-transit processing.

Declarative Visualization Abstraction: An important distinction exists between the operation performed by a service and the algorithm used. Common visualization techniques—such as isocontouring, rendering, or particle tracing—can be accomplished using several different types of algorithms. Some algorithms are optimized for certain data types (e.g., structured grids, explicit grids) on certain hardware types (e.g., GPU or multicore CPU) and have a lower memory footprint or minimize communication. A declarative abstraction provides a separation from the intentions of the scientists and the actual algorithm used by the service. Given the declarative intention from a scientist, separate from a specific algorithm, coordination with the workflow system is then possible to select the proper algorithm that will produce the desired result and optimize performance.

5   Connecting Abstractions to Applications

Both KSTAR and fusion whole device modeling benefits from a data access abstraction. Access to data is generally the first significant challenge in developing a visualization capability, especially for in situ environments. A simple implication of a data access abstraction is a service that can read data from anywhere in the memory hierarchy (i.e., file or in situ data access use the same interface). Generally, it is straightforward to obtain output files from previous runs or test runs from current scientific campaigns. Development, testing, validation, and scaling against files is generally much easier than trying to do live analysis in a running campaign. The data access abstraction makes it possible to easily switch between files and in situ. This was particularly useful for KSTAR where the data were being moved across the globe. The ability to develop services and then switch the access mode from file to streams without needing to change anything else made the development and testing more efficient. This abstraction enabled the codesign of these services between the visualization and middleware teams.

The composability and interpretation of data was used in fusion whole device modeling. This workflow consisted of several different feature extraction services. As each service extracted features from the simulation output, the data stream was annotated with VizSchema to describe the relationship among the underlying data. This allowed a single implementation of a rendering service to support several different use cases. The workflow system chained these service together and placed them for execution on the computing resources. The rendering service used the VizSchema provided in the stream to properly interpret the data and then rendered images. The portability abstraction was also used by the fusion example. The rendering service and the isocontouring service used the VTK-m library, which provides portable performance across multiple processor architectures.

6   Conclusion and Vision for the Future

Rapidly changing computer architectures, the increasing cost of data movement relative to compute, and the move to automated workflow systems is a significant challenge to extracting insight from scientific data. However, a move to service-oriented visualization allows decoupling the complexity of all these tasks. Our abstractions provide a road map for visualization services that can take full advantage of the immense power of modern computing systems, while affording the flexibility to be connected in arbitrary ways by application scientists.

We envision a future in which application scientists will make use of visualization services without depending on outside expertise for workflow composition. The ability to specify intentions for visualization and analysis on data, along with priorities and timelines for when results are necessary will become a mandatory feature of visualization packages. We envision that these declarative intentions will automatically be converted into a set of services via natural language processing. The statements of priorities and deadlines will form constraints that can be validated as satisfiable using performance models. Negotiations with the user might be necessary if there are conflicting requirements; deadlines might need adjusting, or additional resources might be required. The workflow system will then take this information and construct a graph of requisite services and orchestrate its execution. Services will use data access and interpretation schemas to understand and appropriately process in-flight data. The workflow system will use dynamic monitoring to update the performance models and make real-time modifications to service behavior and execution. As the data size and complexity increases and services require more time, the granularity of service execution can be adjusted (e.g., from every tenth cycle to every hundredth cycle) or the algorithm used by the service can be changed (e.g., use a faster but lower quality rendering algorithm).

In order to support the tier 1 abstractions, efforts must be made to agree on standard methods for data access (e.g., a publish/subscribe model). Several schemas and data models are actively being used and developed, but ontologies are needed to ensure flexibility and the interoperability of services. The access and interpretation of data greatly reduces the barriers to service composition by workflows systems. Research efforts addressing tier 2 abstractions have been significant, but these challenges have not all been resolved, and continued work is needed. Great strides have been made in performance portable algorithms, and these needs will continue into the foreseeable future. Declarative interfaces between the user and algorithm implementations will allow the users to specify requirements and the visualization service can select the correct algorithm for the type and amount of data, and the specified time frame. Performance models for a wide range of algorithm classes, workloads and data types are needed that provide time and cost estimates so that services can be scheduled and placed on resources.

Collectively, there are rich sets of capabilities for addressing these challenges. The work required to support the VaaS abstractions involves codesign and multidisciplinary collaboration to ensure that implementations for interfaces are available. Adoption of these abstractions, and the standardization of these interfaces will enable rich visualization ecosystems. This ecosystem will make it easier for application scientists to use visualization in their campaigns. It will also make it easier for visualization scientists to deploy methods and techniques into workflows and help extract understanding from the large amounts of scientific data.

Acknowledgment. This research was supported by the DOE SciDAC RAPIDS Institute and the Exascale Computing Project (17-SC-20-SC), a collaborative effort of DOE Office of Science and the National Nuclear Security Administration. This research used resources of the Argonne and Oak Ridge Leadership Computing Facilities, DOE Office of Science User Facilities supported under Contracts DE-AC02-06CH11357 and DE-AC05-00OR22725, respectively, as well as the National Energy Research Scientific Computing Center (NERSC), a DOE Office of Science User Facility operated under Contract No. DE-AC02-05CH11231.

References

1. Infrastructure as a service (2018). https://webobjects.cdw.com/webobjects/media/pdf/Solutions/cloud-computing/Cloud-IaaS.pdf
2. ADIS: Adaptive data interfaces and services. https://gitlab.kitware.com/vtk/adis. Accessed 10 June 2020
3. Ayachit, U., et al.: Paraview catalyst: Enabling in situ data analysis and visualization. In: Proceedings of the First Workshop on in Situ Infrastructures for Enabling Extreme-Scale Analysis and Visualization, pp. 25–29. ACM (2015)
4. Ayachit, U., et al.: Performance analysis, design considerations, and applications of extreme-scale in situ infrastructures. In: ACM/IEEE International Conference for High Performance Computing, Networking, Storage and Analysis (SC16). Salt Lake City, UT, USA (2016). https://doi.org/10.1109/SC.2016.78. LBNL-1007264
5. Ayachit, U., et al.: The sensei generic in situ interface. In: 2016 Second Workshop on In Situ Infrastructures for Enabling Extreme-Scale Analysis and Visualization (ISAV), pp. 40–44 (2016). https://doi.org/10.1109/ISAV.2016.013
6. Bauer, A., et al.: In situ methods, infrastructures, and applications on high performance computing platforms. In: Computer Graphics Forum, Vol. 35, pp. 577–597. Wiley Online Library (2016)
7. Binyahib, R., et al.: A lifeline-based approach for work requesting and parallel particle advection. In: 2019 IEEE 9th Symposium on Large Data Analysis and Visualization (LDAV), pp. 52–61 (2019)
8. Camp, D., et al.: Parallel stream surface computation for large data sets. In: IEEE Symposium on Large Data Analysis and Visualization (ldav), pp. 39–47. IEEE (2012)
9. Childs, H., et al.: Extreme scaling of production visualization software on diverse architectures. IEEE Comput. Graph. Appl. **30**(3), 22–31(2010). https://doi.org/10.1109/MCG.2010.51.
10. Childs, H., et al.: Visualization at extreme scale concurrency. In: Bethel, E.W., Childs, H., Hansen, C. (eds.) High Performance Visualization: Enabling Extreme-Scale Scientific Insight. CRC Press, Boca Raton, FL (2012)
11. Choi, J.Y., et al.: ICEE: Wide-area in transit data processing framework for near real-time scientific applications. In: 4th SC Workshop on Petascale (Big) Data Analytics: Challenges and Opportunities in conjunction with SC13, vol. 11 (2013)
12. Choi, J.Y., et al.: Coupling exascale multiphysics applications: methods and lessons learned. In: 2018 IEEE 14th International Conference on e-Science (e-Science), pp. 442–452 (2018). https://doi.org/10.1109/eScience.2018.00133
13. Dominski, J., et al.: A tight-coupling scheme sharing minimum information across a spatial interface between Gyrokinetic turbulence codes. Phys. Plasmas **25**(7), 072,308 (2018). https://doi.org/10.1063/1.5044707.
14. Dorier, M., et al.: Damaris/viz: A nonintrusive, adaptable and user-friendly in situ visualization framework. In: LDAV-IEEE Symposium on Large-Scale Data Analysis and Visualization (2013)

15. Dragoni, N., et al.: Microservices: yesterday, today, and tomorrow. CoRR abs/1606.04036 (2016). http://arxiv.org/abs/1606.04036
16. Duque, E.P., et al.: Epic-an extract plug-in components toolkit for in situ data extracts architecture. In: 22nd AIAA Computational Fluid Dynamics Conference, p. 3410 (2015)
17. Fabian, N., et al.: The paraview coprocessing library: a scalable, general purpose in situ visualization library. In: 2011 IEEE Symposium on Large Data Analysis and Visualization (LDAV), pp. 89–96. IEEE (2011)
18. Fogal, T., et al.: Freeprocessing: transparent in situ visualization via data interception. In: Eurographics Symposium on Parallel Graphics and Visualization: EG PGV:[proceedings]/Sponsored by Eurographics Association in Cooperation with ACM SIGGRAPH. Eurographics Symposium on Parallel Graphics and Visualization, vol. 2014, p. 49. NIH Public Access (2014)
19. Hang, D.: Software as a service. https://www.cs.colorado.edu/~kena/classes/5828/s12/presentation-materials/dibieogheneovohanghaojie.pdf
20. Joy, K.I., et al.: Streamline integration using MPI-hybrid parallelism on a large multicore architecture. IEEE Trans. Vis. Comput. Graph. **17**(11), 1702–1713 (2011). https://doi.org/10.1109/TVCG.2010.259
21. Kim, M., et al.: In situ analysis and visualization of fusion simulations: lessons learned. In: Yokota, R., Weiland, M., Shalf, J., Alam, S. (eds.) ISC High Performance 2018. LNCS, vol. 11203, pp. 230–242. Springer, Cham (2018). https://doi.org/10.1007/978-3-030-02465-9_16
22. Klasky, S., et al.: A view from ORNL: Scientific data research opportunities in the big data age. In: 2018 IEEE 38th International Conference on Distributed Computing Systems (ICDCS), pp. 1357–1368. IEEE (2018)
23. Kress, J., et al.: Visualization and analysis requirements for in situ processing for a large-scale fusion simulation code. In: 2016 Second Workshop on In Situ Infrastructures for Enabling Extreme-Scale Analysis and Visualization (ISAV), pp. 45–50. IEEE (2016)
24. Kress, J., et al.: Comparing the efficiency of in situ visualization paradigms at scale. In: Weiland, M., Juckeland, G., Trinitis, C., Sadayappan, P. (eds.) ISC High Performance 2019. LNCS, vol. 11501, pp. 99–117. Springer, Cham (2019). https://doi.org/10.1007/978-3-030-20656-7_6
25. Kress, J., et al.: Opportunities for cost savings with in-transit visualization. In: ISC High Performance 2020. ISC (2020)
26. Labasan, S., et al.: Power and performance tradeoffs for visualization algorithms. In: Proceedings of IEEE International Parallel and Distributed Processing Symposium (IPDPS), pp. 325–334. Rio de Janeiro, Brazil (2019)
27. Larsen, M., et al.: Performance modeling of in situ rendering. In: Proceedings of the International Conference for High Performance Computing, Networking, Storage and Analysis SC 2016, pp. 276–287. IEEE (2016)
28. Larsen, M., et al.: The ALPINE In Situ Infrastructure: ascending from the Ashes of Strawman. In: Proceedings of the In Situ Infrastructures on Enabling Extreme-Scale Analysis and Visualization, pp. 42–46. ACM (2017)
29. Lawrence Livermore National Laboratory: Blueprint. https://llnl-conduit.readthedocs.io/en/latest/blueprint.html. Accessed 30 June 2020
30. Lian, M.: Introduction to service oriented architecture (2012). https://www.cs.colorado.edu/~kena/classes/5828/s12/presentation-materials/lianming.pdf
31. Liu, Q., et al.: Hello adios: the challenges and lessons of developing leadership class i/o frameworks. Concurr. Comput. Pract. Exp. **7**, 1453–1473. https://doi.org/10.1002/cpe.3125

32. Lo, L., et al.: Piston: a portable cross-platform framework for data-parallel visualization operators. In: EGPGV, pp. 11–20 (2012)
33. Malakar, P., et al.: Optimal scheduling of in-situ analysis for large-scale scientific simulations. In: Proceedings of the International Conference for High Performance Computing, Networking, Storage and Analysis, p. 52. ACM (2015)
34. Malakar, P., et al.: Optimal execution of co-analysis for large-scale molecular dynamics simulations. In: Proceedings of the International Conference for High Performance Computing, Networking, Storage and Analysis, p. 60. IEEE Press (2016)
35. Meredith, J., et al.: A distributed data-parallel framework for analysis and visualization algorithm development. ACM Int. Conf. Proc. Ser. (2012). https://doi.org/10.1145/2159430.2159432
36. Meredith, J., et al.: EAVL: the extreme-scale analysis and visualization library. In: Eurographics Symposium on Parallel Graphics and Visualization, pp. 21–30. The Eurographics Association (2012)
37. Moreland, K., et al.: Dax toolkit: A proposed framework for data analysis and visualization at extreme scale. In: 2011 IEEE Symposium on Large Data Analysis and Visualization (LDAV), pp. 97–104 (2011)
38. Moreland, K., et al.: VTK-M: accelerating the visualization toolkit for massively threaded architectures. IEEE Comput. Graph. Appl. **36**(3), 48–58 (2016)
39. Oak Ridge National Laboratory: ADIOS2: The ADaptable Input/Output System Version 2 (2018). https://adios2.readthedocs.io
40. Oldfield, R.A., et al.: Evaluation of methods to integrate analysis into a large-scale shock shock physics code. In: Proceedings of the 28th ACM international conference on Supercomputing, pp. 83–92. ACM (2014)
41. Pugmire, D., et al.: Scalable computation of streamlines on very large datasets. In: Proceedings of the ACM/IEEE Conference on High Performance Computing (SC 2009), Portland, OR (2009)
42. Pugmire, D., et al.: Parallel integral curves. In: High Performance Visualization-Enabling Extreme-Scale Scientific Insight. CRC Press/Francis-Taylor Group (2012). https://doi.org/10.1201/b12985-8
43. Pugmire, D., et al.: Towards scalable visualization plugins for data staging workflows. In: Big Data Analytics: Challenges and Opportunities (BDAC-2014) Workshop at Supercomputing Conference (2014)
44. Pugmire, D., et al.: Performance-Portable Particle Advection with VTK-m. In: Childs, H., Cucchietti, F., (eds.) Eurographics Symposium on Parallel Graphics and Visualization. The Eurographics Association (2018). https://doi.org/10.2312/pgv.20181094
45. Rivi, M., et al.: In-situ visualization: State-of-the-art and some use cases. Brussels, Belgium, PRACE White Paper; PRACE (2012)
46. Tchoua, R., et al.: Adios visualization schema: a first step towards improving interdisciplinary collaboration in high performance computing. In: 2013 IEEE 9th International Conference on eScience (eScience), pp. 27–34. IEEE (2013)
47. The HDF Group: Hdf5 users guide. https://www.hdfgroup.org/HDF5/doc/UG/. Accessed 20 June 2016
48. Whitlock, B., Favre, J.M., Meredith, J.S.: Parallel in situ coupling of simulation with a fully featured visualization system. In: Kuhlen, T., et al. (eds.) Eurographics Symposium on Parallel Graphics and Visualization. The Eurographics Association (2011). https://doi.org/10.2312/EGPGV/EGPGV11/101-109
49. Wong, P.C., et al.: The top 10 challenges in extreme-scale visual analytics. IEEE Comput. Graph. Appl. **32**(4), 63 (2012)

50. Yenpure, A., et al.: Efficient point merge using data parallel techniques. In: Eurographics Symposium on Parallel Graphics and Visualization (EGPGV), pp. 79–88. Porto, Portugal (2019)

51. Yun, G., et al.: Development of Kstar ECE imaging system for measurement of temperature fluctuations and edge density fluctuations. Rev. Sci. Instrum. **81**(10), 10D930 (2010)

Performance Improvements on SNS and HFIR Instrument Data Reduction Workflows Using Mantid

William F. Godoy$^{(\boxtimes)}$, Peter F. Peterson, Steven E. Hahn, John Hetrick, Mathieu Doucet, and Jay J. Billings

Computer Science and Mathematics Division, Oak Ridge National Laboratory, Oak Ridge, TN 37830, USA
godoywf@ornl.gov
https://csmd.ornl.gov/group/research-software

Abstract. Performance of data reduction workflows at the High Flux Isotope Reactor (HFIR) and the Spallation Neutron Source (SNS) at Oak Ridge National Laboratory (ORNL) is mainly determined by the time spent loading raw measurement events stored in large and sparse datasets. This paper describes: (1) our long-term view to leverage SNS and HFIR data management needs with our experience at ORNL's world-class high performance computing (HPC) facilities, and (2) our short-term efforts to speed up current workflows using Mantid, a data analysis and reduction community framework used across several neutron scattering facilities. We show that minimally invasive short-term improvements in metadata management have a moderate impact in speeding up current production workflows. We propose a more disruptive domain-specific solution: the No Cost Input Output (NCIO) framework, we provide an overview, the risks and challenges in NCIO's adoption by HFIR and SNS stakeholders.

Keywords: SNS · HFIR · Neutron scattering · Metadata · Data indexing

W. F. Godoy et al.—Contributed Equally.

This manuscript has been co-authored by UT-Battelle, LLC, under contract DE-AC05-00OR22725 with the US Department of Energy (DOE). The US government retains and the publisher, by accepting the article for publication, acknowledges that the US government retains a nonexclusive, paid-up, irrevocable, worldwide license to publish or reproduce the published form of this manuscript, or allow others to do so, for US government purposes. DOE will provide public access to these results of federally sponsored research in accordance with the DOE Public Access Plan (http://energy.gov/downloads/doe-public-access-plan).

The original version of this chapter was revised: The author's name in the reference 21 was changed to S. Hahn. The correction to this chapter is available at https://doi.org/10.1007/978-3-030-63393-6_38

J. Nichols et al. (Eds.): SMC 2020, CCIS 1315, pp. 175–186, 2020.
https://doi.org/10.1007/978-3-030-63393-6_12

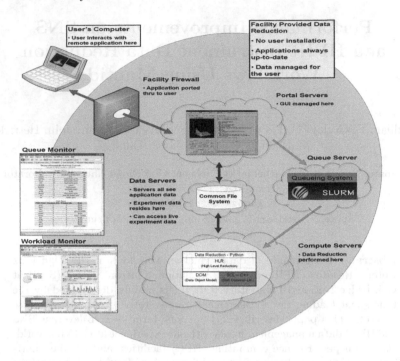

Fig. 1. Schematic representation of the SNS portal services provided at ORNL for showing how user can access their neutron data remotely, from Campbell *et al.* [4].

1   Introduction

Oak Ridge National Laboratory (ORNL) hosts two of the largest neutron source facilities in the world: the Spallation Neutron Source (SNS) and the High Flux Isotope Reactor (HFIR), which produced nearly 67,000 beamline hours to run 780 experiments for 758 unique users during Fiscal Year 2019 [1].

The Research Software Engineering (RSE) group in the Computer Science and Mathematics Division (CSMD) is a stakeholder in providing and supporting a wide variety of data management and computing resources to SNS and HFIR users [2–4]. As shown in Fig. 1, users can reduce, view, analyze and download their data using ORNL's computing resources and software stack. These internal data reduction workflows present several optimization challenges that are an ongoing effort in our data management research and development tasks [5].

Event based measurement and processing of neutron scattering data [6,7] is a recent technique used to collect raw event information at SNS and HFIR instruments. Collection is done either using a live stream [5] or file storage systems for archival purposes, both of which are the entry point for the post-processing data reduction workflows for subsequent analysis and visualization either "in-situ" or "post hoc" [8]. Performance of event-based data reduction workflows is mainly determined by the time spent loading raw measurement events stored in large and sparse datasets. Currently, datasets produced by SNS and HFIR instruments are stored using the standard NeXus [9] schema that is built on top of the self-describing serial HDF5 [10] binary file format. At the engine level of the data reduction workflows is Mantid [11], a framework for data reduction and analysis used at several neutrons facilities across the world. Mantid presents a data management and processing model that transforms raw event data from the NeXus stored files into meaningful reduced quantities of interest to domain scientists, *e.g.* statistics.

In addition to world-class experimental neutron facilities, ORNL hosts state-of-the-art high performance computing (HPC) facilities such as Summit [12], currently the second fastest supercomputer in the world, and the Compute and Data Environment for Science (CADES) [13]. Ongoing efforts have shown that the data life cycle services provided at the neutron sciences facilities can be leveraged with available HPC computing resources [4,17]. Moreover, the direction of computing at the U.S. Department of Energy has been influenced by the extreme heterogeneity in programming models, runtime systems and predictive tools; which must adapt to the evolving scientific computing needs [14].

The purpose of this paper is to provide our views and plans to leverage the current status of data management services at SNS and HFIR with the lessons learned from our experience with HPC resources. There are several reasons to improve the current status quo of data management services. One recent motivation is that science is increasingly moving towards connected instruments, Artificial Intelligence (AI) [18] and heterogeneous computing resources [14]. As a result, AI establishes a research need for understanding and addressing potential I/O bottlenecks that would slow down data processing from acquisition to dynamic workflows. The expectation is to enable AI algorithms to be smoothly integrated into the decision making process that runs the neutrons experiment. The latter is an active research area at ORNL neutrons and computing facilities [19].

The outline of this paper is as follows: Sect. 2 introduces an overview of the current data processing workflows at SNS and HFIR; including a description of the annotated NeXus data and the challenges in data management tasks using the current Mantid framework. Section 3 provides a brief summary of our short-term efforts on metadata management strategies to improve the performance of current neutrons data reduction workflows [21]. Our long-term view is later discussed in Sect. 4. We describe the proposed domain-specific solution: the no-cost input output (NCIO) data framework to provide performance and intelligent I/O at SNS and HFIR. Finally, Sect. 5 provides the conclusions and summary of our views on the direction to enable an overall better user-experience at ORNL's neutrons facilities.

2   Neutrons Data at ORNL Facilities

This section describe the current status and methodologies used to process the data generated at SNS and HFIR facilities. We briefly describe the NeXus data format and the data reduction tasks done in the Mantid framework.

2.1 The NeXus Format

Raw event-based data at SNS and HFIR is stored using the self-describing NeXus [9] file format which uses the HDF5 [10] library as an underlying technology for annotation and storage. NeXus is a rich-metadata data format that follows a strict hierarchy using HDF5's data organization concepts of groups, datasets and attributes to identify each collection of raw event based data from a neutron scattering experiment.

Table 1. File metadata entries for raw event based neutron data using the hierarchical NeXus schema [9].

Data Type	Entry Name
group	/entry
attribute	/entry/NX_class
	...
group	/entry/DASlogs
attribute	/entry/DASlogs/NX_class (NXlog)
group	/entry/DASlogs/BL6:CS:DataType
attribute	/entry/DASlogs/BL6:CS:DataType/NX_class
dataset	/entry/DASlogs/BL6:CS:DataType/average_value
dataset	/entry/DASlogs/BL6:CS:DataType/average_value_error
	...
group	/entry/bank5_events
attribute	/entry/bank5_events/NX_class (NXevent_data)
dataset	/entry/bank5_events/event_id
dataset	/entry/bank5_events/event_index

As shown in Table 1, each hierarchy level in the NeXus schema maps to a "group" in the underlying HDF5 dataset. Groups are described with a "NX_class" string attribute to identify the group's type according to source of the data. Two representative groups are shown for: i) logs, "NX_class=NXlog", and ii) bank event data entries, "NX_class=NXevent_data", which represent the majority of the processed group data type on data reduction workflows at ORNL. Actual value entries such as arrays or single values are represented as scientific datasets (SDS) entries, or "NX_class=SDS" in the NeXus schema.

2.2 Mantid Processing of NeXus Datasets

NeXus files are processed using the Mantid framework for data analysis and visualization [11]. Mantid is used as a backend to several SNS and HFIR instruments data reduction workflows by providing a single and unified "LoadEventNexus" function call for each raw event based NeXus file. "LoadEventNexus" returns an in-memory Mantid structure called an "EventWorkspace" which is designed for time-of-flight event histograms [6,7]. A schematic representation of the "Load-EventNexus" workflow is illustrated in Fig. 2. Depending on instrument needs, different stages of "LoadEventNexus" could potentially become an I/O bottleneck on their own.

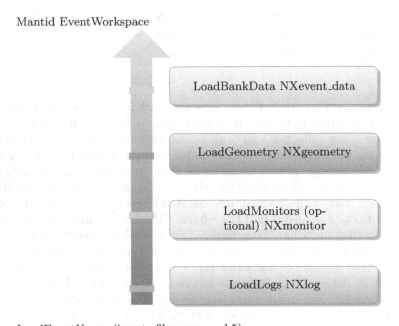

Fig. 2. Mantid's LoadEventNexus algorithm steps for processing entries of an input NeXus file generating a Mantid EventWorkspace data structure.

3 Short-Term Performance Improvements

Proper metadata indexing is essential for efficient data management search and information discovery. As reported by Zhang *et al.* [20], in-memory metadata indexing is essential for search in large scientific datasets stored in self-describing formats. As part of our efforts to improve the I/O performance in SNS and HFIR instrument data reduction workflows, we introduced modifications to the metadata generation and search in Mantid's NeXus loader. In essence, the hierarchical metadata generation and search on NeXus datasets has been replaced with efficient in-memory binary-tree indexing strategy. Since the goal of this section is to illustrate one of the many data management challenges at ORNL neutrons facilities, we refer the reader to our previous work in [21] for full details on this effort.

Table 2. Overall wall-clock times comparison and speed up from applying the proposed in-memory index data structure on production data reduction workflows for SNS and HFIR instruments.

Instrument Workflow	Wall-clock time current index(s)	Wall-clock time improved index(s)	Speed up
GP-SANS	58.9	41.8	29%
Bio-SANS	100.2	80.9	19%
EQ-SANS	99.0	88.0	11%

The impact of this minimally invasive approach is shown in Fig. 3. The CPU profiling information is presented as flame graphs [23] for the Mantid NeXus "LoadEventNexus" function, for: (a) the existing implementation on Mantid, and (b) using the proposed in-memory index binary-tree structure. The x-width in Fig. 3 indicates the relative amount of time spent on each function; while the y-block-structure illustrates the calls to different libraries (represented in colors) in the stack which go deep into the HDF5 and native system I/O calls. A simple comparison indicates that the relative CPU time spent on tasks related to metadata management have been largely reduced inside Mantid's NeXus loader, by minimizing expensive search and memory management operations.

The overall impact on wall-clock times of production data reduction workflows at SNS and HFIR instruments is quantified in Table 2. Results for three small-angle scattering instruments are presented: a time-of-flight instrument, EQ-SANS [24], in which information from each raw event is used to reduce the data; and two monochromatic instruments, Bio-SANS and GP-SANS [25], in which event data is traditionally not used.

Nevertheless, it is important to point out that further improvements imply more invasive, thus disruptive, approaches if we want to tackle critical I/O bottlenecks in the overall data life cycle at ORNL's neutrons facilities.

4   Long-Term View: NCIO

Oak Ridge National Laboratory (ORNL) hosts state of the art computing facilities such as Summit [12], currently the second fastest supercomputer in the world, and the Compute and Data Environment for Science (CADES). Previous efforts [4,17] have shown that the data life cycle services provided at ORNL's neutron science facilities can be leveraged with the available world-class computing resources. In order to take advantage of these resources, we need to introduce new infrastructure that can adapt quickly to the user demands and be able to exploit available hardware resources.

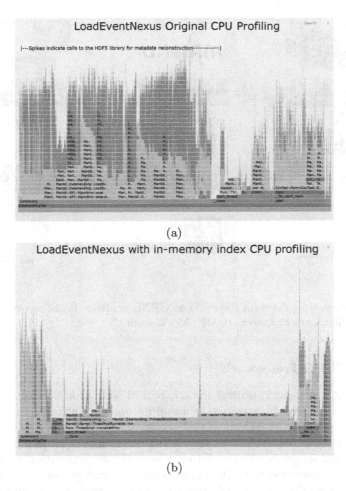

Fig. 3. Mantid's LoadEventNexus CPU profiling flame graph representation from [21] for (a) current hierarchical index reconstruction implementation, (b) improvements after introducing an efficient in-memory metadata index.

We summarize a list of requirements for the proposed infrastructure in no particular order:

– **Performance**: improve current I/O bottlenecks
– **Portability**: across different hardware architectures and configurations, in particular HPC systems
– **Domain-specific**: provide interfaces to enhance stakeholder communication
– **Pluggable architecture**: to allow interoperability with different underlying technologies and data management research tasks
– **Modern software practices**: for reliable data management operations and deployment.

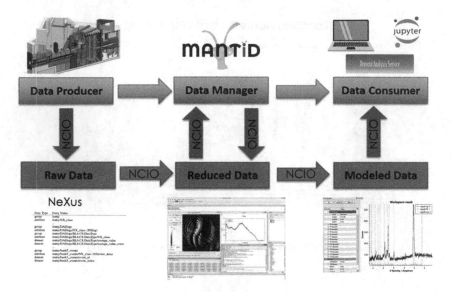

Fig. 4. NCIO role in the data life cycle at ORNL neutrons facilities expanding The Consumers Managers Producers (CMP) Model from [3].

4.1   The NCIO Framework

We proposed a new input output library, named NCIO for No-Cost Input Output. We see the current status quo as an opportunity to introduce new capabilities to customize data management tasks combining domain-specific abstractions and available HPC resources. Our view is that performance in data management involves several stages in how the data is managed from generation at the facility data producer instruments to the final domain scientist consumers. The role of NCIO is presented in Fig. 4 which expands on Donaldson *et al.* [3] illustration of the Consumers Managers Producers (CMP) model applied at ORNL neutrons facilities. Therefore, we propose a unified approach for efficient data reduction, analysis and transport at the different stages of the data life cycle.

Similarly, NCIO must have an independent domain-specific interface that is abstracted away as possible from underlying technologies that facilitate the annotation and storage of data. As explained by Sprinkle *et al.* [15], "when using domain-specific approaches developers construct solutions from concepts representing things in the problem domain, not concepts of a given general-purpose programming language". Fowler [16] states: "The key bottleneck in software development is communication between developers and those for whom they're developing". Hence, by introducing domain-specific software and methodologies we expect to improve the overall communication and productivity of the domain scientists and the developers at ORNL facilities. This is not a new concept and similar efforts of domain-specific interface standardization can be found in physical simulation schema-based data libraries [9,26].

NCIO Architecture

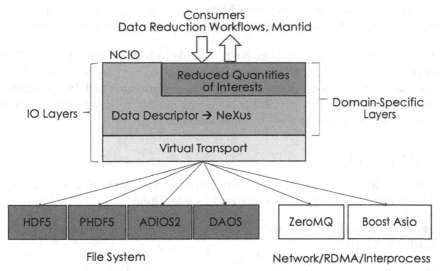

Fig. 5. Schematic representation of NCIO's architecture showing how consumers must interact only with the domain-specific "business" layer, while the IO layer should allow for multiple underlying technologies.

NCIO must have a flexible and "pluggable" architecture. The latter will allow us to research and develop suitable data management solutions based on SNS and HFIR instruments' specific business needs. Figure 5 illustrates the proposed layered architecture of NCIO.

We put emphasis in the separation between the domain-specific "business" and the "IO" layers as they cover different aspects in the data management life cycle:

1. **"IO layer"**: this interface abstracts away the general semantics of underlying technologies that facilitates the access to the raw data bytes. It includes the NeXus-based data descriptor layer and the virtual transport layer.
2. **"Domain-specific business layer"**: this interface provides access to specific instrument needs. Semantics is based on each SNS and HFIR instrument quantities of interest *e.g.* histograms.

Our view is that NCIO will standardize interactions between domain scientists and their instrument data by providing simple interfaces based on familiar concepts. NCIO will remove the requirement to users to pick up more general interfaces such as those provided by the underlying technologies in Fig. 5.

As shown in Fig. 5, NCIO lowest layer will enable interoperability with a wide variety of underlying I/O technologies which are suitable for different file systems and network technologies [10,22,28]. Interoperability itself has been recently provided in HDF5 (using a Virtual Object Layer) [10], while it was a design requirement in ADIOS2 [22]. Thus, the consumer benefits from these libraries application programming interfaces (APIs) serving as a proxy to several underlying technologies to integrate several I/O capabilities at a lower development cost.

It is of particular interest that NCIO is able to interact with ORNL's HPC modern file systems [27]. NCIO must be flexible enough to be deployed with the proper configuration options that enable performance in HPC production systems. At the same time, NCIO must adapt quickly to novel HPC hardware and software paradigms as they become available [12].

4.2   NCIO Risks

Like in any disruptive technology, there are associated risks that we will cover in this section. These can be summarized in a few items:

- Lack of community acceptance
- Unstable interfaces
- Reliance on underlying technologies
- Minimal performance impact

Our plan is to carefully address each potential risk without minimizing their consequences. In particular, we will strive for establishing effective communication practices across NCIO stakeholders: facility users, Computational Instrument Scientist and Research Software Engineers. Nonetheless, NCIO must adhere to modern software engineering practices to ensure a quality product. Last but not least, NCIO must serve as an adaptable research framework to continue explore different data management strategies as novel computing resources are available.

5   Conclusions

We outline our view and plans to leverage the current data management methodologies and operations at Oak Ridge National Laboratory (ORNL) neutrons science world-class facilities: the High Flux Isotope Reactor (HFIR), and the Spallation Neutron Source (SNS). While we showed that our short-term efforts to manage the produced annotated metadata more efficiently have a moderate impact in the search and discovery of information; a more disruptive long-term approach is proposed: the no-cost input output (I/O), NCIO, framework. We outline our rationale so the reader is convinced that introducing a pluggable architecture and unified domain-specific capability will result in a sustainable infrastructure that enhance the business needs at ORNL such as: operations, communication, and provide leverage to HFIR and SNS stakeholder with available high-performance computing (HPC) resources at ORNL to provide a scalable data management framework. NCIO is expected to provide services that are customized to the users' data management needs rather than having them to adapt to particular underlying technologies.

Acknowledgements. A portion of this research used resources at the SNS, a Department of Energy (DOE) Office of Science User Facility operated by ORNL. ORNL is managed by UT-Battelle LLC for DOE under Contract DE-AC05-00OR22725.

References

1. Oak Ridge National Laboratory, Neutron Sciences. https://neutrons.ornl.gov/
2. Oak Ridge National Laboratory, Neutron Sciences Data Management. https:// neutrons.ornl.gov/users/data-management
3. Donaldson, D.R., Martin, S., Proffen, T.: Understanding perspectives on sharing neutron data at Oak Ridge National Laboratory. Data Sci. J. **16**, 35 (2017). https://doi.org/10.5334/dsj-2017-035
4. Campbell, S., Miller, S., Bilheux, J., Reuter, M., Peterson, P., Kohl, J., Trater, J., Vazhkudai, S., Lynch, V., Green, M.: The SNS and HFIR web portal system for SANS. J. Phys. Conf. Ser. **247**, 012013 (2010). https://doi.org/10.1088/1742-6596/247/1/012013
5. Shipman, G., et al.: Accelerating data acquisition, reduction, and analysis at the spallation neutron source. In: 2014 IEEE 10th International Conference on e-Science, Sao Paulo, pp. 223–230 (2014). https://doi.org/10.1109/eScience.2014.31
6. Granroth, G.E., An, K., Smith, H.L., Whitfield, P., Neuefeind, J.C., Lee, J., Zhou, W., Sedov, V.N., Peterson, P.F., Parizzi, A., Skorpenske, H., Hartman, S.M., Huq, A., Abernathy, D.L.: Event-based processing of neutron scattering data at the Spallation Neutron Source. J. Appl. Cryst. **51**, 616–62 (2018). https://doi.org/10.1107/S1600576718004727
7. Peterson, P.F., Campbell, S.I., Reuter, M.A., Taylor, R.J., Zikovsky, J.: Event-based processing of neutron scattering data. Nucl. Instrum. Methods Phys. Res. Sect. A: **803**, 24–28 (2015)
8. Childs, H., Ahern, S.D., Ahrens, J., et al.: A terminology for in situ visualization and analysis systems. Int. J. High Perform. Comput. Appl. (2020). https://doi.org/10.1177/1094342020935991
9. Konnecke, M., Akeroyd, F.A., Bernstein, H.J., Brewster, A.S., Campbell, S.I., Clausen, B., Cottrell, S., Hoffmann, J.U., Jemian, P.R., Mannicke, D., Osborn, R., Peterson, P.F., Richter, T., Suzuki, J., Watts, B., Wintersberger, E., Wuttke, J.: J. Appl. Cryst. **48**, 301–305 (2015)
10. The HDF Group. Hierarchical Data Format, version 5, 1997–2020. http://www.hdfgroup.org/HDF5/
11. Arnold, O., et al.: Mantid-Data analysis and visualization package for neutron scattering and μ SR experiments, Nucl. Instrum. Methods Phys. Res. Sect. A: vol. 764, 156–166, ISSN 0168–9002 (2014). https://doi.org/10.1016/j.nima.2014.07.029
12. Oak Ridge Leadership Computing Facility, Summit supercomputer. https://www.olcf.ornl.gov/summit/
13. The Compute and Data Environment for Science (CADES). https://cades.ornl.gov/
14. Vetter, J.S., et al.: Extreme heterogeneity 2018 - productive computational science in the era of extreme heterogeneity. In: Report for DOE ASCR Workshop on Extreme Heterogeneity, United States. https://doi.org/10.2172/1473756
15. Sprinkle, J., Mernik, M., Tolvanen, J.P., Spinellis, D.: Guest editors' introduction: What kinds of nails need a domain-specific hammer? IEEE Software **26**(4), 15–18 (2009). https://doi.org/10.1109/MS.2009.92

16. Fowler, M.: A pedagogical framework for domain-specific languages. IEEE Softw. **26**, 13–14 (2009). https://doi.org/10.1109/MS.2009.85
17. Stansberry, D., Somnath, S., Breet, J., Shutt, G., Shankar, M.: DataFed: towards reproducible research via federated data management. In: 2019 International Conference on Computational Science and Computational Intelligence (CSCI), Las Vegas, NV, USA, 2019, pp. 1312–1317 (2019). https://doi.org/10.1109/CSCI49370.2019.00245
18. Stevens, R., Taylor, V., Nichols, J., Maccabe, A.B., Yelick, K., Brown, D.: AI for Science. Technical report. https://doi.org/10.2172/1604756
19. Garcia-Cardona, C., Kannan, R., Johnston, T., Proffen, T., Page, K., Seal, S.K.: Learning to predict material structure from neutron scattering data. IEEE Int. Conf. Big Data (Big Data) **2019**, 4490–4497 (2019)
20. Zhang, W., Byna, S., Niu, C., Chen, Y.: Exploring metadata search essentials for scientific data management. In: 2019 IEEE 26th International Conference on High Performance Computing, Data, and Analytics (HiPC), Hyderabad, India, 2019, pp. 83–92 (2019). https://doi.org/10.1109/HiPC.2019.00021
21. Godoy, W.F., Peterson, P., Hahn, S., Billings, J.J.: Efficient Data Management in Neutron Scattering Data Reduction Workflows at ORNL. In: International Workshop on Big Data Reduction held with 2020 IEEE International Conference on Big Data (accepted)
22. Godoy, W.F., Podhorszki, N., *et al.*: ADIOS 2: The Adaptable Input Output System. A framework for high-performance data management, SoftwareX, Volume 12, 2020, 100561, ISSN 2352-7110, https://doi.org/10.1016/j.softx.2020.100561
23. Gregg, B.: The Flame Graph. Queue 14, 2 (March-April 2016), 91–110 (2016). https://doi.org/10.1145/2927299.2927301
24. Zhao, J.K., Gao, C.Y., Liu, D.: The extended Q-range small-angle neutron scattering diffractometer at the SNS. J. Appl. Cryst. **43**, 1068–1077 (2010)
25. Berry, K.D., et al.: Characterization of the neutron detector upgrade to the GP-SANS and Bio-SANS instruments at HFIR", Nuclear Instruments and Methods in Physics Research Section A: Accelerators, Spectrometers, Detectors and Associated Equipment, Volume 693, 2012, Pages 179–185, ISSN 0168-9002, https://doi.org/10.1016/j.nima.2012.06.052
26. Huebl, A., et al.: openPMD 1.0.0: A meta data standard for particle and mesh based data (2015). https://doi.org/10.5281/zenodo.33624
27. Liu, J., et al.: Evaluation of HPC application i/o on object storage systems. In: 2018 IEEE/ACM 3rd International Workshop on Parallel Data Storage & Data Intensive Scalable Computing Systems (PDSW-DISCS), Dallas, TX, USA, pp. 24–34 (2018). https://doi.org/10.1109/PDSW-DISCS.2018.00005
28. Lofstead, J., Jimenez, I., Maltzahn, C., Koziol, Q., Bent, J., Barton, E.: DAOS and Friends: A Proposal for an Exascale Storage System. In: SC 2016: Proceedings of the International Conference for High Performance Computing, Networking, Storage and Analysis, Salt Lake City, UT, pp. 585–596 (2016). https://doi.org/10.1109/SC.2016.49

Experimental/Observational Applications: Use Cases That Drive Requirements for AI and HPC Convergence

Software Framework for Federated Science Instruments

Thomas Naughton[✉], Seth Hitefield, Lawrence Sorrillo, Nageswara Rao,
James Kohl, Wael Elwasif, Jean-Christophe Bilheux, Hassina Bilheux,
Swen Boehm, Jason Kincl, Satyabrata Sen, and Neena Imam

Oak Ridge National Laboratory, Oak Ridge, TN 37831, USA
naughtont@ornl.gov

Abstract. There is an unprecedented promise of enhanced capabilities
for federations of leadership computing systems and experimental science
facilities by leveraging software technologies for fast and efficient operations. These federations seek to unify different science instruments, both
computing and experimental, to effectively support science users and
operators to execute complex workflows. The FedScI project addresses
the software challenges associated with the formation and operation of
federated environments by leveraging recent advances in containerization
of software and softwarization of hardware. We propose a software framework to streamline the federation usage by science users and it's provisioning and operations by facility providers. A distinguishing element of
our work is the support for improved interaction between experimental devices, such as beam-line instruments, and more traditional high-
performance computing resources, including compute, network, storage
systems. We present guiding principles for the software framework and
highlight portions of a current prototype implementation. We describe
our science use case involving neutron imaging beam-lines (SNAP/BL-3,
Imaging/CG-1D) at the Spallation Neutron Source and High Flux Isotope Reactor facilities at Oak Ridge National Laboratory. Additionally,
we detail plans for a more direct instrument interaction within a federated environment, which could enable more advanced workflows with
feedback loops to shorten the time to science.

Keywords: Federation · Science instruments · Software stack

T. Naughton et al.—Contributed Equally.
This manuscript has been co-authored by UT-Battelle, LLC, under contract DE-AC05-
00OR22725 with the US Department of Energy (DOE). The US government retains
and the publisher, by accepting the article for publication, acknowledges that the US
government retains a nonexclusive, paid-up, irrevocable, worldwide license to publish or reproduce the published form of this manuscript, or allow others to do so, for
US government purposes. DOE will provide public access to these results of federally
sponsored research in accordance with the DOE Public Access Plan (http://energy.
gov/downloads/doe-public-access-plan).

J. Nichols et al. (Eds.): SMC 2020, CCIS 1315, pp. 189–203, 2020.
https://doi.org/10.1007/978-3-030-63393-6_13

1   Introduction

There is an increasing interest in science workflows [6] that integrate both experimental instruments and high-performance computing (HPC) infrastructure (e.g., supercomputers, storage systems, networks). A *Science Federation* is a union of distributed, scientific instruments (computing & experimental) that creates a co-operative system for users/operators of complex workflows. Often the orchestration within these workflows becomes increasingly difficult due to unique elements of HPC environments and the level of localized expertise needed to make effective use of the resources. As workflows expand beyond a single administrative domain, the challenges increase because of differing site policies – the more distributed environment is not managed by a single entity. The operators of individual facilities optimize only locally, which can lead to misalignment, such as when a supercomputer is allocated while the wide-area network reservation is unavailable or a beamline time slot is not currently active. When an activity requires coordination across sites, setup can take weeks, during which time critical scientific work may be delayed.

The software infrastructure needed to enable science federations requires tools and methods be developed to enable different facilities to contribute resources, which can be leveraged by science users in an effective manner. This requires software interfaces be created to help abstract the underlying systems into a more consistent user-friendly form. Additionally, the users and operators of the distributed system may have poor visibility into the overall system performance and need monitoring & diagnostic capabilities. Lastly, this operating environment should reduce the setup time from month/years to hours/days so that incorporating resources into an experiment is not too time consuming. Additionally, the interaction of different instruments will require interfaces to "steer" experiments to make the overall process more agile. This is to reduce the time requirements, but also to enable more dynamic workflows that can adapt to changing resource availability and task priority/urgency.

The software infrastructure needed to enable science federations is distinct from a *workflow engine* that is primarily concerned with performing tasks for a specific scientific investigation. Workflow engines sit a layer above the federation and use federation interfaces to more easily provision distributed resources based on user input, resource availability and system health. While workflow engines are useful for expressing and automating science workflows, our federation software stack is focused on providing interfaces to help manage the distributed, heterogeneous resources and instruments in the system. This federation stack can be used in conjunction with a workflow engine to more easily perform scientific investigations across distributed environments.

Given this motivation we have begun work developing the Federated Science Instruments (FedScI) software stack that can be used to support connecting instruments at the Spallation Neutron Source (SNS) and High Flux Isotope Reactor (HFIR) to federated computational resources. In this paper, we describe early work on a framework for the federation of scientific instruments. We include details about a science application from SNS/HFIR that we use to ground our work with a real-world use case with neutron imaging scientists in mind. We also describe our current plans to incorporate virtual instruments for exploring more dynamic and interactive controls within our testbed environment.

2   Science Use-Case

Neutron radiography and computed tomography cover a broad range of scientific applications at the Spallation Neutron Source (SNS) and the High Flux Isotope Reactor (HFIR), e.g., Spallation Neutrons and Pressure Diffractometer [7] at SNS, Neutron Imaging Facility [4] at HFIR. Challenges often arise when data has limited statistics (fast measurements, limited view of the sample due to sample environment in the way, etc.) thus making the data normalization, reconstruction, difficult. In many cases, iterative reconstruction, a computer-intensive method, is required to obtain high fidelity mapping of the linear attenuation coefficient in the sample (which is used to quantify changes as a function of space and/or time). The lack of access to a platform that can draw computing resources when needed hinders scientific discovery. Moreover, neutron beam time is expensive and inadequate live feedback leads to less than optimized measurements. Ideally, access to a Science Federation will allow the scientific team to make informed decision for better scientific productivity at the neutron beamline.

For example, at the reactor, 3D computed tomography (CT) of kinetics such as water uptake in roots requires scans that last less than an hour, thus producing data sets that have very poor signal-to-noise ratios. Reconstruction is impossible when attempting to reconstruct the data in 3D with low computing methods such as the filtered-back projection. These measurements can only be reconstructed using advanced reconstruction method such as the iterative reconstruction (a computer-demanding technique). Over 2 days, several tens of CT scans are acquired and increase the complexity due to the large data sets that need to be reconstructed and compared to each other.

At the SNS, complexity arises from the capability to measure multiple CT scans at different wavelengths (up to 3000 CT scans over several days). However, there is currently no capability that allows reconstruction of low SNR data (similar to HFIR CT scans of kinetic events). The uniqueness of the SNS source is that it is capable of detecting microstructure in crystalline samples. This is called the Bragg edge technique, and unlike HFIR which measures the linear attenuation coefficient on each voxel, it requires heavy modeling and fitting of the Bragg edges to interpret the non-scalar (up to 6 unknowns per voxel) information on each voxel. This technique, when developed to its fullest, will provide 3D strain mapping of superalloys such as additively manufactured components. Indeed, today microstructure information is mainly done using electron backscattered diffraction (EBSD) or other destructive techniques that can be time-consuming and costly.

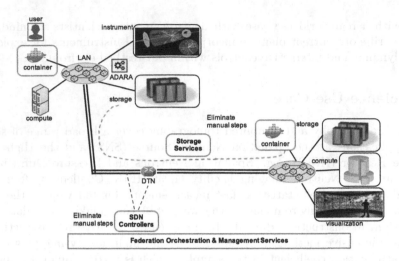

Fig. 1. Compute mobility with SNS/HFIR workflows to leverage federated resources.

Compute Mobility. Productivity is a crucial element for science workflows. The time for end-users to run tests on the experimental instrument is limited (time-share notified in advance on monthly/weekly basis) and is costly. Therefore, minimizing the time spent in setup and analysis is critical for achieving maximal benefit of the reservation time for the scientists and experimental resources. As such, the instrument scientists often pre-stage software on SNS resources in advance of beamline allocations to help expedite work upon arrival. However, this limits the set of resources where the workflow can operate as it assumes the software pre-installed. The workflow involves stages where visualization is needed during the post-processing of data for inspection while reviewing results and making choices for future parameters for subsequent instrument runs. The instrument scientists at SNS/HFIR have developed a workflow that leverages Jupyter notebooks to aid the post-processing and visualization [5]. This improves the interactivity of the data processing and allows for fast customization.

The federation of scientific resources offers more options for scientific exploration. For example, our initial review of the HFIR workflows identified areas where the data processing was not tied to a specific hardware resource, assuming appropriate network and storage is made accessible. The model of a pool of federated resources that can be dynamically connected through software-defined networking enables new opportunities to reduce the processing time using compute resources available elsewhere in the federation. The required analysis software can be bundled into compute containers that can run wherever the data can be made available via the dynamic network and storage methods. This fits well with the Jupyter notebooks, which can be packaged into containers and deployed to run on the federated resources (Fig. 1). This captures the time saving needed for the software pre-staging and the compute mobility of the containerized application increases the set of resources where parts of the workflow can operate.

3   Framework Design

3.1   Overview

Connecting multiple, diverse scientific instruments (computing and experimental) together offers many potential advantages to science users, but also requires that additional software infrastructure be provided to make the distributed heterogeneous environment useful. While it is feasible for end-users to install client software and tools to access a federated set of resources, it is unlikely that a single monolithic software stack will be deployed by every resource provider. Therefore, we assume a modular software framework that can be customized at the different resource provider sites to reduce their barrier of entry to the federation. This involves intelligent management and coordination interfaces at the federation level.

Additionally, we need methods to incorporate experimental instruments into workflows with more agile interfaces that allow for dynamic capabilities to reduce the time to science (e.g., workflows with feedback loops). However, we recognize there is a need to create testbeds for experiments before deploying software at real world instruments. Therefore, we include in our framework the ability to create virtualized instruments to investigate interfaces for controlled steering of scientific experiments.

In this section, we describe the Federated Science Instruments (FedScI) software framework that is being created to help streamline connecting and using federated resources. We include details about the design and review assumptions that guide the work.

3.2   Roles

There are effectively three roles defined within the FedScI framework. These roles are mainly differentiated by 1) the level of awareness (details) of the distinct resources comprising the federated environment and 2) the responsibilities for providing or managing said resources. How these roles are filled for a specific federation is flexible. Each role may be filled by an individual person, group, or organization, but in some instances a single person, group, or organization may conceivably fill multiple roles for the federation.

- *Science Users* are chiefly concerned with running their scientific experiments as efficiently and productively as possible. Having a federated network including both the user's computational and experimental resources reduces overhead for the user and compresses the overall time for generating results. Some users may still need to specify which resources are best suited for their experiments but should find default selections based on the input adequate. Ideally, the *Science User* would not need to provide configurations for different resources in the federation and the resources would simply be available for use.

- *Resource Providers* are mainly interested in making resources available to the federation in an effective and easy to use manner, while still maintaining facility policies for security and accounting. As such, facilities are also interested in knowing what, if any, new capabilities are needed in order to support federated environments (i.e., requirements for mechanisms/services). Providers are responsible for running the components and services that expose the given resources to the federation for science users to access.
- *Federation Maintainers* provide the overall federation stack and are responsible for bridging the gaps between the *Science Users* and the *Resource Providers*. Their goal is making the distributed system as useful and efficient as possible. Another goal is to present the federation to *Science Users* in a way that minimizes the learning curve for using different resources without introducing unnecessary user constraints. This role is responsible for supporting varied users and providers by providing a flexible, plugin based software architecture that allows the *Science User* and *Resource Providers* to easily contribute to the overall federation.

3.3   Software Architecture

The FedScI software stack is comprised of several core components and services that provide the requisite functionality for building science federations. It is designed using a plugin based architecture so the software stack can be easily extended and customized in order to support specific requirements or provide specific resources to different federations. Some components (for example the plugin management, messaging, and logging) are shared throughout the entire stack and provide the base functionality for different services. Each role mentioned in the previous section is responsible for running various services in the software stack to establish the overall federation. Figures 2 and 3 shows a diagram of the FedScI software architect with the different services and components that comprise the software stack and the roles responsible for executing those pieces.

There are two main services that must be running for any science federation: the *manager* and the resource *providers*. The *manager* service coordinates all actions with the distributed resources in the federation and serves as the main entry point for controlling the federation. In addition, this service is run by the *Federation Maintainers*. The *provider* services connect the associated instruments (sensors, compute, storage, or networking) to the federation and serve as a bridge for routing command and control to the instrument from the federation manager. *Resource providers* start the provider service for their specific instruments.

Federation Manager: The federation manager service is the heart of the FedScI software architecture. It handles all coordination throughout the entire federation including starting and stopping resources based on system events or user input. This effectively acts as a surrogate for all actions within the federation.

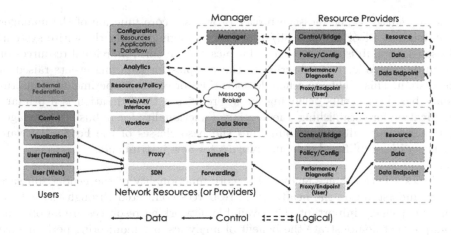

Fig. 2. The FedScI software architecture diagram detailing various services and components and the roles in the federation responsible for running each piece.

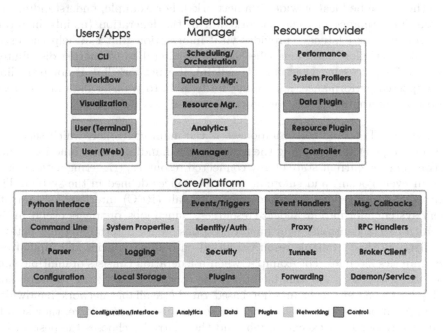

Fig. 3. The FedScI software stack.

The manager itself consists of several modules including: a message broker, performance analyzer, global data store, main controller, and various command and control interfaces. It is implemented using a plugin based approach that allows for easy extension of the manager for either future or custom capabilities for specific federations.

Message broker - The message broker provides a core function of the manager as it handles all of the publish/subscribe messaging within the entire system. Messages are published with defined topics and, in turn, individual resources or the main controller can subscribe to those topics for handling events raised in the system. This ability to schedule operations or control experiments or instruments based on events occurring anywhere within the federation is a primary justification for establishing a federation. Functionality for publishing messages and registering callbacks is built into the base classes of the FedScI software stack, which simplifies developing plugins for new instruments.

Analytics - Performance analysis is a core functionality of the FedScI software stack; understanding the health of all resources connected through the federation is extremely important. The available networking resources are an obvious example that demonstrate the benefit of analytics and monitoring performance within the federation. The federation is a distributed system by nature, so all communication and data transfers need to happen over many different networks (whether those be local or wide area networks). For example, understanding the current performance of each network link in the federation (mainly in terms of bandwidth and latency) provides vital information that can help the users (or main controller) determine whether transferring data to another distributed resource for processing is actually beneficial. If a network link is not providing the expected performance, it may not be feasible to transfer data and instead choose an alternate resource for processing data.

Controller - The final core component is the main controller, which serves as the central point for managing the federation. It handles several functions, such as tracking the current state of any connected resources, triggering actions once certain events occur, and enforcing resource polices defined in the system. The controller also provides a remote procedure call (RPC) interface for users to query system information, allocate resources, launch jobs, or trigger events in the federation. The controller is ultimately responsible for determining how actions are distributed to available resources based on defined policies and input from the analytics modules. For example, when a federation consists of multiple similar resources (like computing facilities), the controller can decide to route data and jobs to one site over another based on the available network bandwidth or computational system load. From the science user's perspective, they simply request a resource for executing jobs and the controller chooses the best option based on the system state, the defined policies, and the job characteristics.

Other - Other functions that are provided by the manager service include a data store, logging mechanism, configuration parser, and various user interfaces. The data store is for storing information global to the federation, which could include data such as performance values, current system statuses, or current configurations. A central logging mechanism allows the federation maintainers to trace the overall execution of the federation and more easily identify and debug any issues that may be occurring in the system. The configuration parser allows users to provide configuration files that define properties of the federation such as the required resources, resource policies, network topology, expected system performance, system security, and enabled modules. User command and control interfaces also use the plugin functionality provided in the software stack's shared base classes to allow for new interfaces to be easily developed. Some simple interfaces such as a command line interface and web interface can be provided in the software stack for easy management of the federation.

Resource Providers: The resource provider service in the software stack implements a base framework for connecting given resources and instruments to a federation. The base implementations provide the needed functionality for connecting to the federation manager (broker and the RPC interface), handling events (callbacks) and commands, logging, configuration parsing. Like the manager service, the provider service uses a plugin based architecture that allows for easy extension and customization. Each resource that is connected to a federation will have a unique set of constraints and environments, so each provider will likely need customization to support the specific requirements of that resource. This approach also allows the resource provider to run multiple modules within the service, including: the main control and command bridge, performance and diagnostics tools, data endpoints, data managers, the resource manager, and any user endpoints. Each provider service could also include multiple similar modules, such as multiple data endpoints or resource managers.

The *resource provider* roles are responsible for executing the provider service to make their resource available to the federation. As mentioned previously, each resource will likely require some customization in order to connect it to the federation, however the plugin architecture greatly simplifies this. Some resources may share similarities allowing reuse of different control modules between the different software stacks. Since the provider service uses a dynamic configuration, different modules can be easily enabled and disabled for each resource.

Control Bridge - While the resource provider service will be unique for each resource, one of the main required components is the control bridge. The control bridge serves as the main connection to the federation and is responsible for handling command and control from the federation manager and routing to the appropriate modules (resource manager, data endpoints, etc.). It is also responsible for both publishing resource events to the federation and creating callbacks and subscribing to events occurring on other resources in the system. This bridge is also responsible for handing active control of connected resources, including both computing resources and scientific instruments. This active command and control channel allows for dynamic, near real-time experiments to execute using the federated resources and reducing the overall time for producing results.

Diagnostics - Each provider service must also include a performance and diagnostic module that determines the current health and capabilities of the monitored resource and reports this status to the analytics module in the federation manager. The diagnostics module periodically characterizes the current status of the provided resource and publishes this information to the analytics module. It also possesses the ability to execute different stress tests and diagnostics on demand for debugging and testing purposes.

Understanding the current system's loads and the health of available resources is critical for the efficient operation of the federation. Because of the distributed nature of the science federation, many different environmental factors could influence the operation of resources, which may force the federation manager to migrate jobs or data to other available resources.

For example, suppose a federation consists of multiple compute facilities with different levels of capability and network connectivity. If the primary compute facility is under extremely high loads due to other users and experiments, the diagnostics modules notify the federation manager so it can make more informed decisions on job placement. It may be more beneficial to shift work to a less capable compute resource simply because the load on the primary resource would create unreasonable wait times for job completion.

Messaging. Messaging is a fundamental function of the software stack because the federation is, by definition, a distributed system. Not all communication between different components and services in the system requires the same type of messaging pattern, so the stack implements multiple patterns for different scenarios rather than attempting to force a single pattern to fit for all communications in the system. This approach allows the use of existing platforms, which are well suited for each messaging pattern. The FedScI framework wraps these existing capabilities with base classes to provide easy access to messaging for modules and plugins.

The three types of messaging patterns implemented within the FedScI stack include: publish/subscribe (asynchronous) events, remote procedure calls (synchronous), and bulk data transfers.

- *Publish/Subscribe* - One of the main messaging patterns within the federation is asynchronous publish/subscribe events or notifications. This pattern provides the basis for hooking different events and performing associated actions within the federation that allows for a more dynamic configuration for federation. These events can be consumed by the federation manager or even the different resource providers. Within a scientific workflow, there are multiple different types of events that can occur during an experiment, including: new data being available at a sensor, completed data transfer, or completed analyzing a dataset. Users can choose to hook events to trigger actions based on those events. For example, the federation may be configured to initiate a data transfer and spin up computational resources when new data is produced by a sensor, so the resources are already provisioned once the data transfer is complete.
- *Remote Procedure Call* - While the asynchronous messaging pattern could be used to implement command and control in the federation, using a synchronous remote-procedure-call (RPC) method provides a better and more

simple structure for these operations. Many control operations in the federation can be implemented using a blocking, synchronous approach. Examples of this include the federation manager starting or stopping resources within the federation, or querying the current state of the connecting provider services. This pattern fits any communication (especially commands and operations) where the caller is always expecting some return value (if even the operation takes a few seconds).

– *Bulk Data* - The bulk data transfer pattern is specific for handling all of the scientific data that is produced, processed, and stored during the course of experimentation using the federation. Many scientific experiments can be extremely data intensive, producing massive amounts of data that need to be processed with high performance computing. The sheer amount of data that can be produced would quickly overwhelm the publish/subscribe and RPC messaging patterns. Because of this, the federation stack provides support for multiple bulk data transfer methods which are highly optimized for transferring data between different facilities. Examples of this include the Globus stack [3] and the ADIOS frameworks [1].

Challenges. While this work is currently in progress, a key difficulty we anticipate involves the need to interoperate with existing facility resource management systems and site policies. We can not assume a totally new environment will be deployed at every endpoint, but instead must leverage existing infrastructure at the facilities and supplement missing pieces as needed. This means we will need to write the framework software that joins these pieces together. This will require connecting heterogenous systems consisting of different computing architectures, network capabilities and administrative domains. In addition to the standard HPC services (compute, network, storage) we must also provide support of interoperability with existing control systems for experimental instruments, e.g., EPICS. Our framework strives to provide a structure whereby we may begin to fill the software gaps related to the aggregation of HPC & experimental resources into a system of federated science instruments.

4   Virtual Beamlines

In order to move toward a more agile environment, we need to link compute resources with a more responsive instrument interface. We anticipate the compute elements can leverage newly emerging queues at HPC centers for preemption or fixed submit time (bound on whether will/will-not get run, to help quasi-urgent processing workloads). However, additional interfaces and connections are needed at the instrument level to facilitate a more direct linkage. As such, we are investigating an instrument gateway that could be used to connect an experimental resource into the federation.

We expect that the production instrument gateways will be a slow adoption, and therefore in the interim we are exploring "virtualized" beamlines to assist in prototyping. The virtual instruments can run much of the same software stack but are devoid of the actual physical resources/apparatuses, so we must implement mock procedures to emulate expected instrument behavior. For example, we can "produce" live images using previously captured historical datasets, at fixed output rates, to emulate standard detector procedures. The fidelity of the science is low with these dataset "replays," but the software procedure realism is high and in some cases the exact same software stack is run in our virtual testbed environment.

4.1 EPICS

The Experimental Physics and Industrial Control System (EPICS) is an open-source toolkit for the design of distributed control systems [2]. The toolkit was started over 30 years ago (circa 1989) between the LANL Ground Test Accelerator and the ANL Advanced Photon Source. The software is now used by numerous facilities around the world.[1]

EPICS includes software/firmware to interface/interact with hardware and electronics devices (e.g., detectors, motors, sensors, magnets). The toolkit includes support for storing and processing system state in a variety of patterns to create open or closed loop controls. This includes the ability to read and write status values, calculate control functions and other device I/O operations. The toolkit also includes various network protocols for accessing the distributed elements (e.g., locate/identify (publish/subscribe) system state, callback/notify on state change). There are also graphical and text-only user interfaces for operators to monitor and control devices, and archive/browse historical data.

There are four key elements used in the EPICS system. The *Input/Output Controllers (IOCs)* encapsulate software modules to process/serve hardware devices (or other IOCs) and can range from real-time firmware controllers to software pieces (e.g., scripts, python, C/C++, etc.). The state of the "live" system is stored in *Process Variables (PVs)*, which are "named data with attributes". These PVs can be of two datatypes: simple native types (float/integer/boolean/strings) or array types ("waveforms", 1-D vectors of native types). The primary internal messaging among items in EPICS is done via a custom *Channel Access (CA)* communication protocol. (Recent EPICS versions extend the system with an additional *PV Access (PVA)* communication protocol, which further supports the use of simple data structures and selective publish/subscribe services for individual data elements.) Lastly, there are clients used to interface with the various IOCs and PVs using either command-line tools or graphical displays. All of the clients are loosely coupled and are completely

---

[1] Some EPICS deployments in USA include: SNS, ANL/APS, BNL, SLAC, LANL, JLAB/CEBAF, LBNL, Fermilab D0, Keck & Gemini Telescopes; and some international deployments: Australian Square-Kilometer Array Pathfinder (ASKAP) and Synchroton; Canadian Light Source; DESY, BESSY, in Germany; PSI/SLS in Switzerland; Ganil, SACLAY in France; Diamond Light Source and ISIS in England; KEK, J-Parc in Japan; IHEP in China; NSRRC in Taiwan; PLS in South Korea.

detachable without causing the underlying control system to stop functioning, i.e., if a client detaches or fails then the IOC-based controls will continue to operate uninterrupted.

The EPICS system is widely used for the experiment controls at SNS/HFIR. For example, the neutron imaging instruments we are working with expose the "Run Control" via an EPICS interface that allows for the standard operations, e.g., Start/Stop, Pause/Resume, etc. A screen capture of this interface is shown in Fig. 4.

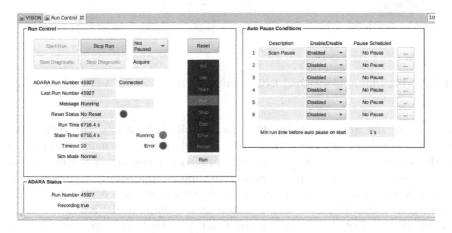

Fig. 4. Screen capture of EPICS based control interface for neutron imaging instrument at SNS.

4.2   FedScI EPICS Bridge

The direct controls for a beamline are something that must be tightly controlled to ensure proper safety, both for human individuals and for scientific equipment/sample materials. The EPICS system has been created to provide a reliable, modular and effective control system for such experimental scientific devices. As such, we believe it offers a good basis for creating a connection to a federation, to compose more advanced workflows and interfaces while still keeping proper control at the local science instruments. We can precisely select only the subsystems and PVs for which we export status and information into the federation, and more importantly which ones we might open up to access for external "steering" feedback or control from workflows or other entities within the federation.

By creating a "Bridge" between the EPICS software IOCs and the Science Federation, we can expose and leverage many of the available capabilities of the EPICS control system from within the beamlines. Initially, access to the beamline systems would be strictly read-only. For example, by providing read access to the right PVs, we could determine status information like whether an "Experiment is Running", or what is the current "Sample Temperature." Additionally, one of the key metrics for experiment completion, at least at the SNS, is expressed

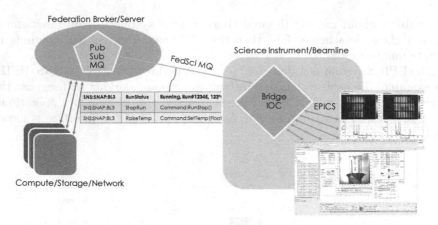

Fig. 5. Illustration of a FedScI EPICS bridge device to create a *virtual beamline.*

in terms of the amount of "proton charge collected" versus a targeted total amount. This kind of metric could be exposed to provide more direct details on the ongoing experiment status and progress. Knowing how close a given experiment is to completion can provide a unique opportunity to preemptively stage any data post-processing resources (network, storage or compute) *before* the run actually finishes. A change to a given beamline PV's state could be applied to signal other services in the federation that the experimental run is nearing completion, to identify compute reservations that need to be obtained, or to make a network data transfer bandwidth reservation. These PVs could be used to trigger federated workflows to analyze either live/intermediate data or final post-mortem data results. We plan to tie this type of information into the FedScI messaging system via publish/subscribe capabilities, for use by other components/entities in the federation.

This EPICS-to-Federation Bridge also provides a potential mechanism for identifying "steerable parameters," i.e., EPICS PVs in the beamline control system that could be externally *written to* via requests originating from the federation. Subscriptions could be made for processing such external directives/commands, to execute locally-controlled subroutines or adjust key operating parameters at the beamline instrument. The specific local Bridge details/configuration settings would provide tight control over precisely which aspects of the beamline could be externally controlled and how/when. Incorporating the Federation Bridge as part of a dual-sided EPICS IOC within the beamline control system enables a simple and easy interface for local facility adoption, that integrates smoothly into the existing local infrastructure.

Ultimately, we believe this approach will provide a very low entry point for facility configuration, as it is exposing pieces of the native infrastructure that are already in use at the experimental facilities. This offers easy customization and incremental design by both federation users and instrument scientists alike. It also enables clear and understandable control points for connecting to other federation resources (Fig. 5).

5   Conclusion

The aggregation of distributed scientific instruments into federations is an ongoing challenge. A key component of this challenge is the creation of services and software interfaces that can help to streamline the use of federations, both by the science users and resource providers. We described our current plans for a software framework that endeavors to support the users and providers of federations, while balancing needs for flexibility to fit the existing infrastructure and policies at the different facilities.

The work is being driven by a science use case from SNS/HFIR that involves neutron imaging beam-lines. We are using software containers to enable compute mobility of the analysis applications that process results from the instruments. Additionally, we are exploring ways to make instruments more dynamically accessible. Our approach for creating a more agile interface to experimental instrumentation is being explored through the creation of a virtual instrument prototype based on the widely used EPICS control system. The approach leverages EPICS' software control interface (an IOC) to create a software "bridge" between the instrument and the federation. This lowers the hurdles for adoption and enables a small incremental start, whereby we may choose key instrument state variables (PVs) and capabilities to expose for possible steering experiments. This also empowers instrument scientists and federation maintainers to quickly copy and extend the bridge for additional features or other beamlines/facilities. Ultimately, this work seeks to provide a more interactive instrument status and control interface to the federation that can be used to trigger more dynamic scientific workflows, both during and after experiments.

Acknowledgements. This research used resources of the Oak Ridge Leadership Computing Facility at the Oak Ridge National Laboratory, which is supported by the Office of Science of the U.S. Department of Energy under Contract No. DE-AC05-00OR22725. This research is support by the ORNL Laboratory Directed Research & Development program.

References

1. ADIOS: Adaptable IO System. https://www.olcf.ornl.gov/center-projects/adios
2. EPICS - Experimental Physics and Industrial Control System. https://epics.anl.gov/
3. Globus - Data Transfer with Globus. https://www.globus.org/data-transfer
4. Neutron Imaging Facility (Imaging — CG-1D — HFIR). https://neutrons.ornl.gov/imaging
5. iMars3D: Preprocessing and reconstruction for the Neutron Imaging Beam Lines. https://github.com/ornlneutronimaging/iMars3D.git
6. Liu, L., Özsu, M.T. (eds.): Encyclopedia of Database Systems. Springer, New York (2018). https://doi.org/10.1007/978-1-4614-8265-9
7. Spallation Neutrons and Pressure Diffractometer (SNAP — BL-3 — SNS). https://neutrons.ornl.gov/snap

Automated Integration of Continental-Scale Observations in Near-Real Time for Simulation and Analysis of Biosphere–Atmosphere Interactions

David J. Durden[1]([✉]), Stefan Metzger[1,2], Housen Chu[3], Nathan Collier[4], Kenneth J. Davis[5], Ankur R. Desai[2], Jitendra Kumar[4,6], William R. Wieder[7,8], Min Xu[4], and Forrest M. Hoffman[4,9]

[1] National Ecological Observatory Network Program, Battelle, Boulder, CO 80301, USA
{ddurden,smetzger}@battelleecology.org
[2] Department of Atmospheric and Oceanic Sciences, University of Wisconsin, Madison, WI 53706, USA
desai@aos.wisc.edu
[3] Lawrence Berkeley National Laboratory, Berkeley, CA 94702, USA
hchu@lbl.gov
[4] Oak Ridge National Laboratory, Oak Ridge, TN 37831, USA
nathaniel.collier@gmail.com, {jkumar,forrest}@climatemodeling.org, xum1@ornl.gov
[5] Department of Meteorology and Atmospheric Science, and Earth and Environmental Systems Institute, The Pennsylvania State University, University Park, PA 16802, USA
kjd10@psu.edu
[6] Bredesen Center, University of Tennessee, Knoxville, TN 37996, USA
[7] Climate and Global Dynamics Laboratory, National Center for Atmospheric Research, Boulder, CO 80307, USA
wwieder@ucar.edu
[8] Institute of Arctic and Alpine Research, University of Colorado, Boulder, CO 80309, USA
[9] Department of Civil and Environmental Engineering, University of Tennessee, Knoxville, TN 37996, USA

Abstract. The National Ecological Observatory Network (NEON) is a continental-scale observatory with sites across the US collecting standardized ecological observations that will operate for multiple decades. To maximize the utility of NEON data, we envision edge computing systems that gather, calibrate, aggregate, and ingest measurements in an integrated fashion. Edge systems will employ machine learning methods to cross-calibrate, gap-fill and provision data in near-real time to the NEON Data Portal and to High Performance Computing (HPC) systems, running ensembles of Earth system models (ESMs) that assimilate the data. For the first time gridded EC data products and response functions promise to offset pervasive observational biases through evaluating,

© Springer Nature Switzerland AG 2020
J. Nichols et al. (Eds.): SMC 2020, CCIS 1315, pp. 204–225, 2020.
https://doi.org/10.1007/978-3-030-63393-6_14

benchmarking, optimizing parameters, and training new machine learning parameterizations within ESMs all at the same model-grid scale. Leveraging open-source software for EC data analysis, we are already building software infrastructure for integration of near-real time data streams into the International Land Model Benchmarking (ILAMB) package for use by the wider research community. We will present a perspective on the design and integration of end-to-end infrastructure for data acquisition, edge computing, HPC simulation, analysis, and validation, where Artificial Intelligence (AI) approaches are used throughout the distributed workflow to improve accuracy and computational performance.

Keywords: Data-model integration · Eddy-covariance · Environmental observatory · National Ecological Observatory Network (NEON) · Edge computing systems · High performance computing · Earth system models · Land surface models · Model benchmarking · International Land Model Benchmarking (ILAMB)

1   Introduction

Advanced computational resources and new algorithmic developments have extended our environmental understanding over the past few decades. Now, an unprecedented volume of standardized observational data products (ODPs) are being realized through the National Ecological Observatory Network (NEON). NEON collects environmental and biological data with in situ sensors, observational sampling, and aerial overflights. Core components of NEON infrastructure are 47 tower sites, where eddy-covariance (EC) sensors are used to determine the surface–atmosphere exchange of momentum, heat, water, and carbon dioxide to assess interactions at the soil–vegetation–atmosphere interface. This continental-scale data set, having numerous contextual observations available in near-real time, affords new data-model integration opportunities to leverage such observations for new scientific understanding and to potentially enable viable ecological forecasting capabilities. This paper explores several ways that continued development of data-model integration, through new measurements, synthesized ODPs, and access to near-real-time data, contributes to improved scientific understanding of ecosystem processes and advances efforts to constrain uncertainty in Earth system models (ESMs) and subsequent benchmarking. First, we provide a background for the potential of data-model integration, the state of ESMs and benchmarking, and the growth of network-scale observations. Next, we discuss our vision for integrating network observations to improve model predictive capabilities, minimize prediction uncertainties, and advance forecast accuracy with scale-aware ODPs and near-real time data. Lastly, the roadmap to accomplishing our stated goals is outlined with considerations of emerging technologies that have the potential to broaden our goals.

1.1   Improving Scientific Understanding Through Data-Model Integration

Data-model integration is quickly becoming a fundamental component in efforts to evaluate and enhance our capabilities to simulate Earth system processes (Fer et al. 2018). Data-model integration improvements can be realized through improved parameterization of initial conditions, data assimilation techniques to inform model states or parameters during simulations, and comprehensive benchmarking of model structure and evaluation against observations (Dietze et al. 2014; Zobitz et al. 2011). Network-scale observations of ecosystem functions, such as surface-atmosphere exchange (SAE) of energy, water vapor, and trace gases, have historically (Stöckli et al. 2008) and continue to lead to novel advances in model performance (Fer et al. 2018).

Improved Model Optimization and Benchmarking

Additional Contextual Observations. Optimized model parameterization or constraints via data assimilation typically targets periods or conditions when model uncertainty is greatest. Enhanced access to numerous contextual observations can inform underlying model processes or elucidate missing information. Data assimilation constrains model predictions by comparing model output with ODPs, determining probabilistic differences, and advancing ensemble members with informed posteriors. The improved availability of repeated and interoperable in-situ, reanalysis, and remote sensing data with quantified uncertainty for weighting in assimilation and model benchmark scoring is expected to facilitate tuning process representations in ESMs and inform data providers of ODP requirements that are still unmet (Hoffman et al. 2017; Collier et al. 2018).

Resolving Scale Mismatch Between Simulations and Observations. Terrestrial ecosystem processes are widely recognized to be heterogeneous at spatial scales well below those resolved by most ESMs resulting in a spatial representativeness uncertainty when evaluating/informing models with single point observations (e.g., Riley and Shen 2014). Scaling has been shown to be non-linear with vegetation cover (e.g., Launiainen et al. 2016) and sensitive to resolution, scaling method, and the magnitude of heterogeneity (Wang et al. 2016; Liu et al. 2016). SAE observations based on the eddy-covariance (EC) flux technique (e.g., Aubinet et al. 2012) are one example of a process-scale benchmark for assessing the performance of ESMs (e.g., Fox et al. 2009; Williams et al. 2009; Schwalm et al. 2010; Schaefer et al. 2012) that suffers from such scale mismatch. Using site-based EC measurements for model benchmarking is thus complicated by biases arising from unmet assumptions on the observations. These include the limited and varying spatial representativeness of the observations at model grid scale (e.g., Chen et al. 2011; Griebel et al. 2020), and the observations violating the conservation of energy (e.g., Mauder et al. 2020). Both of these biases increase with spatial heterogeneity, which complicates regional-scale model benchmarking and improvement (e.g., Metzger 2018; Xu et al. 2020). Therefore, spatial scaling of site-based flux observations to ESM grid scales using multi-scale observations is needed to reduce uncertainties in flux estimates and constrain model benchmarking.

From Hindcasting to Forecasting. Ecosystem models are key to synthesizing process understanding, examining simulated ecosystem functioning against observations at local to regional scales, and can provide the scientific basis for field measurement campaigns (Dietze et al. 2014). The Predictive Ecosystem Analyzer (PEcAn) framework is a powerful ecoinformatics framework that utilizes Bayesian data assimilation techniques to inform models with ODPs. As such, PEcAn is a prime example of the synergistic improvements realized through data-model integration for both model parameterization and observational data requirements to reduce uncertainty (LeBauer et al. 2013; Dietze et al. 2013; Kattge et al. 2011). Access to low latency, repeated, and interoperable ODPs with quantified uncertainty is facilitating a movement to near-term ecological forecasting. These forecasts are envisioned to inform land-use decision makers with the most accurate predictions of ecosystem function via iterative model assessment and improvement through comparison with near-real-time data (Dietze et al. 2018). Similar model evaluation and benchmarking of ESMs can be realized; however, this approach likely involves a large number of perturbed parameter ensembles (PPE) of models or machine learning-based surrogate models running on high performance computing (HPC) systems.

1.2   Earth System Models and Benchmarking

Earth system models (ESMs) are designed to simulate the coupled multiscale, multiphysics processes associated with interactive dynamics, physics, chemistry, and biology across the land, ocean, sea ice, land ice, and atmosphere that drive the Earth's climate system (Randall et al. 2018). Originally conceived as models of physics and dynamics, focused primarily on atmosphere and ocean processes, early global climate models evolved into ESMs with the inclusion of terrestrial and marine ecosystem processes, atmospheric chemistry, and human system interactions (Bonan and Doney 2018; Flato 2011). Research with these coupled ESMs has demonstrated that the carbon cycle responds to climate but also that large nonlinear climate feedbacks are produced by the biosphere (Friedlingstein et al. 2001, 2006; Arora et al. 2013). Terrestrial ecosystems in ESMs are represented by a variety of vegetation types, an amount of leaf area, functioning of stomata in leaves, and carbon and nutrient pools that interact with energy and water cycles (Bonan 2016). Relatively simplistic representations of vegetation and soil processes in land surface models (LSMs), typically contained within coupled ESMs, capture the mean state behavior of plants and soils over large spatial scales on annual time scales. However, process understanding limits the ability to reduce errors and biases when compared with observational data at local scales (Schimel et al. 1997).

Forecasting ecosystem responses to environmental forcing is important for resource management and understanding impacts of rapid climate change or land use change (Clark et al. 2001; Foley et al. 2005; Luo et al. 2011). While long-term EC flux measurements help to constrain energy, water, and carbon cycles for individual biomes (Baldocchi et al. 2001), more rapid integration of these data with models—employing data assimilation and benchmarking tools for uncertainty quantification, parameter optimization, and structural optimization—will improve understanding of these processes and lead to more mechanistic representations in models and more accurate ecosystem forecasts (Williams et al. 2009; Raupach et al. 2005).

LSMs rely on a collection of process representations, called parameterizations, embodied in numerical algorithms that employ many often-uncertain parameters to approximate the evolution of carbon, water, and energy in the natural world (Bonan 2019). Data assimilation methods are commonly used to calibrate and evaluate model accuracy and parameter uncertainty (Luo et al. 2011). Raupach et al. (2005) presented methods for assimilating diverse data and separating observational from model errors to produce more accurate forecasts of the global carbon cycle. These methods have been applied across scales, from global inversions (e.g., Ricciuto et al. 2008) to individual tree stands (e.g., Moore et al. 2008; Ricciuto et al. 2011), with a variety of approaches, including Kalman filters or ensemble Kalman filters (e.g., Quaife et al. 2008), other maximum likelihood techniques, and least squares optimization methods (e.g., Prihodko et al. 2008). Sophisticated data assimilation packages that ingest EC flux measurements are now being coupled directly to complex forward land surface models for use on HPC systems (Fox et al. 2018; Bastrikov et al. 2018). Perturbed physics ensembles (also called perturbed parameter ensembles) or PPEs employ thousands of ensemble simulations to develop an understanding of the sensitivity or importance of individual parameters or to quantify the impacts of their uncertainties on feedbacks, extremes, or model skill (Fischer et al. 2011; Sanderson et al. 2010). Conducting large numbers of ensemble simulations to search for optimal parameter combinations for complex ESMs has become so computationally intensive that in some cases surrogate models are being developed and used in place of running LSMs directly (Li et al. 2018; Lu et al. 2018). For example, Ricciuto et al. (2018) analyzed the sensitivity of five key carbon variables to 68 model parameters in the US Department of Energy's (DOE's) Energy Exascale Earth System Model (E3SM) land model using a global sensitivity analysis on 96 FLUXNET sites. Lu et al. (2018) further optimized 8 of 68 parameters of the E3SM land model using surrogate-based global optimization. Executing these direct or surrogate simulations is one part of the challenge; evaluating model results in a systematic fashion is another.

Systematic evaluation of model results, through comparison with observational data, is important for quantifying model fidelity (Randerson et al. 2009). As ESMs become more complex, routine assessment of model performance must be performed for verification of new parameterizations, evaluation of impacts on other model components, and validation of simulations under changing environmental conditions. The land modeling community has developed a variety of evaluation approaches for terrestrial carbon cycle models (Cadule et al. 2010;

Blyth et al. 2011; Abramowitz 2012; Anav et al. 2013; Piao et al. 2013). Some benchmarking approaches are based on an expected, pre-defined level of performance (Abramowitz 2005; Best et al. 2015), but most systematic benchmarking strategies produce a skill score based on a direct model-data comparison. Lack of standardized evaluation metrics and methods have limited adoption of model benchmarking and use of a wide diversity of observational data sets.

The International Land Model Benchmarking (ILAMB) project was organized to engage the research community in the development of standardized and internationally accepted benchmarks for land model performance. The ILAMB community aims to strengthen linkages among experimental, remote sensing, and climate modeling communities in the design of new model tests and new measurement programs, and supports the design and development of open source benchmarking tools through international workshops and working group activities (Hoffman et al. 2017). With support primarily from the US Department of Energy, community ILAMB activities have resulted in creation of an ILAMB benchmarking software package for evaluation of LSMs that incorporate biogeochemical cycles (Collier et al. 2018; Hoffman et al. 2017). The ILAMB package produces graphical and tabular diagnostics across a range of biogeochemistry, hydrology, radiation and energy, and forcing variables. It scores multi-model performance for period mean, bias, root-mean-square error (RMSE), spatial distribution, interannual coefficient of variation, seasonal cycle, and long-term trend. The design philosophy and details of its implementation and methodology are described by Collier et al. (2018). Efforts are underway to directly link ILAMB to PEcAn for more rapid assessment of site-level simulations over diurnal time scales. Being an open source and extensible package with a scalable design, so that it can run on the largest HPC systems, makes it a good choice for evaluating the results of ensemble simulations aimed at parameter optimization and uncertainty assessment.

1.3   Network-Scale Observations

Network-scale flux tower observations—such as those available from FLUXNET (Baldocchi et al. 2001), AmeriFlux (Novick et al. 2018), ICOS, TERN, or NEON (Metzger et al. 2019a)—are revolutionizing ecosystem science by providing observations that cover large spatial areas across a broad variety of ecoclimatic zones. The proliferation of standardized and interoperable flux network ODPs through cross-network collaboration and integration strengthens the ability of observations to explain measured environmental variability. For instance, NEON provides data to AmeriFlux, which along with ICOS and TERN, feed into FLUXNET. However, limitations exist on standardized measurements across networks, and substantial latency can be incurred for fully quality controlled data sets with quantified uncertainties.

NEON is a continental-scale observatory with sites across the US that will operate for multiple decades. NEON produces data products, software, and services to facilitate research on the impacts of climate change, land-use change, and invasive species. NEON collects environmental and biological data with in-situ sensors, biometric observations, and aerial overflights. One of NEON's core components is its 47 tower sites, where EC sensors are used to determine the SAE of momentum, heat, water, and carbon dioxide to assess interactions at the soil–vegetation–atmosphere interface. These data are streamed from tower sites to a central NEON headquarters facility. There, calibration coefficients are applied, quality assurance and quality control are performed, and additional processing algorithms are applied to derive higher level data products. The resulting ODPs are served on the NEON data portal, currently with about a one month latency. The latency of biometric and airborne remote sensing data varies by ODP. One unique aspect of NEON ODPs is the standardization of sensor infrastructure, biometric protocols and algorithms for processing. This standardization and ubiquitous availability of "contextual" observations with respect to SAE processes, position NEON ODPs as a perfect test suite for ESM hypothesis testing and benchmarking.

2   Visions to Improve Model Performance with Network-Scale Observations

2.1   Scale-Aware Observational Data Products for ESM Evaluation

Improved understanding of model-data interfaces enables maximizing the usefulness of ODPs for ESM improvement. For data-model integration, we commonly rely on half-hourly intervals as the lowest common timestep denominator. That is, we expect both ODPs and models to capture in half-hourly slices the dynamics emerging from environmental processes at a much broader range of scales. From the observational perspective, inconsistencies arise when we interpret continuous, nonlinear environmental processes and non-symmetrical observation techniques through discrete data processing and analytics that assume linearity and Gaussianity. Resultant half-hourly ODPs may be biased on the order of several 10% due to space/time ambiguity associated with scaling (Xu et al. 2017), violation of energy conservation (Mauder et al. 2020), etc.: our models might perform better or worse than we think because we already know that our current ODP reference is off. Here we explore how we could rectify the situation by creating half-hourly ODPs that capture environmental processes at scales consistent with expectations for data-model integration.

A Complementary Benchmarking Framework. To resolve the scale mismatch between simulations and observations, participants of the DOE-funded 2019 RUBISCO-AmeriFlux Working Group Meeting (Hawkins et al. 2020) conceived a scale-aware benchmarking framework that complements top-down ODP constraints with bottom-up ODP process information across DOC, DOE, NASA and NSF projects (Fig. 1). The proposed approach will enable consistent regional-scale evaluations of carbon, water, and energy cycles in ESMs. At the center of the framework is the ILAMB package, which facilitates benchmarking ESMs in a modular fashion. The NCAR-NEON Community Land Model (CLM5) implementation is one example of an enhanced ESM module for use with ILAMB. Participants of the NSF-funded 2019 NCAR-NEON Workshop conceived an implementation of CLM5 that leverages an unprecedented range of contextual observations to constrain model uncertainty. In the past e.g. plot-based biometric observations, high-resolution airborne remote sensing, gas phase and water phase isotopes, replicate soil properties, as well as aquatic properties in adjacent lakes and streams have not been uniformly available at the flux tower network scale. With the advent of NEON these contextual observations are routinely available alongside traditional flux tower data from all 47 NEON terrestrial field sites, in standardized format via the NEON Data Portal and Application Programming Interface (API; Metzger et al. 2019a). A particular science focus of the NCAR-NEON CLM5 implementation is error characterization, including model structure, parameters, initial conditions, meteorological forcing, and observational error.

Large-scale observations of the atmospheric composition and its variation across time and space provide a first principal constraint on the benchmarking framework (e.g., Tans et al. 1990; Gurney et al. 2003; Battle et al. 2000; Pacala et al. 2001). The strength of this top-down ODP constraint is that it provides a direct measure of atmospheric stocks, though attribution to surface processes remains challenging (e.g., Houweling et al. 2017). These top-down constraints are available from tall towers (e.g., Miles et al. 2012; Andrews et al. 2014), airborne (e.g., Sweeney et al. 2015; Miller et al. 2016; Barkley et al. 2019) and spaceborne observations (e.g., Chen et al. 2020). One example is NASA's Atmospheric Carbon and Transport (ACT) - America campaign, which measured atmospheric carbon concentrations, trace gases and meteorological conditions via aircraft in five campaigns spanning all four seasons from 2016–2019 (Davis et al. 2019). ACT-America's airborne measurements are temporally sparse, but spatially extensive, covering four seasons and major ecoregions of the central and eastern United States. These flights are designed to provide regional-scale, seasonal constraints on carbon exchange rates by mapping out carbon and related trace gases (Baier et al. 2020) within synoptic weather systems (Pal et al. 2020), complementing the temporally-rich but relatively spatially sparse tower observations and spatially comprehensive column averaged space-borne observations.

Network-scale flux tower observations such as available from FLUXNET (Baldocchi et al. 2001), AmeriFlux (Novick et al. 2018) or NEON (Metzger et al. 2019a) provide the second principal constraint on the benchmarking framework. The strength of this bottom-up constraint is that SAE observations provide a direct and independent benchmark for assessing the process-scale performance of ESMs, though scale mismatch and surface energy imbalance remain challenging. Here, we seek to improve model benchmarking with flux tower data through two synergistic bottom-up approaches, an "extensive" and an "intensive" approach. The extensive bottom-up approach annotates AmeriFlux data with spatial attributes (e.g., land cover, vegetation indices, etc.; Chu et al. 2020). Thanks to comparatively weak data requirements this approach is readily applied to 200+ AmeriFlux sites. Site spatial representativeness can now be assessed by comparing spatial attributes in the flux surface source area vs. the target domain, such as a model grid cell. This approach facilitates shortlisting spatially representative sites (e.g., sites with similar plant functional type and vegetation characteristics between the flux source area and target domain) for initial model benchmarking, and improved model representation of compound ecosystems. The extensive approach also serves as a prior to identify and prioritize the sites where the intensive approach is deemed necessary, which we explore in more detail in the following section.

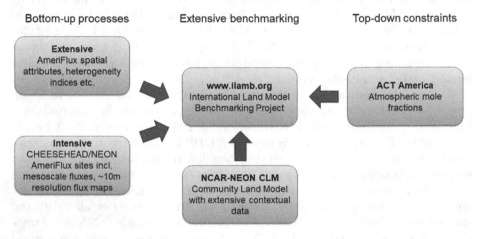

Fig. 1. Scale-aware benchmarking framework that complements bottom-up process information with top-down constraints across DOC, DOE, NASA and NSF projects. Presented during the AGU 2020 Fall Meeting NCAR-NEON Town Hall (Metzger et al. 2019b)

Scale-Equivalent Observational Benchmarks. In contrast to the shortlisting employed in the extensive bottom-up approach, the intensive bottom-up approach aims to fully utilize the variability inherent to changing flux tower sample characteristics. The aim here is to develop scale-aware ODPs from point and line observations for improved model benchmarking at equivalent space and time resolutions. This is achieved by fully incorporating the source area dynamics in source area-to-target-area upscaling (Fu et al. 2014; Metzger et al. 2013a; Ran et al. 2016; Xu et al. 2017). These approaches show great merits in providing space-time explicit flux ODPs that model predictions could be readily benchmarked against at designated grid cells. Furthermore, the Environmental Response Function (ERF) Virtual Control Volume (VCV) spatio-temporal data assimilation system shows promise to also close the surface energy imbalance frequently observed at flux towers (Metzger 2018; Xu et al. 2020), which to date hamstrings data synthesis and model-data fusion with a pervasive bias (e.g., Cui and Chui 2019; Mauder et al. 2020; Stoy et al. 2013).

While ERF promises complete data utilization it has comparatively strong data requirements. This includes EC high-frequency data, which are currently limited to AmeriFlux Core ($N = 14$) and NEON ($N = 47$) sites, and Ameri-Flux Tech Team site visits ($N = 40$–50). Specifically, surface and meteorological controls on the fluxes change at minute timescales through transience of source areas, the passing of clouds, etc. Thus, performing ERF analyses at minute- and decameter-resolution allows separating meteorological and surface controls on the fluxes in unprecedented clarity: spectral averaging and source attribution of high-frequency data combined with machine learning connect fluxes to meteorological and surface properties, and ultimately transfer the joint information to the model grid scale. The utilization of high-frequency wavelet flux calculations produces response variable observation with large sample sizes and high signal-to-noise ratio. Thus, providing ample data for the boosted regression trees technique to extract the key driver-response relationships (Metzger et al. 2013a). Results include half-hourly flux maps and propagated uncertainties, alongside estimates of the spatial mean and land-cover specific fluxes and their variation across space (Fig. 2). Figure 2 illustrates the mapped projection of turbulent sensible heat flux, the transfer of heat inducing a change in temperature, throughout the day across a 30 km × 30 km grid centered on the AmeriFlux Park Falls tall tower site. The derived spatially attributed fluxes from ERF are observed to transition from negative to positive as the surface warms during the day, with clear hot- and cold-spots observable due to the landscapes heterogenuous ecosystem. By including mesoscale motions in a continuous, fixed-frame representation of all hot- and cold-spots within a model grid cell ERF-VCV reduces advective errors by at least one order of magnitude, which effectively closes the surface energy balance (Xu et al. 2020). Where ESMs do not explicitly represent site heterogeneity, we integrate flux maps to probability density functions and from there to statistical measures of location and dispersion (Metzger 2018). We will add these to the ILAMB database of regional simulations to design new, probability-based model benchmarking metrics/scores, and inform the weighting of observations in the data assimilation, uncertainty quantification, and site-level validation processes.

The flux maps are accompanied by a set of non-linear response functions, jointly extracted from ground, airborne, and spaceborne data (Fig. 3). These will serve as benchmarks for diagnosing calibrated models and attributing remote sensing data to surface processes. Ultimately, they allow designing new benchmarking metrics/scores based on ERF-observed vs. ESM-modeled driver-response relationships/surfaces (e.g., Koven et al. 2017).

The promise of scale-aware model benchmarking is that we can better ascribe differences between models and observations to process, parameter, driver, and random error (Dietze 2017), to which we might otherwise falsely attribute scale-related differences. In short: to what extent can we better evaluate or benchmark models with flux data when we consider a flux product that fully matches the scale of the model output and considers the mixing of spatial and temporal variability that occurs at many flux tower sites? The approach outlined here

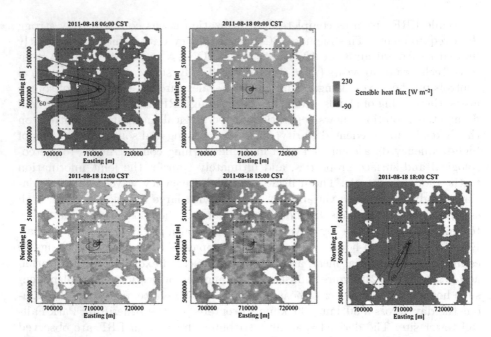

Fig. 2. Flux source area variations over time at the AmeriFlux Park Falls tall tower 122 m measurement height, modified after (Metzger et al. 2013b). The transient source areas are superimposed over the fixed-frame ERF-derived grids of turbulent sensible heat flux. Reprinted from *Agricultural and Forest Meteorology*, Volume 255, Stefan Metzger, Surface-atmosphere exchange in a box: Making the control volume a suitable representation for in-situ observations, Pages 68–80, Copyright (2018), with permission from Elsevier.

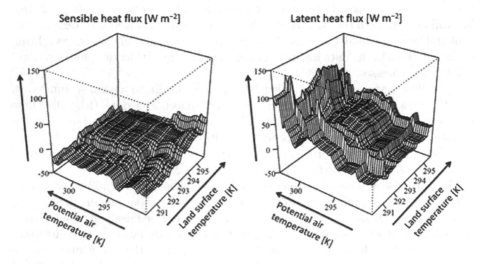

Fig. 3. Multi-dimensional flux response functions at the AmeriFlux Park Falls tall tower 122 m measurement height, modified after (Metzger et al. 2013b).

provides a framework to partition observational uncertainty into scale-related and instrument-related components. Benchmarking or data assimilation is not possible without proper characterization of uncertainty in both observation and model. A systematic approach is essential to make forward progress. A systematic application of a scale-aware benchmark also allows for identification of "ideal" sites or a complementary suite of measurements necessary for an observational site to be considered a high-quality benchmark.

To this last point, recent field experiments have exploited the "super-site" concept to better evaluate the mix of measurement types, extent, and frequency to develop a robust scale-aware benchmark. For example, the Chequamegon Heterogeneous Ecosystem Energy-balance Study Enabled by a High-density Extensive Array of Detectors 2019 (CHEESEHEAD19) field project deployed a quasi-random extensive set of EC flux towers within a "model grid", coupled with a range of airborne and ground based sampling of surface and atmospheric properties and expansive collection of satellite remote sensing imagery (Butterworth et al. 2020). Campaigns like this or the proposed NCAR-NEON super-site project provide a window into the capability of scale-aware benchmarks. They provide a framework for future experimental design of long-term super-sites or identification of core observables necessary to develop scale-aware benchmarks at other sites.

Similarly, nesting sub-grid models within global gridded ESMs provides another opportunity to incorporate scale dependencies within the model. The NOAA Climate Process Team (CPT) Coupling of Land and Atmospheric Subgrid Parameterizations (CLASP) is evaluating how large eddy simulations (LES) and parameterizations can be used to enhance representation of subgrid processes in a model. Such approaches further enhance the value of a scale-aware benchmark.

These experiments and developments thus provide a testbed for evolving the scale-aware benchmark approach. With these, we can start to ask: how much can we relax the high frequency and high resolution data requirements of the ERF approach and still reliably estimate grid-resolved fluxes and uncertainty? How does varying combinations of EC, concentration gradient, tower-mounted imaging, and new sensing techniques expand the reach of the methods into different trace gas fluxes or with higher accuracy? Can ERF also be used to map and predict state variables like biomass, leaf area, canopy chemistry, near-surface temperatures, and other sources of subgrid variability that facilitate space-time consistent ESM inputs and outputs? What are new ways to benchmark models once a space and time resolved benchmark or subgrid model is available? Is the information value of the benchmark limited to the single "grid-cell" of the land-surface model or is the spatial/temporal correlation structure useful for propagating the benchmark to other locations? A number of open research questions and exciting directions are currently foreseen, such as space/time gap-filling and partitioning to resolve issues inherent to current approaches, including confounding space/time transience with biophysical processes.

To summarize, ERF-derived ODPs fully match the scale of ESM inputs and outputs, and comply with previously unmet observational assumptions. The results are half-hourly flux maps of a model subgrid domain that facilitate consistent integration among multi-scale observations and models at flux tower sites. Individual flux pixels even provide a direct link to plot-scale surface observations, such as soil plots and biometric observations. Furthermore, in-situ response function benchmarks improve model diagnosis and remote sensing data interpretation. These scale-aware properties promise unequalled realism for integrating observations and models through overcoming long-standing differences in perception across disciplines.

2.2   Near-Real Time Data Accessibility for ESM and Benchmarking

SAE ODPs for evaluating ESM are currently either available from individual sites in near-real-time, or from many networked sites with latencies on the order of 6 months to 1 year. Due to its central collection and processing structure NEON has the opportunity to push the boundaries of near-real-time data availability to facilitate ecological forecasting, data assimilation into ESMs, and ESM benchmarking. Currently, the vast majority of NEON's 53 terrestrial instrumented systems (TIS) data products are available with a 1-month latency via the NEON data portal (https://data.neonscience.org/) and API (https://data.neonscience.org/data-api/) due to a monthly publication cycle. However, NEON SAE processing pipeline improvements are in development to reduce data latency to 1–5 days. To our knowledge, this would be the largest EC tower data set provided in near-real-time globally.

A pilot project envisioned from the aforementioned NCAR-NEON workshop developed a workflow to grab NEON data from the API, perform some quality assurance and quality control, gap-fill data, partition fluxes, and package data in a netCDF data format that is ingestible by CLM5, ILAMB, and PEcAn. The workflow is being hosted on Github (https://github.com/NEONScience/NCAR-NEON), has been containerized (https://quay.io/repository/ddurden/ncar-neon-ddurden), and is deployable via command line for integration with job schedulers or workflow managers. The NEON data pipeline is transitioning to a microservices-based Pachyderm architecture (https://www.pachyderm.com/), a version control system for data that preserves data provenance. In the Pachyderm pipeline, any new commit to data, metadata, or processing code triggers the reprocessing of downstream derived products. Integration of ODP generation for model-data fusion into this architecture promises near-real time data access with full provenance. Work with the scientific community still remains to address where community modeling and benchmarking data sets should be hosted and determine the essential ODPs to be provided both for driving models and evaluating/benchmarking.

To support rapid and scalable assessment and benchmarking of LSM results, a Land Model Testbed (LMT) system is being developed through a pilot project at ORNL (Fig. 4). Aimed at delivering a workflow for very large ensemble simulations, the LMT provides software infrastructure for running multiple

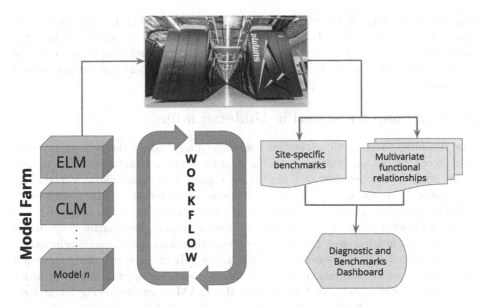

Fig. 4. A Land Model Testbed (LMT) workflow for running and evaluating large numbers of ensemble simulations for multiple LSMs on the Summit supercomputer system and dynamically provisioned cloud resources is being developed at ORNL. Site-specific benchmarks for EC super-sites and new functional relationship metrics are being incorporated into ILAMB, and a dynamic user interface is being developed to give users better control over how model-data comparison results are displayed through an interactive dashboard.

models on the Summit supercomputer system and dynamically provisioned cloud computing resources. New site-specific benchmarks for EC super-sites and new functional relationship metrics are being incorporated into ILAMB to support assessment of large ensembles and PPE simulations. An interactive dashboard is being designed to give users control over how benchmarking results and graphical diagnostics are displayed. Interfaces are also being developed around ILAMB for activation (executing an analysis) and linking to diagnostic results following the evolving Coordinated Model Evaluation Capabilities (CMEC) standards. CMEC interfaces will further enable connections to NOAA's Model Diagnostics Task Force that promotes development of process-oriented diagnostics for climate and weather forecasting models (Maloney et al. 2019). These improvements are key to informing parameterization improvements to address long-standing model biases and to delivering credible projection results for assessing climate change impacts and vulnerabilities for stakeholders and policy-makers (Eyring et al. 2019).

The LMT, combined with NEON's near-real time SAE ODPs, offers a truly scalable approach for rapidly conducting ecological forecasts on HPC systems and evaluating model performance as new measurements are made. We envision integrating the multi-scale observations from NEON's distributed edge computing systems with multiple LSMs running in the LMT framework on centralized HPC systems and distributed cloud computing resources. This data-model integration approach will advance ecological research and improve mechanistic understanding of Earth system processes important for environmental sustainability.

3   Roadmap to Scientific Understanding

The roadmap to extracting scientific understanding through data-model integration is contingent on multiple working groups working toward common underlying goals of maximizing our predictive capabilities, minimizing uncertainty associated with our predictions, and advancing our forecast accuracy with near-real-time data. Near-real-time data cyber-infrastructure is on the verge of being realized for multiple flux tower networks, and is opening new pathways to near-term ESM benchmarking, parameter optimization, and data-fusion techniques.

The 2019 RUBISCO-AmeriFlux Workshop (Hawkins et al. 2020) planned roadmap lays the foundation for the bottom-up scaling approaches to produce scale-aware ODPs and ingest them into the ILAMB benchmarking framework (Fig. 5). For the extensive bottom-up approach initial data processing is complete, and the manuscript by Chu et al. (2020) introduces the results and newly available spatial attributes to the community at large. Our planned goal for 2020 is to produce a shortlist of homogeneous sites for initial model benchmarking, with additional milestones through 2021 (Fig. 5). For the intensive bottom-up approach, the group is working on integrating the ERF-VCV data sets into ILAMB. At this time, the group has successfully ingested the NEON NetCDF file format into ILAMB, and is compiling the Metzger et al. (2019a) 30 min flux grids into these files. Planned goals for 2020 include regional ILAMB evaluations and site-level validations to design performance scores, with additional milestones through 2023 (Fig. 5). We further envision a hybrid "simplified high-res mapping" bottom-up approach to reduce ERF-VCV data requirements for use at all AmeriFlux sites, which is currently ahead of schedule.

The bottom-up approaches are complemented by the top-down syntheses of aircraft campaign data from ACT-America, an array of terrestrial ecosystem models, posterior flux estimates from atmospheric inverse flux estimates and AmeriFlux observations. The expected outcome is spatially and temporally comprehensive evaluation of the performance of these ecosystem models and inversion posteriors. This evaluation will provide insight into the process limitations of these models and the existing seasonal, regional biases in the inversion systems. The improved understanding will be used to improve the prior flux estimates used in atmospheric inversions, and to improve the process representation in regional to continental scale simulations of terrestrial carbon fluxes.

Through the convergence of high throughput computational frameworks processing EC data and applying machine learning algorithms to develop scale-aware ODPs with multiple instances of ESMs running on HPC, we can make substantial strides to our understanding of Earth systems processes across spatiotemporal scales that have previously restricted such studies. The advancement

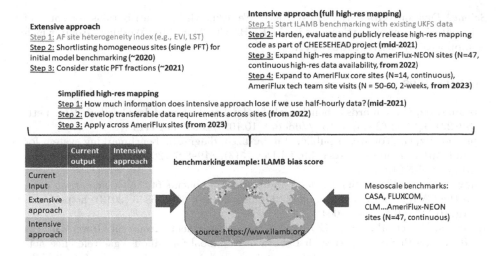

Fig. 5. Status and roadmap of the bottom-up scaling approaches. Blue font indicates areas of currently active work. (Color figure online)

of ecosystem understanding is not confined to the described work though. The development of the Waggle, an open sensor platform for edge computing, by the Array of Things (AoT) opens the door to enhanced distributed data collection, advanced reactive measurements, and manipulative studies (Beckman et al. 2016). NEON has the observational infrastructure, such as sufficient power and network connectivity at tower sites and advanced command and control capabilities, to utilize such compute infrastructure in the future.

Acknowledgements. The National Ecological Observatory Network is a project sponsored by the National Science Foundation and managed under cooperative agreement by Battelle. Some of this material is based upon work supported by the National Science Foundation (Grant DBI-0752017). We acknowledge contributions for some of this material from participants of NSF-sponsored joint NCAR and NEON workshop, Predicting life in the Earth system – linking the geosciences and ecology, and the continued efforts in post-workshop working groups. Any opinions, findings, and conclusions or recommendations expressed in this material are those of the authors and do not necessarily reflect the views of the National Science Foundation. Portions of this research were sponsored by the Laboratory Directed Research and Development Program of Oak Ridge National Laboratory and used resources of the Oak Ridge Leadership Computing Facility (OLCF) at Oak Ridge National Laboratory, which is managed by UT-Battelle, LLC, for the U.S. Department of Energy under contract DE–AC05–00OR22725. Additional support was provided by the Reducing Uncertainties in Biogeochemical Interactions through Synthesis and Computation Science Focus Area (RUBISCO SFA), which is sponsored by the Regional and Global Model Analysis (RGMA) activity of the Earth & Environmental System Modeling (EESM) Program in the Earth and Environmental Systems Sciences Division (EESSD) of the Office of Biological and Environmental Research (BER) in the U.S. Department of Energy Office of Science. Some contributions to this research were supported by NASA's Earth

Science Division (Grant NNX15AG76G). We acknowledge contributions for some of this material from all participants in the RUBISCO-AmeriFlux Working Group, which is supported by the RUBISCO SFA.

References

Abramowitz, G.: Towards a benchmark for land surface models. Geophys. Res. Lett. **32**(22), L22702 (2005). https://doi.org/10.1029/2005GL024419

Abramowitz, G.: Towards a public, standardized, diagnostic benchmarking system for land surface models. Geosci. Model Dev. **5**(3), 819–827 (2012). https://doi.org/10. 5194/gmd-5-819-2012

Anav, A., et al.: Evaluating the land and ocean components of the global carbon cycle in the CMIP5 earth system models. J. Clim. **26**(18), 6801–6843 (2013). https://doi. org/10.1175/JCLI-D-12-00417.1

Andrews, A., et al.: CO_2, CO, and CH_4 measurements from tall towers in the NOAA Earth System Research Laboratory's Global Greenhouse gas reference network: instrumentation, uncertainty analysis, and recommendations for future high-accuracy greenhouse gas monitoring efforts. Atmos Meas Tech **7**(2), 647 (2014). https://doi.org/10.5194/amt-7-647-2014

Arora, V.K., et al.: Carbon-concentration and carbon-climate feedbacks in CMIP5 earth system models. J. Clim. **26**(15), 5289–5314 (2013). https://doi.org/10.1175/ JCLI-D-12-00494.1

Aubinet, M., Vesala, T., Papale, D.: Eddy Covariance: A Practical Guide to Measurement and Data Analysis. Springer, Dordrecht (2012). https://doi.org/10.1007/978-94-007-2351-1

Baier, B.C., et al.: Multispecies assessment of factors influencing regional and enhancements during the Winter 2017 ACT-America Campaign. J. Geophys. Res. Atmos. **125**(2), e2019JD031339 (2020). https://doi.org/10.1029/2019JD031339

Baldocchi, D., et al.: FLUXNET: a newtool to study the temporal and spatial variability of ecosystem-scale carbondioxide, water vapor, and energy flux densities. Bull. Am. Meteorol. Soc. **82**(11), 2415–2434 (2001). https://doi.org/10.1175/1520-0477(2001)082%3C2415:FANTTS%3E2.3.CO;2

Barkley, Z.R., et al.: Forward modeling and optimization of methane emissions in the south central United States using aircraft transects across frontal boundaries. Geophys. Res. Lett. **46**(22), 13564–13573 (2019). https://doi.org/10.1029/ 2019GL084495

Bastrikov, V., MacBean, N., Bacour, C., Santaren, D., Kuppel, S., Peylin, P.: Land surface model parameter optimisation using in situ flux data: comparison of gradient-based versus random search algorithms (a case study using ORCHIDEE v1.9.5.2). Geosci. Model. Dev. **11**(12), 4739–4754 (2018). https://doi.org/10.5194/gmd-11-4739-2018

Battle, M., et al.: Global carbon sinks and their variability inferred from atmospheric O_2 and $\delta13C$. Science **287**(5462), 2467–2470 (2000). https://doi.org/10. 1126/science.287.5462.2467

Beckman, P., Sankaran, R., Catlett, C., Ferrier, N., Jacob, R., Papka, M.: Waggle: an open sensor platform for edge computing. In: 2016 IEEE SENSORS, pp. 1–3. IEEE (2016). https://doi.org/10.1109/ICSENS.2016.7808975

Best, M.J., et al.: The plumbing of land surface models: benchmarking model performance. J. Hydrometeor. **16**(3), 1425–1442 (2015). https://doi.org/10.1175/JHM-D-14-0158.1

Blyth, E., et al.: A comprehensive set of benchmark tests for a land surface model of simultaneous fluxes of water and carbon at both the global and seasonal scale. Geosci. Model. Dev. **4**(2), 255–269 (2011). https://doi.org/10.5194/gmd-4-255-2011

Bonan, G.B.: Ecological Climatology: Concepts and Applications, 3rd edn. Cambridge University Press, New York (2016). https://doi.org/10.1017/CBO9781107339200

Bonan, G.B.: Climate Change and Terrestrial Ecosystem Modeling. Cambridge University Press, New York (2019). https://doi.org/10.1017/9781107339217

Bonan, G.B., Doney, S.C.: Climate, ecosystems, and planetary futures: The challenge to predict life in Earth system models. Science **359**(6375), eaam8328 (2018). https://doi.org/10.1126/science.aam8328

Butterworth, B.J., et al.: Connecting land-atmosphere interaction to surface heterogeniety in CHEESEHEAD 2019 (2020, in preparation)

Cadule, P., et al.: Benchmarking coupled climate-carbon models against long-term atmospheric CO_2 measurements. Glob. Biogeochem. Cycles **24**(2), GB2016 (2010). https://doi.org/10.1029/2009GB003556

Chen, B., et al.: Assessing eddy-covariance flux tower location bias across the Fluxnet-Canada research network based on remote sensing and footprint modelling. Agric. Forest Meteorol. **151**(1), 87–100 (2011). https://doi.org/10.1016/j.agrformet.2010.09.005

Chen, Z., Liu, J., Henze, D.K., Huntzinger, D.N., Wells, K.C., Miller, S.M.: Linking global terrestrial CO_2 fluxes and environmental drivers using OCO-2 and a geostatistical inverse model. Atmos. Chem. Phys. Discuss **2020**, 1–24 (2020). https://doi.org/10.5194/acp-2020-285

Chu, H., et al.: Footprint representativeness of eddy-covariance flux measurements across AmeriFlux sites (2020, in preparation)

Clark, J.S., et al.: Ecological forecasts: an emerging imperative. Science **293**(5530), 657–660 (2001). https://doi.org/10.1126/science.293.5530.657

Collier, N., et al.: The international land model benchmarking (ILAMB) system: design, theory, and implementation. J. Adv. Model. Earth Sy. **10**(11), 2731–2754 (2018). https://doi.org/10.1029/2018MS001354

Cui, W., Chui, T.F.M.: Temporal and spatial variations of energy balance closure across FLUXNET research sites. Agric. Forest Meteorol. **271**, 12–21 (2019). https://doi.org/10.1016/j.agrformet.2019.02.026

Davis, K.J., et al.: ACT-America: L3 merged in situ atmospheric trace gases and flask data. Eastern USA (2019). https://doi.org/10.3334/ORNLDAAC/1593

Dietze, M.C., LeBauer, D.S., Kooper, R.: On improving the communication between models and data. Plant Cell Environ. **36**(9), 1575–1585 (2013). https://doi.org/10.1111/pce.12043

Dietze, M.C., et al.: A quantitative assessment of a terrestrial biosphere model's data needs across North American biomes. J. Geophys. Res. Biogeosci. **119**(3), 286–300 (2014). https://doi.org/10.1002/2013JG002392

Dietze, M.C., et al.: Iterative near-term ecological forecasting: needs, opportunities, and challenges. Proc. Natl. Acad. Sci. **115**(7), 1424–1432 (2018). https://doi.org/10.1073/pnas.1710231115

Eyring, V., et al.: Taking climate model evaluation to the next level. Nat. Clim. Change **9**(2), 102–110 (2019). https://doi.org/10.1038/s41558-018-0355-y

Fer, I., Kelly, R., Moorcroft, P.R., Richardson, A.D., Cowdery, E.M., Dietze, M.C.: Linking big models to big data: efficient ecosystem model calibration through Bayesian model emulation. Biogeoscience **15**(19), 5801–5830 (2018). https://doi.org/10.5194/bg-15-5801-2018

Fischer, E.M., Lawrence, D.M., Sanderson, B.M.: Quantifying uncertainties in projections of extremes-a perturbed land surface parameter experiment. Clim. Dyn. **37**(7), 1381–1398 (2011). https://doi.org/10.1007/s00382-010-0915-y

Flato, G.M.: Earth system models: an overview. WIREs Clim. Change **2**(6), 783–800 (2011). https://doi.org/10.1002/wcc.148

Foley, J.A., et al.: Global consequences of land use. Science **309**(5734), 570–574 (2005). https://doi.org/10.1126/science.1111772

Fox, A., et al.: The REFLEX project: comparing different algorithms and implementations for the inversion of a terrestrial ecosystem model against eddy covariance data. Agric. Forest Meteorol. **149**(10), 1597–1615 (2009). https://doi.org/10.1016/j.agrformet.2009.05.002

Fox, A.M., et al.: Evaluation of a data assimilation system for land surface models using CLM4.5. J. Adv. Model. Earth Syst. **10**(10), 2471–2494 (2018). https://doi.org/10.1029/2018MS001362

Friedlingstein, P., et al.: Positive feedback between future climate change and the carbon cycle. Geophys. Res. Lett. **28**(8), 1543–1546 (2001). https://doi.org/10.1029/2000GL012015

Friedlingstein, P., et al.: Climate-carbon cycle feedback analysis: Results from the C^4MIP model intercomparison. J. Clim. **19**(14), 3373–3383 (2006). https://doi.org/10.1175/JCLI3800.1

Fu, D., et al.: Estimating landscape net ecosystem exchange at high spatial-temporal resolution based on landsat data, an improved upscaling model framework, and eddy covariance flux measurements. Remote Sens. Environ. **141**, 90–104 (2014). https://doi.org/10.1016/j.rse.2013.10.029

Griebel, A., Metzen, D., Pendall, E., Burba, G., Metzger, S.: Generating spatially robust carbon budgets from flux tower observations. Geophys. Res. Lett. **47**(3), e2019GL085942 (2020). https://doi.org/10.1029/2019GL085942

Gurney, K.R., et al.: TransCom 3 CO_2 inversion intercomparison: 1. Annual mean control results and sensitivity to transport and prior flux information. Tellus B **55**(2), 555–579 (2003). https://doi.org/10.3402/tellusb.v55i2.16728

Hawkins, L.R., Kumar, J., Luo, X., Sihi, D., Zhou, S.: Measuring,monitoring, and-modeling ecosystem cycling. EOS Trans. AGU **101** (2020). https://doi.org/10.1029/2020EO147717

Hoffman, F.M., et al.: International land model benchmarking (ILAMB) 2016 workshop report. Technical report DOE/SC-0186, U.S. Department of Energy, Office of Science, Germantown, Maryland, USA (2017). https://doi.org/10.2172/1330803

Houweling, S., et al.: Global inverse modeling of CH_4 sources and sinks: an overview of methods. Atmos. Chem. Phys. **17**(1), 235–256 (2017). https://doi.org/10.5194/acp-17-235-2017

Kattge, J., et al.: TRY - a global database of plant traits. Glob. Change Biol. **17**(9), 2905–2935 (2011). https://doi.org/10.1111/j.1365-2486.2011.02451.x

Koven, C.D., Hugelius, G., Lawrence, D.M., Wieder, W.R.: Higher climatological temperature sensitivity of soil carbon in cold than warm climates. Nat. Clim. Change **7**(11), 817–822 (2017). https://doi.org/10.1038/nclimate3421

Launiainen, S., et al.: Do the energy fluxes and surface conductance of boreal coniferous forests in Europe scale with leaf area? Glob. Change Biol. **22**(12), 4096–4113 (2016). https://doi.org/10.1111/gcb.13497

LeBauer, D.S., Wang, D., Richter, K.T., Davidson, C.C., Dietze, M.C.: Facilitating feedbacks between field measurements and ecosystem models. Ecol. Monogr. **83**(2), 133–154 (2013). https://doi.org/10.1890/12-0137.1

Li, J., Duan, Q., Wang, Y.P., Gong, W., Gan, Y., Wang, C.: Parameter optimization for carbon and water fluxes in two global land surface models based on surrogate modelling. Int. J. Climatol. **38**(S1), e1016–e1031 (2018). https://doi.org/10.1002/joc.5428

Liu, S., et al.: Upscaling evapotranspiration measurements from multi-site to the satellite pixel scale over heterogeneous land surfaces. Agric. Forest Meteorol. **230**, 97–113 (2016). https://doi.org/10.1016/j.agrformet.2016.04.008

Lu, D., Ricciuto, D., Stoyanov, M., Gu, L.: Calibration of the E3SM land model using surrogate-based global optimization. J. Adv. Model. Earth Syst. **10**(6), 1337–1356 (2018). https://doi.org/10.1002/2017MS001134

Luo, Y., et al.: Ecological forecasting and data assimilation in a data-rich era. Ecol. Appl. **21**(5), 1429–1442 (2011). https://doi.org/10.1890/09-1275.1

Maloney, E.D., et al.: Process-oriented evaluation of climate and weather forecasting models. Bull. Am. Meteorol. Soc. **100**(9), 1665–1686 (2019). https://doi.org/10.1175/BAMS-D-18-0042.1

Mauder, M., Foken, T., Cuxart, J.: Surface-energy-balance closure over land: a review. Boundary-Layer Meteorol. (2020). https://doi.org/10.1007/s10546-020-00529-6

Metzger, S.: Surface-atmosphere exchange in a box: making the control volume a suitable representation for in-situ observations. Agric. Forest Meteorol. **255**, 68–80 (2018). https://doi.org/10.1016/j.agrformet.2017.08.037

Metzger, S., et al.: Spatially explicit regionalization of airborne flux measurements using environmental response functions. Biogeoscience **10**(4), 2193–2217 (2013a). https://doi.org/10.5194/bg-10-2193-2013

Metzger, S., et al.: From NEON field sites to data portal: a community resource for surface-atmosphere research comes online. Bull. Am. Meteorol. Soc. **100**(11), 2305–2325 (2019a). https://doi.org/10.1175/BAMS-D-17-0307.1

Metzger, S., et al.: Synthesized observations and processes for plot- to landscape-scale research. In: NCAR and NEON Town Hall TH13M, 2019 American Geophysical Union (AGU) Annual Fall Meeting, CA, USA, San Francisco (2019b)

Metzger, S.: Spatio-temporal rectification of tower-based eddy-covariance flux measurements for consistently informing process-based models. In: 2013 American Geophysical Union (AGU) Annual Fall Meeting, CA, USA, San Francisco (2013b)

Miles, N.L., et al.: Large amplitude spatial and temporal gradients in atmospheric boundary layer co2mole fractions detected with a tower-based network in the U.S. Upper Midwest. J. Geophys. Res. Biogeosci. **117**(G1) (2012). https://doi.org/10.1029/2011JG001781. https://agupubs.onlinelibrary.wiley.com/doi/abs/10.1029/2011JG001781. https://agupubs.onlinelibrary.wiley.com/doi/pdf/10.1029/2011JG001781

Miller, S.M., et al.: A multiyear estimate of methane fluxes in Alaska from CARVE atmospheric observations. Glob. Biogeochem. Cycles **30**(10), 1441–1453 (2016). https://doi.org/10.1002/2016GB005419

Moore, D.J.P., Hu, J., Sacks, W.J., Schimel, D.S., Monson, R.K.: Estimating transpiration and the sensitivity of carbon uptake to water availability in a subalpine forest using a simple ecosystem process model informed by measured net CO_2 and H_2O fluxes. Agric. Forest Meteorol. **148**(10), 1467–1477 (2008). https://doi.org/10.1016/j.agrformet.2008.04.013

Novick, K.A., et al.: The AmeriFlux network: a coalition of the willing. Agric. Forest Meteorol. **249**, 444–456 (2018). https://doi.org/10.1016/j.agrformet.2017.10.009

Pacala, S.W., et al.: Consistent land-and atmosphere-based US carbon sink estimates. Science **292**(5525), 2316–2320 (2001). https://doi.org/10.1126/science.1057320

Pal, S., et al.: Observations of greenhouse gas changes across summer frontal boundaries in the Eastern United States. J. Geophys. Res. Atmos. **125**(5), e2019JD030526 (2020). https://doi.org/10.1029/2019JD030526

Piao, S., et al.: Evaluation of terrestrial carbon cycle models for their response to climate variability and to CO_2 trends. Glob. Change Biol. **19**(7), 2117–2132 (2013). https://doi.org/10.1111/gcb.12187

Prihodko, L., Denning, A.S., Hanan, N.P., Baker, I., Davis, K.: Sensitivity, uncertainty and time dependence of parameters in a complex land surface model. Agric. Forest Meteorol. **148**(2), 268–287 (2008). https://doi.org/10.1016/j.agrformet.2007.08.006

Quaife, T., et al.: Assimilating canopy reflectance data into an ecosystem model with an Ensemble Kalman Filter. Remote Sens. Environ. **112**(4), 1347–1364 (2008). https://doi.org/10.1016/j.rse.2007.05.020

Ran, Y., et al.: Spatial representativeness and uncertainty of eddy covariance carbon flux measurements for upscaling net ecosystem productivity to the grid scale. Agric. Forest Meteorol. **230**, 114–127 (2016). https://doi.org/10.1016/j.agrformet.2016.05.008

Randall, D.A., et al.: 100 years of Earth system model development. Meteor. Monogr. **59**, 12.1–12.66 (2018). https://doi.org/10.1175/AMSMONOGRAPHS-D-18-0018.1

Randerson, J.T., et al.: Systematic assessment of terrestrial biogeochemistry in coupled climate-carbon models. Glob. Change Biol. **15**(9), 2462–2484 (2009). https://doi.org/10.1111/j.1365-2486.2009.01912.x

Raupach, M.R., et al.: Model-data synthesis in terrestrial carbon observation: methods, data requirements and data uncertainty specifications. Glob. Change Biol. **11**(3), 378–397 (2005). https://doi.org/10.1111/j.1365-2486.2005.00917.x

Ricciuto, D., Sargsyan, K., Thornton, P.: The impact of parametric uncertainties on biogeochemistry in the E3SM land model. J. Adv. Model. Earth Syst. **10**(2), 297–319 (2018). https://doi.org/10.1002/2017MS000962. https://agupubs.onlinelibrary.wiley.com/doi/abs/10.1002/2017MS000962. https://agupubs.onlinelibrary.wiley.com/doi/pdf/10.1002/2017MS000962

Ricciuto, D.M., Davis, K.J., Keller, K.: A Bayesian calibration of a simple carbon cycle model: the role of observations in estimating and reducing uncertainty. Glob. Biogeochem. Cycles **22**(2) (2008). https://doi.org/10.1029/2006GB002908

Ricciuto, D.M., King, A.W., Dragoni, D., Post, W.M.: Parameter and prediction uncertainty in an optimized terrestrial carbon cycle model: effects of constraining variables and data record length. J. Geophys. Res. Biogeosci. **116**(G1) (2011). https://doi.org/10.1029/2010JG001400

Riley, W.J., Shen, C.: Characterizing coarse-resolution watershed soil moisture heterogeneity using fine-scale simulations. Hydrol. Earth Syst. Sci. **18**(7), 2463–2483 (2014). https://doi.org/10.5194/hess-18-2463-2014

Sanderson, B.M., Shell, K.M., Ingram, W.: Climate feedbacks determined using radiative kernels in a multi-thousand member ensemble of AOGCMs. Clim. Dyn. **35**(7), 1219–1236 (2010). https://doi.org/10.1007/s00382-009-0661-1

Schaefer, K., et al.: A model-data comparison of gross primary productivity: results from the North American Carbon Program site synthesis. J. Geophys. Res. Biogeosci. **117**(G3) (2012). https://doi.org/10.1029/2012JG001960

Schimel, D.S., VEMAP Participants, Braswell, B.H.: Continental scale variability in ecosystem processes: models, data, and the role of disturbance. Ecol. Monogr. **67**(2), 251–271 (1997). https://doi.org/10.1890/0012-9615(1997)067[0251:CSVIEP]2.0.CO;2

Schwalm, C.R., et al.: A model-data intercomparison of CO_2 exchange across North America: results from the North American Carbon Program site synthesis. J. Geophys. Res. Biogeosci. **115**(G3) (2010). https://doi.org/10.1029/2009JG001229

Stöckli, R., et al.: Use of FLUXNET in the community land model development. J. Geophys. Res. Biogeosci. **113**(G1) (2008). https://doi.org/10.1029/2007JG000562

Stoy, P.C., et al.: A data-driven analysis of energy balance closure across FLUXNET research sites: the role of landscape scale heterogeneity. Agric. Forest Meteorol. **171**, 137–152 (2013). https://doi.org/10.1016/j.agrformet.2012.11.004

Sweeney, C., et al.: Seasonal climatology of co2 across North America from aircraft measurements in the NOAA/ESRL global greenhouse gas reference network. J. Geophys. Res. Atmos. **120**(10, 5155–5190 (2015). https://doi.org/10.1002/2014JD022591. https://agupubs.onlinelibrary.wiley.com/doi/abs/10.1002/2014JD022591. https://agupubs.onlinelibrary.wiley.com/doi/pdf/10.1002/2014JD022591

Tans, P.P., Fung, I.Y., Takahashi, T.: Observational constraints on the global atmospheric CO_2 budget. Science **247**(4949), 1431–1438 (1990). https://doi.org/10.1126/science.247.4949.1431

Wang, Y.Q., Xiong, Y.J., Qiu, G.Y., Zhang, Q.T.: Is scale really a challenge in evapotranspiration estimation? A multi-scale study in the Heihe oasis using thermal remote sensing and the three-temperature model. Agric. Forest Meteorol. **230**, 128–141 (2016). https://doi.org/10.1016/j.agrformet.2016.03.012

Williams, M., et al.: Improving land surface models with FLUXNET data. Biogeoscience **6**(7), 1341–1359 (2009). https://doi.org/10.5194/bg-6-1341-2009

Xu, K., Metzger, S., Desai, A.R.: Upscaling tower-observed turbulent exchange at fine spatio-temporal resolution using environmental response functions. Agric. Forest Meteorol. **232**, 10–22 (2017). https://doi.org/10.1016/j.agrformet.2016.07.019

Xu, K., Sühring, M., Metzger, S., Durden, D., Desai, A.R.: Can data mining help eddy covariance see the landscape? A large-eddy simulation study. Boundary-Layer Meteorol. **176**(1), 85–103 (2020). https://doi.org/10.1007/s10546-020-00513-0

Zobitz, J.M., Desai, A.R., Moore, D.J.P., Chadwick, M.A.: A primer for data assimilation with ecological models using Markov Chain Monte Carlo (MCMC). Oecologia **167**(3), 599 (2011). https://doi.org/10.1007/s00442-011-2107-9

Toward Real-Time Analysis of Synchrotron Micro-Tomography Data: Accelerating Experimental Workflows with AI and HPC

James E. McClure[1(✉)], Junqi Yin[2], Ryan T. Armstrong[3],
Ketan C. Maheshwari[2], Sean Wilkinson[2], Lucas Vlcek[2], Ying Da Wang[3],
Mark A. Berrill[2], and Mark Rivers[4]

[1] Virginia Tech, Blacksburg, VA 24060, USA
mcclurej@vt.edu
[2] Oak Ridge National Laboratory, Oak Ridge, USA
[3] University of New South Wales, Sydney, Australia
[4] Center for Advanced Radiation Sources, University of Chicago, Chicago, IL, USA

Abstract. Synchrotron light sources are routinely used to perform imaging experiments. In this paper, we review the relevant computational stages, identify bottlenecks, and highlight future opportunities to streamline data acquisition for experimental microscopy workflows. We demonstrate our preliminary exploration with an end-to-end scientific workflow on Summit based on micro-computed tomography data. Computational elements include: 1) reconstruction of volumetric image data; 2) denoising with deep neural networks; and 3) non-local means based segmentation and quantitative analysis.

Keywords: Micro-tomography · Deep learning · Image processing · High-performance computing · Scientific workflows

1 Introduction

Synchrotron-based X-ray micro-computed tomography (μCT) is often used to obtain 3D images of complex microscopic structures. In recent years, growth in photon intensity and data collection rates have outpaced the growth in computational and I/O performance [6,7,35]. Due to this mismatch computation has

Notice: This manuscript has been authored by UT-Battelle, LLC, under contract DE-AC05-00OR22725 with the US Department of Energy (DOE). The US government retains and the publisher, by accepting the article for publication, acknowledges that the US government retains a nonexclusive, paid-up, irrevocable, worldwide license to publish or reproduce the published form of this manuscript, or allow others to do so, for US government purposes. DOE will provide public access to these results of federally sponsored research in accordance with the DOE Public Access Plan (http://energy.gov/downloads/doe-public-access-plan).

© Springer Nature Switzerland AG 2020
J. Nichols et al. (Eds.): SMC 2020, CCIS 1315, pp. 226–239, 2020.
https://doi.org/10.1007/978-3-030-63393-6_15

increasingly become a bottleneck in the associated experimental workflows. This trend necessitates adoption of scalable image processing methods so that experimental data can be analyzed in a reasonable length of time. The emergence of fast micro-tomography, which is used to image transient phenomena, is particularly linked with rapid data generation rates. Multiple computational stages are required to process the raw data from the synchrotron beamline and perform the analyses needed to inform scientific inquiry. Real-time data processing capabilities are driven by the desire to adjust experiments on the fly to improve the value and quality of data collected. Such workflows are extensible to the study of a wide variety of physical phenomena, and are actively used to support inquiries based on digital rock physics. Digital rock physics refers to a broad class of first-principles based methods that are used to study how the complex microstructure of geologic materials influences physical behavior in those systems. While these methods have mature applications in geosciences, in principle the same general approaches can be extended to other complex systems where microstructure has a predominant impact on system behavior, e.g. biological tissues, fuel cells and other engineered systems. In this paper we consider the computational requirements for end-to-end digital rock physics workflows, including data collection, data movement, data processing, storage and simulation.

Traditional image processing workflows can involve a wide range of tasks. Common examples include noise removal [9,12,14,15,18,33], artifact removal [3,34,37], image segmentation [16,19,25,29,31], edge detection [10,17], isosurface construction [4,23], and others. Many possible algorithms exist to carry out each task, and the impact on data quality and the associated computational requirements can vary considerably. For applications in digital rock physics, it is also common to perform additional quantitative analysis and to use μCT data to perform direct numerical simulations of physical processes [2,8,27]. Nearly all of these cases present intriguing applications for artifical neural networks (ANNs). The capacity for ANNs to streamline experimental workflows hinge on several factors: (1) to improve data quality based on the use of "smart" algorithms; (2) to add value by augmenting workflows to incorporate additional capabilities; (3) to carry out equivalent computational analyses while reducing the computational costs of applied algorithms; and (4) to reduce or eliminate manual aspects of data processing such that human intervention is less pervasive within computational workflows. In this work, we review computational aspects needed to generate results based on digital rock approaches that rely on synchrotron μCT and identify opportunities for future improvement.

2   Data Acquisition

It is well-known that data generation rates associated with synchrotron light sources have outpaced the growth in computing power. The associated computational challenges are well-illustrated based on experimental workflows for fast μCT. We consider fast μCT based on the experimental workflow that is in place at the GSECARS beamline at the Advanced Photon Source, Argonne National

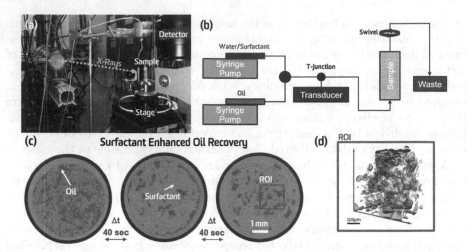

Fig. 1. Experimental setup for the GSECARS beamline at the Advanced Photon Source (a). The flow system used to inject either a single fluid or multiple fluids (b). Example radiographs collected during surfactant flooding of oil saturated Mt. Gambier limestone (c). 3D Region of interest (ROI) rendering of residual oil during surfactant flooding (d).

Laboratory. Among the capabilities of fast μCT is to image dynamic processes, such as the movement of fluids within geological materials [1,5]. The data considered in this work are based on multiphase flow through porous media, and were collected using the procedure summarized in Fig. 1. The physical sample is placed into a core-holder and connected to an experimental apparatus that is used to control fluid flow through the sample. The experimental conditions can be programmed remotely from a computer so that the desired flow dynamics can be realized without directly interacting with the sample while it is being imaged. Each three-dimensional image is generated based on a sequence of 900 radiographs that capture the photon intensity after the beam passes through the sample. The detector size was 1920×1200 pixels, which determines the size of the reconstructed image. Between each radiograph a precise motorized system rotates the sample approximately one-half degree. Based on the intensity of the light source and the photon wavelength it is possible to model the photon attenuation attributed to the sample for each radiograph. A three-dimensional image can then be constructed by formulating an inverse problem to approximate the internal structure of the sample based on the observed sequence of radiographs. The reconstruction step corresponds to the first computational stage required in tomographic experiments. For fast μCT this procedure is repeated in succession to obtain a sequence of 3D images such that transient phenomena occurring within the sample can be observed directly. For the data collected in this work, approximately 40 s were required to collect the 900 radiographs used to reconstruct a single 3D volume. A sequence of 75 3D volumes were collected in a single

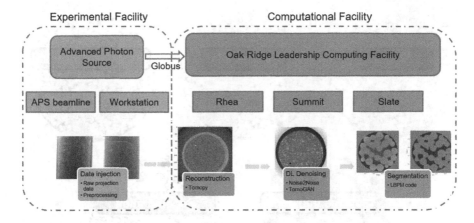

Fig. 2. Summary of computational elements involved in APS-OLCF synchrotron microscopy workflow. Multiple different software tools are used to reconstruct and analyze the data; computational tasks within the workflow are performed on local workstations or remotely on HPC resources.

fast μCT experiment with a duration of one hour. For each volume the total size of each reconstructed volume is 16.5 GB. The associated data generation rate for the experimental setup depicted in Fig. 1 is therefore 1.2 TB/h. Each 3D volume is composed from 16-bit integer data with $1620 \times 1620 \times 1200$ voxels. For the purposes of this work algorithms are implemented to operate directly on the volumetric data.

3   Summary of Computational Stages

Microscopic imaging approaches are inherently dependent on computational methods that perform data processing. The workflow used here is illustrated in Fig. 2. Data processing was carried out both at the APS experimental facility and the OLCF. Data transfers between the two facilities were performed using Globus as the front-end, with ESnet supporting the underlying data movement. Within the OLCF, three computational resources were used to (1) Summit was used to support computational benchmarking; (2) Rhea was used to visualize results; and (3) Slate was used as a workflow orchestration tool. Particular computational tasks are described in more detail in the following subsections.

3.1   Tomographic Reconstruction

Tomographic reconstruction is applied to infer the three-dimensional microstructure of the sample based on the information contained in the radiographs. The performance measurements reported in this work rely on the reconstruction algorithm *gridrec*, which formulated to reconstruct a three-dimensional map of the material structure that best predicts the set of observed radiographs [13, 28].

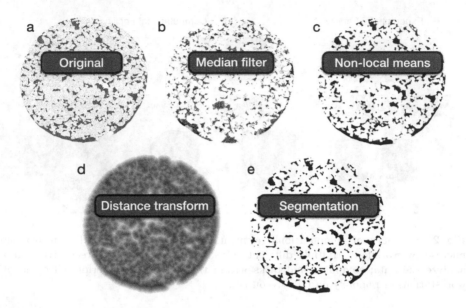

Fig. 3. Summary of steps within conventional image segmentation pipeline for synchrotron micro-tomography data for Benntheimer sandstone: (a) reconstructed volumetric data contains noise that must be removed before quantitative analyses can be performed; (b) median filter is a common technique that allows the removal of noise that also tends to preserve edges; (c) the non-local means algorithm is among the best methods to reduce noise while preserving image features; (d) distance transform can be used to introduce spatial context into segmentation pipelines; (e) segmented data obtained using segmentation pipeline available within the LBPM software.

The underlying computational paradigm is based on Fourier transform methods [24]. While many other reconstruction algorithms have been developed, *gridrec* is the primary algorithm that has been in use for fast μCT data over the last two decades.

3.2   Conventional Image Processing

While the basic material structure is often visually-evident from reconstructed data, significant post-processing is required to make quantitative inferences. The majority of this effort is devoted toward (1) enhancing the signal-to-noise ratio; (2) removing image artifacts such as rings; and (3) image segmentation. Conventional image processing methodologies are typically combined into a data processing pipeline, which often requires manually tuning for algorithm parameters. In digital rock workflows the end goal for image processing steps is often to segment the reconstructed data into a discrete set of components that correspond to the distinguishable fluid and solid materials within the sample. Detailed reviews on segmentation pipelines are available [26,32,36]. In this work, we consider a segmentation workflow that is composed from the following algorithms:

(1) median filter is applied to perform initial noise reduction and generate a rough segmentation; (2) the non-local means filter is applied to remove noise; and (3) the distance transform is applied to inform the weight structure and perform final thresholding and iso-surface construction; The segmentation routine is available in the open-source LBPM software package.

The segmentation pipeline implemented within LBPM is illustrated in Fig. 3, with the reconstructed volumetric data used as the input. Target and background values are specified to identify the intensity values for the region of interest, which are determined based on histograms from the image data. The data is then rescaled to the interval $[-1, 1]$. A median filter is used to perform initial noise reduction, and a rough segmentation is generated by thresholding the resulting data. A multi-scale algorithm is then applied to further reduce noise in the image. The original image data is projected onto a coarse mesh by averaging the voxels in a local region. In this work, the resolution for the coarse mesh was decreased by a factor of two, meaning that the total number of voxels in the coarse mesh is reduced by a factor of eight. The non-local means algorithm is applied to the coarse mesh to further reduce noise, update the coarse segmentation, and recompute the distance transform. The distance transform determined using the coarse mesh is projected onto the original fine mesh using linear interpolation and the original input data is reprocessed using the coarse mesh data to provide additional spatial context. This multi-scale representation plays a similar role to that of skip-connections in U-net, but within an algorithm that has no trainable parameters. Non-local means is applied on the fine mesh, using the distance from the coarse mesh data to skip calculations that are performed in parts of the domain that are far from an interface. The distance transform is then recomputed on the fine mesh, which is used to determine the final segmentation. The distance transform is also used for quantitative analysis based on (1) iso-surface construction using a double-connected edge list (DCEL) data structure; and (2) computation of scalar geometric invariants using the constructed isosurface. The entire segmentation and analysis pipeline is implemented in distributed memory using MPI. By distributing the computations over multiple compute nodes, time-to-solution can be significantly reduced for segmentation and analysis of large images.

3.3 Denoising with Deep Learning

Deep learning techniques have been widely applied to image denoising. Given the success of deep convolutional neural networks (CNN) in image feature extraction, most deep learning denoising models are CNN based. Several generative adversarial networks (GAN) have also been developed for this task, where the generative network is used to generate denoised samples and the discriminator network is trained to distinguish the generated samples from high quality input samples (considered as ground truth). Once the loss of the discriminator is minimized in this zero sum game, the generator can then effectively denoise the low quality input samples. Compared with traditional approaches for image denoising, GAN based denoising can reduce the number of manual steps needed

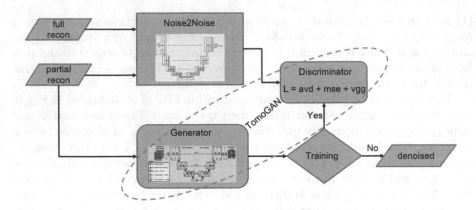

Fig. 4. Deep learning denoising workflow.

to process data, since traditional approaches often rely on hand-tuning for algorithm parameters.

In our deep learning denoising workflow, as shown in Fig. 4, two deep learning models are employed to optimize the processing efficiency: 1) Noise2Noise model [20], which can learn to restore images without ground truth data; 2) TomoGAN [21, 22], which is a generalized adversarial network (GAN) based model that has demonstrated success in dealing with X-ray imaging. The core neural network architecture of both models includes the popular UNet for image reconstruction [30]. Our workflow is implemented as follows,

1. prepare paired input data of high (full reconstruction) and low (partial reconstruction) quality;
2. train Noise2Noise model on above paired data;
3. train TomoGAN on paired data of low quality input and Noise2Noise output (served as ground truth);
4. inference based on TomoGAN model with low quality reconstruction data.

There is a one time cost associated with training both Noise2Noise and TomoGAN models, which is incurred when the experimental conditions or material structure change. Once the models are trained, inferencing with low quality reconstruction can significantly speed up the process in production.

Practical applications of deep learning for denoising must be considered in terms of the overall workflow. Particular attention must be paid to the effect on image quality and the associated effects on the workflow outputs. For example, for GAN-based noise removal the larger- scale microstructures are captured well, but the finer spatial frequencies have a tendency to be washed out. The preservation of fine-scale features is a persistent challenge associated with removal of image noise even using conventional methods, since it is difficult to distinguish noise from fine-scale structural information. The non-local means algorithm is often preferred for applications where noise removal must be applied without destroying fine-scale features [39]. GAN approaches can be further developed

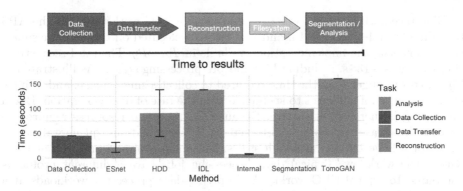

Fig. 5. Time required for each stage of the fast micro-tomography workflow considered in this work.

to exploit frequency-domain information to better preserve information about smaller structures in an image [38]. Hybrid approaches that combine deep learning with traditional image processing strategies are also possible. In applications where data quality is of central importance, strategies to augment existing workflows with AI must consider the quantitative impact on the workflow outputs. It is common to apply multiple algorithms in such workflows, and it is natural to incorporate AI-based approaches where enhancements to data quality and user productivity can be realized.

4 Performance Benchmarking

Computational benchmarking was performed on the Summit supercomputer and on local workstations at the GSECARS beamline. Each IBM AC922 Summit compute node is equipped with two 22-core Power9 CPU and six NVIDIA Tesla V100 GPU. The compute nodes are interconnected with Mellanox EDR Infiniband (100 Gb/s) and connected to a 250 PB IBM Spectrum Scale filesystem a peak read speed of 2.5 TB/s. Data transfers to the OLCF data center were performed using ESnet, a high-performance scientific research network that links the US DOE national laboratories and other facilities. Globus was used to transfer files from the synchrotron beamline to the OLCF filesystem and measure the associated data transfer rates [11]. Measurements were also performed for data transfers between local workstations at the GSECARS beamline, and for data copies from local workstations to 4 TB hard drives. Data transfer times are reported in Fig. 5, along with accompanying measurements for data collection and other computational elements of the data processing pipeline. Error bars are based on the minimum and maximum bandwidth and the collected file size, which is 3.9 GB. Measured data transfer rates are reported in Table 1. Transfers were organized into batches, with multiple images transferred in each batch. Data movement between the ALCF and OLCF facilities did not present a barrier to the overall workflow, with the associated costs being less than other computational tasks within the pipeline.

The reconstruction step was executed using a local workstation at the APS beamline from 4–8 June 2018, and was later re-executed on the Summit super-computer using the implementation available in *TomoPy*. The total reconstruction time was ~138 s, including I/O and pre-processing stages. As illustrated in Fig. 5, this is longer than the time required to collect a single image, and a single workstation is not sufficient to keep pace with the rate of data generation. Batch processing is therefore attractive. Because the time and resources required to process data was short compared to typical HPC simulations, queue wait times were not a large barrier, although still significant in comparison to other tasks within the workflow. Typical data processing jobs have a different profile as compared to typical HPC workloads, applying data processing workloads at a large-scale could have a significant impact on the behavior of the HPC scheduler. In the present context the interaction was complementary, but this might not be the case if large numbers of data processing jobs were queued simultaneously.

The segmentation pipeline was executed in parallel using Power9 CPU cores on the Summit supercomputer. 3D images were distributed using a $5 \times 8 \times 8$ process grid with 240^3 voxels allocated to each processor. One level of refinement was used, meaning that the coarse mesh corresponded to 120^3 voxels per proces-sor. The associated parameters required manual hand-tuning to yield acceptable segmentation results, which did represent a barrier to real-time data processing. Once segmentation parameters were determined for a particular experimental setup, acceptable segmentations could be obtained for many volumetric images ($\mathcal{O}(100)$ or more, usually corresponding to several hours of experimental data collection). Batch processing capabilities on the HPC resources can be used to accelerate the parameter tuning procedure by reducing time-to-solution for parameter sweeps. From the workflow perspective, additional study is warranted to identify optimal parameters more efficiently. Based on the distributed memory implementation, the turnaround for segmentation was ~99 s, on par with other computational tasks. The justification for HPC resources is very strong, since this remains more than $2\times$ the data generation rate. Without the distributed memory implementation, the segmentation pipeline would have presented a seri-ous bottleneck.

Deep learning methods are of interest as an alternative mechanism to reduce noise and otherwise enhance data quality for experimental data. The required training and inference times for *Noise2Noise* and *TomoGAN* are listed in Table 2. Training times are reported for $6\times$ V100 GPU, corresponding with the resources for a single compute node. The one-time cost for each type of material on train-ing both Noise2Noise and TomoGAN models requires a couple of hours on 1 Summit node. This can be further reduced via data parallel training (already implemented in the code). While training is a one-time cost, this is significant in comparison to the overall workflow. Considerable benefits could be realized in situations where trained networks could be re-used many times for data collected from a particular instrument. It is not inconceivable that custom networks could be developed to process data for particular experiments, although such applica-tions would have a dramatic impact on the overall workflow. Additional study is

Table 1. Data transfer rates measured during 4–8 June 2018 visit to APS

Source	Destination	Data transfer rate
Workstation 1	Workstation 2	490–620 MB/s
Workstation 2	Hard drive	30–95 MB/s
Workstation 2	OLCF Atlas	130–350 MB/s

Table 2. Required training time for deep learning networks.

Method	Compute	Time
Noise2Noise training	6 V100	~81 min
TomoGAN training	6 V100	~50 min
TomoGAN inferencing	1 V100	~160 s

needed to understand the extent to which pre-trained networks can be re-used for general data processing, and how deep learning workflows could be integrated into experimental facilities to support novel scientific applications. With the pre-trained model, inferencing on a streaming data sample can be completed in less than 3 min and most time will be spent on the partial reconstruction. While this is longer than then 99 s for the segmentation pipeline, inference required significantly fewer computational resources. Additional studies are needed to understand issues pertaining to data quality, particularly for cases where image processing is being used to support quantitative measurements.

Based on the results reported in Fig. 5, the time required for computational stages is approximately 5× what is required to collect data. This means that the minimum lag time between collecting data and generating results is five to fifteen minutes. A pipelined data analysis routine can be constructed to ensure that this gap does not grow as the experiment progresses. This is illustrated graphically in Fig. 6. Note that the time required for transfer data is shorter than the time required to collect data, so there is not a data transfer bottleneck. Reconstruction, segmentation and analysis routines can execute in parallel using distributed computing resources. For practical reasons, it is attractive to aggregate the processing steps for multiple images together, since manual steps were needed to move the data using Globus. Since data is collected rapidly, fully automated workflows have excellent potential to boost productivity.

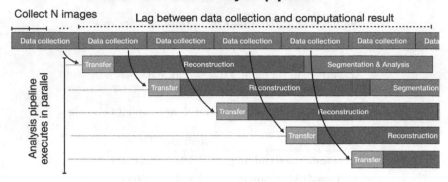

Fig. 6. Distributed computing can be used to pipeline data analysis routines such that the lag time between data collection and results does not grow as the experiment progresses.

5   Summary

The computational steps required to support experimental synchrotron micro-tomography were reviewed in the context of a digital rock physics workflow. Relying on a combination of high performance computing and deep learning methods, a full analysis pipeline can be executed in near real-time. Near real-time processing provides the opportunity to adjust experimental conditions to ensure that high-quality data is being collected. Problems in the experimental setup can be diagnosed in a more comprehensive and efficient way, and challenges associated with the post-processing of large volumes of experimental data can be mitigated. Near real-time processing of synchrotron-based micro-tomography data presents a significant yet tractable computational problem. Effective applications of parallel and distributed computing can offset the imbalance between data collection and processing speed, but such interventions are certainly necessary. We find that distributed computing resources are sufficient to provide near real-time execution for fast uCT. Pipelined execution of workflows allow data processing to proceed such that results are available to inform experiments with a reasonable turnaround, approximately fifteen minutes based on batch queues. Since the data processing jobs are short-running compared to most HPC simulation jobs, they can be efficiently backfilled. Interactive queues are necessary to visualize simulation results, but often only a subset of data must be visualized. Manual steps within the data processing workflow, such as parameter tuning, present a significant barrier. Opportunities to apply machine learning as a way to reduce or eliminate manual intervention are therefore attractive. Compelling advantages of AI include the possibility to improve performance and/or reduce the computational costs associated with noise removal, as well as the possibility to incorporate elements involving automated data annotation and anomaly detection.

Increased adoption of automated workflows and the use of workflow management software could provide a significant payoff for experimental facilities. To obtain high quality image data, multiple computational steps and several different algorithms are often combined to remove noise and otherwise enhance image quality. Due to the fact that user workflows often involve customized routines, eliminating manual steps is non-trivial but crucial. Since workflows often have quantitative outputs, AI techniques should be assessed within the context of the overall workflow so that their effect on these outputs can be properly understood. Workflow automation is also necessary to alleviate data processing bottlenecks by reducing the amount of manual steps, and by enabling more scalable deployment of user workflows. Efforts should also target computational reproducibility and incorporate metadata collection into workflows. Since a shortage of labeled data is often a constraint on the training of neural networks, automated creation of metadata can offer a significant payoff for future AI.

Acknowledgment. This research used resources of the Advanced Photon Source, a U.S. Department of Energy (DOE) Office of Science User Facility operated for the DOE Office of Science by Argonne National Laboratory under Contract No. DE-AC02-06CH11357. An award of computer time was provided by the Frontier Center for Accelerated Application Readiness and the Summit Director's Discretionary Program. This research also used resources of the Oak Ridge Leadership Computing Facility, which is a DOE Office of Science User Facility supported under Contract DE-AC05-00OR22725.

References

1. Armstrong, R.T., Georgiadis, A., Ott, H., Klemin, D., Berg, S.: Critical capillary number: desaturation studied with fast x-ray computed microtomography. Geophys. Res. Lett. **41**(1), 55–60 (2014)
2. Armstrong, R.T., McClure, J.E., Berrill, M.A., Rücker, M., Schlüter, S., Berg, S.: Beyond Darcy's law: the role of phase topology and ganglion dynamics for two-fluid flow. Phys. Rev. E **94**, 043113 (2016)
3. Barrett, J.F., Keat, N.: Artifacts in CT: recognition and avoidance. RadioGraphics **24**, 1679–1691 (2004)
4. de Berg, M., Cheong, O., van Kreveld, M., Overmars, M.: Computational Geometry: Algorithms and Applications, 3rd edn. Springer, Santa Clara (2008). https://doi.org/10.1007/978-3-540-77974-2
5. Berg, S., et al.: Real-time 3D imaging of Haines jumps in porous media flow. Proc. Natl. Acad. Sci. **110**(10), 3755–3759 (2013)
6. Bicer, T., et al.: Real-time data analysis and autonomous steering of synchrotron light source experiments. In: 2017 IEEE 13th International Conference on e-Science (e-Science), pp. 59–68 (2017)
7. Blaiszik, B., Chard, K., Chard, R., Foster, I., Ward, L.: Data automation at light sources. In: AIP Conference Proceedings, vol. 2054, no. 1, p. 020003 (2019)
8. Boek, E.S., Venturoli, M.: Lattice-Boltzmann studies of fluid flow in porous media with realistic rock geometries. Comput. Math. Appl. **59**(7), 2305–2314 (2010). Mesoscopic Methods in Engineering and Science
9. Buades, A., Coll, B., Morel, J.-M.: A non-local algorithm for image denoising. In: CVPR, pp. 60–65 (2005)

10. Canny, J.: A computational approach to edge detection. IEEE Trans. Pattern Anal. Mach. Intell. **8**(6), 679–698 (1986)
11. Chard, K., Tuecke, S., Foster, I.: Globus: recent enhancements and future plans. In: Proceedings of the XSEDE16 Conference on Diversity, Big Data, and Science at Scale, XSEDE 2016, New York, NY, USA. Association for Computing Machinery (2016)
12. Davidoiu, V., Hadjilucas, L., Teh, I., Smith, N.P., Schneider, J.E., Lee, J.: Evaluation of noise removal algorithms for imaging and reconstruction of vascular networks using micro-CT. Biomed. Phys. Eng. Expr. **2**(4), 045015 (2016)
13. Dowd, B.A., et al.: Developments in synchrotron x-ray computed microtomography at the national synchrotron light source. In: Bonse, U. (ed.) Developments in X-Ray Tomography II, vol. 3772, pp. 224–236. International Society for Optics and Photonics, SPIE (1999)
14. du Plessis, A., Broeckhoven, C., Guelpa, A., le Roux, S.G.: Laboratory x-ray micro-computed tomography: a user guideline for biological samples. GigaScience **6**(6), 04 (2017). gix027
15. Huang, T., Yang, G., Tang, G.: A fast two-dimensional median filtering algorithm. IEEE Trans. Acoust. Speech Sig. Process. **27**(1), 13–18 (1979)
16. Iassonov, P., Gebrenegus, T., Tuller, M.: Segmentation of x-ray computed tomography images of porous materials: a crucial step for characterization and quantitative analysis of pore structures. Water Resour. Res. **45**(9) (2009)
17. Kanopoulos, N., Vasanthavada, N., Baker, R.L.: Design of an image edge detection filter using the SOBEL operator. IEEE J. Solid-State Circuits **23**(2), 358–367 (1988)
18. Karnati, V., Uliyar, M., Dey, S.: Fast non-local algorithm for image denoising. In: 2009 16th IEEE International Conference on Image Processing (ICIP), pp. 3873–3876 (2009)
19. Korzynska, A., Strojny, W., Hoppe, A., Wertheim, D., Hoser, P.: Segmentation of microscope images of living cells. Pattern Anal. Appl. **10**(4), 301–319 (2007)
20. Lehtinen, J., et al.: Noise2Noise: learning image restoration without clean data. In: Dy, J., Krause, A. (eds.) Proceedings of the 35th International Conference on Machine Learning, volume 80 of Proceedings of Machine Learning Research (PMLR), pp. 2965–2974, Stockholmsmässan, Stockholm, Sweden, 10–15 July 2018
21. Liu, Z., Bicer, T., Kettimuthu, R., Foster, I.: Deep learning accelerated light source experiments (2019)
22. Liu, Z., Bicer, T., Kettimuthu, R., Gursoy, D., De Carlo, F., Foster, I.: Tomogan: low-dose synchrotron x-ray tomography with generative adversarial networks: discussion. J. Opt. Soc. Am. A **37**(3), 422–434 (2020)
23. Lorensen, W.E., Cline, H.E.: Marching cubes: a high resolution 3D surface construction algorithm. In: Proceedings of the 14th Annual Conference on Computer Graphics and Interactive Techniques, SIGGRAPH 1987, pp. 163–169. ACM, New York (1987)
24. Marone, F., Stampanoni, M.: Regridding reconstruction algorithm for real-time tomographic imaging. J. Synchrotron Radiat. **19**(6), 1029–1037 (2012)
25. Perciano, T., et al.: Insight into 3D micro-CT data: exploring segmentation algorithms through performance metrics. J. Synchrotron Radiat. **24**(5), 1065–1077 (2017)
26. Porter, M.L., Wildenschild, D.: Image analysis algorithms for estimating porous media multiphase flow variables from computed microtomography data: a validation study. Comput. Geosci. **14**, 15–30 (2010)

27. Ramstad, T., Idowu, N., Nardi, C., Oren, P.-E.: Relative permeability calculations from two-phase flow simulations directly on digital images of porous rocks. Transp. Porous Media **94**(2, SI), 487–504 (2012)
28. Mark, L.: Rivers. tomoRecon: High-speed tomography reconstruction on workstations using multi-threading. In: Stock, S.R. (ed.) Developments in X-Ray Tomography VIII. vol. 8506, pp. 169–181. International Society for Optics and Photonics, SPIE (2012)
29. Roerdink, J.B.T.M., Meijster, A.: The watershed transform: Definitions, algorithms and parallelization strategies. Fundam. Inf. **41**(1,2), 187–228 (2000)
30. Ronneberger, O., Fischer, P., Brox, T.: U-Net: Convolutional Networks for Biomedical Image Segmentation. In: Navab, N., Hornegger, J., Wells, W.M., Frangi, A.F. (eds.) MICCAI 2015. LNCS, vol. 9351, pp. 234–241. Springer, Cham (2015). https://doi.org/10.1007/978-3-319-24574-4_28
31. Schlüter, S., Weller, U., Vogel, H.-J.: Segmentation of x-ray microtomography images of soil using gradient masks. Comput. Geosci. **36**(10), 1246–1251 (2010)
32. Schlüter, S., Sheppard, A., Brown, K., Wildenschild, D.: Image processing of multiphase images obtained via x-ray microtomography: a review. Water Resour. Res. **50**(4), 3615–3639 (2014)
33. Ushizima, D., et al.: Statistical segmentation and porosity quantification of 3D x-ray micro-tomography. In: Proceedings of SPIE, vol. 8185, no. 09 (2011)
34. Vo, N.T., Atwood, R.C., Drakopoulos, M.: Preprocessing techniques for removing artifacts in synchrotron-based tomographic images. In: Müller, B., Wang, G. (eds.) Developments in X-Ray Tomography XII, vol. 11113, pp. 309–328. International Society for Optics and Photonics, SPIE (2019)
35. Wang, C., Steiner, U., Sepe, A.: Synchrotron big data science. Small **14**(46), 1802291 (2018)
36. Wildenschild, D., Sheppard, A.P.: X-ray imaging and analysis techniques for quantifying pore-scale structure and processes in subsurface porous medium systems. Adv. Water Resour. **51**, 217–246 (2013). 35th Year Anniversary Issue
37. Xie, S., et al.: Artifact removal using improved GoogLeNet for sparse-view CT reconstruction. Sci. Rep. **8**, 6700 (2018)
38. Yang, G., et al.: Dagan: deep de-aliasing generative adversarial networks for fast compressed sensing MRI reconstruction. IEEE Trans. Med. Imaging **37**(6), 1310–1321 (2018)
39. Zhang, H., Zeng, D., Zhang, H., Liang, Z., Ma, J.: Applications of nonlocal means algorithm in low-dose x-ray CT image processing and reconstruction: a review. Med. Phys. **44**, 03 (2017)

Unsupervised Anomaly Detection in Daily WAN Traffic Patterns

Scott Campbell[✉], Mariam Kiran, and Fatema Bannat Wala

Lawrence Berkeley National Laboratory, Energy Sciences Network (ESnet), Berkeley, CA, USA
{scottc.mkiran,fatemabw}@es.net

Abstract. Growth in large-scale experiments using high capacity reliable networking as part of their design is creating a need for better monitoring and analysis of observed traffic. Network providers need intelligent solutions that can help quickly identify and understand anomalous behaviors at the network edge, allowing reactions to unexpected traffic or attacks on facilities and their peerings. However, due to lack of labeled data in network traffic analysis and user diversity, we introduce novel methods that process very large network datasets quickly for outlier identification.

In this paper, we leverage artificial intelligence (AI), network research, and edge computing to collect and train unsupervised classification algorithms using streaming data pipelines from multiple months of network flow records. Once trained, individual classifiers quickly observe and flag alerts in hourly behaviors. Our work describes building the data pipeline as well as addressing issues of false positives and workflow integration.

Keywords: Network anomaly detection · NetFlow data ·
Unsupervised clustering methods · K-means · Gaussian mixture models

1 Introduction

Large experimental facilities, with their high-speed networks and traffic production rates, face enormous data movement challenges in supporting distributed science workflows. In these wide area networks (WANs), service providers need reliable solutions that can help quickly identify and understand anomalous behaviors at the network edge in near real-time, raising alarms and identifying unexpected attacks [3]. Many traditional approaches used in the security community for quickly identifying anomalous behaviors in a large wide area network designed for big data flows, relies on either performance metrics collected from tools like perfSONAR [9] or characterizing data volume observed in a particular period [19]. There is a need to develop efficient ways in which anomalous behaviors can be recognized quickly in large data volumes in near real-time based on the WAN network traffic patterns and high packet flow rates.

This is a U.S. government work and not under copyright protection in the U.S.;
foreign copyright protection may apply 2020
J. Nichols et al. (Eds.): SMC 2020, CCIS 1315, pp. 240–256, 2020.
https://doi.org/10.1007/978-3-030-63393-6_16

Network traffic classification has been extensively studied over the years [23], but classifying flows based on their behaviors, applications, and quality of service is a formidable task. Machine learning solutions can automate some of these efforts and find patterns to classify 'normal' versus 'abnormal' behaviors, providing some insight to security professionals in identifying potential network threats. Most network intrusion detection systems (NIDS) use flow statistics and features to build outlier detection algorithms, such as using random forest trees [24], fingerprinting [17], and behavioral comparisons. These rely on an offline analysis of large network traces (or network flow data) by using clustering to group similar flows together. For example, in studying network traffic entropy [20] found varying patterns of inbound and outbound traffic on weekdays versus weekends on real internet service providers (ISPs). Similar characteristics could be identified in common host connections, flow sizes, and topology used.

Identifying behavior patterns among hosts and how they connect to various endpoints is a common preliminary approach for anomaly detection in network communications [6]. Various dedicated solutions focus on identifying important features such as packet payload, port numbers, protocols [8,21], and classification techniques to help identify potential threats [25]. However, the lack of labeled data sets makes it difficult for one to cluster results without knowing what each of the classes represents and measure the accuracy of classifiers where minimal information is available [12].

In this paper, we propose to explore unsupervised network traffic classification information, based on K-means and Gaussian methods, to address the issues of unsupervised machine learning for WAN-security. We develop novel methods to recognize anomalies in each method, by estimating how far the data point is from each cluster and density information. Specifically, our major contributions are as follows:

- We propose a novel anomaly finding approach that works with unsupervised clusters to identify potential outliers. With K-means we calculate the furthest data point from all clusters and in Gaussian models, we calculate the least density of data points in each cluster.
- We provide a detailed analysis of two classification techniques - K-means and Gaussian Mixture Models (GMM), used for the benefit of network traffic classification. We observed that feature selection affects the anomalies found.
- Our analysis is done on 3 real WAN data centers from January to May 2020, where we study weekend, weekday traffic patterns.
- We built an extremely efficient data pipeline by pre-processing data for the machine learning algorithms to use, offline training of the clusters, and online-anomaly detection.

The rest of the paper is organized as follows: Section 2 describes the background and literature review, Sect. 3 describes the key points and the motivation for this work. Section 4 provides the details on the overall methodology conducted, the data sets used, the feature extraction and the machine learning approaches explored. Section 5 gives the details of the primary analysis conducted for data set visualization. Section 6 illustrates the findings and results. Finally, Sect. 7 presents the discussion and conclusion of the research.

2   Related Work

Understanding network behavior patterns are crucial to network management and security tasks. Network traffic classification research has developed many approaches using statistical, supervised, and unsupervised machine learning techniques to categorize traffic patterns to understand activity across site endpoints, hours, days, and months.

Understanding security incidents is a classical challenge in network research. However, processing large amounts of network flow capture in meaningful time is itself a formidable challenge. Researchers have provided some solutions such as summary tools for identifying distributions of packet features (IP addresses and ports) [14], detecting volume surges, or changes in origin-destination [13] to help isolate anomalies or flow arrival time and packet types [17]. Techniques from statistical or machine learning solutions have been extensively provided to help summarize 'normal' and 'abnormal' traffic behaviors, but often are designed for specific data sets and network environments [1]. With the growing complexity of networks and devices themselves, network service providers need intelligent solutions that can quickly identify and understand anomalous behaviors at the network edge, raising alarms to prevent unexpected network attacks on their sites or peerings.

Networks sample packets using monitoring tools, extracting features that describe the behavior [16,18]. Feature selection can play a significant role in the anomalies identified [10,22]. Most current work maps traffic profiles to applications or protocols used [21]. Others have used machine learning to find day and night patterns to identify potential DDOS attacks, but in all cases, lack of labeled data makes it difficult to assess the accuracy of the results [7,8,11].

Recent methods used Gaussian Mixture Models to characterize NetFlow data into two categories elephant and mice flows [11], but showed that flow characteristics differ across the sites involved. Deep learning approaches have achieved accuracy of up to 96% for clustering [15], but require labeled data.

Compared to current solutions, this paper provides an end-to-end solution for identifying anomalous traffic patterns from multiple sites and leverages unsupervised machine learning algorithms to help raise alarms. Our work builds a data pipeline from individual NetFlow recorders, processes these as quick Splunk data summaries and runs machine learning code to identify potential anomalies. We also perform offline training and online detection using techniques - K-means, Gaussian Mixture Models - to show how the classifiers show different performances.

3   Key Points and Motivation

This section discusses our assumptions and study motivation.

3.1   Assumptions

Our goal is to build lightweight classifiers that will identify potential anomalies in network traffic. We take one hour blocks of sampled NetFlow records and apply statistical and counting measurements as summaries to feed to the classifiers. Our work relies on the following assumptions:

- **Building 'normal' behavior classifiers.** Deviations from normal traffic behaviors or stable measurements can be identified and are interesting to both the network engineering and security groups because of their unusual characteristics. These deviations are identified via testing against models trained with traffic observed from normal situations. Examples of deviations might be bursts of new addresses or ports (both in or out of a site) as well as more subtle changes like the shape of data measurements. How we identify these is to a large degree the motivation for this work. Due to the lack of labeled data and a diverse set of users, we base our approaches on [14] where using summarizing techniques we will create hourly patterns to train our classifier as normal behaviors.
- **Hourly summaries can help identify morning and afternoon patterns.** This assumption relies on the hypothesis that network usage differs during regular working hours when the users are expected to be more vigilant versus hours in the evening. Since our data sets primarily consist of the research-based WAN network traffic, the chances of observing distinct patterns in the hourly summaries in our training data sets are low.
- **Offline training for classifiers.** We expect to be able to train the classifier using unsupervised clustering methods (mainly K-means and GMM) using a data set known to exhibit normal network traffic patterns. Hence, once the classifier learns what the normal traffic behavior looks like, it can then decide if a given test data set exhibits normal patterns or if it contains anomalous behavior.
- **Online access to the trained clusters to find patterns on the fly.** We expect that once the classifier is trained offline using the datasets known to have normal traffic patterns, it can then be used in near real-time to detect a given pattern exhibiting any abnormal behavior on-the-fly. The classifier then assesses how far the given test pattern falls from the normal clusters within a given threshold.

3.2   Intuition Behind Our Methods

Research WANs Versus Commodity WANs. For the initial experiment, we chose a dataset based on network traffic from the DOE Open Science HPC Facilities. We illustrate our approach with real NetFlow traffic traces from a DOE research WAN (ESnet, www.es.net), across 3 data centers between the months of January and May 2020. The expectation is that the traffic profile for these facilities will have less interactive human activity (such as web browsing) which exhibits a strong diurnal weekday pattern [2], and a far greater proportion of long duration, high volume data transfers than would be expected in Commodity traffic [4].

Network Traffic Monitoring Tools. Traffic traces are collected via tools such as Simple Network Management Protocol (SNMP), sflow, and Netflow. Some (like SNMP) can be used to collect time-stamped information on CPU, memory utilization, and interface counters at end-points. Sflow and NetFlow records provide a local router view and provide details of fine-grained traffic view including key features such as protocols (e.g. TCP, UDP, etc.), interfaces, source, and destination IP addresses and even flow speeds [5].

Unsupervised Clustering Methods for Anomaly Finding. ESnet has a unique perspective with regard to the behavior of network traffic in and around large multiuser facilities. Anomaly detection in data sets can be used for both security as well as traffic engineering. The selection of data sources is dedicated high-performance computing within three large scale office of science computing sites named Site-1, Site-2, and Site-3 for paper anonymity.

3.3 Unsupervised Clustering Algorithms

In this section, we review the clustering algorithms we use to build our classifiers for unlabelled traffic data. In particular, reviewing K-means and Gaussian mixture models.

K-means Clustering Technique. Given a set of data blobs, the K-means algorithm can quickly label these into clusters such a way to closely match relevant data points together. This is calculated based on iterations of distances between the clusters to form circular shapes.

Why is this Good? K-means is a good approach to explain how data sets with seemingly unrelated features can be grouped, just based on their empirical distances.

Gaussian Mixture Models (GMMs). Gaussian mixture models work to find multi-dimensional Gaussian probability distributions that best fit training data. Based on calculating density estimation and probability that a data point belongs to a cluster, this method works well to generalize non-uniform data.

Why is this Good? In K-means, there is no intrinsic probability measure or uncertainty in the clusters. GMMs are better to characterize different shapes of the data which do not exist as clear circles.

4   Methodology

We propose to develop an end-to-end traffic classification mechanism that will work in three phases (Fig. 1): First, the Trace collection phase uses data pipelines that create hourly summaries of NetFlow records for each site from the routers.

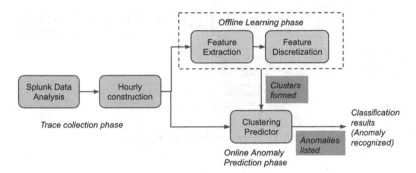

Fig. 1. Overall methodology of recognizing anomalies in Netflow characteristics.

Second, an offline learning phase will use clustering methods to group similar traffic flows together. To verify this behavior we will divide our data into training and test data and compare the results found by the classifier. And lastly, we will deploy these classifiers with the pipelines to perform online clustering as data is collected. We use 3 data centers as we anticipate different traffic patterns.

4.1   Trace Collection: Building Streaming Data Pipelines

Phase one consists of trace collection and data reduction. ESnet sees, in aggregate, between 20–50 million net flow records per hour on average which follow a classic weekday, diurnal pattern. As shown in Fig. 2, this data is gathered through a set of flow collectors and sent to a splunk instance which indexes and stores the records in a performance searchable format. Flow data at ESnet is sampled at 1:1000 before being sent to a collection which plays an important role in the type of analysis that is possible. Values that can be approximated by large sample sets work well, but exact enumerations are not possible. For example, looking at the exact number of packets to port 80/tcp, or if a specific IP has been seen are not possible with sparsely sampled data, but estimating the ratio of 80/tcp vs. 443/tcp is possible.

To analyze the classification techniques we used data sets from three DOE data center sites, we will be referencing them as Site 1, Site 2, and Site 3 in this paper. For this, the raw data is filtered for site Autonomous System Number and or network subnet to define a site or region of interest. In an effort to reduce the effects of random scanning and background noise/radiation an additional filter was imposed which removed records containing less than 64 bytes.

This filtering reduces the data volume down to around 1.3 million records per hour. The data summary process walks through this data, breaks it into one-hour blocks, and generates a set of summary statistics based on counting and heuristics for each block. The reduction in data volume for the summary data set (millions of flow records down to one set of statistical/count measurements) lets us process large windows of data for the model building and comparison in very little time.

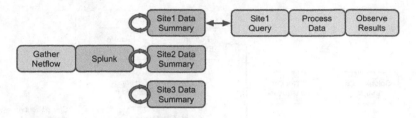

Fig. 2. Workflow for data analysis.

Data summary consists of the one-hour measurement blocks, features concerning byte counts, packet counts, unique server IP, and unique server port are broken out into direction (inbound vs. outbound) as well as protocol (TCP, UDP, and ICMP). The standard deviation for byte and packet counts are broken out similarly. Flow records are combined based on the heuristic that the lowest port represents the service which is based on the classic fixed service port and ephemeral client-side port. This is not always true in terms of dynamically generated services and data transfers (for example Globus GridFTP), but since we are looking at aggregate behavior across a large number of sessions these ephemeral services should average out.

A feature is a property of a data sample, where average, mean, median, and standard deviation can also be features. Unsupervised feature extraction helps identify patterns from features in trace data.

Table 1. Features unsupervised clustering from hourly NetFlow summaries.

Type of feature	Feature description
Byte Count (TCP, UDP, ICMP)	Integer
Packet Count Inbound (TCP, UDP, ICMP)	Integer
Packet Count Outbound (TCP, UDP, ICMP)	Integer
Std Dev Bytes Inbound (TCP, UDP, ICMP)	Float
Std Dev Bytes Outbound (TCP, UDP, ICMP)	Float
Std Dev Packets Inbound (TCP, UDP, ICMP)	Float
Std Dev Packets Outbound (TCP, UDP, ICMP)	Float
Unique Server IP Inbound recorded this hour	Integer
Unique Server IP Outbound recorded this hour	Integer
Unique Server Port Inbound recorded this hour	Integer
Unique Server Port Outbound recorded this hour	Integer
Hour	Date-hour
Weekday	Date-wday

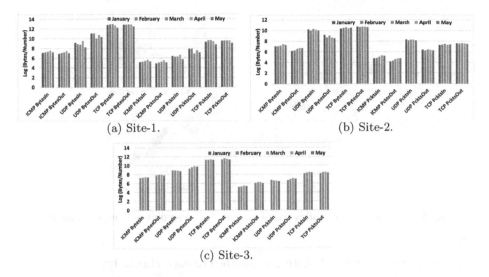

(a) Site-1.   (b) Site-2.

(c) Site-3.

Fig. 3. Traffic Distribution across all sites in months Jan-May 2020.

Training and Test Data. We use January and February 2020 data as training data, and March-May 2020 as test data. The TCP, UDP, and ICMP patterns are shown in Fig. 3 over the 5 months.

4.2   Offline Learning in Classifiers

For phase two, we use K-means and GMM methods to train our classifiers into unsupervised clustering methods. Figure 4 shows how the clusters are formed on training data. The test data is then grouped into one of the clusters.

4.3   Online Anomaly Finding

In phase three, we use K-means and GMM models to perform anomaly findings. Because of the lack of labeled data, we cannot specifically identify an anomaly unless all anomalies are grouped in particular clusters. To counter this, we define an anomaly that falls far from the 'normal' behavior in the training data sets. This is calculated in each clustering technique separately as shown in Eqs. 1, 2. We calculate an anomaly based on how far the data point is from the centroid and the density of the cluster. K-means assumes circular clusters, where we calculate centroid and radius of the original clusters. In GMM, we use Gaussian distribution to calculate the probability of each data point and list the least probability as a possible anomaly.

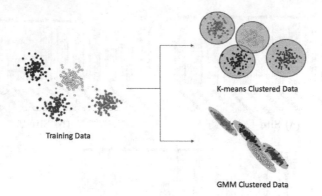

Fig. 4. Calculating anomalies based on how far the point is from the cluster.

In K-means, we can calculate the distance to each cluster by,

$$J = \sum_{j=1}^{k} \sum_{i=1}^{n} \left\| x_i^{(j)} - c_j \right\|^2 \tag{1}$$

where clusters of k groups can assign data points based on the euclidean distance function. The higher the distance from all clusters, the higher the probability of the data point to be anomalous.

For calculating anomalies with GMMs, we use the expectation and maximization method to calculate the probabilities of a data point belonging to a cluster. This probability can be defined as,

$$w_j^{(i)} = \frac{g_j(x)\phi_j}{\sum_{l-1}^{k} g_l(x)\phi_l} \tag{2}$$

where $g_j(x)$ represents the multivariate Gaussian of each cluster and ϕ_j represents the prior probabilities. These can be printed out to denote an average probability that they belong to a cluster. We use a threshold of -0.5 to denote that this is a very low probability that the data point belongs to a cluster and label these as anomalies.

5 Preliminary Analysis

We visualize the data using PCA (Principal Component Analysis) and t-SNE (t-Distributed Stochastic Neighbor Embedding) to represent a high-dimensional dataset (38 features, shown in Table 1) in a low-dimensional space of 2, 3 dimensions. Figure 5 shows the Site-1, Site-2 and Site-3 divided into training and test visuals. The sub-figures show different behaviors in the months, particularly in test data, impacted with COVID-19 work changes.

In contrast to PCA which simply maximizes the variance, t-SNE creates a reduced feature space where similar samples are modeled by nearby points and dissimilar samples are modeled by distant points with high probability. We got optimum results and the KL divergence was minimum for the 3 dimensions reduction (n = 3) of the original data set with t-SNE algorithm with perplexity =40 and 300 iterations. For Site-3 we see a tight clustering for weekdays, but from March-May'20, it shows a diverse traffic profile in Fig. 5, showing that the profile does change and would be picked up as anomalous.

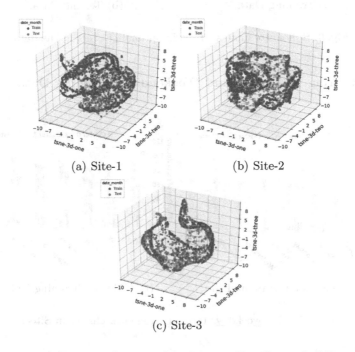

(a) Site-1   (b) Site-2

(c) Site-3

Fig. 5. TSNE visualization of Training vs Test Data of all Sites.

6   Experimental Results and Discussions

6.1   Silhouette Analysis for Optimal Clustering

We perform a silhouette analysis to study the optimal number of clusters in the training and test data sets. This informs the unsupervised clustering results. Figure 6 shows these measures of how close each point is in one cluster to points in neighboring clusters with the maximum value gives the optimum number of clusters. We find that optimal clusters in Site-1 are 3, Site-2 and Site-3 is 2 for training. We also performed a similar analysis for test data, showing that there is considerable variability in characteristics.

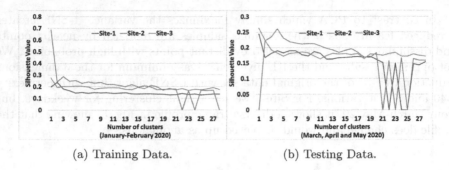

(a) Training Data.   (b) Testing Data.

Fig. 6. Silhouette analysis to gain optimal clusters in the data.

6.2   Clustering Weekdays and Weekends in Training Data

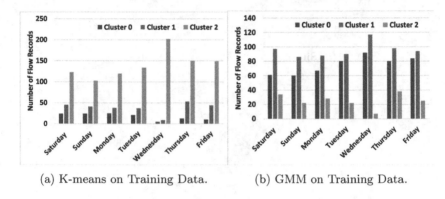

(a) K-means on Training Data.   (b) GMM on Training Data.

Fig. 7. Listing weekdays recognized in each cluster in Site-1.

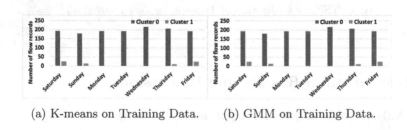

(a) K-means on Training Data.   (b) GMM on Training Data.

Fig. 8. Listing weekdays recognized in each cluster in Site-2.

We listed how the days were being recognized in each of the clusters. Figure 7 shows that K-means and GMM both cluster data differently and there are no distinct patterns between the weekdays. Comparatively in Figs. 8 and 9, we do find that there are individual clusters that can identify specific days of the week

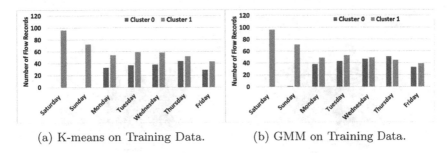

(a) K-means on Training Data.   (b) GMM on Training Data.

Fig. 9. Listing weekdays recognized in each cluster in Site-3.

such as Tuesdays in Cluster 0 in Site-2, and Saturdays in Cluster 1 in Site-3. However, since these also appear in other clusters, it is difficult to run test data and measure this assumption. This shows that the clusters selected in training data are insufficient to recognize individual days in the test data across all sites.

6.3 Identifying Outliers in Test Data

Figure 10 shows the representation of the test data sets with the training data clusters based on K-means and GMM results. In Fig. 10b, we witness that some behaviors in April and May are recognized as anomalies. As GMM calculates anomalies based on ellipsoid density, it recognizes lesser anomalies that K-means which uses only centroids and cluster density to calculate anomaly boundaries. In Fig. 10d, most of the March and May data sets are recognized as anomalous behaviors, in Fig. 10f, nearly all March and May are recognized as anomalies.

The results are summarized in Fig. 11 which shows total anomalies in each site's behavior. GMM is able to recognize fewer anomalies and we know from background information that there were no anomalies recorded in the real dataset. This is an unsupervised technique that lists how many records fall outside the common clusters formed in the training data sets, and because the behavior patterns changed in the months of March onwards these fall outside the clusters formed.

6.4 Impact of Selected Feature Discretization Using Domain Knowledge

Feature discretization takes a subset of features (knowledge-informed) in the data summary object for training and testing rather than the entire object. This not only gives a much better focus on the type of anomaly to look for, but also allows the analyst to better understand *what* specifically has changed in testing.

Specific feature selection is typically driven by the combination of fields that contain data related to the characteristic to measure and are informed by feedback from a domain expert. Individual fields are defined in Table 1 and can be categorized into data volume (bytes and packets), connections (host, port,

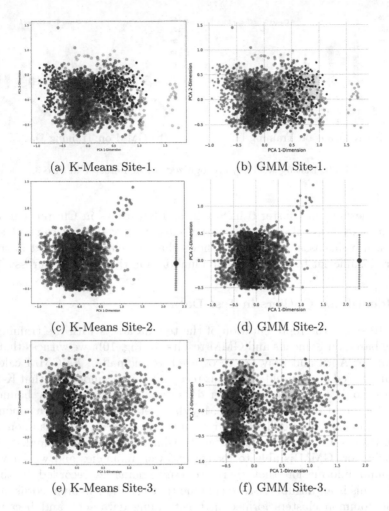

(a) K-Means Site-1.   (b) GMM Site-1.

(c) K-Means Site-2.   (d) GMM Site-2.

(e) K-Means Site-3.   (f) GMM Site-3.

Fig. 10. Plotting all sites training and test data. Colors present: March (green), April (blue), May (red). Others colors (yellow, purple) are training data clusters. (Color figure online)

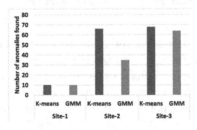

Fig. 11. Total anomalies at each Site during March–May '20.

direction), and descriptive statistics of the data volume. An example would be the count of unique outbound network addresses. This can be captured by the features: 'ServIPOut' (for TCP, UDP, ICMP). A more complex example might have many more fields. Training and test groups are generated using the same ratios as for K-means and GMM.

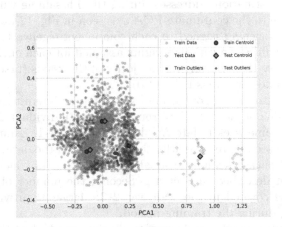

Fig. 12. Feature discritization sample showing training (blue), test (orange) data. (Color figure online)

Training data is normalized via MinMax to prevent biases in clustering from large values, then data dimensionality is further reduced via PCA. After running through GMM we end up with a set of matrices that hold (amongst other things) labels for cluster assignment as well as predict the posterior probability of each data point. Since cluster assignment is driven by the probability that a data point belongs to a cluster, a simple threshold test can be used to identify low likelihood events.

Outlier Detection. Represented graphically, a 2D view of train and test clusters can be seen in Fig. 12. Here training data is in blue diamonds and test data in orange circles. The usual color per cluster is not used here since we are looking at the probability of assignment to any cluster rather than the actual cluster membership. Outliers for test data are in red triangles and for completeness outliers in the training data, are in green squares. As mentioned above, outliers identify when the assignment probability returned by GMM clustering is below a threshold. More detailed information about Fig. 12 will be found in the next section.

Addressing Field Decomposition. Knowing that there are outlier elements in the test data can be informative - in this case, we can identify the outliers as outgoing IP services since both the x-axis (PCA-1) and y-axis (PCA-2) are composed of these features. To get greater details it is necessary to examine the PCA eigenvectors in more detail.

```
index: ['ServIPOut: 1', 'ServIPOut: 6, 'ServIPOut: 17']
X: eigenvalue:  0.035  percent:  0.5484  coeff:  [-0.979 -0.188 -0.074]
Y: eigenvalue:  0.022  percent:  0.3407  coeff:  [-0.085  0.047  0.995]
                 residual percent:  0.11081
```

Here 'ServIPOut: 1', 'ServIPOut: 6', 'ServIPOut: 17' represent the count of unique external destination addresses during the 1 h sample window. In terms of how they relate to the coordinate PCA axis seen in Fig. 12 we look at the set of weights or coefficients assigned to each component eigenvector in the figure. The text above defines the various weights assigned for each of the values, so in this case we can see that the singular majority of the x-axis (first component) is ICMP (-0.979) and the y-axis is UDP (0.995).

The outlier test data centroid around $x = 0.85$ is an interesting artifact worth understanding. The outlier test data represents two individual UDP scans that happened in the same week in late April directed at Site-1. Examining the original flow data we see two reasons why this ended up in the data. First, the byte sizes for the per packet scanning was above the threshold which defined background radiation described in Sect. 4.1. Second, the number of addresses and destination ports covered in the scan was 2–3× larger than what is typically seen in scanning during the training period.

In order to automate the analysis of traffic data, we look at the set of assignment probabilities returned from the training model. Looking at average and variance for the set provides a naive measurement of how good the model fits the test data in a general sense, while skewness and kurtosis provide a measure of asymmetry and the presence of outliers from a normal distribution.

7   Conclusions

In this paper, we analyzed traffic profiles and used these to predict anomalous traffic patterns. In security research, we assume that daily patterns are enough to recognize anomalous behaviors as we classify based on the hour of the day. However, with the changes in COVID working patterns, this assumption did not hold as most behaviors in the test data were labeled as anomalies, even when they were not.

Further our unsupervised clustering technique proved useful to find outliers in unlabelled data sets. GMM was able to provide better results than K-means which assumed a more uniform circular pattern of characteristic profiles, finding more false anomalies.

In the future, we will be deploying additional online classifiers to collect anomalies at each site's edge. Further, these techniques will be adapted to work with lower-level granular data. For example to find the reasons why certain data points are considered outliers such as a new site appearing or a unique transfer size which has never been done before. Our results show the potential to be deployed across many other ESnet network peerings and points of presence in DOE.

Acknowledgements. This work was supported by the U.S. Department of Energy, Office of Science Early Career Research Program, under LAB 16-1625 for Large-scale Deep Learning for Intelligent Networks FP00006145.

References

1. Ahmed, M., Mahmood, A.N., Hu, J.: A survey of network anomaly detection techniques. J. Netw. Comput. Appl. **60**, 19–31 (2016). http://www.sciencedirect.com/science/article/pii/S1084804515002891
2. Benson, T., Akella, A., Maltz, D.A.: Network traffic characteristics of data centers in the wild. In: SIGCOMM conference on Internet measurement (2010)
3. Campbell, S.: ESnet wan security project updates. In: Internet2 Technology Exchange (2018)
4. Campbell, S., Lee, J.: Prototyping a 100g monitoring system. In: Euromicro International Conference on Parallel, Distributed and Network-Based Processing (2012)
5. Claise, B.: Cisco systems netflow services export version 9. Internet Engineering Task Force [IETF] (2004)
6. Dewaele, G., et al.: Unsupervised host behavior classification from connection patterns. Int. J. Netw. Manag. **20**(5), 317–337 (2010). https://onlinelibrary.wiley.com/doi/abs/10.1002/nem.750
7. Erman, J., Arlitt, M., Mahanti, A.: Traffic classification using clustering algorithms. In: SIGCOMM Workshop on Mining Network Data, pp. 281–286. ACM (2006). https://doi.org/10.1145/1162678.1162679
8. Erman, J., Mahanti, A., Arlitt, M., Cohen, I., Williamson, C.: Semi-supervised network traffic classification. In: International Conference on Measurement and Modeling of Computer Systems, pp. 369–370. ACM (2007). https://doi.org/10.1145/1254882.1254934
9. Zhang, J., Ilija Vukotic, R.G.: Anomaly detection in wide area network meshes using two machine learning algorithms. Future Gener. Comput. Syst. **93**, 418–426 (2019)
10. Kim, H., Claffy, k., Fomenkov, M., Barman, D., Faloutsos, M., Lee, K.: Internet traffic classification demystified: myths, caveats, and the best practices. In: Conference on emerging Networking Experiments and Technologies, December 2008
11. Kiran, M., Chhabra, A.: Understanding flows in high-speed scientific networks: a netflow data study. Future Gener. Comput. Syst. **94**, 72–79 (2019). http://www.sciencedirect.com/science/article/pii/S0167739X18302322
12. Kohout, J., Pevný, T.: Unsupervised detection of malware in persistent web traffic. In: IEEE International Conference on Acoustics, Speech and Signal Processing, pp. 1757–1761 (2015)
13. Lakhina, A., Crovella, M., Diot, C.: Diagnosing network-wide traffic anomalies. In: Proceedings of the 2004 Conference on Applications, Technologies, Architectures, and Protocols for Computer Communications, pp. 219–230. ACM (2004). https://doi.org/10.1145/1015467.1015492
14. Lakhina, A., Crovella, M., Diot, C.: Mining anomalies using traffic feature distributions. SIGCOMM Comput. Commun. Rev. **35**(4), 217–228 (2005). https://doi.org/10.1145/1090191.1080118
15. Lopez-Martin, M., Carro, B., Sanchez-Esguevillas, A., Lloret, J.: Network traffic classifier with convolutional and recurrent neural networks for internet of things. IEEE Access **5**, 18042–18050 (2017)

16. Nguyen, T.T.T., Armitage, G.: Training on multiple sub-flows to optimise the use of machine learning classifiers in real-world IP networks. In: IEEE Conference on Local Computer Networks, pp. 369–376 (2006)
17. Nguyen, T.T.T., Armitage, G.: A survey of techniques for internet traffic classification using machine learning. IEEE Commun. Surv. Tutor. **10**(4), 56–76 (2008)
18. Nguyen, T.T.T., Armitage, G., Branch, P., Zander, S.: Timely and continuous machine-learning-based classification for interactive IP traffic. IEEE/ACM Trans. Netw. **20**(6), 1880–1894 (2012)
19. Sommer, R., Paxson, V.: Outside the closed world: on using machine learning for network intrusion detection. In: IEEE Symposium on Security and Privacy (2010)
20. Tari, R.M.: On the move to meaningful internet systems. In: Confederated International Conferences on the Move to Meaningful Internet Systems, vol. 2 (2007)
21. Zander, S., Nguyen, T., Armitage, G.: Automated traffic classification and application identification using machine learning. In: IEEE Conference on Local Computer Networks, pp. 250–257 (2005)
22. Zhang, H., Lu, G., Qassrawi, M.T., Zhang, Y., Yu, X.: Feature selection for optimizing traffic classification. Comput. Commun. **35**(12), 1457–1471 (2012). http://www.sciencedirect.com/science/article/pii/S0140366412001259
23. Zhang, J., Xiang, Y., Wang, Y., Zhou, W., Xiang, Y., Guan, Y.: Network traffic classification using correlation information. IEEE Trans. Parallel Distrib. Syst. **24**(1), 104–117 (2013)
24. Zhang, J., Zulkernine, M.: Anomaly based network intrusion detection with unsupervised outlier detection. In: IEEE International Conference on Communications, vol. 5, pp. 2388–2393 (2006)
25. Zhao, J., Huang, X., Sun, Q., Ma, Y.: Real-time feature selection in traffic classification. J. China Universities Posts Telecommun. **15**, 68–72 (2008). http://www.sciencedirect.com/science/article/pii/S1005888508601582

From Smart Homes to Smart Laboratories: Connected Instruments for Materials Science

Mathieu Doucet$^{(\boxtimes)}$ (iD)

Oak Ridge National Laboratory, Oak Ridge, TN 37831, USA
doucetm@ornl.gov

Abstract. The current focus on artificial intelligence and machine learning in the scientific community has the potential to greatly speed up discovery. In this article, we explore what a "smart facility" would mean for materials science. We propose to capture meta-data at every step of an experiment, including materials synthesis, sample production and characterization, simulation, and the analysis software used to extract information. Although most of this information is captured in various institutional systems and staff logbooks, more insight could be obtained by connecting this information through a system that allows automation. AI-enabled processes built on such a system would have the potential of making experiment planning easier and minimize the time between experiment and publication.

Keywords: FAIR data · Machine learning · Artificial intelligence · Smart facilities · Connected instruments

1 Introduction

We live in a society where the devices that support our daily activities are increasingly connected. Several vendors are offering platforms that allow us to remotely control household devices, from light bulbs to doorbells, some of which use machine learning for greater efficiency. In contrast, instruments that support materials science are mostly disconnected. The life cycle of a well-planned scientific experiment is an endeavor that requires the use of several devices in an intrinsically connected process. Recognizing this is essential for scientific user facilities like neutron and x-ray facilities, where sample preparation is generally not done on site.

M. Doucet—Contributed Equally.
This manuscript has been co-authored by UT-Battelle, LLC, under contract DE-AC05-00OR22725 with the US Department of Energy (DOE). The US government retains and the publisher, by accepting the article for publication, acknowledges that the US government retains a nonexclusive, paid-up, irrevocable, worldwide license to publish or reproduce the published form of this manuscript, or allow others to do so, for US government purposes. DOE will provide public access to these results of federally sponsored research in accordance with the DOE Public Access Plan (http://energy.gov/downloads/doe-public-access-plan).

J. Nichols et al. (Eds.): SMC 2020, CCIS 1315, pp. 257–268, 2020.
https://doi.org/10.1007/978-3-030-63393-6_17

Establishing a common data framework for analytics is both particularly important and challenging for science. The sources of information that support scientific discovery are often very diverse, coming from complementary methods to address particular issues. In contrast, smart home systems easily generate a large amount of training data through the simple fact that we interact with these systems on a daily basis. If the picture of every single person ringing the doorbell is taken, or if every tweak of our smart thermostat is captured, it is much easier to develop training data. Although scientific data is more complex and diverse, there is something to be learned from the approaches followed by industry to develop consumer systems. Several efforts are underway to develop connected systems involving large numbers of data sources beyond a simple household. Those efforts cover areas such as smart neighborhoods interacting with a local electricity grid [1] to intelligent transportation systems [2]. Using artificial intelligence (AI) and machine learning to support scientific user facilities has recently been the topic of a roundtable of domain experts organized by the U.S. Department of Energy [3]. In this position paper, we use the example of interfacial studies of energy storage materials as a use case for envisioning an integrated and analytics-ready system to support materials science and help scientists plan experiments more precisely and interpret data more efficiently.

2   The Experiment Life Cycle: An Example from Electrochemistry

A scientific endeavour is inherently one of planned execution. One postulates a hypothesis, devises a verification experiment, conducts that experiment, and draws conclusions that will inform the next step to be taken. All these activities are recorded to ensure the correctness of the final interpretation. To this day, the paper logbook has a special place in science. Not only do scientists capture their work in them, laboratory instruments often have their own dedicated logbook to record how they were used and by whom. Compounding the problem of making sense of all these logbook entries, science is intrinsically collaborative. Verifying a given hypothesis may require the work of several researchers, in multiple laboratories and using a variety of instruments, each with their own way of capturing data and notes. Even in an era where most scientific activities require a computer, the paper logbook is still the most common way of capturing the thoughts of scientists, and therefore the relationships between the different pieces of information gathered in this collaborative process. Capturing this information in a data system would provide rich meta-data to help automate and speed up the extraction of science from measurements.

The study of energy storage materials using neutron reflectometry lends itself well to this discussion, as it is a research topic that touches several disciplines and exemplifies the challenges outlined above. Specular reflectometry [4] allows us to study the layered structure of thin films as a function of depth at the nanometer scale. Neutrons, being sensitive to light elements and having a low absorption cross-section for most elements, are an excellent probe for *in situ* characterization of energy materials [5–9]. This is especially true because challenges in energy storage involve materials interfaces. A good example is the study of the solid-electrolyte interphase (SEI) formation, the protective layer that forms at the surface of an anode as it is cycled, the full understanding of which remains a challenge [10].

Studies of electrode materials involve multiple fabrication and characterization steps, even in cases where the primary measurements are made using neutron reflectometry. Figure 1 depicts the life cycle of a typical neutron study of anode materials. The thin films are grown in a magnetron sputtering system where high voltage power, vacuum condition, and gas environment are controlled. Depositing a layer of material requires acquiring or fabricating a target for the deposition system, and the amount of deposited material is estimated using an embedded quartz microbalance. Once a film deposition is complete, it is characterized using either neutron or x-ray reflectometry to assess quality before use in the planned *in situ* experiment.

During an *in situ* electrochemistry experiment using neutron reflectometry, the thin film sample under study is placed in an electrochemical cell and hooked up to a potentiostat. Neutron reflectivity is then measured as a function of the state of charge of the cell in a series of constant voltage steps. The interpretation of the results involves the analysis of both the neutron and electrochemistry data. The latter is used as a constraint to inform the modeling of the former.

In parallel to the reflectometry measurements, sister samples are assembled in coin cells to be cycled in chemical laboratory potentiostats. This allows researchers to gather electrochemical data and cycle cells over a time period much longer than the two or three days generally allotted to a typical neutron reflectometry experiment. Such sister samples are used to perform complementary measurements to assess the stoichiometry at the electrode surface. For instance, a test electrode assembled in a coin cell can be brought to a given state of charge, disassembled, and studied with x-ray photoelectron spectroscopy (XPS) to identify the types of chemical species contributing to the SEI as a function of state of charge. The final conclusions of a study of energy storage materials using neutron reflectometry will therefore rely on a global interpretation of both the data acquired during the neutron measurements and the complementary data acquired in the chemical laboratory. The proper interpretation of all this data crucially relies on the expertise of scientists in both the chemical and scattering fields, and requires precise bookkeeping to properly map this rich data landscape.

Thin films are generally modelled as a stack of layers, each with a thickness, a scattering length density (SLD) value that relates to the composition of the layer, and a roughness parameter that characterizes the interface between two adjacent layers [4]. The films prepared prior to an experiment always have a certain degree of variability that depends on the operating conditions of the deposition system. We aim at producing multiple identical samples, but each layer may have a slightly different thickness or composition from sample to sample. When conducting studies of energy storage materials, this variability of the prepared thin films is important and needs to be taken into account. Variations within a single experiment deserve more attention. This is especially true because a potentially large number of sister samples may be used for various purposes throughout an experiment. The quality of each film must therefore be understood to ensure that the proper conclusions are drawn. Although these

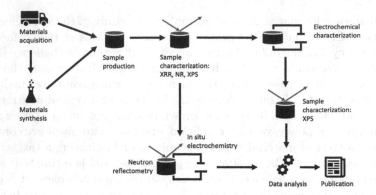

Fig. 1. Overview of the life cycle of a study of energy storage materials using neutron scattering. A typical neutron scattering experiment is usually the culmination of a long process of materials acquisition, sample production and characterization, and careful planning. All these activities are generally captured in separate systems and would benefit from being linked.

issues generally do not prevent us from achieving our scientific goals, each of these need to be dealt with. What are the parameters that made a sample different? Was the microbalance in proper working order during the deposition? Who made the sample? What was the quality of the vacuum when the samples were made? What was made in the chamber before this sample and did it leave impurities behind? Finding answers to those questions would be greatly more efficient if tools were in place to cross-correlate our measurements, help in the data analysis, and help recognize outliers.

Scientific data does not exist in isolation. Capturing and understanding how data sets relate to each other is important in order to draw sound conclusions. Machine learning is a particularly good tool to find correlations in rich data, but whether it is analyzed by hand or through a machine learning enabled process, the relevant data needs to be captured first. All these questions could be readily answered if all the information kept in our logbooks were captured in a linked data system. The information in our logbooks capture both intent and data interpretation. They not only shed light on what we tried to achieve, but how we achieved it and whether it succeeded. In essence, it is crucial meta-data that needs to be linked to the measurement data itself. Capturing the end-to-end scientific life cycle is essential in accelerating scientific discoveries.

3   A Data Infrastructure to Map the Scientific Method

The FAIR principles [11] of Findable, Accessible, Interoperable, and Reusable data are now well established in the scientific community. The challenge in capturing the end-to-end scientific process resides in determining what requirements need to be fulfilled to adhere to the FAIR principles. Modern instruments, especially in the context of scattering user facilities like the Spallation Neutron Source

(SNS) and the High Flux Isotope Reactor (HFIR) at Oak Ridge National Laboratory, already attempt to capture instrument parameters when acquiring data. Although such an approach succeeds at capturing a measurement completely, it rarely captures either intent or the full description of the sample and its state. The emphasis is on the measurement device, and information about the measured sample and its environment is often lacking.

In the electrochemistry use case described above, in the context of experiments conducted at SNS, although the measurement is completely described, the information about which sample was measured is missing. Such information is only captured in a logbook at the instrument. In addition, the electrochemical information [12] (the applied potential and the measured current as a function of time) is also captured in a separate system. That data, crucial to the interpretation of the neutron measurements, is not at all linked to the reflectometry data. It has to be copied from a separate system, interpreted separately, and cross-linked through file names and entries in the experiment logbook. In this situation, data interpretation is time consuming and the typical time to publication is on the order of a year.

Analysis based on machine learning models trained on previous measurements could also help us control experiments more efficiently, a process that would improve in efficiency as researchers learn more about the system under study. The shortcomings in combining related data sets also make it such that it is nearly impossible to use previous measurements to help automate an experiment. While data sources are available to make live decisions about how to conduct an experiment possible, the lack of integration makes it impossible. Capturing the scientific process as it develops would allow us to have all the knowledge necessary when the neutron experiment starts. This would not only allow better experiment planning, but it would also allow researchers to modify their experiment as it proceeds. As the electrochemical and neutron data are acquired, a smart system could use this information to identify important experimental parameters such as identifying which state of charge to investigate and how long to measure them for.

Several minimal requirements can be identified to fully capture a multi-technique experiment of the likes of electrochemical studies involving neutron reflectometry. The following is not intended to be a complete list of what a smart laboratory should provide, but points out gaping holes in the current way scientific data is captured.

3.1   Capturing Sample Provenance and Custody Chain

Smart and connected laboratories need to embrace provenance from the moment an experiment begins. We pointed out the fact that an experiment really starts when acquiring materials to synthesize samples. Scientists reporting results in the literature often specify the vendors from which they acquired materials. This is important for reproducibility. Reporting and utilizing such information could be made easier by realizing that much of the scientific activities are supported by operational processes that hold such valuable information. Materials are acquired through a business process where vendor information is captured. This information is linked to a specific project through a funding account number. Furthermore, larger laboratories like ORNL have databases of chemicals, complete with custody information. All this valuable information is usually lost once the acquired material is put to use. Without breaking privacy rules, it would be possible to capture such information to help automate interpretation further down the scientific process.

Sample fabrication would also benefit from a record system to follow a sample's use. User facilities like SNS and HFIR already have systems in place to record all samples to be measured. Each sample is precisely described and tagged with a unique identifier and a bar code before being allowed to be used. This information is generally, but not always, captured in the neutron data files produced at ORNL. The same should be done for materials synthesis and sample production. For a given sample measured at SNS, researchers should be able to look up where it came from, how it was produced, and with which materials. Once a sample is uniquely identified, it would be possible to look up whether it has been measured using other experimental techniques.

For this to be feasible, capturing the custody chain is essential. This goes beyond simply knowing which employee handled a sample. If each instrument and glove box were uniquely identified with a bar code, it would be possible to follow a sample from the moment it came out of the sputtering chamber all the way to when it was disposed of. Such information can be crucial. If a glove box has a higher water content, or if a previous user left impurities in a vacuum chamber, those are all information that can improve the interpretation of a measurement and prevent wrongful conclusions.

3.2 Complete Recording of Experimental Data and Processing

Most scattering user facilities are focused on developing the infrastructure needed to support the instruments they provide to their community. In order to develop an infrastructure that maps the end-to-end process of a scientific experiment, we need to ensure that all the relevant data necessary to interpret the measurements are properly stored and readily accessible.

User programs already lend themselves well to developing such an infrastructure. The SNS and HFIR facilities have several linked systems in place to support their program. The allocation of beam time to users is done through a peer-reviewed experiment proposal process. Before being approved, users submit a technical description of their experiment, including which ancillary devices they may need. They also need to describe the samples they will study. Once they arrive at the facility, they need to check in their samples, which will each be labelled with a unique bar code to ensure proper processing and disposition once the experiment has ended. In this case each experiment's unique identifier is used to link data together.

At ORNL beam lines, neutron data is stored on a facility file system in the NeXus standard format [13]. The NeXus format is a good example of a data format that aims at completeness in capturing scattering experiments. NeXus is developed by an international collaboration of facility scientists and software engineers to provide a common data format for neutron, x-ray, and muon experiments. It is used by the neutron facilities at ORNL and around the world. The NeXus files contain the neutron data itself and time series logs of all the process variables describing the instrument during the measurement process. Those include motor positions, information about velocity selectors, and data acquisition information describing how the measurement proceeded. It also can accommodate information related to the experiment itself, such as the experiment identifier and the sample identifier.

Once written to disk, each data file is submitted to a post-processing workflow [14]. This workflow takes care of coordinating jobs to catalog the raw data, process the data to be ready for consumption by the end-user, and catalog the processed data. The cataloging is done through a service developed in-house [15]. It captures the data location and meta-data, which it makes available to other applications. In a second step, the neutron data undergoes a transformation process (called data reduction in the neutron community) that takes the data in instrument coordinates and produces data in physics units that can be analyzed by community software. Although standards do exist, such as the CanSAS format [16] for small-angle scattering data, most data sets are not self-described, often saved in multi-column ASCII formats. Those data sets are also cataloged. Capturing this workflow is crucial in our vision of a fully integrated system where the output of each step in an experiment process is available to the next.

What is often missing from the data captured in NeXus files is complementary data acquired *in situ*. In our electrochemistry example, this means that the current and voltage information acquired while cycling our cell during the reflectometry measurements is not captured in the raw data file. This data is generally written to disk on the computer that runs the potentiostat software and needs to be transferred manually. This data should be stored on a central system with enough information to tie it to the experiment. At a minimum it should be linked through the experiment's unique identifier, and it should be formatted in a way that is usable for consumption in analytics processes such as those used to establish a machine learning training set.

The modeling and analysis results should also be treated as data sources and captured. To be useful in machine learning processes, these would need to be captured with full provenance information. The same principles should be applied to all software used to produce data. In addition to capturing models that represent the measured data, one would need to capture how such models were obtained, including which modeling software was used, and which starting parameters were used. Fully capturing the provenance trail of how the data was analyzed is crucial in establishing fully connected instruments in a smart facility. Establishing standard formats for interoperability is also crucial. This is in addition to *ex situ* characterization data that may have been acquired before the experiment takes place. All this data should be properly captured and linked to enable end-to-end analytics.

3.3 Semantic Processing to Capture Intent and Results to Inform Interpretation

Mapping domain knowledge and experimental results to a graph network of domain data could accelerate discovery. So far we have stressed that a complete recording of instrument data and provenance is crucial to establishing smart facilities. To be useful in the context of automated analytics, capturing all the data produced to support a given study is necessary but in itself insufficient. That data needs to be enriched with relationship information that links the various data sets together and gives them context. This means more than tying together all the data from a given experiment with a unique identifier.

An often overlooked aspect of laboratory experiments, especially those conducted at user facilities, is the human factors of the process. Although visiting researchers plan their experiments in advance, setting up a new experiment once getting to the facility is always hectic even for seasoned practitioners. The consequence is that asking users to enter meta-data information is often difficult. Proper incentives in the form of an easier and more complete data analysis is probably not enough to ensure data completeness.

For this reason, we foresee that a second step to data ingestion providing automated enrichment is necessary. Such a process would greatly be helped by establishing processes to map the complex knowledge relationships between existing results and data. In addition to capturing experimental data and capturing a rich description of the relationship between data, establishing context based on previous results is important.

There are several examples of semantic analysis of publication data that could provide a foundation for such an effort. The SemMedDB database of semantic predications for medical publications is a great example from the medial field [17]. Closer to our electrochemistry example, Springer Nature and researchers from Goethe University recently published a book reviewing recent publications on lithium-ion batteries that was entirely written with machine learning [18]. The approach followed a workflow that involved clustering, extracting, and summarizing algorithms applied to scientific literature. Coupling such an approach to meta-data rich experimental data could greatly speed up measurement interpretation. This would also enable us to integrate with external sources of information such as the Materials Project [19,20].

4   AI-Enabled Smart Beamlines

The environment we have outlined above would greatly minimize the time needed between the conception of an experiment and publication of results. More importantly, it would allow for the use of artificial intelligence and machine learning at multiple points in the process. A fully connected neutron reflectometer, for instance, would allow the use of machine learning to inform experiment planning in real time. The complete archive of existing neutron and characterization data, along with simulation data, could more easily be combined to develop machine learning models in advance of the allocated beamtime. In the case of electrochemistry, this could mean that we would be able to use machine learning to interpret both the electrochemistry and reflectometry data as it is acquired to identify states of charge of interest, where longer or more detailed measurements would be beneficial. Such an approach would allow us to better leverage the simulation work that is usually done as a separate effort [10]. The study of electrode materials using reflectometry is usually a multi-step process that alternates between driving current into the system to reach a specific state of charge, followed by a neutron reflectometry measurements at that state of charge once equilibrium is reached. Being able to use machine learning to interpret the electrochemistry data to better identify the states of charge to be measured would immensely improve the impact of such measurements. The work of Browning and coworkers [8] (see their Fig. 6) shows a good example where the current and voltage curves show changes that do not have corresponding reflectometry measurements. In this case, a better integration between a time-resolved measurement of neutron data and the electrochemical processes involved would provide important data that is currently missed. For this to be possible, several capabilities need to be put in place.

4.1 Access to Flexible Workflows

The ability to dynamically configure workflows is needed to allow for AI-enabled beamlines. Figure 2 depicts an example of a workflow for a smart reflectometry beamline. In addition to the automated data reduction currently available, an infrastructure is needed to plug in data analysis processes. In the case of reflectometry, this would include automated processes for the extraction of thin film structure parameters. This data would need to be fully captured in our data infrastructure. This modeling step would be followed by a machine learning process leveraging previously obtained data to obtain both a structural interpretation of the system and a suggestion for the subsequent measurement. Putting such an infrastructure in place would allow for a more automated experimental procedure where data-informed decisions are made on the fly, and where experiment planning blends in with experiment execution.

4.2 Smart Laboratory as a Data Hub

To seamlessly integrate instruments, the scientific data they produce, and workflows to allow automated measurements based on prior knowledge, a shared infrastructure between laboratories needs to be put in place. Several projects that aim at integrating data sources into a federated system, like DataFed [21] and PaNOSC [22], have started to tackle these issues. Although enabling individual devices to access central storage and leverage compute resources is essential, the ultimate goal would be for instruments to recognize the resources they have access to according to the context they are in. This is especially true for sample environment devices that move from laboratory to laboratory. Analogous to the Google Assistant's *Home Graph* [23] that maps out devices defined by type and traits within a house, we envisage a laboratory setting where functionality and

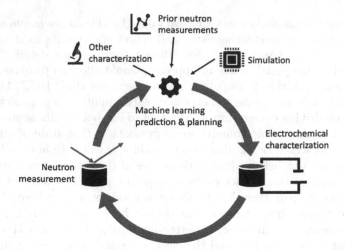

Fig. 2. Overview of a smart beamline workflow. The key aspect of a smart workflow is the live feedback during acquisition. A fully integrated workflow would allow the experiment to be guided by prior information obtained from complementary characterization methods, simulation, as well as previous neutron measurements.

resources can automatically be made available by the simple fact of connecting an instrument to a particular laboratory. In the case of neutron reflectometry, the act of adding the potentiostat to the beamline within the context of a given experiment would enable workflows and easy access to pre-trained machine learning models. As more information is put into the system, and as more researchers use the system and thus put knowledge into it, more capabilities would automatically be made available according to how the system has been used in the past. Over time, we envisage the infrastructure around a given instrument to be able to help users in planning and executing experiments based on prior knowledge and the context of each laboratory setting.

5   Conclusion

Experiment data following the FAIR data principles, stored in a scientific data infrastructure and connected by provenance information captured along with meta-data augmented by automated semantic processing, is necessary to take full advantage of previous knowledge and maximize the impact of scientific research. The national laboratories and their scientific user facilities have a unique opportunity to create an infrastructure that supports the end-to-end scientific life cycle. With expertise in place and a wide variety of instruments covering all areas of science, they are in an ideal position to lead to way.

The benefits of developing smart laboratories go beyond the specific case outlined here. A fully integrated system of connected instruments would open up a world of possibilities we have not discussed. Once the AI-enabled beamlines we described become a reality, we can imagine major changes in the model for user experiment proposal and planning. The same knowledge network and analytics processes used to accelerate the interpretation of experiments could be used to plan them. Users would be able to simulate their experiments before submitting their proposal and therefore help the review process. The output of simulated experiments could be used as templates for running the measurements.

The infrastructure outlined here would also greatly help the peer-review process and reproducibility of published literature. Once all the necessary data is captured, the end-to-end provenance trail should be assigned a Digital Object Identifier (DOI) to be required as supplementary material when submitting manuscripts for publication. The recent focus on artificial intelligence and machine learning has pointed out the importance of improving our data landscape. We believe that taking a step back to explore how we capture the whole life cycle of scientific endeavours has the potential to accelerate science discoveries even more.

Acknowledgements. A portion of this research used resources at the SNS, a Department of Energy (DOE) Office of Science User Facility operated by ORNL. ORNL is managed by UT-Battelle LLC for DOE under Contract DE-AC05-00OR22725. The picture painted in this paper is the result of years worth of discussions with scientists in the fields of chemistry, physics, and computer science. In particular, I would like to thank Sudharshan Vazhkudai for discussions on data infrastructure and FAIR data, Rama Vasudevan for discussions on cross-facility data analytics, Jay Billings for discussions on machine learning, Dale Stansberry for discussions on data provenance, and Gabriel Veith for discussions on applying this approach to chemistry laboratories. I would like to thank John Hetrick and Jim Browning for discussing this manuscript and the overall vision.

References

1. Buckberry, H., Burke, J., Starke, M., et al.: Smart technologies enable homes to be efficient and interactive with the grid ORNL/TM-2020/1507 (2020). https://doi.org/10.2172/1615193
2. Intelligent Transportation Systems Joint Program Office, Strategic Plan 2020–2025, FHWA-JPO-18-746 (2020). https://www.its.dot.gov/stratplan2020/
3. Ratner, D., Sumpter, B., Alexander, F., et al.: BES roundtable on producing and managing large scientific data with artificial intelligence and machine learning (2019). https://doi.org/10.2172/1630823
4. Sivia, D.S.: Elementary scattering theory for X-ray and neutron users. Oxford University Press (2011). https://doi.org/10.1093/acprof:oso/9780199228676.001.0001
5. Veith, G.M., Doucet, M., Baldwin, J.K., et al.: Direct determination of solid-electrolyte interphase thickness and composition as a function of state of charge on a silicon anode. J. Phys. Chem. C **119**(35), 20339–20349 (2015). https://doi.org/10.1021/acs.jpcc.5b06817
6. Fears, T.M., Doucet, M., Browning, J.F., et al.: Evaluating the solid electrolyte interphase formed on silicon electrodes: a comparison of ex situ X-ray photoelectron spectroscopy and in situ neutron reflectometry. Phys. Chem. Chem. Phys. **18**, 13927–13940 (2016). https://doi.org/10.1039/C6CP00978F

7. Veith, G.M., Doucet, M., Sacci, R.L., et al.: Determination of the Solid Electrolyte Interphase Structure Grown on a Silicon Electrode Using a Fluoroethylene Carbonate Additive. Sci. Rep. **7**, 6326 (2017). https://doi.org/10.1038/s41598-017-06555-8

8. Browning, K.L., Browning, J.F., Doucet, M., et al.: Role of conductive binder to direct solid-electrolyte interphase formation over silicon anodes. Phys. Chem. Chem. Phys. **21**(31), 17356–17365 (2019). https://doi.org/10.1039/C9CP02610J

9. Browning, K.L., Sacci, R.L., Doucet, M., et al.: The study of the binder poly(acrylic acid) and its role in concomitant solid-electrolyte interphase formation on Si anodes. ACS Appl. Mater. Interfaces **12**(8), 10018–10030 (2020). https://doi.org/10.1021/acsami.9b22382

10. Wang, A., Kadam, S., Li, H. et al.: Review on modeling of the anode solid electrolyte interphase (SEI) for lithium-ion batteries NPJ Computational Materials 4:15 (2018). https://doi.org/10.1038/s41524-018-0064-0

11. Wilkinson, M., Dumontier, M., Aalbersberg, I., et al.: The FAIR Guiding Principles for scientific data management and stewardship. Sci. Data **3**, 160018 (2016). https://doi.org/10.1038/sdata.2016.18

12. Elgrishi, N., Rountree, K.J., McCarthy, B.D., et al.: A practical beginner's guide to cyclic voltammetry. J. Chem. Educ. **95**, 197–206 (2018). https://doi.org/10.1021/acs.jchemed.7b00361

13. Könnecke, M., Akeroyd, F.A., Bernstein, H.J., et al.: The NeXus data format. J. Appl. Cryst. **48**, 301–305 (2015). https://doi.org/10.1107/S1600576714027575

14. Shipman, G., Campbell, S., David Dillow, D., et al.: Accelerating data acquisition, reduction, and analysis at the spallation neutron source. In: IEEE 10th International Conference on eScience (2014). https://doi.org/10.1109/eScience.2014.31

15. Parker, P.G., Ren, S.: ONCat (ORNL Neutron Catalog) (2018). https://doi.org/10.11578/dc.20200513.5

16. http://www.cansas.org/formats/canSAS1d/1.1/doc/index.html

17. Kilicoglu, H., Shin, D., Fiszman, M., Rosemblat, G., Rindflesch, T.C.: SemMedDB: a PubMed-scale repository of biomedical semantic predications. Bioinformatics **28**(23), 3158–60 (2012). https://doi.org/10.1093/bioinformatics/bts591

18. Writer, B.: Lithium-ion batteries: a machine-generated summary of current research. Springer, Heidelberg (2019). https://doi.org/10.1007/978-3-030-16800-1

19. Jain, A., Ong, S.P., Hautier, G., et al.: Commentary: the materials project: a materials genome approach to accelerating materials innovation. APL Materials **1**, 011002 (2013). https://doi.org/10.1063/1.4812323

20. Zhao, S., Qian, Q.: Ontology based heterogeneous materials database integration and semantic query. AIP Adv. **7**, 105325 (2017). https://doi.org/10.1063/1.4999209

21. Stansberry, D., Somnath, S., Breet, J. DataFed: Towards Reproducible Research via Federated Data Management 2019 International Conference on Computational Science and Computational Intelligence (CSCI), pp. 1312-1317 (2019). https://doi.org/10.1109/CSCI49370.2019.00245

22. Götz, A., Bodera Sempere, J., Campbell, A. et al.: Enabling Open Science for Photon and Neutron Sources, Proceedings of ICALEPCS2019, PROCEEDING-2020-029, 2085 (2019)

23. https://developers.google.com/assistant/smarthome/overview

Machine Learning for the Complex, Multi-scale Datasets in Fusion Energy

R. Michael Churchill[1]([⊠]), Jong Choi[2], Ralph Kube[1], C.S. Chang[1], and Scott Klasky[2]

[1] Princeton Plasma Physics Laboratory, Princeton, NJ 08540, USA
rchurchi@pppl.gov
[2] Oak Ridge National Laboratory, Oak Ridge, TN 37830, USA

Abstract. ML/AI techniques, particularly based on deep learning, will increasingly be used to accelerate scientific discovery for fusion experiment and simulation. Fusion energy devices have many disparate diagnostic instruments, capturing a broad range of interacting physics phenomena over multiple time and spatial scales. Also, fusion experiments are increasingly built to run longer pulses, with a goal of eventually running a reactor continuously. The confluence of these facts leads to large, complex datasets with phenomena manifest over long sequences. A key challenge is enabling scientists/engineers to utilize these datasets, for example to automatically catalog events of interest, predict the onset of phenomena such as tokamak disruptions, and enable comparisons to models/simulation. Given the size, multiple modalities, and multi-scale nature of fusion data, deep learning models are attractive, but at these scales requires utilizing HPC resources. Many ML/AI techniques not fully utilized now will demand even more HPC resources, such as self-supervised learning to help fusion scientists create AI models with less labelled data, and advanced sequence models which use less GPU memory at the expense of increased compute. Additionally, deep learning models will enable faster, more in-depth analysis than previously available, such as extracting physics model parameters from data using conditional variational autoencoders, instead of slower techniques such as Markov chain Monte Carlo (MCMC). Comparison to simulation will also be enhanced through direct acceleration of simulation kernels using deep learning. These ML/AI techniques will give fusion scientists faster results, allowing more efficient machine use, and faster scientific discovery.

1 Introduction

Plasma phenomena contain a wide range of temporal and spatial scales, often exhibiting multi-scale characteristics[50]. In fusion energy plasmas, many disparate diagnostic instruments are simultaneously used in order to capture these various spatiotemporal scales, and to cover the multiple physics present in these plasmas (see Figs. 1 and 2). In addition, fusion experiments, such as ITER, are

© Springer Nature Switzerland AG 2020
J. Nichols et al. (Eds.): SMC 2020, CCIS 1315, pp. 269–284, 2020.
https://doi.org/10.1007/978-3-030-63393-6_18

increasingly built to run longer pulses, with a goal of eventually running a reactor continuously. The confluence of these facts leads to large, complex datasets with phenomena manifest over long sequences. In addition, simulation plays an important role in verifying the underlying physics of experimental observations, to aid in achieving efficient machine operation and designing future reactors. A key challenge is enabling scientists/engineers to utilize these long sequence datasets to automatically catalog events of interest, predict the onset of phenomena such as tokamak disruptions [53], and enable comparisons to models/simulation. In this paper we discuss multiple machine learning research directions with the singular goal of enabling fusion scientists to leverage machine learning tools in order to work more effectively with these complex multi-scale diagnostic datasets, and to ultimately accelerate the pace of knowledge discovery in fusion energy sciences.

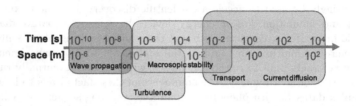

Fig. 1. Example temporal and spatial scales of different broad physics phenomena in fusion plasmas, based on Ref. [50]

Fusion tokamaks. The tokamak is the leading fusion energy device concept, with several large tokamaks at sites across the globe. The U.S. Department of Energy (DoE) funds two major domestic tokamak facilities (the DIII-D tokamak in San Diego, CA and the NSTX-U spherical tokamak in Princeton, NJ), and also funds U.S. fusion researchers to collaborate with the major international tokamaks. There is also a significant investment in building and preparing for ITER, a next-generation tokamak being built in the south of France, which is scheduled to begin operation in 2025. Maximizing the scientific output from these machines in the quest for fusion energy maximizes the return on investment made by the U.S.

The typical workflow for fusion scientists is to run an experimental shot (anywhere from a few seconds to hundreds of seconds on current devices), and then apply a variety of filters, transforms, and models to raw, measured data, to extract physically relevant quantities. The techniques used can range from simple fitting to more sophisticated Integrated Data Analysis (IDA) techniques [21], which bring together multiple diagnostics in a Bayesian manner. Reduced representations are sought especially in high temporal resolution diagnostics, since manually reviewing the data is nearly impossible. These reduced representations are visually inspected by scientists, to verify correct operation of diagnostics and recognize physics information of interest. Reduced physics information is

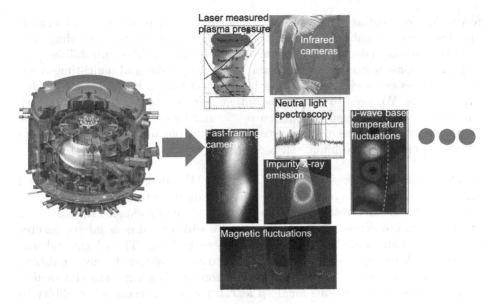

Fig. 2. Examples of the many disparate diagnostics used to measure various plasma quantities and phenomena in tokamaks.

often stored in a database, and written observations recorded in online group logbooks. This metadata store is useful for future work on discovering physics from experimental shots, but the quality and quantity of remarks is variable and wholly dependent on the researchers themselves. A principled way of identifying and storing the metadata on plasma events during a shot could greatly help scientists with uncovering patterns, and forming greater insights from experimental shots.

The data generation rates of tokamaks is large and fast, with ITER projected to generate 50 GB/s of information dense, raw diagnostic data. Ingesting important data in reasonable times can aid researchers in making informed decisions on how to guide and setup the next experiments. For scenarios where compute resources are lacking on-site, early concept implementations of streaming data to remote compute resources has been implemented [13,16]. Both ingesting the data locally, or leveraging remote compute resources, needs fast and meaningful analysis to aid faster feedback to fusion scientists, to make use of this information for adjusting the next experimental shots. For remote, the ability to send only data that is interesting makes the streaming more efficient. Remote sites also need algorithms for ingesting the data in automated ways.

In addition to this manual input by scientists, automated machine control algorithms are used locally on site to drive the experiment, to avoid instabilities and achieve maximum performance. The most pressing issue facing fusion tokamaks is a instability known as a disruption, which is a sudden loss of control causing a termination of the plasma, leading to potentially large destructive forces and/or heating on the containment vessel and protective wall materials. There are a number of different root causes for disruptions, including edge radiation, too high density, and magnetohydrodynamic (MHD) instabilities [10], requiring sophisticated models to cover the multi-physics and multi-timescales. Next-step devices such as ITER and beyond will have a low tolerance for disruptions [53]. We need to ensure disruptions can be avoided by planning with simulation and experimental experience [23], and by using accurate predictions of oncoming disruptions to allow steering away from unstable operation, and triggering mitigation techniques if necessary.

Machine learning for fusion Machine learning (ML) algorithms have been used for decades, including in fusion energy[9,57], to automate tasks and learn complicated non-linear relationships between data. Traditionally, classic ML algorithms (such as Random Forest, SVM, etc.) were used, which requires as inputs features of data that human analysts would define, often by hand. The advent and success of deep learning presents an opportunity to create systems for accomplishing fusion science tasks that were not possible before on sufficiently fast time scales, or at all. One of the reasons for deep learning's great success is the ability to learn multiple filters for high-dimensional data, in many cases avoiding the need for humans to do feature extraction [37]. In a sense, deep neural networks learn their own set of features (often called representations, which we will use interchangeably). This allows the deep learning algorithms to learn directly from raw (or lightly processed) data, without hand crafted features, for example using directly the pixels from a camera image to predict whether a cat is in the picture, instead of having humans to specify filters to extract features such as ovals (for eyes) and triangles (for ears). In fusion physics, this same concept of using deep neural networks to learn the filters/transforms necessary to accomplish a task is shown in Fig. 3. This can remove some of the impetus from the fusion physicists to exactly specify useful features based on physics models, potentially extracting more utility from the information rich raw data produced by tokamak diagnostics.

In the following sections we will detail several ML/AI algorithms and methods, focused around deep neural networks, which can have a significant impact on use cases both in the fusion energy field and in various other scientific domains. We detail how these use cases often dictate such ML/AI methods, and the use of High Performance Computing (HPC) resources to train these ML/AI models.

2   ML/AI for Fusion Use Cases

2.1   Deep Neural Networks Architectures for Multi-scale Data

In order to meet the needs of fusion scientists with the various use cases in Sect. 1 concerning prediction and automated tagging of data, we need deep neural networks which can handle multi-scale data. Sequence models which are sensitive to events over long sequences (associated with multi-scale data) are being developed to overcome the limitations of more traditional recurrent neural networks

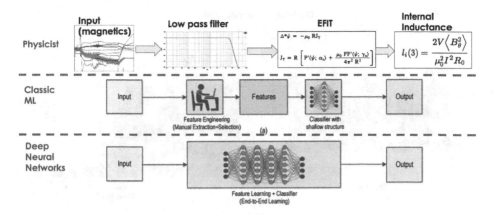

Fig. 3. Schematic comparison of models ("physicist"), classic or shallow machine learning reliant on hand-crafted features, and deep learning which allows working with high-dimensional data without feature engineering. Physicists will often use models with a number of filters or transforms applied to measured data (for example, deriving internal inductance from magnetic sensor measurements). Classic machine learning would take in these model parameters or "features" to learn to make predictions. Deep learning, in contrast, allows learning directly on the raw data ("end-to-end" learning). Adapted from Ref. [55]

(RNN), including Long Short Time Memory networks (LSTM) sequence models, which are prone to forget events occurring over long sequences [3]. Here we point out several areas of development to better enable training these models on HPC, and deployment on the edge for use in real-time processing.

An exemplary fusion use case is that of accurately predicting oncoming disruptions, such that real-time controllers can be used to adjust actuators to avoid or mitigate the disruption. As the physics involved in the cause and evolution of a disruption are not completely understood, a data-driven approach which can utilize as much information from available diagnostics is attractive. Over the years many classical ML algorithms have been applied on reduced features from diagnostics [46,52], including recently with deep LSTM architectures, which additionally made use of spatial information [24,33]. Our recent work went a step further, using raw data from a 2-D high-temporal resolution diagnostic (Electron Cyclotron Emission imaging, ECEi), achieving good results for disruption predictions on the DIII-D tokamak[17,18]. A deep convolutional neural network with dilated convolutions, the Temporal Convolutional Network (TCN) [3], was used to work with the long, multi-scale sequences of the ECEi data (see Fig. 4). The TCN architecture has a structure or inductive bias that aids in separating scales while being parameter efficient, and allows for fast parallel training on distributed GPU systems. Despite the success, many simplifications had to be made, such as downsampling and undersampling resulting in a reduction from the original 10 TB ECEi dataset to 100 GB. This was done in order to meet the GPU memory limitations, and to run in a reasonable amount of time (2 days),

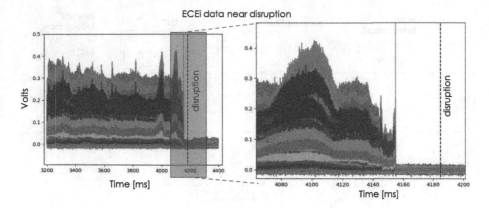

Fig. 4. Temporal sequences of individual channels of the 2-D ECEi diagnostic on the DIII-D tokamak, near a disruption

despite using distributed training with data parallelism on 16 GPUs. In the following we discuss several techniques that will further improve the accuracy for these problems by enabling the use of more data, longer sequences, and larger networks.

Scaling up Neural Network Training. Training TCN architectures using synchronous data parallel training on larger GPU resources such as Summit at the Oak Ridge Leadership Computing Facility (OLCF) will allow expanding the amount of data and model sizes used. However, a significant difficulty in scaling up data parallel schemes to large numbers of GPUs is that as the effective batch size becomes large, there is a well known task-dependent critical batch size beyond which the stochastic gradient descent optimization scheme simply doesn't learn much [38]. Additionally, data parallelism limits the size of the model that can be used, set by GPU memory. To solve this problem, and increase the size of the model we are able to train, a hybrid data/model parallelism can be used, where model parallelism (splitting model layers among separate GPUs) is used within a node (intra-node), and data parallelism is used between nodes (inter-node) [6]. Beyond this main thrust, a newly released library from Microsoft called DeepSpeed [44] shows promise for training with HPC. DeepSpeed is advertised to enable training trillion parameter models, using ZeRO (Zero-Redundancy Optimizer) [44], which focuses on data parallelism, but being more memory efficient by partitioning the weights, gradients, and optimizer parameters among the processes and communicating when necessary, instead of replicating all of them as is typically done in data parallelism.

Efficient sequence models. Some recent alternative architectures which more easily work with long sequences compared to TCN show promise, as they require much less memory, with the tradeoff of needing increased compute. This could more easily allow the use of large GPU resources available in current petascale and future exascale supercomputers for training these machine learning models.

The first of these is the Deep Equilibrium model (DEQ) [4]. The DEQ method instead has a single, weight-tied layer, f_θ, and solves the root finding problem of $g_\theta(\mathbf{z}_{out}; \mathbf{x}_{in}) = f_\theta(\mathbf{z}_{out}; \mathbf{x}_{in}) - \mathbf{z}_{out} = 0$ iteratively using Newton or quasi-Newton approximation methods:

$$\mathbf{z}^{j+1} = \mathbf{z}^j - \alpha B g_\theta(\mathbf{z}^j; \mathbf{x}_{in}) \tag{1}$$

where j is the iteration index, α the step size, and B the inverse Jacobian. Equation 1 is the forward pass of the neural network. The backward pass to update the networks weights is done in a manner which does not require storing the solver iteration information, avoiding explicit differentiation through the root-finding algorithm (allowing that piece to be black-box). The result is that the DEQ method is very memory efficient, not requiring the storing of gradients for multiple layers. The cost is increased computational time spent in the root-finding algorithm. Another architecture which promises the ability to work with long sequences while being memory efficient is the recent Reformer architecture [34]. This builds off the popular Transformer architecture [51], which is often used in natural language processing tasks. Transformers unfortunately have the drawback of requiring a lot of memory. The keys to the memory efficiency of the Reformer architecture are replacing dot-product attention with locality-sensitive hashing, and using reversible layers to avoid storing gradients. While more memory efficient, the Reformer is also computationally faster than Transformer architectures, though there are reports time to accuracy is still slower [54].

Moving to the edge. Even when larger sequence models can be trained, they must meet the computational, memory, and latency requirements when deployed at the edge. For example, disruption predictions require <10ms latency to ensure mitigation actions can be taken, and the edge accelerator used for inference must be able to work in the nuclear environment of fusion devices. Beyond identifying the hardware (GPU, FPGA, specialty accelerators like Neural Processing Units, etc.), use of neural network compression with tools such as Distiller [1] can greatly reduce the memory and computational requirements for edge accelerators.

2.2   Working with Multi-modalities

The combination of multiple diagnostics (in machine learning parlance often referred to as multiple modalities) offers the potential to capture complicated multi-physics sequences of events for more robust predictions. For example, disruptions have a number of different physics root causes, which may be more accurately predicted using diagnostics more sensitive to those physics, e.g. bolometry diagnostic for impurity radiation induced disruptions. There are various techniques to allow combining modalities into a single network, or spliced (often referred to as "fused") at different levels (see Fig. 5). This not only makes use of shared network weights for efficiency, but also enables the network to make use of correlations among diagnostics, with the potential to improve accuracy. However, caution must be used as some modalities anti-correlate, and can have a negative impact on accuracy depending on where injected. Naturally the increased complexity and data will require increased compute resources.

The question of what level to fuse multiple modalities in neural networks is dependent on data set and network, with many permutations possible. One option that is more computationally efficient than brute force training all permutations is to use a combinatorial optimization process to try fusing at different levels, optimizing to avoid competing modalities [49]. Another technique, feature-wise linear modulations (FiLM) uses learnable parameters at each level, so that the fusion is automatically learned during the training of the network [22,43]. For example, two modalites, say an ECEi signal and bolometer signal, normally would have their output z of some intermediate layers fused by simple concatenation $\mathbf{z} = [\mathbf{z}_{ecei}, \mathbf{z}_{bolo}]$, e.g. the late 'fusion' in Fig. 5(b). FiLM layers instead perform an affine transformation at each layer, $\mathbf{z} = \gamma(\mathbf{z}_{ecei}) \odot \mathbf{z}_{bolo} + \beta(\mathbf{z}_{ecei})$, where γ and β are the learnable parameters, as seen in Fig. 5(c). This offers a more principled way to fuse multiple modalities. With all of these techniques, even while more efficient, the needed compute will increase with increasing number of modalities, making HPC attractive for training.

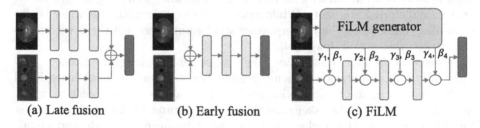

(a) Late fusion   (b) Early fusion   (c) FiLM

Fig. 5. Example layout to include FiLM generator parameters, incorporating multi-modalities such as ECEi and bolometry to enhance disruption predictions. Adapted from Ref. [22]

2.3   Working with Small Labelled Training Sets

One of the difficulties in using deep learning for supervised learning is the requirement to have a lot of labelled data, usually manually labelled by experimentalists. Often this is impractical due to the time required of the experimentalist, or in situations where multiple examples can not be tolerated, such as disruptions on ITER. While transfer learning [47] can serve to learn a new task with a small dataset, it still normally requires that the neural network be trained on an initial, larger labelled dataset. An often more common scenario is that we don't have such a large labelled dataset to begin with. In these scenarios, with a sufficient amount of unlabelled data, we can use a technique known as self-supervised learning to pre-train a neural network by simply having it look at the unlabelled data and attempt to predict future time points, such that the neural network learns the underlying data distribution. This greatly increases the amount of data to process, again leading to an increased need for HPC compute. With the representations learned from this master pre-trained network, we can train a new network for a particular supervised learning task but with much fewer examples than normally needed [56]. Self-supervised pre-training can also boost accuracy when working with large labelled datasets (albeit a smaller boost than with the smaller labelled datasets).

With fusion diagnostic data, unlabelled data is usually plentiful. Even in scenarios like the startup of ITER, where we must avoid too many disruptions, the slow ramp up to high power scenarios will give a large database of typical, unlabelled data which can be used in a self-supervised manner. Self-supervised learning can also be useful in generic scenarios where fusion scientists want to find other instances in historic data of a potentially new phenomena, such as a new flavor of Alfven Eigenmodes in NSTX-U data.

Most of the recent research on self-supervised learning for sequences focuses on natural language processing [20], however there are various techniques available for more continuous, scientific data, for example the wav2vec model [48], which is used for speech recognition from audio time-series signals. The main idea is to encode each section of the input, $\mathbf{x}$, using a neural network, g_{enc}, into a lower-frequency feature representation $\mathbf{z}_i = g_{enc}(\mathbf{x}_{t>t_i, t \leq t_{i+1}})$, then predict future times in this feature space, i.e. predict $\mathbf{z}_{i+k}$ using $\mathbf{z}$ ranging from the current $\mathbf{z}_i$ back to $\mathbf{z}_{i-r}$, where r represents the user-specified receptive field. A context network is used to aggregate several past feature representations, $\mathbf{c}_i = g_{context}(\mathbf{z}_i, ..., \mathbf{z}_{i-r})$. Instead of calculating the mean squared error from the real and predicted $\mathbf{z}_{i+k}$, a contrastive loss [41] is used, which attempts to distinguish the true sample, $\mathbf{z}_{i+k}$, from a number of other samples $\tilde{\mathbf{z}}$ drawn from the signal which are not $\mathbf{z}_{i+k}$ (distractor or negative samples):

$$\mathcal{L}_k = -\sum_i \left(\log \sigma(\mathbf{z}_{i+k}^T h_k(\mathbf{c}_i)) + \lambda \underset{\tilde{\mathbf{z}} \sim p_n}{\mathbb{E}} \left[\log \sigma(-\tilde{\mathbf{z}}^T h_k(\mathbf{c}_i)) \right] \right) \qquad (2)$$

σ is the sigmoid function, h_k an affine transformation, and $\sigma(\mathbf{z}_{i+k}^T h_k(\mathbf{c}_i))$ represents the probability that $\mathbf{z}_{i+k}$ is the true sample. p_n is the probability distribution from which the distractor samples are drawn, typically taken to be a uniform distribution. Training in this manner results in the networks g_{enc} and $g_{context}$ which can produce feature and context vectors $\mathbf{z}_i$ and $\mathbf{c}_i$ from new labelled data, which in turn can be used to train a neural network on a new supervised task.

2.4   Working with Streaming Data

Real value for fusion scientists can be had from receiving analysis and simulation results quickly, so that they can get near real-time feedback on machine performance and steer the experiment accordingly. Work is ongoing in creating the infrastructure to enable streaming data from fusion experiments to remote compute resources [13,36]. As part of this infrastructure, techniques for reducing the data size to send are being researched, for example compression or sending only areas of highest contrast. In general, whether researchers are local or remote, they derive enormous benefit from tools helping them deal with the deluge of data, such as algorithms for fast identification of known and unknown (anamolous/novel) events, and parameter estimation to systematically compare models to experimental data.

Anomaly/Novelty detection A number of anomaly detection algorithms are available for time-series data that could be applied [2]. Deep neural networks have increasingly been used for anomaly detection, due to their capacity and potential to learn the underlying data distribution [12]. A useful general method is to learn representations from unlabelled data, and then continually monitor new data to see if it deviates significantly from the common representations to determine if an anomaly/novelty is present. This can be accomplished using the latent space representations from the self-supervised learning algorithms in the previous section, or with related architectures such as autoencoders. A variant known as the Vector Quantised- Variational AutoEncoder (VQ-VAE) [42] has the typical encoder and decoder networks, but assumes discrete, categorical posterior and prior distributions. While often used for generative modeling (e.g. creating synthetic audio), the learned latent space distribution of the VQ-VAE is also very useful. The VQ-VAE has had some upgrades, dealing with using hierarchical representations (VQ-VAE-2, multiple encoders/decoders, at different scales) [45], and to more efficiently work with large embedding latent spaces (DVQ) [32]. Using such networks should improve the detection of anomalies/novelties through better representation of the previously observed data distribution. The application of these anomaly/novely techniques can be at the fusion machine (the edge), to reduce the data needed to stream over to remote compute centers, or at the remote analysis side, to quickly allow remote scientists to identify time points which merit further scrutiny. The outputs from these VQ-VAEs can be saved to a database to give scientists enhanced metadata within an automated logbook, with entries marking time points of interest. We can also gain information by combining these VQ-VAE predictions across diagnostics, to better understand these predictions. If only a single diagnostic predicts anomaly, this may be the result of instrument issues, and if predictions from multiple diagnostics were anomalous, this would give increased likelihood of a fundamentally different plasma operating regime (both cases useful information for scientists).

Parameter Estimation. Beyond anomaly/novelty detection for enabling scientists to quickly recognize time slices of importance, neural networks can also greatly aid in the problem of comparing experimental diagnostic data to analytical physics models, allowing efficient and speedy parameter estimation in a Bayesian manner. A fusion application example of parameter estimation is extracting model parameters for tearing mode stability, Δ' and ω_c, from the 2D ECEi data from KSTAR [14]. As an extension, Integrated Data Analysis (IDA) techniques [21] allow bringing together multiple diagnostics to estimate model parameters in a systematic way, producing with it uncertainty information. In fusion, often Bayesian inference for parameter estimation is done using the MCMC algorithm [29] or its variants like Hamiltonian MCMC, however this is slow and can often require hours for estimating a single set of parameters. This is not scalable given there are potentially millions of time slices in long-pulse experimental shots. There are multiple recent works using neural networks to speed up this Bayesian inference, using various Bayesian neural networks techniques [30], autoregressive normalizing flows [26], conditional VAE (CVAE) [25], and simply training a neural network on a large dataset generated from assumed priors [15]. The conditional VAE, for example, works by learning the model parameters used to generate synthetic data, and thereby being able to produce a distribution of model parameters based on new inputs. These networks enable fast analysis, which can be very beneficial for fusion scientists needing to quickly compare to established physics models. Consideration for inference time is not as stringent for real-time control settings, but need to be accomplished on the edge for determining streaming, or at remote compute sites in the time in between experimental discharges. This research, comparing experiment to models, is a step towards more sophisticated comparisons of experiment to simulation directly, when likelihoods are difficult to calculate [11,19]. These techniques would be very powerful for fusion energy, as simulations are often required to have a faithful model of the plasma dynamics.

3 Working with Simulations

Simulations form an important part of understanding experimental observations, especially as diagnostics can not measure everywhere or everything inside fusion devices. Simulations for fusion physics range from simple reduced models to large-scale simulations run on extreme-scale HPC machines such as Summit. Even with the advent of exascale computers, accelerating simulation kernels can be beneficial to enable richer, higher-fidelity physics potentially not possible otherwise. Neural networks are capable of learning high-dimensional, nonlinear surrogates of simulation kernels, and are increasingly being applied in simulation settings to do so [5,7,8,31,39].

An example of this is seen in work using an encoder-decoder neural network to accelerate the Fokker-Planck collision operator [27] in the massively parallel particle-in-cell code XGC [35]. In order to more accurately simulate the boundary area of tokamaks, XGC needs to simulate multiple impurity ion species. The collision operator scales quadratically with the number of ion species, and can quickly become a bottleneck if simulating multiple charge states of heavy impurities such as tungsten. The encoder-decoder network was trained to ingest kinetic particle distribution functions, and output the result of the collision operator [40]. Relative conservation error on the order 10^{-4} has been so far achieved in the model training, and still improving. The neural network approach also allows better convergence globally, in regions with very high collisionality which may not converge well with the current Picard iteration solver. The main advantage of course is the neural network approach reduces the time to solution by orders of magnitude. Combining the neural network approaches with traditional iterative solvers may provide a path for acceleration, with still achieving the low convergence error needed for accurate simulations.

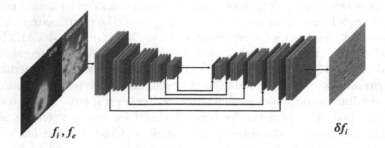

f_i, f_e δf_i

Fig. 6. Encoder-decoder neural network architecture for the integro-differential Fokker-Planck collision operator, which replaces the Picard iteration solver used in XGC

Deep learning has the potential to aid in various other facets of traditional HPC simulations beyond kernel acceleration, including physics-based reduced or surrogate models [28], and simulation-based inference [19]. This will greatly enhance the connection of experiment to simulation and theory, providing even more insights into fusion science.

4   Conclusion

Many powerful machine learning tools are available and being developed which can aid fusion scientists in understanding and working with complex diagnostic datasets. The critical problem of accurate disruption predictions was mentioned several times and is a key example. Current ML models and simulations still fall short of the needed disruption prediction accuracy, which is a critical and urgent need the tokamak fusion community faces as it prepares for ITER operation and beyond. The ML techniques discussed in this paper have the potential to achieve the needed accuracy to ensure safe operation of tokamaks such as ITER. These machine learning techniques can also be applied in a range of tasks, such as creating an "automated logbook" using a neural network to identify phenomena of interest, creating tremendous value in helping physicists sift through the data intelligently. Also, they can be utilized throughout areas of tokamak control, streaming of diagnostic data to remote compute centers for near real-time feedback, and to compare experiment to models.

References

1. NervanaSystems/distiller: Neural Network Distiller by Intel AI Lab: a Python package for neural network compression research. https://nervanasystems.github.io/distiller. https://github.com/NervanaSystems/distiller

2. Ahmad, S., Lavin, A., Purdy, S., Agha, Z.: Unsupervised real-time anomaly detection for streaming data. Neurocomputing **262**, 134–147 (2017). https://doi.org/10.1016/j.neucom.2017.04.070

3. Bai, S., Kolter, J.Z., Koltun, V.: An empirical evaluation of generic convolutional and recurrent networks for sequence modeling. arXiv e-prints arXiv:1803.01271 (2018). URL http://arxiv.org/abs/1803.01271

4. Bai, S., Kolter, J.Z., Koltun, V.: Deep equilibrium models. arXiv e-prints arXiv:1909.01377 (2019). http://arxiv.org/abs/1909.01377

5. Bar-Sinai, Y., Hoyer, S., Hickey, J., Brenner, M.P.: Learning data-driven discretizations for partial differential equations. Proc. Natl. Acad. Sci. U. S. A. **116**(31), 15344–15349 (2019). https://doi.org/10.1073/pnas.1814058116. http://www.ncbi.nlm.nih.gov/pubmed/31311866

6. Ben-Nun, T., Hoefler, T.: Demystifying parallel and distributed deep learning: an in-depth concurrency analysis. arXiv e-prints arXiv:1802.09941 (2018). URL http://arxiv.org/abs/1802.09941

7. Berg, J., Nyström, K.: A unified deep artificial neural network approach to partial differential equations in complex geometries. arXiv::1711.06464 (2017). https://doi.org/10.1016/j.neucom.2018.06.056. http://dx.doi.org/10.1016/j.neucom.2018.06.056

8. Beucler, T., Pritchard, M., Rasp, S., Gentine, P., Ott, J., Baldi, P.: Enforcing analytic constraints in neural-networks emulating physical systems. arXiv::1909.00912 (2019). URL http://arxiv.org/abs/1909.00912

9. Bishop, C.M., Roach, C.M., von Hellermann, M.G.: Automatic analysis of JET charge exchange spectra using neural networks. Plasma Phys. Control. Fusion **35**(6), 765–773 (1993). https://doi.org/10.1088/0741-3335/35/6/010. http://iopscience.iop.org/0741-3335/35/6/010

10. Boozer, A.H.: Theory of tokamak disruptions. Phys. Plasmas **19**(5), 058–101 (2012). https://doi.org/10.1063/1.3703327. http://aip.scitation.org/doi/10.1063/1.3703327

11. Brehmer, J., Mishra-Sharma, S., Hermans, J., Louppe, G., Cranmer, K.: Mining for dark matter substructure: inferring subhalo population properties from strong lenses with machine learning. Astrophys. J. **886**(1), 49 (2019). https://doi.org/10.3847/1538-4357/ab4c41. http://dx.doi.org/10.3847/1538-4357/ab4c41

12. Chalapathy, R., Chawla, S.: Deep learning for anomaly detection: a survey. arXiv e-prints arXiv:1901.03407 (2019). http://arxiv.org/abs/1901.03407

13. Choi, J.Y., et al.: Stream processing for near real-time scientific data analysis. In: 2016 New York Sci. Data Summit, pp. 1–8. IEEE (2016). https://doi.org/10.1109/NYSDS.2016.7747804. http://ieeexplore.ieee.org/document/7747804/

14. Choi, M.J., et al.: Improved accuracy in the estimation of the tearing mode stability parameters (Δ' and w c) using 2D ECEI data in KSTAR. Nucl. Fusion **54**(8), 083010 (2014). https://doi.org/10.1088/0029-5515/54/8/083010. http://stacks.iop.org/0029-5515/54/i=8/a=083010?key=crossref.88a6457ca7434ceddf6b6be95522512a

15. Chua, A.J., Vallisneri, M.: Learning bayesian posteriors with neural networks for gravitational-wave inference. Phys. Rev. Lett. **124**(4), 041–102 (2020). https://doi.org/10.1103/PhysRevLett.124.041102

16. Churchill, R., et al: A framework for international collaboration on ITER using large-scale data transfer to enable near real-time analysis. In: IAEA, Fusion Data Process, p. 2019. Tech. Meet, Validation, Anal (2019)

17. Churchill, R., Tobias, B., Zhu, Y.: The DIII-D Team: deep convolutional neural networks for multi-scale time-series classification and application to tokamak disruption prediction using raw, high temporal resolution diagnostic data. Phys. Plasmas **27** (2020)

18. Churchill, R.M.: The DIII-D Team: deep convolutional neural networks for multi-scale time-series classification and application to disruption prediction in fusion devices. Second Work. Mach. Learn. Phys. Sci. (NeurIPS 2019) (2019). http://arxiv.org/abs/1911.00149

19. Cranmer, K., Brehmer, J., Louppe, G.: The frontier of simulation-based inference. arXiv e-prints arXiv:1911.01429 (2019). http://arxiv.org/abs/1911.01429

20. Devlin, J., Chang, M.W., Lee, K., Toutanova, K.: BERT: pre-training of deep bidirectional transformers for language understanding. arXiv e-prints arXiv:1810.04805 (2018). http://arxiv.org/abs/1810.04805

21. Dinklage, A., Dreier, H., Fischer, R., Gori, S., Preuss, R., Toussaint, U.V.: Integrated data analysis for fusion: a Bayesian tutorial for fusion diagnosticians. In: AIP Conference Proceedings, vol. 988, pp. 471–480. AIP (2008). https://doi.org/10.1063/1.2905117. http://aip.scitation.org/doi/abs/10.1063/1.2905117

22. Dumoulin, V., et al: Feature-wise transformations. Distill. **3**(7), e11 (2018). https://doi.org/10.23915/distill.00011.   https://distill.pub/2018/feature-wise-transformations

23. Ferraro, N., Lyons, B., Kim, C., Liu, Y., Jardin, S.: 3D two-temperature magnetohydrodynamic modeling of fast thermal quenches due to injected impurities in tokamaks. Nucl. Fusion **59**(1), 016,001 (2019). https://doi.org/10.1088/1741-4326/AAE990

24. Ferreira, D.R.: Applications of deep learning to nuclear fusion research. arXiv e-prints arXiv:1811.00333 (2018). http://arxiv.org/abs/1811.00333

25. Gabbard, H., Messenger, C., Heng, I.S., Tonolini, F., Murray-Smith, R.: Bayesian parameter estimation using conditional variational autoencoders for gravitational-wave astronomy. arXiv e-prints arXiv:1909.06296 (2019). http://arxiv.org/abs/1909.06296

26. Green, S.R., Simpson, C., Gair, J.: Gravitational-wave parameter estimation with autoregressive neural network flows. arXiv e-prints arXiv:2002.07656 (2020). http://arxiv.org/abs/2002.07656

27. Hager, R., Yoon, E., Ku, S., D'Azevedo, E., Worley, P., Chang, C.: A fully non-linear multi-species Fokker-Landau collision operator for simulation of fusion plasma. J. Comput. Phys. **315**, 644–660 (2016). https://doi.org/10.1016/J.JCP.2016.03.064. https://www.sciencedirect.com/science/article/pii/S0021999116300298?via%3Dihub

28. Han, J., Ma, C., Ma, Z., Weinan, E.: Uniformly accurate machine learning-based hydrodynamic models for kinetic equations. Proc. Natl. Acad. Sci. **116**(44), 21983–21991 (2019). https://doi.org/10.1073/pnas.1909854116. http://www.pnas.org/lookup/doi/10.1073/pnas.1909854116

29. Hogg, D.W., Foreman-Mackey, D.: Data analysis recipes: using Markov Chain Monte Carlo. Astrophys. J. Suppl. Ser. **236**(1), 11 (2018). https://doi.org/10.3847/1538-4365/aab76e. http://stacks.iop.org/0067-0049/236/i=1/a=11?key=crossref.0a2b61f395b98c90f2d746466846903c

30. Hortua, H.J., Volpi, R., Marinelli, D., Malagò, L.: Parameters estimation for the cosmic microwave background with bayesian neural networks. arXiv e-prints arXiv:1911.08508 (2019). http://arxiv.org/abs/1911.08508

31. Hsieh, J.T., Zhao, S., Eismann, S., Mirabella, L., Ermon, S.: Learning neural PDE solvers with convergence guarantees. arXiv::1906.01200 (2019). http://arxiv.org/abs/1906.01200
32. Kaiser, Ł., et al.: Fast decoding in sequence models using discrete latent variables. In: 35th International Conference Machine Learning ICML 2018, vol. 6, pp. 3743–3752 (2018). http://arxiv.org/abs/1803.03382
33. Kates-Harbeck, J., Svyatkovskiy, A., Tang, W.: Predicting disruptive instabilities in controlled fusion plasmas through deep learning. Nature **568**(7753), 526–531 (2019). https://doi.org/10.1038/s41586-019-1116-4.http://www.nature.com/articles/s41586-019-1116-4
34. Kitaev, N., Kaiser, Ł., Levskaya, A.: Reformer: the efficient transformer. arXiv e-prints arXiv:2001.04451 (2020). http://arxiv.org/abs/2001.04451
35. Ku, S., Hager, R., Chang, C., Kwon, J., Parker, S.: A new hybrid-Lagrangian numerical scheme for gyrokinetic simulation of tokamak edge plasma. J. Comput. Phys. **315**, 467–475 (2016). https://doi.org/10.1016/j.jcp.2016.03.062. http://linkinghub.elsevier.com/retrieve/pii/S0021999116300274
36. Kube, R., Churchill, R., Choi, J.Y., Wang, R., Klasky, S., Chang, C.S.: Leading magnetic fusion energy science into the big-and-fast data lane. In: Proceedings 19th Python Science Conference (2020). https://conference.scipy.org/proceedings/
37. LeCun, Y., Bengio, Y., Hinton, G.: Deep learning. Nature **521**(7553), 436–444 (2015). https://doi.org/10.1038/nature14539. http://www.nature.com/articles/nature14539
38. McCandlish, S., et al.: An empirical model of large-batch training. arXiv e-prints arXiv:1812.06162 (2018). https://arxiv.org/pdf/1812.06162.pdf
39. Meneghini, O., et al.: Self-consistent core-pedestal transport simulations with neural network accelerated models. Nucl. Fusion **57**(8), 086,034 (2017). https://doi.org/10.1088/1741-4326/aa7776. http://stacks.iop.org/0029-5515/57/i=8/a=086034?key=crossref.bd8ca2032ac2046a3a270c0b80762b50
40. Miller, M.A., Churchill, R.M., Chang, C.S., Hager, R.: Encoder-decoder neural network for solving the nonlinear Fokker-Planck-Landau collision operator in XGC. In: Workshop Integr. Deep Neural Model. Differ. Equations (ICLR 2020) (2020)
41. van den Oord, A., Li, Y., Vinyals, O.: Representation learning with contrastive predictive coding. arXiv (2018). http://arxiv.org/abs/1807.03748
42. van den Oord, A., Vinyals, O., Kavukcuoglu, K.: Neural discrete representation learning. Adv. Neural Inf. Process. Syst. 2017-Decem, 6307–6316 (2017). http://arxiv.org/abs/1711.00937
43. Perez, E., Strub, F., De Vries, H., Dumoulin, V., Courville, A.: FiLM: visual reasoning with a general conditioning layer. In: 32nd AAAI Conference Artificial Intelligence AAAI 2018, pp. 3942–3951. AAAI press (2018)
44. Rajbhandari, S., Rasley, J., Ruwase, O., He, Y.: ZeRO: memory optimization towards training a trillion parameter models. arXiv e-prints arXiv:11910.02054 (2019). http://arxiv.org/abs/1910.02054
45. Razavi, A., van den Oord, A., Vinyals, O.: Generating diverse high-fidelity images with VQ-VAE-2. arXiv e-prints arXiv:1906.00446 (2019). http://arxiv.org/abs/1906.00446
46. Rea, C., Granetz, R.S.: Exploratory machine learning studies for disruption prediction using large databases on DIII-D. Fusion Sci. Technol. pp. 1–12 (2018). https://doi.org/10.1080/15361055.2017.1407206. https://www.tandfonline.com/doi/full/10.1080/15361055.2017.1407206
47. Ruder, S.: Transfer Learning - Machine Learning's Next Frontier (2017). http://ruder.io/transfer-learning/

48. Schneider, S., Baevski, A., Collobert, R., Auli, M.: wav2vec: unsupervised pre-training for speech recognition. arXiv e-prints arXiv:1904.05862 (2019). http://arxiv.org/abs/1904.05862

49. Standley, T., Zamir, A.R., Chen, D., Guibas, L., Malik, J., Savarese, S.: Which tasks should be learned together in multi-task learning? arXiv e-prints arXiv:1905.07553 (2019). http://arxiv.org/abs/1905.07553

50. Subcommittee, F.I.: FESAC ISOFS subcommittee final report. Technical report, FES (2002). https://www.cs.odu.edu/~keyes/scales/reports/fsp_2002b.pdf

51. Vaswani, A., et al: Attention is all you need. arXiv e-prints arXiv:1706.03762 (2017). http://arxiv.org/abs/1706.03762

52. Vega, J., et al.: Results of the JET real-time disruption predictor in the ITER-like wall campaigns. Fusion Eng. Des. **88**(6–8), 1228–1231 (2013). https://doi.org/10.1016/J.FUSENGDES.2013.03.003. https://www.sciencedirect.com/science/article/pii/S0920379613002974?via%3Dihub

53. de Vries, P.C., et al.: Requirements for triggering the ITER disruption mitigation system. Fusion Sci. Technol. **69**(2), 471–484 (2016). https://doi.org/10.13182/FST15-176. https://www.tandfonline.com/doi/full/10.13182/FST15-176

54. Wallace, E.: Eric Wallace on Twitter (2020). https://twitter.com/Eric_Wallace_/status/1235907651193548801

55. Wang, J., Ma, Y., Zhang, L., Gao, R.X.: Deep learning for smart manufacturing: methods and applications. J. Manuf. Syst. **48**, 144–156 (2018). https://doi.org/10.1016/J.JMSY.2018.01.003. https://www.sciencedirect.com/science/article/pii/S0278612518300037

56. Weng, L.: Self-supervised representation learning (2018). https://lilianweng.github.io/lil-log/2019/11/10/self-supervised-learning.html

57. Windsor, C., et al.: A cross-tokamak neural network disruption predictor for the JET and ASDEX Upgrade tokamaks. Nucl. Fusion 45(5), 337–350 (2005). https://doi.org/10.1088/0029-5515/45/5/004. http://stacks.iop.org/0029-5515/45/i=5/a=004?key=crossref.170e4cfeab7836eaf142634f3e851578

Data Federation Challenges in Remote Near-Real-Time Fusion Experiment Data Processing

Jong Choi[1(✉)], Ruonan Wang[1], R. Michael Churchill[2], Ralph Kube[2],
Minjun Choi[4], Jinseop Park[4], Jeremy Logan[1], Kshitij Mehta[1],
Greg Eisenhauer[3], Norbert Podhorszki[1], Matthew Wolf[1], C. S. Chang[2],
and Scott Klasky[1]

[1] Oak Ridge National Laboratory, Oak Ridge, TN 37830, USA
choij@ornl.gov
[2] Princeton Plasma Physics Laboratory, Princeton, NJ 08536, USA
[3] Georgia Institute of Technology, Atlanta, GA 30332, USA
[4] National Fusion Research Institute, Daejeon, South Korea

Abstract. Fusion energy experiments and simulations provide critical information needed to plan future fusion reactors. As next-generation devices like ITER move toward long-pulse experiments, analyses, including AI and ML, should be performed in a wide range of time and computing constraints, from near-real-time constraints, between-shot analysis, and to campaign-wide long-term analysis. However, the data volume, velocity, and variety make it extremely challenging for analyses using only local computational resources. Researchers need the ability to compose and execute workflows spanning edge resources to large-scale high-performance computing facilities.

We present *Delta*, a system to address data analysis challenges, including AI/ML, in fusion science, by leveraging the ADIOS I/O library and middleware, to support executing science workflows over the wide area network for near-real-time streaming. We discuss the data federation challenges in performing remote workflows, focusing on on-going research work in (1) managing, reducing, and streaming data to minimize I/O and data movement overheads, (2) decompressing and reorganizing data for analysis, and (3) executing workflows for automated data analysis. We introduce examples for deep-learning based data analysis for the fusion domain and demonstrate how we use *Delta* to construct end-to-end workflows for a fusion device in Korea, connecting a remote DOE facility in

J. Choi et al.—Contributed Equally.
This manuscript has been co-authored by UT-Battelle, LLC, under contract DE-AC05-00OR22725 with the US Department of Energy (DOE). The US government retains and the publisher, by accepting the article for publication, acknowledges that the US government retains a nonexclusive, paid-up, irrevocable, worldwide license to publish or reproduce the published form of this manuscript, or allow others to do so, for US government purposes. DOE will provide public access to these results of federally sponsored research in accordance with the DOE Public Access Plan (http://energy.gov/downloads/doe-public-access-plan).

J. Nichols et al. (Eds.): SMC 2020, CCIS 1315, pp. 285–299, 2020.
https://doi.org/10.1007/978-3-030-63393-6_19

the USA. The capability demonstrated by this project is the basis for improving the state of the art for near-real-time data federation amongst remote facilities.

Keywords: Data federation · Fusion · Data streams · Remote data analysis

1 Introduction

As scientific experiments have gotten bigger and complex, scientists have had to rely more on concurrent, online, high-performance computing resources to analyze, reduce, and/or visualize the data streams. Such experiments may depend on hundreds or thousands of high-resolution, high-speed sensors to carefully collect the required data. Even further, there has emerged a new class of federated experiments that bring this experimental data together with large-scale simulation and the associated analysis capabilities to gain fast and accurate understanding of complex phenomena. However, the logical, time-scale, and physical discrepancies between the experiment site and high-computing facilities require scientists to explicitly spend time to manage their data, resources, and execution patterns in the distributed setting, while still trying to find time to do their science.

Plasma science, and fusion energy research in particular, have already made the transition into exploring these sorts of federated and hybrid experimental/computational environments. As next generation devices like ITER [17] move toward long-pulse experiments, not only will the amount of data increase, but there will also be an intense focus on this federation of experimental and simulation results. In particular, ITER has announced the intention that no run should occur on the physical facility without first having a full set of simulated results to compare against. Any deviations from predicted plasma behavior should be monitored and such monitoring should trigger additional analysis/simulation to identify causes of deviations. If significant deviations can be identified and assessed rapidly during an experiment, then such information can contribute to the optimization of the experimental plan and ultimately contribute to the timely realization of the ITER mission.

In this context, the workflows needed for timely and autonomous delivery of the analytics become extremely important. There are a host of new, next-generation compute-intensive AI and ML analyses that will need to be run over a wide range of time (e.g., near-real-time, between-shot) and computing (e.g., edge device, GPU accelerator) constraints. However, the data volume, velocity, and variety make it extremely challenging for AI/ML analysis using only local computational resources. Therefore, researchers need the ability to compose and execute workflows spanning edge resources to large-scale high performance computing facilities.

Currently, constructing such a capability is labor-intensive and distracting from the core science investigation. We represent a team of computer science and fusion scientists who are experiencing such data federation challenges. In our research and development of software tools to support current and future workflows aimed at next-generation devices such as ITER, we have identified what we view as core challenges and the capabilities that are needed to address them. We present a framework for aDaptive rEaL Time Analysis, *Delta* for short, as our progress that addresses such data federation challenges for remote fusion experiment analysis. Specifically, we design *Delta* to provide services and runtime support for the following core capabilities: 1) Temporal analysis, 2) Feature detection, 3) Data reduction/compression, and 4) Data movement and access. All of these are identified as a critical, generic tasks needed to support federated fusion data analysis.

This infrastructure for *Delta* is constructed using our Adaptable I/O System (ADIOS) [12] as a backbone, which offers a high-performance data management solution for HPC storage as well as an online data management based on a publish/subscribe abstraction [8,13]. We take advantage of ADIOS' publish/subscribe interface in which users can federate data producers (sensors or simulations) and consumers (analysis or visualization application).

In this paper, our contribution is in identifying these core capabilities and in offering experimental validation of this approach for real scientific investigations. In Sect. 2, we discuss two fusion experiments and their data, which motivate our research. One of which is a multi-national collaboration between the KSTAR facility in South Korea, researchers at Princeton Plasma Physics Laboratory, and contributors from Oak Ridge National Laboratory as well as the NERSC Computing Center. In Sect. 3, we demonstrate how we use *Delta* to attempt to support the temporal and spatial evolution of the plasma within the device during long-pulse experiments to simulated results and online analytic pipelines.

An additional concern that we address in our *Delta* experiments has to do with the introduction of AI/ML methods into the federated computing pipeline. In many ways, AI/ML methods represent a fourth pillar to the traditional approaches to science of experiment, theory, and simulation. As such, we found that there were unique constraints and considerations that needed to be respected in order to fully integrate AI/ML methods into *Delta*. Although utilizing a previously-trained model may not be very different from other analytics methods, an ML algorithm we use in this paper (the variational auto-encoder, VAE), which allows for efficient compression and generation of surrogate data representations, combines training and model usage in novel ways. The experience of integrating these features into the capability matrix of *Delta* has offered lessons that we believe can be applicable to other areas of science as well. Some of these connections will be discussed in Sect. 4.

1.1 Related Work

We briefly discuss existing work prior to *Delta* in the field of remote data federation and AI/ML applications for data streams.

Remote Data Federation: Data federation for stream data processing over a wide-area network has been an active research area for the last decades. In our previous work, WASP [5], we explored our initial research on how to use data streams to remotely federate data from KSTAR and fusion simulation with the previous ADIOS version. In this paper, we extend our work with new data transport engines, called DataMan and SST, by leveraging a newer version of ADIOS and focus on demonstrating data federation between KSTAR in Korea and one of DOE HPC sites, NERSC, in the USA.

Amazon Lambda [2] and Apache OpenWhisk [1] utilizes the cloud platform to ingest data collected from distributed sensors or the internet at scale. Our work focus more on performing mission-critical analysis for science, targeted toward near-real-time support.

While Codor [20] and Globus [7] focused on utilizing multi-institute computing resources, integrating remote computing sites and data facilities has been a new trend as the big data challenge emerges. More recently, Cray announced the next interconnect network, Slingshot [3], which will include the capability to connect remote third-party data centers with HPC centers.

AI/ML Applications for Streams: As data volume grows at an exceeding rate, several floating-point lossy data compressors, such as ZFP [11], SZ [6], and MGARD [4], have been actively researched and applied in many science applications. Researchers start looking at deep learning methods for data compression as well. While most lossy compression methods are broadly based on numerical solutions for regression, interpolation, and decompositions, data compression with deep learning is mostly based on developing a generative process for the data provided by users. A family of generative deep learning models, such as Variational Autoencoders (VAE) and Generative Adversarial Network (GAN), has been developed to reconstruct missing parts of an image or compress image data. PixelRNN [16], WaveNet [15], and realtime adaptive compression [19] are some of the examples. In our paper we explore vector quantization based VAE, VQ-VAE [14], for our fusion data compression.

2   Remote Fusion Experiment

ITER [17] is the largest, next-generation international experimental fusion reactor currently being built in France, aiming to begin operation with first plasma in December 2025. ITER will make a huge impact on how fusion scientists process and federate experimental data for online analysis by integrating their workflow using local and remote compute resources. In this section, we describe the current fusion experiments and data challenges by using the cases of two current machines, KSTAR and NSTX-U, to give an overview of fusion data challenges.

2.1   KSTAR Fusion Experiment and Workflows

The Korea Superconducting Tokamak Advanced Research (KSTAR) [10] is a medium-sized tokamak (or a fusion reactor). This fusion device confines a plasma whose core temperature may exceed 50 million degrees for up to 5 min. Achieving such long plasma confinement times with available technology requires the use of superconducting magnet coils and KSTAR is one of only a hand full superconducting tokamaks ever built. Operating with such uniquely long pulses, KSTAR data is a relevant target to develop federated data analysis systems for.

Numerous scientific diagnostics interrogate the plasma and its supporting machinery in plasma discharges and generate a variety of data streams. For plasma diagnostics, designed to investigate physical processes occurring in the fusion plasma, read-outs of high-dimensional data on a microsecond time-scale is required. Electron Cyclotron Emission Imaging (ECEI) diagnostics for example measure the intensity of emissions by free electrons in the plasma. This information allows to recover fluctuations of the electrons temperature, which in turn gives physicists important information on the macro- and micro-scale dynamics of the confined fusion plasma. Modern ECEI systems, as the one installed in KSTAR, measure the emission intensity using hundreds of spatial channels with Megahertz sampling rates. Generating a data stream of about 5 GByte per second, this diagnostic produces a fast, high-dimensional data stream that makes it challenging to analyze in near real-time.

A common analysis workflow for ECEI time series data is spectral analysis routines which compare ECEI channel pair combinations. Since short-time Fourier transformations are used for this workflow, the time series data for this workflow can be divided in millisecond long chunks. Furthermore all channel pair combinations can be treated separate from one another. That is, the input data for this algorithm consists of numerous relatively small data chunks which can all be analyzed independent from one another. Such workflows are typically performed manually by fusion scientists in a batch-wise fashion some time after a given plasma shot. While this workflow involves the calculation of standard spectral quantities, performing it on the large amount of available ECEI data render it a substantial task.

We envision federated data analysis systems that perform such a prototypical workflow with little configuration. The system should allow to offload the data analysis to HPC systems that can handle fast, high-dimensional incoming data stream and perform the analysis in near real-time to facilitate decision making.

2.2 NSTX-U Fusion Experiment and Workflows

National Spherical Torus Experiment - Upgrade (NSTX-U), a magnetic fusion device that is operated by the Princeton Plasma Physics Laboratory (PPPL), provides another examplary analysis workflow that can be enhanced using federated compute resources.

One of the diagnostics installed in NSTX-U is the so-called gas-puff imaging (GPI) system. This diagnostic measures light emissions from the edge of the confined plasma using a fast framing 2d camera that captures 80-by-64 pixel frames at a rate of about 400,000 frames per second. A particularly interesting phenomena that can be studied by GPI is the motion of plasma filaments with excess pressure that transport a significant amount of hot plasma towards the main chamber walls. As such they may affect confinement performance and erode material surfaces. When observed in the two-dimensional view of the GPI, these filaments present their circular cross-section, usually referred to as blobs.

To better understand this blobby transport, physicists study statistics of the blobs observed in the plasma discharges, including their cross-field sizes, amplitudes and velocities. All of these are readily calculated from GPI data. Modern algorithms rely either on manually selected filters or use machine learning algorithms to detect blobs in single frames and compile statistics on their extent and their dynamics.

Now NSTX-U plasma discharges last only a few seconds and the GPI diagnostic only collects data for a fraction of that time, typically about 500 MBytes per discharge. Blob detection can be performed in individual frames and is therefore parallelizable in a similar way as the ECEI workflow. To compile the motion of plasma blobs in a given discharge however, the positions of blobs in the entire sequence of images is required. In other words, the data needs to be made available in full and in order. This, together with the fact that we are using a neural network based architecture to detect blobs motivates us to treat this workflow as a machine learning toy model for the context of federated data analysis.

The requirements posed by these two workflows allow us to derive capabilities we want from a federated workflow system. While this list should not be seen as exhaustive, the workflows described above capture a broad range of requirements for other workflows.

Capabilities to drive future federated fusion experiments

- Reliably transfer large volumes of data with high velocity from data production site to HPC resources with minimum overhead (e.g., memory-to-memory)
- Facilitate execution of data analysis routines with as few as possible changes to existing codes
- Adaptively adjust data analysis and compression techniques in real-time to be reactive to analysis results and network performance

---

3   *Delta*: Supporting Federated Data Today

We present the *Delta* framework as a concrete example on how federated data analysis workflows may be implemented and facilitated with ADIOS. We also discuss how recent AI/ML methods can be incorporated in such a framework.

3.1   ECEI Analysis with *Delta*

Delta is a python framework that facilitates federated data analysis workflows. In particular, it is used to analyze data from the KSTAR ECEI diagnostic in near real-time by using remote high-performance computing resources at Cori, NERSC. While we aim to facilitate general federated data analysis workflows with *Delta* in the future, it has been designed around the task to perform a suite of spectral analysis on time-series of imaging data from KSTAR's ECEI diagnostic. We choose this task because it can be seen as a prototype workflow for analysis of other diagnostic data, such as probes or magnetic flux sensors, and because the ECEI diagnostic produces a high-velocity data stream.

Figure 1 illustrates the network topology that *Delta* targets, KSTAR and NERSC as the experimental and compute site and as well as an additional storage backend that feeds live-streams of analyzed data into visualizers. As a framework for distributed computing, *Delta* is comprised of multiple components that connect the individual sites with one another. At KSTAR, a `generator` sources and streams sequential tranches of ECEI data to NERSC. This stream is received by a `middleman` running on the NERSC Data Transfer Node (DTN) and forwarded to a `processor` on Cori. This processor uses a `dispatcher`, a thread for asynchronous I/O, and uses MPI to execute a user-defined suite of spectral analysis on compute nodes. Analyzed data is stored in a storage backend, such as a database. Data visualizers can then ingest this data and make it available to researchers in near real-time.

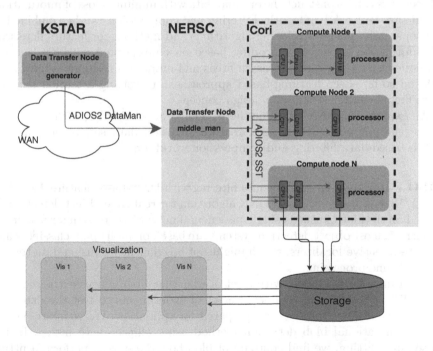

Fig. 1. Where does *Delta* live? *Delta* consists of multiple distributed components (generator, middleman, and processor) and ADIOS provides remote data federation. More details can be found in [9].

Delta consists of multiple distributed components and more comprehensive discussion of achieved performance on the architecture can be found in [9].

The ECEI workflow consists of calculating spectral quantities, the cross-phase, cross-correlations, coherence and cross-power for $18,336$ unique channel pair combinations from the 192 channels of the diagnostic on 500 time chunks consisting of $10,000$ data points per channel. Launching this analysis on Cori, where the processer runs on 32 compute nodes, *Delta* performs the ECEI workflow in $339 \, s$. To set this runtime in context, performing this workflow using a naive single-core implementation takes multiple hours.

3.2 Adaptable Data Transfers Using Data Compression and Filtering

One of the challenges in remote data federation for near real-time processing is how to reduce the amount of data to transfer over a wide-area network. Data filtering and compression are two of the most common practices for remote processing. If one can accurately detect specific features of interest in the data stream, we can filter out unnecessary parts and send only the necessary data for remote processing. With lossy compression, if one can compress data for sending and receivers can reconstruct the original data with minimum loss of information, we can save network bandwidth. Filtering and compression can be combined or used separately. While developing algorithms and methods for feature detection and information preserving encoding based on conventional machine learning techniques have been active research areas and numerous techniques have been deployed so far, deep learning-based approaches are getting attention recently for its flexible and customizable design concept.

We explore two DNN-based methods, YOLO and VQ-VAE, with the NSTX (before the upgrade) GPI images, real-world fusion data set, to demonstrate AI/ML-based data filtering and compression workflows.

YOLO Filtering. We explore data filtering with DNN-based feature detection. YOLO [18] is a state-of-the-art DNN algorithm for real-time object detection. It is based on the idea of using a single-pass neural network regression for detection. In contrast, most object detection systems are based on multi-pass classifiers and compute-intensive localizers, which might not be efficient for fusion data toward near real-time processing.

We train a YOLO model with a set of examplar blob images extracted from the NSTX GPI data and conducted a set of experiments to test the detection performance against the data set prepared for validation. We compare YOLO with a conventional blob detection method using ellipse curve fitting. In the ellipse curve fitting, we find contours of blob boundaries and perform a fitting to find ellipse parameters to fit each contour into an ellipse shape. In contrast, YOLO divides the whole region into multiple subblocks and performs a one-pass regression to decide whether a chunk contains an object of interest, which is a blob in our case. Figure 2 demonstrate how YOLO can detect blobs compared with ellipse fitting based blob detection. We extend our test to check whether the model we built can be used for the out-of-sample data. Table 1 shows various accuracy measurements for four different data sets we prepared. Except for Set A, which is the in-sample data, Set B-D are out-of-sample data. The performance result shows that YOLO detection performance remained closely similar even for the out-of-sample datasets.

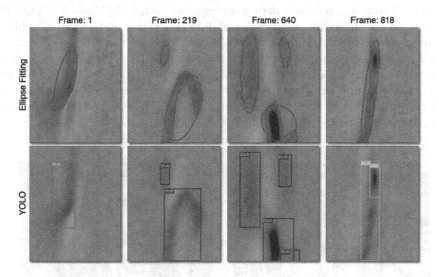

Fig. 2. Blob detection demonstrated with NSTX GPI images, comparing conventional ellipse fitting with DNN-based YOLO.

Table 1. Performance of YOLO with NSTX GPI data set.

	Recall (%)	Precision (%)	Accuracy (%)
Set A	96.8	93.2	95.2
Set B	96.0	90.8	97.2
Set C	93.7	87.8	96.6
Set D	91.7	80.8	98.9

VAE Compression. Next, we explore how we can use DNN to build a generative model that can efficiently find a compressed representation of data from which users can reconstruct the data. We use VQ-VAE [14], a variant of Variational autoencoder (VAE) families, as a reduced representation finder. While conventional VAEs focusing on finding Gaussian distribution as a latent representation, VQ-VAE employs vector quantification to capture a more discrete nature of features in the data.

The core of the VQ-VAE algorithm is to find an underlying latent representation of encoding data, which can be decoded with a minimum loss of information. In the context of data compression, the latent representation can be considered as a reduced form of data. By sending this reduced representation, a receiver can reconstruct the original data with a certain degree of information loss. Compared with conventional lossy data compressions, such as ZFP and SZ, VQ-VAE is generative as it recovers the process of data generation and is customizable as the network architectures and parameters are tuned for the user's data set.

Figure 3 demonstrate how VQ-VAE can learn NSTX GPI images and reconstruct. The errors measured by Root Mean Square Error (RMSE) show about 22% errors without any treatment. With a noise filter applied, we further lowered the errors around 12%. In this experiment, we achieved 8x data compression ratio. We leave more extensive comparison studies for the next work.

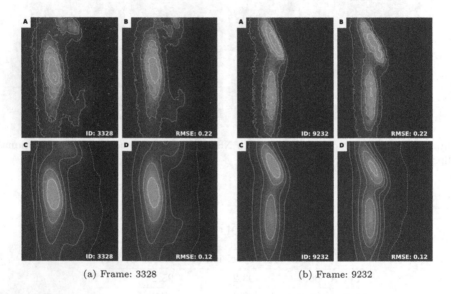

(a) Frame: 3328   (b) Frame: 9232

Fig. 3. Demonstration of VQ-VAE reconstruction with NSTX GPI images. (A) original NSTX GPI image, (B) reconstructed image by VQ-VAE, (C) original image with Gaussian denoising treatment, and (D) reconstructed VQ-VAE image followed by Gaussian denoising. Frame numbers and Root Mean Square Error (RMSE) metrics are shown on the bottom-right corner.

3.3   Remote Data Federation Services with ADIOS

ADIOS [12] is an HPC I/O library designed to provide I/O services to users, such as data management, transport, and transforms. We leverage ADIOS to build our framework, *Delta*. ADIOS supports remote data federation with a convenient and unified data interface that allows scientists to handle data and its metadata both as files and data streams.

To transport data as streams, ADIOS provides a plug-in approach; ADIOS provides multiple engines users can choose depending on the need. We use two main ADIOS engines, called SST and DataMan, which can be used for a wide-area network transport. We briefly introduce SST and DataMan engine used in this paper and provide experiment results to demonstrate how we use ADIOS for remote analysis.

Scalable Staging Transport (SST).   SST is a flexible data transport engine in ADIOS. It is designed to utilize a wide range of network protocols, such as RDMA, TCP, and UDP, widely used for both high-performance HPC networks and long-haul wide-area network connections. This flexibility is an important feature, especially for remote data processing. With SST, users can switch network protocols easily to adapt to different network environments.

On the other hand, data flow control is another important aspect in data stream processing. It is common the speed of data generation and processing is different. Without caching or buffering, either the generator or the receiver needs to wait simply by wasting valuable CPU cycles and resources. SST provides a buffering policy for users to control, such as changing buffer size or applying rules when a buffer is full or not.

DataMan.   While SST is an engine for the best flexibility, DataMan is another ADIOS engine mainly focusing on performant data transport over a wide area network. DataMan is specifically optimized for long-distance low-latency data movement, leveraging the ZeroMQ library for asynchronous messaging.

Experiments.   First, we measure the bandwidths between KSTAR and NERSC. We have two connection points in NERSC. We can connect to NERSC through the NERSC DTNs, a set of dedicated nodes for wide-area data transfer. NERSC also allows users to connect directly to Cori compute nodes as an experimental feature. Figure 4 shows the bandwidths, measured by iperf3, a) between KSTAR and NERSC DTN and b) between KSTAR and NERSC Cori compute node, with a varying number of parallel streams, up to 8.

In both cases, we observed variances in the throughput between KSTAR and NERSC due to the congestion. Also, there are large differences in throughput for sending from Korea to NERSC DTN or directly to Cori compute nodes. It implies we need a transport mechanism adaptively adjust throughput developing on the dynamic network conditions. DataMan is currently implemented adaptive performance, and further improvement is under development.

In Fig. 5, we performed the ECEI workflow (Fig. 1) with 2 different scenarios; (a) 2-node scenario where we send ECEI data from KSTAR directly to Cori compute node. We use DataMan between KSTAR and Cori, and (b) 3-node scenario where we send ECEI data to a middle man running on a NERSC

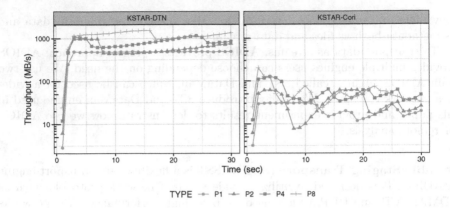

Fig. 4. Network performance between KSTAR and NERSC DTN nodes (left) and between KSTAR and Cori compute node (right), measured by iperf3 with up to 8 parallel streams. The Y axis (throughput) is log scaled.

DTN node, which receives data from KSTAR and concurrently forwards to the ECEI analysis processes running on Cori compute nodes. We use DataMan for KSTAR-NERSC DTN over wide area network and SST between NERSC DTN and Cori compute node communication. Although we deployed an extra process (middleman) in our 3-node scenarios, we were able to finish ECEI analysis task earlier than using 2-node scenario. ADIOS's transport engine enabled us to achieve flexible workflow composition and execution.

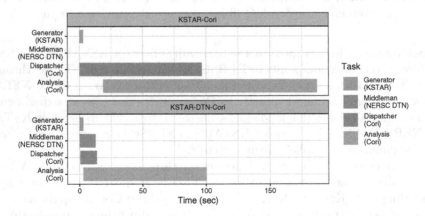

Fig. 5. Timelines of tasks performed in two cases; (a) 2-node scenario (KSTAR-Cori) and (b) 3-node scenario (KSTAR-DTN-Cori). We used ADIOS DataMan engine for both KSTAR-Cori and KSTAR-DTN transport. ADIOS SST engine was used intra NERSC transportation, DTN-Cori.

4   Toward Plasma Science of the Future

We have explored how we can support the next-generation data analysis challenges in fusion science, based on the real-world data and workflows obtained through our collaboration with KSTAR and NSTX-U, which we believe can be applicable to the upcoming ITER challenges. We summarize key capabilities identified for the success of the future fusion analysis workflow.

First, an adaptive workflow system with intelligence is required. This will allow the system to adjust to the state of the network and/or receiver agent responsiveness, by for example sending coarser or reduced data when the system lacks the network fidelity to accomplish the streaming, and returning to complete full dataset transfers when possible. With the current ECEI workflow with *Delta*, we found optimal network transfer could result in sent data chunks lost if the receiver agent was overwhelmed and not able to keep pace. Adaptivity built into the framework will allow intelligent, automated throttling (through data coarsening, or delayed network transfer) depending on the data stream and user needs, which for some streams will require complete datasets (such as the GPI workflow), and for others can accept data loss (such as the ECEI workflow).

Second, extending on the concept of adaptivity for data streaming, a flexible yet tightly integrated workflow execution will be enormously beneficial in terms of data monitoring and workflow automation. This enables reactive workflow components, where additional, more expensive higher-tiered analyses can be spun up based on an anomaly/novelty detected in lower-tiered analysis on data streams. For example, a sudden change in the correlation between certain ECEI channel pairs could indicate the presence of magnetohydrodynamics (MHD) mode activity, which could automatically trigger simulations into the current MHD stability limits based on magnetic and kinetic plasma profiles diagnostics. Instead of waiting for the scientist to manually comb through the data and run the simulations themselves, the results would be present and the scientists notified to draw their attention to such time points of interest.

Third, incorporating next-generation analysis, including additional AI/ML, which can take advantage of hardware-based acceleration can be a game-changer for how fusion scientists analyze their experiments. Automating and accelerating the tasks fusion scientists must perform in time for more immediate feedback will allow scientists to extract richer insights from their experimental and simulation data. Interfacing humans and AI/ML in this way can be greatly beneficial, but must be researched and explored in the context of fusion science, to determine best practices and needs, for example if techniques found in continual learning are needed to update machine learning models as new tasks and data distributions present themselves.

5   Conclusion

Fusion experiments pose unique data federation challenges. Not only the volume, velocity, variety of data the fusion experiments produce, but also the time constraint for between-shot or near-real-time analysis makes performing data analysis workflows challenging. In addition, utilizing remote high-performance computing resources is being explored to perform compute-intensive, state-of-the-art analysis at scale and/or to couple with impromptu simulation runs on an HPC machine for making timely decisions for the next shot. Indeed, constructing and executing such analysis pipelines combined with multiple remote sources is challenging and efficient data federation for remote data processing is necessary.

We present *Delta* as a framework to facilitate fusion data analysis using remote computing resources, taking advantage of ADIOS' publish/subscribe interface where users can federate data producers (sensors or simulations) and consumers (analysis or visualization application) regardless of their locations. By using real-world fusion data and analysis workflows from KSTAR and NSTX-U as a use case, we demonstrate how we use *Delta* and ADIOS for real-world fusion analysis workflows to federate experiment data and remote resources over wide area networks and introduce recent AI/ML methods to be applicable for fusion data streams.

Building on this framework, and the ideas and principles underlying it can provide fusion scientists extended remote computing capabilities to accelerate their current workflows, and make possible workflows not currently employed or even imagined today. AI/ML can play a key enabling role in this regard, offering the promise of faster, better analysis to provide scientists deeper insights and guidance.

Acknowledgement. This research was supported by the Department of Energy's SciDAC RAPIDS Institute and the HBPS SciDAC Partnership, as well as the Exascale Computing Project (17-SC-20-SC), a collaborative effort of U.S. Department of Energy Office of Science and the National Nuclear Security Administration. This material is based upon work supported by the U.S. Department of Energy, Office of Science, Office of Fusion Energy Sciences, under AC02-09CH11466. This research used resources of the Argonne and Oak Ridge Leadership Computing Facilities, DOE Office of Science User Facilities supported under Contracts DE-AC02-06CH11357 and DE-AC05-00OR22725, respectively, as well as the National Energy Research Scientific Computing Center (NERSC), a U.S. Department of Energy Office of Science User Facility operated under Contract No. DE-AC02-05CH11231. The research at KSTAR was conducted as part of KSTAR R&D Program of National Fusion Research Institute of Korea (EN2001-11).

References

1. Apache OpenWhisk: Open source serverless cloud platform. https://openwhisk.apache.org/
2. AWS Lambda - serverless compute - Amazon Web Services. https://aws.amazon.com/lambda/
3. Slingshot: The interconnect for the exascale era. Technical report, Cray Inc. (2019)
4. Ainsworth, M., Tugluk, O., Whitney, B., Klasky, S.: MGARD: a multilevel technique for compression of floating-point data. In: DRBSD-2 Workshop at Supercomputing (2017)

5. Choi, J.Y., et al.: Stream processing for near real-time scientific data analysis. In: 2016 New York Scientific Data Summit (NYSDS), pp. 1–8. IEEE (2016)
6. Di, S., Cappello, F.: Fast error-bounded lossy HPC data compression with SZ. In: 2016 IEEE International Parallel and Distributed Processing Symposium (IPDPS), pp. 730–739. IEEE (2016)
7. Foster, I., Kesselman, C.: Globus: a metacomputing infrastructure toolkit. Int. J. Supercomput. Appl. High Perform. Comput. **11**(2), 115–128 (1997)
8. Klasky, S., et al.: A view from ORNL: scientific data research opportunities in the big data age. In: 2018 IEEE 38th International Conference on Distributed Computing Systems (ICDCS), pp. 1357–1368 (2018). https://doi.org/10.1109/ICDCS.2018.00136
9. Kube, R., et al.: Leading magnetic fusion energy science into the big-and-fast data lane (2020). https://doi.org/10.25080/issn.2575-9752
10. Lee, G., et al.: Design and construction of the KSTAR tokamak. Nucl. Fusion **41**(10), 1515 (2001)
11. Lindstrom, P., Isenburg, M.: Fast and efficient compression of floating-point data. IEEE Trans. Vis. Comput. Graph. **12**(5), 1245–1250 (2006)
12. Liu, Q., et al.: Hello ADIOS: the challenges and lessons of developing leadership class I/O frameworks. Concurr. Comput. Pract. Exp. **26**(7), 1453–1473 (2014)
13. Logan, J., et al.: Extending the publish/subscribe abstraction for high-performance I/O and data management at extreme scale. Data Eng. Bull. (2020)
14. van den Oord, A., Vinyals, O., et al.: Neural discrete representation learning. In: Advances in Neural Information Processing Systems, pp. 6306–6315 (2017)
15. van den Oord, A., et al.: WaveNet: a generative model for raw audio. arXiv preprint arXiv:1609.03499 (2016)
16. van den Oord, A., Kalchbrenner, N., Kavukcuoglu, K.: Pixel recurrent neural networks. arXiv preprint arXiv:1601.06759 (2016)
17. Rebut, P.H., et al.: ITER: the first experimental fusion reactor. Fusion Eng. Des. **30**(1–2), 85–118 (1995)
18. Redmon, J., Divvala, S., Girshick, R., Farhadi, A.: You only look once: unified, real-time object detection. In: Proceedings of the IEEE Conference on Computer Vision and Pattern Recognition, pp. 779–788 (2016)
19. Rippel, O., Bourdev, L.: Real-time adaptive image compression. In: Proceedings of the 34th International Conference on Machine Learning, vol. 70, pp. 2922–2930. JMLR.org (2017)
20. Thain, D., Tannenbaum, T., Livny, M.: Distributed computing in practice: the condor experience. Concurr. Comput. Pract. Exp. **17**(2–4), 323–356 (2005)

Deploying Computation: On the Road to a Converged Ecosystem

Software Defined Infrastructure for Operational Numerical Weather Prediction

Sadaf R. Alam[1](✉), Mark Klein[1], Mauro Bianco[1], Roberto Aielli[1],
Xavier Lapillonne[3], Andre Walser[3], and Thomas C. Schulthess[1,2]

[1] Swiss National Supercomputing Centre, ETH Zurich, 6900 Lugano, Switzerland
{alam,klein,bianco,aielli,schulthess}@cscs.ch
[2] Institute for Theoretical Physics, ETH Zurich, 8093 Zurich, Switzerland
[3] Federal Office of Meteorology and Climatology MeteoSwiss, Zurich, Switzerland
{Xavier.Lapillonne,Andre.Walser}@meteoswiss.ch
https://www.csscs.ch, https://www.meteoswiss.admin.ch

Abstract. In 2015, CSCS and the Swiss national weather and climate service (a.k.a. MeteoSwiss) have deployed the first GPU accelerated HPC system for numerical weather prediction (NWP), which has been in operation since Spring of 2016. As part of the lifecycle management, an eight-times more performant system that can support an upgraded model had to be developed, but at constant cost. This new system is scheduled to go into operation later in 2020. The performance of viable GPUs at a given price has not been sufficiently increasing in recent years. With a fixed budget envelope, the traditional design for operational NWP with two, fully redundant and self-contained systems, was no longer viable to support operations of the 2020–2024 model. We have solved the challenge with a software defined infrastructure concept from cloud infrastructure technologies, and designed a single system with builtin redundancies that would meet reliability requirements with only 1.5 x the number of (expensive) compute nodes needed for the operational NWP. Specifically, concept of network tenants is introduced to define a production, a failover/research-and-development (R&D) and a system test-and-development tenant. Moreover, operational resiliency metrics are ensured via transparent migration of components, similar to cloud environments but with subtle differences to ensure bare-metal performance and scaling of MeteoSwiss simulations. In the paper, we will describe the process for designing and operating a cloud-technology driven, high-availability operational HPC service in a cost-effective manner.

Keywords: High performance computing (hpc) · Cloud computing · Numerical weather prediction (nwp) · Software defined infrastructure · Software defined networking · Resiliency

© Springer Nature Switzerland AG 2020
J. Nichols et al. (Eds.): SMC 2020, CCIS 1315, pp. 303–317, 2020.
https://doi.org/10.1007/978-3-030-63393-6_20

1   Introduction

IT infrastructure for parallel HPC applications is characterised by high performance processing units or servers, low latency and high bandwidth interconnect technology to serve scalable applications, and parallel file systems to sustain compute and memory intensive workloads. Numerical weather prediction (NWP) applications are among the class of scalable, compute and memory intensive workloads that have been benefiting from the architectural and operational design features of high-end HPC or supercomputing ecosystems to deliver at-scale performance in a cost-effective manner. Typically, national supercomputing IT infrastructures serve multiple scientific domains for research and are designed for delivering a quality of service (QoS) that can be accomplished with a batch scheduling system. In other words, there is no guarantee on an immediate or time critical response times. Furthermore, to deliver an optimal performing environment, these systems periodically go through scheduled downtime for maintenance. The NWP service provider communities have historically addressed these quality of service expectations by designing fully dedicated and self-contained IT infrastructure for ensuring response times or periodic generation of simulation results, and by creating fully redundant IT-infrastructures (often called production and failover for 2N redundancy).

Service delivery concepts in public and cloud computing environments encompass various aspects. On-demand computing, auto-scaling, high availability, multi-tenancy for isolation and security are just to name a few. Notwithstanding the financial aspects of these service delivery options, the underpinning technologies in hardware and software can greatly benefit NWP services. Specifically, the concepts of high availability of services through live migration of applications and periodic, on-demand access to resources are concepts that distinguish a shared research IT infrastructure of a supercomputing centre from a shared, multi-tenant, virtualised, software defined infrastructure of cloud computing. We attempt to identify similarities and differences between a dedicated IT infrastructure for NWP service, shared research supercomputing facilities and cloud computing. The dedicated NWP IT infrastructure is over-provisioned, much like a cloud environment, to accommodate on-demand and exclusive access, with high availability. However, unlike a multi-tenant cloud environment, the workload is periodic and predictable. The payload is unlike cloud applications and requires features of a highly performance and scalable bare-metal HPC clusters. If CapEx and OpEx are not limiting factors, a dedicated HPC cluster plus its failover counterpart can continue providing performance and dual (2N) redundancy that is a common place for operational national weather forecasting services without the complexity of software stack for cloud computing.

Processing requirements for operational NWP services have been increasing at a much faster rate than computing and memory performance capabilities. In 2015, CSCS and the Swiss national weather and climate service (a.k.a. MeteoSwiss) have deployed the first GPU accelerated HPC system for numerical weather prediction (NWP), which has been in operation since Spring of 2016. These systems delivered a 40x improvement over its predecessor systems that was introduced in 2012 by exploiting high memory bandwidth and computing capabilities of GPUs. A great deal of investment in the development and acceleration of the application software, namely the "Swiss" implementation of COSMO, attributed to delivery and success of the solution. As part of the life-cycle management, in 2019 an eight-times more performant system that can support an upgraded model had to be developed, but at constant cost. This new system is scheduled to go into operation later in 2020. The performance of viable GPUs at a given price has not been sufficiently increasing in recent years. With a fixed budget envelope (CapEx and OpEx), the traditional design for operational NWP with two, fully redundant and self-contained systems, was no longer viable to support the 2020–2024 model generation. We have solved the challenge with a software defined infrastructure concept from cloud infrastructure technologies, and designed a single system with built in redundancies that would meet reliability requirements with only 1.5 x the number of (expensive) compute nodes needed for the operational NWP. We achieved an N+7 redundancy for the computing services while maintaining a 2N redundancy for storage services in a transparent manner to the end user by exploiting programmable feature of the infrastructure.

In the paper, we will describe the process of designing and operating high-availability operational HPC service in a cost-effective manner. Section 2 provides background to usage of HPC for NWP applications and workflows over the years and recent developments for the convergence of cloud and high performance computing technologies. Section 3 describes the core hardware and software components of the system that contribute to performance and service delivery expectations. Section 4 provides results from the operational setup. Future outlook for exploiting cloud technologies is detailed in Sect. 5.

2   Background

A broad overview of data processing and computing for weather and climate simulations is beyond the scope of the paper. The focus is the operational workflow, specifically for MeteoSwiss (the Swiss national weather and climate service), which can serve as a representative model for different regional and national short and medium term forecasting institutions. Likewise, an overview of cloud computing as provisioned by public cloud providers like AWS, Azure among others is not considered here. Attention is given to topics that are considered somewhat complementary to a typical service delivery model of a national, open research supercomputing platform.

2.1   HPC in Operational Workflows for NWP

The workflow for an operational weather forecasting system comprises of multiple steps including data assimilation, data processing, ensemble generation, simulation, forecast generation, etc. The distinguishing features are generation of products and services in a time constrained manner, which are then used by downstream customers. Operational weather forecasting services are offered by different institutions such as European Centre for Medium-Range Weather Forecasts (ECMWF) [2], Australian Bureau of Meteorology [15], etc. to name a few. Each site has fairly substantial and redundant supercomputing e-infrastructure. For instance, ECMWF current operational environment is composed of two identical Cray XC40 clusters, each has 20 cabinets of compute nodes and supporting storage ecosystem. The Australian Bureau of Meteorology has a similar setup with redundant components to ensure resiliency for delivering 24 × 7× 365 operational service level agreements (SLAs). Each operational site is unique though to fulfill its programmatic objectives. Similarly, MeteoSwiss IT infrastructure is aligned with its own mission objectives and its investment profile.

The workflow of MeteoSwiss system is shown in Fig. 1. Different number of ensembles and resolutions are run in different time steps. The validity period of an output is critical and can only be accepted by the downstream applications within a certain time frame. These downstream applications often make time critical decisions based on the outcome. Data processing and computing requirements for a new model often depend on two factors: resolution of a model and number of ensembles. For instance, in 2016, MeteoSwiss moved from a 2 km single-trajectory model to a 1km single-trajectory plus a 2km ensembles resulting in 40x increase in performance requirements. Similarly, for the 2020 model, MeteoSwiss requirements are increased by factor 8x due a combination of factors such as increase in resolution and ensembles to meet the demanding needs of forecasting and downstream applications. Details are shown in Fig. 2.

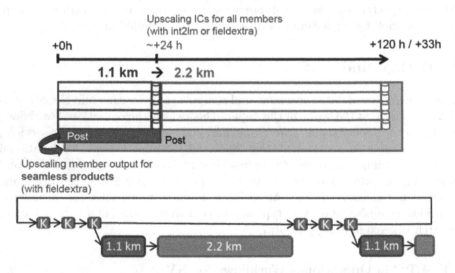

Fig. 1. Workflow for MeteoSwiss comprises different steps highlighting simulation setup. Number of ensembles vary, 40 for K or KENDA (1.1km), 11 for COSMO-E (1.1km) and 21 for COSMO-E (2.2km). Presented by A. Walser (MeteoSwiss) titled "COSMO-E Update" at the COSMO General Assembly meeting, 2018, http://www.cosmo-model. org/content/consortium/generalMeetings/general2018/default.htm. Note that the time shown are simulated times for the forecast.

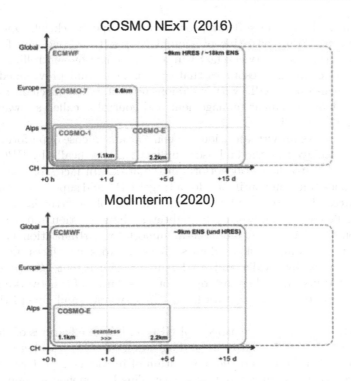

Fig. 2. Comparison of the two models, current (COSMO NExT) and upcoming (Mod-Interim) showing increased resolution for operational configuration. Presented by D. Leuenberger (MeteoSwiss) titled "ModInterim: On the way to a new operational COSMO configuration" at the COSMO User Workshop 2019, https://wiki.c2sm.ethz. ch/COSMO/EventsCUW2019. The two models show significant changes for Alps for forecasts ranging from 1 day to 5 d. Meanwhile, there are changes to the resolution of mid-range European and global models by ECMWF. Collectively, there is an increase both in terms of data ingested by ECMWF and subsequently computation, which is estimated to be a factor of over 7 going from 2016 COSMO NExT to 2020 COSMO ModInterim.

2.2   Convergence of Cloud and High Performance Computing

On-demand and auto-scaling are among the features highlighted by public cloud service providers. The remarkable aspect is delivery of these services without dedicated IT infrastructure for a wide range of customers, with diverse business and operational sensitivities. Often the concept of multi-tenancy is used to describe levels of isolation where applications share IT resources like CPU, GPU, memory, storage and network. This is accomplished through different virtualisation techniques and essentially a virtual system is build on top of the physical infrastructure, like a virtual machine (VM). A VM is decoupled from the underlying hardware and can therefore be launched and migrated from one physical infrastructure to other without a disruption to services. Software defined infrastructure (SDI) is often referred to a provisioning scheme where configuration of a system is defined in software, for instance, OpenStack [9]. OpenStack is defined as a platform consisting of a number of software packages for delivering Infrastructure-as-a-Service (IaaS) in a data centre by controlling compute, storage, and networking resources that are managed and provisioned through standard, open-source APIs with common authentication mechanisms. In the networking domain, similar management and control is called software defined networking (SDN) [14].

Software stacks for virtualisation can come at an expense of performance that needs to be achieved by the end-user application, specifically by HPC applications where close-to-the-metal performance matters. In fact, HPC applications are often hand-tuned and optimised for a target HPC and supercomputing infrastructure. Recently, however, different devices are enabling virtualisation natively, to ensure different service types and qualities such as isolation and performance. In addition to CPUs or servers where support for virtualisation has become a commonplace, component vendors such as network interfaces and switches and GPU devices by Nvidia and AMD support single root I/O virtualisation (SR-IOV). For instance, there are open source solutions for networking such as Cumulus [6] as open software stack for network switches and Open Ethernet [4] by Mellanox.

In short, the performance aspects of HPC and service features of cloud computing are converging for hardware and software. Machine learning (ML) applications are said to be behind the momentum of introducing performance sensitive features to the cloud computing stacks. This has opened up opportunities, particularly, for operational weather and climate workflows where isolation for performance and security, plus on-demand and on-time delivery of service are key Quality of Service (QoS) requirements. SDI technologies can therefore be adopted for delivering operational QoS with selected multi-tenancy features in a cost effective manner within a shared environment as we demonstrate with the recent MeteoSwiss platform.

3   Implementation Details

Designing a platform to deliver performance and the necessary QoS for all aspects of the 2020 MeteoSwiss model comprised of multiple efforts. These include designing a system architecture (with performance expectations and cost constraints), operational integrity to deliver QoS and service level agreements (SLAs), and application development and tuning for the new hardware target (CPUs, GPUs, memory, network and storage). Maintaining end users and customer (MeteoSwiss) operational interfaces was a high priority i.e. design features should be transparent to platform users. Table 1 compares the IT infrastructure for 2016 and 2020 platforms (note that investment or CapEx for 2020 is higher).

Table 1. Comparison of 2016 and 2020 MeteoSwiss platforms for delivering COSMO NExT and ModInterim respectively performance and operational expectations.

Component	Total 2016	Total 2020	Difference
GPUs	192 Nvidia K80s (dual K40 or 384)	144 Nvidia V100	Reduction of 48 GPU devices or 240 GPUs
Compute nodes	24	18	Reduction of 6 nodes
Post processing nodes	10	15	Increase of 5 nodes
Login nodes	6	6	No change
High speed network	4 InfiniBand switches	7 100 Gbs Ethernet switches	Increase of 3 switches
Storage	2 Lustre file systems	2 Lustre file systems	No change
Racks	2 racks	3 racks	Increase of 1

3.1 Functional Specifications-System Architecture

The functional requirements for the MeteoSwiss workflow includes:

- Compute nodes: these are dense GPU nodes that run the bulk of the NWP application workflow and file I/O.
- Post processing nodes: these nodes perform majority of post processing operations running both multi-threaded and serial I/O intensive applications.
- Operational storage: this supports applications running on operation compute and post processing nodes.
- High speed network (HSN): this is required for MPI and I/O workload performance and connectivity.
- Operating environment: this include the **validated environment** for applications in the production workflow including a secure OS, network and GPU drivers, and resource management and scheduling system (with custom MPI task to GPU mappings).
- Programming environment: the **validated environment** e.g. compilers and libraries for operational suite must be available and functional.

The above are typically described as components that are needed in the emergency operation mode because the MeteoSwiss IT infrastructure supports additional research and development (R&D) tasks. In fact, the failover system is normally used as an R&D platform for developing future models while the operational platform is dedicated for regular and periodic delivery of forecasts.

The building blocks for the architecture are shown in Fig. 3 highlighting production, R&D and test and development system (TDS) as unique clusters. While some components like storage and interconnect are fully redundant, the underlying architecture is provisioned and managed as a single infrastructure. Attention has been given to the isolation of production cluster tenant (to fulfill functional and performance SLAs) and to automate failover process of hardware components.

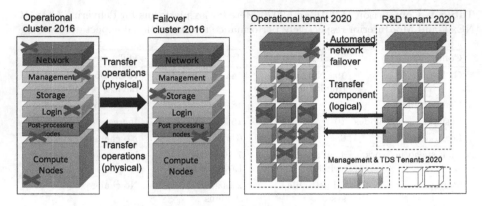

Fig. 3. Architecture comparison for current and future operational MeteoSwiss systems. In the current (2016) system, full operation is moved to the failover cluster in case of planned and unplanned events. The future (2020) operational model allows for failing over components. Three key advantages of 2020 system includes N+6 redundancy of computing components as opposed to 2N, a software-defined failover of network components and a management/system TDS tenant. Failed parts (denoted by X) can be repaired and return to service in the R&D tenant.

3.2 Operational Specifications-Software Defined Infrastructure

The high level $24 \times 7 \times 365$ operational specifications for the cluster include:

- **Minimum number of computing nodes and GPUs** must be fully operational for delivering operational model (resolution and ensembles).
- **Minimum number of post-processing nodes** must be fully operational for delivering operational model (resolution and ensembles).
- Operational storage must fulfill **functional and performance** requirements for applications running on compute and post processing nodes.
- HSN for compute and post processing nodes must deliver **functional and performance** requirements.
- Internet connectivity: a **secure network connection** must be available to transfer observational data and models to the cluster and to extract products from the cluster.
- Availability of validated operating and programming environment for the operational suite.

Historically, clusters to deliver operational services have been constructed as two identical clusters, where one would serve as production and other as a failover for 2N redundancy. Processes are then set in place to migrate services (note that no HPC applications are being migrated) in case of scheduled and unscheduled down times, from one cluster to another. In contrast, our proposed scheme maintains an operational cluster (operational tenant) without service downtime by migrating components from other, much smaller R&D cluster (R&D tenant) (no migration of applications). These clusters are tenants in a two-tenant IT infrastructure where there is a level of sharing (described below) while maintaining full isolation as separately provisioned clusters. In short, creation of the cluster is not a one time operation but rather a programmable workflow for maintaining its dimensions to fulfill MeteoSwiss operational requirements while managing incident and changes (scheduled and unscheduled) to the IT infrastructure.

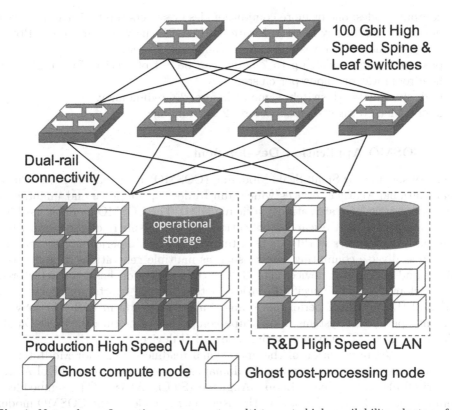

Fig. 4. Network configuration to support multi-tenant, high availability clusters for the MeteoSwiss operations. A high-level of redundancy for networking components ensures HSN performance for parallel, MPI applications and storage. Ghost nodes prevent a need for manual configuration and management, where a node from one tenant can be added to the production Slurm cluster with its image and file mounts in a programmable manner, without privileged (root) access.

Only network level virtualisation is considered for the MeteoSwiss operational system allowing sharing and isolation of multiple cluster tenants. Four virtual networks are created namely production, R&D or failover, system TDS and management. Figure 4 depicts the high speed network design to support HPC applications on production and R&D tenants. Each compute server and post-processing server has a dual-rail setup, which is bonded to support failover and performance for MPI and storage traffic. We use RDMA over Converged Ethernet (RoCE) is a network protocol that leverages Remote Direct Memory Access (RDMA) capabilities to accelerate communications between applications hosted on clusters of servers and storage arrays [7]. Programmability and automation are keys for exploiting a software defined infrastructure. The following failure scenarios are considered for automatically maintaining the operational cluster profile (by migrating nodes and failing over redundant components):

- compute nodes: one or more compute nodes or servers (up to 7) can be taken out of service for any issue (software, CPU, GPU, network card, etc.). Previously, the headroom was one node within each cluster.
- post processing nodes: up to 7 nodes can be out of service. Previously, the headroom was one node per cluster.
- high speed network switch: same as before, 2N redundancy.
- operational storage: same as before, 2N redundancy.

3.3   COSMO Application Development

The Consortium for Small-Scale Modeling (COSMO) members are seven European national weather services which aim to develop, improve and maintain a non-hydrostatic local area atmospheric model [1]. The COSMO model is used for both operational and research applications by the members of the consortium and many universities worldwide [11]. In order to sustain performance portability across diverse computing targets such as multiple generations of multi-core CPUs and accelerator devices like GPUs, the application has been refactored by developing domain specific libraries. Details of such efforts are provided in [11] and [13] including performance and scaling results from both MeteoSwiss current operational systems and a supercomputing platform called Piz Daint, which is a Cray XC50 system with Nvidia GPU devices.

During the preparation of the operational readiness phase for ModInterim, one of the key step was to replace the domain specific library from STELLA [12] to GridTools [3,8]. STencil Loop LAnguage (STELLA) is a C++ embedded-domain specific library that allows the user to write code for the COSMO model that is agnostic of the target hardware architecture. The GridTools (GT) framework is a set of libraries and utilities to develop performance portable applications for weather and climate simulations not bound to the COSMO model. Its design goals are to allow to better engineer the application and improve code reusability. In GT, stencil operations on regular and block-structured grids (as are commonly found in the weather and climate application field) are central. GT provides a useful level of abstraction to enhance productivity and obtain excellent performance on a wider range of computer architectures with respect to STELLA, since GT provides a better separation between front-end and back-end, thus allowing new back-ends to be introduced relatively quickly. GT also provides means to perform efficient halo-update operations to run in distributed memory architectures. The development and integration of GT with COSMO was critical in achieving performance expectation from the new generation of

Nvidia GPUs namely Volta and the new high bandwidth and low latency inter-connect called NVLink [5]. Specifically, the timelines of the operational workflow that is depicted in Fig. 1 required completion of each member of COSMO-E sim-ulation within a fixed time window. Hence, there were strict performance goals that must be achieved for the 24 × 7 operating environment with multiple ensem-bles over and over again. The software defined infrastructure setup can, in no way, deteriorate performance behaviour of computing, networking and storage (file I/O) operations for the MeteoSwiss operational suite.

4   Results

A number of failure scenarios are evaluated to ensure the desired level of redun-dancy within the operational time constraints. Moreover, extensive tuning is per-formed with the GridTools-based implementation of COSMO, in order to ensure performance constraints can be maintained within the strictly time-constrained window in operations.

4.1   Resiliency Expectations

The expected resiliency of the system in case of different failure scenarios is listed in Table 2. These scenarios are compared with existing 2N failover cluster setup (2016 operational system) and N+X setup for 2020 operational configuration. Except for the facility related scenarios, which are similar for both systems within the data centre, the 2020 system allows for more fine-grain failover options.

Table 2 does not specify the user or admin intervention i.e. whether some sce-narios require no human-in-the-loop, an unprivileged intervention by operational users, or a privileged, system admin alerts and access controlled operations. Majority of network level operations are fully automated as the open software stacks and APIs of the switch allow for implementing the logic for maintaining the QoS of the operational tenant. Failure or performance regression of compute and post processing nodes can be triggered by a script that is executed by the MeteoSwiss operator where a replacement node can be reconfigured on-demand for the operational slurm cluster. System admins receive alerts for failures and regressions. They are required to intervene for immediate recovery of service for issues that are not covered in the Table 2.

4.2   Performance Expectations

The most computationally intensive component of the NWP forecast workflow is the COSMO model simulation. The target timings, see Table 3, have been set depending on the estimated time of the other components and the requirement for the time critical products. When designing the new system the benchmark used were based on the COSMO-E (1.1 km) and COSMO-E (2.2 km) forecast component, while the data assimilation component KENDA was not included. In the original implementation of the assimilation code for GPU several parts

Table 2. An analysis of failure and performance regression scenarios comparing a 2N redundant system and a system with N+X redundant components. Note that single failures of components are considered. The 2020 system allows for combined failure scenarios where an operational tenant can continue to operate without physically parts unlike the predecessor 2016 system. Failure management times are recorded by induced and simulated failures to ensure service recovery times are within the SLAs.

Failing component or regression	Impact 2016 platform	Impact 2020 platform	Management of operational Resiliency 2016 vs. 2020
Full rack	None (one rack failure)	none (one rack failure out of 3 in total)	move to failover cluster (2016) vs. operational cluster tenant recreated with remaining spare components (2020)
Single GPU node	none	none	utilize spare node within cluster (automated)
Multiple GPU nodes (operational cluster)	none (limit 3)	none (limit 7)	move to failover cluster (2016) vs. cluster tenant claims spare GPU nodes (2020)
Single PP node	none	none	move to failover cluster (2016) cluster tenant claims spare PP nodes (2020)
Multiple PP nodes (operational cluster)	none (limit 2)	none (limit 7)	move to failover cluster (2016) cluster tenant claims spare PP nodes (2020)
Single login node	none	none	spare node available all the time
Multiple login nodes (operational cluster)	none (limit 2)	none (limit 2+)	cluster failover triggered for 2016 and 2020 (*new feature: login nodes can be re-provisioned for 2020*)
Operational storage	none	none	cluster failover triggered for 2016 and 2020
Operational switch (core/spine)	none	none	cluster failover triggered for 2016, automated for 2020
Operational switch (leaf)	N/A	none	automated for 2020
Management switch	none	N/A	cluster failover triggered for 2016, separate VLAN of operational switch in 2020
Management nodes	none	none	cluster failover triggered for 2016, 2+1 redundancy before failover in 2020
Facility	100%	100%	single data centre

were still running on CPU, requiring constant data transfer between the CPU and the GPU. On the old, 2016 COSMO-NExT model, running on the previous generation system called Kesch, there was a single 1 km model-trajectory running on 72 GPUs. With a relatively small MPI sub-domain per GPU this was not an issue (fitting into the GPU memory). However, in the new 2020 Mod-Interim setup on the current system, the 1 km system runs on 8 GPUs. MPI sub-domain per GPU become a critical bottleneck (72 K40 to 8 V100 GPUs). Initially, performance measurements on the KENDA components appeared to be about 2x slower then the target timing as shown in Table 3.

The model was carefully optimized regarding data movement in the assimilation part, which enabled reduction of run time in this part from 46% to below 9% of the total KENDA run time. The model was further adapted so that KENDA assimilation could run in single precision. Additional optimizations in the OpenACC code as well as the transition from the STELLA dycore to the GridTools dycore led to further performance improvements. These optimisation steps achieved very close to the target timings required for the ModIterim operational targets. The remaining differences between the target timings and the optimized COSMO timing are compensated by additional improvements in the workflow. This part of the optimisation depend on close-to-metal performance features of CPU, GPU, memory hierarchies and I/O subsystems including inter and intra-node MPI latencies and bandwidth.

Table 3. Optimization of COSMO component to achieve ModInterim performance targets. All timings are in seconds.

Component	Target	After optimisations	Before optimisation
KENDA	640	660	1380
COSMO-E (1.1 km)	3300	3310	3590
COSMO-E (2.2 km)	2700	2730	2970

5   Future Work

Convergence of cloud and HPC technologies has opened up several opportunities to rethink delivery of NWP services, not only for cost-efficiencies on dedicated IT infrastructure but also for future, on-demand and auto-scale distributed research infrastructure. Here are a few near- to mid-term possibilities:

- **Containerised HPC workloads**: the containers technology for HPC has been investigated over the past few years [10]. The workflow can have several advantages namely reproducibility with underlying changes to programming environments and ability to spawn workflows at cloud facilities.
- **Containerised workflow**: the next steps after successful containerisation of compute, data and IO intensive workloads, is the containerisation of the entire NWP workflow including a number of pre- and post-processing and

analysis applications. Such a containerised workflow could potentially allow for the migration to public and private cloud installations that support OCI and HPC resource management systems.

– **Multi-tenancy and Infrastructure-as-code**: the current installation enables sharing of multiple network interfaces to allow failover of components. Users of production and failover systems see isolated clusters. These concepts can be extended to a public or private cloud environment that allow for creating HPC clusters in non-dedicated environments.

– **On-demand, auto-scaling and highly resilient services**: These are currently unsupported functionality at many HPC centers due to the investment and operational constraints of dedicated IT infrastructure. With containerised workflows and software defined infrastructure, it would be feasible to deploy clusters for NWP on non-dedicated cloud infrastructure on-demand, extend them as needed and to have multiple failover options to improve resiliency (taking into consideration both technical/performance and financial considerations).

Acknowledgments. We would like to thank the GridTools developer team for developing the infrastructure software for enabling COSMO to run efficiently on GPUs. Additionally we would like to thank Felix Thaler and Hannes Vogt from their dedication in porting the COSMO to use GridTools libraries. This work has been partially funded by the PASC program in Switzerland.

References

1. Consortium for small-scale modeling. http://www.cosmo-model.org/
2. ECMWF's high performance computing facility (HPCF). https://www.ecmwf.int/en/computing/our-facilities/supercomputer
3. Gridtools. https://github.com/GridTools/gridtools
4. Open Ethernet Switch Software. https://www.mellanox.com/open-ethernet
5. Nvidia tesla v100 gpu architecture whitepaper. https://www.nvidia.com/content/dam/en-zz/Solutions/Data-Center/tesla-product-literature/volta-architecture-whitepaper.pdf
6. Open networking software for the modern data center. https://cumulusnetworks.com/
7. Roce v2 considerations. https://community.mellanox.com/s/article/roce-v2-considerations
8. Afanasyev, A., et al.: Gridtools: a framework for portable weather and climate applications (Submitted)
9. Basnet, S.R., Chaulagain, R.S., Pandey, S., Shakya, S.: Distributed high performance computing in openstack cloud over sdn infrastructure. In: 2017 IEEE International Conference on Smart Cloud (SmartCloud) (2017)
10. Benedicic, L., Cruz, F.A., Madonna, A., Mariotti, K.: Sarus: highly scalable docker containers for hpc systems. In: Weiland, M., Juckeland, G., Alam, S., Jagode, H. (eds.) ISC High Performance 2019. LNCS, vol. 11887, pp. 46–60. Springer, Cham (2019). https://doi.org/10.1007/978-3-030-34356-9_5

11. Fuhrer, O., et al.: Towards a performance portable, architecture agnostic implementation strategy for weather and climate models. Supercomput. Front. Innov. **1**(1), 45–62 (2014)
12. Gysi, T., Osuna, C., Fuhrer, O., Bianco, M., Schulthess, T.C.: Stella: A domain-specific tool for strucutred grid methods in weather and climate models. In: Proceedings of the International Conference for High-Performance Computing, Networking, Storage and Analysis (2015), https://doi.org/10.1145/2807591.2807627
13. Osuna, C., etal.: Operational numerical weather prediction on a GPU-accelerated cluster supercomputer (2016), https://www.ecmwf.int/node/16818
14. Ranjbar, A., Antikainen, M., Aura, T.: Domain isolation in a multi-tenant software-defined network. In: 2015 IEEE/ACM 8th International Conference on Utility and Cloud Computing (UCC) (2015)
15. West, C.: Weathering the storm - lessons learnt in managing a 24x7x365 hpc delivery platform. In: Cray User Group Meeting (CUG) (2018)

OpenSHMEM I/O Extensions for Fine-Grained Access to Persistent Memory Storage

Megan Grodowitz[1]([✉]), Pavel Shamis[1], and Steve Poole[2]

[1] Arm Research, Austin, TX, USA
{Megan.Grodowitz,Pavel.Shamis}@arm.com
[2] Los Alamos National Lab, Los Alamos, NM, USA
swpoole@lanl.com

Abstract. Application workflows use files to communicate between stages of data processing and analysis kernel executions. In large-scale high performance distributed systems, file based communication significantly penalizes performance by introducing overheads such as meta-data access, contention for file locks, and slow speed of spinning disks. Using files as system wide persistent storage also hinders fine-grained access to data when files are stored on block devices handled through the I/O software stack. To address speed and granularity, we employ persistent memory (PMEM) devices, which provide DRAM-like speeds and byte granular access combined with persistent storage capabilities. To address file and I/O software stack overheads, we deploy an Arm-based Mellanox Bluefield SmartNIC with attached NVDIMM-N modules. Both Smart-NIC and PMEM introduce API design and system software integration challenges. We address this with the design and implementation for an innovative client-server software architecture with a client API extension to the OpenSHMEM library. We benchmark the implementation using a workflow of invocations of OpenSHMEM kernels on a persistent data set. Compared to the same workflow using a network file I/O client, our solution shows no degradation of performance as the number of clients increases. We accelerate startup and shutdown phases of each kernel by reducing the time to move file data in and out of OpenSHMEM process memory to the speed of one-sided memory access. We also support the creation of many small files with minimal overhead. OpenSHMEM workflows can leverage these changes to create more, shorter lived kernels with lower penalty. This API can replace file I/O with code that appears and behaves similar to other OpenSHMEM remote memory accesses.

Keywords: SmartNIC · RDMA · OpenSHMEM · Persistent memory · Non-volatile memory · Fault tolerance · PMEM · PGAS

© Springer Nature Switzerland AG 2020
J. Nichols et al. (Eds.): SMC 2020, CCIS 1315, pp. 318–333, 2020.
https://doi.org/10.1007/978-3-030-63393-6_21

1   Introduction

Traditional high performance distributed applications use program data stored in RAM for computation while relying on file I/O to disk-based storage to ensure data persistence. The slow speed of file I/O compared to memory means that data-intensive computations suffer under this model when data persistence is ensured. The emergence of SmartNIC programmable network cards in the hardware stack allow a new mechanism to provide persistent data access to applications. In particular, we can use SmartNIC hardware to accelerate the I/O needs of workflows.

A workflow model is common in data analysis applications; workflows use file I/O as a universal communication medium between independent application kernels. For example, a common type of graph analytics workflow executes stages of analysis kernels on a large persistent graph; the result of each stage determines the actions of the next stage [5]. Workflow models are robust in the event of power failure, since the data and workflow meta-data are stored in persistent files. Other conveniences of file based persistent data include ubiquitous language compatibility, ability to rewind and redo stages, and ability to move computations between systems.

Workflow models are convenient, but distributed file I/O incurs overheads from such factors as slower disk hardware, meta-data updates, and ordering and visibility of shared reads and writes. Emerging non-volatile (NVM or NVMe) and persistent memory (PMEM) provide higher speed disk hardware. In this work, we use the term PMEM to mean *byte addressable* devices with DRAM-like speeds. We use NVM to mean non-volatile memory in general; NVM disks means *block addressable* NVM. To accelerate file access, large system designs increasingly place NVM disks throughout a system close to the network fabric to relieve file system pressure [6].

In this work, we add the hardware capability of a SmartNIC loaded with PMEM to provide workflows with low overhead, in-network access to persistent data. The hardware is exposed to applications through an API to setup and access data using one-sided remote operations. The API is supported by a lightweight server that can run on a SmartNIC.

This paper makes the following contributions:

- An OpenSHMEM [1] interface allows applications to define persistent distributed data sets that support byte-level access over RDMA networks.
- An OpenSHMEM interface that enables dynamic connections to a remote PGAS address space using a server-client API while preserving OpenSHMEM memory semantics.
- A PGAS storage server implementation based on the UCX network library [12,14] for RDMA SmartNIC appliance with NVDIMM-N PMEM storage
- Performance evaluation using a server running on a Mellanox Bluefield SmartNIC with NVDIMM-N PMEM and an OpenSHMEM application running on a Marvell ThunderX-2 platform.

Section 2 describes where this work fits into the scope of other work in high performance application support for large persistent memory spaces. Section 3 describes how this I/O interface is implemented as a client-server design. Section 4 provides results and analysis of testing the implementation using an OpenSH-MEM benchmark that executes a basic workflow model. Finally, Sect. 5 summarizes results and conclusions.

2   Background

There are several notable works on APIs for distributed byte-addressable non-volatile memory. The OpenFAM API [4] is an OpenSHMEM-inspired API that provides access to non-volatile memory storage. Nevertheless, this work does not present the implementation or performance evaluation of the API. In [10], Rivas-Gomez et al. present a persistent co-arrays implementation based on the MPI Storage Windows [9] concept using NVMe SSDs over the distributed GPFS file system. Dorozynski et al. [2] demonstrate how byte-addressable non-volatile RAM can be used for application checkpointing using persistent memory simulation using DRAM. In [13], Shan et al. explore a Linux kernel-based approach for implementing distributed persistent shared memory and present an evaluation based on persistent memory simulation using DRAM. Similarly, Lu et al. [7] explore an user-space distributed persistent file system implementation and evaluates it using persistent memory simulation using RAM. Burst buffers [6] is another file system based approach that implements a layer in a file system that can absorb bursts of I/O communication using fast persistent memory storage. Our implementation contrasts these prior studies in the following two ways. First, our implementation puts PMEM storage and data layout strictly within OpenSHMEM semantics. Second, our evaluation uses NVDIMM-N memory and a Mellanox Bluefield SmartNIC.

3   Design

We have implemented a client API and a server to support the API. This implementation demonstrates partitioned persistent data access over fabrics supported by the UCX library.

We extended the OpenSHMEM communication library, which provides semantics to define a strictly symmetric space across all processes in a computation. High performance applications can take advantage of the assumption of symmetry to avoid consensus and translation overheads. OpenSHMEM applications communicate between processes using *processing element (PE)* numbers. Each PE has a unique number and can perform remote memory operations (such as put and get) to memory on other PEs using the PE number and a remote memory address.

Our OpenSHMEM I/O extension presents PMEM devices to applications via a symmetric file space or "fspace". Memory regions on PMEM devices are given their own OpenSHMEM PE numbers, transparently granting fspace data the existing OpenSHMEM remote memory access (RMA) semantics. Unlike the core OpenSHMEM model, the fspace extension does not require all PE numbers be assigned during library initialization (shmem_init). Instead, any OpenSHMEM PE can, at any time after shmem_init, connect as a client to an fspace server via host IP and port. That connection initiates an exchange of remote memory access keys that are assigned on the client PE to new, unique remote PE numbers. The client PE then accesses persistent fspace data with OpenSHMEM RMA operations, using the fspace PE numbers and memory addresses assigned to fspace files.

This I/O model leverages the existing strength of OpenSHMEM's global view of memory partitions accessed by PE number, but breaks symmetry for fspace data to avoid an unscalable requirement that every file be accessible to every PE in a symmetric manner. Files can be laid out across any striped subset of fspace PEs, so files are not created with the same semantics as shmem_malloc. These changes are in line with ongoing evolution of the OpenSHMEM standard to support more dynamic process groupings, i.e. the OpenSHMEM teams extension.

3.1 Client-Side Interface

The client API was completely defined prior to implementation. Very few API modifications happened during implementation. So, this is not an "organic" API design. None of the operations are collective operations.

Connect & Disconnect. Client connections purposefully break the OpenSH-MEM notion of global PE numbering. For example, one client PE may connect and view an fspace as remote PEs 16–31, whereas another client PE may view the same fspace as PEs 32–47. Global numbering can be addressed later in extensions to design collective connections. In this version, connections are non-collective so that systems can integrate low-compute devices, such as SmarNICs, in a heterogeneous fashion and control I/O access through subsets of PEs that are "near" to fspace servers.

shmem_fspace_conx_t structure provides a host address and port for the fspace server.

shmem_fspace_t shmem_connect(shmem_fspace_conx_t* conx) connects to an fspace. On successful connection, a handle to the fspace is returned. The program can test the returned handle against SHMEM_FSPACE_NULL to check if the connection was successful.

int shmem_disconnect(shmem_fspace_t fspace) disconnects from the fspace, closes any open files on the client, and releases server and client resources. This is called automatically for all connected fspace during shmem_finalize

Fspaces & Files. shmem_fspace_t is an opaque handle to an fspace. A client PE receives this handle when it connects to an fspace server. The fspace connection operation adds a unique range of PE numbers to the client. These PE numbers are used to access file data in the fspace.

shmem_fp_t structure represents an open file in an fspace. The structure contains fields describing a subset of PEs in fspace, a file size in bytes, a base address used for remote memory operations, a contiguous unit size for striped files, and event timestamps for last open, last flush to persistence, and last modification to size or layout.

Files are laid out symmetrically with respect to a subset of fspace PEs. Say file X is stored on PE 16–19 as indicated by the shmem_fp_t. If a client PE can access file X data at remote address A on remote PE 16, then there is data for file X at remote address A on PEs 17,18,19 as well.

Fspace files are not POSIX compliant, nor do they provide I/O streams. There is no notion of current file pointers or seek operations. The client uses a base address and offset calculations to do remote operations on file data. Fspace files enforce read/write ordering and visibility between processes through existing OpenSHMEM semantics.

So, Files are a hybrid memory allocation and file; they provide memory speed access similar to a remote heap, combined with minimal lightweight synchronization and meta-data management suitable for network edge devices. Streaming I/O and POSIX compliance could be interesting future work.

Open, Close, & Stat. Just as with connections, file open and close commands are performed per PE. These routines are not collective operations. They do provide some basic synchronization around file access so that PEs do not need to use other OpenSHMEM synchronization mechanisms in order to use fspace files.

shmem_fp_t* shmem_open(shmem_fspace_t fspace, const char *fname, size_t fsize, int pe_start, int pe_stride, int pe_size, int unit_size, int *err) opens a file in an fspace. This call has the most dynamic behavior in the API and acts as a hybrid of a traditional file open operation and a symmetric memory allocator.

The string fname is used as a unique key to identify the file. If the string matches a file that already exists in the fspace, all other size and layout arguments are ignored, and the returned shmem_fp_t structure will reflect the existing file attributes. So, if a PE opens a file, any subsequent PEs that open the same file will get a reference to the same memory.

If fname does not match any existing file in the fspace, the server attempts to allocate fsize bytes symmetrically across pe_size PEs in the fspace, starting with pe_start with a stride of pe_stride. The data is allocated in chunks of unit_size in a round robin fashion across PEs, as is done in Ceph [15]. If the indicated layout is not available or is invalid, the server will attempt to allocate the requested number of bytes in any manner. The actual layout is returned in shmem_fp_t. The client may set any layout argument to −1 to allow the server to set that value.

If fname indicates a valid file path visible to the fspace server (but not necessarily visible to the PE), the fspace server will use that path as the backing file. Data will be loaded from that path into the allocated file space, and stored back to that path when the file is flushed from the fspace. Files remain in the fspace until the PE explicitly removes them or when the server removes them. When a file is open by any PE, that file cannot be moved or shrunk by any other PE or the server. These actions would invalidate that PE's mapping of the file.

int shmem_close(shmem_fp_t* fp, int ioflags) closes the file and releases server side resources for the calling PE. The ioflags argument indicates modifiers regarding what to do with file data on close. See Table 1 below.

int shmem_fp_stat(shmem_fp_t* fp) updates the attributes in the shmem_fp_t structure. The routine will always return the same or newer attributes for a file, so timestamps will not go backward, nor will size go down.

I/O Flags, Flushing and Synchronization. Routines to close, flush, or truncate files accept flags to modify behavior for flushing file data and synchronizing operations when multiple PEs have opened the same file.

Table 1. I/O Flags used for close, truncate, or flush

DEALLOC	Remove the file from the fspace
POP_FLUSH	Flush the file to the point of persistence
DEEP_FLUSH	Write back the file from PMEM to the path indicated by the file name
WAIT	Wait for all other clients to close the file, then perform the operation

A PE can request to deallocate the file and remove it from the fspace on close. This will fail if other PEs currently have the file open.

The wait flag is a novel feature of this interface. This flag provides a mechanism for file routines to act as collective synchronization points between PEs. A PE can close, flush, or truncate a file using the wait flag. This indicates to wait for all other PEs to close the file, then perform the operation. Using wait, applications do not need to use other synchronization structures like barriers, or provide other PE grouping, like teams.

Flush operations are particularly important in implementations such NVDIMM-N where the PMEM device uses both volatile and non-volatile memory. In this case, flushing the file to a point of persistence incurs overhead while data from volatile memory is backed up to non-volatile state. In other hardware, even if writes are guaranteed persistent at the memory module level, there may not be a way to guarantee that a write over RDMA has reached the point of persistence on a remote host. In that case, the POP_FLUSH would be more like a quiet operation, but would involve the fspace server to ensure persistence of data at a remote memory module.

Flush, Extend, & Truncate. A PE can move or resize files stored in the fspace as long as these operations do not invalidate open file handles on other PEs.

int shmem_fp_flush(shmem_fp_t* fp, int ioflags) flushes a file to a persistent state, to backing storage, or out of fspace, depending on flags. The PE will block until the operation is complete.

int shmem_ftrunc(shmem_fp_t* fp, size_t bytes, int ioflags) resizes the file to the indicated size. The file may change location during this operation, so the PE should check the file address and layout after truncate.

int shmem_fextend(shmem_fp_t* fp, size_t bytes) increases file size to the indicated new size if space allows. The file may change location during this operation, so the PE should check the file address and layout after truncate.

3.2   Server Daemon

The server is designed to wait for PE client-initiated actions while consuming as little resource as possible. It uses the UCX client-server and streaming protocols to establish listeners on ports using IP over IB (IPoIB), so the implementation can use one InfiniBand fabric for control and data.

Server Actions. The server passively waits for control traffic for file open, file close, flush, stat, extend or truncate operations. Control requests cause the server to return from the ucp_wait command, where it sleeps in a low power state using the WFE instruction [11].

When a PE opens a file, the server receives an open request and sets up a region of PMEM and potentially loads data from a backing file. After passing back the file handle information, the server is not involved in file access operations. The server tracks all open file handles on PEs so that truncate, extend, and flush operations do not invalidate open file handles. If a PE disconnects from the server, the server will release that PEs file handle.

The server implements the flush command by iterating over file data to issue the DC CVAC instruction available on Arm v8 and newer. This instruction pushes a cache line to the point-of-coherency. Arm v8.2 provides a new instruction DC CVAP that implements flush to point-of-persistence semantics, but it is not available on Arm Cortex-A72. For the Mellanox Bluefield SoC (Arm Cortex-A72) implementation, the point-of-coherency is also the point-of-persistence. Therefore, we can safely use DC CVAC instruction. Currently, our implementation does not track which data in the file has changed since the last flush, and flushes all cache lines for a file.

3.3   Server Subspaces

The server internally implements subspaces of the fspace to accommodate client requests for file layouts. These subsets are similar to the OpenSHMEM v1.5

teams concept, but only exist on the server. They are dynamically created in response to file open requests. When a client requests a file layout, the server will try to allocate the file in an existing subspace with that layout. If this fails, the server will try to create a new subspace with the requested layout. If this fails, the server will allocate the file in any available space that has room. The resulting subspace layout is sent back to the PE client in the file handle.

3.4   Client-Server Mechanisms for Remote Access of Fspace Data

When a PE connects to an fspace, it receives the meta-data required to access remote PMEM. This includes UCX remote access keys and remote addresses to support one-sided remote operations.

Pseudo Addressing by Client PE. The fspace design break the OpenSH-MEM notion of PE address space symmetry for similar reasons that design breaks global PE numbering. A client PE is not required to have symmetric data to fspace PEs. Otherwise, connecting to an fspace would require a PE to allocate ranges of local memory just to provide some alignment with remote file data. Instead, a client PE allocates ranges of addresses to use for fspace access when it connects.

Allocation is a trivial local operation since a PE number is supplied during any remote access. Each PE number maps uniquely to either another computational PE or exactly one fspace PE. So, a client PE assigns pseudo-address ranges on a per fspace basis. To resolve a remote memory access, the client PE uses the remote PE number to select the correct mapping of supplied address to actual remote address.

Client PE Uses Fspace PE, Server Subspace To Resolve Access. For fspace PEs, the client PE only maintains pseudo address mappings for the subspaces that it requires, not the whole fspace. The fspace server lazily creates subspaces (RDMA mapped symmetric PMEM regions) to support different file layouts. A PE lazily maps symmetric subspaces to pseudo-addresses only when it opens a file in that subspace.

Suppose a client PE has opened a file with a base address A, size S, located on PE 6 and 8 in an fspace assigned to remote PEs 6–10. The client PE is ensured that all accesses to address ranges A to $A + S \div 2$ on PE 6 and 8 will access data for this file.

Suppose the client PE accesses A on PE 8 with an OpenSHMEM put operation. The client PE resolves PE 8 to an fspace. Then, the client resolves A to exactly one subspace, which will be striped over PE 6 and 8, since all fspace file layouts are subspace layouts. The client PE resolves A to its subspace by range lookup of A within the fspace. Then translation through the subspace local base pointer and remote address results in an issue to remote access of address $A - B + A'$ using subspace rkey R.

Note that the file is never part of the control logic. This is intentionally done to support existing OpenSHMEM remote access routines, which take only PE number and address arguments. As a consequence, there is a client-side calculation to resolve the address to the corresponding subspace, i.e., file layout. So, the more file layouts that a client generates within an fspace, the more overhead is incurred during remote access to resolve the address. However, there is zero added access time overhead for accessing many small files within a subspace. Also, there is no semantic requirement for the server to provide file layout as requested. So, address resolution overhead can be tuned on the server side by restricting the total number of subspaces.

Regarding file permissions under this model, any kind of data access control would need to be done at the subspace level and not the file level. We leave data protection concerns to other work.

3.5   Software Implementation Details

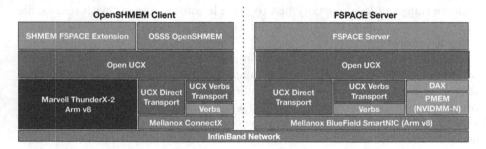

Fig. 1. OpenSHMEM client and server software-hardware stacks for our implementation.

Figure 1 provides a high-level overview of our software stack implementation. The client implementation is integrated into the OSSS OpenSHMEM library [8] implementation. OSSS is the open source reference implementation of Open-SHMEM API driven by Los Alamos National Laboratory in collaboration with Stony Brook National Laboratory. We chose OSSS because it is a lightweight, easily extensible implementation of the current OpenSHMEM standard directly on top of the UCX communication library.

The fspace server is implemented using the UCX library; it stands alone from OpenSHMEM. UCX is an open source communication middleware library that provides high performance communication services over shared memory, InfiniBand/RoCE, and TCP. UCX exposes point-to-point one-sided communication semantics that closely matches the OpenSHMEM API. The library is well tested on Arm v8 platform and is supported by Mellanox, AMD, Arm, IBM, and Nvidia.

The server interface to PMEM is built on the DAX file system mechanisms in the Linux kernel. A file system (e.g. EXT4) is created on a PMEM device and mounted with the DAX option. Files are created in the file system and then memory mapped into a process. The DAX option causes the memory mapping to generate a range of virtual addresses that resolve directly to the PMEM device. By contrast, a memory-mapped file in a non-DAX file system resolves to a buffer in the Linux block cache, which is periodically sync-ed back to the block storage device. To allow remote access to this memory-mapped file, the server registers the memory-mapped region for RDMA access using the UCX library. To enable RDMA memory registration in combination with the DAX file system, we use UCX's on-demand memory registration features. This is the only memory registration mechanism that works in combination with the DAX file system.

4   Implementation Results

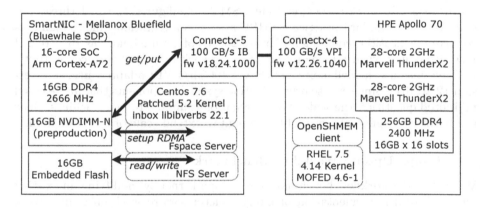

Fig. 2. Experimental setup

To test our implementation, we constructed a testbed of two systems, shown in Fig. 2. On the left, a Mellanox Bluefield SmartNIC development platform ("Bluewhale") runs NFS and fspace servers. On the right, an HPE Apollo 70 system runs the OpenSHMEM client code.

The Bluefield software stack includes CentOS Linux 7.6.1810 and a customized 5.2.1 Linux kernel. The kernel was patched with the most recent fixes for PMEM support on Arm so that the NVDIMM hardware type presented by the firmware at boot would load the PMEM Linux driver and present the device as both storage and memory. We used the CentOS distribution libibverbs-22.1--3.el7 as the user space RDMA driver interface.

The Bluefield hardware stack includes a SoC with 16 Cortex-A72 processing cores, a 16GB embedded flash drive, 16GB of DDR4 and a 16GB DDR4

NVDIMM-N preproduction module. To install the NVDIMM-N module, we installed a patched firmware version on the Bluefield BMC to enable recognition of the NVDIMM-N save pin so that it would be presented to the OS as persistent DIMM type. The NVDIMM-N JEDEC standard describes an energy backed byte addressable module; it uses DRAM technology with onboard flash so that data can be flushed from volatile to non-volatile memory by several mechanisms. The NVDIMM-N module is connected to a separate battery power module in the chassis so that data can be flushed from volatile to non-volatile in the event of power failure. This SmartNIC is built on a ConnectX-5 100GB/s InfiniBand adapter, firmware version 18.24.1000.

The HPE Apollo 70 system runs Red Hat Enterprise Linux Server 7.5 based on 4.14.0–49.el7 Linux kernel. We installed the Mellanox OFED 4.6-1.0.1.1 driver distribution for InfiniBand drivers and user library support. The client Open-SHMEM application is built against our modified version of the OSSS reference implementation of OpenSHMEM, which uses the UCX v1.5 library as the low level communication layer.

The HPE Apollo 70 system is equipped with two 28-core pre-production Marvell ThunderX2 SoCs clocked at 2GHz. Each core is SMT-configurable allowing up to 4 threads. For these experiments, SMT is configured to run 1 thread per core, which is standard practice for HPC system configurations due to high per-core communication requirements. It has 256GB of main memory as 16×16 GB DDR4 modules, with 8 memory channels per socket. For network connectivity, we have installed a Mellanox ConnectX-4 100Gb/s VPI adapter, firmware version 12.26.1040. Since we use preproduction system components that are released in limited quantities, the scale of our evaluation is limited to two machines. Once the hardware is generally available, we plan to extend scale of the evaluation.

4.1 Graph Update Workflow Benchmark

We designed a workflow benchmark for a graph kernel by modifying an existing OpenSHMEM implementation of integer bucket sort to work on graph edges. This type of sort is described as a part of a workflow for analyzing distributed graphs using linear algebra primitives [3]. In that work, the edges are distributed across all of the processing elements in an OpenSHMEM application.

A semantic graph data structure is defined as $G = (V, E)$, where G is the graph, V is the set of vertices, and E is the set of edges. Each edge is defined as $E = (V_1, V_2)$, where V_1 and V_2 are two vertices in the graph connected by the edge. Any graph can be represented as a matrix of size VxV, where each matrix element (V_i, V_j) represents an edge between vertex V_i and V_j.

In practical settings, a large graph data set receives regular updates. Analysis steps are re-run on the data as it changes. So, our workflow benchmark generates a large random graph, sorts the edges, then updates the edges, then sorts the updated edge set, and so on. This is not done in a single execution. Each step is a separate program execution using a data set that persists between executions. We implement the benchmark using the proposed OpenSHMEM extensions base-lined against traditional POSIX I/O on a network mounted file system (NFS).

- Application 1: generate graph $G = (V, E)$ on N_{pe} processes and sort edges
  - Each PE randomly generates E/N_{PE} edge tuples edge set E.
  - All E are sorted onto PEs based on NxM matrix decomposition.
  - Each PE writes its subset of E in binary format to a large shared graph file at a fixed offset based on PE ID. Each PE also stored meta-data in that file to indicate how many edges are in the subset.
- Application 2: N_{pe} processes modify edge set
  - Each PE reads meta-data from its location in the graph file to determine how many edges are in the PE subset.
  - Each PE randomly overwrites some number of existing edges in the file with new randomly generated edges.
- Application 3: read graph and sort edges
  - Each PE reads in edges from its portion of the shared graph file.
  - All E are sorted onto PEs based on NxM matrix decomposition.
  - Each PE writes its subset of E in binary format to a large shared graph file at a fixed offset based on PE ID.

Applications 2 and 3 then repeat.

4.2 Benchmarking Requirements and Baseline for Data Persistence

The experiments model a scenario where a system has one or more dedicated storage nodes serving as a data recovery point for power failures. As an application runs, it writes data, then flushes the data to files to ensure that data will persist through a power outage. The benchmark results do not do many small individual writes to files, even though our API supports this. This behavior would overly penalize a traditional filesystem baseline. Data is modified in OpenSHMEM client main memory, then copied to remote persistent storage in bulk transactions.

Using the OpenSHMEM I/O extension, the application copies data into fspace files. Then it calls the `shmem_fp_flush` routine to move the data to a persistent state, which blocks until the server has flushed all of the file data. In our testbed, we have NVDIMM-N modules, so the flush operation blocks until all data from volatile data has been backed to the onboard NVM. All of the benchmark results include costs for flushing data.

To guarantee data persistence on NFS after a bulk write, the program must ensure that the data is written all the way to physical block device on the NFS server. The mechanisms to do this for NFS are not as straightforward. Linux provides an `fsync()` function and an `O_SYNC` option for opening files. According to the documentation, either of these should be sufficient to commit all writes to disk before returning from a write call. However, in practice, because these mechanisms are defined for local disk, and do not have specific language for network file operations, there is some ambiguity about how these semantics apply to NFS. To ensure that NFS behaves exactly as expected, we use the sync mount option for our NFS mount point, which forces all writes to complete before returning from the write call. We leave NFS caching enabled.

We mount NFS over the same IB fabric, using the same IPoIB connection as the fspace server uses for command traffic. So, the comparison is made using the same network.

4.3 Performance Evaluation

Results are presented here for running the graph generation and decomposition workflow on a single node connected to a file server node.

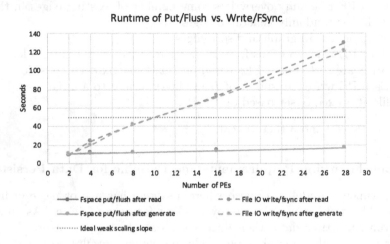

Fig. 3. Runtime comparison for writing out graph tuple data

The first metric showing the usefulness of the fspace interface is the total time taken to move the resulting decomposed tuple data over the network and ensure that it is stored such that no data loss occurs during power disruption. Figure 3 shows the runtime on 2 to 28 PEs of only the write and flush of the graph tuple data. Some applications in the workflow write the data after doing in-memory edge generation, while other applications write the data after reading it. There is little difference between these lines, though at the higher core count, the file I/O to NFS suffers a small performance hit after a large read. An investigation indicates that this is likely an effect of leaving NFS caches enabled, but the effect was not consistent between runs, and so is considered noise in the network file system interaction layers.

Comparing to file I/O, the OpenSHMEM put/flush interface does not suffer much performance degradation as core count increases. The ideal weak scaling slope is shown as a straight line (slope = 0) which would indicate that adding new PEs to the computation will allow new work to be done without slowing down the overall runtime. The OpenSHMEM fspace put/flush runtimes show a 1.6X slowdown between 2 and 28 cores versus an ideal 1x slowdown. It should be noted that there is currently a performance penalty for the OpenSHMEM

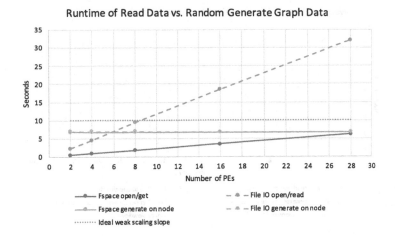

Fig. 4. Runtime comparison for reading in graph tuple data

flush function that does not affect fsync. The OpenSHMEM flush function does not currently track which parts of a file have been updated. Instead, the flush operation must flush each cacheline in a separate operation. Since we use a fixed size file for all runs, each call to flush will operate over the entire file. By comparison, the file I/O synchronous write only operates on the actual data being written.

As stated above, all writes and puts are bulk data transfers. So, in the case of 28 PEs accessing the file on NFS, this runtime is largely the sum of 28 large transfers of contiguous data that should be friendly to the I/O stack, and not many thousands of small random accesses. Yet, the runtime scales roughly linearly with core count, with a slowdown of 12X between 2 and 28 cores, showing little ability to overlap or optimize bulk writes to separate blocks in the file.

The runtime for the parallel read/get by all PEs of the tuple data is compared in Fig. 4. The read/get runtime is compared to the runtime needed to randomly generate edge data. On-chip edge data generation is typically considered to be a much faster option than reading graph data from a file. For traditional file access, any PE count over about 6 would be better served by randomly generating graph data. However, when using the fspace interface, it is faster to get the data than to generate it.

In terms of scaling, both of the read mechanisms scale roughly linearly with number of PES. However, the get interface of the OpenSHMEM fspace method has a much lower overhead, since it allows transferring data over RDMA. By comparison, the runtime for file I/O includes all of the time needed to interact with the kernel and file system layers on both the local and remote node.

The runtime of reads and writes is shown to be much faster for the Open-SHMEM fspace interface. Figure 5 shows how this slowdown affects the entire application. Other than the read and write phases, the applications spend the most time in two other sections, the local sorting of tuples and the all to all com-

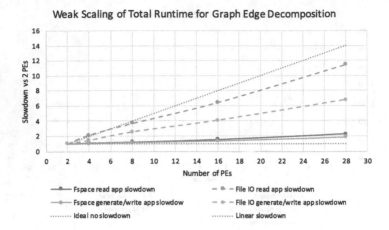

Fig. 5. Scaling comparison to show slowdown of total application

munication to move tuples onto the correct PE. These sections have the same runtime no matter the I/O method.

Figure 5 shows that the time spent in I/O dominates the total runtime when reading and writing to files. The read app here is slower than the write app because it both reads and writes the data.

5   Conclusions

The OpenSHMEM I/O API design exposes disaggregated persistent memory to client application kernels using the OpenSHMEM processing element abstraction. Using this API, applications can access persistent memory storage over RDMA networks on any number of PMEM devices. Our implementation is built over the UCX high performance library, and so is highly portable and performant across Linux based systems. To the best of our knowledge, this is the first work demonstrating distributed storage implementation using SmartNIC hardware in combination with NVDIMM-N persistent memory. We demonstrate the usability of this method with a lightweight API and server implementation. We demonstrate that this methodology provides data persistence guarantees at the same or higher speed than NFS caches over the same network fabrics. Also, this method does not suffer from performance degradation of traditional filesystem access for increasing numbers of clients accessing a shared file.

Acknowledgments. The authors would like to thank the United States Department of Defense and Los Alamos National Laboratory for their continued support of this project. In addition, we would like thank Gilad Shainer and Wang Wong from Mellanox Technologies for providing us BlueField development platform and enabling NVDIMM support in BIOS. We thank Luis E. Peña and Curtis Dunham from Arm for their reviews of the paper.

References

1. Chapman, B., et al.: Introducing openshmem: Shmem for the pgas community. In: Proceedings of the Fourth Conference on Partitioned Global Address Space Programming Model. pp. 1–3 (2010)
2. Dorożyński, P., et al.: Checkpointing of parallel mpi applications using mpi one-sided api with support for byte-addressable non-volatile ram. Procedia Comput. Sci. **80**, 30–40 (2016)
3. Hughey, C.: Tumbling down the graphblas rabbit hole with SHMEM. In: Pophale, S., Imam, N., Aderholdt, F., Gorentla Venkata, M. (eds.) OpenSHMEM 2018. LNCS, vol. 11283, pp. 125–136. Springer, Cham (2019). https://doi.org/10.1007/978-3-030-04918-8_8
4. Keeton, K., Singhal, S., Raymond, M.: The OpenFAM API: a programming model for disaggregated persistent memory. In: Pophale, S., Imam, N., Aderholdt, F., Gorentla Venkata, M. (eds.) OpenSHMEM 2018. LNCS, vol. 11283, pp. 70–89. Springer, Cham (2019). https://doi.org/10.1007/978-3-030-04918-8_5
5. Kogge, P.M.: Graph analytics: complexity, scalability, and architectures. In: 2017 IEEE International Parallel and Distributed Processing Symposium Workshops (IPDPSW). pp. 1039–1047. IEEE (2017)
6. Liu, N., et al.: On the role of burst buffers in leadership-class storage systems. In: 2012 IEEE 28th Symposium on Mass Storage Systems and Technologies (MSST). pp. 1–11. IEEE (2012)
7. Lu, Y., Shu, J., Chen, Y., Li, T.: Octopus: an rdma-enabled distributed persistent memory file system. In: 2017 USENIX Annual Technical Conference (USENIXATC 17). pp. 773–785 (2017)
8. Pritchard, H., Curtis, A., Welch, A., Fridley, A.: Open shmem reference implementation. Technical Reports, Los Alamos National Lab. (LANL), Los Alamos, NM (United States) (2016)
9. Rivas-Gomez, S., Fanfarillo, A., Narasimhamurthy, S., Markidis, S.: Persistent coarrays: integrating mpi storage windows in coarray fortran. In: Proceedings of the 26th European MPI Users' Group Meeting. p. 3. ACM (2019)
10. Rivas-Gomez, S., Gioiosa, R., Peng, I.B., Kestor, G., Narasimhamurthy, S., Laure, E., Markidis, S.: Mpi windows on storage for hpc applications. Parallel Comput. **77**, 38–56 (2018)
11. Shamis, P., Lopez, M.G., Shainer, G.: Enabling one-sided communication semantics on arm. In: 2017 IEEE International Parallel and Distributed Processing Symposium Workshops (IPDPSW). pp. 805–813. IEEE (2017)
12. Shamis, P., et al.: Ucx: an open source framework for hpc network apis and beyond. In: 2015 IEEE 23rd Annual Symposium on High-Performance Interconnects. pp. 40–43. IEEE (2015)
13. Shan, Y., Tsai, S.Y., Zhang, Y.: Distributed shared persistent memory. In: Proceedings of the 2017 Symposium on Cloud Computing. pp. 323–337. SoCC 2017, ACM, New York, N USA (2017). https://doi.org/10.1145/3127479.3128610
14. The Unified Communication X Library. http://www.openucx.org
15. Weil, S.A., Brandt, S.A., Miller, E.L., Long, D.D., Maltzahn, C.: Ceph: A scalable, high-performance distributed file system. In: Proceedings of the 7th Symposium on Operating Systems Design and Implementation. pp. 307–320 (2006)

Distributed Transaction and Self-healing System of DAOS

Zhen Liang[1]([✉]) [iD], Yong Fan[1] [iD], Di Wang[2] [iD], and Johann Lombardi[3] [iD]

[1] Intel China Ltd. GTC, No. 36 3rd Ring Road, Beijing, China
{liang.zhen,fan.yong}@intel.com
[2] Intel Corporation, Santa Clara, CA, USA
di.wang@intel.com
[3] Intel Corporation SAS, 2 Rue de Paris, 92196 Meudon Cedex, France
Johann.lombardi@intel.com

Abstract. The Distributed Asynchronous Object Storage (DAOS) is an open source scale-out storage system designed from the ground up to support Storage Class Memory (SCM) and NVMe storage in user space. DAOS uses an optimized two-phase commit protocol to guarantee atomicity of distributed I/O. This protocol is tightly coupled with the self-healing system of DAOS, in contrast with traditional two-phase commit protocol that is blocking when coordinator fails, this protocol can proceed in presence of failure, and it also has shorter transaction response time than the traditional protocol, these characteristics are important for massively distributed and low latency storage system like DAOS. This paper introduces the distributed transaction and self-healing system of DAOS, and presents the performance benefits of the transaction protocol.

Keywords: DAOS · Distributed storage system · Distributed transaction · Two-phase commit · SCM · Self-healing · Data recovery · Rebuild

1 DAOS Introduction

Distributed Asynchronous Object Storage (DAOS) [1] is a complete I/O architecture that aggregates Storage Class Memory(SCM) and Non-Volatile Memory Express (NVMe) storage distributed across the fabric into globally accessible object address spaces, providing consistency, availability, and resiliency guarantees without compromising performance. It presents a key-value storage interface and provides features such as transactional non-blocking I/O, a versioned data model, and global snapshots.

In order to unleash the full potential of new hardware technologies, the new stack provides byte-granular shared-nothing interface, it can support massively distributed storage for which failure will be the norm while preserving low latency and high bandwidth access over the fabric.

© Springer Nature Switzerland AG 2020
J. Nichols et al. (Eds.): SMC 2020, CCIS 1315, pp. 334–348, 2020.
https://doi.org/10.1007/978-3-030-63393-6_22

1.1 DAOS System Architecture

DAOS takes advantage of next generation technologies like SCM and NVMe. It bypasses all of the Linux kernel I/O, runs end-to-end in user space, and avoids system calls during I/O.

As shown in Fig. 1, DAOS is built over three building blocks. The first one is persistent memory and the Persistent Memory Development Toolkit (PMDK) [14]. DAOS uses it to store all internal metadata, application or middleware key index, and latency sensitive small I/O. DAOS uses a hybrid approach to optimize the trade-offs between cost, performance, and capacity, this requires the second building block, NVMe SSDs and the Storage Performance Development Kit (SPDK) [13] software, to support large streaming I/O. The DAOS service can submit multiple I/O requests via SPDK queue pairs in an asynchronous manner from user space, and create persistent memory indexes for data in SSDs. Libfabric [12] and an underlying high performance fabric is the third build block for DAOS. It is a library that defines the user space API of OFI, and exports fabric communication services to application or storage services. The transport layer of DAOS is built on top of Mercury [11] with a Libfabric/OFI plugin.

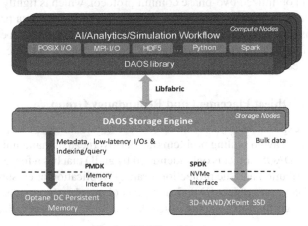

Fig. 1. DAOS architecture

1.2 Data Protection and Distributed I/O

In order to prevent data loss, DAOS provides both replication and erasure coding for data protection and recovery. When data protection is enabled, DAOS objects are stored across multiple storage nodes for resilience. If a failure happens on a storage device or server, DAOS objects are still accessible in degraded mode, and data redundancy is recoverable from replicas or parities.

DAOS distributed I/O for data protection is a primary-slave model: The primary server forwards client requests to slave servers. This model is slightly different from a traditional one. As shown in Fig. 2, the primary server forwards the RPC and RDMA descriptor to slave servers. All servers will then initiate an RDMA request and get the data directly from the client buffer. DAOS chooses this model because the fabric bandwidth between client and server is much higher than the bandwidth between servers in most HPC environments.

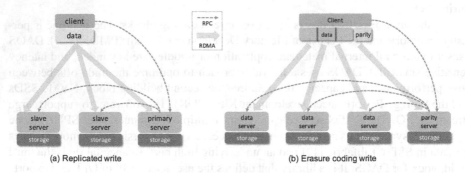

(a) Replicated write   (b) Erasure coding write

Fig. 2. DAOS distributed I/O

DAOS uses an optimized two-phase commit protocol, which is tightly coupled with self-healing system, to ensure atomicity of the distributed I/O for data protection. The main focus of this paper is introducing how this protocol overcomes the blocking problem of two-phase commit, supports low transaction response time and reduces the number of messages between servers as presumed commit protocol [5].

1.3   Algorithmic Object Placement and Redundancy Group

DAOS storage is exposed as objects that allow user access through a key-value or key-array API. In order to avoid scaling problems and the overhead of maintaining per- object layout metadata, a DAOS object is only identified by an ID that has a few encoded bits to describe data distribution and the protection strategy (replication or erasure code, stripe count, etc.). DAOS passes object ID and storage pool membership to a pseudo-random based placement algorithm to compute object layout, this process is called algorithmic object placement [4].

Layout of a distributed object can consist of N redundancy groups, each redundantly storing a subset of object data. For replication, each member of a redundancy group stores one replica of the same object shard, whereas for erasure coding, a redundancy group is equivalent to a parity group. The distributed transaction described in this paper only applies to I/O against one redundancy group, thus a redundancy group is the equivalent of transaction group within context of this paper.

1.4   Self-healing System

In a distributed storage system, rectification of system faults is important because Mean Time Between Failures(MTBF) of the system decreases when the system scales to more storage nodes, if the storage system does not have a robust self-healing system, it is difficult to guarantee its availability and scalability. The self-healing system should be able to detect failure and handle data reconstructing without human intervention.

The self-healing system of DAOS consists of two components: health monitoring system and rebuild system. DAOS is using SWIM [2], a gossip-like protocol, as the core protocol of its health monitoring system. When the health monitoring system detects failure of a storage node, it reports the failure to the highly replicated RAFT [3] based pool service, which can globally activate the second component, rebuild service, on all storage servers. The rebuild service can independently discover objects impacted by the fault by running placement algorithm against its local objects, and determine which objects have replicas or parity on the failed server. These components are scheduled for data reconstruction or replication to fallback servers in the background, even as application I/O are still inflight. Details of the self-healing system will be introduced in section-3 of this paper (Fig. 3).

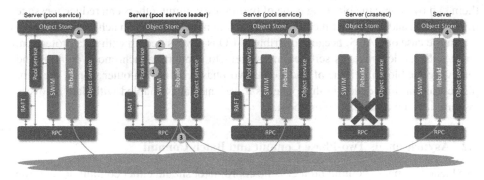

Fig. 3. Workflow of DAOS self-healing system

2   Distributed Transaction of DAOS

DAOS has both replication and erasure coding as built-in data protection strategies. Writes to an object can be distributed to multiple object shards stored on different storage nodes. Atomicity of distributed writes should be guaranteed, otherwise reads from different servers can be inconsistent and data is unrecoverable on failure. The main focus of this paper is presenting an optimized two-phase commit that can guarantee atomicity of distributed I/O while decreasing the response time of traditional protocol.

2.1   Two-Phase Commit

The two-phase commit(2PC) protocol [8] is a type of atomic commitment proto-col(ACP). It is a distributed algorithm that coordinates all the members that participate in a distributed atomic transaction on whether to commit or abort the transaction. A two-phase commit transaction always needs a coordinator to drive transaction status transition among members. The coordinator can either be a dedicated process, or one of the transaction members. Within the context of this paper, transaction coordinator is also a member, it is algorithmically chosen from transaction members by running a pseudo random based function with object ID or key as random seed.

In execution of a distributed transaction, the two-phase commit protocol consists of two phases [16]:

- Prepare phase: a coordinator requests all participants to prepare for the transaction and reply vote-commit or vote-abort. If all participants voted "commit" then the transaction is "committable".
- Commit phase: based on voting of the participants, the coordinator decides whether to commit (only if all members have voted "commit") or abort the transaction, and notifies the result to all the participants.

There are a few variants of two-phase commit [9], including presumed abort(PrA), presumed commit(PrC) [5], easy commit [6], and three-phase commit [7] etc. Some of them can overcome the blocking issue of two-phase commit, others can reduce message transmission and response time of transaction, but none of them can achieve both goals.

In the case of DAOS, because distributed I/O is always tied up with data protection, so DAOS can leverage its self-healing system to support asynchronous commit and resolving the blocking issue of traditional two-phase commit. In other words, the two-phase commit introduced in this paper is a variant that is coupled with data recovery system, it is not a standalone protocol.

2.2 Asynchronous Two-Phase Commit and Batch Commit

In a basic two-phase commit protocol, the coordinator should either commit or abort the transaction before replying to client (Fig. 4.a), the response time of transaction includes two network round-trips between servers. With asynchronous commit, the coordinator can reply to the client when all members replied vote-commit for the operation (Fig. 4.b), which is called "prepared", and afterwards commit the transaction asynchronously. If any participant cannot prepare the operation, DAOS aborts the transaction synchronously.

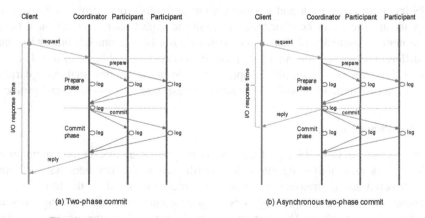

(a) Two-phase commit   (b) Asynchronous two-phase commit

Fig. 4. Synchronous and asynchronous two-phase commit protocols

Asynchronous two-phase commit has similar response time as PrC two-phase commit protocol, but it is different with PrC in essence:

- In PrC two-phase commit protocol, coordinator should log every transaction that has started to prepare, because missing transactions are presumed to have committed. In asynchronous commit protocol of DAOS, coordinator does not log the transaction before dispatching the vote request, instead it logs the write after dispatching vote request, and other participants log the write after receiving the vote request. It means asynchronous commit protocol can save one log write and reduce the latency of transaction.
- In the asynchronous two-phase commit protocol, the logged writes on participants and coordinator are the same, they are also deemed as transaction log records. A transaction will be aborted if it is not logged by either coordinator or participant, details will be introduced in Sect. 2.5.

In the asynchronous commit protocol, transaction coordinator can reply to client before sending out the commit request. It means if clients submit many transactions against the same transaction group, the coordinator can commit them in a batch. In this approach, DAOS can significantly reduce communications between servers while also reducing persistent memory transactions by batching status changes into a single transaction. Figure 5 is an example of batched commit. In order to support asynchronously batched commit, the coordinator should cache transactions IDs that are ready to commit, or are committable, and commit them periodically or when the number of outstanding committable transactions exceeds a threshold.

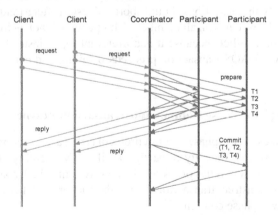

Fig. 5. Batched commit of asynchronous two-phase commit

To make this protocol practical, two issues should be addressed: 1) How a non-coordinator handles read if transaction status of data is "prepared" and 2) How to complete the transaction status transition if a member fault happened before the asynchronous commit. Solutions for these issues will be introduced in following sub-sections.

2.3 Read Protocol

Asynchronous two-phase commit of DAOS can significantly reduce latency of completing a transaction. However, it also increases complexity of the read protocol. With asynchronous commit, the writer sees write completion immediately after all members are prepared. If a reader waits long enough for the transaction to be committed asynchronously, the request can be handled normally. However, if a reader attempts to read while the asynchronous commit is in flight, the status of the transaction could be either "prepared" or "committed". In this case, it is not safe for the non-coordinator to handle the read because different servers could provide inconsistent data. So a non-coordinator should only return a special error code to the client which, instead of reporting the error to application, re-resubmits the I/O request to the coordinator that has the authoritative state of the transaction cached, either "committable" or "abort" if any members could not complete the local transaction. The coordinator can either return the correct data back to the client, or prioritize commit or abort of the transaction so other members can service reads.

2.4 Transaction Conflict

DAOS I/O can support three types of write operations: insert, update, and upsert (update or insert). Upsert of DAOS can be applied unconditionally, however, insert and update should be executed with condition check, for example, trying to insert an already existent key should fail. In order to reduce response time of RPCs, distributed I/O of DAOS does not serialize execution on primary and slaves nodes, so if two conflicting conditional operations arrived at two nodes in different order, they can end up with different execution results. In this case, both transactions should abort and restart after a random time interval until one successfully executes on all members. This paper will not include content about resolving transaction conflicts because it is a irrelevant topic, instead, the next section will introduce how a DAOS transaction proceeds if failure and conflict happen at the same time.

2.5 Non-blocking Two-Phase Commit and Transaction Resync

One of the main issues of two-phase commit protocol is that a transaction will be blocked on coordinator failure, significantly impacting availability, usability and scalability of large storage system. DAOS relies on its self-healing system, which can detect failure in bounded time and reconstruct transaction data in the background, to avoid the blocking characteristics of two-phase commit.

When a DAOS server failure happened, it can be detected by the health monitoring system (Sect. 3.1), which runs SWIM protocol, in a deterministic bound. If the coordinator was alive and received the failure event, it should return "retry" error code to the client, which can choose a fallback server to replace the failed one and re-submit the I/O transaction.

However, if the transaction coordinator failed and the storage system wants to avoid transaction blocking, then surviving members of the transaction group have to run an extra protocol to progress status of the uncommitted transaction. But if the race described in previous section and coordinator failure happen at the same time (Sect. 2.4), this process is difficult to proceed because there is no bounded time for the coordinator coming back. In the example in Fig. 6, C0/P0, which is both transaction coordinator and participant, made a different decision than other members on T1 because T1 conflicts with T0, but crashed before sending the "abort" to other members. In this case, the transaction cannot be synchronously aborted because the coordinator is gone, and nobody can even know this transaction should be aborted. In a traditional two-phase commit protocol, transaction cannot proceed before the coordinator comes back. However, bringing a server back could take unbounded time, particularly if it requires administrator, so the transaction is blocked by the failure.

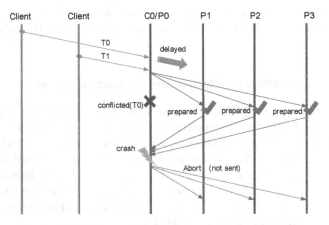

Fig. 6. Conflicting operation and transaction member failure

This is a well-known issue, DAOS resolves it by running two independent protocols: 1) resync protocol, surviving members of the transaction group should run this protocol to get agreement on status of inflight transactions, then commit or abort them; 2) rebuild protocol of self-healing system, it reconstructs data on a fallback node for all committed transactions. The rebuild protocol will be introduced in later sections, this section only focuses on resync protocol:

- If at least one of the surviving members decides to abort or has no logged vote, then the transaction group can proceed and abort the transaction, because vote of the failed one has no impact on the final decision of the transaction group.
- If the failed participant voted "abort" and it has already shared the vote with at least one of the group members, then the transaction group can also proceed and abort the transaction.
- However, if all the surviving members did vote-commit in the prepare phase, and the failed participant is the only one with "abort" vote and it crashed before sharing, the surviving members can also reach agreement and commit the transaction. It seems odd but is safe with the support of the self-healing system. Based on assumption of synchronous abort, it means neither surviving members nor client knows about the "abort" vote from the failed participant, so the self-healing system can reconstruct

data and overwrite the "abort" decision. This makes sense if the abort decision was made for an I/O error but it could also indicate a race. In the latter case, the fact that the failed participant decided to abort a transaction (C0/P0 decided to abort T1 in Fig. 6) implies others may have already decided or will decide to abort the other transaction (T0 in Fig. 6) because they already voted "prepared" for T1. So the transaction group can reach agreement and allow T1 to commit and the unseen "abort" decision will be overridden by self-healing system.

In summary, the resync protocol collects transaction votes from surviving members and makes decision without waiting for the failed member, it is not a standalone protocol because it relies on self-healing system to reconstruct committed data and even override the diverged decision. Neither transaction members nor clients will see inconsistent result with this protocol, because resync can only override abort decision if it is not known by others.

2.6   Transaction Coordinator Selection and Transaction Resync

As described in Sect. 1.3, DAOS uses pseudo-random based algorithm to generate the layout of objects. It also uses pseudo-random hash to select transaction coordinator. When a client starts an I/O against a transaction group, it can hash the object ID and map it to one of the members as the coordinator. A transactional write request has to be sent to coordinator, while read requests can be sent to any member of the transaction group, as discussed in Sect. 2.3. DAOS server uses the same pseudo-random hash to choose transaction leader, it means that for the same I/O transaction, client and servers always choose the same node as transaction coordinator.

If the transaction coordinator fails, a new coordinator must be selected by hashing object ID against and mapping to one of the surviving members. The new coordinator should immediately gather all outstanding transactions from other members, and try to commit or abort them (resync protocol), instead of caching their status in volatile memory again. This is because user data is more vulnerable after failure, those committable data should be committed so the self-healing system can reconstruct and restore the data redundancy.

The new coordinator has to be chosen from surviving members and it cannot be the fallback node in reconstructing, because only surviving members have logs for uncommitted transactions. The new coordinator can iterate log entries and request other members to move the transaction to the second phase, either commit or abort. It should be noted that some transactions might not be logged by the new coordinator, in this case they cannot be committed or aborted. It also means the original coordinator did not reply to the client, because (old) coordinator can reply only if all members confirmed "prepared" and stored the transaction in log whereas the new coordinator does not have the transaction log. So the client will eventually get a timeout from the request, and resend the request to the new coordinator and complete the transaction. If the client is also gone, then these orphan transactions will be eventually reclaimed by a background service of DAOS.

3   Self-healing System of DAOS

The self-healing system of DAOS is not just for recovering data on failure, but can also eliminate the blocking constraint of regular two-phase commit protocol. It can help the failed server to catch up transaction status when it returns, or reconstruct committed transactions on a fallback server if the original one cannot be restored. The self-healing system consists of two components: health monitoring system and rebuild protocol. This section will introduce both of them.

3.1   Health Monitoring System

DAOS uses SWIM as the health monitoring protocol. SWIM is a gossip-like protocol where node running it randomly pings a peer in the cluster and tries to share the known failures with the peer. If a node cannot reach a peer, then this node will put the peer on suspected list. After a certain timeout, if it still did not get any status update about the suspected peer, it should mark it as dead and propagate this information to other peers by random pings.

SWIM implementation of DAOS allows a server to register a notification callback, whenever a node is deemed as dead by SWIM, DAOS pool service will be notified by the callback, it can evict the dead node from the membership table, and propagate the new membership table to all nodes in the cluster. Each node receives the membership update should run "rebuild protocol" to reconstruct data for the failed node.

SWIM protocol can detect a failure in bounded time, a DAOS server running SWIM should abort message against faulty node after detecting the failure, and proceed transaction by switching to a fallback server or running resync protocol in the background, instead of blocking.

3.2   Rebuild Protocol

Rebuild protocol is the core algorithm of the DAOS self-healing system. The rebuild service of a storage node starts to run this protocol after receiving the membership update indicating a node is "down".

This protocol includes "scan" and "pull" phases. In the scan phase, a storage server scans object IDs stored in local persistent memory, independently calculates the layout of each object, and then finds out all the impacted objects by checking if the failed node is within layouts. In this phase, the rebuild service also sends IDs of these impacted object to algorithmically selected fallback servers. The fallback servers then enter the "pull" phase to reconstruct data. In this phase, fallback servers reconstruct data for impacted objects by pulling data from nodes that have redundant data of these objects, and writing the reconstructed data to the local object store.

When a storage node completes any of these two phases, it should report status to the pool service. When the pool service receives both scan and pull completions from all nodes, it can announce rebuild is globally completed by propagating the membership table again, this time the failed node is marked as "out".

As shown in Fig. 7, there is no global barrier between the scan phase and pull phase, these phases can overlap on different nodes. For example, node3 has already started to

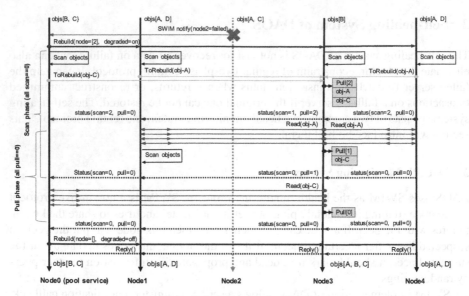

Fig. 7. Rebuild protocol of DAOS

pull data while node1 is still scanning. It means that a storage node may report false completion because it could get more object IDs after it reported "pull" completion, if a remote peer is still in scan phase and it can send object IDs to this node time to time. Therefore, the phase transition of rebuild protocol can be described like:

- A storage node should report "scan" completion once it scanned its local objects and sent out all impacted object IDs.
- A storage node should report "pull" completion each time it completed data reconstruction for all currently received objects, it means a node can report "pull" completion more than once, because after reporting, it may still receive object IDs from remote peers.
- The pool service can only trust the "pull" completions after it received all "scan" completions, because no one will provide objects for rebuild once all nodes have completed scan, then no one will report false "pull" completion anymore.

The essential of DAOS object placement algorithm is a pseudo random based hash that can distribute objects to everywhere in the storage system, so a storage node can belong to thousands or more redundancy groups. During the rebuilding process, objects impacted by the failure are distributed to nearly all the nodes, so there is no central place to perform data or metadata scans or data reconstruction. In addition, storage model of DAOS is multi-tenancy and user can create many storage pools on the same set of storage nodes, so this gives another level of rebuild declustering because objects within different pools have different layouts. In other words, the I/O workload of the rebuild service will be fully declustered and parallelized.

3.3 Cascading Failure Rebuild

Rebuild protocol of DAOS is also based on a two-phase commit protocol. Most of the work is done in the "prepare" phase that includes both "scan" and "pull". The commit phase only propagates the membership table to complete rebuild. Again, the major issue of two-phase commit is that it is a blocking protocol. DAOS is using rebuild system to eliminate the blocking of two-phase commit I/O. Since the rebuild system itself is also based on two-phase commit protocol, how can DAOS handles cascading failure without blocking the current rebuild protocol? An obvious approach is restarting the rebuild process for cascading failure where all members scan object store again to detect objects impacted by the new failure. However, in a large system with thousands of storage nodes, restarting could happen frequently because MTBF is relatively short and possibility of cascading failure is high. Tracking and resuming rebuild progress becomes a big challenge in this case in order to make progress and move to a clean status.

DAOS is using a very simple approach to avoid the blocking and restarting rebuild protocol: it simply queues the new failure, ignores all the impacts of new failure and continues the rebuild for the original failure, only handling the new one after completing the original. To explain this, two roles are defined for a storage node while running rebuild protocol:

- Contributor: a contributor should detect all local objects being impacted by the failure and is the data source for data recovery.
- Puller: a puller is the fallback node that is responsible for reconstructing data, it receives object IDs from contributors, and reconstructs data for these objects by pulling data from contributors and writing to local storage.

Although a node can be both puller and contributor (node3 of Fig. 7), they are separated in this section to simply the description. When a cascading failure happens during rebuild:

- If the newly failed node is a contributor and its data is still available on other nodes, then rebuild can proceed because other nodes can provide everything being provided by the new faulty node, the rebuild service can just switch to degraded mode and pull data from other places. On the other hand, if no other node can provide the same information as the new faulty node, it means that data is unrecoverable after cascading failure. In such cases, the rebuild protocol should also proceed because there is nothing it can do.
- If the new faulty node is a puller, then the data being reconstructed on that node is gone again but will be reconstructed by the queued rebuild task for cascading failure, so there is no necessity to start over.

Based the description above, rebuild protocol of DAOS allows the data rebuild process to proceed even there is a cascading failure, so the system would neither block nor restart the rebuild process. These characteristics ensure the protocol is scalable in a large scale storage system.

4   Asynchronous 2-Phase Commit Performance Results

This section shows the performance differences by running IOR with and without asynchronous commit. Since one of the major goals of this protocol is reducing latency and increasing throughput of small I/O size transaction, the benchmark used 256 bytes as the transfer size to avoid the noise of bulk transfer. The results also include data points from unsafe, non-transactional or one-phase writes, which have no commit, thus the I/O is deemed as complete as long as all members are prepared.

The benchmarks have been run on Intel's DAOS prototype cluster "boro". Both client and storage nodes use Intel Xeon E5-2699 v3 processor and they are equipped with Intel Omni-Path 100 adapters. There is no persistent memory or NVMe SSD on these nodes, so data was written to tmpfs though libpmemobj of PMDK [10], which still calls flush and drain instructions even its backend is tmpfs based emulation. This does not impact the conclusion because the goal of this benchmark is showing benefits of protocol with reduction of network transmissions and cache flushes. The object in the benchmark was 3-way replicated, so the transaction group has three severs. There was a single client in the benchmark, it ran one rank for the latency test, and 16 ranks for the throughput test.

There are three bars in each part of the diagram:

- The first bar is two-phase commit that does synchronous commit, it shows the performance of the basic two-phase commit protocol.
- The second bar is one-phase distributed I/O, it skips the commit phase to represent the baseline performance of the benchmark when there is no overhead of transaction protocol.
- The third bar represents the performance result of asynchronously batch commit protocol, comparing it with the first bar can show the performance gain from running this protocol.

Figure 8.a shows I/O latency of asynchronous two-phase commit reduced 35% while comparing with regular two-phase commit, and Fig. 8.b shows small I/O throughput of asynchronous two-phase commit increased 40%.

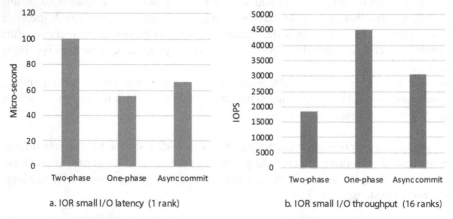

a. IOR small I/O latency (1 rank)   b. IOR small I/O throughput (16 ranks)

Fig. 8. IOR latency and throughput (3-way replication)

5 Conclusion

Two-phase commit protocol of DAOS is tightly coupled with its self-healing system and can avoid the unbounded blocking phenomena of a traditional implementation of two-phase commit protocol, thus increasing the availability of system. In addition, because it allows a committable transaction to move to the commit phase even in the case of multiple failures that includes both the coordinator and participant, so it can support asynchronous commit and decrease transaction response time significantly. It can also support batch commit for transactions belonging to the same transaction group, reducing the message transmissions between servers and the number of persistent memory transactions, thereby improving the overall throughput of the storage cluster.

6 Future Work

The transaction protocol introduced in this paper is only for atomicity of a replicated or erasure coding I/O against one redundancy group, it can also be extended to transactions that modifies multiple redundancy groups of arbitrary number of objects. This extension cannot simply determine transaction order by arriving order anymore but has to rely on MVCC and a global logical clock to define transaction order and control the consistency of data accessed by multiple concurrent transactions. The enhanced protocol is not described in this paper due to limited space available.

References

1. Breitenfeld, M.: DAOS for Extreme-scale Systems in Scientific Applications (2017) https://arxiv.org/pdf/1712.00423.pdf
2. Abhinandan, D., Indranil, G., Ashish, M.: SWIM: Scalable weakly-consistent infection-style process group membership protocol. In: DSN 2002 Proceedings of the 2002 International Conference on Dependable Systems and Networks. pp. 303–312 (2002)
3. Diego, O., John, O.: In Search of an Understandable Consensus Algorithm (2014) https://www.usenix.org/system/files/conference/atc14/atc14-paper-ongaro.pdf
4. Sage, A., Weil, S., Brandt, Ethan, A., Miller, L., Carlos, M.: CRUSH: controlled, scalable, decentralized placement of replicated data. In: SC'06: Proceedings of the 2006 ACM/IEEE Conference on Supercomputing. (2006) https://doi.org/10.1109/sc.2006.19
5. Butler, L., David, L.: A new presumed commit optimization for two phase commit. In: VLDB 1993: Proceedings of the 19th International Conference on Very Large Data Bases. pp. 630–640 (1993)
6. Suyash, G., Sadoghi, M.: EasyCommit: a non-blocking two-phase commit protocol. In: International Conference on Extending Database Technologies, At Vienna, Austria (2018) https://doi.org/10.5441/002/edbt.2018.15
7. Yousef, J.A., George S.: Three-Phase Commit. Encyclopedia of Database Systems. Springer, Boston, MA (2009) https://doi.org/10.1007/978-0-387-39940-9
8. George, S., Kathryn, B., Andrew, C., Mohan, C.: Two-phase commit optimizations and trade-offs in the commercial environment. In: Proceedings of IEEE 9th International Conference on Data Engineering (1993) https://doi.org/10.1109/icde.1993.344028

9. Liu, M.L., Agrawal, D., El Abbadi, A.: The performance of two phase commit protocols in the presence of site failures. Distr. Parallel Databases **6**, 157–182 (1998)https://doi.org/10.1023/a:1008639314265
10. Andy, R.: APIs for persistent memory programming (2018). https://storageconference.us/2018/Presentations/Rudoff.pdf
11. Mercury Homepage: https://mercury-hpc.github.io/documentation/
12. Libfabric Homepage: https://ofiwg.github.io/libfabric/
13. SPDK Homepage: https://spdk.io/
14. PMDK Homepage: https://pmem.io/pmdk/
15. DAOS Homepage: https://github.com/daos-stack/daos
16. Two-phase commit Wikipedia: https://en.wikipedia.org/wiki/Two-phase_commit_protocol

Truly Heterogeneous HPC: Co-design to Achieve What Science Needs from HPC

Suma George Cardwell[✉], Craig Vineyard, Willam Severa, Frances S. Chance, Frederick Rothganger, Felix Wang, Srideep Musuvathy, Corinne Teeter, and James B. Aimone

Sandia National Laboratories, Albuquerque, NM 87123, USA
sgcardw@sandia.gov
https://www.sandia.gov

Abstract. Future high-performance computing (HPC) platforms increasingly depend on heterogeneous node architectures to meet power and performance requirements. While modern HPC design largely incorporates GPUs with CPU resources, there is potential to further integrate novel forms of computing. The ability to leverage efficient, non-conventional computing technologies would be a fundamentally disruptive development in advancing HPC. Neuromorphic computing is such an emerging technology, which would interest the HPC community, due to its potential for implementing large-scale calculations with an extremely low power footprint. We will explore the example of mapping the connectome of the brain to illustrate advantages of using a heterogeneous system that incorporates neuromorphic hardware.

Keywords: Neuromorphic computing · Heterogeneous HPC

1 Overview

Recently there has been a trend toward incorporating multiple classes of processors on a single HPC board. Embracing this heterogeneity has been invaluable in moving towards exascale computing, with significant reliance on general purpose graphics processing units (GPGPUs) to more efficiently implement large-scale problems that rely on dense linear algebra. More attention has been given to linear algebra accelerators, such as systolic arrays (i.e., Google's Tensor Processing Unit) to achieve further efficiencies for suitable computations. Unsurprisingly, this shift in HPC configuration has also expanded the scope of applications for which HPC is relevant to include many current computationally-expensive artificial intelligence (AI) tasks such as deep artificial neural networks (ANNs). However this broadening of HPC components has been limited to conventional processor approaches. Here we present a vision for what we refer to as truly heterogeneous HPC, whereby HPC systems include both conventional components (e.g., CPUs, GPUs, systolic arrays) and non-conventional components, such as neuromorphic hardware and processing-in-memory (PIM) devices.

© National Technology & Engineering Solutions of Sandia, LLC 2020
J. Nichols et al. (Eds.): SMC 2020, CCIS 1315, pp. 349–365, 2020.
https://doi.org/10.1007/978-3-030-63393-6_23

These emerging technologies promise substantial benefits in efficiency as shown in Fig. 1, especially in terms of power requirements, but also require a distinct approach to computation. These architectures are extremely parallel, with different trade-offs between precision and speed than are typically encountered in von Neumann systems. The use-cases for neuromorphic hardware are actively evolving. For instance, while the long-term impact of neuromorphic computing likely lies in future brain-derived algorithms [2]; much of the recent focus has been on accelerating ANNs [54, 56] and it is increasingly recognized to be capable for numerical computing applications [3, 55]. It is not immediately obvious whether neuromorphic approaches are critical for scientific applications that have driven HPC development to date. Computing technologies have evolved to solve large physics models. Similarly, large-scale machine learning approaches such as ANNs, bolstered by GPUs, have outperformed alternatives. However, the scientific computing ecosystem is beginning to change. As data collection begins to outpace theory in fields such as neuroscience, medicine, and climatology, we increasingly find ourselves in a world where the simulation of physics models is less important than deriving insight from extremely large volumes of complex data. To illustrate this shift and how it would drive the eventual requirements of a truly heterogeneous HPC platform, we work through a specific scientific example: mapping and interpreting the connectome of the brain as illustrated in Fig. 2. The connectome example is both salient (the US Government and EU continue to spend significant funds on it) and representative of an emerging class of data-intensive scientific endeavors where classical modeling and analytics are only part of the solution. Within this example, we highlight how incorporating the scientific exploration of data changes computing needs, and show that a system combining the strengths of traditional CPUs/GPUs with emerging neuromorphic technology will be invaluable and disruptive for HPC systems.

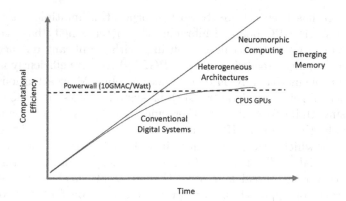

Fig. 1. The computational efficiency of modern general-purpose processors has hit a power wall [18, 24], leading to the search for novel architectures and emerging devices. The metric used for performance is Multiply Accumulates per Watt (GMAC/Watt).

Connectomics and Electron Microscopy data

Mapping the connectome of a brain and deriving new understanding of the underlying neural circuit function as shown in Fig. 2 requires addressing a number of key challenges. Scaling electron microscopy (EM) techniques to handle a volume the size of an entire brain [31,42] comes with the challenge of analyzing the massive amounts of associated data. The first reconstruction of the *C. elegans* nervous system [60] was performed almost entirely by human-hand, requiring more than 10 years to map approximately 300 neurons and 7000 connections between them [29]. For comparison, a *Drosophila melanogaster* (fruit fly) brain comprises on the order of 100,000 neurons [65] while a mouse brain is estimated at 70 million neurons [26]. The raw data for one cubic millimeter of mouse visual cortex is on the order of 2 petabytes [64]. While advances in high-throughput EM [63,64] and automated segmentation and reconstruction algorithms [30] signify the 'coming of age' of EM, interpreting newly-available, high-resolution whole-brain connectomes will require overcoming significant computational challenges. As larger volumes from both invertebrate [20,51,62,65] and mammalian [19,53,64] brains become available with increasingly dense reconstructions and more complete identification of different cell types and synaptic connections, so will the need for semi-automated and increasingly sophisticated analysis.

In this paper, we focus on how a heterogeneous platform may be leveraged to address the computational challenges associated with processing and analysis of the EM imagery, including segmentation and analysis of the resulting connectome graph. First, emerging technology may be used to accelerate current state-of-the-art methods for EM imagery analysis. The use of flood-filling networks for image segmentation and reconstruction [30] of large-volume EM constitutes state-of-the-art today (e.g. see [34,51,62]). While these networks perform with significantly better accuracy compared to alternative approaches, they are also computationally expensive. Some of our existing approaches to developing neuromorphic systems may be leveraged to implement these networks at significantly lower computational cost.

Another challenge for fully realizing the potential of high-throughput EM is analyzing the connectome to draw meaningful conclusions regarding the organization and function of neural circuits. Larger-scale connectomes with online tools for visualization and analysis have only recently become widely available

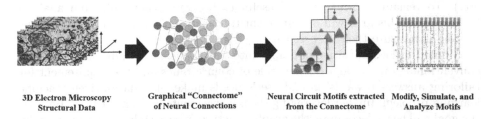

3D Electron Microscopy   **Graphical "Connectome"**   **Neural Circuit Motifs extracted**   **Modify, Simulate, and**
Structural Data   **of Neural Connections**   **from the Connectome**   **Analyze Motifs**

Fig. 2. Pipeline needed to map the Brain Connectome from 3D EM Structural Data to extracting neural circuit motifs and analyzing it. EM Image reproduced from [65]

(for examples, see https://microns-explorer.org [19,53] and https://neuprint.
janelia.org [15]). Analysis of the associated neural graphs thus far have been
largely limited to statistics describing the input/output connectivity of specific
cell types [50,53,65] within individual volumes. Analysis of graphs combined
with functional data [10,67], or across multiple specimens [61] are less common and will likely require more sophisticated semi-automated approaches. Our
approaches to accelerating AI algorithms on neuromorphic hardware can be
extended to accelerate the process of identifying meaningful graph motifs contained within these images, thereby facilitating meaningful interpretations of the
data.

2   Algorithmic Approach

Many scientific domains, ranging from astrophysics to materials science, leverage large scale data collection and a series of AI analyses to extract scientifically
meaningful data. Image processing, or very similar data processing, is often the
first step of such scientific analysis pipelines, and many of the successful AI
techniques being developed today impact this stage. The convolutional neural
network component of this AI pipeline is a well-established algorithm that has
broad applicability, and the process of identifying the computationally expensive
parts of these neural networks and tailoring them for hardware acceleration is an
immediately approachable research challenge. The algorithmic approach will be
primarily to identify critical computational kernels that are suitable for neuromorphic hardware implementation and that can be extracted from an overall AI
pipeline. Below we describe approaches that can leverage neuromorphic architectures and enable the acceleration of EM image analysis with lower computational
cost.

2.1   Deep Graph Decomposition

Deep learning methods, as applied to analyze graph structure, is still a developing
field, for example the work on graph neural networks (GNN) in recent years (see
[66] for a review). In contrast to more commonly studied social or information
graphs, however, the data extracted from EM image analysis admits a higher
degree of complexity in its structure (e.g. cortical microcircuits, high fan-in/out,
etc.). To remain informative and useful to the researcher, subgraph analysis
techniques in this area will be important to specify salient neural circuit motifs,
as well as measure their occurrence.

   While the decomposition of graphs into subgraphs is typically the purview of
conventional graph analytics, the scale of connectomes and the requirement for
tailoring answers towards an end-user's needs makes it a data-driven machine
learning problem, further leveraging the advancements in deep learning. Because
the goal will be to decompose the graph structure from EM data into functionally
relevant subgraphs, we refer to the approach as Deep Graph Decomposition,
or DGD.

Supporting this approach are recent developments in graph embedding, such as graph2vec, structural-rnn, or LINE, which enable effective vector representations that may be useful in identifying critical, repeating features in graphs [28,38,58]. This is analogous to the role of convolution filters used for image processing problems or acquiring dictionary elements for sparse coding. The learned filters in either of these domains are effectively data-driven feature extractors. More specific to image processing, these filters may combine and stack into a layered hierarchy. For our subgraph task, we are specifically interested in patterns that carry critical information about the composition (i.e. rate of occurrence) in the larger graph, and we hypothesize that these can be determined either directly (via inference) or indirectly (via network introspection).

Embedding methods such as DeepWalk, which use random walks from graph vertices to generate representational signatures, may better leverage heterogeneous architectures [43]. Previous work [55] shows that neuromorphic systems can be highly efficient at computing diffusive random walks on graphs. By categorizing and counting the types of walks that are observed, we can extract an approximation of the common connectivity patterns within a given graph. In contrast with more conventional, state-of-the-art algorithms for subgraph counting (e.g. ESCAPE [44]), the motivating trade-off is to be able to extend beyond the limited subgraph sizes (e.g. up to five vertices) of exact methods. This leads to the scalability and subgraph complexity needed to analyze EM data, where there will be expected variability within equivalence-classes of neural circuit motifs. Neuromorphic systems are uniquely suited as a computational platform to map and scale graphs because of parallelism, local connections, and efficiency gains.

2.2 Neuromorphic Scaling of 3D Convolutional Neural Networks

Deep learning methods, particularly convolutional neural networks used in EM segmentation, are becoming increasingly common within scientific experimental workflows. Researchers in several fields have been able to use deep learning to help shift effort away from time-intensive tasks (e.g. hand-labeling images) or to help mitigate technical bottlenecks (e.g. when storing large-scale raw data is prohibitive). Large-scale applications, such as the use of flood-filling networks to segment neural EM data, require a considerable amount of compute power, often utilizing a heterogeneous CPU/GPU system. This compute requirement is complicated by the inclusion of 3D convolutional layers – a standard 2D convolution strides a 2D window (filter) across the x and y dimensions of an image, whereas a 3D convolution strides a 3D cube across the x, y, and z dimensions of a 3D image or a stack of 2D images. These 3D convolutions are well-suited for stacked frames (such as those found in EM data or video) or other 3D imaging (such as MRI images). Despite possible acceleration via Fourier methods, these algorithms require more compute and more memory than the common 2D counterpart.

The most straightforward approach to making neural networks more efficient is to tailor algorithms to require less precision, in both weights and activation functions, along with hardware capable of benefiting from this low-precision.

High-performing neural networks traditionally use 32-bits or more precision for activation functions (e.g. rectified linear units) and weights. However, the high precision afforded by these representations is costly both in computation and communication. To address the challenge of big data science applications such as EM, the scale of today's neuromorphic systems is vastly insufficient. For instance, the first layer of the flood-filling network would likely require over one billion neurons, well beyond the largest neuromorphic platforms available today. It requires further design trade-offs, such as fixed precision weights or limited connectivity. We envision that future large-scale systems as described in Sect. 3 will rise up to these challenges.

3   Hardware Architecture

As digital systems saturate in terms of power efficiency, it is clear that the future of computing is heterogeneous. Moore's law is slowing, and recently neural networks have regained popularity. This has led to renewed focus on emerging technologies, such as neuromorphic computing. Inspired by the brain, neuromorphic architectures leverage properties such as massive parallelism, sparse activity, and event-driven computing. Prof. Carver Mead pioneered neuromorphic engineering in the late1980 s using silicon devices to mimic biology. These were analog circuits that utilized sub-threshold dynamics of CMOS transistors to emulate biological systems. Today, neuromorphic systems encompass digital as well as mixed-signal approaches. Recently, several large-scale neuromorphic projects have paved the way to demonstrating problems at scale on these systems. Spiking neuromorphic hardware fabricated in cutting-edge technology nodes is rapidly progressing to a billion neurons from vendors such as Intel (Pohoiki Springs/Loihi). Recent developments in non-conventional devices like nanoscale memristors that are CMOS-compatible show promising solutions to modeling dense synaptic memory.

3.1   Analog Neuromorphic Computing

Researchers at Sandia have shown that analog in-memory computations have a fundamental scaling advantage over digital memories. Analog crossbars have been projected to reduce energy and latency by three orders of magnitude compared to an optimized digital Application Specific Integrated Circuit (ASIC) [1]. Different classes of devices show promise, including TaOx Resitive RAM (ReRAM) and conventional floating-gate SONOS. The analog ReRAM shows the most promise when compared to digital SRAM-based ASICs, with better performance in area, energy, and latency [1]. However, the algorithms used to train and learn on these devices are not optimized for their behavior. In-memory analog kernels are subject to analog noise. This variability can be leveraged by incorporating hardware characteristics as features while training [9,46]. Furthermore, these systems tend to have lower bit precision. Co-designing multi-precision algorithms for these devices and integration with conventional CMOS approaches will be crucial to unleashing their potential. Other approaches in analog and mixed-signal CMOS chips include large-scale mixed-signal ICs like DYNAP-SEL [37], Neurogrid [8], and analog CMOS floating-gate based reconfigurable approaches like GT's learning enabled neuron IC [11] and Field Programmable Analog Arrays [23]. For a detailed overview see [59].

3.2 Digital Neuromorphic Computing

Developments in large-scale digital neuromorphic chips have shown the promise of these systems at scale. Table 1 highlights the digital neuromorphic front-runners. University of Manchester's SpiNNaker chip (130 nm CMOS) represents a more configurable approach, with programmable ARM cores and an interconnect fabric optimized for spiking communication [22]. This platform is flexible to different neuron and synapse models. IBM's TrueNorth chip was the first neuromorphic chip with a million neurons [35]. Intel's Loihi is fabricated in 14 nm FinFET technology with 128 neuromorphic cores and with an integrated learning engine on-chip [16].

The SpiNNaker and Loihi architectures lend themselves well to scaling and are front runners in the race to achieving billion neurons. The million ARM core SpiNNaker system aims to simulate a billion neurons and Intel recently announced the Poihiki Springs system with 100 million neurons [39]. Plans on building the next generation of SpiNNaker2 chips in 22 nm FDX CMOS are currently underway [27]. Both systems support learning on-chip, are configurable, and have a dedicated software stack to program the hardware. These systems also support research communities, which is key to the adoption of such emerging technologies.

Table 1. Current large-scale digital neuromorphic systems. Energy per event as reported from [59]

Platform	Technology	Neurons (chip)	Synapses (chip)	On-chip learning	Energy per event
Loihi	14 nm	128 K	128 M	Yes	23.6 pJ
TrueNorth	28 nm	1 M	256 M	No	45 pJ
SpiNNaker	130 nm	16 K	16 M	Yes	43 nJ

3.3 Integrating Neuromorphic Computing with Conventional HPC: Optimizing System Architecture

The fundamental principle guiding architecture design is to match the structure of the physical machine to the algorithm. This leads us to focus on two secondary principles: heterogeneity and information distance.

Heterogeneity – No single machine structure will best fit every algorithm, even within the specific domain of neural-inspired algorithms. The mix of available core types still represents a commitment to a particular range of algorithms. Alternately, different installations could choose different combinations of 'plug-and-play' hardware modules to target specific sets of algorithms.

Information Distance – Data movement is the key limit in modern systems. Individual transistors are already extremely efficient, requiring on the order of 1e− neurons and digital communication 17 J of energy to switch, not far above the thermal noise limit of $\sim 40kbT = 2e{-}19$ J. However, communication is orders of magnitude costlier, requiring around 1 pJ to move data across a chip. The cost of computation is dominated by Joules/(bit*meter). That is, energy cost scales with the distance information must move. Consequently, the focus would be to use neuromorphic accelerator kernels that process in memory and minimize data movement. A full system design will consist of the following levels:

- **Core**: A single processing block. This may be either analog or digital.
- **Package:** A collection of cores assembled on a single die, or perhaps a vertically-integrated stack of dies. The package may be heterogeneous, containing several different types of cores, and perhaps mixing digital with analog cores. A key question is how heterogeneous cores communicate with each other. We make the simplifying assumption that cores always connect to a digital network and follow a standard protocol. This protocol will be designed to scale up to system and cluster levels.
- **System**: Neuromorphic packages may be integrated with conventional components (GPUs, CPUs, memory banks) on a compute node. Each package could have dual-ported memory, such that it can be accessed on the main system bus, or it may be accessed solely through the neuromorphic network protocol, in which case a bridge device will be visible to the rest of the system.
- **Cluster**: Specifies how to scale-up systems which include neuromorphic components to work efficiently at the petascale or exascale (machines that occupy an entire warehouses or data-centers). Interesting questions include whether there is any impact on the design of a cluster system due to the presence of neuromorphic components. For example, will it move event packets over the main network backbone, or will there be a separate neuromorphic network fabric?

To achieve this objective, high-level architecture simulations will be needed to search the design space for good matches to specific algorithms. Tools that optimize the system architecture to minimize costs such as energy, area, and time will be key. This is analogous to the SWaP (size, weight, and power) constraints often cited in neuromorphic applications, but here we are less concerned about spatial restrictions and more concerned with throughput. Developing tools that help evaluate mixed-precision, highly heterogeneous architectures incorporating neuromorphic components will be key to enable adoption of these novel neuromorphic processors. We discuss strategies for co-design by using analytical modeling tools in Sect. 4.1 and using Joint Neural Architecture and Hardware Search in Sect. 4.2.

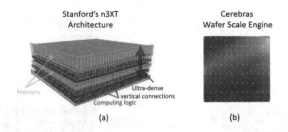

Fig. 3. Novel Approaches in development (a) 3D memory and compute architecture. Breakthroughs will allow very high density memory cells to be built. Image reproduced from [6]. (b) Wafer-Scale Systems such as Cerebras' Wafer Scale Engine promise high bandwidth and low latency [13].

3.4 Novel Approaches in Fabrication

Novel approaches in fabrication include building three-dimensional architectures and wafer-scale integrated circuits as shown in Fig. 3. Early demonstration of 3D memory has been promising, and dense integration with CMOS processing units will yield further advantages. Stanford's Nano-Engineered Computing Systems Technology (N3XT) program offers insight into 3D architectures via their simulation framework for highly integrated ultra dense (monolithic) 3-D integration of thin layers of logic and memory devices [5,6].

Wafer-scale processors dramatically reduce communication overhead for large-scale systems but are very challenging owing to thermal as well as process yield issues. *BrainScaleS* is an example of a wafer-scale neuromorphic system with analog circuits to emulate point neurons and digital communication (digital interconnect network) fabricated in 180 nm [52]. Current wafer-scale accelerator chips like *Cerebras's* Wafer Scale Engine demonstrate that wafer-scale approaches are feasible at lower technology nodes with considerable innovation in fabrication and packaging of these systems [13].

4   Co-Design of Heterogeneous Architectures

While algorithm-hardware co-design is critical for achieving high performance and energy efficiency, there is a practical challenge in linking design at these different scales. In terms of hardware development, a bottom-up approach is typically followed, whereby architectural designs are assumed and potentially-accelerated algorithms are sought after the fact. Similarly, because most real-world AI research focuses on task performance, the implications of algorithm design choice on potential hardware acceleration are often considered once an approach is set. To achieve the overall objective, both algorithmic and hardware optimizations need to be incorporated into a design as illustrated in Fig. 4. Sandia has developed an open-source python based tool called Fugu [4], that enables designing Spiking neural networks while being hardware agnostic.

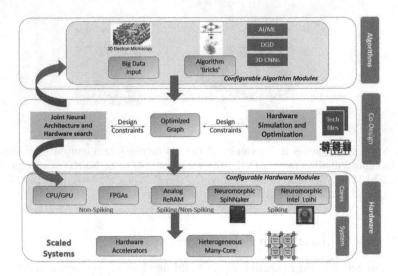

Fig. 4. Co-design of Algorithms and Architectures is critical for heterogeneous HPC systems.

4.1 Analytical Modeling

Exploration of accelerator designs has ushered in a new 'Golden Age in Computer Architecture' [17]. A spectrum of computer architecture design tools have emerged to facilitate research into these new computational architectures. This ranges from analytical assessments to high fidelity simulations. The analytical approaches assess the steps which must occur for a given neural network to be computed given the architectural choices of a target platform. This includes calculating how the computation must be decomposed to pass through the computational units, how many memory accesses are required for retrieving input values and weights as well as storing results, and how communication structures facilitate these data movements. These counts are then multiplied by appropriate costs attributed to a targeted node technology (e.g. how much energy a multiplication or memory access requires). Effectively, this forecasts how a neural network maps onto a target architecture. Example analytical approaches include Modeling Accelerator Efficiency via Spatio-Temporal Resource Occupancy (MAESTRO) and Eyeriss Eyexam [14,32]. Other analytical tools focus upon assessing properties of a hardware architecture such as the utilization of resources and identifying what is an optimal dataflow strategy for the architecture. An example is the Timeloop tool [41]. More accurate, but slower tools offer cycle accurate simulation capabilities. This increased fidelity often incorporates component models to attain the cycle accurate analysis and sometimes couples with executable hardware description level simulations. Examples include Systolic CNN AcceLErator Simulator (SCALE Sim) and Nvidia Deep Learning Accelerator (NVDLA) [40,49]. The above techniques have largely focused on ML accelerator approaches such as systolic arrays and CNN accelerators. Additional interest is in how emerging neuromorphic architectures may also be modeled. For example, NeMo utilizes the Rensselaer's optimistic simulation system (ROSS) in a discrete event simulation tool to provide a functional simulation of the IBM TrueNorth spiking neuromorphic architecture [45]. Other capabilities seek to account for the performance of emerging device technologies such as CrossSim and PUMA [1,7]. Effectively, this spectrum of analytical modeling capabilities help enable co-design and the assessment of the impact of incorporating emerging ML accelerator and neuromorphic architectures into truly heterogeneous HPC systems.

4.2   Joint Neural Hardware and Architecture Search

Currently, the deep learning community increasingly leverages systematic parameter exploration of the algorithm space, but it generally does not explicitly consider the interaction of algorithms with its hardware implementation. Hyperparameter optimization techniques are often used to systematically explore sets of parameters, such as learning rates, kernel widths, and layer sizes to help tune neural network structures to optimize algorithm performance in new domains. Hardware constraints can also be viewed as hyperparameters that can be optimized for.

4.3   Learning Algorithms for Neuromorphic Hardware

In contrast to standard artificial neural network (ANN) training methods, neuromorphic hardware increasingly utilizes brain-inspired, local-learning rules to update weights between nodes. Standard ANNs implemented on CPUs are often trained using extended versions of gradient descent [47] learning algorithms. Although these ANNs have proven quite effective at specific tasks, even surpassing human performance on some, such as image processing [48], natural language processing [33], and playing games [36,57], there are drawbacks to these networks. Weight adjustments require both a forward and a back-propagation pass through the entire network. This makes them computationally expensive to train. They require enormous amounts of labeled data for training and they can be quite rigid and fail in unexpected and catastrophic ways [21]. Many, techniques have been developed to address these problems. However, such solutions only treat the symptoms, not underlying issues.

The ability of biological brains to quickly synthesize, process, and act on large or small amounts of unlabeled data, while consuming very small amounts of power, have inspired scientists and engineers from many fields. Brains use a different approach for learning. In local learning, such as Hebbian learning [25] or spike time dependent plasticity (STDP) [12], the weights are adjusted between the pre and post synaptic neurons based on their activity.

Local learning may have substantial computational benefits. It enables learning with spikes without contrived methods to estimate gradients. It is intrinsically parallel; learning does not need a signal to be forward and then back-propagated though a network. And it is relatively unsupervised; weights are strengthened via correlated activity, not, via a backpropagated error signal. Techniques to effectively utilize local learning in deep networks is an active research topic in neuroscience and computer science. The realization of local learning will likely unleash the next generation of adaptive, low-power, deep neural networks. Neuromorphic hardware is ready to capitalize on these new algorithms.

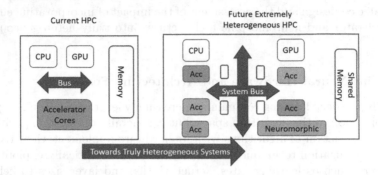

Fig. 5. Future of heterogeneous high performance computing

5   Future of HPC: Truly Heterogeneous Architectures

Lower costs of fabrication and testing have encouraged development of synchronous digital approaches in the past, but sub-10 nm development of CMOS circuits is significantly more expensive. Now, the industry is trending towards more specialized hardware as opposed to general-purpose processors. This is truly a 'Golden Age for Computer Architecture', with new innovations required from devices to architectures. With AI/ML algorithms as compelling use cases for these architectures, co-design of hardware and algorithms will be crucial. The future of HPC is heterogeneous and will fundamentally change the role of computing in science. Neuromorphic computing is an emerging technology that can impact HPC in the next 5–10 years. Over the next few decades other technologies like quantum computing, photonics, newer devices and fabrication techniques will be potentially impactful as well.

We discussed the example of brain connectomics using serial electron microscopy (EM) to construct the 'connectome' (i.e., the graph of neurons and connections between them) of progressively larger volumes of brain tissue. Producing terabytes of data per day, image analysis of EM data already demands an HPC approach. However, the ultimate goal of EM mapping of the brain is to extract computational understanding of its structure in order to advance neuroscience. Neuromorphic technologies, specifically, provide both low-power and configurable acceleration of such challenging AI algorithms. If designed into a heterogeneous system with other accelerators and conventional computing devices, this technology can augment and extend the capabilities of traditional HPC platforms as shown in Fig. 5.

Relevance to DOE and HPC

It is worth noting that the recent advances in EM methodologies have continued to draw the interest of BRAIN Initiative stakeholders, including NIH and NSF, as well as potential new investments from DOE. Today, most AI algorithms are designed independently of hardware considerations, with algorithm performance the dominant criterion for a successful AI approach. As a result, the extreme computational costs of emerging AI technologies, especially in deep learning, have led to an explosion of proposed ANN accelerators. These accelerators are largely conventional CMOS approaches tailored to accelerate core linear algebra operations. Future AI solutions, such as those integrated into high-throughput scientific pipelines, will leverage both deep learning-based ML approaches and other AI algorithms that may not be ideally suited for the current generation of deep learning accelerators. Our proposed co-design strategy has two requirements: 1) the cumulative performance of an AI system is critical, not simply the acceleration of any particular kernel and 2) hardware acceleration cannot come at the expense of algorithm performance. EM image analysis is an attractive 'test' application space for a heterogeneous system. Image processing of 3D electron microscopy data using deep neural networks already has a well-established approach as its solution (flood-filling networks), yet the decomposition of deep neural connectivity graphs at increasingly large scales is still relatively nascent and more effective approaches remain to be discovered. The field needs approaches to acceleration that can maintain performance without significantly increasing computational cost. This application space is particularly attractive because it illustrates the data analytics pipeline in a number of scientific research areas and highlights the challenges associated with both ultra-large scale data and still rapidly-evolving AI and ML techniques.

Acknowledgment. The authors acknowledge financial support from the DOE Advanced Simulation and Computing program and Sandia National Laboratories' Laboratory Directed Research and Development Program. Sandia National Laboratories is a multi-mission laboratory managed and operated by National Technology and Engineering Solutions of Sandia, LLC, a wholly owned subsidiary of Honeywell International, Inc., for the U.S. Department of Energy's National Nuclear Security Administration under contract DE-NA0003525. This paper describes technical results and analysis. Any subjective views or opinions that might be expressed in the paper do not necessarily represent the views of the U.S. Department of Energy or the United States Government. SAND Number: SAND2020-8238 C.

References

1. Agarwal, S., et al.: Designing an analog crossbar based neuromorphic accelerator. In: 2017 Fifth Berkeley Symposium on Energy Efficient Electronic Systems & Steep Transistors Workshop (E3S), pp. 1–3. IEEE (2017)
2. Aimone, J.B.: Neural algorithms and computing beyond Moore's law. Commun. ACM **62**(4), 110–110 (2019)

3. Aimone, J.B., Hamilton, K.E., Mniszewski, S., Reeder, L., Schuman, C.D., Severa, W.M.: Non-neural network applications for spiking neuromorphic hardware. In: Proceedings of the Third International Workshop on Post Moores Era Supercomputing, pp. 24–26 (2018)
4. Aimone, J.B., Severa, W., Vineyard, C.M.: Composing neural algorithms with fugu. In: Proceedings of the International Conference on Neuromorphic Systems, pp. 1–8 (2019)
5. Aly, M.M.S., et al.: Energy-efficient abundant-data computing: The n3xt 1,000 x. Computer 48(12), 24–33 (2015)
6. Aly, M.M.S., et al.: The n3xt approach to energy-efficient abundant-data computing. Proc. IEEE 107(1), 19–48 (2018)
7. Ankit, A., et al.: Puma: A programmable ultra-efficient memristor-based accelerator for machine learning inference. In: Proceedings of the Twenty-Fourth International Conference on Architectural Support for Programming Languages and Operating Systems, pp. 715–731 (2019)
8. Benjamin, B.V., et al.: Neurogrid: a mixed-analog-digital multichip system for large-scale neural simulations. Proc. IEEE 102(5), 699–716 (2014)
9. Bennett, C.H., et al.: Evaluating complexity and resilience trade-offs in emerging memory inference machines. arXiv preprint arXiv:2003.10396 (2020)
10. Bock, D.D., et al.: Network anatomy and in vivo physiology of visual cortical neurons. Nature 471(7337), 177–182 (2011)
11. Brink, S., et al.: A learning-enabled neuron array ic based upon transistor channel models of biological phenomena. IEEE Trans. Biomed. Circ. Syst. 7(1), 71–81 (2012)
12. Caporale, N., Dan, Y.: Spike timing-dependent plasticity: a hebbian learning rule. Annu. Rev. Neurosci. 31, 25–46 (2008)
13. Cerebras: (2020). URL https://www.cerebras.net/
14. Chen, Y.H., Yang, T.J., Emer, J., Sze, V.: Eyeriss v2: a flexible accelerator for emerging deep neural networks on mobile devices. IEEE J. Emerg. Select. Top. Circ. Syst. 9(2), 292–308 (2019)
15. Clements, J., et al.: neuprint: Analysis tools for em connectomics. BioRxiv (2020)
16. Davies, M., et al.: Loihi: A neuromorphic manycore processor with on-chip learning. IEEE Micro 38(1), 82–99 (2018)
17. Dean, J., Patterson, D., Young, C.: A new golden age in computer architecture: empowering the machine-learning revolution. IEEE Micro 38(2), 21–29 (2018)
18. Degnan, B., Marr, B., Hasler, J.: Assessing trends in performance per watt for signal processing applications. IEEE Trans. Very Large Scale Integr. (VLSI) Syst. 24(1), 58–66 (2015)
19. Dorkenwald, S., et al.: Binary and analog variation of synapses between cortical pyramidal neurons. bioRxiv (2019)
20. Erichler, K., et al.: The complete connectome of a learning and memory centre in an insect brain. Nature 548(7666), 175–182 (2017)
21. Eykholt, K., et al.: Robust physical-world attacks on deep learning visual classification. In: Proceedings of the IEEE Conference on Computer Vision and Pattern Recognition, pp. 1625–1634 (2018)
22. Furber, S.B., Galluppi, F., Temple, S., Plana, L.A.: The spinnaker project. Proc. IEEE 102(5), 652–665 (2014)
23. George, S., et al.: A programmable and configurable mixed-mode FPAA soc. IEEE Trans. Very Large Scale Integr. (VLSI) Syst. 24(6), 2253–2261 (2016)
24. Hasler, J., Marr, H.B.: Finding a roadmap to achieve large neuromorphic hardware systems. Front. Neurosci. 7, 118 (2013)

25. Hebb, D.O.: The Organization of Behavior: a Neuropsychological Theory. J. Wiley; Chapman & Hall, New York (1949)
26. Herculano-Houzel, S., Mota, B., Lent, R.: Cellular scaling rules for rodent brains. Proc. Natl. Acad. Sci. **103**(32), 12138–12143 (2006)
27. Höppner, S., Mayr, C.: Spinnaker2-towards extremely efficient digital neuromorphics and multi-scale brain emulation. In: Proc. NICE (2018)
28. Jain, A., Zamir, A.R., Savarese, S., Saxena, A.: Structural-RNN: deep learning on spatio-temporal graphs. In: Proceedings of the IEEE Conference on Computer Vision and Pattern Recognition, pp. 5308–5317 (2016)
29. Jain, V., Seung, H.S., Turaga, S.C.: Machines that learn to segment images: a crucial technology for connectomics. Curr. Opin. Neurobiol. **20**(5), 653–666 (2010)
30. Januszewski, M., et al.: High-precision automated reconstruction of neurons with flood-filling networks. Nat. Meth. **15**(8), 605–610 (2018)
31. Kornfeld, J., Denk, W.: Progress and remaining challenges in high-throughput volume electron microscopy. Curr. Opin. Neurobiol. **50**, 261–267 (2018)
32. Kwon, H., Pellauer, M., Krishna, T.: Maestro: an open-source infrastructure for modeling dataflows within deep learning accelerators. arXiv preprint arXiv:1805.02566 (2018)
33. LeCun, Y., Bengio, Y., Hinton, G.: Deep learning. Nature **521**(7553), 436–444 (2015)
34. Li, P.H., et al.: Automated reconstruction of a serial-section Em drosophila brain with flood-filling networks and local realignment. Microsc. Microanal. **25**(S2), 1364–1365 (2019)
35. Merolla, P.A., et al.: A million spiking-neuron integrated circuit with a scalable communication network and interface. Science **345**(6197), 668–673 (2014)
36. Mnih, V., et al.: Human-level control through deep reinforcement learning. Nature **518**(7540), 529–533 (2015)
37. Moradi, S., Qiao, N., Stefanini, F., Indiveri, G.: A scalable multicore architecture with heterogeneous memory structures for dynamic neuromorphic asynchronous processors (dynaps). IEEE Trans. Biomed. Circ. Syst. **12**(1), 106–122 (2017)
38. Narayanan, A., Chandramohan, M., Venkatesan, R., Chen, L., Liu, Y., Jaiswal, S.: Graph2vec: learning distributed representations of graphs. arXiv preprint arXiv:1707.05005 (2017)
39. Newsroom, I.: Intel Scales Neuromorphic Research System to 100 Million Neurons 18th March 2020 . URL https://newsroom.intel.com/news/intel-scales-neuromorphic-research-system-100-million-neurons/#gs.7xo39i. Accessed 13 June 2020
40. NVDLA: (2020). URL http://nvdla.org/index.html
41. Parashar, A., et al.: Timeloop: A systematic approach to dnn accelerator evaluation. In: 2019 IEEE International Symposium on Performance Analysis of Systems and Software (ISPASS), pp. 304–315. IEEE (2019)
42. Peddie, C.J., Collinson, L.M.: Exploring the third dimension: volume electron microscopy comes of age. Micron **61**, 9–19 (2014)
43. Perozzi, B., Al-Rfou, R., Skiena, S.: Deepwalk: Online learning of social representations. In: Proceedings of the 20th ACM SIGKDD International Conference on Knowledge Discovery and Data mining, pp. 701–710 (2014)
44. Pinar, A., Seshadhri, C., Vishal, V.: Escape: efficiently counting all 5-vertex subgraphs. In: Proceedings of the 26th International Conference on World Wide Web, pp. 1431–1440 (2017)

45. Plagge, M., Carothers, C.D., Gonsiorowski, E., Mcglohon, N.: Nemo: A massively parallel discrete-event simulation model for neuromorphic architectures. ACM Trans. Model. Comput. Simul. (TOMACS) **28**(4), 1–25 (2018)

46. Rothganger, F., Evans, B.R., Aimone, J.B., DeBenedictis, E.P.: Training neural hardware with noisy components. In: 2015 International Joint Conference on Neural Networks (IJCNN), pp. 1–8 (2015)

47. Rumelhart, D.E., Hinton, G.E., Williams, R.J.: Learning representations by back-propagating errors. Nature **323**(6088), 533–536 (1986)

48. Russakovsky, O., et al.: Imagenet large scale visual recognition challenge. Int. J. Comput. Vis. **115**(3), 211–252 (2015)

49. Samajdar, A., Zhu, Y., Whatmough, P., Mattina, M., Krishna, T.: Scale-sim: Systolic cnn accelerator simulator. arXiv preprint arXiv:1811.02883 (2018)

50. Scheffer, L.K.: Graph properties of the adult drosophila central brain. bioRxiv (2020)

51. Scheffer, L.K., et al.: A connectome and analysis of the adult drosophila central brain. BioRxiv (2020)

52. Schemmel, J., Fieres, J., Meier, K.: Wafer-scale integration of analog neural networks. In: 2008 IEEE International Joint Conference on Neural Networks (IEEE World Congress on Computational Intelligence), pp. 431–438. IEEE (2008)

53. Schneider-Mizell, C.M., et al.: Chandelier cell anatomy and function reveal a variably distributed but common signal. bioRxiv (2020)

54. Schuman, C.D., et al.: A survey of neuromorphic computing and neural networks in hardware. arXiv preprint arXiv:1705.06963 (2017)

55. Severa, W., Parekh, O., Carlson, K.D., James, C.D., Aimone, J.B.: Spiking network algorithms for scientific computing. In: 2016 IEEE International Conference on Rebooting Computing (ICRC), pp. 1–8. IEEE (2016)

56. Severa, W., Vineyard, C.M., Dellana, R., Verzi, S.J., Aimone, J.B.: Training deep neural networks for binary communication with the whetstone method. Nat. Mach. Intell. **1**(2), 86–94 (2019)

57. Silver, D., et al.: Mastering the game of go with deep neural networks and tree search. Nature **529**(7587), 484 (2016)

58. Tang, J., Qu, M., Wang, M., Zhang, M., Yan, J., Mei, Q.: Line: large-scale information network embedding. In: Proceedings of the 24th International Conference on World Wide Web, pp. 1067–1077 (2015)

59. Thakur, C.S., et al.: Large-scale neuromorphic spiking array processors: a quest to mimic the brain. Front. Neurosci. **12**, 891 (2018)

60. White, J.G., Southgate, E., Thomson, J.N., Brenner, S.: The structure of the nervous system of the nematode caenorhabditis elegans. Philos. Trans. R Soc. Lond. B Biol. Sci. **314**(1165), 1–340 (1986)

61. Witvliet, D., et al.: Connectomes across development reveal principles of brain maturation in c. elegans. bioRxiv (2020)

62. Xu, C.S., et al.: A connectome of the adult drosophila central brain. BioRxiv (2020)

63. Xu, C.S., Pang, S., Hayworth, K.J., Hess, H.F.: Enabling fib-sem systems for large volume connectomics and cell biology. bioRxiv, p. 852863 (2019)

64. Yin, W., .: A petascale automated imaging pipeline for mapping neuronal circuits with high-throughput transmission electron microscopy. bioRxiv, p. 791889 (2019)

65. Zheng, Z., et al.: A complete electron microscopy volume of the brain of adult drosophila melanogaster. Cell **174**(3), 730–743 (2018)
66. Zhou, J., et al.: Graph neural networks: A review of methods and applications. arXiv preprint arXiv:1812.08434 (2018)
67. Zhou, P., et al.: Ease: Em-assisted source extraction from calcium imaging data. bioRxiv (2020)

Performance Evaluation of Python Based Data Analytics Frameworks in Summit: Early Experiences

Benjamín Hernández[1]([✉]), Suhas Somnath[1], Junqi Yin[1], Hao Lu[1], Joe Eaton[2], Peter Entschev[2], John Kirkham[2], and Zahra Ronaghi[2]

[1] Oak Ridge National Laboratory, Oak Ridge, TN, USA
hernandezarb@ornl.gov
[2] NVIDIA, Santa Clara, CA, USA

Abstract. The explosion in the volumes of data generated from ever-larger simulation campaigns and experiments or observations necessitates competent tools for data wrangling and analysis). While the Oak Ridge Leadership Computing Facility (OLCF) provides a variety of tools to perform data wrangling and data analysis tasks, Python based tools often lack scalability, or the ability to fully exploit the computational capability of OLCF's Summit supercomputer. NVIDIA RAPIDS and Dask offer a promising solution to accelerate and distribute data analytics workloads from personal computers to heterogeneous supercomputing systems. We discuss early performance evaluation results of RAPIDS and Dask on Summit to understand their capabilities, scalability, and limitations. Our evaluation includes a subset of RAPIDS libraries, i.e., cuDF, cuML, and cuGraph, and Chainer's CuPy, and their multi-GPU variants when available. We also draw on the observed trends from the performance evaluation results to discuss best practices for maximizing performance.

Keywords: Performance evaluation · Python · Data analytics · GPU · multi-threaded

1 Introduction

Data-analytics driven scientific discovery is rapidly transforming the landscape of practically all scientific domains. The explosion in the volumes of data generated from ever-larger simulation campaigns and experiments or observations

B. Hernández et al.—Contributed Equally.

This manuscript has been co-authored by UT-Battelle, LLC, under contract DE-AC05-00OR22725 with the US Department of Energy (DOE). The US government retains and the publisher, by accepting the article for publication, acknowledges that the US government retains a nonexclusive, paid-up, irrevocable, worldwide license to publish or reproduce the published form of this manuscript, or allow others to do so, for US government purposes. DOE will provide public access to these results of federally sponsored research in accordance with the DOE Public Access Plan (http://energy.gov/downloads/doe-public-access-plan).

J. Nichols et al. (Eds.): SMC 2020, CCIS 1315, pp. 366–380, 2020.
https://doi.org/10.1007/978-3-030-63393-6_24

necessitates correspondingly competent tools for data wrangling and analysis. At the core of this explosion lies software and hardware infrastructure able to process massive volumes of data at large-scale.

Data analysis tools and services utility will be determined based on the scientific productivity of their users. Feature improvement in these tools that harness the capabilities of pre-exascale and exascale computer systems is essential. Equally important is a comprehensive understanding of user and system requirements, and limitations of the current data analysis tools, to quantify their impact in these computer systems.

According to the Python Software Foundation, the Python language has had sustained user growth in the last few years. Its 2019 survey reports that in 59% of the cases, Python is being used for data analysis with NumPy [27], Pandas [12], Matplotlib [8] and SciPy [26] the most popular data science Python packages [5]. Similarly, in the OLCF User Survey 2019 [11], users emphasized the need for support of Jupyter [9] and Python-related software and capabilities. Particularly, *"optimized numpy packages, which is a must-have for scientific applications"*. For the interested reader, Raschka et al. [19] provide an up-to-date overview of Python based frameworks for machine learning, scientific computing, distributed big data and data analytics, including software and hardware acceleration approaches using these frameworks.

While a variety of Python software modules are available for OLCF users to perform data wrangling and data analysis tasks, these modules often lack scalability, i.e. the ability to fully use the computational capability of OLCF's Summit supercomputer. RAPIDS [14] and Dask [21] offer a promising solution to scale up and scale out data analytics workloads on heterogeneous supercomputing systems. RAPIDS is a fast evolving suite of Python libraries and C/C++ APIs to execute end-to-end data science and analytics pipelines entirely on GPUs. It uses CUDA based libraries for low-level compute optimization and offers support for multi-node and multi-GPU deployments with Dask. RAPIDS offers nearly out-of-the box, drop-in replacements for libraries such as Pandas, SciPy Signal, and scikit-learn [18] or provides similar functionality as NetworkX [6] libraries [14].

In this work, we describe the efforts of the OLCF's Advanced Data and Workflow Group and NVIDIA to deploy and evaluate RAPIDS and Dask on Summit. The process of testing and evaluation of RAPIDS and Dask is critical to inform technical and user facing aspects and to make the best use of Summit's resources. It is also of importance to work with NVIDIA to provide feedback, report issues and develop, extend or optimize key features of these data analytics frameworks. We report preliminary results from evaluating cuDF, cuML, cuGraph and CuPy libraries and their multi-GPU or multi-node variants when available.

2 Technical Overview

OLCF's Summit supercomputer, based on POWER9 architecture, has unique hardware features that require further investigation beyond scientific computing workloads [25]. In particular, we are interested in studying the interplay between Summit's hardware and NVIDIA RAPIDS to scale-up and scale-out OLCF's users' data analysis workloads. In the following paragraphs we provide an overview of Summit's hardware and NVIDIA RAPIDS advances aimed at enabling large scale data analytics.

2.1 OLCF Summit

Summit has 4, 608 IBM Power System AC922 nodes each with six NVIDIA Volta V100 (16 GB memory) GPUs with 96 GB of HBM2 memory per node providing over 95% of the floating point capability of the system [24]. Powerful sequential performance is provided by two POWER9 CPUs paired with 512 GB of main memory per node. The NVLink 2.0 interface provides intranode data movement across GPUs and CPUs at 50 GB/s [20] and internode communication occurs at 25 GB/s. On the other hand, Summit's I/O subsystem is composed of two layers - the in-system layer and the parallel file system layer. The in-system layer uses node-local SSDs providing 26.7 TB/s for read operations and 9.7 TB/s for write operations. The parallel file system layer provides I/O at 2.5 TB/s [17].

2.2 NVIDIA RAPIDS

NVIDIA RAPIDS uses a single data exchange format that is based on Apache Arrow for all input and output to workflow operations. This format supports the DataFrame representation and operations which form the core component of RAPIDS cuDF. The intent of cuDF is to mimic the popular Pandas API as closely as possible. In addition to operations on DataFrames, cuDF provides GPU accelerated data readers for several popular on-disk data formats, such as CSV, ORC, Parquet, and JSON-lines. The combination of GPU accelerated data readers, parallel parsers, GPU accelerated data wrangling operations, and API mimicking the Pandas package enables cuDF to directly addresses some of the most time-consuming aspects of data analytics, namely the ETL (extract transform and load) phase.

The cuML package in RAPIDS implements GPU accelerated machine learning methods, again mimicking the API of the popular scikit-learn package. The cuGraph package in RAPIDS provides NetworkX-like API for graph analytics workloads. It is important to emphasize that cuGraph by itself is only a set of graph analytics methods while cuDF handles data format conversions, data loading and wrangling.

Finally, Chainer's CuPy is a NumPy-compatible, open source matrix library [16]. While CuPy is not a library under the RAPIDS framework, it is built on top of CUDA-related libraries such as CUB, cuBLAS, cuDNN, cuRAND, cuSOLVER, cuSPARSE, cuFFT and NCCL to take full use of the GPU architecture. CuPy also includes compatibility with RAPIDS and Dask for memory management and multi-GPU, multi-node workload distribution.

3   Performance Evaluation

The main objective of RAPIDS performance evaluation was to understand the interplay between RAPIDS and Dask for memory management, workload distribution and performance. These are important features that OLCF users should know about to provide appropriate job resources when running GPU based distributed analytics workloads on Summit.

At the time of this study, RAPIDS v.0.14 source code was the latest version available while RAPIDS 0.14 official binaries supported x86 architecture only. Therefore, we developed build scripts to compile RAPIDS for ppc64le architecture, implemented job scripts to interface it with Summit's compute nodes and fine-tuned configurations with help from NVIDIA. We recommend consulting [7], which is a repository that serves as a preamble to understand concepts around execution of Dask, Dask-CUDA and RAPIDS jobs on Summit.

3.1   cuDF

We evaluated the performance of Dask-cuDF[1] for performing a variety of operations such as reading csv files, calculating the number of unique elements in an integer column, performing groupby and merge operations. These operations were tested for various combinations of number of GPUs and sizes of DataFrames whose data were contained in csv files of sizes 1 GB, 2.5 GB, 5 GB, 10 GB, and 25 GB. Each csv file consisted of 260 floating point columns and one integer column and the data for these columns were generated according to a random normal distribution. We varied the chunk size [2] for reading the file to observe its effect on the time to read the csv file. For the merge operation, the main DataFrame was merged with another that was roughly ten times smaller. Additionally, we separately studied the effect of varying the number of partitions that the DataFrame was broken into on the time taken to compute the unique, merge, and groupby operations. The performance of Dask-cuDF was compared against other DataFrame packages such as cuDF, Pandas, and Dask-DataFrame. In the case of Dask-DataFrame, the Dask workers were each assigned to one CPU core. For Dask-cuDF, each Dask-CUDA worker was given a single GPU. In the case of Dask-cuDF and Dask-Dataframe, we used "persist" instead of "compute" on the results [3], which lowered computation time since results are not returned to the python client. Each test was run six times and the mean and standard deviation for each measurement are reported in the figures.

Figure 1 shows the time taken to read csv files, perform the unique, groupby and merge operations using Dask-cuDF as a function of number of GPUs and DataFrame sizes. Figure 1(a) shows that it takes less time to read csv files when increasing the number of GPU workers. However, the higher than expected load time is likely caused by using small datasets based on the available GPU memory,

---

[1] In RAPIDS 0.14 multi-gpu/multi-node support was provided by Dask-cuDF. In newer versions, scale-out support has been added into cuDF GitHub repository and Dask-cuDF repository has been archived.

and as a result underutilized GPUs. If deployment is possible on Summit, a more efficient pipeline would include loading data using GPUDirect Storage (GDS) [13], which will be integrated into future releases of cuDF. Figure 1(b) shows that the time required to perform the unique operation on the integer-valued column generally increased as the number of GPU workers were increased. Figure 1(c) shows generally increasing time required to perform the groupby operation as the number of GPU workers are increased. In the case of 10 GB and 25 GB files, the groupby time decreased when the number of GPUs were increased from 1 to 3. Performance of groupby-aggregates were improved in a recent change [15] that will be added in the next release of RAPIDS (0.16). Figure 1(d) shows that the time required to perform the merge operation also generally increased as the number of GPUs are increased. Overall, the read_csv operations show some strong scaling trends (negative slope) while the merge, unique and groupby operations show poor strong scaling, that may be in part attributed to communication bandwidth and will be addressed in the future with the use of UCX [23]. Furthermore, the overall time to perform the unique, groupby, and merge operations appear to have dropped by 1 to 2 orders of magnitude by using "persist" instead of "compute" for the results.

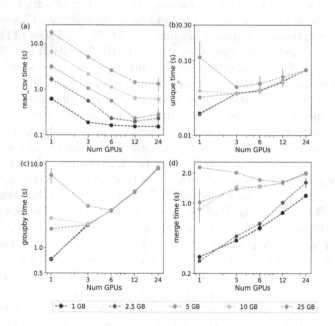

Fig. 1. Time taken to (a) read csv files of various sizes, perform (b) unique, (c) groupby and (d) merge operations using Dask-cuDF as a function of number of GPUs and DataFrame size. The default chunk size and numbers of DataFrame partitions were used

Figure 2 shows a comparison in the times required to perform the aforementioned operations for Dask-cuDF, cuDF, Dask-Dataframe and Pandas when using a single node of Summit. Pandas used a single python process while cuDF used a single GPU. Figure 2(a) shows that the time taken to read csv files rises proportionally as the size of the file is increased in all packages, except for Dask-Dataframe. Figure 2(b) shows that despite having multiple GPU or CPU workers Dask-cuDF and Dask-DataFrame were two orders of magnitude slower than either Pandas or cuDF, which are comparably fast at performing the unique operation. However, Dask-cuDF appears to take almost constant for the unique operation regardless of the dataframe size. Figure 2(c) shows that cuDF is the fastest at performing the groupby operation followed by Dask-cuDF and Dask-DataFrame for large files. However, Pandas is roughly 1–1.5 orders of magnitude slower than cuDF regardless of the data size. Figure 2(d) shows that both cuDF and Dask-cuDF are roughly 1 to 2 orders of magnitude faster than Pandas and Dask-DataFrame are 1–2 orders of magnitude slower than Pandas at performing the merge operation.

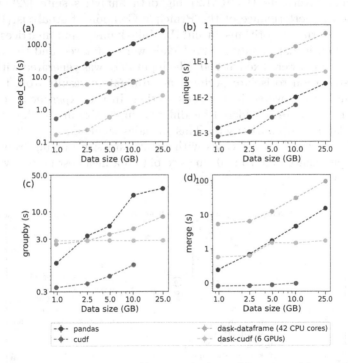

Fig. 2. Time taken to (a) read csv files and perform (b) unique (c) groupby and (d) merge operations as a function of DataFrame size using pandas, Dask-DataFrame, cuDF, and Dask-cuDF. A full node of Summit was used in the case of Dask-DataFrame and Dask-cuDF

These trends present a mixed bag that could be explained by the fact that cuDF and Dask-cuDF are in their early stages of development but are showing performance and stability improvements with each newer version. Furthermore, certain operations can be performed swiftly on GPUs, especially if forking is not involved in the operations. Though cuDF and Pandas are sometimes much faster than Dask-DataFrame and Dask-cuDF, these packages are unable to handle large datasets or scale beyond one process or node to take advantage of distributed computing. Overall, the results observed show some minor jitter which is expected on large shared production systems like Summit with fluctuations in the network and I/O loads [25]. Next steps include running the Dask-cuDF benchmarks with UCX to reduce communication overhead; the numbers presented in this paper are based on the TCP protocol. Additional performance improvements for groupby and I/O will also be added in the next release of cuDF.

3.2   cuML

Methodologies similar to those outlined in the Collaboration of Oak Ridge, Argonne and Livermore (CORAL2) big data analytics suite [22] were used to evaluate the performance of the Principle Component Analysis (PCA) and K-means clustering algorithms in cuML. Tall-skinny input matrices that are commonly seen in data analytics workloads were employed and the number of columns (features) were fixed at 250. The input data was generated with random normal distribution to isolate performance evaluation results from the impact of I/O, which was covered in previous section. In the experiment setup, various usage modes were considered for different input size in an effort to provide recommendations to cuML users. This includes single-GPU, multi-GPU, and multi-node (multi-GPU) use-cases with input data size ranging from 1 GB to 96 GB. Experiments were run 10 times to obtain a mean estimation with first 3 dropped as warm-ups.

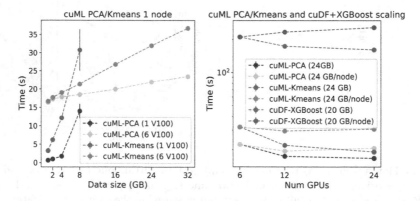

Fig. 3. cuML PCA and Kmeans, and XGBoost on Dask-cuDF performances: (left) single-GPu, multi-GPU, and (right) multi-node.

The left side subplot in Fig. 3 shows that a single GPU could process a little over 4 GB data for PCA and Kmeans. With unified memory support enabled, cuML could handle input matrices as large as 8 GB for PCA but with a performance penalty of about 70% for this type of tall-skinny matrices. For input data size smaller than 4 GB, the computational load was not high enough to benefit from employing multiple GPUs. However, for data sizes larger than 8 GB, using all 6 V100 GPUs on a single Summit node starts to show a performance boost in terms of throughput (GB/s). One Summit node was able to accommodate 32 GB input data for PCA and Kmeans, respectively, with a throughput of 13.6 GB/s for PCA and 8.7 GB/s for Kmeans.

In terms of multi-node performance, both strong and weak scaling were examined, as shown in right-hand side subplot in Fig. 3. In addition to PCA and Kmeans in cuML, we also considered XGBoost by providing input matrices via Dask-cuDF given the popularity of the XGBoost method. For the cuML version we used, the tested algorithms did not demonstrate strong scaling for the tall-skinny matrices that were 20 or 24 GB in size. On the other hand, the throughput displays weak-scaling with $75-80\%$ efficiency up to 24 V100s when keeping input size fixed per node. With rapid developments in cuML releases and underlying communication of Dask, the scaling trend is expected to improve.

3.3 cuGraph

To evaluate the performance of cuGraph, we performed several common graph operations and examined the impact of using Rapids Memory Manager (RMM). The performance of cuGraph was compared against igraph [1]. We compared two traversal and three structure-discovering operations between cuGraph and igraph for different graph sizes. Detailed information regarding the graphs used in this study are listed in Table 1. For breadth-first search (BFS) and single source shortest path (SSSP) algorithms, we randomly selected 64 vertices as the source vertices. In the case of K core computation, we iterated the "K" parameter from 2 to 32. The experiments were performed using a single GPU and run-time statistics are reported based on 10 runs.

Table 1. Graph used for CuGraph evaluation

Graph name	$|V|$	$|E|$	Data Size
coPapersDBLP	540,486	30,491,458	192MB
cit-Patents	3,774,768	16,518,948	250MB
com-LiveJournal	3,997,962	69,362,378	475MB
Hollywood-2009	1,139,905	113,891,327	772MB
Europe_osm	50,912,018	108,109,320	906MB
Soc-LiveJournal1	4,847,571	68,993,773	965MB
ljournal-2008	5,363,260	79,023,142	1.2GB
com-Orkut	3,072,441	234,370,166	1.7GB
uk-2002	18,520,486	298,113,762	4.7GB

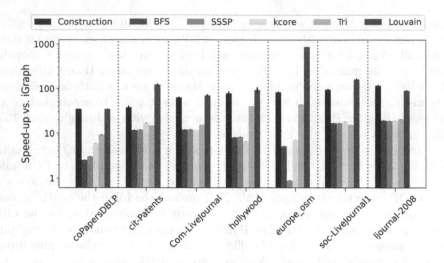

Fig. 4. Speedup of cuGraph vs igraph.

As shown in Fig. 4, cuGraph demonstrated a significant speedup on graph construction and most graph operations over igraph. The result shows operations that involve vertex-centric computation has the most speedup (up to 870X). We observed that cuGraph does not scale as well on SSSP and BFS for bounded degree graphs, which may due to the large number of synchronization steps. (europe_osm contain more uniform degree distribution).

In addition to comparisons against igraph, we tested the effectiveness of RMM for accommodating larger graphs. Figure 5(b) shows the end to end runtime for the Louvain method using different sizes for the RMM pool. We did not observe significant impact of the pool size on either the load & construction or graph operations. The data suggested that when graph size is smaller than the GPU memory, using a pool size equal to half the GPU memory does not impact the performance much. Additional tests are needed for larger graphs that do not fit within the GPU memory. In the version of cuGraph we evaluated (version 0.14), we observed that cuGraph has significantly improved the quality of their Louvain clustering algorithm from their previous versions. In Fig. 5(a), we see that cuGraph generates the modularity that is compatible if not better than other serial/parallel implementations of Louvain method. With the above result, we are confident that cuGraph has become a very stable and fast tool for single GPU based graph analysis.

3.4   CuPy

CuPy offers a large set of NumPy-like capabilities, however, we considered the Singular Value Decomposition (SVD) function for this study since it exposes key complexities in terms of memory management (several allocations and deallocations) and computation. In particular, given a matrix x of size $m \times n$, CuPy uses

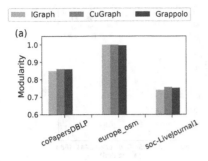
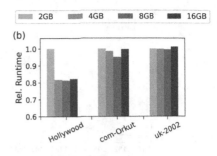

Fig. 5. Additional statisitcs of cuGraph: (a) Output quality of Louvain method in igraph, cuGraph and other parallel library. (b) Impact of RMM pool size on cuGraph run-time.

cuSOLVER to solve the SVD that returns two matrices, u and v, of size $m \times m$ and $n \times n$, and a vector s containing the singular values of x. On the other hand, experiments were run 10 times with first 3 dropped as warm-ups and, the mean and standard deviation for each measurement are reported in the figures.

CuPy's SVD memory management was evaluated by running the SVD algorithm on one GPU with randomly generated values for the input matrix values and the matrix size was varied as shown in Table 2. CuPy-Dask configuration used one Dask-CUDA worker per GPU and the input matrix was partitioned into different chunk sizes [2]. The objective of this test was to determine the largest problem one GPU could handle, its performance under different workload and chunk sizes.

Table 2. Different matrix sizes used for CuPy's SVD evaluation

Matrix size	Data size (MB)
$10\,K \times 1\,K$	76
$20\,K \times 1\,K$	152
$40\,K \times 1\,K$	305
$80\,K \times 1\,K$	610
$160\,K \times 1\,K$	1220
$320\,K \times 1\,K$	2441
$640\,K \times 1\,K$	4883

Figure 6 shows SVD's time-to-solution took a few seconds for different workloads and chunk sizes. In general, a chunk size of $8K \times 8K$ delivered consistent behavior across mid-size matrices and best performance for larger matrices (e.g. $640K \times 1K$ or 4883 MB). In addition, Fig. 6 shows that CuPy was unable to perform SVD for matrix sizes larger $40K \times 1K$ while CuPy-Dask

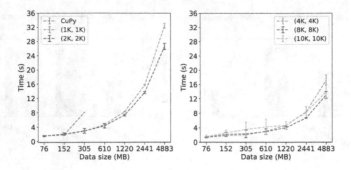

Fig. 6. SVD timings with CuPy and CuPy-Dask using different chunk sizes.

configuration overcame this limitation. For the interested reader, a similar performance evaluation for solving SVD with NumPy-Dask was reported in [10].

The workload distribution experiment consisted of performing a general scalability evaluation, strong scaling and weak scaling tests. We used CuPy-Dask configuration to distribute the SVD workload using synthetic matrices (Table 2) partitioned by the chunk size that delivered best performance in the previous experiment, i.e. $8K \times 8K$. For these experiments, the SVD computation was distributed on one to six GPUs wherein each Dask-CUDA worker was given a single GPU.

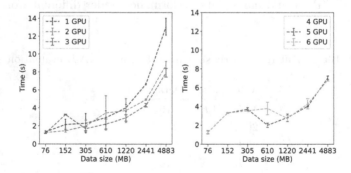

Fig. 7. CuPy-Dask's SVD overall scalability results for a single node of Summit

The general scalability test showed performance trends similar to our first experiment (Fig. 7), i.e. increasing the workload size also increased run-times. In particular, adding more GPUs for a given workload did not necessarily improve runtimes significantly (e.g. - matrix of size $160K \times 1K$ or 1220 MB). Poor performance for matrix sizes below 1GB can be explained by low GPU occupancy. Furthermore, it was not possible to compute matrices larger than $640K \times 1K$ or 4883 MB even by using more GPUs due to limitations in the current cuSOLVER 10.x [4].

For the strong scaling test, we used the largest workload, i.e. a matrix size of $640\,K \times 1\,K$ or 4883 MB while varying the number of GPUs. For the weak scaling test, we increased the workload by a factor of two as in Table 2, starting with a matrix size of $20\,K \times 1\,K$ or 152 MB.

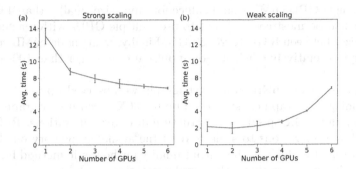

Fig. 8. CuPy-Dask's SVD performance on one Summit node. a) Strong scaling performance. b) Weak scaling performance.

Figure 8 reports strong and weak scaling results. Though the strong scaling plot shows a curve with negative slope, as expected for strong scaling tests, the steepness of the slope or efficiency decreases substantially after two nodes. The weak scaling plot shows that the computation time remained roughly constant, as expected for weak scaling tests, up to 3–4 GPUs, but then increased past 4 GPUs. The performance trends in Fig. 8(b) could be explained by the increasing communication overhead due larger workload distribution across increasing number of GPUs.

4 Conclusions

In this study, we evaluated a subset of the NVIDIA RAPIDS family of packages on the Summit supercomputer. In parallel to this study, we explored operational and technical aspects such as compilation, installation, bug reporting, integration with the LSF scheduler and job configuration. Based on the needs of OLCF users for Python-based data wrangling and machine learning, we limited our study to NVIDIA RAPIDS' cuDF, cuML, cuGraph and Chainer's CuPy, and their distributed equivalents in combination with Dask when available. We evaluated the performance of certain functions in each package as a function of (randomly generated) input data sizes and the number of GPUs (where applicable) against counterparts in other similar software. Jitter and minor inconsistencies in performance were observed for operations on Summit for a variety of factors that have been discussed previously. Nonetheless, we observed similar performance trends on Summit, at node level, and on a NVIDIA DGX-1.

Dask-cuDF (now referred to simply as cuDF) displayed no clear relationships between times required to perform the operations as a function of number of

GPUs. Note that we called persist instead of compute on the delayed / lazy Dask computations, which may be attributed to improved wall times. Overall, Dask-cuDF was generally 1–3 orders of magnitude slower than pandas, Dask-DataFrame, or (single-GPU) cuDF for the version of RAPIDS we evaluated.

cuML was in general 1–2 orders of magnitude faster than scikit-learn on Summit. Single-GPU cuML would suffice for input size smaller than 4 GB. Similarly, it would be most cost-efficient to use multiple GPUs within a single node for data sizes between 8 GB to 20–30 GB. Finally, multi-node cuML could perform analytics relatively efficiently on input datasets larger than 100s of GB on Summit.

When comparing cuGraph against igraph, we observed up to 76X speedup for file loading and graph construction; up to 130X speed up for graph-traversal operations; and 870X speedup for structure discovery operations. RMM facilitated cuGraph operations to scale beyond the available memory on the GPUs very effectively. In addition, the output quality for heuristic method has become compatible if not better than other implementation.

The SVD algorithm in CuPy was evaluated for a variety of data sizes and GPUs by taking advantage of Dask for parallelism. The best performance was obtained for matrix chunk sizes of $8\,K \times 8\,K$. CuPy-Dask was found to be as much as 9X faster than Numpy-Dask for the SVD operation.

NVIDIA RAPIDS is continuously evolving, efficiency and performance is expected to improve further from that which was observed in this study in subsequent versions. Besides the obvious performance benefits of using RAPIDS instead of other counterparts, we expect RAPIDS' user-friendly and familiar Python API to improve the productivity of OLCF users' for data analytics workloads. We plan on developing documentation on the usage and best practices based on this study to efficiently utilize the Summit's computational resources.

Acknowledgments. This research used resources of the Oak Ridge Leadership Computing Facility (OLCF) at the Oak Ridge National Laboratory, which is supported by the Office of Science of the U.S. Department of Energy under Contract No. DE-AC05-00OR22725.

References

1. Csardi, G., Nepusz, T., et al.: The igraph software package for complex network research. InterJ. Complex Syst. **1695**(5), 1–9 (2006)
2. Dask Development Team. Chunks - DASK (2020). https://docs.dask.org/en/latest/array-chunks.html. Accessed 26 May 2020
3. Dask Distributed. Managing computation (2016). https://distributed.readthedocs.io/en/latest/manage-computation.html#dask-collections-to-futures. Accessed 22 Sep 2020
4. Econtal. sgesvd_buffersize int32 overflow with CUDA (2019). https://github.com/cupy/cupy/issues/2351. Accessed 26 May 2020
5. Python Software Foundation and JetBrains. Python software foundation survey (2019). https://www.jetbrains.com/lp/python-developers-survey-2019. Accessed 26 May 2020

6. Hagberg, A., Swart, P., Chult, D.S.: Exploring network structure, dynamics, and function using networkx. Technical report, Los Alamos National Lab. (LANL), Los Alamos, NM (United States) (2008)
7. Hernández, B.: Recipes to build, install and execute NVIDIA RAPIDS framework on Summit supercomputer (2020). https://github.com/benjha/nvrapids_olcf. Accessed 26 May 2020
8. Hunter, J.D.: Matplotlib: a 2D graphics environment. Comput. Sci. Eng. **9**(3), 90–95 (2007)
9. Kluyver, T.,et al.: Jupyter notebooks-a publishing format for reproducible computational workflows. In: ELPUB, pp. 87–90 (2016)
10. Lu, H., Hernández, B., Sommath, S., Yin, J.: Nvidia rapids on summit supercomputer: early experiences. In: Nvidia GPU Technology Conference (2020)
11. Martin, A.M., Townsend, K.P., Miller-Bains, K., Burr E.M.: 2019 Oak Ridge Leadership Computing Facility User Survey. Findings and Recommendations. Technical report, Scientific Assessment & Workforce Development, February 2020
12. McKinney, W., et al.: pandas: a foundational python library for data analysis and statistics. Python High Perform. Sci. Comput. **14**(9), (2011)
13. NVIDIA. GPUDirect Storage: A Direct Path Between Storage and GPU Memory (2019). https://developer.nvidia.com/blog/gpudirect-storage/. Accessed 14 Sept 2020
14. NVIDIA. Open GPU Data Science-RAPIDS 2020. https://rapids.ai. Accessed 26 May 2020
15. NVIDIA. Optimize groupby-agg in dask_cudf (2020). https://github.com/rapidsai/cudf/pull/6248
16. Okuta,R., Unno, Y., Nishino, D., Hido, S., Loomis, C.: Cupy: a numpy-compatible library for Nvidia GPU calculations. In: Proceedings of Workshop on Machine Learning Systems (LearningSys) in the Thirty-first Annual Conference on Neural Information Processing Systems (NIPS) (2017)
17. Oral, S., et al.: End-to-end i/o portfolio for the summit supercomputing ecosystem. In: Proceedings of the International Conference for High Performance Computing, Networking, Storage and Analysis, SC 2019, New York, NY, USA. Association for Computing Machinery (2019)
18. Pedregosa, F.: Scikit-learn: Machine learning in python. J. Mach. Learn. Res. **12**, 2825–2830 (2011)
19. Sebastian, R., Joshua, P., Corey, N.: Machine learning in python: Main developments and technology trends in data science, machine learning, and artificial intelligence. Information **11**(4), 193 (2020)
20. Roberts, S., Mann, C., Marroquin, C.: Redefining IBM power system design for coral. IBM J. Res. Dev. **64**(3/4), 1–10 (2020)
21. Rocklin, M.: Dask: parallel computation with blocked algorithms and task scheduling. In: Huff, K., Bergstra, J., (eds.) Proceedings of the 14th Python in Science Conference, pp. 130–136 (2015)
22. Schmidt, D., Yin, J., Matheson, M., Messer, B., Shankar, M.: Defining big data analytics benchmarks for next generation supercomputers (2018)
23. Shamis, P., et al.: UCX: an open source framework for HPC network APIs and beyond. In: IEEE 23rd Annual Symposium on High-Performance Interconnects, pp. 40–43 (2015)
24. Vazhkudai, S.S.: The design, deployment, and evaluation of the coral pre-exascale systems. In: Proceedings of the International Conference for High Performance Computing, Networking, Storage, and Analysis, SC 2018. IEEE Press (2018)

25. Vergara Larrea, V., et al.: Scaling the summit: deploying the world's fastest super-computer. In: Weiland, M., Juckeland, G., Alam, S., Jagode, H. (eds.) ISC High Performance 2019. LNCS, vol. 11887, pp. 330–351. Springer, Cham (2019). https://doi.org/10.1007/978-3-030-34356-9_26
26. Virtanen, P., et al.: Scipy 1.0: fundamental algorithms for scientific computing in python. Nat. Meth. **17**(3), 261–272 (2020)
27. van der Walt, S., Colbert, S.C., Varoquaux, G.: The numpy array: a structure for efficient numerical computation. Comput. Sci. Eng. **13**(2), 22–30 (2011)

Navigating the Road to Successfully Manage a Large-Scale Research and Development Project: The Exascale Computing Project (ECP) Experience

Kathlyn Boudwin[1]([✉]), Douglas Collins[1], Cathleen Lavelle[2], and Julia White[1]

[1] Oak Ridge National Laboratory, Oak Ridge, TN 37831, USA
{boudwinkj,collinsdn,whitejc}@ornl.gov
[2] Brookhaven National Laboratory, Upton, NY 11973, USA
lavellec@bnl.gov

Abstract. The road to successful management of a large research and development (R&D) project requires comprehensive and flexible capabilities to foster effective and timely communication, tracking, and decision-making. Best practices developed and employed by the Exascale Computing Project (ECP) afford a comprehensive example of management practices that benefit this type of a large-scale, physically dispersed R&D project. This article will summarize the ECP's hybrid approach to project management, which incorporates principles of the Department of Energy (DOE) order for the management of large capital asset projects (DOE O 413.3b) and elements of industry-standard Agile practices, as well as the tools that promote extensive collaborative endeavors.

Using a hybrid approach to managing project elements is a key tenet within the ECP and is implemented in part by ensuring that information such as detailed technical plans and achievements, budget and cost information, milestone creation, and progress metrics are readily accessible to all participants. The functionality to enable this broad, dynamic access is provided by a variety of essential and flexible tools, which the ECP has found to be invaluable in managing work and communicating with project team members and stakeholders. The strong integration of R&D efforts results in a dynamic environment in which frequent input from management, collaborators, and stakeholders is essential.

This overall approach provides the guidelines and policies, processes, information, tools and services, and output that are necessary for the effective management of large, complex projects. Such an approach may also be applied to smaller, less complex projects for a similar outcome.

K. Boudwin et al.—Contributed Equally.
This manuscript has been authored by UT-Battelle, LLC, under contract DE-AC05- 00OR22725 with the US Department of Energy (DOE). The US government retains and the publisher, by accepting the article for publication, acknowledges that the US government retains a nonexclusive, paid-up, irrevocable, worldwide license to publish or reproduce the published form of this manuscript, or allow others to do so, for US government purposes. DOE will provide public access to these results of federally sponsored research in accordance with the DOE Public Access Plan (http://energy.gov/downloads/doe-public-access-plan).

J. Nichols et al. (Eds.): SMC 2020, CCIS 1315, pp. 381–393, 2020.
https://doi.org/10.1007/978-3-030-63393-6_25

1 Introduction

Planning and executing the ECP presents a considerable project management challenge because of (1) its scale, (2) the R&D focus on applications that meet mission needs, (3) the software tools needed for capable computing platforms, and (4) the integration of ECP applications, software, and hardware innovations into the DOE high performance computing (HPC) facilities. The long-range (multiyear) plans of an ECP R&D team include intermediate progressive steps toward final deliverables. The strong integration of R&D efforts between the technical focus areas results in a dynamic environment in which frequent input from collaborators and stakeholders is essential. These dynamics are consistent with an iterative, incremental development approach in which subsequent requirements and feature sets are likely determined or finalized with input from the results of previous activities and refinement of information about future computer architectures. This requirement to be "agile" while maintaining a more traditional earned value performance baseline against which to assess progress leads to a hybrid approach allowing for both practices.

In addition to its scale and focus, project complexities include two direct funding sources and multiple distributed participants (over 1000 participants from 15 national laboratories as well as subcontracted effort from 75 universities and 60 companies) requiring considerable integration and coordination. The project's complexity extends to the development and implementation of the plan for measuring and monitoring performance and progress, including the need for a hybrid approach that incorporates principles of the standard DOE Earned Value Management System (EVMS) [1] and elements of industry-standard Agile [2] practices. EVM is a technique for measuring project performance and progress in an objective manner. It combines measurements of scope, schedule, and costs and works best when these elements are well defined. Agile practices include adaptive planning and evolutionary development. Many performance measurement approaches currently used in the ECP are unique but may also be useful to small, less complex projects.

2 Background

In 2009, the DOE began to anticipate the need for exascale computing as part of the solution to many of the nation's, and even the world's, most challenging problems. In fiscal year 2016, a 7 year combined effort (2017–2023) by the Office of Science's (SC's) Advanced Scientific Computing Research (ASCR) program and the National Nuclear Security Administration's (NNSA's) Advanced Simulation and Computing (ASC) program was begun to prepare and uplift the high performance computing community toward capable exascale platforms, software, and applications. The ECP is a multi-institution project and is structured into three technical focus areas to address requirements for Applications Development (AD), Software Technology (ST), and Hardware and Integration (HI). The project incorporates the principles of DOE's Order 413.3b [3] , the order for Program and Project Management for the Acquisition of Capital Assets, and other DOE project management practices. Even though ECP produces no capital asset, the DOE required the project to be managed under this order and tailored to fit the requirements as a best practice for managing this large and complex project. The ultimate question is whether an R&D project operating under the guidance of DOE Order 413.3b, such as ECP, can determine its goals and desired outcomes, measure progress toward those outcomes, manage project communications, and provide interim results to all stakeholders so that at the end of a specified period those outcomes can be realized. To do so, the ECP has adopted a hybrid approach to traditional EVM practices that incorporates Agile methodologies. Additionally, ECP has embraced a set of tools that enable project participants to manage work and communicate broadly through the use of dashboards, reports, and collaboration areas.

This paper will highlight some of the unique aspects of the ECP project management practices and tools which may be applied to other R&D projects regardless of their size or complexity. The blending of traditional EVMS and Agile project management principles will be explored and noteworthy practices highlighted in an effort to inform early career project managers as well as seasoned practitioners. A unique case study will further highlight how a variety of performance tracking approaches ranging from level of effort to decomposition of work into small pieces (i.e., stories) can be used to effectively manage project work. Lastly, a robust set of project management tools used to provide a tightly integrated tracking and reporting management system will be cataloged and lessons learned shared.

3 Implementing a Hybrid Approach in an Earned Value Environment

The application of an iterative, or agile, approach to project management in a traditional EVMS environment can be challenging and, at the same time, crucial to effective project performance monitoring and reporting. Traditional EVMS techniques provide a useful methodology for planning and measuring project performance. Standard performance measurement principles employed in a traditional EVMS include planning and decomposing work scope, developing a performance measurement baseline (i.e., scope, schedule, cost, quality, risk) using actual costs incurred and recorded, assessing accomplishments with objective metrics and key performance parameters, analyzing variances, forecasting impacts, estimating completion, and reporting. There are many benefits of an EVMS, including the integration of scope, cost, and schedule. It provides tools for assessing cost and schedule performance and assesses the impacts of performance on the project objectives. Changes to the plan are carefully identified, analyzed, and incorporated into the baseline plan with formal change control and approval processes. Forecasting estimates to completion is an important aspect of an EVMS and is critical when communicating project forecasts for completion with cost and schedule objectives.

In today's project environment, it is possible that many projects have software/R&D scope that requires an Agile methodology to effectively monitor and track performance within an EVMS. To complicate this issue, many such projects inherently contain uncertainty and therefore are difficult to measure in a traditional EVMS. Scope requirements may not be well defined in the planning and execution phases of a project. Software development activities cannot be easily measured using objective performance measurement techniques due to the complex nature and uncertainty of the work. The 12 principles of the Agile Manifesto [2] provide guidelines for a workable solution to managing the software development and R&D portion of the work scope. Three key Agile principles are

- "welcome requirements, even late in development. Agile processes harness change for the customer's competitive advantage,"
- "working software is the primary measure of progress," and
- "continuous attention to technical excellence and good design enhances agility[4]."

The Agile Manifesto [4] summarizes the important elements of applying Agile principles and methodologies, stating "individuals and interactions over processes and tools, working software over comprehensive documentation, customer collaboration over contract negotiation, responding to change over following a plan." The first Agile concept (e.g., "individuals and interactions" is in contrast to the second traditional concept (e.g., "processes and tools") [2] . By using a hybrid approach, it is possible to meet the needs of many projects that have a mix of hardware/software or design/R&D activities within the same project. EVMS can be tailored to follow the principles of EVMS and include Agile principles and practices. An example of this approach is assessing story points (stories are similar to steps in Primavera (a project portfolio scheduling software)/points give weights to the stories) to develop an EV-based assessment.

The hybrid approach incorporates Agile methods in a traditional EVMS framework to meet performance measurement requirements by integrating traditional reporting requirements with R&D/software work scope requirements.

EVMS can be tailored to follow the principles of earned value and include Agile practices. The approach permits agile methods, where applicable, and integrates the results with traditional earned value. An example is to assess story points to develop an EV-based assessment of story point accomplishments. Plan Value represents the total number of story points planned and Velocity represents the number of story points completed per time unit. The cumulative number of story points completed is analogous to EV.

Performance measurement methodologies [weighted milestones, Level of Effort (LOE)] are also accepted practices for progress measurement on these types of projects that include scope uncertainty. Monitoring milestones at a lower level of a work breakdown structure (WBS) is informative, consistent with EVM principles, and an accepted practice on a hybrid project. Monitoring milestones in an agile environment can be applied by calculating the ratio of (story points completed)/(total story points in a release) – a good measure of percentage complete in a hybrid approach.

Forecasting using EV data is a critical aspect of EV performance measurement. An approach in the hybrid application is based on average velocity (story points) representing the estimate to complete (ETC) in dollars. The estimate at complete (EAC) = historical average velocity (i.e., completed story points) × number of iterations in the release × labor cost of team. A key assumption is that the ratio of (story points completed)/(total story points in a release) is a good measure of the actual percent complete.

The NDIA Agile and EVM Guide calculates EAC as Actual cost plus (velocity x remaining backlog) as follows [5, 6].

PLATINUM CARD

EVM FOR AGILE DEVELOPMENT

Total Allocated Budget — EAC

MR (for rate impacts, R&O liens) — BAC

PMB

VELOCITY X
REMAINING BACKLOG
ETC $_{Cum}$

Schedule Variance

(Actual Cost)

Cost Variance

Projected Slip

RELEASE PLAN
(BCWS $_{Cum}$)

REMAINING BACKLOG
(BCWR $_{Cum}$)

BURN UP CHART STATUS
(BCWP $_{Cum}$)

$

Time   Time Now   Completion Date

The WBS framework in place for the project can be used to summarize the project performance using JIRA (an issues management software) to track progress on milestones at the lowest level of the WBS and summarize to a higher level WBS element. The EV methodologies should always be documented in the Project Management Plan.

The hybrid approach has been used on one-of-a-kind or state-of-the-art projects. A good example is the implementation of controls software on a scientific accelerator beamline project. [7] As discussed, the traditional EVMS methodology does not provide the needed flexibility for assessing performance on work that has changing requirements, continued refinement/revisions to scope, uncertainty, and coding/testing (a basic characteristic of software and R&D projects). The hybrid approach is an effective methodology for measuring project performance for these types of projects, as it addresses the needs and nature of software/R&D project work scope by applying Agile methodology for measuring performance within the framework of the traditional project measurement and reporting structure of EVMS.

4 Case Study: Implementing a Hybrid Approach for ECP

The ECP delivers products and outcomes centered on applications, software, and the integration across applications and software for specific hardware technologies or exascale[1] system instantiations. The outcome of the ECP is the accelerated delivery of a capable and sustainable exascale computing ecosystem to provide breakthrough solutions addressing the nation's most critical challenges in scientific discovery, energy assurance, economic competitiveness, and national security. The ECP is designed to create more valuable and rapid insights from a wide variety of applications ("capable"), which requires a much higher level of inherent efficacy in all methods, software tools, and ECP-enabled computing technologies to be acquired by DOE national laboratories ("ecosystem").

---

[1] Ability to perform 10^{18} operations per second

To deliver on its mission and achieve its vision of capable exascale computing, the ECP is organized into three major integrated technical focus areas, each with specific technical objectives within the project, as summarized below. The WBS also includes the project management focus area which provides the management and support services to the project.

Work Breakdown Structure (WBS)

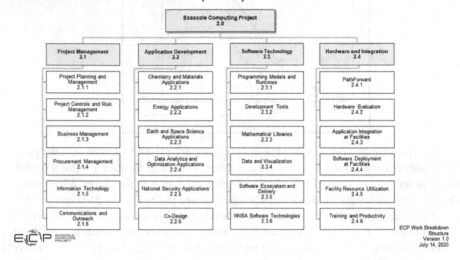

Exascale Computing Project 2.0			
Project Management 2.1	Application Development 2.2	Software Technology 2.3	Hardware and Integration 2.4
Project Planning and Management 2.1.1	Chemistry and Materials Applications 2.2.1	Programming Models and Runtimes 2.3.1	PathForward 2.4.1
Project Controls and Risk Management 2.1.2	Energy Applications 2.2.2	Development Tools 2.3.2	Hardware Evaluation 2.4.2
Business Management 2.1.3	Earth and Space Science Applications 2.2.3	Mathematical Libraries 2.3.3	Application Integration at Facilities 2.4.3
Procurement Management 2.1.4	Data Analytics and Optimization Applications 2.2.4	Data and Visualization 2.3.4	Software Deployment at Facilities 2.4.4
Information Technology 2.1.5	National Security Applications 2.2.5	Software Ecosystem and Delivery 2.3.5	Facility Resource Utilization 2.4.5
Communications and Outreach 2.1.6	Co-Design 2.2.6	NNSA Software Technologies 2.3.6	Training and Productivity 2.4.6

ECP Work Breakdown Structure Version 1.0 July 14, 2020

4.1 Application Development (AD)

Developing exascale-capable applications are a foundational element of the ECP and the vehicle for delivery of mission need on the targeted exascale systems. The ECP launched its mission need application projects, each targeting a specific exascale challenge problem—to address a high-priority strategic problem of national interest that is intractable without performant or efficient use of exascale computing resources. These applications span chemistry, materials, energy, earth and space science, data analytics and optimization, and national security. The AD focus area will create or enhance the predictive capability of these applications through algorithmic and software advances via co–design centers and targeted development of requirements-based models, algorithms, and methods. In addition, the AD focus area provides systematic improvement of exascale system readiness and utilization and demonstration and assessment of effective software integration.

4.2 Software Technology (ST)

Applications are built on underlying software technologies. As a result, software technologies play an essential supporting role in application efficacy on computing systems. The ECP's ST effort is developing an expanded and vertically integrated software stack that includes advanced mathematical libraries, extreme-scale programming environments, development tools, visualization libraries, and the software infrastructure to support large-scale data management and data science for science and security applications. The ST efforts complement and integrate into the broader scientific software ecosystem that includes capabilities from industry and the broader HPC R&D community.

4.3 Hardware and Integration (HI)

The HI focus area ensures a capable exascale computing ecosystem by integrating the ECP applications, software, and hardware innovations into the DOE HPC facilities (hereafter referred to as the "Facilities"). The scope of HI includes support for US HPC computer industry ("vendor") R&D focused on innovative architectures for competitive exascale system designs, hardware evaluation, tested exascale software products and an automated testing capability deployed and integrated at Facilities, accelerated application readiness on targeted exascale architectures, access to resources at the Facilities, and training on key ECP technologies to accelerate the software development cycle and optimize productivity of application and software developers.

The HPC systems (including testbeds and datacenter site preparation) are procured as separate DOE projects and therefore are not formally within the ECP's scope. HPC system procurements will be executed as projects by the DOE national laboratories hosting the systems. Acquisition and deployment of production systems will follow DOE SC and NNSA policies and procedures for major scientific computing facility upgrades. The fact that DOE HPC system procurements occur outside ECP's formal scope means that intimate integration and co-dependency with DOE computing facility operations and procurements are critical to the success of the ECP.

4.4 Assessing Performance Measurement

As described above, ECP has adopted a hybrid approach to assessing performance measurement. Each ECP focus area has chosen a performance measurement method that best matches their work scope and method of accomplishment. The various methods chosen include using stories to allow for progress measurements with long duration activities, refinement of baselined activities to allow for agile development, using weighted milestone achievement with short duration activities, and LOE for management activities (Fig. 1).

AD teams plan and execute work in a manner that is typically different from more traditional software development and construction projects. The inherent research component makes fine-grained planning impractical as the scope and schedule of future tasks are often dependent on the results of current tasks. Several concurrent activities are usually being executed by people working on the project part-time; therefore, accurately estimating start and end dates of the tasks required to complete the activities is a challenge. Rather than artificially schedule interdependent pieces of work, each subproject has defined the major technical goals as activities in the formal schedule. These activities tend to be longer in duration than those typically used for determining EV, so each activity is broken into smaller pieces of work using features of both the Agile and traditional project management systems, which allow for subtasks to be "earned"

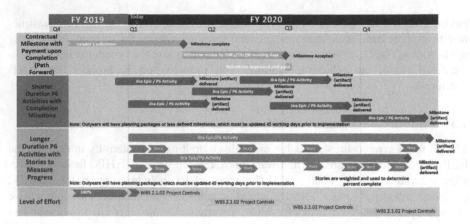

Fig. 1. ECP uses different performance measurement methodologies to measure progress.

as they are completed but are not scheduled with a start and finish date. Thus, while the activity may be of long duration, subtasks (stories/steps) can be used to provide progress indicators using the percent complete method. Each story/step has a value, and upon completion, this value is earned, and a percentage of the total value assigned to the activity is also earned.

ST teams plan and execute work in a manner that is more typical of agile software projects but tailored to meet the unique requirements of software development subprojects of the magnitude and complexity of ECP, along with satisfying mandatory requirements for traditional EV project management. The methodology chosen provides agility with a cadence of more planning fidelity as time proceeds. With this methodology, a baseline plan with high-level definitions is developed. Each year the plan is refined to include four to six activities, each of which is of relatively short duration and is assigned a budget, a start and end date, a high-level description, and completion criteria. Eight weeks prior to the start of an activity, a high-fidelity description of an execution strategy, refined completion criteria, and staffing details are developed. In this way, ST has both a long-term plan and a method for agilely adjusting as necessary.

HI teams use a weighted milestone approach, with each subproject dividing work into 3 month increments and ending in an observable milestone. Each activity has a summary, description, execution plan, completion criteria, and planned start and finish dates. Once completed, each activity is earned. The HI work scope also includes vendor milestones, which are earned when contractual milestones are completed. This produces only schedule variances as the milestone payment is fixed via the contract with the vendor.

Due in part to the complexity of ECP, but also inherent to software development R&D scope, an organizing principle for the ECP is to ensure all staff can see and have ready access to the detailed technical plans for all project areas. Furthermore, the database for detailed plans must be continuously viewed and updated by the ECP staff, which is consistent with Agile project management principles. To achieve the requirement for plans, interactions, and information to be shared with ECP contributors and stakeholders, a suite of tools was acquired and further developed to support this requirement.

5 Tools

Integration is a key operational tenet within the ECP and is implemented in part by ensuring that information such as detailed technical plans and achievements are readily accessible to all participants. A hybrid approach to project management almost necessitates the need for an equally flexible suite of project management tools. The functionality to enable this broad, dynamic access is provided by a suite of tools described here, which the ECP has found to be invaluable in managing work and communicating with teams. The tools must allow the end user the ability to status work without the overhead of a complex project management interface, but also provide the robustness of a tool that can assimilate large amounts of data and display the resulting information in a highly consumable reporting structure. The strong integration of research, development, and deployment efforts results in a dynamic environment in which frequent input from collaborators and stakeholders is essential.

Integration for a project of this size must allow considerable coordination among geographically and institutionally dispersed team members to operate efficiently. Challenges to delivering this functionality include requirements gathering over a broad set of partners; disparate institutional cyber security requirements; implementation of an intuitive training program to bring participants up to speed quickly; tool procurement and deployment costs; and maintenance of a consistent, common database with real-time data analytics and dashboarding. Portability, scalability, and flexibility are also key requirements for the tool suite given the ever-changing environment and the need to repurpose the tools to other DOE projects.

Within 6 months of the project's initiation, the ECP IT team identified tool requirements; evaluated, procured and deployed a suite of tools; and trained over 400 IT and project team members. Critical to this effort was the early identification of key sponsors and stakeholders and the collection of clear requirements in each of the development areas (e.g., project management, collaboration, workflow automation, and reporting). Several project management and digital workflow management tools (e.g., Deltek ERP, MS Project, ServiceNow, Trac)[2] were evaluated against criteria including ease-of-use, user interface, reporting and analytics capabilities, security, and total cost of ownership, to name a few. While each of these tools provided compelling reasons to pursue further, the ECP IT team found that the Atlassian suite of tools were most closely aligned to its key selection criteria. The Agile suite of tools contains project management (Atlassian Jira), collaboration (Atlassian Confluence), and workflow automation (Atlassian Service Desk) tools that required minimal customization. The ECP IT application development team used the Atlassian suite and Agile development and work planning methods to effectively deploy the project management tools to the ECP staff. The use of daily standups, Kanban board task management, effective team collaboration and communication, self-driven teams, continuous deployments with key customer-identified features, and metrics driven decision making were all critical components for the deployment

---

[2] The co-author has experience with these tools and found them to be very effective and in many cases, industry leading in the project management and IT service management fields. Several factors were considered during tool evaluation and the selection of the Atlassian suite no way reflects negatively on the capabilities these tools offer.

of these tools. The Atlassian tools were augmented by project management industry standard scheduling (Primavera P6) and cost analysis (Deltek Cobra) tools to supply a comprehensive yet intuitive end user experience. Interfaces were developed that would allow project team members to input deliverable status into the Jira tool which would then be automatically converted (and subsequently tracked) in the Primavera P6 scheduling tool where seamless reporting occurs. These tools were rounded out with robust persistent chat (Slack) and video-teleconferencing (Zoom for Gov) tools that could be easily deployed and scaled to meet project user requirements.

Team members follow their own institutional cyber security and access control requirements, which rarely align across organizations. The ECP information technology group teamed with cyber security counterparts at partner institutions to develop and maintain a comprehensive cyber security plan for the ECP tools. The plan addressed data classifications in the ECP IT systems and how this data is protected, how access controls (e.g., audit frequency, password refresh intervals) provide entry into the IT systems, and the network monitoring tools and web security policies used to control and govern the ECP IT infrastructure. By identifying the ECP data classifications and brokering a relationship with the partner cyber security experts early in the project, the ECP IT architecture has remained relatively unchanged since the initial deployment.

The tools are housed on an Amazon Web Service (AWS) instance. AWS provides security, affordability and reliability. This instantiation was established through a contract with Apnatomy, LLC. This Atlassian expert partner is thoroughly familiar with the tool functionality and deployment methods, which expedited the implementation. The tool suite was deployed using base functionality to quickly evaluate the tool's performance, while meeting project requirements. The team chose to minimally customize the tools, reducing overhead associated with implementing patches and update compatibility. ECP-specific training modules were created and deployed by Apnatomy. The content was provided using a combination of live instructor-led training and videos that could be accessed at any time for future use.

As the ECP continues to evolve and expand, it becomes even more important for the entirety of the project team to work from a common database and be able to quickly see project performance against its baseline goals and objectives. A key component of the tool suite is a set of dashboards and reports that can be easily accessed and configured, such as the cumulative monthly milestone reports shown in Fig. 2. A lesson learned was that by using clearly defined user groups, access to subprojects, collaboration areas, reports, and dashboards is controlled more efficiently than by traditional ad hoc user groups. Having specified owners of these groups who can quickly determine group memberships is another key component for user access controls. Data integrity and availability have been traditional challenges for database architects and administrators. Web-hosted services such as AWS provide security and availability for data that is leading in the industry. The disaster recovery and failover benefits were key considerations for choosing a cloud-hosted datacenter architecture. The Atlassian tools with an overlay of business information tools such as EazyBI provide a simple but effective real-time reporting structure that can be accessed 24 × 7 on a need-to-know basis. Project information is dynamic, and the reliance on static reporting is drastically reduced. The ECP identifies and meets reporting needs while maintaining a rich database of information that can be shared with other project stakeholders. Information that has been historically captured in emails is now captured in a tightly integrated set of tools.

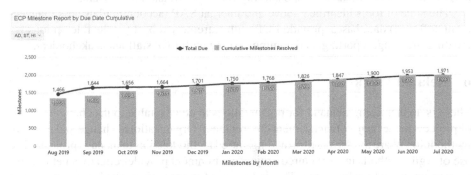

Fig. 2. ECP milestone reports by due date (cumulative).

Capturing lessons learned and the application of those lessons is a key component of any DOE project. As such, the transference of project management tools to similar projects is an important consideration when scoping tool selection criteria. The suite of tools and their underlying configurations are easily ported to other projects with minimal development and system administrative effort. Defined processes for maintaining out-of-the-box configurations is crucial to maintaining tool portability to other projects. With the exponential growth of the project, the ECP IT team has provided a scalable, economic, and flexible solution. Using automated scripts and logical business process workflows, the tools accommodate changing user requirements and additional database loads through a thoughtful architectural design. The suite of tools is flexible in accommodating a specific, but unique, set of business processes ranging from the tracking of project changes to the onboarding and offboarding of project personnel. Once the underlying architecture has been decided, additional functionality can be added with minimal effort.

The team is continually challenged by expenditures related to the ECP IT solutions. Tool bundling, outyear planning, and the use of cloud-hosted services provide an attractive cost-per-user pricing model for a well-rounded set of tools. Processes are implemented to deactivate stale accounts and offload modules and add-ons not being used. By using AWS, cost savings were realized by throttling performance requirements based on usage instead of the traditional data models that are based on flat rate fees, regardless of usage. These measures help to maintain an affordable product offering that has remained relatively constant throughout the project.

Tools to manage project deliverables, collaborate real time, report on project deliverables, and automate repeatable processes are all needed to make the project perform efficiently and to deliver on the DOE's goals and objectives. By gathering a clear set of requirements and identifying key stakeholders (e.g., sponsors, users, cyber security experts) early in the deployment process, a streamlined deployment of tools is easily obtainable for a project of this complexity. Additionally, using industry-leading approaches such as cloud architectures and Agile development, while maintaining standard system configurations, will deeply reduce future issues related to patch and update compatibilities while helping to reduce the overall cost of product ownership. Lastly, using tools that are easily portable to other projects leverages past lessons learned while helping to maintain fiduciary responsibility for the DOE and its sponsors.

The suite of tools identified above and internal SAP (accounting/business management software) data bases, provide ECP with extremely robust yet flexible options for creating, tracking, reporting, and communicating with ECP staff and stakeholders.

6   Related Work

There is an increasing demand for organizations to be adaptable to the changing needs of projects in the project management environment. Organizational change and adaptive methodologies are the drivers to providing varied methodologies to manage projects. The use of Agile methods in a structured project environment provides effective methods for measuring project performance. This is the case for projects in which a component of the project scope that does not typically benefit from traditional metrics for budgetary performance or for tracking deliverables. Monitoring budgetary performance and deliverables is typically required by senior leadership and the customer. Project leaders need reliable report submittals that track and forecast cost and schedule performance throughout the project life cycle. EVM adapted for Agile methods, called the hybrid approach, can provide performance metrics based on the EV of work performed on a monthly basis. In addition, this performance methodology is designed to generate estimates of work completion planned in the future based on past performance. It is recognized that a systems approach to managing project performance should be structured to meet the project objectives and customer reporting expectations and be flexible enough to accommodate work scope that typically lends itself to an Agile methodology but resides in a traditional project environment (hybrid project). Agile applied to a hybrid project is a valued methodology for meeting the project performance measurement needs and customer reporting requirements within a more structured project management environment.

7   Conclusion

The ECP is a challenging project because of its scale and R&D focus. The combination of traditional and Agile methodologies for determining progress with the right set of tools provides ECP the ability to determine goals and desired outcomes, measure progress toward these outcomes, manage project communications, and provide interim results. The hybrid approach is an effective methodology for measuring performance for this type of project, as it addresses the needs and nature of software/R&D project work scope by applying an Agile methodology within the framework of traditional project measurement and reporting structure of EVMS. The lessons learned by ECP can be tailored and applied to similar but smaller or less complex R&D projects.

Acknowledgements. This work was supported by the Exascale Computing Project (17-SC-20-SC), a collaborative effort of the U.S. Department of Energy Office of Science and the National Nuclear Security Administration.

A special thanks to Jonathan Wilson, ECP IT lead and Jason White, founder Apnatomy, LLC.

References

1. National Defense Industrial Association, Integrated Program Management Division: Earned Value Management Systems EIA-748-C Intent Guide. Arlington, Virginia, 29 April 2014
2. Manifesto for Agile Software Development. https://agilemanifesto.org/
3. DOE O 413.3B Chg 5 (MinChg), Program and Project Management for the Acquisition of Capital Assets
4. 12 Principles Behind the Agile Manifesto. https://www.agilealliance.org/agile101/the-agile-manifesto/
5. Project Management Institute Global Standard, The Standard for Earned Value Management
6. National Defense Industrial Association (NDIA), titled An Industry Practice Guide for Agile on Earned Value Management Programs
7. Brookhaven National Laboratory: National Synchrotron Light Source II 2020 Strategic Plan, September 2019

Memory vs. Storage Software and Hardware: The Shifting Landscape

Jay Lofstead[✉]

Sandia National Laboratories, Albuquerque, USA
gflofst@sandia.gov

Abstract. With emerging workflows incorporating both modeling and simulation scale-up workloads along with large scale data analytics and machine learning scale-out workloads, new machine architectures that can support both simultaneously is essential. New memory technologies, such as the persistent memory modules supported by the latest Intel chips offer a persistent storage device accessible on the memory bus. This newly available technology niche offers an opportunity to multipurpose a memory/storage tier. Further, with traditional storage moving to solid state technology, where to divide between memory and storage is less clear. NVMe and other high-performance storage devices offer extreme storage performance at increasingly affordable prices allowing them to masquerade as slow memory. Which of these devices should be considered memory and which storage varies with the workload. The software infrastructure to better support these hybrid technologies is crucial for widespread adoption.

To achieve the vision of hybrid use memory/storage tier(s), multiple system software components will have to be changed. The node operating system must be able to reassign the hardware into different roles and issues with purging and pre-staging data with persistent on-node stores must be addressed. Additional possibilities for compute node area shared resources must also be considered for a complete solution. This paper explores the variety of potential possibilities and the challenges with achieving this vision while laying out a plan to achieve the goals.

1 Introduction

Traditionally the performance differences between memory and storage devices have been orders of magnitude clearly delineating device purposes. With the introduction of NAND-flash devices, application developers and storage researchers each embraced the technology to expand their domain's capabilities. With the NVMe standard commonly moving these devices onto the PCI bus, the impact on application developers and storage researchers has been profound. Both groups saw a technology capable of revolutionizing their domain. The "right" way to use this technology and how to "properly" provision and allocate it has caused differing priorities to generate opposed answers. With persistent memory (PMEM) devices

---

Under the terms of Contract DE-NA0003525, there is a non-exclusive license for use of this work by or on behalf of the U.S. Government.

on the memory bus offering even higher performance and load/store access, the "right" way to think about the devices has gotten harder.

While these hardware changes are moving into the mainstream, traditional scale-up HPC workloads are being asked to live alongside scale-out analytic and machine learning tools that work best with different hardware configurations. New platforms are being asked to run both scale-up and scale-out workloads. Projected exascale applications are expected to be ensembles of applications and analytics components, from both scale-up and scale-out models, at the same time. To accelerate the time to science, application and storage developers each focus on their own priorities.

Application developers and users focus on how much compute can they get out of a machine. In very coarse, raw terms, compute is measured in FLOPS. More memory can yield more localized computation yielding more FLOPS. PMEM offers a way to get more memory per node offering greater potential for more FLOPS at a cost more affordable than DRAM.

Storage developers are focused on IOPS and bandwidth. The IOPS show the number of operations performed per second. Bandwidth is the raw data transfer capability. PMEM offers high IOPS and bandwidth making it a seemingly ideal storage technology. The drawback for PMEM, in the short term, may be the memory bus rather than block-oriented storage interfaces requiring rethinking storage software stacks. These conflicting desires between application and storage developers prompts rethinking how technology is deployed on HPC machines.

While the persistence properties of flash storage and PMEM devices suggest they are most ideally used as storage, this property may be the least interesting device property. Using the devices as cheaper, higher capacity memory may make persistence a penalty since erasure may require more than a reboot or a power cycle. The benefit of expanding memory capacity may outweigh the storage performance benefits. This paper explores these technologies and the impacts on applications, storage, infrastructure management, and machine procurement.

Throughout the rest of the paper "memory" and "storage" are frequently written with quotes. This is to emphasize that the devices or operating modes referenced may be for a particular purpose, but it might not be the purpose the manufacturer primarily intends the hardware to fit. This fluidity is the foundation of new opportunities for research and development.

The rest of the paper is structured as follows. First, in Sect. 2, an evaluation of devices typically classified as memory and how they work in this shifting landscape. In Sect. 3, is a discussion of the impacts new persistent storage devices have impacted research and production storage as well as machine procurement. Section 4 discusses the pertinent persistent memory characteristics that make this technology unusually interesting. Next in Sect. 5 is a discussion of a hybrid machine and the impacts of persistent memory. Finally in Sect. 6 conclusions are made.

2   The Shifting Memory Landscape

Modern compute memory started with registers and main memory. Then cache was inserted close to the CPU to shorten the time to read/write with main memory. Ultimately, the caching facilities split into layers and separate caches for data and instructions. This has proven crucial for compute performance given the differences between external and internal clock rates for CPUs and the delay when storing and retrieving data from main memory. Multi-core CPUs have driven a need for larger and larger caches to keep the cores processing as much as possible.

With the introduction of high bandwidth, on package memory, another layer is inserted into the memory hierarchy. Figure 1 illustrates what a current memory hierarchy looks like. By moving from left to right, the performance decreases and the capacity increases. Also, the price per byte decreases moving left to right in the figure.

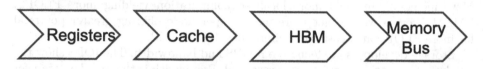

Fig. 1. Memory Hierarchy

While the memory bus seems like an inappropriate item to list with the other three entries, it represents the possibility of two different technologies deployed in varying quantities. First are the traditional volatile DRAM devices. Alternatively are the persistent memory devices. The possibilities of no devices of either or both types are all viable models. In some cases, the memory bus outside the CPU package may become optional.

With the arrival of the multi-core era with internal and external clock speed differences already dominant, one might have asked, "why aren't we doing on package memory instead?" Unfortunately, the manufacturing process for a CPU core is different from what is used to make DRAM. Requiring multiple processes for a single chip is not feasible. Putting multiple "chiplets" into the package was infeasible at the time as well. Instead, the next best option was to add additional cores with the hope that the caches could keep them fed sufficiently that processing performance is significantly better.

High-bandwidth, on package memory (HBM) products demonstrate that the manufacturing issues related to additional on package memory have been solved. Manufacturers are still in a profit taking phase making the technology expensive. The additional challenges related to yield and bits per pin may limit the ultimate potential driving the need for more off package memory.

Persistent memory offers a different option that is less expensive than DRAM or HBM with nearly the performance of DRAM [12]. PMEM paired with HBM may offer the right financial solution to accelerating compute workloads. Price, performance, functionality, and usability all matter.

2.1 How is "Memory" Used?

To best think about memory, think about what assumptions systems and applications developers make when thinking about a memory device and memory function.

Consider a proto-typical scale-up HPC application, big physics, that applies physics-based calculations across a large data structure. The normal communication patterns are less important than the data access and persistence patterns employed.

Assumption 1: Data only Lives as Long as the Application. Application developers work under the assumption that whatever is stored in memory will be deleted automatically on application exit. Things like cleaning up dynamically allocated data structures is unnecessary if the application is exiting since the OS will reclaim those resources. This is done both out of laziness and for performance. Cleaning up a large, complex data structure can noticeably delay application exit when the memory free operations all invoke a system call to return the freed resources.

Assumption 2: Knowledge for Understanding the Data Format is Encoded in the Application. With one known exception outlined below, application developers seek to get the greatest cache efficiency for the greatest performance. This requires packing data as tightly and efficiently as possible. Stated differently, the application is coded such that it understands the tightly packed data bits rather than the bits including any information about what follows.

Assumption 3: Writing and Reading Environment Identical. With DRAM performance identical for writing and reading (assuming either both in cache or all the way to main memory operations), optimizing for one over the other is not considered when writing applications. Instead, a developer may optimize to minimize the sum of both even if that skews writing or reading strongly.

Assumption 4: Writing/Reading is "Fast" Compared to Storage. Memory operations, from both a memory and a storage perspective, are far cheaper than storage traditionally. Instead of using sub-optimal storage IO patterns, spending some time manipulating memory pays off in significant IO performance improvements. Given a choice, programmers will choose orders of magnitude more memory operations than storage operations and achieve greater performance.

3 The Shifting Storage Landscape

Modern computing storage has employed disk and tape for decades. Improvements in capacities and performance as well as innovations in storage software and interconnect infrastructures have enabled growing storage systems to meet application needs. Gary Grider pointed out around 2015 that disk performance was not keeping up with capacity making a situation where buying sufficient disk to get the desired performance yielded an excess in capacity. In essence, in procurements, buying adequate disk quantities based on bandwidth requirements guaranteed capacity requirements were exceeded.

As part of Grider's assertions about disk, solid state storage in the form of NAND-flash SSDs offered far greater performance, but with far less capacity. Purchasing, if buying SSDs instead of disks, switched to buying capacity and getting bandwidth for free. Balancing these two technologies as proposed with "burst buffers" [2] introduced storage software complexities, but offered performance and capacity at a net lower cost. This kind of staging data in a fast tier before moving to a disk tier goes back to at least 1996 [16] in data staging research. Hierarchical storage certainly goes back decades further.

The price/performance/capacity balance that burst buffers addressed from a hardware perspective is shifting again. QLC flash, particularly with 3D NAND, moves the price for capacity of flash much closer to disk [9,13,15]. These advances have already eliminated the 10K and 15K RPM HDDs and will continue to erode the HDD market. Getting sufficient HDDs in parallel to offer the same performance as flash reveals that the cost difference is far smaller than it might appear, particularly when considering total cost of ownership. This shift cannot happen overnight as manufacturing capacities for flash are far too small to wholesale replace HDDs at this time, but the shift is continuing as more devices and purchasers opt for flash over HDDs. Skeptics may look and be concerned about write endurance for these devices. For a projected 5-year lifetime, these devices can serve without replacement. Projections based on write volumes per day show that in spite of the limited lifetimes, they will last as long as the compute system for the specified usage [10]. Based on the workflow examples, devices with as short as 0.1 drive writes per day could suit a 5-year lifetime offering substantial performance and lower cost of ownership.

Figure 2 illustrates the storage hierarchy today. Note that like with the memory hierarchy, the memory bus is not strictly a storage device, but is a stand-in for devices that can work on the memory bus at speeds reasonable for a "memory" device. Discussions of where burst buffers fit into this picture is more a matter of where burst buffer software is deployed. With the node-local design used on Summit [22] at Oak Ridge Leadership Computing Facility being one design and centralized nodes as sold by Cray as their DataWarp [8] product, the design of a burst buffer is more of a storage layer rather than a storage layer using a particular technology or in a particular location. Ultimately, as the price of higher performance storage devices drop for capacity, burst buffers will disappear to be replaced by near-compute storage for medium-term data storage. Data lakes as used by Internet scale companies are a reasonable model. Data needs to be accessible faster than tape will use slower, but higher capacity disk using technologies like shingled magnetic recording [1] and/or energy-assisted magnetic recording (e.g.., HAMR and MAMR).

Fig. 2. Storage hierarchy

3.1 How is "Storage" Used?

The example big physics application is still a good model to help think about storage from the application developer's perspective. In general, the application developer uses storage to save a snapshot of their model periodically based on the application progression. Because of how this data is later used, different assumptions are made and the data is managed differently from the in memory image.

Assumption 1: Data Lifetimes Exceed the Application's Lifetime. Writing data to storage is expensive. Developers project some percentage of application runtime and limit their data output to approximately hit those targets. This offers an acceptable balance between compute progress and analysis capabilities. Writing data more frequently will take too much time. Writing data less frequently limits the ability to gain scientific insights. Finding this balance is not an easy task and is generally a guess with innovations and adjustments made in analysis trying to compensate if insufficient data can reasonably be saved. In all cases, the intent is that some future analysis will take the data and process it without the big physics application still running at the same time. Complicating this balance is the need for resilience-related defensive output based on MTBF for the system. This data may or may not be usable for analysis purposes. In many cases, developers have significant overlap between analysis output contents and defensive output contents.

Assumption 2: Knowledge to Understand Data Format and Types Encoded with the Data. A key insight for this is the data consumption by analysis applications. Using standard applications generally means the data is stored in a standard format the application can read and then the analysis operations can be performed. The implication of this is that the standard data formats, such as HDF5 [6], netCDF [17], and ADIOS' BP format [11] all encode metadata with the data so that these data consumers can take an arbitrary output and still process it without having to write custom data interpretation code. This encoding metadata as part of the data is nearly unique to storage. The secondary purpose of this formatting is to enable data to survive memory layout changes in the application. When the application re-reads data, it will know how to organize it in memory to suit the current application expectations.

Assumption 3: Writing Architectural Assumptions may Not Hold When Reading. While little-endian formats have almost exclusively taken over as the dominant in memory image, standard storage formats cannot rely on this unless it can be guaranteed that little-endian (or big-endian) formats are the only format they will support. For memory, the compiler will generate code that properly matches how the CPU manipulates data.

Assumption 4: Writing/Reading is "Slow" Compared to Memory. Storage systems have historically relied on "slow" devices as motivation to do things like data re-arrangement [20]. The performance differences made this tradeoff worthwhile offering net better performance.

SSDs and NVMe devices have changed this picture forcing a rethinking of IO libraries to avoid stealing too much performance for "optimizations" that do not yield sufficient benefit.

4   Persistent Memory Characteristics

PMEM's load/store access is the most important characteristic. It means that conventional programming models for addressing memory can work directly with PMEM devices with only slight modifications. These modifications are limited to a change to the allocation such that a programmer can specify what kind of memory to use and then the compiler being smart enough to generate proper code to access PMEM vs. DRAM properly. This small change makes it extremely simple for a programmer to adopt not just for the simple API, but also because the programming model is what they are accustomed to already.

But for a storage system, is persistence the most important characteristic? From the operational semantic contract storage APIs have with programmers, it must be. But how does this affect HPC-related applications where multiple nodes running a single task are standard?

Typical node-level storage issues remain with PMEM devices. Unless the PMEM can be accessed while the node is offline, data access can be lost. While centralizing storage was done to address reliability issues for storage devices, it also serves to make data resilience easier to implement. No longer will a single node going down affect data availability. Systems like Scalable Checkpoint Restart (SCR) [14] offer a model for mitigating the risks of node local storage while enjoying the performance benefits. However, SCR has yet to become a standard tool on HPC systems nor has it been widely adopted by HPC application in spite of the proven benefits. NVMe devices already can serve the niche of high performance node local storage. The additional benefits vs. financial costs may make PMEM adoption a difficult argument.

Given the conflicting benefits of either load/store access vs. persistence, how should these devices be allocated and used?

4.1   Considering PMEM (Scale-Up)

For scale-up machines using large quantities of thin nodes, the memory bus may be empty and may not even have any sockets on the node board. This is one of the "swim lanes" for expected exascale machines [18]. For these cases, the additional cost of the memory slots must also be considered. For fat node machines, sufficient memory slots should exist that some of them could be dedicated to PMEM devices lowering the up front costs.

In the presence of existing technology, PMEM still makes good sense. The SATA bus used by most disks or SSDs today is too slow to be useful. The interconnect to a different node may be as much as 10× faster. Even saturating the SATA bus is not fast enough to make using it viable. NVMe devices can offer performance beyond all but the newest interconnect while still offering more of a traditional storage model with blocks as the primary storage unit. However the additional costs of NVMe devices must be factored into the storage system cost to justify their purchase. With storage being allocated, generally, something like 10% of the machine budget, price/performance trade-offs are important.

Referring back to Fig. 1 and Fig. 2, what devices are placed in the Memory Bus block becomes an interesting question. PMEM is a strong candidate in the presence of HBM since it can offer additional capacity at a cheaper cost. However, the storage benefits are also strong. Given these conflicting use cases, how should it be used?

5   The Hybrid Machine

Consider an exascale machine with expected workload mixes. For most cases, the expectation is that an ensemble will run concurrently rather than a single application occupying the whole machine at once. Today's analysis components are strongly incorporating scale-out tools to augment existing functionality. With a scale-up application running in concert with scale-out analysis tools, the best hardware configuration for each component varies.

5.1   Consider Persistent Memory

Persistent memory's characteristics offer a way to address both application needs of additional memory as well as storage's needs of a fast, persistent store. Given this dichotomy, the following questions are relevant.

Question 1: Is It Slow Memory or Fast Storage? For the nodes hosting the application, using PMEM as slow memory makes the most sense. However, for the nodes hosting analysis components, having high capacity, fast storage may make more sense.

Question 2: Does Persistence Matter? One of the questions the storage community wrestled with when SSDs became affordable enough to deploy on HPC machines (as part of the storage hierarchy) was the importance of persistence. Seeing these as storage devices, many people considered persistence a key characteristic. For those working on data staging, they saw something that was probably better as a storage device. Some applications people, particularly those that already were using out of core computations, SSDs offered fast storage (or very slow memory) to accelerate their applications. For these applications people, the persistence was a detriment. Because SSDs have a required erase operation before a block can be reused, unless it is an enterprise-class device with sufficient over provisioning, writing slows to half speed over time. PMEM devices avoid this cost.

For Summit and Sierra, the amount of writes before falling off this cliff is larger than the vast majority applications need to write in a write phase and is not an issue. We expect apps to write ≤15% of GPU memory. The devices can absorb this before falling off of the write cliff.

Question 3: If it is Across a Fast Interconnect, Does that Matter? For storage operations, the device location is unimportant. HPC storage software is largely written assuming data will move from the source node to some other location for persistence. It may migrate through multiple locations, but ultimately, it does migrate off node. For memory, the interconnect is still slow. The GenZ [4] architecture assumes distributed memory across the interconnect factoring in slow memory into the hardware model. In this case, the location and whether or not it is a memory or a storage device is irrelevant. Other similar approaches include CAPI/OpenCAPI (Open Coherent Accelerator Processor Interface) [19], CCIX (Cache Coherent Interconnect for Accelerators) [3], and CXL (Compute Express Link) [21].

Question 4: Does it Have to be Natively Byte Addressable? Consider cache lines vs. blocks or pages. Isn't everything byte addressable through a suitable API? Memory operations cause a cache line to be loaded into the cache or a cache line to be flushed back to main memory. Storage has a native block-sized access granularity, but still offers byte-addressibility through APIs like the standard C open/read/write/close POSIX calls.

In short, whether or not the device offers byte-level addressibility is not a valid question anymore. Instead, the question is the cost of fine grained access compared to the native access granularity. PMEM, as it lives on the memory bus, will offer cache line sized access granularity. While this is smaller than typical 512-byte or larger blocks, it is sufficient to deal with memory access performance with standard DRAM. This makes the native access granularity uninteresting as a defining characteristic.

5.2   Pop Quiz! Memory or Storage?

Organizing Data for Highest Density? No matter the kind of device the data is stored on, this is a traditional memory function. This is even true for some disk-based operations.

Organizing Data in an Archive/Long-Term Reuse Format? Typically, this is a storage characteristic. Recall that HDF5, netCDF, and ADIOS BP files all use this technique to make data easily accessible for arbitrary future data users.

Application Writing Checkpoint to Disk Using a raw Memory Dump? A checkpoint-restart output that is a strict memory dump rather than annotating the data is treating the storage device as memory by effectively doing a memory copy through an appropriate API.

There is one notable production exception: The European Center for Medium Range Weather Forecasting (ECMWF) changed their models to always keep data in a network transmission format [7]. That means there is less data density for compute and the storage format requires a custom to ECMWF interface to interpret the written format. For them, this simplification and de-optimization has served to make their code easier to write and the data easier to consume. A programmer only needs to read the block from storage and send that directly down the network. Also, computation needs only read the block and then can compute on it directly. The additional coding overheads and slowdown in memory access due to less data density was seen as less important than simplifying the data management environment. Further, the performance penalties have not been severe enough to justify rethinking this approach with the center continuing to meet forecast generation goals without difficulty.

5.3   What Do Apps People See?

Considering the above information, clearly, most scale-up applications people see PMEM as a slow memory device that can offer them additional compute memory to supplement the limited HBM deployed on the machines. The persistence is not something that is relevant at all. The benefit is that PMEM offers higher performance memory access than anything across the interconnect. Further, they get the convenient CPU load/store programming model they are accustomed to using eliminating the need to learn a new API to use the new hardware.

The key opportunity afforded by PMEM is the feasibility of out-of-core computations for applications that may have chosen to spread to other nodes historically. They can get additional memory capacity on a single node avoiding the interconnect communication overheads. Until HBM becomes inexpensive enough to eliminate the need for any out of package memory-like device, this model makes marginally large enough HBM a workable model. A careful OS model could place nearly all of the OS code and modules into the PMEM space opening more HBM for the computation.

Since out-of-core computing is a well known compute model, there is only a small learning curve. In simplistic terms, a programmer just needs to add a loop to move memory blocks from HBM to PMEM and vice versa after computation rounds.

5.4   What Do Storage People See?

Node-local storage devices, such as NVMe, have demonstrated the value of having persistent storage close to the compute. The performance when writing and reading to these devices enables meeting machine forward progress requirements with less difficulty than larger interconnects and higher bandwidth on shared storage. In this environment, PMEM is clearly fast storage. Systems like SCR [14] offer an existing, proven approach easily adapted to use PMEM rather than other node-local storage devices.

Opportunity: Can extend remote storage onto the node Auto-migrate off node for better resilience over time

5.5   Who Wins?

Winning the right to define how a type of technology is not really the goal. Instead, consider why the big machines exist and where PMEM can offer the most benefit. In general, we buy machines for computation. Whatever best supports computation throughput is what we will use. In the case of PMEM, the typical memory-oriented API offers a convenient, familiar programming model that does not impose any special requirements.

But there are other considerations to keep in mind. For the proposed exascale machine with an ensemble of application and analysis components running simultaneously, making PMEM into a memory device is not as easy a decision. For data staging between ensemble components, PMEM offers a convenient hardware interface with additional persistence guarantees. For analysis components that favor close storage, PMEM offers a convenient technology to address those needs. But this really points out that depending on the particular code use case, how PMEM is best used varies.

6   Memory vs. Storage: Bottom Line

Overall, it is clear that data lifetimes are not a particularly interesting difference. Instead, the performance can offer advantages to both memory operations or storage operations, as needed. With the endian-ness issues mostly standardized now, the need to encode data to account for different endian-ness is nearly gone. The performance differences between the fastest and slowest part of either the memory or storage tier is still vast. (Registers vs. PMEM or PMEM vs. disk or even tape). That means that PMEM for memory uses is unlikely to be suitable as a primary memory for compute while disk is no longer viable as the primary data repository for persistent storage.

Overall, data encoding might be the only meaningful difference between data intended for memory or storage. However, keep in mind that pesky ECMWF example eliminates even this consideration.

6.1 What Do We Need to Do?

For PMEM, if memcpy is the desired IO API, what primitives do we need to implement this effectively? To address the need for long-term stored bytes to be interpretable in the future, it is all but certain that some data encoding or annotation is required. Some new implementation of memcpy that offers the encoding and decoding would be ideal.

When using a machine with both HBM and PMEM, how does a programmer know if something is in HBM or PMEM? How much do they care? In reality, it is likely the programmer will use particular variables solely with one type or the other to limit confusion. However, there is the still the data swap operation. One solution to the data swapping is something like Kokkos [5]. This offers a simple programming model that makes explicit operations to transition data from one kind of media or storage location to another. Should those two logical location be in a single device, Kokkos defaults to a no-op. This kind of approach would be required.

For storage-oriented block devices and APIs that assume this hardware implementation, what changes will be made to take into account PMEM, if any? At a raw level, simply changing the block movement from read/write operations to memcpy operations may both be the quick fix as well as a viable long term solution.

Most importantly is the question of when will there be broad CPU support for PMEM beyond the few Intel parts? How long until AMD, Power, and ARM support PMEM. Is RISC-V possible as well? This will require market demand and good programming tools to drive usage and therefore demand.

One challenge storage developers encountered about a decade after they started using asynchronous IO to accelerate data movement while carefully avoiding application communication patterns was asynchronous collectives. The application writers discovered that there were times during the application execution where inter-node data movement could occur without disturbing the application's communication. Unfortunately, this was precisely the same times that the storage developers had used to perform asynchronous IO operations. With the adoption of asynchronous collectives, does this mean that all asynchronous operations simply become synchronous again because there is insufficient time to allow all asynchronous operations to complete during these interconnect quiet phases? Finding the right balance when storage wants to move 10s of GB and applications want to move a few MB, but both trying to do it asynchronously, is an open question.

6.2   Why Do We Care?

In summary, PMEM offers an opportunity to have a hybrid machine with devices that can serve as either slow memory or as fast, node local storage. With resource management systems updated to acknowledge these devices and change their deployment dynamically, we can have machines that suit both scale out memory intensive operations as well as scale up read intensive applications at the same time. HBM is still a bit too expensive, but 100% on package is the goal when we can afford it. Capacity limitations due to physical constraints may be a stronger limiting factor than cost in the foreseeable future.

A potentially surprising outcome of this analysis is that on node NVMe for thin nodes is too heavyweight. This might also be true for fat nodes. The additional performance and convenient interface to PMEM devices may do to NVMe devices what SSDs did to disks.

Until we get widespread support beyond just Intel, this is challenging to achieve. Unfortunately, Intel chose a confusing name by reusing Optane for PMEM effectively hiding the part from potential customers. With the big 5 cloud companies driving hardware development choices far more than any supercomputing application today, it may prove challenging to impossible for PMEM to get the market inroads necessary for wide-spread support. To make this work, showing the benefits for cloud workloads would help tremendously.

JEDEC ratified NVDIMM-P that will provide mixed DRAM/Flash DIMMs and will work with any DDR-5-capable CPU.

Intel's Optane is an Intel-specific NVDIMM-T spec.

NVDIMM-N exists today but is DRAM that backs up to on-board Flash upon unscheduled power-off and does not expose the backing Flash.

NVDIMM-F is defined (byte-addressable Flash) but potential products have not been announced.

Acknowledgments. Sandia National Laboratories is a multimission laboratory managed and operated by National Technology and Engineering Solutions of Sandia, LLC., a wholly owned subsidiary of Honeywell International, Inc., for the U.S. Department of Energy's National Nuclear Security Administration under contract DE-NA0003525. SAND2019-8513 PE

References

1. Amer, A., Holliday, J., Long, D.D., Miller, E.L., Pâris, J.F., Schwarz, T.: Data management and layout for shingled magnetic recording. IEEE Trans. Magn. **47**(10), 3691–3697 (2011)
2. Bent, J., et al.: On the non-suitability of non-volatility. In: 7th USENIX Workshop on Hot Topics in Storage and File Systems (HotStorage 15). USENIX Association, Santa Clara, CA, July 2015. https://www.usenix.org/conference/hotstorage15/workshop-program/presentation/bent
3. Consortium, C., et al.: Cache coherent interconnect for accelerators (ccix) (2017). http://www.ccixconsortium.com

4. Consortium, G.Z., et al.: Gen-z overview. Technical Report (2016). http://genzconsortium.org/wp-content
5. Edwards, H.C., Trott, C.R., Sunderland, D.: Kokkos: enabling manycore performance portability through polymorphic memory access patterns. J Parallel Distrib. Comput. **74**(12), 3202–3216 (2014)
6. Folk, M., Heber, G., Koziol, Q., Pourmal, E., Robinson, D.: An overview of the HDF5 technology suite and its applications. In: Proceedings of the EDBT/ICDT 2011 Workshop on Array Databases, pp. 36–47 (2011)
7. Gopalakrishnan, S.G., et al.: Toward improving high-resolution numerical hurricane forecasting: influence of model horizontal grid resolution, initialization, and physics. Weather Forecasting **27**(3), 647–666 (2012)
8. Henseler, D., Landsteiner, B., Petesch, D., Wright, C., Wright, N.J.: Architecture and design of cray datawarp. Cray User Group CUG (2016)
9. Krass, P.: Data-center storage costs too high? try the latest SSDs. https://www.techproviderzone.com/cloud-and-data-centers/data-center-storage-costs-too-high-try-the-latest-ssds. Accessed 15 Sep 2020
10. LANL, NERSC, SNL: Crossroads workflows. https://www.lanl.gov/projects/crossroads/_internal/_blocks/xroads_workflows_20190204.pdf. Accessed 15 Sep 2020
11. Lofstead, J., Zheng, F., Klasky, S., Schwan, K.: Adaptable, metadata rich IO methods for portable high performance IO. In: 2009 IEEE International Symposium on Parallel and Distributed Processing, pp. 1–10. IEEE (2009)
12. Mason, T., Doudali, T.D., Seltzer, M., Gavrilovska, A.: Unexpected performance of intel® optane™ dc persistent memory. IEEE Comput. Archit. Lett. **19**(1), 55–58 (2020)
13. Mellor, C.: How long before SSDs replace nearline disk drives? https://blocksandfiles.com/2019/08/28/nearline-disk-drives-ssd-attack/, Accessed 15 Sep 2020
14. Moody, A., Bronevetsky, G., Mohror, K., De Supinski, B.R.: Design, modeling, and evaluation of a scalable multi-level checkpointing system. In: SC'2010 Proceedings of the 2010 ACM/IEEE International Conference for High Performance Computing, Networking, Storage and Analysis, pp. 1–11. IEEE (2010)
15. Nimbus: Exadrive. https://nimbusdata.com/products/exadrive/. Accessed 15 Sep 2020
16. Oldfield, R.A., Womble, D.E., Ober, C.C.: Efficient parallel I/O in seismic imaging. Int. J. High Perform. Comput. Appl. **12**(3), 333–344 (1998)
17. Rew, R., Davis, G.: Netcdf: an interface for scientific data access. IEEE Comput. Graph. Appl. **10**(4), 76–82 (1990)
18. Shalf, J., Dosanjh, S., Morrison, J.: Exascale computing technology challenges. In: Palma, J.M.L.M., Daydé, M., Marques, O., Lopes, J.C. (eds.) VECPAR 2010. LNCS, vol. 6449, pp. 1–25. Springer, Heidelberg (2011). https://doi.org/10.1007/978-3-642-19328-6_1
19. Stuecheli, J., et al.: IBM power9 opens up a new era of acceleration enablement: opencapi. IBM J. Res. Dev. **62**(4/5), 8:1–8:8 (2018)
20. Thakur, R., Gropp, W., Lusk, E.: Data sieving and collective I/O in romio. In: Proceedings Frontiers 1999 Seventh Symposium on the Frontiers of Massively Parallel Computation, pp. 182–189. IEEE (1999)
21. Van Doren, S.: Abstract - hoti 2019: Compute express link. In: 2019 IEEE Symposium on High-Performance Interconnects (HOTI), p. 18 (2019)
22. Wells, J., et al.: Announcing supercomputer summit. Technical Report, Oak Ridge National Lab. (ORNL), Oak Ridge, TN (United States) (2016)

ALAMO: Autonomous Lightweight Allocation, Management, and Optimization

Ron Brightwell[✉], Kurt B. Ferreira, Ryan E. Grant, Scott Levy, Jay Lofstead,
Stephen L. Olivier, Kevin T. Pedretti, Andrew J. Younge, Ann Gentile,
and Jim Brandt

Sandia National Laboratories, Albuquerque, New Mexico, USA
{rbbrigh,kbferre,regrant,sllevy,gflofst,slolivi,ktpedre,ajyoung,
gentile,brandt}@sandia.gov

Abstract. Several recent workshops conducted by the DOE Advanced
Scientific Computing Research program have established the fact that
the complexity of developing applications and executing them on high-
performance computing (HPC) systems is rising at a rate which will
make it nearly impossible to continue to achieve higher levels of performance and scalability. Absent an alternative approach to managing this
ever-growing complexity, HPC systems will become increasingly difficult
to use. A more holistic approach to designing and developing applications and managing system resources is required. This paper outlines a
research strategy for managing the increasing the complexity by providing the programming environment, software stack, and hardware capabilities needed for autonomous resource management of HPC systems.
Developing portable applications for a variety of HPC systems of varying scale requires a paradigm shift from the current approach, where
applications are painstakingly mapped to individual machine resources,
to an approach where machine resources are automatically mapped and
optimized to applications as they execute. Achieving such automated
resource management for HPC systems is a daunting challenge that
requires significant sustained investment in exploring new approaches
and novel capabilities in software and hardware that span the spectrum from programming systems to device-level mechanisms. This paper
provides an overview of the functionality needed to enable autonomous
resource management and optimization and describes the components
currently being explored at Sandia National Laboratories to help support this capability.

© National Technology & Engineering Solutions of Sandia, LLC 2020
J. Nichols et al. (Eds.): SMC 2020, CCIS 1315, pp. 408–422, 2020.
https://doi.org/10.1007/978-3-030-63393-6_27

1   Introduction

Leadership-class high-performance computing (HPC) systems have become too complex to manage every critical resource across the entire infrastructure. Mapping an application to the resources in a system has become both inefficient and manual, requiring locality management and resource utilization to be done by hand. Processes are manually assigned to cores explicitly by user pinning, and this assignment remains unchanged throughout the lifetime of the job execution. Discovering a reasonable mapping is usually tedious process, typically done through trial-and-error, with no understanding of whether the result is optimal. This situation will worsen as future heterogeneous systems with complex node types and a wider variety of system architectures become a reality in a post-Moore era.

Mapping an application to the resources of an HPC machine must be done in an automated fashion that lessens the burden on the application programmer, employing many aspects of autonomous computing [21,26]. In order for autonomous resource management and optimization to be most effective, a holistic approach that spans the entire software stack must be employed. For example, a programming model and system that does not allow for dynamic adaptivity to the underlying resources will not be able to take full advantage of automated resource management. Likewise, asynchronous task-based programming systems cannot be fully exploited on systems where resources are fixed and unable to adapt.

Several key capabilities are required in order to enable autonomous resource management. First, resources must be dynamically discovered and changes to resources must be realized in an event-driven fashion. The system must develop an understanding of how best to use the available resources. This capability involves several aspects, including measuring how resources are being used, developing cost models that accurately reflect the overheads, providing flexible resource management policies, and determining appropriate responses to constantly changing resource needs. The current approach to doing offline performance analysis and optimization needs to be automated and remove the application programmer from the process as much as possible.

Developing these capabilities is a daunting task that will require significant sustained investment in exploring new approaches and novel capabilities in software and hardware. This white paper describes some of the components of a software stack being explored at Sandia that are necessary, but not sufficient, to enable autonomous resource management and optimization for HPC systems. Our intent is to use these components as research vehicles to support collaboration within the broader HPC research community to take steps toward enabling automated resource management and optimization of resources for HPC applications and systems.

2   Autonomous Operating System Design

Current leadership-class HPC systems are made up of a collection of individual servers each running a local operating system (OS) such as Linux, with a given server's OS having little or no particular insight into what the other servers in the system are doing. Given the primary purpose of these systems is to run tightly-coupled parallel applications across large fractions of the distributed servers, this situation is unfortunate. As a result of the lack of coordination and global view at the OS level and the increase in system complexity, many users have come to expect significant and increasing run-to-run variability and unexplained job failures. While this is an inherent problem of our current capabilities rather than an effect of heterogeneity, increasing heterogeneity will only exacerbate these problems as uncoordinated resource allocation decisions across nodes can lead to differing performance. Work in several areas related to global-view autonomous operating systems can help address these issues and lead to a more efficient and productive HPC computing environment.

Given the current state, we have identified three areas of focus in OS design that are critical for the efficiency of HPC in a heterogeneous environment. These areas includes lightweight node-OS architecture, an autonomous global-OS design, and resource allocation usability.

2.1   Lightweight Node OS

First, lightweight kernels are needed to enable predictable and repeatable resource allocation across nodes. A prime example is the ability to create an identical virtual-to-physical address mapping across nodes, which can help alleviate noise and variability due to memory management. This approach becomes more important as hierarchical byte-addressable memory subsystems take hold within the HPC node architectures, leading to nondeterministic caching and memory latency scenarios.

Today it is commonplace for a highly-tuned HPC application to be unable to take full advantage of the hardware concurrently on several leadership-class supercomputers. This situation is due to both the limitations of parallelism Amdahl's law, but also due to the additional heterogeneity found in emerging node architectures, and the ability for applications individually utilize each component. As node-level heterogeneity becomes evermore prevalent, this inefficiency will only increase. One important aspect of lightweight kernels that can help alleviate this hardware inefficiency is the ability to provide additional isolation between individual hardware resources, be it cores, memory, accelerators, network devices, or other I/O operations. This isolation would allow for nodes to be co-scheduled and jobs packed more efficiently by running dissimilar tasks, part of different workflow execution mechanisms, entirely in isolation. While this scenario of job packing has become commonplace in the cloud and industry, such mechanisms introduce significant interference that is unacceptable to the performance and predictability of our HPC applications. With efficient resource specialization provided by a lightweight OS, many of these challenges of performance isolation could be improved.

2.2   Global OS

Second, global system monitoring is needed to gather a real-time view of system operation, including system thermals, power usage, network utilization, and error events such as memory and network failures. On today's leadership-class HPC systems, when a job runs slowly it is often difficult to determine what went wrong and where inefficiencies are. Frustratingly, the information needed to explain the failure is often present deep within the system but only accessible to root-level system administrators. While significant gains can be made in system engineering to help address these symptoms, several open research questions remain in how to enable mult-resolution system monitoring to support both real-time analysis of system operation and detailed analysis and optimization of longer-time scale behavior.

Sandia has developed its Lightweight Distributed Metric Service (LDMS) [1] for high fidelity monitoring of large-scale HPC resources. In conjunction with this work, Sandia has performed extensive work in the area of global state and on-the-fly analysis of system and sub-system resource utilization, including use of windowed resource utilization information to trigger changes in application behavior to more closely match available resources given current contention for shared resources (e.g., storage and network) [7]. This work is extensible to the shared node resource use case where tasks could be mapped onto available compute node resources that are in a topologically advantageous position given current and/or anticipated communication needs. Monitored system state data, currently comprising greater than ten terabytes per day on some of the largest HPC systems, lends itself to Machine Learning (ML) and Artificial Intelligence (AI) techniques to identify the most significant data and their effects on performance. Sandia has promising results in using such techniques for runtime detection of network congestion [17] and identification of abnormal application behavior including root-cause analysis [33].

Recent work on using databases at the OS level is a promising approach for managing global state in a consistent way that can be queried and updated with powerful database query languages [19]. The content and fidelity of data being stored to such a database must be carefully tuned to provide the appropriate amount of detail for making both real-time and long-term decisions on performance and failures without introducing unnecessary analysis complexity or latency. We must also design new mechanisms and algorithms to both analyze data on a component and sub-system level and act on resultant decisions at a global level.

Once analysis and actionable decisions can be made efficiently on HPC systems, a fully scoped global operating system layer is needed to coordinate across a large and diverse infrastructure created by a heterogeneous HPC system. While several distributed OSs have been proposed, such systems are not in use today. This situation is largely due to the lack of an appropriate design that fits the problem without additional overhead. Instead, a middle ground in design is needed where a higher-level entity than a node is aware of the resource availability and allocation state across nodes, so that more intelligent and coordinated decisions can be made.

This global OS has several design characteristics that are important for autonomous resource management of large-scale heterogeneous systems. Traditional schedules take a strict approach to scope, either owning the total global system explicitly as with batch job schedulers like SLURM, PBSPro, or LSF, or they take an implicit yet localized and unmanaged resource management through the OS itself. Instead, a more comprehensive and structured scheduling system is needed, whereby loose resource management decisions can be made at a higher level, whereby it can be refined as it is passed down to group and eventually a node-level resource manager. In this mechanism, the global OS can make broad strokes for system allocation with predictable performance, and those decisions can be refined and implemented in greater details at the lowest levels. For instance, if a local lightweight kernel were able to interact with and interpret a global scheduling decision for a given application, then core pinning and memory management can be done efficiently by the OS-level best able to implement it autonomously.

While global-to-local resource management refinements can happen autonomously, a similar feedback mechanism must also be possible. For instance, if a localized node OS detects a fault with a device that is necessary for the efficient completion of a task (e.g., an accelerator), then that information needs to be quickly sent upstream to a group or global viewpoint. With such information at hand, the global OS can autonomously act to augment a job's capabilities by allocating resources elsewhere and de-provision the specific node with a fault. Furthermore, this de-provisioning could happen only towards jobs that are actually impacted by the fault itself. For instance, a global scheduling decision could be made to still allocate a CPU-bound analysis task that doesn't require a GPU on a node that has a GPU fault, effectively increasing overall system throughput.

2.3   Resource Management Usability

With the additional capabilities of autonomous hierarchical scheduling of heterogeneous resources comes the additional requirement of enabling capabilities for both users and applications. Today, this is often more than the number of cores, the expected runtime, and the amount of memory to be utilized. Instead, users need to include specific details, such as which accelerators to use, how to pin the cores, and how to organize the memory caching mechanisms for hierarchical memory subsystems. Furthermore, applications have to very carefully manage the use of system storage. This explicit mapping of resources culminates in long and heroic porting processes for HPC applications moving to new resources to manually manage scale and efficiency. Such application placement is currently static and unable to adapt to failures or slowdowns during runtime.

With a an autonomous global OS resource management policy, users may no longer be required to specify the full extent of their resource requirements.

Instead, users could provide a deadline, their full software ecosystem to be executed, and a list of hints to the autonomous resource management system. It then becomes the job of the system to efficiently and autonomously allocate and manage system resources to meet the specific requirements.

While this hands-off approach for users may be exceeding attractive to more adaptive AMT runtime models like Darma, Legion, Parallex HPX-5, or others [3,18,35], supporting traditional bulk synchronous parallel models, specifically MPI, should also be supported. This approach will avoid the need for additional porting effort of legacy applications while providing additional features to users and applications capable of using them.

Another key aspect of autonomous resource management usability is the ability to specify a runnable software environment as a single entity. While this functionality is available today to some extent in HPC with containers [36] and virtual machines [22], such usage is currently explicit and not well integrated into scheduling decisions. Mechanisms are still needed for the usage of containerized HPC to be transfered and managed implicitly within an autonomous system. Furthermore, additional capabilities and library standardization is required to make container usage ubiquitous to users. For instance, users should only need to reference the desired container image, and the global OS will handle performance considerations, device utilization, and efficient storage mechanisms at runtime.

3   Autonomous Allocation of Lightweight Threads

The hybrid programming needed to exploit available hardware parallelism on current node architectures typically combines message passing with either heavyweight threading (e.g., OpenMP over pthreads) on manycore CPUs or single-instruction multiple-thread execution (e.g., Nvidia CUDA) on GPUs. As compute units on each node increase and diversify, issues of load balancing and resource management become more important. It is precisely these issues that require a more flexible approach to threading, facilitated by programming models like the tasking model introduced in OpenMP 3 and extended to accelerator offload in later versions of OpenMP. This task-based approach focuses the application developer's effort on decomposition of their program into a set of functional tasks and identifying dependencies between the tasks. The threading runtime system takes on the burden of scheduling the tasks as lightweight threads to make optimal use of the available execution resources.

Coupling full-empty bit synchronization made the Tera MTA/Cray XMT architecture a particularly useful tool for applications with irregular data accesses such as graph processing. Such applications are now a key part of data-driven scientific computing, and the Sandia Qthreads runtime library [34] for lightweight threading implements full-empty bit synchronization in software to support workloads in that space. Qthreads also serves as the on-node tasking layer for Cray's implementation of its Chapel programming language [8], which aims to advance parallel programming productivity beyond the constraints of legacy programming languages like Fortran and C++. In contrast, Sandia's

Kokkos [10] and Darma [20] are performance portability libraries for C++ programmers targeting on-node parallelism and inter-nodes asynchronous multitask (AMT) parallelism, respectively. While originally Kokkos only offered data parallel execution patterns, these are now supplemented by the new task-DAG pattern. Data parallelism within the tasks is translated into efficient OpenMP loops and CUDA kernels. Darma maps user-defined tasks onto one of several AMT frameworks or virtual transports (VT).

The key challenge for threading runtime systems is to make optimal scheduling decisions in increasingly heterogeneous node environments. The scheduling decisions must determine when and where to execute tasks to maximize spatial and temporal locality among related tasks while also maintaining load balance. Promising approaches have included user annotations to convey information to the runtime and profiling based on performance counters. The ultimate solution likely comprises online learning techniques to adaptively adjust task scheduling for the particular combination of workload and available resources at execution time.

4   Autonomous Allocation of Network Resources

Current networks have a variety of hardware features that enable allocation, sharing and prioritization of resources on a node and at the network switch. One of the major capabilities is assigning service levels to traffic to prioritize some traffic types or even specific traffic streams over those of other jobs on the system [15]. For example, at a high level, it is possible to prioritize MPI traffic over a network versus I/O traffic or other application types. It is also possible to prioritize certain types of MPI traffic over other MPI traffic, like prioritizing collectives over large point to point transfers to guarantee good latency for collectives.

Autonomous allocation of network resources is a difficult problem as current generation communication APIs like MPI and PGAS implementations typically attempt to claim ownership of all node-side networking resources at initialization time from underlying network interfaces [2]. Negotiating between multiple communication libraries on a single node, or multiple jobs using the same communication library is difficult as it is not clear what resources will be needed and when. Delayed requests for network resources can cause significant delays for the operations that need additional resources on the fly. This situation leads to performance variation that is observable by users. A better solution would be to anticipate network resource needs and pre-allocate negotiated resources only when they are needed by an application. A first step in this direction is the prediction of resource needs that leads to application length allocations of these resources. Returning resources to a common pool is possible, but predicting when such resources should be released is an additional challenge that must be addressed.

Sandia is in a unique position to address these challenges as it currently has projects underway that can help address some of the fundamental reasons behind the current motivation to register resources in a greedy manner. One of these solutions is to approach the underlying network interfaces and operation in a more structured and receiver-side focused manner. By having receiver-side management of data placement and abstracting sender-side data placement interfaces, resources can be better managed without unnecessary resource subscription. For example, in current systems for a direct memory placement interface like Remote Direct Memory Access (RDMA), the sender-side must request that the receiver allocate pinned physical memory and send the physical address of that memory back to the sender before data can be sent. This approach requires allocating resources on the receiver-side with no guarantees as to when or even if those resources will be used by the sender. Allocating these resources as close as possible to when they will be used and allowing the receiver more flexibility in allocating and deallocating said resources is the key to efficiency. An autonomous solution to this allocation is possible both from a centralized arbiter for a system as well as a locally managed autonomous allocation scheme.

5   Autonomous Allocation of Storage Resources

Extreme scale capability platforms are enabling a second operating mode. Instead of a single, large-scale application run, a collection of cooperating components, each optimized to use specific hardware and programming approaches, will run in concert to accomplish the compute tasks. This data flow model requires specific capabilities to best enable this processing model. Workflows, in general, need the same kinds of infrastructure to offer the kinds of functionality both users and the science demand.

First, each of these components have particular processing cycles that are almost certainly not identical to their upstream and downstream components. To deal with this processing mismatch, data must be effectively staged between components. Existing data staging work done by Sandia and others has shown how, with dedicated resources, data staging operations can enable online processing rather than requiring using persistent storage for the staging location. Existing work as focused on the challenges of disk-based storage with the inherent seek and rotational latencies as well as low bandwidth per device when compared to the interconnect ingress. Modern storage systems are using solid state devices deployed such that the interconnect is the slowest part of the path from compute to storage. This shift allows rethinking how to best use these resources to address workflow requirements. While this is true, the solid state storage is also being deployed in smaller capacities right now leading to the inability to use this storage for data staging as much as desired. New approaches that take into account the current and future interconnect performance, various levels of the memory/storage hierarchy, and cost/capacity/concurrency must be considered.

Second, in addition to just determining how to use the various kinds of storage devices in various locations within the machine, effectively sharing these resources is crucial to effective platform usage. Currently, storage resources are largely unmanaged. Burst buffer resources are managed in some resource managers, but the allocation is not taking into account potential oversubscription and how to interleave simultaneous users. Leveraging Sandia's experience in storage systems and data staging (cite) gives us a strong position from which to investigate how to best address this problem. An additional wrinkle that may be a problem with this idea as well is that solid state storage, unlike disk, has a cost associated with erasing. With disk, erases happen while writing for no additional cost. For flash, an erase costs as much as a write and is required before overwriting a dirty block or page. While enterprise-class devices offer additional resources to try to manage this issue, cheaper consumer grade devices do not making it into a universal problem. Offering a way to use cheaper components on future platforms can reduce costs allowing limited budgets be spent on more important resources.

Third, data is not all created equal and is not all of the same value. For example, an extra checkpoint output is unnecessary and can be eliminated. Further, looking at a double precision floating point number, the last several digits of the exponent or mantisa contribute in only a tiny way, such as no more than $1/2^{10}$ of the actual value. While this tiny contribution may be important for final analysis, it is unimportant for a first pass data exploration phase. By splitting data such that only the most important half of a double precision floating point value is stored together, data density can be improved with a near trivial loss in precision that only affects the analysis while the lower precision pieces are the only part read. Instead, if we can address this kind of data priority or utility more effectively, we can better address how to most effectively use smaller, more expensive storage resources. Sandia's work on the ASCR SIRIUS SSIO project was a first step towards incorporating these features into storage management.

Finally, long term data management is also a consideration. We need to determine how to best annotate and track data as it is moved to the archive. While we currently manage files using a standard POSIX namespace, we do not have adequate tools and support to do simple queries, such as, "what files are related to project B61?" Additional, richer questions, such as "what simulation runs from CTH during 2012 experienced crumbling?" are completely impossible. This latter query is more interesting in that it is looking at the data features themselves to better select what data is desired for retrieval. Additional efforts to explore how to not only tag and manage data, but also to deal with queries for things related to data contents are woefully inadequate. Sandia's current EMPRESS system (cite) is a good first step towards addressing this long term data use problem. Additional efforts to build an appropriate system are desperately needed. Existing tools and efforts by others have all proven to have significant flaws making those solutions incapable of addressing the needs that Sandia and other labs have.

6   Autonomous Allocation of Power and Energy

Power consumption of future supercomputing systems is expected to be a major challenge. Contracts on power usage with utilities typically have bounds placed upon them that incur significant penalties when power consumption lies outside of an agreed upon power band. As such, the allocation of resources of a system must also take into account a power profile. Without an autonomous allocation of resources, maintaining contract compliant power bounds is both difficult and requires a significant amount of person effort in order to keep the system running well while also obeying power requirements.

Autonomous control of power consumption on a system wide basis is not yet a feature on large systems, but the required building blocks for such a system are close to completion. First, we have portable power control and monitoring APIs like Power API [14], a community initiative that Sandia initiated. Power-capping mechanisms exist on many current-generation supercomputers, but they are based on a node- or job-level solution that has no centralized allocation mechanism. Individual jobs may be power capped today, but the management of the system as a whole for power capping is not current practice and such allocation schemes have not been developed. Before autonomous control can be utilized, strategies for allocating power caps on systems must be further refined from the current state-of-the-art from the research community. As job-level mechanisms exist, this is an optimization problem similar to those approached by the real-time computing scheduling research community and such work can be leveraged for solutions in the power consumption allocation solution area.

A very challenging, but also potentially groundbreaking approach, is to predict future power usage on supercomputers. This approach has a potential to significantly reduce operating costs with power utilities if such predictions can be accurate and provide several hours worth of lead time. Prediction is a follow-on activity from autonomous allocation as the autonomous system can make decisions at a known speed and can schedule jobs on the system in a consistent manner versus having system administrators trying to manage overall power usage. This situation means that the autonomous system is already making some predictions about individual job usage and therefore it should be possible to extend this mechanism to the system as a whole. There is a prime opportunity for machine learning to be utilized in observing and predicting power usage based on a history of many jobs worth of power measurements. In addition, an autonomous system should also be capable of adjusting job-level power caps to ensure the highest level of science output from the system within the required power bounds.

7   Autonomous Management of Resilience

Studies have shown that hardware faults are commonplace on current HPC systems [4,9,11,16,23–25,27–32]. As HPC systems approach exascale, increases in component count and complexity are projected to lead to significantly more frequent failures. As a result, efficient resilience mechanisms will continue to be an important on next-generation systems.

In addition to increases in size and complexity, current projections also suggest that future systems will be more heterogeneous than current systems. Advances in GPUs, memory devices (e.g., high-bandwidth memory, NVDIMMs), and storage (e.g., solid-state drives) mean that the challenge of efficiently configuring resilience mechanisms will be significantly more challenging. The development of autonomous services that manage resilience mechanisms has the potential to significantly reduce the burden on application developers and to improve system utilization by reducing time redoing work lost to failures.

Historically, resilience on extreme-scale HPC systems has been addressed with two mechanisms: Error Correcting Codes (ECC) and coordinated Checkpoint/Restart (CR). ECCs detect and correct errors in memory by adding parity symbols to data stored in memory. Each time the contents of a memory location is read, the ECC is used to determine whether corruption has occurred. CR reduces the amount of work that an application loses when a failure occurs. The basic idea behind CR is for the system to periodically (with or without application involvement) save its current state to persistent storage. When a failure occurs, application processes roll back to the last valid checkpoint and resume their computation from that point. Although coordinated CR offers very strong guarantees of failure recovery, writing checkpoints and restarting after a failure are expensive operations.

7.1   Failure Prediction

Correctly configuring the interval between checkpoints is a significant challenge for HPC users. They may not always have access to the necessary data or knowledge to be able to properly determine how frequently to checkpoint their application. Moreover, determining the optimal checkpoint interval depends on the probability of an error occurring in the future, which may be difficult to determine. Failure probabilities can only be established retrospectively; there is no way to definitively establish the probability density function for errors on a running system. As a result, users frequently rely on their intuition to establish a "reasonable" interval.

Autonomous management of checkpoint/restart has the potential to reduce the burden on users and to improve overall system utilization. For example, to mitigate the impact of potentially imprecise checkpoint intervals an autonomous system can leverage existing research on failure prediction, see e.g., [5,12], to proactively take checkpoints or migrate processes to a spare node when failures are imminent.

Sandia has performed extensive work in the areas of HPC log analysis in conjunction with system wide, high fidelity, component and sub-system state monitoring [6]. Analysis of system and scheduler logs in conjunction with global system monitoring data can enable early detection of problems and more accurate characterization of probability distributions of future errors. By leveraging detailed failure data, an autonomous system can potentially adjust the configuration of resilience mechanisms to improve system utilization.

7.2   Scheduling Resilience Activities

Obtaining efficient system utilization for failure mitigation methods requires mechanisms that are well-tuned to the target application's programming model, failure rates and global synchronization characterization. For example, combining uncoordinated checkpointing with bulk-synchronous parallel (BSP) applications can significantly increase the application's time-to-solution [13]. Autonomous management of resilience activities (e.g., taking a checkpoint) has the potential to increase system utilization by scheduling resilience activities to minimize the application performance impact based on ever-changing system and application input state.

7.3   Heterogeneous Architectures

Different hardware components exhibit different resilience characteristics, which may change over time, and may require different strategies for mitigating these errors. For example, CPUs have a long history of integrating powerful error detection and correction features while GPUs have traditionally provided significantly less protection. As HPC systems become more heterogeneous, the task of managing resilience becomes increasingly challenging for users. An autonomous systems that is tightly integrated with the OS/runtime can reduce the burden on users and make informed resilience decisions based on the current mix of system resources that are currently being used and age/wear of the current system.

7.4   Programming Models

Traditionally, HPC systems have been used to run BSP applications. However, new programming models, e.g., AMTs, are growing in importance. The resilience implications of these programming models can be very different. Managing the differences between these programming models autonomously would remove this burden on users and allow them to focus on their scientific simulation rather than requiring the considerable expertise needed to ensure application progress in the current failure state of the system.

8   Conclusion

This paper has described software stack components and capabilities currently being explored at Sandia that could be integrated nto a larger set of components to enable autonomous resource management and optimization for HPC applications and systems. Given the current complexity of HPC systems and the expectation that components, systems, and applications will only continue to become more complex and difficult to use, the ability to provide a software stack that automatically and continually maps the system to the application will be required. However, achieving this goal will require significant exploration of novel capabilities and approaches, which in turn must be supported by a sustained program investment involving expertise from across the entire HPC community.

References

1. Agelastos, A., et al.: The lightweight distributed metric service: A scalable infrastructure for continuous monitoring of large scale computing systems and applications. In: SC 2014 Proceedings of the International Conference for High Performance Computing, Networking, Storage and Analysis, pp. 154–165 (2014)
2. Barrett, B.W., et al.: The Portals 4.2 networking programming interface. Technical Report, Technical report SAND2018-12790, Sandia National Laboratories (SNL-NM) (2018)
3. Bauer, M., Treichler, S., Slaughter, E., Aiken, A.: Legion: Expressing locality and independence with logical regions. In: SC 2012 Proceedings of the International Conference on High Performance Computing, Networking, Storage and Analysis, pp. 1–11. IEEE (2012)
4. Bautista-Gomez, L., Zyulkyarov, F., Unsal, O., McIntosh-Smith, S.: Unprotected computing: A large-scale study of DRAM raw error rate on a supercomputer. In: Proceedings of the International Conference for High Performance Computing, Networking, Storage and Analysis. SC 2016, pp. 55:1–55:11 (2016)
5. Bouguerra, M.S., Gainaru, A., Gomez, L.B., Cappello, F., Matsuoka, S., Maruyam, N.: Improving the computing efficiency of HPC systems using a combination of proactive and preventive checkpointing. In: 2013 IEEE 27th International Symposium on Parallel and Distributed Processing, pp. 501–512. IEEE (2013)
6. Brandt, J., et al.: Quantifying effectiveness of failure prediction and response in HPC systems: Methodology and example. In: 2010 International Conference on Dependable Systems and Networks Workshops (DSN-W), pp. 2–7 (2010)
7. Brandt, J., Devine, K., Gentile, A., Pedretti, K.: Demonstrating improved application performance using dynamic monitoring and task mapping. In: 2014 IEEE International Conference on Cluster Computing (CLUSTER), pp. 408–415 (2014)
8. Chamberlain, B., Callahan, D., Zima, H.: Parallel programmability and the Chapel language. Int. J. High Perform. Comput. Appli. **21**(3), 291–312 (2007). https://doi.org/10.1177/1094342007078442
9. Di Martino, C., Kalbarczyk, Z., Iyer, R.K., Baccanico, F., Fullop, J., Kramer, W.: Lessons learned from the analysis of system failures at petascale: The case of Blue Waters. In: International Conference on Dependable Systems and Networks (2014)
10. Edwards, H.C., Trott, C.R., Sunderland, D.: Kokkos: Enabling manycore performance portability through polymorphic memory access patterns. J. Parallel Distrib. Comput., **74**(12), 3202–3216 (2014). http://www.sciencedirect.com/science/article/pii/S0743731514001257
11. El-Sayed, N., Stefanovici, I.A., Amvrosiadis, G., Hwang, A.A., Schroeder, B.: Temperature management in data centers: Why some (might) like it hot. In: Proceedings of the 12th ACM SIGMETRICS/PERFORMANCE Joint International Conference on Measurement and Modeling of Computer Systems. SIGMETRICS 2012, pp. 163–174. ACM (2012). https://doi.org/10.1145/2254756.2254778
12. Engelmann, C., Vallee, G.R., Naughton, T., Scott, S.L.: Proactive fault tolerance using preemptive migration. In: 2009 17th Euromicro International Conference on Parallel, Distributed and Network-based Processing, pp. 252–257. IEEE (2009)
13. Ferreira, K.B., Widener, P., Levy, S., Arnold, D., Hoefler, T.: Understanding the effects of communication and coordination on checkpointing at scale. In: Proceedings of the International Conference for High Performance Computing, Networking, Storage and Analysis. SC 2014, pp. 883–894 (2014)

14. Grant, R.E., Levenhagen, M., Olivier, S.L., DeBonis, D., Pedretti, K.T., Laros III, J.H.: Standardizing power monitoring and control at exascale. Computer **49**(10), 38–46 (2016)
15. Grant, R.E., Rashti, M.J., Afsahi, A.: An analysis of QOS provisioning for sockets direct protocol vs. IPOIB over modern InfiniBand networks. In: 2008 International Conference on Parallel Processing-Workshops, pp. 79–86. IEEE (2008)
16. Hwang, A.A., Stefanovici, I.A., Schroeder, B.: Cosmic rays don't strike twice: Understanding the nature of DRAM errors and the implications for system design. ACM SIGPLAN Notices **47**(4), 111–122 (2012)
17. Jha, S., et al.: Measuring congestion in high-performance datacenter interconnects. In: 17th USENIX Symposium on Networked Systems Design and Implementation (NSDI 20), Santa Clara, CA, pp. 37–57. USENIX Association, Feburary 2020
18. Kaiser, H., Brodowicz, M., Sterling, T.: ParalleX: An advanced parallel execution model for scaling-impaired applications. In: 2009 International Conference on Parallel Processing Workshops, pp. 394–401. IEEE (2009)
19. Kepner, J., et al.: TabulaROSA: Tabular operating system architecture for massively parallel heterogeneous compute engines. CoRR abs/1807.05308 (2018). http://arxiv.org/abs/1807.05308
20. Sandia National Laboratories: Darma (2019). https://darma.sandia.gov
21. Lalanda, P., McCann, J.A., Diaconescu, A.: Autonomic Computing. Springer-Verlag, London (2013)
22. Lange, J., et al.: Palacios and Kitten: New high performance operating systems for scalable virtualized and native supercomputing. In: 2010 IEEE International Symposium on Parallel and Distributed Processing (IPDPS), pp. 1–12. IEEE (2010)
23. Levy, S., Ferreira, K.B., DeBardeleben, N., Siddiqua, T., Sridharan, V., Baseman, E.: Lessons learned from memory errors observed over the lifetime of Cielo. In: SC'2018 International Conference for High Performance Computing, Networking, Storage and Analysis, November 2018
24. Li, X., Huang, M.C., Shen, K., Chu, L.: A realistic evaluation of memory hardware errors and software system susceptibility. In: Proceedings USENIX Annual Technical Conference (ATC 2010), pp. 75–88 (2010)
25. Li, X., Shen, K., Huang, M.C., Chu, L.: A memory soft error measurement on production systems. In: 2007 USENIX Annual Technical Conference on Proceedings of the USENIX Annual Technical Conference. ATC 2007, pp. 21:1–21:6 (2007). http://dl.acm.org/citation.cfm?id=1364385.1364406
26. Parashar, M., Hariri, S. (eds.): Autonomic Computing: Concepts, Infrastructure, and Applications. Taylor & Francis, Inc., New York (2007)
27. Schroeder, B., Gibson, G.A.: A large-scale study of failures in high-performance computing systems. In: Dependable Systems and Networks (DSN 2006), June 2006
28. Schroeder, B., Pinheiro, E., Weber, W.D.: DRAM errors in the wild: A large-scale field study. Commun. ACM, **54**(2), 100–107 (2011)
29. Siddiqua, T., Papathanasiou, A., Biswas, A., Gurumurthi, S.: Analysis of memory errors from large-scale field data collection. In: 2013 IEEE Workshop on Silicon Errors in Logic-System Effects (SELSE) (2013)
30. Sridharan, V., et al.: Memory errors in modern systems: The good, the bad, and the ugly. In: Proceedings of the Twentieth International Conference on Architectural Support for Programming Languages and Operating Systems. ASPLOS 2015, pp. 297–310 (2015)
31. Sridharan, V., Liberty, D.: A study of DRAM failures in the field. In: Proceedings of the International Conference on High Performance Computing, Networking, Storage and Analysis. SC 2012, pp. 76:1–76:11 (2012)

32. Sridharan, V., Stearley, J., DeBardeleben, N., Blanchard, S., Gurumurthi, S.: Feng shui of supercomputer memory: Positional effects in DRAM and SRAM faults. In: Proceedings of SC13 International Conference for High Performance Computing, Networking, Storage and Analysis. SC 2013, pp. 22:1–22:11. ACM (2013)

33. Tuncer, O., et al.: Diagnosing performance variations in HPC applications using machine learning. In: Kunkel, J.M., Yokota, R., Balaji, P., Keyes, D. (eds.) ISC 2017. LNCS, vol. 10266, pp. 355–373. Springer, Cham (2017). https://doi.org/10.1007/978-3-319-58667-0_19

34. Wheeler, K.B., Murphy, R.C., Thain, D.: Qthreads: An API for programming with millions of lightweight threads. In: 2008 IEEE International Symposium on Parallel and Distributed Processing Workshops, pp. 1–8, April 2008

35. Wilke, J.J., et al.: The DARMA approach to asynchronous many-task programming. Technical Report, Sandia National Lab. (SNL-CA), Livermore, CA (United States) (2016)

36. Younge, A.J., Pedretti, K., Grant, R.E., Brightwell, R.: A tale of two systems: Using containers to deploy HPC applications on supercomputers and clouds. In: 2017 IEEE International Conference on Cloud Computing Technology and Science (CloudCom), pp. 74–81. IEEE (2017)

Scientific Data Challenges

Smoky Mountain Data Challenge 2020: An Open Call to Solve Data Problems in the Areas of Neutron Science, Material Science, Urban Modeling and Dynamics, Geophysics, and Biomedical Informatics

Suzanne Parete-Koon[1]([✉]), Peter F. Peterson[1], Garrett E. Granroth[1],
Wenduo Zhou[1], Pravallika Devineni[1], Nouamane Laanait[1], Junqi Yin[1],
Albina Borisevich[1], Ketan Maheshwari[1], Melissa Allen-Dumas[1],
Srinath Ravulaparthy[1], Kuldeep Kurte[1], Jibo Sanyal[1], Anne Berres[1],
Olivera Kotevska[1], Folami Alamudun[1], Keith Gray[2], Max Grossman[2],
Anar Yusifov[2], Ioana Danciu[1], Gil Alterovitz[3], and Dasha Herrmannova[1]

[1] Oak Ridge National Laboratory, Oak Ridge, TN 37831, USA
paretekoonst@ornl.gov
[2] BP plc, London, UK
[3] US Department of Veterans Affairs, Presidential Innovation Fellows Program,
Washington D.C., USA
https://smc-datachallenge.ornl.gov/

Abstract. The 2020 Smoky Mountains Computational Sciences and Engineering Conference enlists research scientists from across Oak Ridge National Laboratory (ORNL) to be data sponsors and help create data analytics challenges for eminent data sets at the laboratory. This work describes the significance of each of the seven data sets and their associated challenge questions. The challenge questions for each data set were required to cover multiple difficulty levels. An international call for participation was sent to students, and researchers asking them to form teams of up to four people to apply novel data analytics techniques to these data sets.

Keywords: Data analytics · Artificial intelligence · Machine learning

---

S. Parete-Koon et al.—Contributed Equally.
This manuscript has been co-authored by UT-Battelle, LLC, under contract DE-AC05-00OR22725 with the US Department of Energy (DOE). The US government retains and the publisher, by accepting the article for publication, acknowledges that the US government retains a nonexclusive, paid-up, irrevocable, worldwide license to publish or reproduce the published form of this manuscript, or allow others to do so, for US government purposes. DOE will provide public access to these results of federally sponsored research in accordance with the DOE Public Access Plan (http://energy.gov/downloads/doe-public-access-plan).

J. Nichols et al. (Eds.): SMC 2020, CCIS 1315, pp. 425–442, 2020.
https://doi.org/10.1007/978-3-030-63393-6_28

1   Introduction

All the data analytics challenges we host represent real world problems in different areas of research. The 2020 challenge solutions could impact unsolved questions in materials science, research on energy conservation in cities, geological studies based on seismic data, research toward matching critically ill medical patients and their physicians with the most helpful clinical trials of novel therapeutics and research toward halting the spread of COVID19.

By requiring the challenge questions for each data set to cover multiple difficulty levels and by allowing students and experts to compcte in separate categories we hope to draw in a diverse set of researchers and perspectives to help solve these questions.

The call for participation was broadly advertised and open to all interested parties. It appeared in scientific and engineering newsletters such as HPC Wire, and was spread by social media. Invitations to participate were also sent to several university computer science department professors and users of Oak Ridge Leadership Computing facility.

In addition to providing and serving the datasets for the challenges, organizers and data sponsors held an interactive webinar to explain the relevance of each challenge task and describe the size and composition of its associated dataset. Subsequently, three online Reddit.com forums were held in the two months before solutions were due, so participants could post questions about the tasks and get answers from each other and the data sponsors. Lastly, to accommodate the student challenge competitors who may not have ever written a scientific paper, the challenge organizers held a best practices in scientific paper writing webinar the week before the solution papers were due.

In this work, each of the challenges has its own section wherein the authors of the challenge describe the motivation and science behind the challenge, the data and its origins, and the reasoning behind the individual challenge questions.

2   Challenge 1: Understanding Rapid Cycling Temperature Logs from the Vulcan Diffractometer

Neutron scattering allows scientists to count scattered neutrons, measure their energies and the angles at which they scatter, and map their final positions. This information can reveal the molecular and magnetic structure and behavior of materials, such as high temperature superconductors, polymers, metals, and biological samples. The Spallation Neutron Source (SNS) facility at the Oak Ridge National Laboratory provides the most intense pulsed neutron beams in the world for scientific research and industrial development.

2.1   Background

The VULCAN diffractometer [1] is designed to understand the fundamental aspects of material behaviors during synthesis, processing, and service. One of the experiments conducted at SNS is designed to generate high intensity neutron pulses for the study of materials, where, over the course of the measurement, the temperature is varied as a function of time [2]. The overall purpose of the neutron measurement is to understand the changes in structure of the material as a function of temperature.

The experiment is conducted as follows: the sample is rapidly heated, then the heat source is turned off allowing the sample to relax and reach an equilibrium. Then the sample is rapidly heated again and the experiment is repeated several times. The goal is to associate neutron events occurring within a certain temperature bin. An event is defined as follows: the event starts when the sample is subjected to rapid heating and it ends right before the next rapid heating occurs. This is called a heat cycle.

2.2 Dataset

The VULCAN Beamline dataset [4] provides the sample measurement, where temperatures are recorded in two physically different places on the sample. These are held in two different hdf5 groups in the data file. Figure 1 depicts Temperature (in Celsius) vs. time (in seconds), a sample measurement on the VULCAN [3] beamline. The total size of the data is 1.06 MB and a and a laptop, workstation or small cluster should be suitable for developing solutions to this challenge.

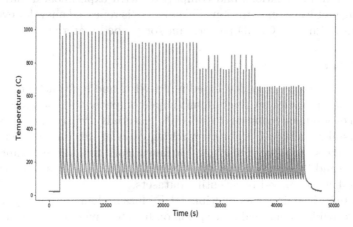

Fig. 1. Temperature vs. time on the VULCAN Beamline

2.3 Challenges of Interest

These questions seek insight into the behavior of the sample as the temperature is varied.

1. The goal is to identify heat cycles pertaining to equivalent temperatures during the same heating or cooling phase. For example, two data points at 800C are in the same group only if both of them are in either the heating or cooling cycle. To that end, you need to identify the beginning and end times of the heat cycle and temperature group it needs to belong to. (The latter part could be thought of as a clustering problem.)

2. How many events are there in each group and how similar are the identified events? A sample input to the question could be attributes of the heat cycle like height, step size etc.
3. Once the heat cycles are identified, how do they vary from one event to the next? A visualization would be great help showcase this variation.

   Note: The dataset consists of two sample measurements that are highly correlated with each other. We suggest the second measurement be used as a validation set.

3   Challenge 2: Towards a Universal Classifier for Crystallographic Space Groups

3.1   Background

State of the art electron microscopes produce focused electron beams with atomic dimensions and allow to capture diffraction patterns arising from the interaction of incident electrons with nanoscale material volumes. Backing out the local atomic structure of said materials requires compute- and time-intensive analyzes of these diffraction patterns (known as convergent beam electron diffraction, CBED). Traditional analyses of CBED requires iterative numerical solutions of partial differential equations and comparison with experimental data to refine the starting material configuration. This process is repeated anew for every newly acquired experimental CBED pattern and/or probed material.

3.2   Dataset

In this data, we used newly developed multi-GPU and multi-node electron scattering simulation codes on the Summit supercomputer to generate CBED patterns from over 60,000 materials (solid-state materials), representing nearly every known crystal structure [5]. The overarching goals of this data challenge are to: (1) explore the suitability of machine learning algorithms in the advanced analysis of CBED and (2) produce a machine learning algorithm capable of overcoming intrinsic difficulties posed by scientific datasets.

The dataset is split across multiple HDF5 files and an accompanying Jupyter Notebook provides a detailed description on how to navigate the file structure to access the data samples and the associated materials properties. Briefly, a data sample from this data set is given by a 3D array formed by stacking three CBED patterns simulated from the same material at three distinct material projections (i.e., crystallographic orientations). Each CBED pattern is a 2D array (512×512 pixels) with float 32-bit image intensities. The dataset is 589 GB and a workstation or small cluster should be suitable for developing solutions to this challenge.

Associated with each data sample in the data set is a host of material attributes or properties which are, in principle, retrievable via analysis of this CBED stack. These properties consist of the crystal space group the material belongs to, atomic lattice constants and angles, chemical composition, to name but a few. Of note is the crystal space group attributed (or label). All possible spatial arrangements of atoms in any solid (crystal) material obey symmetry conditions described by 230 unique mathematical discrete space groups.

3.3   Challenges of Interest

The data challenge tasks revolve around developing and implementing a machine learning (ML) algorithm to predict a material's space group, essentially a classification task. The data set is, however, heavily imbalanced (i.e., number of data samples per class). This imbalance is not an artifact, instead it reflects the reality that most known materials have low symmetry and as such are not uniformly distributed across the 230 space group classes.

The challenges are:

1. Perform exploratory data analysis on both CBED patterns and materials properties to summarize data characteristics.
2. Develop an ML algorithm for space group classification of CBED data.
3. Implement proper ML techniques to overcome data/label imbalance and show how it affects the performance of the ML algorithm in (1).
4. Implement an ML algorithm for multi-task prediction of a space group in addition to other material structural properties and show how it affects the performance of the ML algorithm.

Notes on Challenge Tasks

1. Preliminary task (1) is meant to provide better understanding about both input data (e.g. principle components of input images) and targets (e.g. distribution of space groups).
2. A participant may choose to solve challenges (1), (2) and (3), or (1), (2) and (4). Solving all 4 questions is optional.
3. Regarding approaches to (2), our preference is for ML techniques (e.g. loss-weighting, model ensembles, active learning, decision boundary analysis with GANs, etc.,), in lieu of brute-force data augmentation approaches (e.g. mixup, random erasing, etc.).
4. If a deep learning model is used by the participant, our preference is for the implementation use one of the following three frameworks: MXNet, Pytorch or TensorFlow.
5. Our preference is for the ML algorithms be implemented in one of the following languages: Python, C, C++, and/or Julia.

4   Challenge 3: Impacts of Urban Weather on Building Energy Use

4.1   Background

Recent advances in multi-scale coupling of high-performance computing models provide unique insights into how interdependent processes affect one another. Some of these processes are uniquely observable in urban environments. This data challenge addresses questions at the intersection of the natural environment and urban infrastructure by encouraging participants to examine variations in weather and building energy use, seasonal influences, and the building types most sensitive to weather at daily, monthly, and yearly scales. The dataset for this challenge was generated under a Laboratory Directed Research and Development project aimed at examining the impact of an area's built environment on weather and energy use. Data includes a year of simulated weather data taken at 15-minute intervals in a section of downtown Chicago; the latitude/longitude location for each building in the study area, each building's 2D footprint and height, and a year of building-by-building energy use simulation (EnergyPlus) data run by Joshua New, Mahabir Bhandari, Som Shrestha (ORNL, Energy and Environmental Sciences Directorate), and Mark Adams (ORNL, National Security Sciences Directorate).

4.2   Dataset

The dataset [6] comprises three elements:

1. High resolution, 90m simulated weather data for 1 year at 15-min intervals (with known gaps toward the end of each month). These files are provided in a comma separated value (CSV) format.
2. A mapping of individual buildings with individual IDs, their latitude/longitude location, and height (provided in Excel file).
3. Energy simulation output of these individual buildings, at 15-min intervals for one year (provided in java script object notation (JSON) and other files).

The total data set is 6.35 GB and a laptop, workstation or small cluster should be suitable for developing solutions to this challenge.

4.3   Challenges of Interest

The questions that are of interest for this challenge are:

1. Are there interesting variations in weather and building energy use data for the geographic area?
2. Which buildings in the study are most sensitive to weather (e.g., temperature, humidity, wind, radiation) effects?
3. Are there any interesting visualizations that illustrate the changing dynamics of the simulated urban environment?
4. How can the data best be divided into subsets for meaningful analysis and visualization?
5. How does energy use in each building change through the year?
6. How is energy use different during the coldest and hottest months (e.g., January and July) of the year as compared to during those of less extreme temperature?

Participants are welcome to bring in additional datasets to combine with the provided data to create meaningful insights.

We look forward to presentations using novel methods for interpreting and visualizing this data that draw on machine learning and other big data techniques. We welcome new collaborations to complement the work of understanding climate, infrastructure, and energy use in urban areas from a systems perspective. We hope the participants enjoy the interdisciplinary nature of the dataset and its challenges.

5   Challenge 4: Computational Urban Data Analytics

5.1   Background

Urban environments are complex systems in which social factors, mobility, building energy, and urban climate interact with each other. Large parts of urban energy use are driven by the movement of population through the city. Each day, humans consume energy, whether they are traveling, at home, or in their workplace. Transportation and building energy are two of the top consumers of energy use in the United States. Transportation accounts for 29% of energy use, whereas buildings account for 38–40% of energy use (combined residential and commercial) [25, 26].

There are many factors that influence energy use in any particular building, but one of the major contributing factors is the number of occupants. In this challenge, we provide data that can help model the population's behavior and decision making, and obtain a more accurate representation of energy use in buildings, which nicely builds upon our previously published work [7], where we developed a data-driven transportation model, which determines building occupancy throughout the day in order to create more accurate simulations for building energy.

5.2   Dataset

Due to the tightly coupled nature of urban systems, we provide a wide variety of data for this challenge. All data is from 2017 (or based on 2017 inputs in case of simulations) unless noted otherwise. We hope that with this breadth of available data, every challenge participant will find an area they are particularly passionate about, however it is not a requirement to use all provided data. The size of the dataset is about 2 GB unzipped and a laptop, workstation or small cluster should be suitable for developing solutions to this challenge.

Vehicle Data. Vehicle data provides information on the population's daily trips as well as vehicle types from survey data. It is a simulation snapshot of a transportation simulation that was based on surveyed data.

1. Simulation snapshot for morning commute from TRansportation ANalysis SIMulation System (TRANSIMS): This snapshot contains vehicle traces (in Universal Transverse Mercator Coordinates) at 30-s intervals for one simulated day. At each time step, we also have the link (road segment) ID, driver ID, and vehicle speed.

2. Schedule for morning commute from National Household Travel Survey (NHTS): This is an extract of the official NHTS data [8] which only contains survey responses from Chicago.
3. Vehicle type distribution: Simplified Federal Highway Association (FHWA) classifications of vehicles in Chicago, which was derived from NHTS data.

Emissions Data. To study emissions, we are providing traffic volumes and emissions that were generated using an emissions simulation, by using the traffic simulation outputs. In addition, we provide weather data to enable the study of relations between weather and emissions.

1. Road-level traffic volumes (aggregated from TRANSIMS outputs).
2. Road-level emissions generated using MOVES, an emissions simulator. This simulation is based on traffic volumes and weather patterns throughout a year.
3. Weather data from DarkSky. For this data, we provide instructions on downloading it, as it is free to use but the license agreement does not allow redistribution.

Road Network. A transportation-focused dataset would not be complete without the road geometry. We provide the road network that was used for the simulations, along with some metadata.

1. The road network has the link IDs for each road segment, as well as road type etc.
2. GeoJSON file of the road network used for the TRANSIMS and MOVES runs.
3. Definition of different link types.

Building Data. We provide building footprints and socioeconomic data to provide a better idea of population distribution and demographics, and the type and distribution of buildings throughout the area.

1. Building footprints from Microsoft (2019): All US building footprints [9] and the clipped version for Chicago [10].
2. Land Use data from Chicago Metropolitan Agency for Planning (CMAP): GeoJSON file containing polygon data with land use attributes and a Codebook defining the land use codes
   (a) Socioeconomic data is provided for different *community areas* (neighborhoods, such as "Chicago Heights") [12]:
       i. Population from CMAP/Census (2010).
       ii. Census data summarized to community areas [11].
       iii. Spreadsheet (CSV) of census data by community area.
       iv. GeoJSON of community area polygons.

(b) Community Area Snapshots contain additional information such as employment, travel mode choice, housing types, job types in community (held by residents, available in community), walkabilty, etc. [12].
    i. Spreadsheet (CSV) of Community Area Snapshot data.
    ii. Data dictionary explaining the different fields.

Each of the folders in the provided dataset has a README file with more detailed information on file format and contents.

5.3 Challenges of Interest

One of the main challenges in coupled or integrated systems is the disparity of data sources. For this data challenge, we would like participants to address one of the three following tasks:

- Develop an algorithm to efficiently assign vehicle occupants to nearby buildings.
  1. In [7], we have performed an initial weighted quad tree-based approach to map vehicles to buildings.
  2. The ideal algorithm should be efficient and accurate. Consider the trade-off.
  3. The resulting mapping should be realistic. Consider building size, use type (the vehicle traces are only for commute) etc.
- Perform an area-wide correlation analysis of vehicle emissions.
  1. Determine spatial variation, and variation based on other factors, such as land use of surrounding areas, population, network classification (road type), weather, etc.
  2. Correlate the provided emissions data with other provided datasets.
- Characterize traffic patterns from the simulation.
  1. What are the traffic hot spots? Is there any congestion?
  2. What are the travel times? How do they vary through out the day?
  3. What are busy times? How well do they match the commute pattern from NHTS?
  4. How do speeds vary spatially and temporally?
  5. What are the most popular roads?
  6. Can you draw conclusions about the simulation setup from the output?

We hope that the wide range of questions will provide an interesting challenge for every participant. If participants have their own unique ideas based on using the data we provided, this will also be of interest.

6 Challenge 5: Using Machine Learning to Understand Uncertainty in Subsurface Exploration

In the energy industry, an understanding of subsurface characteristics and structure is crucial to identifying and localizing untapped resources. At a high level, the process of taking an entirely unexplored region of earth and generating an actionable understanding of its structure includes:

1. Seismic data collection: Collect raw signals from the subsurface using techniques similar to sonograms used in hospitals.
2. Seismic data pre-processing: Quality check and clean the collected raw signals.
3. Seismic migration and velocity model construction: Use the raw signals and our understanding of the likely geology of the region to construct a 3D representation of the subsurface.
4. Seismic interpretation: Using the constructed 3D representation, interpret where faults, layers, and other important structural features are in the subsurface.

With each of these steps comes an amount of uncertainty from various sources of potential error: instrument error, human error, modeling error, and more. Despite this, the output of most seismic processing workflows is a single, gold standard, output image. An image which we know cannot possibly be 100% accurate!

It is crucial that future seismic processing workflows start to incorporate uncertainty when estimating the true subsurface structures. Rather than outputting a single interpretation, we should aim to emit a spectrum of possible realizations and an understanding of where uncertainty is high or low.

6.1 Background

Seismic Data Collection. Seismic data collection (i.e., the process of conducting a seismic survey) involves transmitting powerful sound waves into the ground and then recording their echoes at the surface as they bounce off boundaries between layers in the Earth. This process parallels techniques used in x- ray and ultrasound imaging in the medical field to reconstruct structures inside the human body. The figure below depicts a typical offshore seismic survey setup, in which sound waves are transmitted from an air gun behind a survey ship and the return echoes are recorded by a line of hydrophones being towed behind the ship.

During a seismic survey, one or more sources of sound energy are used to transmit waves into the ground. One or more receivers are used to record the reflection of that sound energy at the surface. The raw output generated from a seismic survey is a set of recorded waveforms at each receiver for each source. This recording stores the amplitude of the reflected sound wave at the surface as a function of the time it took to travel to the receiver.

Seismic Data Preprocessing. Pre-processing of our raw seismic data can include a multitude of steps. Broadly, seismic preprocessing aims to clean up and strengthen signals in the seismic data while reducing noise, facilitating later stages of the seismic processing pipeline.

Seismic Migration and Velocity Model Construction. Seismic migration refers to the process by which the seismic waves received at receivers are back-propagated to the source through a simulated version of the seismic medium.

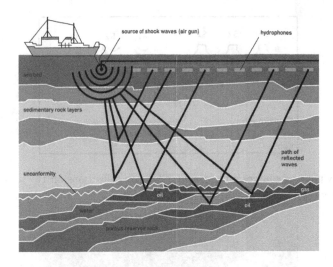

Fig. 2. Seismic Survey [13]

Through knowledge of (1) the source location, (2) the receiver location, (3) the time/amplitude of the received signal, and (4) the medium through which the signal traveled, we can simulate in reverse the propagation of the signal through the subsurface, identify its reflection point, and thereby identify the location of a potential object/reflector of interest in the subsurface.

Note how crucial an accurate estimate of the subsurface velocity of sound waves is in this process. Without an accurate velocity estimate, it is impossible to accurately predict the distance traveled by sound waves in the subsurface in a certain period of time.

While building a velocity model is a critical component for accurate seismic reconstruction, a number of uncertainties are involved in the process. Simply asking two different geophysicists to perform velocity model construction on the same seismic traces can produce drastically different velocity models. Quantifying and visualizing this uncertainty in velocity models will be the prime focus of this data challenge.

One common practice for checking the validity of a given velocity model is through offset pair gathers. Modern seismic surveys generally involve many sources and many receivers. As a result, many pairs of sources and receivers capture reflections off the same reflector in the subsurface (see Fig. 3). This redundancy can be helpful in validating the quality of a velocity model, as an accurate velocity model is expected to produce similar/identical depth estimates for a given reflector no matter which offset pair a reflection is received from.

Gathers generally refer to collecting the depth estimate for a given reflector across many offset pairs and plotting them visually, with depth on the y axis and offset pairs along the x axis. In a gather of an accurate velocity model, geophysicists expect to mostly see horizontal lines, indicating that the depth

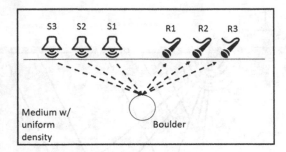

Fig. 3. Many pairs of sources and receivers capture reflections off the same reflector in the subsurface.

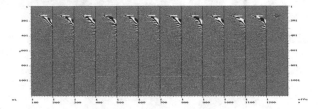

Fig. 4. Reasonably good gathers show mostly horizontal lines, indicating that the depth estimate for a layer is the same across all offset pairs.

estimate for a layer is the same across all offset pairs. See Fig. 4 for several examples of reasonable gathers, indicated by the prevalence of horizontal lines.

Seismic Interpretation. Once a final seismic image is rendered following seismic migration, seismic interpretation—the process of identifying faults, reservoirs, and other features of interest in the imag—begins. This manual labeling is then used in field development and reservoir characterization. See Fig. 5 for an example seismic image with faults manually labeled and emphasized.

Fig. 5. A seismic image with faults manually labeled and emphasized [14]

Dataset. The dataset included in this data challenge serves as a starting point in exploring techniques for quantifying uncertainty in seismic processing workflows. In this dataset we are focused on quantifying and visualizing the uncertainty in our estimations of the density of the subsurface based on how varying those estimates impacts our output 3D volume. At a high level, this dataset consists of a set of synthetic but realistic models of the density of the subsurface, randomly generated based on a single, known, synthetic ground truth. This dataset also includes the final 3D realizations generated using those density models (also called velocity models). These files are stored in the industry standard SEGY format, and an example Jupyter notebook is provided to illustrate how to load and visualize them.

A 3 GB trial dataset is given to help competitors get started. The full dataset is 49 GB. A laptop, workstation, or small cluster should be suitable for developing solutions to this challenge.

6.2   Challenges of Interest

The end goal of this data challenge is to construct an uncertainty map for a given seismic survey, labeling each pixel in a final 2D seismic image with a value between 0.0 and 1.0 indicating how volatile the estimate for that pixel is.

However, we also welcome submissions that include any intermediate work towards that end goal or answers to any of the below challenge questions. Even if you are unable to complete the entire challenge, any submissions that show progress towards this end goal and lay out ideas for how the challenge could eventually be completed will be considered.

1. Given that geophysicists generally use horizontal lines in gathers as a good indicator of velocity model accuracy, build a model (analytical, mathematical, data-driven, or otherwise) to estimate the quality of each velocity model based on its associated gathers.
2. Train a model to label each pixel with an uncertainty value between 0.0 and 1.0 indicating how uncertain any given realization of that part of the subsurface is.
3. Generate a single uncertainty map given all of the velocity models, realizations, and gathers at hand.
4. Generate some form of visualization of this uncertainty map of the subsurface.

7   Challenge 6: Using Artificial Intelligence Techniques to Match Patients with Their Best Clinical Trial Options

The Presidential Innovation Fellows, US Department of Veterans Affairs, and the Oak Ridge National Laboratory Health Data Sciences Institute are coordinating this Data Challenge, which draws on resources across a dozen federal agencies and departments. The related project, Health Tech Sprint, emphasizes the need for open federal data for artificial intelligence (AI) applications as defined by the newly signed OPEN Government Data Act under the Foundations for Evidence-based Policymaking Act (signed Jan 15, 2019).

7.1   Background

Novel therapeutics, such as those under development in clinical trials, are often a treatment option for patients with serious and life-threatening diseases such as cancer. Increasing patient awareness of clinical trials is believed to be a factor in reducing time for participant recruitment, a very large cost category in clinical trials. Thus, applying AI to help patients and their health care providers find clinical trials of novel therapeutics may improve patient care and, by aiding in recruitment, reduce drug development costs.

For AI to be useful in trial matching, both representative patient data and clinical trial eligibility information, ideally in a structured format, are needed. In addition, expert-based guidance on matching patients to trials, including which criteria are matched, is useful for building and testing models.

The AI-able data ecosystem seeks to enable AI by bringing together an ensemble of interlinked datasets with data suitable for AI in a given use case. Having this information in the public domain enables standardization by facilitating testing across different approaches. This challenge features the first such standardized dataset ensemble related to clinical trial matching, with the various interlinked datasets provided.

7.2   Dataset

We provide three datasets to the data challenge participants

1. A subset of eligibility criteria translated into machine-readable code from a selected group of cancer clinical trials.
2. Records based on callers to the NCI's Cancer Information Service that have been enhanced with synthetic data and translated into machine-readable code.
3. Participant records matched against clinical trials for which the eligibility criteria and participant data were previously translated into machine-readable code.

The size of the three datasets is 1.3 MB and a laptop, workstation, or small cluster should be suitable for developing solutions to this challenge. A second version of the third dataset, produced by oncology professionals, serves as a comparison dataset for the matches identified through the application of AI. For more information on the above datasets and potential approaches on usage, please see reference [15].

In addition to the datasets provided, participants are encouraged to use other publicly available datasets. For example, National Cancer Institute (NCI)-funded cancer clinical trials, including API with annotations on disease eligibility criteria for all trials, is available at https://clinicaltrialsapi.cancer.gov.

7.3   Challenges of Interest

Challenge tasks are listed below. However, participants are encouraged to suggest and tackle challenge tasks different from those listed below. Innovative use of the provided data is strongly encouraged.

1. Data representation
   - Develop novel big data structures to represent the clinical trials and the patient data that accommodate the interaction of the three datasets. The ultimate goal is to support thousands of clinical trials being matched with millions of people.
2. Algorithm development
   - Develop novel algorithms for finding the most suitable matches between patients and clinical trials.
3. Visualization/human computer interaction
   - Develop visualization and/or human-computer interaction solutions to enable medical providers to effectively leverage the data for clinical decision support.

Notes on the Challenge Tasks

1. A participant may choose to do any question(s) they prefer. Completing all three questions is optional.
2. Regarding approaches to question 2, our preference is to receive solutions involving machine learning techniques.

8   Challenge 7: The Kaggle CORD-19 Data Challenge

8.1   Background

As governments, policymakers, and scientists across the globe are racing to identify potential vaccines and drugs for SARS-CoV-2, many scientists hope the information needed to identify a vaccine lies in the millions of available research documents. To support mining information from research literature, the White House, along with leading industries, has made a dataset of research publications directly related to the outbreak available to the general public [16]. Some of the most important questions pertaining to the outbreak which were identified by the US NASEM and the WHO, were published as part of a public challenge along with the publication dataset on Kaggle [17].

8.2   Dataset

The entire body of scientific literature is growing at an enormous rate; it is currently estimated at over 100 million publications [20] with an annual increase of more than 5 million articles. The publication set of corona virus-related literature provided for the Kaggle COVID-19 Open Research Data Challenge (CORD-19) have been growing at a rate of thousands of new publications per year (Fig. 6) and the growth has nearly doubled since the start of the current epidemic. Thus, it is not only difficult for scientists to source inspiration and new insights from their own domains, but also other adjacent domains. Since comprehensive reading of the growing scientific literature is now beyond the capacities of any human being, artificial intelligence techniques, including natural language processing and text mining, offer the potential to intelligently parse large bodies of loosely connected text to provide scientists solving some of the world's most pressing challenges with meaningful insights [22–24].

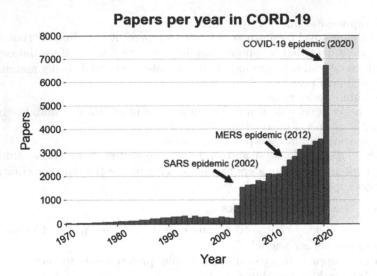

Fig. 6. Growth of papers in the CORD-19 dataset. Figure from [21].

8.3 Challenges of Interest

To kick-start the development of such AI techniques, the Kaggle CORD-19 challenge lists some of the most important questions pertaining to the COVID-19 epidemic, which will require parsing and connecting information provided in the available literature. This list of questions evolves as we learn more about the virus and identify new questions which need to be answered, and includes questions about symptoms, risk factors such as pre-existing conditions, and vaccines and therapeutics currently under investigation. However, answering some of the questions may require going beyond existing CORD-19 publication set. What if an existing vaccine developed for another disease has a potential to also work for COVID-19, but hasn't as of yet been mentioned in COVID-19 related literature? Expanding beyond just the directly relevant literature exacerbates the need for AI techniques.

We invite submissions describing complete or partial solutions to any of the Kaggle CORD-19 Tasks to SMCDC for consideration for a best solution paper award, poster presentation, and publication in the conference proceedings. The SMCDC poster session will give selected researchers perusing the CORD-19 dataset a place to present their work and discuss it with other researchers.

9   Conclusion

In addition to contributing to the solutions of open research questions, we hope these challenges gave participants a taste of the types of data and modeling problems in each of the scientific areas featured in the 2020 Data Challenge.

We also hope these challenges got researchers thinking about how important and difficult it is to account for uncertainty and probability in large scientific datasets.

In total, 52 teams competed to solve the seven data challenges. Of those, 23 teams submitted solution papers. The best solutions were selected for publication by a peer review.

About 90% of the finalists identified themselves as students. According to studies in educational psychology such as [18] and [19], novel intellectual challenges, like those posed by the 2020 Data Challenge, can be highly motivating and promote deeper engagement in tasks and lead to longer-term persistence in academic pursuits like research.

Acknowledgments. This research used resources of the Compute and Data Environment for Science (CADES) at the Oak Ridge National Laboratory, which is supported by the Office of Science of the U.S. Department of Energy under Contract No. DE-AC05-00OR22725"
This research used resources of the Oak Ridge Leadership Computing Facility, which is a DOE Office of Science User Facility supported under Contract DE-AC05-00OR22725.

References

1. https://neutrons.ornl.gov/vulcan
2. Granroth, G.E., et al.: Event-based processing of neutron scattering data at the Spallation neutron source. J. Appl. Crystallogr. **51**(3), 616 (2018)
3. Wang, X.L., et al.: First results from the VULCAN diractometerat the SNS. In: Materials Science Forum, vol. 652, pp. 105–110. Trans Tech Publications (2010)
4. Niyanth, S, Noyan, I.C., Seren, M.H., An, K.: Vulcan Beamline dataset. In: Partly supported by the US Department of Energy (DOE) Office of Energy Efficiency and Renewable Energy, Advanced Manufacturing Office program. This research used resources at the SNS, a DOE Office of Science User Facility operated by Oak Ridge National Laboratory. https://doi.org/10.13139/ORNLNCCS/1604074
5. Laanait, N., Borisevich, A., Yin, J.: A Database of Convergent Beam Electron Diffraction Patterns for Machine Learning of the Structural Properties of Materials. https://doi.org/10.13139/ORNLNCCS/1604074
6. Allen-Dumas, M., New, J. Chicago microclimate and building energy use data. https://doi.org/10.13139/ORNLNCCS/1619243
7. Berres, A., Im, P., Kurte, K., Allen-Dumas, M., Thakur, G., Sanyal, J.: A mobility-driven approach to modeling building energy. In: 5th IEEE Workshop on Big Data Analytics in Supply Chains and Transportation, Los Angeles (2019)
8. https://nhts.ornl.gov/
9. Microsoft building footprints. https://github.com/Microsoft/USBuildingFootprints
10. https://usbuildingdata.blob.core.windows.net/usbuildings-v1-1/Illinois.zip
11. Census data for Chicago community areas. https://datahub.cmap.illinois.gov/dataset/2010-census-data-summarized-to-chicago-community-areas
12. https://datahub.cmap.illinois.gov/dataset/community-data-snapshots-raw-data
13. https://krisenergy.com/company/about-oil-and-gas/exploration/

14. https://www.geoexpro.com/articles/2016/01/super-high-resolution-seismic-data-in-the-norwegian-barents-sea
15. https://digital.gov/2019/02/27/how-a-health-tech-sprint-inspired-an-ai-ecosystem
16. https://www.whitehouse.gov/briefings-statements/call-action-tech-community-new-machine-readable-covid-19-dataset/
17. https://www.kaggle.com/allen-institute-for-ai/CORD-19-research-challenge/tasks
18. Csikszentmihalyi, M.: Flow: The Psychology of Optimal Experience. Harper Perennial, New York (1990)
19. Shernoff, D.J., Hoogstra, L.: Continuing motivation beyond the high school classroom. New Dir. Child Adolesc. Dev. **93**, 73–87 (2001)
20. Khabsa, M., Giles, C.L.: The number of scholarly documents on the public web. PloS One **9**(5), e93949 (2014)
21. Wang, LL., et al.: CORD-19: The Covid-19 Open Research Dataset. arXiv (2020)
22. Wang, K., Shen, Z., Huang, C., Chieh-Han, W., Dong, Y., Kanakia, A.: Microsoft academic graph: when experts are not enough. Quant. Sci. Stud. **1**(1), 396–413 (2020)
23. Wade, A.D., Wang, K.: The rise of the machines: artificial intelligence meets scholarly content. Learned Publishing **29**(3), 201–205 (2016)
24. Saggion, H., Ronzano, F.: Scholarly data mining: making sense of scientific literature. In: 2017 ACM/IEEE Joint Conference on Digital Libraries (JCDL), pp. 1–2 (2017)
25. U.S. Energy Information Administration. Use of energy in the United States-Energy explained. https://www.eia.gov/energyexplained/index.php
26. DOE Office of Energy Efficiency and Renewable Energy efficiency trends in residential and commercial buildings. http://www.osti.gov/servlets/purl/1218835/

Examining and Presenting Cycles in Temperature Logs from the Vulcan Diffractometer

Regan Moreno[1](✉), Chad Steed[2], Katherine Engstrom[2], and Erik Schmidt[2]

[1] University of Tennessee, Knoxville, TN 37996, USA
reganmoriah@gmail.com
[2] Oak Ridge National Laboratory, Oak Ridge, TN 37830, USA
{steedca,engstromka,schmidteh}@ornl.gov

Abstract. As scientific facilities produce more and more data, it is the job of scientists to parse through and present the data in clear, well-formatted, and accurate mediums in order to apply this information to future projects. This was the primary goal when processing the Spallation Neutron Source's challenge data for the VULCAN diffractometer. The diffractometer generates high-intensity neutron pulses towards a material and the changes in temperature over time are recorded. This information can reveal the molecular structure of the material as well as their behavior under certain conditions and duress. As the material was rapidly heated and cooled, we examine the change in temperature, eliminate stagnant data, and divide information into cycles. Doing so provides insight into the composition and behavior of the material, as well as the diffractometer's process.

Keywords: Time series · Data visualization · Neutron science · Data wrangling

1 Introduction

When confronted with the challenge data, our team decided it was a perfect opportunity to experiment with data visualization using the virtual reality headset Magic Leap. Remotely accessible, yet interactive visualization was the primary goal when processing the Spallation Neutron Source's challenge data for the VULCAN diffractometer. The diffractometer generates high-intensity neutron pulses towards a material and the changes in temperature over time are recorded. This information can reveal the molecular structure of the material as well as its behavior under certain conditions and duress. The temperatures and time were recorded as the material was rapidly heated and cooled. The goal of this project was to wrangle this data into appropriate formats and visualize it in a clear, accessible, and informative way, thereby providing further information and concepts to future studies.

J. Nichols et al. (Eds.): SMC 2020, CCIS 1315, pp. 443–450, 2020.
https://doi.org/10.1007/978-3-030-63393-6_29

2 Tools

2.1 Software

Pandas provided an opensource library which we took full advantage of. Pandas provided the data frame structure we use to load in and wrangle the provided information.

Matplotlib/NumPy [4] allowed for simple and internal examination of the data.

Altair is a declarative statistical visualization library for Python based with **Vega:** a high-level grammar of interactive graphics.

Seaborn is a Python based visualization library based on matplotlib and provided a high-level interface for the statistical graphics.

2.2 Hardware

As the team was heavily involved with the Visual Informatics for Science and Technology Advances (VISTA) Lab at Oak Ridge National Laboratory, visualization in a 3D space was a focus and learning opportunity of this challenge. We used the **Magic Leap** virtual reality headset and its connection to Unity and Helio, its built-in browser, to visualize within our homes.

3 Data

The data contained values of the tested materials temperature over time as the diffractometer conducted its tests. It was provided in a HDF5 file [1]. A Python script broke this information down into two.csv files (t1 and t2). All examples listed throughout the paper have been taken from the second set (t2) on suggestion of the challenge authors. Each file contained about sixty-four thousand values of time and temperature as the diffractometer measured the cycles of heating and cooling in the material. All information was then loaded into a Pandas [2] data frame to wrangle with greater efficiency.

4 Technical Approach

Pre- and Post-processing

Approaching time series data is an arduous process, there is a lot of wrangling to be done. One of the first issues we came across were stagnant values at the beginning and the end of the files. These values represented a. The material's resting temperature and b. Its gradual return to resting temperature post heating. The first of these issues could be eliminated so as not to throw off calculations at a later point. The second had to be carefully examined to not disregard the cooling process of the material inside of the cycles, yet not provide false positives during the final cooling. We eliminated these first values by parsing through the values and determining a cutoff temperature of 29 °C. Filtering through the values above that cutoff provided the data we could begin to section off into cycles, remaining aware of the small spices in temperature during cooling.

Another problem we had to be aware of when examining data were small spikes and valleys in the data we needed to disregard when determining the pattern. This was accomplished by identifying cycles with a rolling average window. This is establishing a mean while traversing the data while being conscientious of the weight of certain values. A rolling average with a window of 20 values allowed our team to identify cycles with precision and append the cycle start and end values to the data frame. A rolling average is represented by:

$$SMA = nA_1 + A_2 + \ldots + A_n$$

Pandas allowed this to be easily accomplished as it provided built in functions to take the average between values, calculating the moving range with a window of 20 values to smooth small jumps in data, and then to calculate the differences between those ranges.

```
18    #Calculate the differences between values
19    newData['dtemp'] = newData['temperature'].diff()
20
21    #Calculate the moving range
22    newData['matemp'] = newData['temperature'].rolling(window=20).mean()
23
24    #Calculate the change  in the moving range values
25    newData['dmatemp'] = newData['matemp'].diff()
26
```

Code Listing 1 - Brief Calculations

Then, by setting a Boolean variable, we were able to observe whether we consider the values to be in a cycle by whether they have stopped cooling. We monitor cycle start and stop values by iterating through the information to look for when the rolling average window has begun the next heating process, if it is true, we update the cycle count, mark the starting value of the next rotation, and continue.

```
#Create column to track cycles
cooling = False
start = 0
end = 0
newData['cycles'] = np.nan
cycle_count = 1
#Append to the cycles column if value is starting or ending a cycle

for i in range(len(newData)):
    if not np.isnan(newData.iloc[i]['dmatemp']):
        if not cooling:
            if newData.iloc[i]['dmatemp'] < 0:
                cooling = True
        else:
            if i + 1 == len(newData):
                end = i
                newData['cycles'][start:end+1] = cycle_count
            else:
                if (newData.iloc[i]['dmatemp'] > 0) and (newData.iloc[i + 1]['dmatemp'] > 0):
                    if (i + 2) < (len(newData) - 1) and (newData.iloc[i + 2]['dmatemp'] > 0):
                        end = i - 1
                        # cycles.append([start, end])
                        newData['cycles'][start:end] = cycle_count
                        cycle_count += 1
                        start = end
                        end = start
                        cooling = False

newCycle = newData.groupby('cycles').head(1)
```

Code Listing 2 - Cycle Detection Code

All code was contained within the public GitHub repo of the author [6].

Problem 1
Identify heat cycles pertaining to equivalent temperatures during the heating and cooling phase.

Graphing the data provided a clear view of decreasing plateaus of the high temperatures over time. The base graph [Fig. 1] demonstrates the values of the time series as a blue line, while light orange vertical lines denote the beginning/stopping points of the marked cycles. Doing so allowed the team to then isolate specific cycles to then group together by similarity of temperature height. The Magic Leap then allowed us to overlay individual cycles for comparison. With a focus on this project being on data visualization in a 3D space, this allows the representation of chosen separate cycles to be compared visually.

A suggestion inside the challenge was to compare the cycles by equivalent temperatures during heating and cooling cycles as that may provide insight on the material's response to the rapid temperature changes over time. Choosing a cap of 800 ° Celsius will show that specific temperature being reached 304 times within the second dataset. As shown there were plateaus above 800 throughout the first half of the experiment but from a certain point that height was only reached through intermittent spikes and then never reached again as the cycles top height maxed out at around 650 ° Celsius before the final cooling. The below graph [Fig. 2] was a color histogram using the library Seaborn [5] to pinpoint recurring temperatures up to five decimal places, the range adjusted as needed.

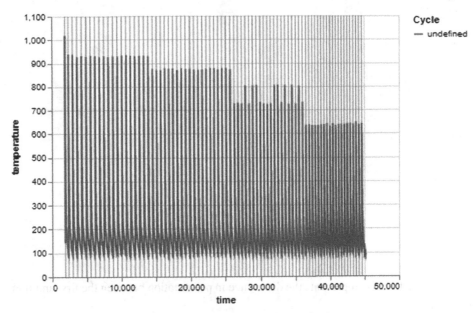

Fig. 1. Cycle detection marked

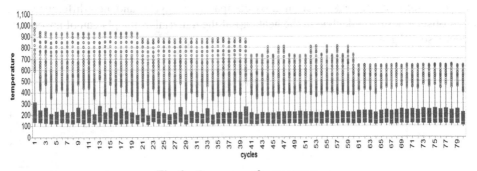

Fig. 2. Frequency of temperature

Problem 2

How many events are there in each group and how similar are the identified events?

There was a total of 80 cycles within the second data set (t2) as identified by our program. Cycles span between 400 and 700 s in length with an average of 541.1457244551898 s in a cycle. Isolating cycles for comparison yields a varying representation of sharp inclines sliding down to a slow return to resting temperature. They vary significantly over time as the peak temperature reached lessens consistently. The below graph is the difference between the first and the second cycle (Fig. 3).

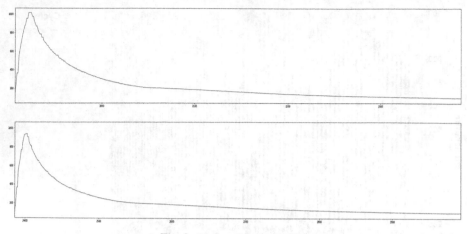

Fig. 3. First and second cycles

The graph below represents the difference in presentation between the first and final cycle.

As we observe, the peak of the cycle lowers significantly after numerous tests. From a time series analysis point of view, this is important as it could provide insight into the degradation of cycle peaks over time. By comparing the cycles and their differences, we can observe a steady decline in the heat cap of the material as the plateau of absorption decreases (Fig. 4).

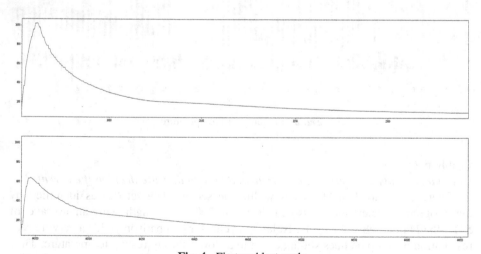

Fig. 4. First and last cycle

5 Results

Using Helio, the Magic Leap built in browser, we pulled up the Altair [3] provided visualization through GitHub. This allows users to access interactive graphs within their homes [Fig. 5]. The graph was interactive to the points of manipulation along the scale and zooming capability. As such, users can isolate a specific cycle for examination, zoom in or out, highlight, or travel along the axis. The Magic Leap headset is also capable of photo and video capture as well as streaming on the live streaming platform Twitch. Live streaming capabilities does increase accessibility, especially during the time of COVID enforced remote work. Augmented reality technology allows the feel of a VISTA lab within our own homes.

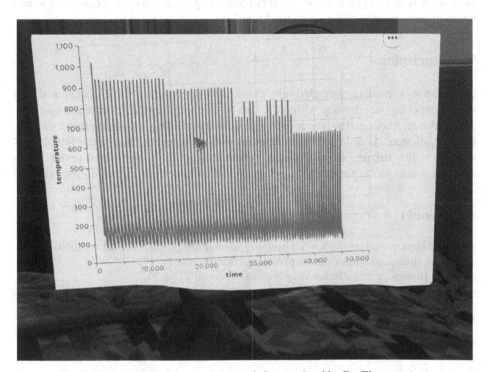

Fig. 5. Observation of the graph in magic leap assisted by Dr. Finnegan (cat)

6 Improvements

Improvements would be focused on data visualization in a 3D space. We ran into some implementation issues with the Magic Leap when it came to maintaining compatibility with game engines like Unity and Unreal. Using Unity to create an interactive 3D visualization that could be openly manipulated was a goal that was unfortunately cut short by the incompatibility. Branching out to possibly use the Microsoft HoloLens 2, as a augmented reality substitute is in the works. The clear goal would be an interactive heat map that could be streamed to audiences of scientists. The presence of the COVID-19 pandemic was an inspiration for ensuring data visualization remained accessible while remote without disregarding the importance of interaction. Using Vega and the built-in browser was an acceptable substitution but branching out into a clearer execution would be an improvement to strive for in the future.

7 Conclusions

Our team took the data, wrangled it by eliminating unnecessary values, calculated, and stored important information within the data frame, and graphed information using the Altair library. Accessed the interactive graphs through the Magic Leap augmented reality headset allowed 2D holographic interaction with the data and shared the interactions through a live stream. This can allow future projects to be visualized remotely yet effectively using a single virtual/augmented reality headset and a streaming service.

References

1. HDF5 Homepage. https://www.hdfgroup.org/solutions/hdf5/. Accessed 27 Jul 2020
2. Pandas Homepage. https://pandas.pydata.org/. Accessed 27 Jul 2020
3. Altair Homepage. https://altair-viz.github.io/. Accessed 27 Jul 2020
4. Matplotlib Homepage. https://matplotlib.org/. Accessed 27 Jul 2020
5. Seaborn Homepage, https://seaborn.pydata.org/. Accessed 27 Jul 2020
6. Personal Github Repo. https://github.com/raygunzapzap/intern. Accessed 27 Jul 2020

Probability Flow for Classifying Crystallographic Space Groups

Jin Pan[⊠]

Antioch, USA
jinpan@alum.mit.edu

Abstract. We present a machine learning approach to classify convergent beam electron diffraction (CBED) patterns and a novel ensemble technique of combining binary classifiers to address label imbalance in the dataset. We train a primary classifier on the full dataset and additionally train $\binom{n}{2}$ binary classifiers on pairs of labels using a weighted loss function that corrects for class imbalance. At test time, we combine the predictions of the primary classifier and binary classifiers using a method we call Probability Flow, leading to a 60.79% top-1 accuracy and a 76.95% top-5 accuracy. All of the source code is available at https://github.com/jinpan/smc_challenge2.

1 Exploratory Data Analysis

A common material analysis method is to use electron microscopes to produce convergent beam electron diffraction (CBED) patterns, and then analyze the patterns using iterative numeric solutions of partial differential equations and comparison with empirical data to determine material properties, such as the crystallographic space group (SG) the material belongs to. This paper explores the suitability of using ML techniques to create a black box classifier to predict SG.

The CBED dataset is comprised of 187,155 patterns, with a 79/11/10 split between training, validation, and testing. These patterns span 16,152 distinct chemical formulas and 200 SGs, but the representation of each SG is imbalanced: the top 20% of SGs represent over 80% of the training data (see Fig. 1), and there is no data for 30 out of the total 230 mathematically distinct SGs. This imbalance reflects the natural reality that most materials belong to a few common SG.

1.1 Image Scaling Function

Each pattern is represented as a $3 \times 512 \times 512$ array of 32bit floats, where each float is a measure of diffraction intensity. The diffraction intensities vary by orders of magnitude based on the distance to the center of the image, so we evaluate model performance on two scaling functions: one that takes a logarithm of all values and one that takes a logarithm and adds brightness according to the distance from the center. We will refer to these scaling functions as "log" and "middle-out".

© Springer Nature Switzerland AG 2020
J. Nichols et al. (Eds.): SMC 2020, CCIS 1315, pp. 451–464, 2020.
https://doi.org/10.1007/978-3-030-63393-6_30

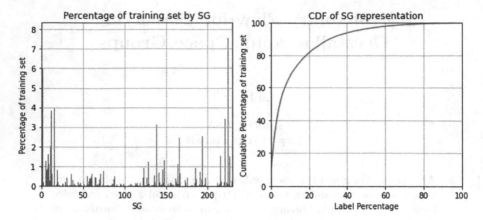

Fig. 1. Left: Percentage of the training set by SG. Right: CDF of SG representation, excluding SGs not seen in the training set. The top 20% of labels represent over 80% of the training set, which is a clear indicator of class imbalance.

To determine how much brightness to add for the second scaling function, we randomly take a sample of 10,000 intensities for each distance to the center (rounding distances down an integer). To efficiently and uniformly sample the data, we create a mapping from integers to points for each of the 362 integral distances from the center. Then we sample 10,000 integers from each of these mappings to produce a set of $362 \times 10,000$ (filename, h5 group, x, y, z) tuples that represent the sample space. We visit the h5 files in sorted order to efficiently sample by minimizing the number of disk seeks[1]. Figure 6 shows the distribution of this sample. From this data, we compute the linear regression of the log intensities as a function of distance from the center (excluding data with a distance exceeding 250) at multiple percentiles. Then, we add intensity to each pixel of each image according to the pixel's distance from the center, where the added intensity is the negative average of slopes from the above linear regressions.

Figure 2 shows the outputs of the two image scaling functions. In contrast to log-scaling, middle-out-scaling brings out more details along the edges of the image, at the cost of increasing what appears to be the noise floor. We expected middle-out to outperform log scaling because normalizing the data at the edges could lead the convolutional filters to activate more uniformly across the image. However, we found image classifiers achieve very similar accuracies on both scaling functions, so we proceed with the simpler log-scaling for the remainder of the paper.

---

[1] On a HDD with a max sustained read rate of 210 MB/s, this sampling of 550GB of data took 90 min, which is within 50% of the theoretical speed. We also evaluated online streaming algorithms for calculating distributions, but found them to run significantly slower than scheduling the exact points to sample ahead of time.

Fig. 2. Left/Middle/Right: no/log/middle-out scaling applied to the CBED stack for Fe8 Ni4 P4 at 100 keV. Without scaling, there are orders of magnitude difference in signal between the center of the slice and elsewhere, making classification difficult. Compared to log scaling, middle out scaling brings out more detail at outer parts of the image: the second band for the left slice is much more visible with middle-out scaling. However, more background noise is introduced as a consequence. Resnet-based image classifiers perform similarly under log and middle-out scaling functions.

2   ML Algorithm for Space Group Classification

In this section, we apply many standard techniques in modern CNN-based image classifiers to develop a strong baseline ML algorithm for SG classification. We start with a robust pretrained resnet-50 model and incrementally tune the training pipeline (focusing on the model architecture, data augmentation, and optimizer parts) to improve validation accuracy.

Most of the exploratory work was done on a single Nvidia GTX 1080 GPU, and many of the design decisions in training are motivated by the available hardware. Specifically, we aimed for a maximum training time of 12 h for any particular model with a target of <4h, to allow for rapid iteration. Unless otherwise indicated, all accuracy and loss numbers given are based on a model trained on the training set and tested against the validation set.

2.1   Transfer Learning

Our initial approach is to utilize transfer learning to train a resnet34 [1] model on stacked CBED images, that were downsized from 512×512 to 128×128 for an input image size of $3 \times 384 \times 128^2$. We start with a resnet34 model that was pretrained on imagenet, replace the final fully connected layer with adaptive pooling, batchnorm, dropout, and fully connected layers, as recommended by fastai for transfer learning [4]. We freeze the pretrained resnet34 parameters and train with cross-entropy loss using an AdamW optimizer [6] and one cycle learning rate annealing [9] for 10 epochs at a max learning rate of 10^{-3}. We then unfreeze those parameters to train the full model for 10 epochs at a max learning rate of 10^{-3}.

This initial approach yields 53.0/71.3% top-1/5 accuracy, with training and validation losses of 0.012/3.3. The extremely low training loss and significant difference between training and validation losses indicates that this approach overfits the training set. We also worry that the model is not making full use

---

[2] The intensities are replicated across the 3 color channels to satisfy the input to the pretrained model.

of all three slices and is just lazily looking at a subset to memorize the training data. To mitigate these issues, we proceed to train a classifier on individual slices, and combine model outputs by averaging softmax activations, a standard test time augmentation method.

The split classifier approach yields a raw 43.2/60.9% top-1/5 accuracy on individual slices, with training and validation losses of 0.093/3.8. Averaging the outputs of the three slices of input together improves the top-1/5 accuracy to 55.5/71.5%. Going forwards, all reported accuracies will be for predictions made on the averaged outputs. The low training loss indicate that simply using a deeper/wider/larger model will not improve generalization accuracy. To quickly try out new approaches, we retire transfer learning in favor of *tabula rasa* learning.

2.2   *Tabula Rasa* Learning

By no longer doing transfer learning, we lose the pretrained convolutional filters, but that is acceptable since 1) the given dataset is fairly large with over 500k images (considering each slice as a separate image) 2) the CBED patterns are very different compared to the imagenet domain. In exchange, we gain the flexibility to tune the architecture and a 3x speedup in training by using a single-channel model.

We modify the resnet34 architecture to accept a single channel image, and reduce the width of each layer by a factor of $64/20 = 3.2$. Model parameters are initialized with Kaiming initialization [2], followed by LSUV initialization [7]. Then we train using a LAMB optimizer[3] [11] with one cycle learning rate annealing for 50 epochs[4] at a max learning rate of 5×10^{-2}, yielding an accuracy of 52.64/69.67% top-1/5 accuracy[5], with training and validation losses of 0.034/7.4. In comparison to transfer learning, training loss is lower and accuracy is lower, which is a sign of overfitting as the model no longer starts from the robust pretrained convolutional filters.

To counteract overfitting, we consider using rotation, mixup [12], and random erasure to augment the data. We rotate on the resized 128×128 images and use bicubic interpolation[6]. Rotational augmentation is also used at test time if and

---

[3] For *tabula rasa* learning, we use a LAMB optimizer (instead of AdamW) to avoid needing to tune discriminative learning rate hyper parameters for the early network layers.

[4] The increase in epochs counteracts most of the speedups from moving to a single-channel model, but we found that we could not train to a similar accuracy with a lower number of epochs at a higher learning rate.

[5] We trained 5 models with different initial random seeds, but otherwise identical parameters, and this reported accuracy is the average of those 5 model accuracies.

[6] Resizing during the training loop turned the CPU into the bottleneck and significantly slowed the training cycle down with low GPU utilization. Nearest neighbor and lanczos interpolation were also considered: nearest neighbor interpolation lead to lower accuracy. Lanczos interpolation lead to similar accuracy, but was slower to compute.

only if it was used during training[7]. Random erasure is done with probability 80%[8] and using the default PyTorch 1.5 hyperparameters. Table 1 shows mixup and random erasure data augmentation lead to the highest accuracy. Rotational augmentation leads to a decrease in test accuracy in each scenario; this could be explained by 1) the CBED scans are taken from a canonical perspective so rotated images are not representative of the test set 2) the rotation interpolation adds noise to the training set.

Table 1. Table of model top-1 accuracy with various data augmentation combinations. All models were trained for 50 epochs at a max learning rate of 5×10^{-2}. Rotational augmentation actually leads to a decrease in model accuracy, which may be explained by CBED scans being taken from canonical perspectives.

Rotation	Mixup	Erasure	Top-1 Acc	Top-5 Acc	Training loss	Validation loss
F	F	F	52.72	69.50	0.034	7.4
T	F	F	50.69	67.26	0.096	5.5
F	T	F	56.31	73.22	1.3	2.7
F	F	T	56.35	71.47	0.28	4.7
T	T	F	53.66	71.20	1.6	2.9
T	F	T	54.19	72.09	1.9	2.8
F	**T**	**T**	**57.07**	**73.80**	**1.5**	**2.6**
T	T	T	53.00	71.74	1.9	2.8

Using mixup and erasure augmentation improves top-1/5 accuracy to 57.24/73.98%[9]. We proceed with mixup and random erasure data augmentation to train a resnet50 model, which improves accuracy to 57.89/74.89%. We also find that introducing a dropout layer (p = 50%) before the final fully connected layer slightly improves accuracy to 58.34/74.38%.

Additionally, we try the resnet-C/D[10] modifications proposed by [3], and replicate their findings that resnet-C outperforms resnet-B with accuracies of 58.35/74.89% and resnet-D outperforms C with accuracies of 58.67/75.02%.

We also evaluate larger models via deepening, widening, and adding resnext grouped convolutions [10]. Deepening the network with the resnet101 architecture slightly increases the accuracies to 58.95/74.80%. However, widening the

---

[7] Rotational augmentation with 72 copies at 5° rotations leads to an approximate 1.0/1.3% increase in absolute top-1/5 accuracy at test time, relative to training with rotational augmentation but testing without any augmentation.

[8] We also considered random erasure with probability 50% and 100%, and 80% lead to the highest validation accuracy.

[9] These figures differ slightly from the table since they are averaged across 5 identically trained models, whereas the table is just a single model.

[10] The above resnet models use the default Pytorch architecture, which is considered resnet-B.

network and adding resnext grouped convolutions lowered accuracies. Figure 3 summarizes the impact on top-1 accuracy of the evaluated modifications.

At this stage, we have applied many general modern techniques in training image classifiers with diminishing returns, so we use the resnet101-D with a 50% dropout layer (and mixup/random erasure data augmentation) as our baseline model and turn our attention to label imbalance.

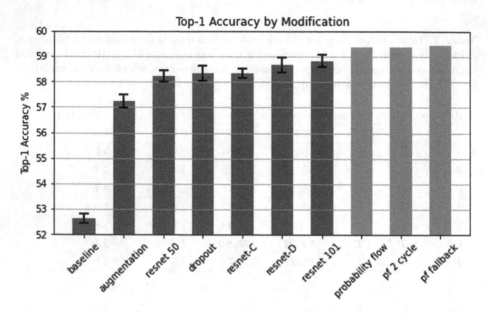

Fig. 3. The impact on top-1 accuracy of the evaluated modifications. Each modification was trained 5 times from different initial random seeds, and the blue bars represent the mean top-1 accuracy. The black bars represent ±1 standard deviation of noise across the 5 samples. Probability Flow (discussed in Sect. 3) significantly improves top-1 accuracy, relative to many other well-established architecture modifications. We only train Probability Flow once because it relies on an ensemble of over 100 classifiers, making it less sensitive to any particular initial random seed (and also more expensive to train). The consistent accuracy of all the probability flow variations demonstrates the overall robustness of this approach.

3   Overcoming Label Imbalance

As discussed in the Exploratory Data Analysis section, the top 20% of SGs represent over 80% of the training data, so there is significant label imbalance. Traditional label imbalance techniques improve recall of minority labels by effectively increasing the cost of an incorrect minority prediction in the loss function. This is commonly achieved by either directly weighting the loss function or artificially increasing the representation of minority labels in the training set [5].

However, the approach of boosting recall for minority labels is inappropriate for this data challenge's goal of a high overall accuracy; we do not want to optimize recall for any particular SG at the expense of another group. Figure 7 shows that over half of the errors for the above resnet101-D model are for groups with good representation in the training set, so simply increasing the loss weight for underrepresented SGs will likely increase those errors. Use of a weighted loss function (such that weights are inversely proportional to training set label representation) sharply reduces top-1/5 accuracy to from $59.07/73.95\%$ to $0.00/0.05\%$, because of the large weights applied to the long tail of rare SGs.

3.1 Probability Flow

We introduce a novel technique for handling label imbalance that we call Probability Flow (PF). With PF, we train a primary classifier that predicts SG with cross entropy loss[11]. Additionally, we train $\binom{n}{2}$ binary classifiers[12] (BC) that predicts one of two SGs, for each pair of SGs. When testing an input, we run the primary classifier on the input and record the top-k predictions and their probabilities. Then for all top-k predictions, we run the $\binom{k}{2}$ BCs to get pairwise probabilities, which are then used to refine the top-k probabilities from the primary classifier, as described in Fig. 4.

Training all $\binom{200}{2}$ BCs is computationally expensive, so we train $\binom{20}{2}$ classifiers for the top 20 most represented SGs in the training set. We note that this technique is particularly effective for imbalanced datasets because training a few classes leads to good coverage of the validation test space. We also evaluate the use of a weighted loss function when training the BCs, such that class weights are inversely proportional to representation in the training set[13]. Figure 5 shows model top-1 accuracy as a function of how many SGs we train BCs for, when refining the top-5 predictions. We observe greater robustness when using the weighted loss functions so we proceed forwards with the weighted BCs, which yields a top-1 accuracy of 59.36% with 15 groups and $\lambda = 75\%$.

We also analyze the impact of multiple flow cycles and find that for k = 5 and using $\binom{15}{2}$ BCs for the top 15 groups, two flow cycles of $\lambda = (50\%, 65\%)$ yields a top-1 accuracy of 59.38%, a minor improvement on a single cycle[14]. Figure 9 shows the accuracy landscape as a function of λ. For k = 4, the best results are with 14 groups and flows of $(35\%, 40\%)$; k = 3: 12 groups and $(25\%,30\%)$; k = 2: 12 groups and $(10\%, 20\%)$.

---

[11] The above resnet101-D model can serve as this primary classifier.

[12] We use resnet50-D models for the binary classifiers (with the above data augmentations) with cross entropy loss. We decided against using resnet101-D for the binary classifiers to reduce compute costs.

[13] Specifically, the weight per class is (mean samples per class) × (number of class samples)$^{-1}$. The first term is a constant that does not mathematically change the weighting function, but is included for numerical stability.

[14] Because the improvement from one to two cycles is minor, we do not explore the impact of three or more flow cycles.

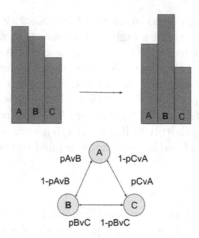

Fig. 4. An example of how PF refines pairwise probabilities. Here, we have the top-$n = 3$ classes (A,B,C) with relative probabilities in the top left as outputted by the main model. The BCs are run on (A,B), (B,C), (C,A) and give probabilities of $pAvB$, $pBvC$, and $pCvA$. Let pA, pB, and pC represent the initial probabilities. Then, $pA' = \lambda\frac{(pAvB)(pA+pB)+(1-pCvA)(pA+pC)}{2} + (1-\lambda)pA$, $pB' = \lambda\frac{(pBvC)(pB+pC)+(1-pAvB)(pB+pA)}{2} + (1-\lambda)pB$, and $pC' = \lambda\frac{(pCvA)(pC+pA)+(1-pBvC)(pC+pB)}{2}+(1-\lambda)pC$ give the updated probabilities (top right), where λ is a parameter for controlling how much probability is flowed. After redistributing probabilities in this example, B has the highest probability so it would be promoted as the model prediction. Intuitively, we can think of a probability flow refine step as taking the probability for each predicted class, scaling it down by λ, splitting it among the other $n-1$ classes according to the binary classifiers' predicted ratios, and redistributing the splits. Figure 8 gives a Python implementation for the general case.

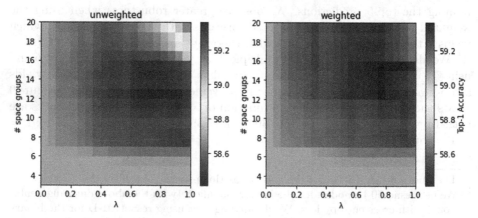

Fig. 5. PF top-1 accuracy when refining the top-5 predictions as a function of the number of SGs that BCs were trained for, and as a function of the flow factor λ. We observe that using a weighted loss function leads to greater robustness: doing so yields lower accuracy variance, higher average accuracy, and higher max accuracy; The max top-1 accuracy of 59.36% is observed at 15 groups and $\lambda = 75\%$.

In many cases, we do not have binary classifiers for all of the top-5 classes from the main classifiers. We can still apply BCs in those cases with an iterative fallback testing approach: we use the k = 5 PF parameters if the top 5 predictions are in the top 15 groups, falling back to the k = 4 parameters if the top 5 predictions are in the top 14 groups, and so on. This iterative fallback approach improves accuracy to 59.44%. Figure 3 shows the impact of PF on top-1 accuracy, relative to other ML techniques and Fig. 10 shows the impact of PF on F1 scores across all the SGs. The modifications do not significantly change PF accuracy, which is a good signal of PF robustness and generalizability.

All BCs are trained with the same learning rate parameters, and there is significant variation in the training loss trajectory. This variation indicates that there is room for improvement by fine tuning learning rates for the binary classifiers based on analysis of the training loss trajectories.

Probability Flow shares some similarities with Outrageously Large Neural Networks [8], but primarily differs in some key areas: 1) the subnetworks use an explicitly defined gating functions and merging functions instead of a learned one and 2) we explicitly train biased binary classifiers and a main classifier.

4   Conclusion

We develop a machine learning algorithm to train a crystallographic space group classifier that uses many modern CNN-based image classification techniques to achieve a top-1/5 accuracy of 60.40/76.95% on the test set[15]. We then apply Probability Flow, a novel ensemble technique for handling label imbalance, which improves top-1 accuracy to 60.79%[16].

4.1   Future Directions

All of the models were trained on 128×128 scans, but the raw data has $16\times$ more data with 512×512 dimensions. The additional resolution could allow the model to learn pick up finer details such as Holz lines to better discriminate between SGs. Training on the full-sized images can transform compute into greater accuracy. Additionally, the data pipeline used converts the raw 32bit floating point intensities into a grayscale 8bit png, which truncates the lower 24 bits and clamps maximum values. It is expected that a pipeline directly feeds the h5 array into the model (without losing information by converting into a u8 int) will perform better.

---

[15] All models were retrained on both the training set and validation set.

[16] We use weighted BCs, run two flow cycles of $\lambda = (50\%, 65\%)$, and use iterative fallback starting with k = 5, which we found to work the best on the validation set.

The CBED data also contains additional information that can be used for multi-task prediction, which has been shown to improve accuracy in other settings. Retraining the models for multi-task prediction would incur a multiplicative cost on top of all the binary classifiers that were trained, which we did not pursue due to the limited compute. However, we surmise that multi-task training will not cannibalize any of the training techniques, and therefore will provide another method to convert compute into accuracy.

We also notice that not all dimensions are equal: the main classifier is significantly more accurate on the first slice than the second or third slice. We tried training separate models for each dimension, but observed lower accuracy on each dimension than with a single classifier trained on all dimensions, and believe this is due to overfitting on the smaller training set. It may be worthwhile to apply transfer learning to create separate classifiers: train a model on all slices, then treat that as a pretrained model to train separate models for the separate dimensions.

A key issue we faced was with the model overfitting to the training set, and we needed strong data augmentation to overcome overfitting. Another way to avoid overfitting is to train an autoencoder and then a classifier using transfer learning on the autoencoder's encoded state. This may obviate the need for mixup and random erasure data augmentation.

We have only scratched the surface of the PF technique and there are many unexplored extensions, such as 1) are there better refining functions? 2) does training binary classifiers with binary cross entropy loss and "null" examples improve accuracy? 3) are there more effective secondary classifiers? 4) can we apply ideas from [8] such as learning a gating/combination function?

A   Appendix

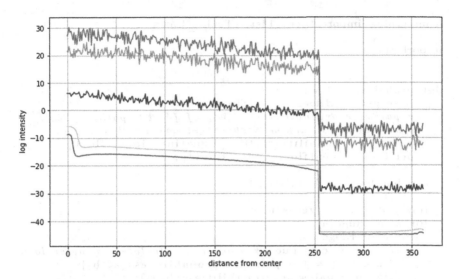

Fig. 6. Log of intensities by distance from the center at 1/50/99/99.9/99.99 percentiles. At all percentiles, there is a decrease in log intensity as a function of distance. The sharp dropoff at 255 is related to the fact that radius of the circle embedded in a 512 × 512 square is 256, and all intensities beyond 255 represent data in the corners outside the circle.

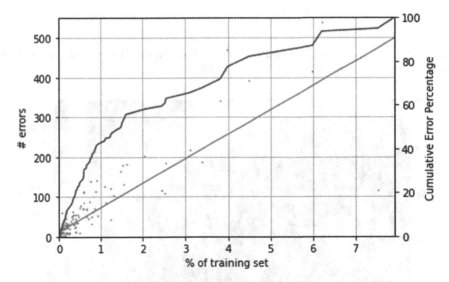

Fig. 7. Graph of the number of classification errors by SG as a function of how well represented the SG was in the training set. On the left y-axis, the blue dots represent individual SGs and the blue line is a linear regression of the number of errors as a function of SG representation: there is a strong positive relationship between training set representation and number of errors, which is explained by the strong correlation of label representation across the training and validation set. On the right y-axis, the green line represents the CDF of the number of errors. Over half of the classification errors are for the 22/200 SGs that represent over 1% of the training set.

```python
from typing import Dict, List, Tuple, Union

import torch


def probability_flow(
    base_probabilities: List[float],
    # pairwise_probabilities is map of (A, B): pAvB,
    # map length should be N choose 2, and A < B
    pairwise_probabilities: Dict[Tuple[int, int], float],
    pct_flow: Union[float, List[float]],
):
  n = len(base_probabilities)

  flow_mat = torch.zeros(n, n)
  for a in range(n):
    for b in range(n):
      if a == b: continue  # diags are calculated in outer loop
      if a < b: p = 1 - pairwise_probabilities[(a, b)]
      else: p = pairwise_probabilities[(b, a)]
      flow_mat[a][b] = p / (n-1)
    flow_mat[a][a] = 1 - flow_mat[a][:].sum()

  if isinstance(pct_flow, float): pct_flow = [pct_flow]
  ps = torch.tensor(base_probabilities)
  for λ in pct_flow:
    ps = λ * ps @ flow_mat + (1-λ) * ps
  return ps
```

Fig. 8. Python implementation of Probability Flow. Figure 4 gives a diagram of the idea for $n = 3$ and some intuition for the calculation.

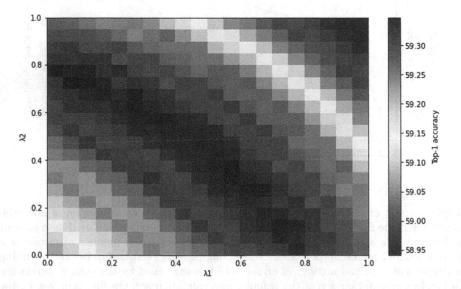

Fig. 9. PF top-1 accuracy with two flow cycles. X axis is the λ for the first flow cycle, and Y axis is the λ for the second.

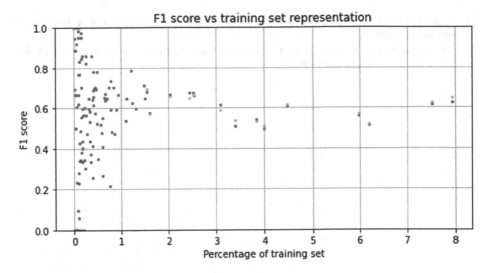

Fig. 10. F1 score of the space groups, by training set representation. Each point represents a single space group, and space groups with a precision or recall of 0 are shown in the plot with a F1 score of 0. Blue points are F1 scores with a single main resnet101-D classifier, and orange points are F1 scores with PF with two flow cycles and iterative fallback. PF improves the F1 score for 9 of the top 15 space groups, with an average change of 0.0022.

References

1. He, K., Zhang, X., Ren, S., Sun, J.: Deep residual learning for image recognition. In: 2016 IEEE Conference on Computer Vision and Pattern Recognition (CVPR), pp. 770–778 (2016)
2. He, K., Zhang, X., Ren, S., Sun, J.: Delving deep into rectifiers: surpassing human-level performance on imagenet classification. In: Proceedings of the 2015 IEEE International Conference on Computer Vision (ICCV). IEEE Computer Society, USA (2015). https://doi.org/10.1109/ICCV.2015.123
3. He, T., Zhang, Z., Zhang, H., Zhang, Z., Xie, J., Li, M.: Bag of tricks for image classification with convolutional neural networks. In: 2019 IEEE/CVF Conference on Computer Vision and Pattern Recognition (CVPR), pp. 558–567 (2019)
4. Howard, J., et al.: Fastai (2018). https://github.com/fastai/fastai
5. Johnson, Justin M., Khoshgoftaar, Taghi M.: Survey on deep learning with class imbalance. J. Big Data 6(1), 1–54 (2019). https://doi.org/10.1186/s40537-019-0192-5
6. Loshchilov, I., Hutter, F.: Decoupled weight decay regularization. In: ICLR (2019)
7. Mishkin, D., Matas, J.: All you need is a good init (2015)
8. Shazeer, N., et al.: Outrageously large neural networks: the sparsely-gated mixture-of-experts layer (2017)
9. Smith, L.N.: A disciplined approach to neural network hyper-parameters: Part 1 - learning rate, batch size, momentum, and weight decay (2018)
10. Xie, S., Girshick, R., Dollár, P., Tu, Z., He, K.: Aggregated residual transformations for deep neural networks. In: 2017 IEEE Conference on Computer Vision and Pattern Recognition (CVPR), pp. 5987–5995 (2017)

11. You, Y., et al.: Large batch optimization for deep learning: training bert in 76 minutes (2019)
12. Zhang, H., Cisse, M., Dauphin, Y.N., Lopez-Paz, D.: Mixup: beyond empirical risk minimization. ICLR 2018 (2017)

Towards a Universal Classifier for Crystallographic Space Groups: A Trickle-Down Approach to Handle Data Imbalance

Sajal Dash[(✉)] and Archi Dasgupta

Department of Computer Science, Virginia Tech, Blacksburg, VA 24060, USA
{sajal,archidg}@vt.edu

Abstract. Convergent Beam Electron Diffraction (CBED) images are 2D diffraction patterns created through the interaction between the fired electron and the atoms of a crystalline structure. Due to the absence of geometric mapping between three-dimensional structures and two-dimensional projections in this process, traditional image processing methods cannot classify CBED images into crystallographic space groups with high accuracy. The problem gets exacerbated by the class imbalance in the dataset. To effectively bridge the gaps in our understanding of solid-state crystalline structures, we must build a classifier capable of classifying diffraction patterns such as CBED images into crystallographic space groups while addressing the class imbalance. In this project, we explore the sources and nature of classification difficulties to gather insight into building a robust classifier. We first built some naive classifiers on the subset of classes by augmenting ResNet50 in various schemes. We developed a novel multi-level classification technique, called Trickle Down Classifier (TDC) to address the class imbalance in scientific datasets. TDC consists of multiple levels of subset classifiers. At each level, TDC trains a classifier to allocate the samples into a subset of classes. TDC forwards samples missed by a component classifier at a particular level to the next level classifier. For the top 20 classes, the TDC performs at an estimated 34% accuracy compared to a naive classifier's 14% accuracy.

Keywords: Data imbalance · Crystallographic space group · Deep learning · High-performance computing

1 Introduction

Accurately identifying the crystallographic space groups of materials is a crucial factor in material development and analysis [9]. Understanding the properties of solid-state crystalline structures can benefit from analyzing Convergent Beam

---

S. Dash and A. Dasgupta—These authors contributed equally to this work.

J. Nichols et al. (Eds.): SMC 2020, CCIS 1315, pp. 465–478, 2020.
https://doi.org/10.1007/978-3-030-63393-6_31

Electron Diffraction (CBED) patterns. Accurate classification of CBED patterns into crystallographic space groups (configurational symmetry in space) reveals the crystal's critical properties since the structure of a crystal determines its physiochemical properties in large part [10,11].

Determination and classification of material structures during electron microscopy experiments have the potential to enable new discoveries and analyses. However, currently, the field of material science research lacks advanced deep learning based techniques to solve classification and data imbalance problems for scientific datasets. In this research, we aim to use deep learning based methods for image classification to build space group classifiers to bridge the gap in our understanding of the solid-state crystalline structures.

We address the problem of classifying CBED images into 230 crystallographic space groups. This classification task faces challenges from multiple sources. The CBED images are created using electron beams passing through atoms of a crystal. The complicated diffraction patterns make the classification task challenging as traditional image recognition techniques do not perform well enough with CBED images. Moreover, the large volume of the dataset (500 GB) and the class imbalance in the dataset where some classes are more representative than others make the classification task more difficult. When all the classification categories in the dataset do not have approximately equal representation, then classification performance decreases significantly [1]. The end goal of our classifier is decoding material properties using deep learning. Unidentified crystals can be classified into one of the space groups to help understand the properties of that material using our proposed techniques. Our novel hierarchical classification technique will also be useful to researchers in any field for tackling overall data imbalance.

To address the associated challenges, we performed exploratory data analysis on both CBED patterns and material properties to summarize data characteristics. We also explored different ML algorithms for space group classification of CBED data and implemented proper ML techniques to overcome data/label imbalance and show how it affects the performance of the ML algorithm.

Dataset. The dataset consists of multidimensional images that are simulations of electron diffraction patterns. Laanait et al. [12] generated CBED patterns from over 60,000 solid-state materials that represent nearly every known crystal structure using multi-GPU and multi-node electron scattering simulation codes on the Summit supercomputer at Oak Ridge National Laboratory.

1.1 Problem Definition

We have identified three challenges associated with this dataset and the classification task.

The first issue associated with this problem is that CBED images are not usual two-dimensional orthogonal projections of three-dimensional objects created by passing visible light rays. Instead, when electron beams pass through atoms of a crystal, a complicated diffraction pattern emerges from the interaction between the toms and the electron beam. Unlike regular images, there is no straightforward geometric relationship between the crystals and corresponding CBED images.

The second issue is the class imbalance in the dataset. The dataset has significant class imbalance with the majority of the classes having only a handful of examples while around 30–40 classes have hundreds to thousands of examples. Making a good classifier that can assign correct labels to the examples from the under-represented classes is difficult.

The third problem is that the dataset we are working with is too large for a single computational unit.

1.2   Proposed Approaches

Our proposed approach for solving these three problems are— (1) Using universal function approximator to address non-geometric mapping of CBED images– we use deep learning models for dealing with the problem intrinsic to CBED images. (2) Developing a novel classifier called *Trickle Down Classifier* for addressing the data imbalance issue, and (3) Using 480 V100 GPUs from Summit supercomputer for tackling the big data aspect of the problem.

1.3   Outline of the Paper

In Sect. 2, we present our exploratory data analysis to discover the nature and the implications of class imbalance in the dataset. In Sect. 3, we explore the viability of deep learning based classifiers as a universal function approximator, where the function of interest maps CBED images to crystallographic space groups. In Sect. 4, we present TDC and other proposed approaches to tackle the class imbalance in the dataset. In Sect. 5, we document our effort to scale out the classifiers using Summit nodes. Section 7, we discuss the limitations of our approaches, and in Sect. 6 we discuss our plan for completing the proposed approaches.

2   Exploratory Data Analysis

We have performed an exploratory data analysis to understand the nature of the data and the potential imbalances across classes. We inspected three datasets, *train*, *test*, and *dev*. Though there are a total of 230 classes, these three datasets have examples from subsets of the classes (Table 1). Only 121 classes have non-zero examples across three datasets.

Table 1. Number of classes with non-zero examples across datasets.

Dataset	Train	Test	Dev	Train ∩ Test ∩ Dev
Number of Classes	200	140	145	121

2.1 Class Frequencies for All Non-Zero Classes

Figures 1, 2, and 3 show distribution of the classes with at least one example in each of these datasets (train, test, and dev). The classes are sorted by their frequencies.

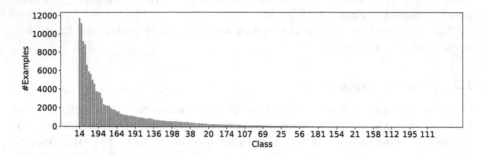

Fig. 1. Frequency distribution of 200 classes in training dataset.

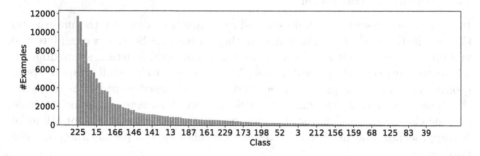

Fig. 2. Frequency distribution of 140 classes in test dataset.

A good number of classes don't have any examples in these datasets. The frequency drops exponentially, and a majority of the classes have very few examples. This imbalance should make classification of those classes relatively more difficult than the top 20/30 classes since classifiers biased toward over-represented classes tend to have better training accuracy.

2.2 A Closer Inspection into Better Represented 20 Classes

We looked into the top 20 highest represented classes from all three datasets to see if the same classes are represented proportionally across datasets.

Figures 4, 5, and 6 show distribution of top twenty classes in each of these datasets (train, test, and dev). The top 20 classes are not exactly same across three datasets, nor they are in the exact same order (Figs. 4, 5 and 6). However,

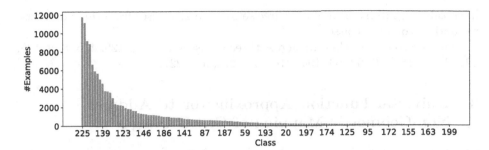

Fig. 3. Frequency distribution of 145 classes in dev dataset.

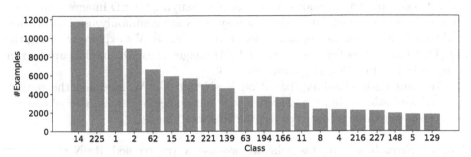

Fig. 4. Frequency distribution of top twenty classes in training dataset.

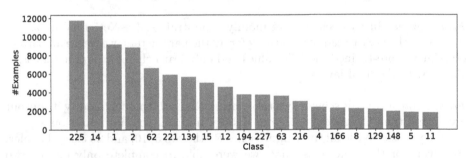

Fig. 5. Frequency distribution of top twenty classes in test dataset.

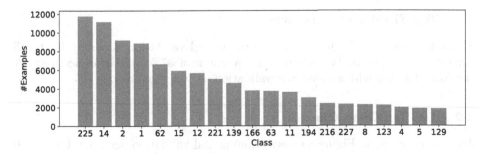

Fig. 6. Frequency distribution of top twenty classes in dev dataset.

if we take the intersection of the three sets of top 22 classes from three datasets, we find 20 common classes.

The top 20 classes that are across three datasets are 1, 2, 129, 4, 5, 8, 9, 139, 12, 11, 14, 15, 166, 62, 63, 194, 216, 221, 225, and 227.

3   Universal Function Approximator to Address Non-Geometric Mapping of CBED Images

CBED images are a non-geometric mapping of 3D structures to 2D diffraction patterns. Hence, traditional computer vision approaches that leverage geometric projections of objects are not very useful in classifying CBED images into space groups. Neural network-based detection systems are commonly used to provide traditional image processing and object recognition [4]. We explore Deep Learning (DL) based classifiers to classify CBED images since DL models are known to be universal function approximators [13].

We built basic classifiers based on ResNet50 [8]. We modified the output layer of ResNet50 to build a classifier with our choice of the number of classes. We considered three schemes to use the ResNet50 model.

Feature Extraction. In this scheme, we use a pre-trained ResNet50 model (trained on ImageNet dataset) and modify its output layer. Then we train the model by starting parameter weights from the weights of the pre-trained model.

Fine Tuning. In this scheme, we modify a pre-trained ResNet50 model as the previous scheme. Instead of relearning for all the parameters, we freeze all parameters at the pre-trained model's values and only learn the new parameters associated with the final layers.

From Scratch. In this scheme, we take a fresh ResNet50 model, modify its output layer, and train the model using our dataset from random initialization.

We propose to use all three approaches for the top 5, 10, and 20 class classifier. However, for the time constraint, we were able to complete only one or two schemes.

3.1   Top Five-Class Classifiers

Feature Extraction. Figure 7 shows training and validation accuracy for top 5 classes in ten epochs. We achieved a maximum of 37% validation accuracy. A random classifier will achieve 20% validation accuracy on average.

3.2   Top Ten-Class Classifiers

Feature Extraction. Figure 8 shows training and validation accuracy for top 10 classes in ten epochs. We achieved a maximum of 35.4% validation accuracy. A random classifier will achieve 10% validation accuracy on average.

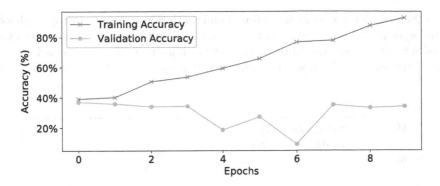

Fig. 7. Top five class classifier using feature extraction method.

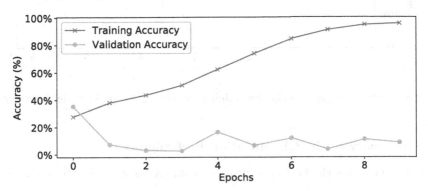

Fig. 8. Top ten class classifier using feature extraction method.

3.3 Top Twenty-Class Classifiers

Feature Extraction. Figure 9 shows training and validation accuracy for top 20 classes in ten epochs. We achieved a maximum of 6.43% validation accuracy. A random classifier will achieve 5% validation accuracy on average. So, a model achieved for the top 20 classes using a feature extraction scheme is almost as bad as a random classifier.

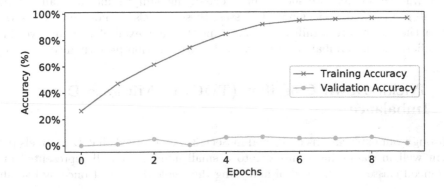

Fig. 9. Top ten class classifier using feature extraction method.

From Scratch. Figure 10 shows training and validation accuracy for top 20 classes in ten epochs. We achieved a maximum of 11.2% validation accuracy. A random classifier will achieve 5% validation accuracy on average. So, a model achieve for top 20 classes using from scratch scheme is twice as good as a random classifier.

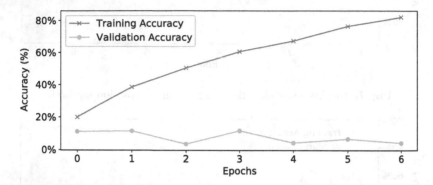

Fig. 10. Top twenty class classifier by training a modified ResNet50 model from scratch

3.4 Summary of the Classification Performances

Table 2 summarizes the best classification accuracy for various subset classifiers.

Table 2. Best classification accuracy achieved using different schemes.

Subset size	Training accuracy	Validation accuracy
5	92.9%	37%
10	95.8%	35.4%
20	96.5%	14%

While DL models are successful in classifying samples into a small number of well-represented and balanced classes, these models do not perform as well when the classes are significantly imbalanced 1. For example, in the five-class classifier, the class imbalance is low, so the classification performance is higher.

4 Trickle-Down Classifier (TDC) to Mitigate Data Imbalance

Through our explorations described in Sect. 3, we observed that DL models perform well in classifying samples into a small number of well represented and balanced classes. So, instead of analyzing the whole dataset at once by training a single model, it might be beneficial to perform incremental analysis. One of the three guidelines for exploring big data analytics proposed by Dash [5] is to perform incremental analysis on data through the innovation of domain-specific merging methodologies. While we can perform incremental analysis on the small group of classes at each increment by training one model for each increment, the challenge is to combine the results in a meaningful way [6]. One way to combine the results could be establishing a sequence among these incremental classifiers in a way such that whenever an earlier model fails to classify an example, a later model can come into play.

Using this insight, we developed a novel classification approach TDC for dealing with imbalanced data. The issue of imbalanced data for classification problems arises when the classes are inequally-represented. Class-imbalance is a pervasive obstacle for classification problems in scientific datasets across all disciplines.

Through our exploratory data analysis phase (Sect. 2), we observed that a few classes have a large number of samples each, while a large majority have a very small number of samples each. It will be easier to classify a sample from the first group of classes compared to the second. We propose the novel *Trickle Down* classifier, which will utilize multiple simple classifiers in a cascade of classification tasks.

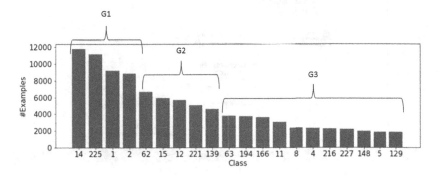

Fig. 11. An example grouping of top 20 classes for TDC.

We first sort the classes by the number of samples in descending order. Then we group consecutive classes with a roughly similar number of samples (Fig. 11). We use this grouping to build multiple levels of subset classifiers, where each level classifies the corresponding groups. The unclassified samples are assigned to a dummy "Rest of the World (RotW)" class and sent downstream to the next classifier level. This downstream flow of unclassified data is where the novel approach gets its name—"Trickle-down Classifier".

For now, we have used similar frequency ranges by visually inspecting into the distribution to group this data. We group classes into several sub-classes according to their cardinality (number of representative samples for the class).

For generalization purposes, we can use some statistical clustering (e.g., groups of classes that have frequency with a maximum of five percent standard deviation within the group). Different levels of TDC consists of a different number of classes.

Figure 11 shows a tentative grouping where we include the four most frequent classes with 8000 or more samples (G1). We build a five-class (class 1, 2, 3, 4, and 5–20) classifier C1 to decide whether a test sample falls within the first four classes or not. The fifth class denotes that the sample needs further classification using less frequent class; we will mark such samples as *rejected*. Then we group the next five classes (G2) having 5000–7999 samples each. We build a six-class classifier C2 to classify the samples rejected by C1. We build an 11-class classifier (C3) for the remaining group of 11 classes (G3). An example rejected by classifier C1 will be passed down to C2, and an example rejected by C2 will be passed down to C3.

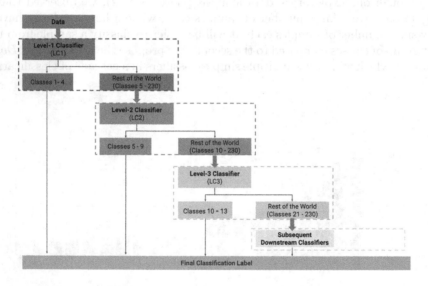

Fig. 12. Proposed Trickle Down model.

Figure 12 illustrates this approach. The benefit of the top-level classifier's ability to classify within the most frequent classes reduces the error for less frequent classes. Since, less frequent classes collectively work as a collective negative class for the classifier built for most frequent classes, error due to class imbalance is reduced.

Classification Performance. Table 3 demonstrates the three component classifiers' (C1, C2, C3) classification performance in terms of validation accuracy. The last row shows the estimated validation accuracy of the TDC classifier.

Classification performances of the three component classifiers are 75.9%, 22.7%, and 15.7%, respectively. The number of validation samples in these three

Table 3. Classification accuracy of the TDC classifier.

Level	Classes	Validation sample size	Validation accuracy
1	1–4	5280	75.9%
2	5–9	3440	22.7%
3	10–20	10029	15.7%
TDC	1–20	18749	$\approx 34\%$

levels are 5280, 3440, and 10029 respectively. So, an estimated accuracy of the trickle-down classifier is $\dfrac{0.76 \times 5280 + 0.23 \times 3440 + 0.16 \times 10029}{5280 + 3440 + 10029} \approx 34\%$ for the top 20 classes.

5 Scaling Out the Classifiers and Hyper-Parameter Selection

Since training ResNet50 model and its variants can take hours to days on a single CPU, we needed to scale out the classifiers. We empirically determined that a batch-size of 480 tentatively gives the best training performance. So, we distributed the training workload across 480 GPUs so that one GPU can process one image at any given time. We used 80 Summit nodes to run these classifiers with a batch size of 480. We used Horovod [15] for distributed deep learning and its communication. Junqi et al. [18] identified and described the best practices for scaling large-scale deep learning applications on Summit and we utilized some insights from their work.

Mini-Batch Size: We observed that increasing the mini-batch size beyond 480 in the distributed deep-learning results in diminishing validation accuracy. We assigned one CBED image per GPU, which brings the number of nodes to 80 (6 GPU per node).

Learning Rate: We used a similar base learning rate as Imagenet training (0.01) for our training. We also experimented with a slower learning rate without much change in the training performance.

Software Platform: We implemented our classifiers using PyTorch and built our classifiers based on PyTorch-Horovod example. We used Horovod for managing communication in distributed deep learning.

6 Future Work

In this section, we discuss other approaches for dealing with data imbalance that we aim to implement in the next phase of this research.

Using other Performance Metrics. Rather than only depending on traditional classification accuracy, we can explore the following performance measures to get more insight into the model's accuracy.

1. Using the default performance metric (accuracy) and modified loss function might be beneficial for dealing with imbalance. We are using neural net/decision tree-based classifiers. The loss function can be customized based on the frequency of the classes.
2. Confusion Matrix: A breakdown of predictions into correct and incorrect predictions in a tabular format.
3. Precision: Fraction of the correct positive prediction count and the total positive prediction count.
4. Recall: Fraction of the correct positive prediction count and the total positive example count.
5. F1 Score (or F-score): A weighted average of precision and recall.

Composite Algorithm. Decision trees perform well on imbalanced data. For image classification, combining two outstanding classifiers, like CNN and XGBoost [2], might be a good idea. We can use CNN to extract compact numeric features and XGBoost as a classifier [14].

Application of Resampling Techniques. We aim to explore resampling techniques to balance the dataset. There are two main methods to sample examples fairly from imbalanced classes:

1. Adding/generating copies of samples from the under-represented class, which is called over-sampling (e.g., synthetic minority over-sampling technique (SMOTE) [1,7]).
2. Deleting instances from the over-represented class, called under-sampling [17].

7   Conclusion

We developed a deep learning based technique for predicting material's crystal structures and introduced a novel approach for solving class imbalance in scientific datasets. Our contribution will be impactful to the materials science field and provide a new hierarchical classification technique to researchers in any field for tackling overall class imbalance in scientific datasets.

In this paper, we describe our novel approach towards developing a universal classifier for crystallographic space groups. We have identified potential sources and implications of class imbalance in the provided dataset, which provided us with insights into how to tackle the imbalance. To overcome the problems arising from non-geometric projections in the scientific data, we used deep learning models as universal function approximators. We proposed a novel classification technique called Trickle Down Classifier (TDC) to tackle class imbalance in the data. We also proposed re-sampling techniques and a composite of deep and traditional "shallow" machine learning models to solve this problem. We have provided a partial implementation of TDC, which we aim to complete in the next phase of the computation. The CBED dataset is large in volume (500GB), and training a large model such as ResNet50 with this large dataset required using high-performance computing (HPC) resources. We scaled out our deep learning models using 480 V100 GPUs of the Summit supercomputer.

So far, we have achieved promising results with the novel approach. To realize the full potentials of the TDC technique, we aim to complete the entire pipeline and test the completed model with a robust test dataset. We also plan to experiment with bucketing the classes at different levels to get the best performance. To build component models, we used a feature extraction scheme on ResNet50; we also aim to build these models using two other schemes. Moreover, we plan to experiment with other deep learning models such as ResNet18 and VGG16.

Decision tree classifiers such as XGBoost [2] tend to perform better in the presence of an imbalanced dataset. We plan to construct features using a CNN and then train an XGBoost model using these features. However, XGBoost is not very scalable as of yet (some extension runs on single GPU, but it is yet to run on multiple nodes). We aim to overcome this problem by inventing a compute pipeline that can distribute workload across different MPI processes and then combine the results. We also plan to extend our work to address classification problems in other research areas where data sources are heterogeneous and real-time classification is crucial for providing responsive actions (i.e., IoT-based smart built environments) [3,16]. Overall, our work will be useful in handling data imbalance in any research area by providing a novel hierarchical classification technique.

Source and Supplementary Materials

The source code, data and supplementary materials explaining the solution approaches are available at https://bitbucket.org/sajal000/spacegroup.

Acknowledgement. Part of this work has benefited from a collaborative work with our friends and collaborators Shubhankar Gahlot, Rohan Dhamdhere, and Mohammad Alaul Haque Monil.

References

1. Chawla, N.V., Bowyer, K.W., Hall, L.O., Kegelmeyer, W.P.: Smote: synthetic minority over-sampling technique. J. Artif. Intell. Res. **16**, 321–357 (2002)
2. Chen, T., He, T., Benesty, M., Khotilovich, V., Tang, Y.: Xgboost: extreme gradient boosting. R package version (4-2), 1–4 (2015)
3. Dasgupta, A., Handosa, M., Manuel, M., Gračanin, D.: A User-centric design framework for smart built environments. In: Streitz, N., Konomi, S. (eds.) HCII 2019. LNCS, vol. 11587, pp. 124–143. Springer, Cham (2019). https://doi.org/10.1007/978-3-030-21935-2_11

4. Dasgupta, A., Manuel, M., Mansur, R.S., Nowak, N., Gračanin, D.: Towards real time object recognition for context awareness in mixed reality: a machine learning approach. In: 2020 IEEE Conference on Virtual Reality and 3D User Interfaces Abstracts and Workshops (VRW), pp. 262–268. IEEE (2020)
5. Dash, S.: Exploring the landscape of big data analytics through domain-aware algorithm design. Ph.D. thesis, Virginia Tech (2020)
6. Dash, S., Rahman, S., Hines, H.M., Feng, W.C.: Incremental blast: incremental addition of new sequence databases through e-value correction. bioRxiv, p. 476218 (2018)
7. Han, H., Wang, W.-Y., Mao, B.-H.: Borderline-SMOTE: a new over-sampling method in imbalanced data sets learning. In: Huang, D.-S., Zhang, X.-P., Huang, G.-B. (eds.) ICIC 2005. LNCS, vol. 3644, pp. 878–887. Springer, Heidelberg (2005). https://doi.org/10.1007/11538059_91
8. He, K., Zhang, X., Ren, S., Sun, J.: Deep residual learning for image recognition. In: Proceedings of the IEEE Conference on Computer Vision and Pattern Recognition, pp. 770–778 (2016)
9. Kaufmann, K., et al.: Paradigm shift in electron-based crystallography via machine learning. arXiv preprint arXiv:1902.03682 (2019)
10. Kaufmann, K., Zhu, C., Rosengarten, A.S., Maryanovsky, D., Harrington, T.J., Marin, E., Vecchio, K.S.: Crystal symmetry determination in electron diffraction using machine learning. Science **367**(6477), 564–568 (2020)
11. Kaufmann, K., Zhu, C., Rosengarten, A.S., Vecchio, K.S.: Deep neural network enabled space group identification in EBSD. Microsc. Microanal. **26**(3), 447–457 (2020)
12. Laanait, N., Yin, J., Borisevich, A.: Towards a universal classifier for crystallographic space groups (2020). https://smc-datachallenge.ornl.gov/challenges-2020/challenge-2-2020/
13. Liang, S., Srikant, R.: Why deep neural networks for function approximation? arXiv preprint arXiv:1610.04161 (2016)
14. Ren, X., Guo, H., Li, S., Wang, S., Li, J.: A novel image classification method with CNN-XGBoost model. In: Kraetzer, C., Shi, Y.-Q., Dittmann, J., Kim, H.J. (eds.) IWDW 2017. LNCS, vol. 10431, pp. 378–390. Springer, Cham (2017). https://doi.org/10.1007/978-3-319-64185-0_28
15. Sergeev, A., Del Balso, M.: Horovod: fast and easy distributed deep learning in tensorflow. arXiv preprint arXiv:1802.05799 (2018)
16. Tasooji, R., Dasgupta, A., Gračanin, D., LaGro, M., Matković, K.: A multi-purpose IOT framework for smart built environments. In: Proceedings of the 2018 Winter Simulation Conference, pp. 4240–4241. IEEE Press (2018)
17. Yen, S.J., Lee, Y.S.: Cluster-based under-sampling approaches for imbalanced data distributions. Expert Syst. Appl. **36**(3), 5718–5727 (2009)
18. Yin, J., et al.: Strategies to deploy and scale deep learning on the summit supercomputer. In: 2019 IEEE/ACM Third Workshop on Deep Learning on Supercomputers (DLS), pp. 84–94. IEEE (2019)

The Macro Impacts of Micro-Climates on the Energy Consumption of Urban Buildings

Samantha Inneo, Daniel Wadler, Jack Schneiderhan, and Ronald Estevez[(✉)]

Stevens Institute of Technology, Hoboken, NJ 07030, USA
restevez@stevens.edu

Abstract. This paper addresses Challenge 3 of the SMC data challenge by leveraging data-driven tools to understand the relationships between our built environment and nature, and how this relationship impacts energy consumption. It presents detailed results to the research questions posed, along with the rationale for the tools used and limitations of the developed solutions.

Keywords: Urban micro-climate · Energy analysis · Spatial visualization

1 Introduction

From the urban heat islands (UHI) of New York City [1], to Chicago's notorious wind-tunnel effect [2], the adverse impact of urban morphology on local climate is undeniable. Recent studies [3] have uncovered links to extreme weather events such as severe thunderstorms, and heat/cold waves. Despite growing concern [4,5], scientific understanding of this phenomenon - both cause and effect - remains limited [6]. This is in part due to the modeling complexities involved, sometimes requiring exascale computing resources [7]. By leveraging recent advances in data science and machine learning, this paper presents a computationally inexpensive, data-driven understanding of the coupling between nature and urban infrastructure. A survey of the literature is discussed in the following section to highlight previous advancements in this research area.

2 Literature Review

The coupling between urban climate and energy has long been the subject of research interests. Vallati et al. [8] for example explored the impact of urban climate on the heating/cooling demand of standalone vs. urban building types. Their findings indicated that urban buildings required notably less energy for heating. This may be explained by the urban heat island (UHI) effect - a byproduct of the pervasive use of heat-absorbing materials such as steel and concrete.

© Springer Nature Switzerland AG 2020
J. Nichols et al. (Eds.): SMC 2020, CCIS 1315, pp. 479–490, 2020.
https://doi.org/10.1007/978-3-030-63393-6_32

This idea served as the basis for work conducted by Arifwidodo et al. [9] which found strong correlations between the presence of UHIs and increased electricity expenses. Subsequent research focused on the impact of urban morphology [11], climatic variations [10], and population trends [12], all of which found correlations between urban morphology, local climate gradients and energy consumption patterns.

From a modeling perspective, researchers at the Oak Ridge National Laboratory [13] conducted studies focused on how variations across weather datasets impact micro-climate simulations, and ultimately energy consumption forecasts. New et al. [7] then leveraged discrete building energy modeling at urban-scale to inform on the dynamics between urban form and climate. While representing significant progress, the computationally intensive nature of these research efforts (some requiring the world's most powerful supercomputer at the time [7]) deter from widespread use. This presents an opportunity to develop computationally inexpensive alternatives. To this end, this paper leverages building energy consumption as an alternative lens through which to investigate the complex multi-scale coupling between nature and urban infrastructure. Specifically, it makes a contribution by investigating the role urban buildings play in shaping the climate around them through the data-driven analysis of variations in their annual energy consumption.

The remainder of the paper details how this was achieved and is structured as follows. Section 3 begins with an overview of the scope of study and an understanding for the type of data used. Section 4 follows with detailed solutions to the research questions posed. It details the exact approaches used, discusses the results and highlights their limitations. Section 5 concludes with a discussion of the broader impacts and future potential of the presented work. Source code and a comprehensive set of all generated visualizations and animations have been open-sourced, and is accessible via our Github page (link in Appendix).

3   Initial Data Collection and Processing

Generated by the Oak Ridge National Laboratory (ORNL) [14], the primary dataset describes the weather, buildings, and energy consumption of the "Chicago Loop" - the second largest commercial business district (CBD) in the US, located in downtown Chicago. The dataset is composed of three sub-datasets, the first of which (herein called *Building-Data*) contained building IDs, longitude and latitude coordinates and structural height for 334 buildings (see Fig. 1a). The second dataset (herein called *Energy-Data*) contained the annual energy consumption of each building. Finally, the third dataset (herein called *Weather-Data*), provided high resolution, 90-meter simulated weather data for the year 2015, at 15-minute intervals (with known gaps toward the end of each month). In addition to the provided datasets, our team sourced additional open datasets to strengthen our data pipeline. Namely, we obtained a building footprint dataset [15] to aid with building visualizations, and an energy benchmarking dataset from the Chicago Data Portal [16] which provided Energy-Star ratings of each building.

Combining our external datasets to *Building-Data* proved rather challenging. Despite having similar building references, the long/lat coordinates differed significantly between datasets. By spatially analyzing our data using the Folium python library [17], we made a fascinating finding. We discovered that the building coordinates provided in *Building-Data* utilized a Lambert Conformal Conic projection (with 90-meter resolution grids). Consequently, the coordinates in *Building-Data* referenced grid cell centroids, as opposed to real world building locations. To address this problem, our team scripted a nearest neighbor algorithm which computed and assign the nearest real world building (using Euclidean distance) to each centriod location. Our approach was validated by randomly sampling nearest neighbor assignments and visually verifying them using two popular web tools, namely Google Maps [18] and Koordinates [19].

(a) Building footprint visualization   (b) Building overlaid with weather sensors

Fig. 1. Data exploration of building (yellow) and weather (red) dataset. (Color figure online)

Exploring the *Weather-Data* dataset revealed a total of 880 sensor points. By combining this data with *Building-Data*, we discovered that the weather data covered a land area about twice the size of that occupied by our buildings (see Fig. 1b). We narrowed the scope of our weather data to match that of our buildings in terms of land area (please refer to Appendix for more details). We created a local SQLite database for the resulting dataset to enable faster data retrieval. With respect to *Energy-Data*, we found data parsing to be particularly challenging because the dataset contained extraneous data in the form of null values. This was addressed using standard data cleaning practices.

3.1   Data Visualization Pipeline

We developed a visualization pipeline (see Fig. 2) to streamline the spatial visualization of our data and results. For any visualization task, we first extracted the necessary WKT (Well-known text) data contained within our SQLite database and transformed it into a shapefile using Mapshaper, an online geographic information system (GIS) service. Next, we converted the shapefile into a Python friendly GeoJSON file format and visualized it using the Kepler.gl python library. In terms of hardware, our team relied on personal laptops to execute the pipeline, the most capable of which had a Core i7 processor and 16GB of RAM. Having briefly discussed the dataset, the next section presents the research questions asked of this dataset, along with our detailed responses for each.

Fig. 2. Data visualization pipeline

4   Research Questions

4.1   Are There Interesting Variations in the Weather and Building Energy Use Data for the Geographic Area?

Approach: Using our visualization pipeline, we mapped all building footprints against multiple energy and weather variables. Color was used as a relative measure for comparisons between buildings, with lighter color shades representing lower use/intensity, and darker shades representing high use/intensity. This gradient-based, color-to-intensity relationship is maintained across all visualizations presented in this paper. For visualizations involving weather, we developed a multithreaded Python script that efficiently summarized *Weather-Data* into daily descriptive statistics (including standard deviation, variance, and mean) and saved the output as a JSON file. We then narrowed the features of our weather dataset using personal intuition. Although approaches such as Principal Component Analysis (PCA) are best suited for feature selection tasks, we did not feel comfortable using it owing to a limited understanding of how it works. This represents an area for improvement in future work. Based on our intuition, we selected temperature, wind speed, long-wave radiation, and relative humidity as the features of interest for this work. To visualize potential micro-climatic effects, we further narrowed our scope to only days which displayed significant variance across our selected features. This was motivated purely by computational expense as an exhaustive exploration would have proved computationally infeasible given our limited computational resources.

Variations in Building Energy Use: Our analysis revealed several variations across both energy use and weather. An interesting trend - which we termed *"two halves of Chicago"* - emerged when we compared both electricity usage and intensity across the entire building stock. According to Fig. 3a, buildings in the northern half generally used more electricity compared to the south. This relationship is, however, reversed with respect to electricity intensity (see Fig. 3b). This implies the existence of two unique urban morphologies, with the north having predominantly tall buildings (hence lower electricity intensity), and the south having relatively shorter, less efficient buildings. Visualizing building heights across the dataset confirmed our suspicions. Please refer to our Github page (link in Appendix) for a more comprehensive set of all generated visualizations for this problem.

(a) Total electricity use   (b) Total electricity intensity

Fig. 3. Comparing relative electricity use and intensity - darker shades represent greater use/intensity

Variations in Weather: Figure 4 illustrates weather gradients observed across Temperature (F), Wind speed (m/s), Long-wave radiation (W/m2) and Relative humidity (%). We discovered that weather gradients typically emerged from one predominant direction and spread across the map. From these plots, it is evident that micro-climatic effects exist and it would be interesting to apply machine learning algorithms in future work to recognize patterns in these variations and begin to correlate them directly to features of the urban morphology.

Limitations of solution: Our analysis relied heavily on physical building variations (e.g. building height) owing to a lack of adequate granularity in our energy

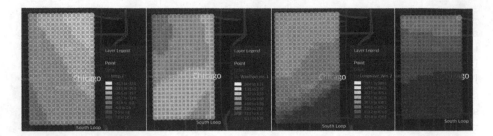

Fig. 4. From left to right - temperature, wind speed, long-wave radiation, and relative humidity visualizations. Darker shades represent greater intensity.

dataset. Additionally, the reduced scope of our weather analysis limited our findings. Future iterations will look to leverage high-performance computing (HPC) resources along with advanced data structures such as HDF5 to enable efficient, detailed analysis. We hypothesize that leveled mappings of annual weather data at 15-minute intervals with energy use data of equal resolution will yield very interesting results regarding the connection between building energy use and micro-climates.

4.2   Which Buildings in the Study Are Most Sensitive to Weather Effects?

Approach: Addressing this question required an understanding of energy use variation across short term events (i.e rain) and seasons (i.e. winter). However, a major shortcoming of our dataset is that it aggregated energy use over an annual cycle, hence it lacked the granularity we needed. This presented an opportunity for "out of the box" thinking. Our resulting approach made one key assumption - that the ratio between heating and cooling energy for all buildings is constant, irrespective of building size. While improbable, we concluded that for any building to violate this relationship, it must be because its sensitivity to weather forced it to use more cooling or heating energy than the "normal ratio" requires.

To test this hypothesis, we divided each building's HVAC consumption based on end use (heating and cooling) and plotted them against each other. Surprisingly, our assumption was indeed correct. Figure 5 (leftmost plot) shows a strong linear relationship between heating and cooling across the entire building stock. Note that this accounts for all building sizes. It also revealed some weather-sensitive outliers. By plotting the building footprints of the outliers, we noticed that the majority of the outliers were located in the bottom half of our map (see middle plot of Fig. 5). This underscored the impact of urban morphologies on energy use. For deeper insights, we then combined our findings with the energy audit dataset we had sourced externally. This revealed that several of the buildings in our outlier set had low Energy-Star ratings (lighter color shades), further strengthening our conclusions that these buildings are most sensitive to weather (see rightmost plot in Fig. 5).

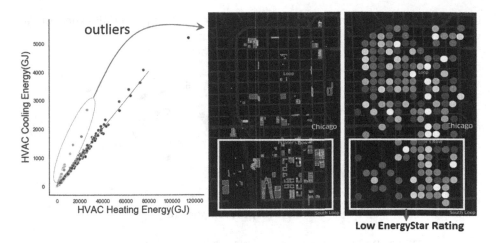

Fig. 5. Identifying buildings most sensitive to weather

Limitations of solution: Although weather sensitivity is indeed one of the potential drivers behind the presented results, it is also likely that our findings are the result of inefficient/faulty HVAC systems in these buildings. Should granular energy data become available in the future, our approach to this problem will be to identify days with extreme weather conditions and compare each building's energy usage on these days to a derived building baseline. This will enable us to perform sensitivity analysis to identify buildings with strong sensitivities.

4.3   How Can the Data Best Be Divided into Subsets for Meaningful Analysis and Visualization?

"Two Halves of Chicago": As highlighted earlier, the Chicago Loop can be separated into two halves based on urban morphology, with the north end comprising mainly of high rise buildings and the south having a comparatively shorter cityscape. Buildings in the north had lower energy intensity compared to the south. Energy intensity is an efficiency metric measured by dividing total annual energy consumed by a building (in gigajoules) by the building's total gross floor area. We hypothesize that given granular building energy use data, meaningful micro-climate analysis can be performed to compare the performance of similar buildings across the geographic divide.

Unsupervised Hierarchical Clustering: We also discovered natural clusters within the dataset using the Hierarchical Density-Based Spatial Clustering of Applications with Noise (HDBSCAN) algorithm, an unsupervised learning approach. This was motivated by the fact that energy consumption data is typically noisy, hence using an algorithm suited to such data was crucial. Additionally, the algorithm treats cluster size as a hyper-parameter, minimizing the chance of induced clustering bias. Using this algorithm, we were able to segment our dataset into 8 main clusters as illustrated in Fig. 6. Although we did not explore further with this approach, we found it to have a lot of potential, especially as we introduce additional datasets to the data pipeline.

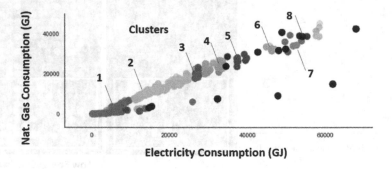

Fig. 6. Building clusters generated using unsupervised learning

Extracting Workdays and Types of Buildings: During our preliminary data analysis, we explored the idea of segmenting based on building function. Moreover, we were interested in sub-setting energy output according to work-days, weekends and holidays. We believed this to be a good line of inquiry given that the Chicago Loop is a commercial business district. This idea motivated additional interest into further sub-setting based on building zoning type (i.e residential or commercial). Although we managed to source relevant datasets to enable all of these, we eventually abandoned these efforts owing to the lack of energy data granularity. The possibility of revisiting this idea using detailed energy data, however, presents a promising avenue for future efforts.

4.4   How Does Energy Use in Each Building Change Throughout the Year?

Approach: Our analysis revealed a clear variation between the energy consumed during the winter months (requiring heating) and the summer months (requiring cooling). It should be noted that Fall and Spring seasons were neglected in this study. On average, buildings in the dataset were found to use 15 times more energy for heating than cooling. Given that heating primarily occurs in winter, we conclude that energy usage peaks during the colder months. We followed this by calculating the normalized weather energy use intensity (EUI) as well as the average energy demand per heating/cooling day. We also computed the average energy demand per heating/cooling day, illustrated in Fig. 7.

Analysis: Figure 7 reveals a trivial, yet important trend - the larger the build-ing, the more energy it uses for heating/cooling (left plot). Additionally, we compared energy intensities of heating (natural gas) and cooling (electricity) (see right plot). From this, we discovered that not only do high rise buildings use comparatively more natural gas than electricity (measured in gigajoules),

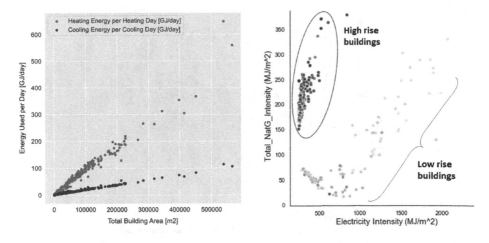

Fig. 7. Energy demand per heating/cooling day(left) and EUI plot (right)

but they tend to be more efficient (hence the tighter cluster of dark colored points in Fig. 7). In contrast, not only did low rise buildings rely more on electricity than natural gas, but most importantly, they exhibited irregular trends with respect to efficiency (see larger spread of lighter colored circles). This was a very interesting finding and potentially points to high rise building benefiting from newer construction and HVAC systems.

4.5 How Is Energy Use Different During the Coldest/Hottest Months as Compared to During Those of Less Extreme Temperature?

Based on the findings presented in Fig. 7, we assume that the coldest months have the highest energy usage, while the hottest months have comparatively lower energy usage (measured in gigajoules). Despite this, the months of extreme temperature will still likely exhibit higher energy usage than in the more temperate months. An analysis of energy used for heating and cooling compared to the overall energy used revealed that some buildings used as much as 69% of their annual energy on heating and cooling (see Fig. 8). These particular buildings will see a significant decrease in the least extreme months.

4.6 Are There Any Interesting Visualizations that Illustrate the Changing Dynamics of the Simulated Urban Environment?

Figure 9 illustrates the urban heat island effect projected over a 3D representation of the Chicago Loop. This figure provides a number of key takeaways. It visually confirms the morphological differences between the two halves of Chicago. But more importantly, it highlights man-made heat zones. Each building is shaded based on its heat rejection energy data. As we can deduce, a

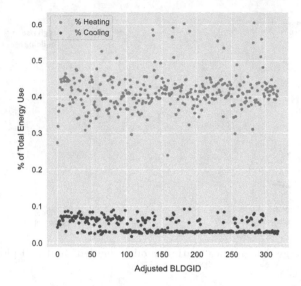

Fig. 8. Breakdown of HVAC energy use over total energy expenditure

heat-zone emerges between the high rise buildings in the north, in stark contrast to the south buildings. Future work will look to leverage wind directional patterns to observe impacts on temperature gradients across the Loop.

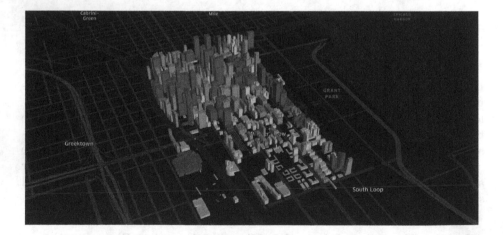

Fig. 9. Visualizing the urban heat island effect using heat rejection data

5   Conclusion

Using detailed data analysis and visualization, the results presented in this paper shed light on some of the complex relationships between nature and urban infrastructure in the downtown Chicago area. Computationally inexpensive in nature, the approach used, along with its findings serve to provide an exploratory step prior to more detailed energy modeling and analysis. It also sets the stage for use of high performance computing resources with more granular data to uncover even more hidden insights and relationships.

Acknowledgments. The authors would like to acknowledge the Pinnacle Scholar Program at the Stevens Institute of Technology for their support of this work. The authors would also like to thank Dr. Philip Odonkor for his mentorship and support of this work.

Support for DOI 10.13139/ORNLNCCS/1619243 dataset is provided by the U.S. Department of Energy, project SMC2020 under Contract DE-AC05-00OR22725. Project SMC2020 used resources of the Oak Ridge Leadership Computing Facility at Oak Ridge National Laboratory, which is supported by the Office of Science of the U.S. Department of Energy under Contract No. DE-AC05-00OR22725.

APPENDIX

This bounding box used to graphically bound our weather data was developed using the following coordinates: (41.858452, -87.641479), (41.858452, -87.617188), (41.891693, -87.641479), (41.891693, -87.617188).

Source code and comprehensive set of visualizations and animations have been open-sourced and can be accessed via our Github page.

Github Link - https://bit.ly/3hGEwo0

References

1. Bornstein, R.D.: Observations of the urban heat island effect in New York City. J. Appl. Meteorol. **7**(4), 575–582 (1968)
2. Kijewski-Correa, T., et al.: Validating wind-induced response of tall buildings: synopsis of the Chicago full-scale monitoring program. J. Struct. Eng. **132**(10), 1509–1523 (2006)
3. Brookhaven National Laboratory: Predicting urban and coastal microclimates. (2019). Retrieved 23 July 2020. https://www.bnl.gov/newsroom/news.php?a=213156
4. Jiang, Y., Han, X., Shi, T., Song, D.: Microclimatic impact analysis of multi-dimensional indicators of streetscape fabric in the medium spatial zone. Int. J. Environ. Res. Public Health **16**(6), 952 (2019)
5. Chapman, S., Watson, J.E., Salazar, A., Thatcher, M., McAlpine, C.A.: The impact of urbanization and climate change on urban temperatures: a systematic review. Landscape Ecol. **32**(10), 1921–1935 (2017)
6. Yang, Q., Huang, X., Li, J.: Assessing the relationship between surface urban heat islands and landscape patterns across climatic zones in China. Sci. Rep. **7**, 9337 (2017). https://doi.org/10.1038/s41598-017-09628-w
7. New, J.R., et al.: Automatic building energy model creation (AutoBEM) for urban-scale energy modeling and assessment of value propositions for electric utilities. Oak Ridge National Lab. (ORNL), Oak Ridge, TN (United States) (2018)

8. Toparlar, Y., Blocken, B., Maiheu, B., van Heijst, G.J.: Impact of urban microclimate on summertime building cooling demand: a parametric analysis for Antwerp, Belgium. Applied Energy **228**, 852–872 (2018)
9. Arifwidodo, S., Chandrasiri, O.: Urban heat island and household energy consumption in Bangkok, Thailand. Energy Procedia **79**(1), 189–194 (2015)
10. Yang, J., et al.: Local climate zone ventilation and urban land surface temperatures: towards a performance-based and wind-sensitive planning proposal in megacities. Sustain. Cities Soc. **47**, 101487 (2019)
11. Allegrini, J., Dorer, V., Carmeliet, J.: Influence of morphologies on the microclimate in urban neighbourhoods. J. Wind Eng. Ind. Aerodyn. **1**(144), 108–117 (2015)
12. Fu, K.S., Allen, M.R., Archibald, R.K.: Evaluating the relationship between the population trends, prices, heat waves, and the demands of energy consumption in cities. Sustain. **7**(11), 15284–15301 (2015)
13. Bhandari, M.S., Shrestha, S.S., New, J.R., Allen, M.R.: Comparison of microclimate simulated weather data to ASHRAE clear sky model and measured data. Oak Ridge National Lab. (ORNL), Oak Ridge, TN (United States) (2017)
14. Dumas, M., New, J.: Chicago microclimate and building energy use data. United States: N. p. (2020). https://doi.org/10.13139/ORNLNCCS/1619243
15. Oak Ridge National Laboratory: Chicago Loop. (2020). Retrieved 23 July 2020. https://evenstar.ornl.gov/autobem/chicago/
16. Chicago Data Portal. Retrieved 23 July 2020. https://data.cityofchicago.org/
17. Folium. Retrieved 23 July 2020. https://python-visualization.github.io/folium/
18. Google Map. Retrieved 24 July 2020. https://www.google.com/maps
19. Koordinates. Retrieved 24 July 2020. https://koordinates.com/

A Framework for Linking Urban Traffic and Vehicle Emissions in Smart Cities

Clark Hathaway[✉] and Sebastian Mobo

University of Tennessee, Knoxville, TN, USA
chathawa@vols.utk.edu, smobo@vols.utk.edu

Abstract. This paper tackles Challenge 4, 'Computational Urban Data Analytics', of the 2020 Smoky Mountains Conference Data Challenge. Specifically, we design and implement an analysis and visualization framework to study traffic emissions across time and space in a urban setting. We use our framework to qualitatively and quantitatively analyze the influence of urban layout on traffic flows in the Chicago Loop area. Our findings allow us to investigate the relationships between traffic congestion, building distributions, and vehicle emissions. Insights from our framework can provide communities with decision-making tools for urban design and smart cities.

Keywords: Vehicle positions · Road network · Building footprints · Vehicle-building mapping

1 Introduction

Urban traffic flows are complex phenomena influenced by a diverse range of factors, such as road network topology, the spatial layout of buildings within the urban environment, as well as human habits and patterns, among others. These traffic flows, in turn, not only consume large amounts of energy, but also impact their local environment by emitting exhaust heat and gases into their surroundings. However, accurately modelling these relationships can be challenging, as it requires many disparate data sets to be not only reconciled, but unified with an interdisciplinary approach. Nonetheless, we believe that an effective solution for fusing these separate data sets into a single coherent analysis of traffic patterns could help guide efforts towards reducing traffic emissions and improving traffic energy efficiency.

Each year, Oak Ridge National Laboratory (ORNL) and the Smoky Mountains Computational Sciences and Engineering Conference (SMC) publish a series of data science challenges, known as the SMC Data Challenge, as an open competition in which large data sets are sponsored and students can register to submit a paper after researching a given challenge. In exploring Challenge 4, *'Computational Urban Data Analytics'* [2], we develop a methodology to understand the relationship between traffic patterns and emissions. Specifically, we use analysis and visualization techniques to study traffic emissions across time

© Springer Nature Switzerland AG 2020
J. Nichols et al. (Eds.): SMC 2020, CCIS 1315, pp. 491–502, 2020.
https://doi.org/10.1007/978-3-030-63393-6_33

and space; we analyze the influence of urban layout on traffic flows; and ultimately we combine these insights to investigate the relationships between traffic congestion, building distributions, and vehicle emissions.

A key problem we are tasked with solving in this challenge is reconciling disparities between data sources. These differences must be addressed to respond to the questions posed by the challenge authors, characterize patterns in the data, and correlate emissions with other variables. In answering the questions set forth by the challenge authors, we hypothesize that if we can develop a useful metric of traffic congestion, we can show a correlation between congestion and emissions. During our research, we develop a suite of data analysis, visualization, and validation tools to aide in the preparation and analysis of the originally provided datasets. The data preparation process can then be universally applied to similarly-structured data.

Through statistical analysis, we test for a correlation between measured traffic congestion and emissions data, and show the existence of a statistically-significant relationship; however, we also reveal inherent limitations to this type of analysis, which can be explored and accounted for in future work.

The rest of this paper is organized as follows: Sects. 2 and 3 characterize the data sets provided to us and outline the preprocessing techniques applied to prepare them for our statistical analysis, respectively; Sect. 4 discusses the methods and models we developed to relate the data; Sect. 5 provides a qualitative and quantitative analysis of the emissions heat map and the vehicle-building mappings when compared to emissions quantities; and Sect. 6 summarizes our methods, the artifacts produced during the research, and our results.

2   Characterization of Original Data

Table 1 summarizes the original data provided as part of Challenge 4 together with the data characteristics (i.e., spatial layout, sampling rate, sampling frequency, and description). For all of these datasets, the region of interest is, specifically, the Chicago Loop area, which is also the central business district for the city of Chicago.

2.1   Traffic Data

The original vehicle positions are obtained from the TRANSIMS traffic simulator [5], which incorporates a fine-grained microsimulator for modelling the movement of individual vehicles. The simulation is run for approximately 24 h, and snapshots are taken at 30-second intervals to record the position of every active vehicle as a *(road, offset, direction)* triplet, where a road corresponds to an edge in the road network and a unique series of line segments in our road network dataset (see Sect. 2.3), while an offset and direction specify a point along those line segments.

The challenge organizers performed an additional pre-processing step before publishing the dataset. The vehicle positions were converted to Universal Mercator Transform (UTM) coordinate pairs by interpolating along roads, as in [1].

Table 1. Description of the original datasets available for the data challenge.

Dataset	Spatial Layout	Sampling Rate	Sample Period	Description
Traffic	Points	30 s	24 h	Sampled vehicle positions from the TRANSIMS traffic simulator over the course of a day
Emissions	Per-Road	Hourly	8 days	Hourly aggregated emission totals from the MOVES-Matrix emissions simulator over multiple days
Roads	Line Segments	N/A	N/A	Sequences of line segments describing local roads
Buildings	Polygons	N/A	N/A	Polygons describing local building footprints

These coordinates were then included alongside the raw simulation output as an alternative representation of vehicle positions.

Notably, this simulation reflects commutes *to* work, but not commutes *from* work; this asymmetry impacts our analysis, as discussed in Sect. 5.2.

2.2   Emissions Data

The original emissions data are generated using the MOVES-Matrix simulator [3], with data spanning two separate simulations: one covering a morning commute on January 9, 2017, and another covering full 24-hour spans from July 4 to July 10, 2017. This data contains measurements of heat emitted from vehicles, simulated on the level of road segments and aggregated on an hourly basis. For our analysis we only use total aggregated emissions for each link and hour, recorded in the dataset in millions of British Thermal Units (MMBtu).

Similarly to the traffic simulation, the emissions simulations only reflect commutes *to* work, and not commutes *from* work.

2.3   Road Network

A dataset covering local roads (also referred to as 'links') within the area of interest was made available by the challenge organizers. In this dataset, each road is described as a sequence of connected line segments, with each segment's endpoints represented as latitude-longitude coordinate pairs. A unique *link ID* is also given to each road, which is used to associate vehicles and emission quantities to individual roads.

2.4   Building Footprints

The building footprints are based on the Microsoft's US Building Footprints dataset [4]. This dataset consists of building footprints identified from satellite imagery using a neural network and transformed into simple polygons in a two-step process. The full set of building footprints identified within the state of

Illinois was pre-filtered by the challenge organizers to include only buildings within the region of interest, producing a final dataset containing approximately 2,600 buildings.

3   Data Preparation

The original traffic simulation data came with incorrect or unfeasible locations for some vehicles. We processed the data to make sure that the vehicles locations are all realistic in the context of our study. To this end, we implemented an algorithmic approach that allowed us to (1) gain an understanding of where vehicles were located at various points in time and (2) adjust those vehicles with unrealistic locations to realistic ones.

The approach consists of two steps. First, by overlaying the vehicle positions on a map of the area, it appears that there are clusters of vehicles in unrealistic locations such as water or railways. Because of this, we use a distance threshold to measure how many vehicles throughout the entire data set are disassociated with their specified link. We set our visualization scripts to render plots as images with resolutions of 400×550 pixels, so we use 30 pixels as the threshold to determine if a vehicle is too far from its link. We apply this threshold to the distance from the link to the vehicle on both the x and y axis, but not to the Euclidean distance. The reason for only evaluating distances on the x and y axes separately is that we also check for coordinates outside the bounds of the image. This algorithm determines that there are no instances of x-coordinates that are out of bounds, while 16.5% of entries have a y-coordinate where this is the case. On further inspection, instances where a coordinate's distance from the link is beyond the given tolerance are almost exclusively in the y-coordinate column in the simulation data. Only 1.2% of the entries have a x-coordinate that exceeded the threshold, while 48.0% have a y-coordinate that did so.

The second part of our approach is the adjustment of the y-coordinates. Because x-coordinates appear to be generally reliable, the process we use to resolve this discrepancy between the vehicle coordinates and the coordinates of their associated link using as follows:

1. If we consider each link a line that naturally extends infinitely in both directions, we assume that the vehicles should be aligned in a way that places them on this line.
2. We use the x-coordinates to compute new y-coordinates such that the new ordered pair obeys the slope and y-intercept derived for each link's line interpretation.
3. In instances where a vehicle's x-coordinate is not between the link's endpoints, we move the x-coordinate to the nearest endpoint so that the new y-coordinate is not be above or below the endpoints. This is necessary as there naturally will be links that are nearly vertical so an x-coordinate beyond the bounding box of the link would project the y-coordinate even farther away in some cases.

As we believe this new data set is more reliable in the examination of traffic patterns, we base our vehicle-to-building mapping algorithm and final correlation analysis on this new data as discussed in Sects. 4.2 and 5.2, respectively.

4 Methodology

As outlined in the challenge, there are often inherent disparities in the sources of large data, and so our methods in addressing these questions ultimately aim to produce associations, or mappings, between the datasets we analyze. These procedures allow us to relate the data to overcome these disparities and produce meaningful analyses of the relationships between variables present across this data.

4.1 Simplification of Building Data

We simplify our original building dataset by reducing each building into an sequential ID, bounding-box, centroid, and area. Aside from speeding up the vehicle-building mapping methods described in Sect. 4.2 and enabling the building emission accumulation described in Sect. 4.4, this also allows us to store buildings in a flat, tabular representation (such as a CSV file).

4.2 Vehicle-Building Mapping

To study how traffic emissions impact nearby buildings, we adapt an agent-based approach [1], in which individual vehicle agents are mapped to nearby buildings. Mapping methods used in such an approach must be efficient and scalable with respect to both agent and building count: for example, our data includes over 100,000 total agents in an area containing more than 2,600 buildings. The original cited approach uses a quadtree-based method to recursively subdivide the mapping region into small cells based on a splitting criteria; our method instead organizes the buildings within the mapping region into a k-d tree, where each building is keyed by the centroid of its footprint, and then uses this tree to efficiently search for the building closest to each agent.

Our implementations of both methods output sets of (vehicle, building, distance) tuples, with one tuple for each vehicle. While developing this implementation, we also developed tools for visualizing these mappings and identifying buildings with many associated vehicles; one such visualization is shown in Fig. 1.

We found that the k-d tree method is slightly more straightforward to implement, and also avoids an issue with the quadtree-based method, where buildings that are seemingly close to an agent are separated from it by unfortunate cell boundary placement and thus excluded from consideration for mapping. Our method, in contrast, always finds the nearest building for each agent, though perhaps at the cost of more comparisons; this has not turned out to be an issue for our dataset size. Both methods were readily parallelizable, and experiments with our data indicate that they have roughly similar performance at our scale.

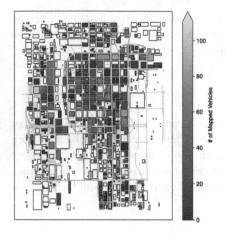

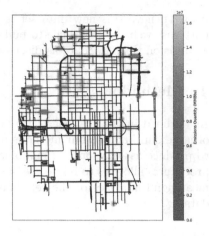

Fig. 1. Distribution of vehicle mapping counts at 10:00. Unfilled outlines indicate buildings with no mapped vehicles.

Fig. 2. Radiated emissions computed from July 04, 2017 simulated emissions data.

4.3 Dispersion of Traffic Emissions

The emissions data, as described in Sect. 2, is organized with slightly different spatial granularity compared to our other data sets: in our data, emissions are only associated with entire road links, whereas other data (such as buildings) are described using geographic coordinates. Therefore, we align the emissions data with our vehicle, building, and road data by discretizing our region of interest into cells and computing emission quantities for each cell: cells containing links are treated as being sources that add emissions to nearby cells, and the strength of these added emissions are inversely proportional to the squared distance between cells. This process models the dispersal of concentrated heat emissions from individual roads into the surrounding environment, and a visualization of the resulting heat maps is shown in Fig. 2.

With these heatmaps in hand, we can then associate emissions with other features in our dataset, such as buildings, for further analysis.

Using these generated heatmaps to begin to characterize patterns in emissions concentrations, we notice there is no obvious variation between different days in the data. When looking at heatmaps for a given hour on two separate days under scrutiny, any variation that exists continues to be unaccounted for visually. Therefore, we also use a metric to determine how different any two heatmaps are, to investigate this numerically.

In this procedure, we consider each heatmap as a vector of emissions quantities, and compute the dot products between pairs of heatmaps that are generated using data from the same hour, but across different days. Numerically, this showed there is no difference between any two heatmaps with this criteria. Figure 3 shows the visual comparison we did prior to developing this procedure.

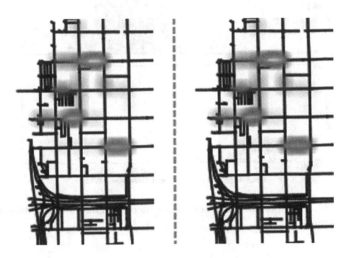

Fig. 3. Comparison of emission quantities at 10:00, between July 04 (left) and July 06 (right)

What this seems to indicate is that the simulator is configured so that it does not consider random variations in traffic flows, vehicle density, or individual vehicles' exhaust output.

4.4 Association of Emissions to Buildings

In order to measure the local impact of traffic emissions on buildings in our region of interest, we first compute a per-building *emission total* by summing radiated heat emissions from nearby roads, as taken from the heat maps developed in Sect. 4.3, over the footprint of each building. We then derive *emission concentrations* by dividing each building's emission total by the area of its footprint; this accounts for large buildings with more space for accumulating emissions. For the purposes of our analysis in Sect. 5.2, we focused on studying emission concentrations rather than non-normalized emission totals.

From these metrics, we identify a clearly distinguishable morning commute period lasting from 08:00 to 11:59. As shown in Fig. 4, emission concentrations for this commute period consistently follow a clear log-normal distribution, with median concentrations close to $10^{3.6}$ MMBtu/m^2; meanwhile, emission concentrations for other times of the day tend to be much lower, with medians less than or equal to approximately $10^{1.1}$ MMBtu/m^2. We could not find an equivalent evening commute period, though this is likely because our simulated data does not include any work-to-home commutes.

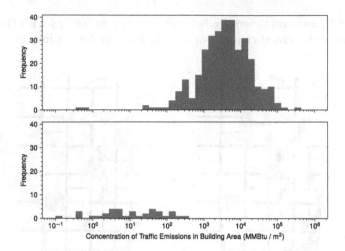

Fig. 4. Distribution of per-building emission concentrations, measured at 10:00 (top) and 17:00 (bottom)

Figure 5 shows the aggregated distribution of emission concentrations over an entire day, with vertical dashed lines indicating median concentration values for individual hours of the day. The morning commute period can be seen not only as the sharp peak near 10^4 MMBtu/m^2, but also in the tight cluster of medians centered in the same location. On the other hand, the more spread out group of medians between 10^0 and 10^2 MMBtu/m^2 correspond to data taken from most other hours of the day.

Interestingly, the data for 12:00 (represented by the lone dashed line near 10^3 MMBtu/m^2 in Fig. 5) proves to be an exception: while emissions at this time are typically much higher than in the other non-morning hours, it nonetheless has lower emission concentrations than those seen during the morning commute period. This uniqueness will be discussed further in Sect. 5.2.

5   Results and Discussion

5.1   Qualitative Analysis of Emission Heatmaps

For a typical day within our emissions data, activity seems to be centered around the hours of 07:00 to 12:00, with very little to no activity for all other hours. During these hours, high-activity areas appear to be concentrated in a region in the west, with hot spots appearing in the northeast and southeast, as shown by Fig. 2.

To quantitatively analyze the spatial correlation between emissions and vehicle distributions, we develop a visualization that overlaps the heatmap with the mapping of vehicle occupants to buildings based on data with the same time. The results show there is increased vehicle exhaust around the buildings that had a

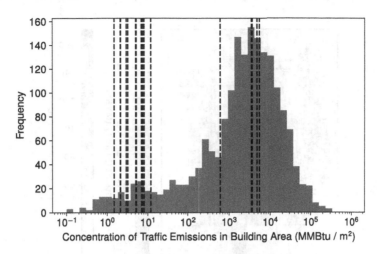

Fig. 5. Distribution of per-building emission concentrations across the entire day; each vertical dotted line indicates the median concentration (or equivalently, the mean of $\log_{10}[\text{concentration}]$) for one hour of the day.

greater count of mappings. Figure 6 shows several areas of high occupant density that also show increased emissions. To measure how strong this correlation was, we develop a statistical approach that will be explored in Sect. 5.2.

5.2   Quantitative Analysis of Per-Building Emission Concentrations

For our analysis of emission concentrations, we develop linear regression models predicting building emission concentrations from transformed and normalized vehicle counts. To be specific, our models take the form:

$$\hat{y} = \beta_1 \sqrt{\frac{x_i}{A_i}} + \beta_0$$

where the quantity x_i represents, for each building i, the count of vehicles x_i mapped to it; this count is then normalized by dividing by the building footprint area A_i, similarly to how building emissions quantities are normalized. We found that applying this normalization makes our models slightly more consistent across time. β_1 and β_0 form our model parameters, which we fit using least-squares. In addition, for each model we compute Pearson correlation coefficients r and two-sided p-values for our estimates of β_1.

For each fitted model, we also select an emission concentration threshold for the purpose of removing outliers; data points with a concentration below this threshold are not considered when fitting the model. We denote this threshold in Figs. 7 and 8 with a dotted line, and mark excluded data points using 'x's.

During the course of our modelling, we initially considered threshold values of 1, 70, and 150 MMBtu/m^2. For the morning commute period, however, threshold

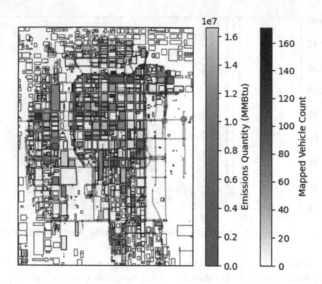

Fig. 6. Heatmap of emissions overlaid on top of building-vehicle mapping counts.

values of 70 and 150 MMBtu/m^2 result in nearly identical models and results; on the other hand, while a threshold value of 1 MMBtu/m^2 fails to eliminate outliers in data for this period, it is usually the only usable threshold value when fitting models for other hours, due to the difference in concentration scales between these two time periods. As such, the rest of this analysis primarily focuses on models fitted using outlier thresholds of 150 MMBtu/m^2.

The models we fit to data from the morning commute period (08:00 to 11:59) show evidence of a weak positive correlation between normalized vehicle counts and emission concentrations, with significance at the $p < 0.01$ level; one of our regression models for this time period can be seen in Fig. 7. The strength of this correlation seems to peak around 09:00, as shown in Table 2.

Meanwhile, we found that our models can not be reasonably fit for hours past 12:00, as our chosen outlier thresholds lead to most, if not all of the data points for these hours being discarded; emission concentrations for these times are simply too low and too sparse for our modelling approach. Even a threshold of 1 MMBtu/m^2 typically leads to all but a dozen or so points being discarded for these hours, resulting in models with wildly inconsistent r- and p-values. As such, we cannot draw conclusions about correlations between vehicle counts and emissions for these hours. This sparsity is likely caused by our source data not reflecting commutes from work, as mentioned in Sect. 2; future work could use a richer dataset to model this portion of the day and provide further insight.

Finally, although we can fit a similar model to our data from 12:00, as seen in 8, the correlation we found was noticeably weaker ($r = 0.119$), as is the evidence supporting it ($p = 0.0317$). Note that the emissions model for this model has been set at 1 MMBtu/m^2, rather than 150 as for the previously shown models.

Table 2. Linear regression model results for the morning commute period and 12:00

Time	r	p
08:00	0.182	$p < 0.001$
09:00	**0.220**	$p < 0.001$
10:00	0.173	0.002
11:00	0.151	0.006
12:00	0.119	0.032

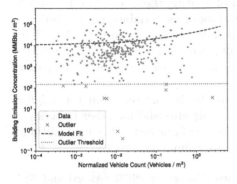

Fig. 7. Regression from vehicle counts to emission concentrations at 09:00 ($r = 0.220$, $p < 0.01$)

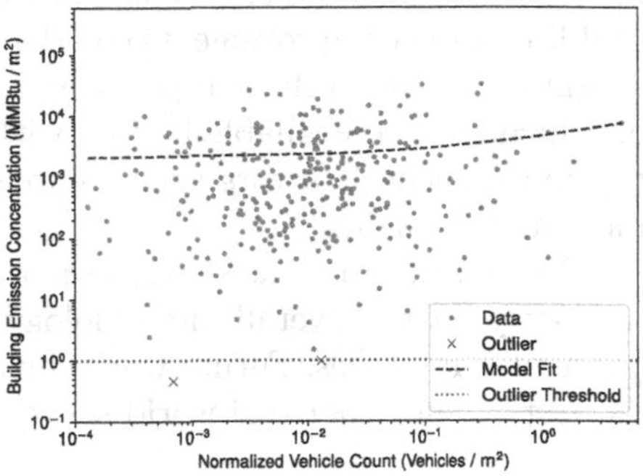

Fig. 8. Regression from vehicle counts to emission concentrations at 12:00 ($r = 0.119$, $p = 0.032$)

As previously mentioned, this is due to the lower emission concentrations found at this time: using a threshold of 150 would lead to our model discarding a large proportion of the data.

The weaker correlation found at 12:00, along with the lower position of the points and fit line for 12:00 within Fig. 8, seem to indicate that the data at 12:00 is distinct from both the morning commute hours and the later hours, and instead exists between these two extremes: although there is still enough activity at 12:00 to allow for analysis as with the morning hours, emissions concentrations are lower and more sparse, as with the evening hours. Figure 5, as discussed in Sect. 4.4, also supports this interpretation, with the median emission concentration lying in the gap between the two clusters representing the morning commute period and the evening hours.

6   Conclusions

In the context of the 2020 SMC Data Challenge, in this work we explore Challenge 4, 'Computational Urban Data Analytics' [2], and investigate the relationships between urban traffic flow and vehicle emissions.

As part of our investigation, we systematically characterize and prepare the datasets provided by the authors of the data challenge; we create a methodology to understand traffic patterns and emissions; we develop algorithmic methods for computing these emissions maps and map both vehicles and emissions to buildings; and provide open-source scripts for conducting the associated analysis and visualizations.

From the results of our analysis we can conclude that the volume of traffic flow has a weak positive correlation with emissions around buildings. This suggests there are additional factors affecting this relationship that could be addressed in future work. For example, the mappings between individual vehicles and buildings could be improved by taking into account all the buildings in the area surrounding a vehicle, instead of limiting the association to a single building. Other improvements could account for other variables, such as building height or mapped vehicle types, which could affect emission concentrations, both of which were unavailable factors within our provided data. These, in addition to environmental factors such as weather and temperature, could yield more meaningful results.

Our results are based on data that had to be curated from the original datasets, yet the overall methodology and tools are valid for other datasets or particular use cases. Future work could validate of our methods with additional datasets from either real-world sources or other simulation tools.

Acknowledgment. Supported by IBM Shared University (SUR) Award and NSF awards IIS 1841758 and CCF 1841758.

The authors wish to thank Silvina Caíno-Lores, Travis Johnston, and Michela Taufer for their mentorship during this project.

References

1. Berres, A., Im, P., Kurte, K., Allen-Dumas, M., Thakur, G., Sanyal, J.: A mobility-driven approach to modeling building energy. In: Proceedings IEEE International Conference on Big Data, Big Data 2019. pp. 3887–3895, Institute of Electrical and Electronics Engineers Inc., (2019)
2. Berres, A., Ravulaparthy, S., Allen-Dumas, M., Kurte, K., Sanyal, J.: Challenge 4: Computational Urban Data Analytics. https://smc-datachallenge.ornl.gov/ challenges-2020/challenge-4-2020/. Accessed 27 July 2020
3. Guensler, R., et al.: Moves-matrix: setup, implementation, and application. In: 95th Annual Meeting of the Transportation Research Board, Washington, DC (2016)
4. Microsoft Corporation: US building footprints. https://github.com/Microsoft/ USBuildingFootprints. Accessed 26 July 2020
5. TRANSIMS Community: Transportation analysis and simulation system (transims). https://sourceforge.net/projects/transims/. Accessed 27 July 2020

A Data-Integration Analysis on Road Emissions and Traffic Patterns

Ao Qu, Yu Wang, Yue Hu, Yanbing Wang, and Hiba Baroud[(✉)]

Vanderbilt University, Nashville, TN, USA
{ao.qu,hiba.baroud}@vanderbilt.edu

Abstract. Understanding human activities and urban mobility patterns is key to solving many urban issues such as congestion and emissions. With the abundant data sets available at different levels of fidelity, one of the main challenges is the sparsity and heterogeneity of data sources. The integration of such data sources is essential to better inform system design and community-level strategies. In this paper, we incorporate a variety of data sources including land use, vehicle emissions and building footprint to comprehensively visualize and analyze traffic patterns in the Chicago Loop area. We first implement and compare three different nearest-neighbor-search algorithms to determine building occupancy assignment, and then perform a spatial-temporal correlation analysis of vehicle emissions focusing on factors such as land use, public transit and demographic. Lastly, we discuss the traffic characteristics from data analysis, such as traffic congestion formation and rush hours etc.

Keywords: Vehicle emissions · Traffic patterns · Nearest neighbor search

1 Introduction

Motivation and Contribution. According to the inventory of U.S. Greenhouse Gas (GHG) Emissions and Sinks 1990–2018, transportation accounted for the largest portion (28%) of total U.S. GHG emissions in 2018 [1]. Amongst all the sources, passenger-cars contribute to nearly 60%. The majority of the use cases are for daily commute. Therefore, it is central to understand the commute patterns of city dwellers, and the integral relationship amongst other factors such as land use, building occupancy, road network and emissions, to consequently inform energy-efficient and sustainable community strategies specifically to each city.

The fundamental problem we address in this paper is the lack of data integration procedures for city-scale traffic impact analysis. Because of the lack of direct data sources for traffic impact analysis such as daily commute schedule

Electronic supplementary material The online version of this chapter (https:// doi.org/10.1007/978-3-030-63393-6_34) contains supplementary material, which is available to authorized users.

© Springer Nature Switzerland AG 2020
J. Nichols et al. (Eds.): SMC 2020, CCIS 1315, pp. 503–517, 2020.
https://doi.org/10.1007/978-3-030-63393-6_34

or block-level emissions, and the inconsistency of the fidelity and scale of various data sources, we design a workflow (Fig. 1) by (1) developing algorithms to realistically assign vehicles' last-seen locations to nearby buildings, (2) preparing grid-based data that incorporates multiple data sources for regression analysis, and (3) conducting feature selection and impact analysis for vehicle emissions. The question of finding the determining factors in the urban areas that contribute to traffic congestion and vehicle emissions is city-dependent, and doing so could potentially help city planners and policy makers target specific areas to estimate and reduce traffic-related emissions. In this paper, we focus on the Chicago Loop area, a major business district in Chicago, IL.

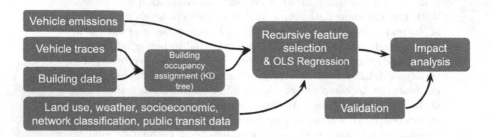

Fig. 1. Workflow for traffic impact analysis.

The main contributions are the following: (1) we estimate a realistic building occupancy schedule by efficiently assigning vehicle occupants to nearby buildings using three nearest neighbor algorithms, with our customized metric, *nearest end point distance*. We demonstrate numerically the superiority of running time and accuracy of our approach by comparing it with others; (2) we propose a method to analyze the impact of city land use, populations, and public transit on vehicle emissions. We integrate various data sources that contribute to vehicle emissions, and perform an area-wide correlation analysis on the selected features using a linear regression model and XGBoost for validation. Specifically, we investigate the impact of land use, population, building occupancy schedule and weather on local vehicle emissions; (3) we lastly characterize traffic patterns by locating the traffic hot spots, popular roads, and rush hours, among others.

Data Sources. Most of the data sources used in this project are provided by Oak Ridge National Laboratory. The data sources are listed following.

1. Commute data: (1) simulated morning commute vehicle traces data at 30 s intervals for one day. The data include road segment (link) ID, driver ID and vehicle speed at each time step. The simulation software is TRansportation ANalysis SIMulation System (TRANSIMS) [2,3]. (2) schedule data for morning commute from National Household Travel Survey (NHTS) [4] and (3) vehicle type distribution data.

2. Emission data: (1) road-level traffic volumes (aggregated from TRANSIMS outputs). (2) Road-level emissions generated using MOVES [5], an emissions simulator.
3. Road network: this data includes link IDs and road type, GeoJSON file of the road network used for the TRANSIMS and MOVES runs, and definition of different link types.
4. Building data: (1) building footprints from Microsoft [6]. (2) Land use data from Chicago Metropolitan Agency for Planning (CMAP) [7], including Geo-JSON file containing polygon data with land use attributes.
5. Socioeconomic data: (1) Population from CMAP/Census (2010) [8], (2) community snapshots (2017) [9] and (3) Chicago commute time (2017) [9].

Additional data was collected. The list with corresponding references are provided below. (1) OpenStreetMap: natural cover data [10], (2) DATA.GOV: Chicago bus routes and Chicago rail system ("L") shapefiles [11], (3) Weather Underground: historical weather data [12], (4) Chicago Data Portal: building height data, Chicago population by census block, and census block boundaries [13].

Related Work. Daily commute has a high impact on city traffic and vehicle emissions. In order to analyze the factors that affect vehicle emissions, we need to understand the commute behaviors in terms of when and where people travel to work, based on survey data such as National Household Travel Survey (NHTS), vehicle traces data and building location information. The highly spatio-temporally varying commute patterns have posed many challenges to modeling building occupancy on a high-resolution level. Studies such as [14,15] develop high-resolution building occupancy models using surveyed time-based data, which underpin further analysis such as building energy demand modeling. In [16], a realistic building occupancy assignment is accomplished using a quadtree based approach to allocate agents' first and last seen locations to nearby buildings. Our paper uses a similar approach but compares and analyzes different agent assignment algorithms along with the quadtree.

Integration of other data sources and modeling techniques are also important to understand the relationship amongst human activities, land use and traffic emissions. For example, meteorological data [17] and social media data [18] are adopted to explore the potential influence of human activities on urban traffic congestion and emissions. Integrated models of land use and transportation are also applied to study city dynamics [19–21]. All of the related works present a comprehensive model for evaluating the effect of human activities on cities' microclimates.

The challenge of assigning vehicle occupants to nearby buildings is essentially a nearest neighbor search (NNS) problem [22]. There are numerous algorithms to solve the NNS problem and they are classified into two types: exact methods and approximation methods. In exact methods, the simplest algorithm is the purely brute force one, which is the most accurate but most computationally demanding of all. This running time can be further improved by employing space partitioning methods, such as KD-tree and Hilbert R-tree [23], which skip computations on some branches and increase efficiency. In approximation methods, the quadtree is widely used due to its superior performance and simple implementation. The details of the quadtree can be seen in [16].

2   Methodology

2.1   Challenge 1: Algorithms to Assign Vehicle Occupants to Buildings

We formulate the building occupancy assignment as a nearest-neighbor-search (NNS) problem. Specifically, we want to assign the last seen locations of vehicles (given by the simulated vehicle trace data) to their nearest buildings (given by the building footprint data) [16]. We apply three search algorithms, brute-force, quadtree, and KD-tree. We compare their performance with respect to efficiency and accuracy. Regarding the building type, we assume that people work in non-residential buildings, and filter out residential buildings based on the land use codes.

We first apply brute-force search algorithm to obtain the baseline running time and accuracy of the building occupancy assignment. Since this algorithm finds the exact solution using a double loop: for each agent find the nearest building, we use the results to benchmark the accuracy of other algorithms. Secondly, we apply the quadtree algorithm used in [16] to assign occupants to buildings. We further introduce the KD-tree algorithm to solve the same problem.

The KD-tree algorithm iteratively bisects the search space and constructs a tree where the leaf nodes correspond to the building locations and the branch nodes correspond to the higher subspaces. If the distance between a vehicle and a subspace is larger than the minimum distance, we can skip this branch of the tree such that the search efficiency can be improved.

For each of the above three algorithms, we assign vehicles based on three distance metrics: *Euclidean distance* (ED), *weighted Euclidean distance* (WD) and our heuristic version *nearest end point distance* (ND). The WD is measured by multiplying the ED with a weight factor proportional to the inverse of building area. The detailed definition has been mentioned in [16]. The ND is the distance from a vehicle to the nearest end point of a building polygon. For vehicle i and building j , ND (d_{ij}) is defined as:

$$d_{ij} = \min_{k \in P_{\text{poly}_j}} \|r_i - r_k\|, \forall i \in V, j \in B \tag{1}$$

where V is the set of vehicle last seen locations and B is the set of building polygons; P_{poly_j} denotes the set of points on the boundary of building polygon j. r_i's are the coordinates of the vehicle location i.

Furthermore, we calculate building capacity by multiplying building size with per capita area and count the number of overload buildings to compare the performance of the three distance metrics.

2.2 Challenge 2: Vehicle Emissions and Correlation Analysis

Data Preparation: Generate Grid-Based Data. We enrich the provided data with data from additional sources (listed in Data sources).

One of the main challenges in conducting traffic emissions analysis and exploring the impact of other factors is data reconciliation. Geographical features are often based on different scopes, such as points, lines, and polygons. To address this problem, we first select a target area that fully covers our study region. Then we introduce a grid-based data integration technique to normalize and aggregate various data sets into $N \times N$ grids as shown in Fig. 2a. Specifically, the feature variables are aggregated as follows. The *population* is the total number of residents in the grid. The *inflow population* is the total number of people commute to the grid area each day. The *Public transit (bus & rail)* and *road types* measure the total length of corresponding bus, rail or road line within the grid. *Land use types* and *natural cover types* are the total area of the corresponding type, and the *foot print area* is multiplied by the number of stories if the building type information is available.

If one line or polygon intersects with more than one square grid, then we assume that the corresponding feature is evenly distributed on this line/polygon. For example, the emission data for a certain square grid is calculated as following:

$$\text{total grid emission} = \sum_{\text{all roads}} \text{road emission} \times \frac{\text{length of road within grid}}{\text{total length of road}}$$

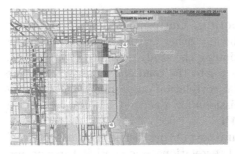

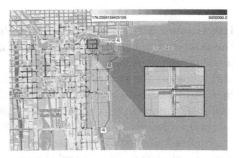

(a) A 12×12 grid example and its rela-   (b) Road emission visualization.
tionship with roads.

Fig. 2. Spatial variation of aggregated emission. Darker red color indicates more emissions. The partially enlarged view in (b) shows that even within a small space, there is a large variation among road links. Thus, the grid-based method as illustrated in (a) is used to reduce the noise. Note: The dark area on the left of (b) doesn't look dark in (a) because roads in that area are actually more sparse and our grids don't cover some of the roads with heavy emission due to the difficulty of incorporating spreading road network into regularly shaped grid. This issue should be minimized when a broader range of data becomes available.

Another way to combine all the data is a road centered method, which defines fixed areas centered around the centroid of each road, and then measures each quantity within every defined area as the independent variables. However, this method is not suitable for our case since the emission data is generated by simulation and contains inherent noise. Emission per unit length is calculated as $\frac{\text{road emission}}{\text{road length}}$ and we observe a large variation in this measure even among roads that are within the same intersection (Fig. 2b). Therefore by averaging all roads in a specific area, the grid-based method effectively reduces the noise.

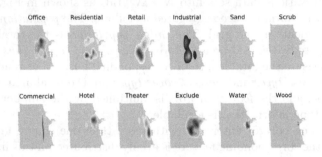

Fig. 3. The spatial distribution of each land use and natural cover type. We can see that different land use type is concentrated in different areas. For example, residential buildings are concentrated in the south while office is more likely to be seen in the north.

Regression Model and Feature Selection. Our primary analysis examines the relationship between vehicle emissions and other factors. We first perform a multivariate regression analysis by partitioning the study area into 12×12 grids, and assessing the contribution of each factor to the road emissions nearby. The first model intends to examine the spatial correlation only, so the time-varying variables are averaged. For example, emissions for a certain grid are calculated as total emissions in a day divided by 24 h.

Figure 3 and 4 show land use and natural cover types distribution using kernel density estimation (KDE) and the spatial correlations among all features within the study area, respectively. From the correlation matrix (Fig. 4), we notice that the correlation coefficients between some features (e.g., population and residential areas) indicate the presence of a strong multicollinearity (Pearson correlation coefficient $\rho \geq 0.7$), which increases the standard errors of the coefficients when doing regression analysis, and in turn may cause some independent variables to be not significant. To address this issue, we employ recursive feature elimination(RFE) to repeatedly remove the least important variables. For spatial correlation analysis of vehicle emissions, we regress the averaged emissions on other variables selected by RFE using an Ordinary Least Squares(OLS) model.

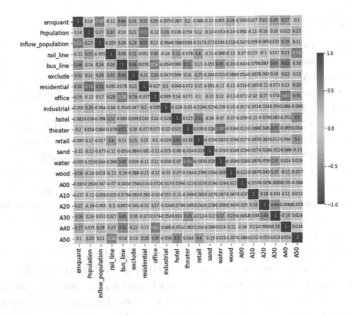

Fig. 4. A matrix showing correlation coefficients between variables

Robustness Testing. Since the number of grid cells may affect the correlation results, we test the robustness of the area division by employing three approaches to validate our result. First, we repeat the same procedure on 8×8, 10×10, and 15×15 grid dividing the same area to check the consistency of the significance of independent variables. Second, we implement the road centered method although some variations in feature importance caused by the inherent data noise are expected. Third, we use tree-based XGBoost regression to calculate the feature importance ranking. The feature importance reported by XGBoost is the average information gain across all decision trees when the feature is used as a splitting node. In each robustness test, we also rank the feature importance of each variable so that we can check whether the variables used in our primary model remain stable.

Temporal Variation. Since the vehicle emissions and some other variables are also time-varying quantities, we intend to investigate the temporal correlation of vehicle emissions as well. To this end, we include features such as weather. Overall, 94.8% of all roads demonstrate an increase in emission from January to July which is clearly an evidence of the presence of seasonal effect. However, we are unable to extract more detailed insights regarding temporal variation. The reason is twofold: first, the current emission data covers only two very short time periods (Jan 9th and July 4th to 10th) and the simulated emission data in July is the same each day. Second, the spatial coverage is too small to include the diversity of weather conditions. We intend to address the temporal correlation in future work when a broader range of data becomes available.

2.3   Challenge 3: Traffic Patterns Characterization

Traffic Hot Spots, Congestion, and Popular Roads. According to INRIX [24], a leading traffic analytics company, traffic hot spots are defined as traffic jams that occur at the same locations along a stretch of road. The measure we use is based on the idea that traffic state can be reflected by the average speed. To identify traffic jams, we apply *speed performance index* (SPI) formerly developed by *Beijing Traffic Management Bureau* (BTMB) to evaluate the traffic condition of each road during each hour [25]. The index, defined as the ratio between the current speed and the maximum possible speed, can be applied here. SPI ranges from 0 to 1 with 1 indicating a very smooth traffic and 0 extremely congested traffic. However, we do not count zero in this study because zero average speed for an hour is more likely a sign of no vehicle passing through. According to BTMB, heavy congestion occurs when $SPI < 0.25$. In our study of hot spots, we first use k-means algorithm to cluster roads into 20 small groups by their spatial locations and calculate the average number of occurrences of heavy congestion for each cluster. We also calculate the ratio between the weekly average speed in a week and maximum possible speed for each road so that we can identify specific hot spots. Popular roads are measured by their traffic volume instead of average speed. We aggregate the traffic volume provided in the simulation data and select the top ranked roads to highlight in the map.

Travel Time. We pre-process the data to eliminate outliers in two steps. First, we select all the commute trips from home to work that are less than 2.5 h (as the rest are obviously outliers, e.g., 10+ hours for a single trip), which cover 99.5% of all the trips. Second, we only keep the trips that start from home between 5:00 and 13:00 since people typically go to work in the mornings. Then to analyse the travel time, we divide the time window between 5:00 and 13:00 into 10-second-intervals. We treat the travel time for each time interval as a random variable, and calculate the mean and the 95% confidence interval based on the travel time of trips occurring in this interval.

Busy Times and Comparison with NHTS. To compare the simulation results and the survey conducted by NHTS, we first average the simulation output from Monday to Friday to compute the average total traffic volume of each hour in a day. The provided NHTS trip distribution is the same for each day so it suffices to make comparison on a one-day distribution. Then, we proceed to obtain the fraction of traffic volume per hour in the busy-time distribution plot (Fig. 9). Note that the busy-time distribution sums up to 1 overtime, and thus can be treated as a probability distribution. Therefore, a commonly used measure, Jensen–Shannon divergence [26], can be used to quantify the resemblance between two probability distributions. Jensen-Shannon divergence is calculated as the entropy of the mixture of two distributions minus the sum of the entropy of each distribution such that a disparity in the two inputs would lead to higher score.

Spatial-Temporal Analysis of Speed. We analyze the spatial temporal variation and summarize our finding in a dynamic visualization. Again, we assume that zero-speed roads imply zero-traffic so those roads are colored green.

3   Results

3.1   Challenge 1: Performance Comparison of NNS Algorithms

The accuracy of quadtree, KD-tree and brute-force algorithms for building occupancy assignment are shown in the first row of Fig. 5. Both KD-tree and brute-force algorithms achieve 100% accuracy because they compute the exact solution to the NNS problem, no matter what distance metric we choose. However, the accuracy of quadtree only improves when the partition is coarser (i.e., the number of leaf nodes becomes smaller), and no-split quadtree becomes equivalent to the brute-force method). In terms of the distance criteria, ND metric can achieve a higher accuracy than WD or ED, this is because ND metric as in Eq. (1) considers the geometric shape of the buildings and not just the centroids, leading to a better approximation of the actual distance. The running time of each of three algorithms is shown in the second row of Fig. (5). Brute-force algorithm has the longest running time when using ED or ND metric. This is due to the double loop structure in the brute-force algorithm which requires going through all the vehicles' last seen locations and all the building locations to find the nearest building for each occupant. KD-tree has a consistently low running time for ED or SD metric, but fails to outperform brute-force when using WD metric. This is because WD requires reconstructing the search tree when each new vehicle location is added, which significantly slows down the computational time for KD-tree. As for quadtree, higher accuracy can be achieved when using lower-fidelity split, but this also increases the running time. The vehicle assignment and the overload buildings are shown in the supplementary materials. The total number of office buildings is 665 and the number of overload buildings is 27, 10, 10 for ED, WD and SD metrics. Considering both the accuracy and the running time, KD-tree with ND metric consistently outperforms brute-force and quadtree.

3.2   Challenge 2: Area-Wide Correlation Analysis of Vehicle Emissions

Regression Analysis. To reduce standard errors caused by feature multicollinearity, we first perform a recursive feature selection (RFE) on the grid-based data. RFE is a method that keeps removing the weakest feature, which also allows us to evaluate the rankings of features. We find that for 12×12 grid, the adjusted R^2 is the highest(0.71) when top 13 features are used in regression model and most of them are statistically significant (Fig. 6). This high adjusted R^2 indicates that a large portion of variance in emission can be explained by the features chosen by the model.

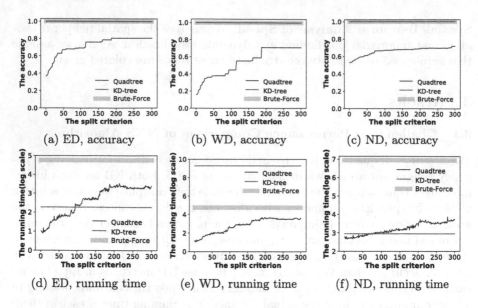

(a) ED, accuracy (b) WD, accuracy (c) ND, accuracy

(d) ED, running time (e) WD, running time (f) ND, running time

Fig. 5. The performance of algorithms based on different distance metrics

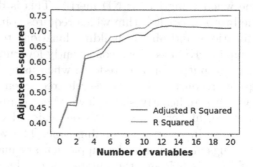

Fig. 6. Adjusted R^2 increases as more features are added to the model

The regression result (Table 1) shows that the main contribution to vehicle emissions comes from inflow population, and some certain types of road including A50 (Vehicular trail, road passable only by four-wheel drive vehicle) and A40 (Local, neighborhood, and rural road, city street), which are positively correlated with vehicle emissions with significance (p-value) $p < 0.001$. Rail line length and vehicle emissions are negatively correlated with p-value $p < 0.001$, which implies the important role of Chicago rail system in alleviating road transportation. One interesting finding is that wood coverage has a strong positive correlation with emissions. One possible interpretation is that wood coverage represents urban parks which are often built near city busy corridors. We also want to emphasize that correlation does not imply causation. Our analysis only explores

Table 1. Vehicle emissions regression analysis and feature rankings. * and *** represent $p < 0.05, p < 0.001$ respectively.

Features	Coefficients	Feature ranking		
		Grid-based OLS	Grid-based XGBoost	Road-centered OLS
Inflow population	62939.816***	1	2	8
Rail line	−52640.761***	4.75	4.25	2
Bus line	40243.822*	4.75	8	7
Office	−35525.439*	10.5	10	9
Water	−31460.252*	12.75	15.75	17
Wood	50688.006***	3.75	7.63	1
A20[1]	27364.166*	10.25	15.13	15
A30[2]	43346.564*	7.5	6	5
A40[3]	70263.346***	6.75	4.75	4
A50[4]	50938.104***	5.5	5	3

[1] Primary road without limited access, U.S. and state highway
[2] Secondary and connecting road, state and county highways
[3] Local, neighborhood, and rural road, city street
[4] Vehicular trail, road passable only by four-wheel drive (4WD) vehicle

the concurrent land use features on vehicle emissions rather than establishing a cause-and-effect relationship.

Validation. To further verify our results of feature selection, we generate three more datasets with different choice of grid size. Then, we calculate the average ranking of each feature based on RFE. We can see from Table 1 that most features presented here, especially those with $p < 0.001$, are consistently top-ranked. Feature importance with XGBoost model and a road-centered model also reports similar ranking, as shown in Table 1. We conclude that our regression model is able to identify the most significant features and the outcome is validated using other methods.

3.3   Challenge 3: Characterize Traffic Patterns

Hot Spot, Congestion and Popular Roads. The visualization in Fig. 7 shows the traffic hot spots and the frequency of heavy congestion for each cluster of roads. The number in the circle indicates on average how many hours the roads around that region are in heavy congestion. The street view images are the six most popular roads ranked by total volume and this result is largely confirmed by the street reviews we find online. An interesting finding is that some very popular roads are not highly congested, which might due to the difference in road design.

Travel Times. Figure (8) visualizes the variation of commute time departing between 5:00 to 13:00 of both NHTS and simulation data. We can clearly see that the mean of the travel time ranges from 0.2 h to roughly 1 h, which is similar

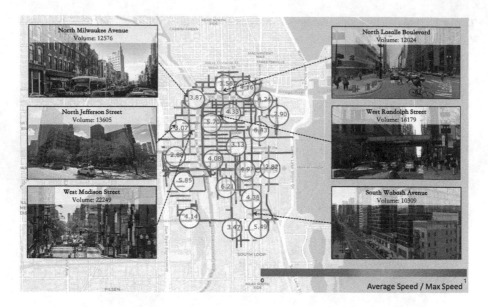

Fig. 7. The variation of travel times throughout the day

to the commute time 58.5 min from a study by Robert Half [27]. In simulation data, the travel time is longest around 7 am and slightly shorter afterwards, possibly because people who have to commute long hours tend to depart early. The travel time between 8 am and 11 am is typically longer than the travel time before 6 am and after 11 am, which might be due to the morning rush hours. In NHTS data, the travel time is highest around 11 am due to the noon peak and decreases afterwards. There is no increasing travel time from 5 am to 7 am in NHTS data as in simulation data, which is caused by the simulation error.

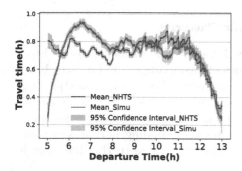

Fig. 8. The variation of travel times throughout the day

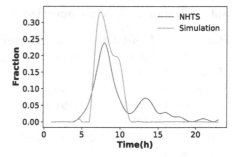

Fig. 9. Busy times according to simulation data and NHTS survey

NHTS Survey Vs Simulation. In general, the simulation has a very similar trend as NHTS with some minor variations. The Jensen-Shannon divergence for these two distributions is 0.38, which indicate a relative similarity between the busy-time distributions. The busy times indicated by both two data sources agree on the morning rush hours (6 am to 10 am). However, there is a second peak in NHTS data after 12 pm which is not found in the simulation. In fact, analyzing on the original simulation data, we find very few trips after 12 pm compared to the NHTS survey. In addition, we observe some unrealistic speeds in the simulation setting. We find that there are about 200 roads with average speeds between 0–1 mph. In fact, excluding the zero speeds, the average speed for all roads is only 8.53 mph. Moreover, we believe that the traffic volume is underestimated. For example, as one of the most popular streets, North Jefferson street is reported to have 8,300 average daily traffic according to Chicago Data Portal. However, in the simulation, the same street has a weekly traffic that is only 13,605.

Spatial-Temporal Variation of Speeds. For this part of the analysis, we plot the speeds on the street map of loop area and generate a GIF to show dynamics (Fig. 10). Basically this visualization aligns with the previous congestion analysis. The speeds are lowest during morning rush hours and roads around the city center tend to have heavy congestion.

Fig. 10. Spatial-temporal variation of speeds. Green indicates high speed or no traffic while red indicates the opposite. (It may require an Adobe reader to load this GIF. Screenshots of this GIF can also be found here: Appendix) (Colour figure online)

4 Conclusions

In this paper, we provide a framework for data reconciliation and urban traffic patterns characterization. Our solutions to the three challenges contribute to the study of commute patterns and urban transportation systems in the following ways. First, we develop a fast and efficient nearest-neighbor search algorithm, KD-tree with nearest-end-point distance metric, to realistically assign the last seen locations of vehicles to the nearby building. This addresses the lack of direct data sources such as building occupancy schedule, and provides more information on when and where people commute to work. Second, we perform an area-wide analysis of land use, populations and public transit on vehicle emissions. We identify that the inflow population and road types significantly correlates to vehicle emissions. These features are validated using an alternative road-centered data generation approach and a XGBoost model, which produces a similar feature importance ranking. Temporally, a seasonal effect on vehicle emissions is observed but further analysis is hindered due to the lack of high resolution data. Lastly, we explore the traffic simulation data and extract some interesting traffic patterns. We conclude that overall this simulation setup is able to reproduce realistic traffic activities. Most of the travel times are realistic. A good match in busy-time distribution is found between the simulation data and NHTS survey, and major streets are indeed occupied with more vehicles. However, the simulation fails to take into account, for example, the commute back to work after lunchtime that NHTS might indicate.

Some limitations of this study are also worth noting. First, we are not able to draw any conclusion of the impact of vehicle types on emissions, due to the lack of diversity in vehicle classifications. Information about vehicle types would also help us design a more realistic algorithm since the vehicle type might implicate the building type that the vehicle owner is more likely to work at. Second, the vehicle emissions analysis focuses on a specific region (Chicago Loop area), and may not well generalize to other cities. We acknowledge that these limitations exist due to the scope of this study, and instead we focus on providing a framework of reconciling data of different types, and analyzing emissions using other more accessible data, which can be applied in broader scenarios.

Acknowledgement. This material is based upon work supported by the National Science Foundation under Grant No. CMMI-1727785 (Hu), CMMI-1853913 (Wang), and USDOT Dwight D. Eisenhower Fellowship program under Grant No. 693JJ31945012 (Wang).

References

1. EPA. Fast Facts U.S. Transportation Sector Greenhouse Gas Emissions 1990–2018 (2018). https://www.epa.gov/greenvehicles/fast-facts-transportation-greenhouse-gas-emissions
2. TRANSIMS. https://sourceforge.net/projects/transimsstudio/
3. Williams, M.D., Thayer, G., Smith, L.: Technical Report LA-UR-9782 (1997)

4. National household travel survey. https://nhts.ornl.gov/
5. EPA. Motor vehicle emission simulator (MOVES) (2014). https://www.epa.gov/moves/latest-version-motor-vehicle-emission-simulator-moves
6. Microsoft. U.S. building footprints (2018). https://github.com/Microsoft/USBuildingFootprints
7. CMAP. Land use data. https://www.cmap.illinois.gov/data/land-use
8. CMAP. 2010 census data summarized to chicago community areas (2010). https://www.cmap.illinois.gov/data/land-use
9. CMAP. Community data snapshots raw data, July 2020 release (2020). https://datahub.cmap.illinois.gov/dataset/community-data-snapshots-raw-data
10. OpenStreetMap. https://www.openstreetmap.org
11. U.S. Government's open data. https://www.data.gov/
12. Weather underground. https://www.wunderground.com/
13. Chicago data portal. https://data.cityofchicago.org/
14. Richardson, I., Thomson, M., Infield, D.: Energy and Buildings **40**(8), 1560 (2008). https://doi.org/10.1016/j.enbuild.2008.02.006. http://www.sciencedirect.com/science/article/pii/S0378778808000467
15. McKenna, E., Krawczynski, M., Thomson, M.: Energy and Buildings **96**, 30 (2015). https://doi.org/10.1016/j.enbuild.2015.03.013. http://www.sciencedirect.com/science/article/pii/S0378778815002054
16. Berres, A., Im, P., Kurte, K., Allen-Dumas, M., Thakur, G., Sanyal, J.: In: IEEE International Conference on Big Data (Big Data), pp. 3887–3895. IEEE (2019)
17. Shiva Nagendra, S., Khare, M.: Transportation Research Part D: Transport and Environment **8**(4), 285 (2003). https://doi.org/10.1016/S1361-9209(03)00006-3. http://www.sciencedirect.com/science/article/pii/S1361920903000063
18. Huang, W., Xu, S., Yan, Y., Zipf, A.: Cities **84**, p. 8 (2019). https://doi.org/10.1016/j.cities.2018.07.001. http://www.sciencedirect.com/science/article/pii/S0264275118302786
19. Bandeira, J.M., Coelho, M.C., Sá, M.E., Tavares, R., Borrego, C.: Science of the Total Environment **409**(6), 1154 (2011). https://doi.org/10.1016/j.scitotenv.2010.12.008. http://www.sciencedirect.com/science/article/pii/S0048969710013112
20. Namdeo, A., Mitchell, G., Dixon, R.: Environmental Modelling & Software **17**(2), 177 (2002). https://doi.org/10.1016/S1364-8152(01)00063-9. http://www.sciencedirect.com/science/article/pii/S1364815201000639
21. Gualtieri, G., Tartaglia, M.: Transportation Research Part D: Transport and Environment **3**(5), 329 (1998). https://doi.org/10.1016/S1361-9209(98)00011-X. http://www.sciencedirect.com/science/article/pii/S136192099800011X
22. Bhatia, N., et al.: arXiv preprint arXiv:1007.0085 (2010)
23. Kamel, I., Faloutsos, C.: In: Proceedings of the Second International Conference on Information and Knowledge Management, pp. 490–499 (1993)
24. INRIX a smart way to drive (2016). URL https://inrix.com/mobile-apps/. INRIX Inc
25. He, F., Yan, X., Liu, Y., Ma, L.: Green intelligent transportation system and safety. Procedia Eng. **100**(137), 11–12 (2016). https://doi.org/10.1016/j.proeng.2016.01.277. http://www.sciencedirect.com/science/article/pii/S1877705816003040
26. Oesterreicher, F., Vajda, I.: Ann. Insts. Stat. Math. **55**, 639 (2003). https://doi.org/10.1007/BF02517812
27. McGhee, J.: Chicago commute is 2rd longest, but less stressful than in many cities (2017)

Data Analysis and Visualization of Traffic in Chicago with Size and Landuse-Aware Vehicle to Buildings Assignment

Alnour Alharin$^{(\boxtimes)}$, Yatri Patel$^{(\boxtimes)}$, Thanh-Nam Doan$^{(\boxtimes)}$, and Mina Sartipi$^{(\boxtimes)}$

University of Tennessee at Chattanooga, Chattanooga, TN 37403, USA
{dyc881,jwb318}@mocs.utc.edu
{thanh-nam-doan,mina-sartipi}@utc.edu

Abstract. Besides vehicles, buildings are one of the main energy users in urban areas. The rate of energy usage of a particular building depends on features such as human activities, the number of people inside, weather, and the surrounding landscape. Such complex interactions makes energy usage of buildings hard to understand. In this work, we analyze the energy usage of Chicago loop under the effects of several features. Through our extensive experiments, we explore the connections between energy usage and these features. Moreover, we proposed an algorithm that assigns vehicles to buildings by considering three parameters: location of the building, its size, and land-use.

Keywords: Urban informatics · Visualization · Vehicle emission

1 Introduction

Global warming is a global challenge for society. It pushes our existence to the edge of a cliff and fosters consequences such as extreme weather and rising sea levels. The primary driver of global warming is greenhouse gases, dominated by carbon dioxide and methane. For this reason, reducing these gases is an essential task. An oft overlooked factor in energy consumption, US buildings use 39% of energy and 38% of CO_2 emission while the two respective figures for Europe are 40% and 36% [2]. Understanding the energy emission of buildings is crucial.

The nature of energy consumption of buildings is complicated due to a large number of variables. Firstly, it depends on the number of people inside buildings. The more people, the more energy it needs. Secondly, energy consumption is highly related to the activities of users inside. For example, lighting is around 16% of electricity usage in U.S. commercial buildings. Thirdly, external conditions such as weather play an important role. Buildings use more energy to warm in winter than fall. Last but not least, traffic is a crucial feature to understand the energy use of buildings [3].

In order to untangle the complexity of how buildings consumer energy, we analyzed the data of Chicago loop, the commercial core of Chicago and the second largest business district in North America. In this work, we use data analysis

© Springer Nature Switzerland AG 2020
J. Nichols et al. (Eds.): SMC 2020, CCIS 1315, pp. 518–529, 2020.
https://doi.org/10.1007/978-3-030-63393-6_35

and visualization to understand traffic patterns and emissions with respect to building usage and weather.

Our contributions can be summarized as follows:

1. Proposing a novel algorithm for vehicles to building assignment that takes into account both the size of the building and its land-use.
2. Utilizing datasets from different sources to study the temporal and spatial patterns of traffic, weather, and emission.
3. Using GIS tools to make temporal and spatial visualizations in both static and dynamic formats.

2   Literature Review

In this section, we survey related works to our paper which can be classified into two categories: i) energy consumption of buildings and ii) urban mobility.

2.1   Energy Consumption of Buildings

Building energy has been researched extensively in recent decades. Crawley et al. [7] focused on simulating the energy consumption of buildings. In this work, they surveyed several simulation programs and a comparison is conducted according to general modeling features: zone loads, building envelopes, and day light and solar infiltration, ventilation and multizone airflow, renewable energy systems, electrical systems and equipment, HVAC systems, HVAC equipment, environmental emissions, economic evaluation, climate data availability, results reporting, validation, and user interface, links to other programs, and occupancy load of buildings. Amasyali et al. [1] examine machine learning methods in predicting building energy consumption. From their work, the short-term, e.g. hourly, and long-term, e.g. yearly, prediction has equal importance for the construction and maintenance of buildings and power grid. Sadineni et al. [10] study the technical point of construction components e.g. walls, roofs of building toward energy efficiency. Castleton et al. [4] focus on making energy efficiency of buildings through green roof.

2.2   Urban Mobility

Urban mobility is a branch of research that focuses on understanding the movement of people within urban areas. Doan and Lim [8] use data from location-based social networks to understand urban mobility. Specifically, they analyze data to illustrate two new factors named area attraction and neighborhood competition. Then, they propose a probabilistic model to incorporate these factors. Through their extensive experiment, they show that these two factors are very important for understanding the movement of people in urban areas. Cho et al. [5] studied the movement of urban dwellers around two important places: home and work. It shows that using these two places can reveal several movement patterns of users such as their habits and movement behaviors. Wei *et al.* [13] wants to optimize traffic by enhancing the vehicle flow through controlling traffic lights. Particularly, they propose a reinforcement learning method to achieve the goal. Through their experiment using real data, it significantly improves on traditional methods. Stiglic *et al.* [11] studies the combination of two modes of transportation: ride-sharing and public transit. From their work, they find out that such integration improves mobility and also encourages people to use public transportation.

3   Datasets

We used 3 different datasets, one main dataset provided by the organizing committee and two other datasets form external sources. The first dataset contains the following information:

1. Vehicles dataset: we have the tracking data (snapshots) for vehicles across the road links, in addition to the average commute data from and to work.
2. Buildings dataset: the footprints of the buildings.
3. Emission dataset: the hourly emission data for 10 different dates.
4. Traffic dataset: road links, their properties and locations.

The second one is available freely online at the city of Chicago's website [6]. The dataset contains traffic volume measurements for different streets across different times of the year (mainly the data was collected in 2006).

The third dataset, which is the Land Use Inventory for Northeast Illinois, is an open source dataset containing the land use codes for all the buildings and land parcels in northeast Illinois [9]. The dataset is collection of land uses which were identified at the parcel level using parcel and assessor data provided by seven northeast Illinois counties, and is published by Chicago Metropolitan Agency for Planning (CMAP).

For each location and date given in the main dataset, we crawled its weather information via DarkSky API.

Data Preprocessing: After we summarized the data into trips, we found that about 7.5% of the vehicle's end points data are outside the area of buildings as shown in Fig. 1. Since this percentage is high enough to be effective on the conclusions that can be drawn from this study, we dropped them and kept the remaining data for our analysis. Moreover, we relied only on the data of weekdays since we have a shortage of data for the weekends.

After analyzing the building dataset given to us, we observed that the dataset lacked the land use codes. In order to combine the dataset published by the CMAP and the dataset provided to us, we used QGIS intersection tools to combine the two datasets [12]. The intersection tool extracts the portion of features from the input and the overlay layer and makes a temporary layer with attributes of the overlapping features from both the input and overlay layers. This temporary layer was then used for further processing for the vehicle assignment.

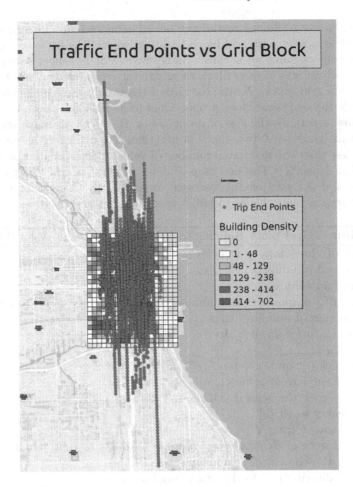

Fig. 1. Trips ending points vs grid blocks

4   Methodology

4.1   Vehicle to Buildings Assignment

This method is an improvement to the approach followed by Berres *et al.* [3] where they used the last seen location of a particular vehicle to assign it to the nearest building. Similarly, we also use the last seen location but instead of assigning the vehicle to one specific building, we assign it to a grid block that contains several buildings. Then, we use the land-use and size of the building to fine tune the assignment. We created a mapping between the land-use of the building and the expected number of vehicles that belong to it. The table is filled based on intuition and data whenever it was available for us. For example, the land-use code 1111 is used for a single family building. We looked for the expected number of vehicles owned by a single family in Chicago area and saved this number in our buildings to the number of vehicles map. Then, to assign a specific vehicle to one of its grid block building, we use the expected number of vehicles to help us make an accurate assignment. For instance, if the building with 1111 land-use was already filled, we assign the considered vehicle to another building in the grid block. We use the size of the buildings to make the number of cars inside the same grid block proportional to its size. For example, if the size of a building A is twice the size of its neighbor B, we try to make the number of vehicles assigned to A two times larger than the one of B as long as this number is less than the maximum number of vehicles as estimated by the land-use (building capacity). The first step of determining the grid block is straight forward since it is based on the last seen location only. Algorithm 1 describes the second step in our vehicles to building assignment approach.

Algorithm 1: Grid Block Building to Vehicles Assignment Algorithm

---

Result: BC: buildings to vehicles assignment
B: set of grid buildings;
V: set of grid vehicles;
Initialize BC: mapping from building to vehicles empty dictionary ;
S = total sum of buildings sizes ;
for *i from 1 to length of B* **do**
    b = B[i] ;
    b_vehicles_number = size(b) * length of V / S ;
    for *j from 1 to b_vehicles_number* **do**
        v = pick the nearest vehicle in V to b ;
        push v to BC[b] ;
        remove v from V ;
        if *length of BC[b] is more than its land-use capacity* **then**
            R = b_vehicles_number - size(BC[b]) ;
            distribute R to the remaining buildings ;
            break;
        end
    end
end

Regarding the size of the grid blocks, we tried different ranges. Our main criteria of judging a good grid blocks segmentation is the average number of buildings. If the number was too high, then the next step of fine tuning the exact building that the vehicles belong to will be harder. On the other hand, choosing a segmentation with a small number of buildings increases the chance of missing the real building. We tried different combinations and ended up with the segmentation shown by Fig. 2. Each grid is of 245 m. X 235.32 m.

4.2 Traffic Analysis

We studied multiple aspects of traffic. First, we analyzed the hourly pattern of traffic across different road links from the provided dataset. Moreover, we used

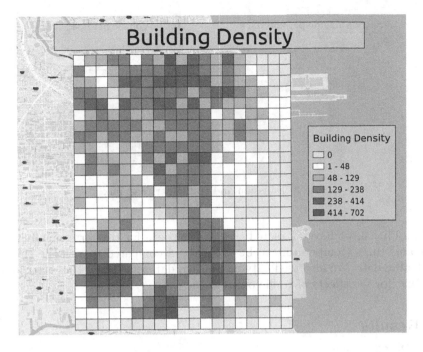

Fig. 2. Density of buildings in Chicago loop

another dataset provided by the city of Chicago to cover more places in Chicago. We also compared the pattern of the provided commute data with the pattern summarized from the snapshots. We converted the snapshots data (data that describe the details of commutes by different vehicles across different links) into a small table of trips that contains: vehicle id, starting and finishing time of the trip, first and last seen locations and then extracted the hourly pattern from it.

Moreover, we performed a hybrid spatial temporal analysis for traffic to examine the effect of location and time. This data is visualized in GIF 1 that shows the spatial distribution of traffic data where the photo changes to show the 24-h of the day.

4.3   Emission Versus Traffic and Weather

In order to compare emission with traffic, we calculated the average hourly pattern of both quantities across the entire dates of the given dataset, and then we plotted them with each other to see the correlation. We classified traffic values into three categories: high, low, and medium. High category includes the values more than one standard deviation above the mean, while low category includes the values lower than one standard deviation from the mean. Other values are considered medium. We applied the same technique on emission data as seen in Fig. 3.

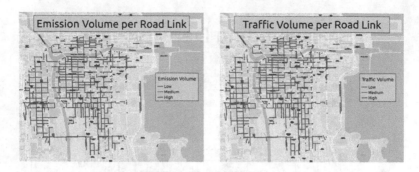

Fig. 3. Emission and traffic per road link

In addition, we have extracted the weather data for the corresponding locations and times (temperature to be exact), and compared it with the emission and traffic data. We also used City of Chicago dataset [6] to get a better understanding for the affects of traffic on weather.

5 Results

5.1 Vehicle to Buildings Assignment

Out of 18K unique vehicles summarized from the snapshots data, we found that about 1K vehicles were not assigned to any grid blocks since they are outside the area covered by buildings. For the remaining vehicles we first tested our assumption about the relationship between land-use and the end locations of vehicles to work snapshots summaries. Figure 5 shows the relationship between the level of traffic and land-use. Notice that we divided land-use into two categories: residential and work areas. Residential areas include residential codes, while work areas consist of commercial, institutional, and industrial buildings. From this figure, we can deduce that the northern part of Chicago loop tends to be more crowded with a high number of work buildings, while the outskirts have more residential places and less traffic.

Since one of the important metrics in the assignment process is the average number of vehicles assigned to each grid block, we can see the histogram of the average number of vehicles in Fig. 6. We observe that the majority grid blocks have relatively lower average number of vehicles assigned to them (less than 50), while we have few grid blocks with high density. It is important to distinguish between the vehicles assigned to a specific grid block and the traffic density of that block, since the traffic density correlates with the number of vehicles at a specific point of time, regardless whether vehicles stopped at that place or not, while we assign the vehicles to grid blocks based on their last seen location only. Secondly, we pair vehicles to specific buildings as stated in the Algorithm 1 using the land-use to specify the capacity of the buildings, and the building size to estimate the number of expected vehicles for that building. When the

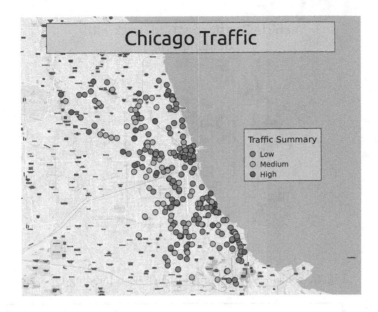

Fig. 4. City of Chicago traffic

estimated number of vehicles exceeds the capacity, we distribute the remaining vehicles to be assigned to the other buildings. We also found that the algorithm is sensitive to the selection of the grids configuration. Choosing a configuration of grid blocks with a high number of buildings increases the rate of assigning a vehicle to a relatively distant building which might not be true since people tend to park near their working place.

5.2   Traffic, Emission and Weather Analysis

When we studied the hourly pattern of traffic from commute survey data in weekdays, we found that it tends to have a peak between 8 to 9 AM as shown in Fig. 7. The same pattern is supported by the snapshot data as we can see in Fig. 8. Note that in this graph the y axis represents the ratio between traffic/emission to its peak over all the data since we are more interested in the pattern rather than the unit of measure. Moreover, we can see the spatial distribution of traffic data for different links in Fig. 3. For the parts closer to the east we used the City of Chicago's data to provide their spatial traffic as shown in Fig. 4. Note that the data was collected in 2006 in scattered points without determining the hour of the day, which makes it less accurate than the given dataset. The shown traffic values represent the average number of cars per link across all the covered period in the dataset. To see temporal and spatial patterns at the same time, we created a GIF that shows the traffic per link in different hours of the day. More details are shown for both emission and traffic in GIF while Fig. 8 shows the hourly pattern for both emission and traffic. We noticed

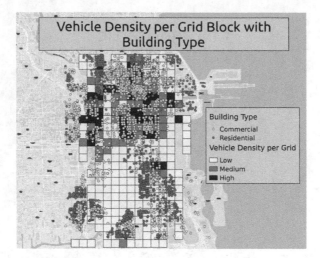

Fig. 5. Vehicle density per grid block with building type

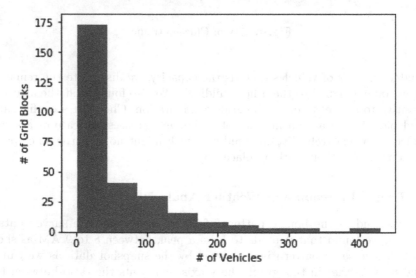

Fig. 6. Histogram of vehicles distribution over grid blocks

that the two quantities are well aligned and this pattern applies for the 5 weekdays given in the dataset (The graph shows the pattern for Monday). On the other hand, a typical day's temperature in Chicago can be seen in Fig. 9. If we compare this with the pattern of traffic/emission in Fig. 8 we can observe two differences: the peak value of temperature is at 2 pm while the peak of emission and traffic is about 3 h earlier. The second difference is that temperature decreases more smoothly compared with emission and traffic.

GIF 1: Traffic and Emission Visualization

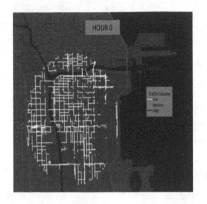
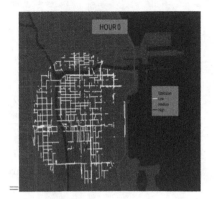

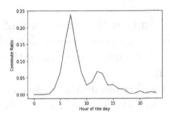

Fig. 7. Commute by hour for a weekday

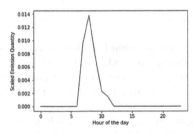
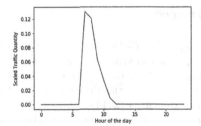

Fig. 8. Emission (left) and Traffic by hour

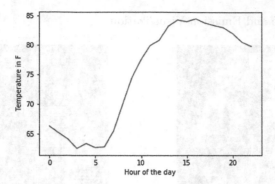

Fig. 9. Temperature of a typical day in August

6 Conclusion and Future Work

In this work, we have examined the energy use of buildings in Chicago loop. To untangle the relation, we propose a novel algorithm for assigning vehicles to buildings. We also study the energy use under the effects of different features such as weather, emission.

For future works, we will examine the higher resolution of data in Chicago. For example, wind and humidity are two more features that have strong impact but are not included in this study due to space limitation. Moreover, integrating the detailed movement of each individual also increases the accuracy of our study.

References

1. Amasyali, K., El-Gohary, N.M.: A review of data-driven building energy consumption prediction studies. Renew. Sustain. Energy Rev. **81**, 1192–1205 (2018)
2. Becerik-Gerber, B., et al.: Civil engineering grand challenges: opportunities for data sensing, information analysis, and knowledge discovery. J. Comput. Civ. Eng. **28**(4), 04014013 (2014)
3. Berres, A., et al.: A mobility-driven approach to modeling building energy. In: 2019 IEEE International Conference on Big Data (Big Data), pp. 3887–3895 IEEE (2019)
4. Castleton, H.F., et al.: Green roofs; building energy savings and the potential for retrofit. Energy Build. **42**(10), 1582–1591 (2010)
5. Cho, E., Myers, S.A., Leskovec, J.: Friendship and mobility: user movement in location-based social networks. In: Proceedings of the 17th ACM SIGKDD International Conference on Knowledge Discovery and Data Mining, pp. 1082–1090 (2011)
6. City of Chicago: Data Terms of Use, 22 July 2020. https://www.chicago.gov/city/en/narr/foia/data_disclaimer.html. Accessed on 23 Jul 2020
7. Crawley, D.B., et al.: Contrasting the capabilities of building energy performance simulation programs. Build. Environ. **43**(4), 661–673 (2008)

8. Doan, T.N., Lim, E.P.: Attractiveness versus competition: towards an unified model for user visitation. In: Proceedings of the 25th ACM International on Conference on Information and Knowledge Management. CIKM 2016, Indianapolis, Indiana, USA, pp. 2149–2154. Association for Computing Machinery (2016)
9. CMAP Data Hub: Land use inventory for northeast Illinois, 2013 - CMAP Data Hub, 23 July 2020. https://datahub.cmap.illinois.gov/dataset/land-use/resource/5716abb3-a432-46b2-ab47-d268de302b94. Accessed on 23 Jul 2020
10. Sadineni, S.B., Madala, S., Boehm, R.F.: Passive building energy savings: a review of building envelope components. Renew. Sustain. Energy Rev. **15**(8), 3617–3631 (2011)
11. Stiglic, M., et al.: Enhancing urban mobility: integrating ride-sharing and public transit. Comput. Oper. Res. **90**, 12–21 (2018)
12. QGIS Development Team et al.: QGIS geographic information system. Open Source Geospatial Foundation Project (2016)
13. Wei, H., et al.: Intellilight: a reinforcement learning approach for intelligent traffic light control. In: Proceedings of the 24th ACM SIGKDD International Conference on Knowledge Discovery & Data Mining, pp. 2496–2505 (2018)

Using Statistical Analysis and Computer Vision to Understand Uncertainty in Subsurface Exploration

Joshua Bae[✉] and Jonathan Sheng

Rice University, Houston, TX 77005, USA
jsb9@rice.edu

Abstract. As part of the 4th annual Smoky Mountains Data Challenge hosted by Oak Ridge National Laboratory, we sought to quantify uncertainty in subsurface exploration of the underground to facilitate decision-making. To provide some context, in the collection of seismic data, sounds waves are transmitted into the ground and their reflections recorded by a receiver. However, due to inconsistencies of the subsurface medium, accurate localization of underground layers is difficult without directly digging down to confirm. To combat this issue, we used several statistical and computer vision to quantify uncertainty of seismic data images by labelling each pixel of a seismic survey (realistic models of subsurface density) to indicate its volatility. After thorough analysis, we could conclude that not one "good" metric exists to accomplish our de- fined goal; uncertainty is defined differently depending on the specific methods one employs. Every uncertainty map that was generated using a unique technique highlighted distinct areas of the seismic surveys. More experimentation and feedback from experts are needed to identify what optimal combination of these (or other) techniques would be best to arrive at the best measurement by which to measure subsurface uncertainty.

1 Background

In the energy industry, it is important to have a solid understanding of subsurface characteristics in order to discover untapped natural resources. Before drilling down to acquire these resources, engineers will conduct a thorough seismic analysis of the area to determine whether it is worth the risk to do so. The process of generating an understanding of the unknown subsurface structures includes the following:

1. Seismic data collection/surveying
2. Seismic data pre-processing
3. Seismic migration & velocity model construction
4. Seismic interpretation

© Springer Nature Switzerland AG 2020
J. Nichols et al. (Eds.): SMC 2020, CCIS 1315, pp. 530–541, 2020.
https://doi.org/10.1007/978-3-030-63393-6_36

Seismic surveys are typically conducted using powerful sound waves being emitted deep into the earth. These sound waves bounce off boundaries between subsurface layers and are recorded at the surface. During this collection of seismic data, one or more sources of sound energy transmit waves while one or more receivers record the reflections of these waves. The locations of these layers can be identified knowing the source location, receiver location, and measurement of how much time has elapsed between the transmission and reception of the signal. Ideally, one can label subsurface boundary layers based on peaks found in the seismic trace (amplitude over time of the signal received). However, noise can often distort the signal, making peaks much more difficult to identify, so signal-processing techniques are employed to denoise the signal as much as possible.

To evaluate every seismic trace, offset pair gathers are used to reduce the uncertainty. Offset pair gathers are produced by many pairs of sources and receivers that record reflections off the same reflector in the given subsurface. This redundancy helps validate the accuracy of a velocity model. These many pairs collect depth estimates for reflectors and plot them so that depth is depicted on the y-axis and offset pairs along the x-axis. Gathers with mostly horizontal lines indicate an accurate velocity model.

In this paper, we analyze subsurface densities and incorporate different methods to quantify and visualize areas of uncertainty. Given how difficult it can be to identify points of uncertainty as there is no certain way to verify our results, we employed a variety of many different statistical and imaging methods to arrive at our most confident conclusion.

2   Related Work

In determining what methods to use for quantifying and visualizing uncertainty, we drew ideas from medical imaging and image comparison measurements. The Kullback-Leibler Divergence approach was inspired by [1], which explains the uses of K-L Divergence in determining uncertainty within medical images.

Another metric we used, Structural Similarity Index [3], is a common image comparison method that compares the similarity between two entities. SSIM uses luminance, contrast, and structure to check image quality, returning a number between −1 to 1 (complete opposite to exact replica, respectively).

As for the use of canny filters [2], academic papers on computer vision provided insight into how we could use edge detection techniques to focus on horizontal striping present in gathers. The use of this popular edge detection technique primarily comes from image processing in the field of artificial intelligence.

3   Contributions

In this paper, we showcase various statistical and computer vision techniques utilized for analyzing subsurface characteristics and the uncertainty around them. We developed a set of metrics that seek to identify exactly where uncertainty is present and then techniques for visually presenting those metrics overlaid on raw data. Specifically, we delve into seismic uncertainty, seeking to further understand subsurface characteristics.

In particular, we evaluated the following methods/metrics for quantifying uncertainty in seismic realizations:

1. Standard Deviation, a common method to determine a metric of uncertainty
2. K-L Divergence, a metric to quantify the statistical distance difference between an actual and observed probability distribution
3. Structural Similarity Index, an image comparison technique to determine the similarities and differences between partitions of the realizations
4. Canny Filtering, an edge detection operator used to detect edges in images based on the intensity of the gradients

All code developed as part of this project is made available open source on Github at https://github.com/agrippa/geo-owl-ogy.

4 Methods

In this section, we expand on the dataset and algorithms used in this work (Fig. 1).

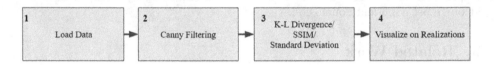

Fig. 1. Workflow schematic of project

4.1 Dataset

There were two datasets available for this project: one small dataset (3 GB) and one large dataset (49 GB). The small dataset is a subset of the files contained in the large dataset. The datasets consist of a set of models of the subsurface density (called density models, realizations, or stacks). For every realization, the plausible density at a given point is generated based on the full seismic survey.

These 2-D realizations were randomly generated and based on a single known ground truth, and can be used to visualize the structures in the subsurface. These realizations are commonly loaded into a 2-D Numpy array (depth (z) dimension of 400 and a horizontal (x) dimension of 1058, with x as your leading dimension and z as your innermost dimension. Figure 2 shows an example of what a stack looks like when visualized in Python.

For each realization, the dataset also includes a file of gathers produced using the same velocity model. A gather is basically an estimate of the density at a given point for a source-receiver pair in the seismic survey. Every single realization is mapped to one of these offset pair gather files, and each file is conveyed in 3-D form as a Numpy array with 39 offset pairs in the survey. The x and z dimensions are the same as the realizations, with an added y-dimension indicating the offset pair. These gathers basically store values measured at the same physical coordinate in the subsurface using different sources and receivers during a seismic survey. Figure 3 shows an example of what several gathers look like when visualized.

All of these files were stored in industry-standard SEGY format, and a Python module was used to load and visualize them.

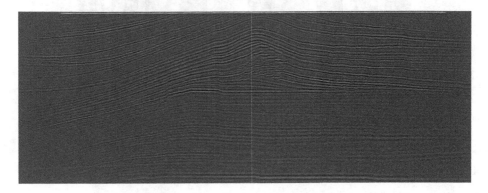

Fig. 2. 2-D realization of subsurface

4.2 Standard Deviation

The goal of our Standard Deviation method was to take the standard deviation across all realizations for each pixel, and use that as a simple uncertainty metric.

First, the standard deviations were calculated through collecting every pixels' values from every realization in the small data set, storing these values in a 1058 × 400 (dimensions of each realization) × number of realizations matrix. The first iteration over the realizations was to collect the means for each pixel; the second iteration was to apply the standard deviation formula.

After the computation, the standard deviations were visualized across every pixel to see where the points of high variation existed on a sample realization. The points of high standard deviation were displayed as varying shades of red on top of a random realization, where the darker shade represented more uncertainty. This method was conducted on the large data set and the canny-filtered realizations (later discussed).

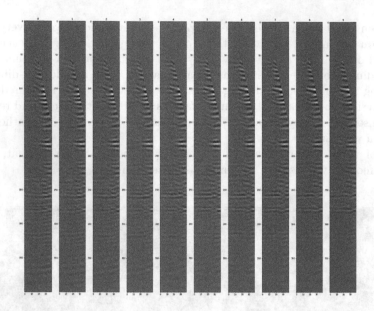

Fig. 3. 3-D gathers based on realization

4.3   Kullback-Leibler Divergence

We also explored the application of K-L Divergence (also called relative entropy) across realizations to highlight areas of general uncertainty by computing the distance between two probabilistic distributions.

For every pixel across all realizations, the set of possible values were first binned into a frequency vector. Then a "true" distribution was computed by finding the most common binned value among the realizations; it was then converted into a probability vector by giving the most common bin a value of 1.0 and all others 0.0. The K-L score for each pixel was then computed by taking the K-L divergence between this "true" distribution and the observed distribution across realizations. We were then able to view an image of the K-L scores superimposed on a sample realization.

To offer some intuition in to this approach, what we are essentially doing is finding the distance between the observed distribution of values and a "true" distribution of values, where the "true" distribution assumes that the most common value bin is also the correct one. For pixels where the possible values are focused in a single bin, the K-L divergence between our fake "true" distribution and the observed distribution will be small. For pixels where there is a wide range of possible pixel values/bins, the K-L divergence will be high because no one bin will be much more frequent than the others.

$$D_{\text{KL}}(P \parallel Q) = \sum_{x \in \mathcal{X}} P(x) \log\left(\frac{P(x)}{Q(x)}\right)$$

Fig. 4. K-L divergence formula (discrete probability distributions P and Q)

4.4 Structural Similarity

The goal of this method was to calculate the structural similarity of a sliding window across every pair of realizations.

At first, we used a sliding window in which there were no overlap, across all pairs. However, this resulted in blocky visuals, not accurately showing the SSIM values at a fine granularity as large blocks of pixels were being assigned a single value (see Fig. 6). Thus, we tweaked our approach to instead use overlapping windows to gather more fine grain information and more accurately assign pixels an SSIM value (Fig. 4).

When using overlapping windows, we ran into performance issues with a step size of 1. As a result, we decided to reduce the time by a factor of 16 by making the horizontal and vertical step size 4, trading off granularity for speed. With every iteration of the sliding window, we calculated the SSIM value of the window between the two files and added each of those values to its respective pixel. Finally, we took the mean of every pixel's SSIM across all realizations and plotted the result. Due to the nature of overlapping, the corners and edges receive less coverage than elements towards the middle of a realization (Fig. 5).

$$\text{SSIM}(x, y) = \frac{(2\mu_x \mu_y + c_1)(2\sigma_{xy} + c_2)}{(\mu_x^2 + \mu_y^2 + c_1)(\sigma_x^2 + \sigma_y^2 + c_2)}$$

Fig. 5. Formula for structural similarity across windows x and y

4.5 Canny Filtering/Gather Image Quality

The techniques previously described have focused entirely on the stacks/ realizations available in this dataset. However, an entirely separate collection of data is also available to us in the gathers of the dataset. These gathers break down the measured values at each physical coordinate by source-receiver pairs, and so they can offer more fine grain information. From the challenge problem description, we know that "in a gather of an accurate velocity model, geophysicists expect to mostly see horizontal lines, indicating that the depth estimate for a layer is the

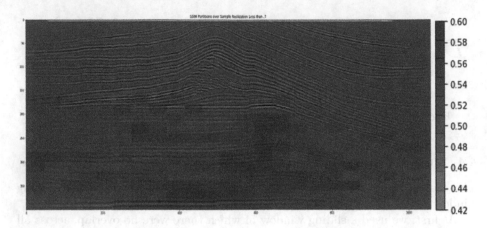

Fig. 6. Areas where mean SSIM values ≤0.6 on a sample realization (deeper red, lower SSIM value). Block-like visuals are evident.

same across all offset pairs" [4]. Therefore, we explored techniques for finding high quality velocity models by finding horizontal lines in gathers. This can enable us to then focus our techniques on only realizations that are most realistic.

The Canny Filtering method proved to be especially useful. After normalizing the gathers' data from the small data set to ensure good illumination, Canny Filter was applied to the images. A Canny Filter is an edge detection operator used to detect edges in images based on the intensity of their gradients.

With the application of the Canny Filter, the Gaussian-smoothed gather images were reduced to just a few white lines edges highlighting the most obvious edges. The smoothing threshold was set for the purpose of noise reduction and to showcase just the most prominent edges. Figure 7 shows an example of what a gather looks like after applying a Canny Filter.

We could then narrow down the number of "good" realizations based on the horizontal consistency of the gathers after applying the Canny Filter. To do this, the 2-norm (Frobenius norm) was calculated between neighboring columns of each gather and summed up. By this metric, a gather containing the greatest number of similar columns of pixels would be given the lowest scores and qualify as a "good" gather.

The Structural Similarity and K-L Divergence techniques mentioned in the previous sections were then re-applied to a tuned dataset consisting of only "good" realizations.

5   Results

5.1   Standard Deviation

Figure 8 shows a sample result from our Standard Deviation method, applied to the large dataset for this challenge problem. In this visualization, overlay

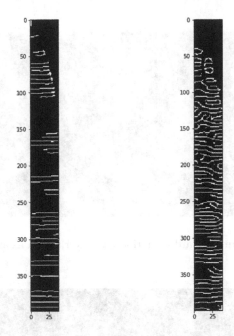

Fig. 7. Example gathers after applying Canny Filters

red on top of pixels whose standard deviation exceeds a certain threshold (2.0). Deeper reds indicate higher standard deviations, lighter/brighter reds indicate lower standard deviations. In general, this method appears to be highlighting areas where the layers in the subsurface are more angled – or very deep portions of the volume.

5.2   K-L Divergence

Figure 9 shows a sample output of our K-L Divergence method applied to the small dataset. It is clear that the uncertainties picked up by this method differ from those highlighted by the standard deviation metric. K-L appears to be picking up on more fine grain uncertainties around the edges of layers in the subsurface as they shift around under different velocity models.

5.3   Structural Similarity

Figure 10 shows a sample output of the Structural Similarity method. In these images the brighter the red, the higher the mean SSIM values while not crossing above a given threshold (0.6). The deeper the red, the lower the mean SSIM value and therefore the more uncertainty. Again, we find this method seems to be highlighting a different area of uncertainty than the previous two methods – particularly focusing on the deeper regions of the volume.

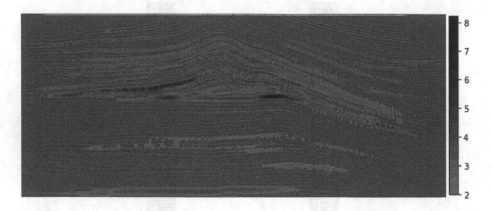

Fig. 8. Areas where standard deviation ≥2.0 overlaid on a sample realization.

Fig. 9. Superimposed image of the good realizations (small data set) after being processed using K-L Divergence

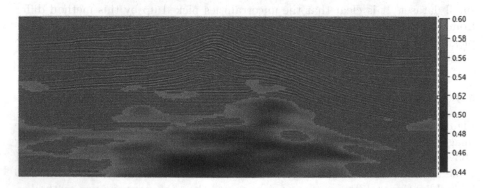

Fig. 10. Areas where mean SSIM values ≤0.6 on a sample realization

5.4   Canny-Filtered Dataset

Finally, we also consider how using a filtered and tuned dataset with the three above methods (Standard Deviation, K-L, SSIM) changes the outputs generated by those respective methods on the challenge's small dataset.

Figure 11 shows the distribution of quality scores across the small data computed using the Canny method applied to gathers files. Based on this distribution, we labeled all realizations/gathers in the small dataset with a score $<= 286,000$ as "good". This reduced the size of our dataset from 59 realizations to 29 realizations. Figures 7 shows an example of a quick spot check to validate that the scores match our intuition about what a "good" and "bad" gather looks like (Fig. 12).

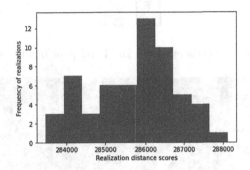

Fig. 11. Histogram visualizing the distributions of realization scores (small dataset) based on gather distances

Figures 13, 14, and 15 show the outputs of our Standard Deviation, K-L Divergence, and SSIM methods applied to the high quality dataset, respectively. We can see that the trimmed dataset has a major impact on the output of the Standard Deviation and SSIM methods, but don't observe much change in the K-L Divergence output.

The Standard Deviation metric is now highlighting less of the image, suggesting that uncertainty has been reduced by focusing on "good" realizations.

The SSIM metric now appears to be mostly highlighting uncertainty in the left side of the volume – the region of highest uncertainty appears to have shifted. At the moment, we do not have an explanation for this change.

6   Discussion and Conclusions

Based on the visualizations delivered by each strategy, each technique seems to be highlighting the image in different ways. Standard deviation indicates broader strokes of uncertainty by coloring in whole regions of the image, while K-L divergence focuses on outlining horizons where the distribution is showing high uncertainty. Meanwhile, the SSIM approach is similar to Standard Deviation in

Fig. 12. Example of two gathers with a good and poor quality score, respectively

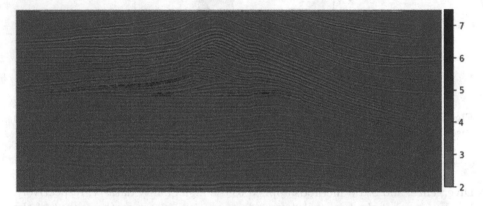

Fig. 13. Areas where standard deviation ≥ 2.0 on a sample realization

Fig. 14. Superimposed image of all realizations (small data set) after being processed using K-L Divergence

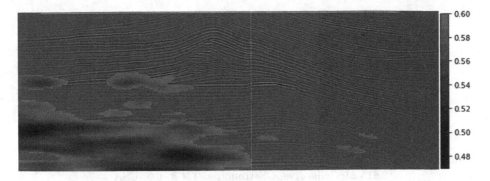

Fig. 15. Areas where mean SSIM values ≤0.6 on a sample realization

that it is highlighting broad strokes of the image but seems to be focusing on a different region.

When focusing on the realizations that were deemed to be "good" by our simple distance metric, we saw that Standard Deviation and SSIM were significantly impacted in their outputs. In general, both seemed to demonstrate lower uncertainties. In the case of Standard Deviation, the same regions are highlighted but to a lesser extent. In the case of SSIM, its focus seems to have shifted entirely.

Given these results, it is difficult to objectively say that a single metric stands out above the rest to serve as basis for correctly quantifying the uncertainty into a certain area. Since the data is sparse on how accurate density models have been in identifying desirable subsurface characteristics, in addition to not having a ground truth, it is difficult to select a clear winner. Instead, it is likely some combination of these techniques (and potentially other unexplored ones) would be the best option as each is able to highlight different types or regions of uncertainty that might be interesting to seismic interpreters.

References

1. Al-Taie, A.A.: Uncertainty estimation and visualization in segmenting uni-and multi-modal medical imaging data. Ulm University, Ulm, Germany (2015)
2. Canny, J.: A computational approach to edge detection. IEEE Trans. Pattern Anal. Mach. Intell. **6**, 679–698 (1986)
3. Wang, Z., et al.: Image quality assessment: from error visibility to structural similarity. IEEE Trans. Image Process. **13**(4), 600–612 (2004)
4. Gray, K., Grossman, M., Yusifov, A.: Using machine learning to understand uncertainty in subsurface exploration. Smokey Mountain Data Challenge Problem Descriptions (2020)

The Heavy Lifting Treatment Helper (HeaLTH) Algorithm: Streamlining the Clinical Trial Selection Process

Misagh Mansouri(✉)🆔, Jeremiah Roland🆔, Sree Nukala🆔, Jin Cho🆔, and Mina Sartipi🆔

Center for Urban Informatics and Progress, University of Tennessee at Chattanooga, 615 McCallie Ave, Chattanooga, TN 37403, USA
misagh-mansouri@utc.edu

Abstract. The Medical diagnosis and screening field has benefited tremendously from the advancement of computer technology and access to data over the past decades. However, due to the complexity of medical diagnosis and medical research, there are still many unknown problems in this field. With the recent emphasis of the national government and academic agencies in open sharing data and advancement of computational tools, e.g. machine learning and artificial intelligence, there is a renewed hope to tackle such complex problems. One of the fields that can benefit greatly from such advancement is the cancer clinical trial matching. This field has gained a lot of attention due to its complexity and the large number of people it affects. The algorithms proposed in this paper aim to assist clinicians and patients in cancer clinical trial matching by reducing the number of eligible trials using a combination of logical conditions and text mining of trial descriptions. Data for this study is provided by the Clinical Trial website which consists of 100 patients' demographic and clinical information. Our preliminary results demonstrate the capabilities of unsupervised learning and conditional logic in reducing the matched trials and suggest further exploration for improvement and optimization of clinical trial matching for clinicians.

Keywords: Clinical trial matching · Agglomerative clustering · Jaccard similarity · Unsupervised learning · Text mining

1 Introduction

One of the astonishing feats of this century is the rapid advancement of medical data and knowledge through clinical studies. With the advancement of computer algorithms and medical devices, we now have access to more data than ever before. This is opening up previously unexplored ways of disease identification and treatment through data science and engineering. Having patient-specific access to data from numerous sensors and data sources allows for intricate and individualized treatment plans to be implemented and advised to patients for

© Springer Nature Switzerland AG 2020
J. Nichols et al. (Eds.): SMC 2020, CCIS 1315, pp. 542–552, 2020.
https://doi.org/10.1007/978-3-030-63393-6_37

illnesses that were once considered incurable. Cancer research in particular is one of the fields that is hoping to take advantage of such novel treatment strategies with a consistent increase in cancer cases. Although the death rate per 100,000 people has decreased since 2010, the total number of deaths from cancer in the U.S. alone has increased from 574,738 in 2010 to 599,099 in 2017 [1], and it is projected to pass 620,000 by 2020 [2]. The number of registered clinical trials has quadrupled from 82,000 studies in 2010 to more than 349,000 in 2020 (reference: clinicaltrials.gov). From these studies, more than 52,000 are currently enrolling patients. However, only one in twenty of cancer patients enroll in clinical trials due to lack of access and complexity of finding the right match for patients [3]. With the expansion of these data sets also comes challenges for clinicians to select the treatment plan that best matches a patient's medical history. Artificial Intelligent (AI) and Machine-learning (ML) algorithms aim to facilitate clinician decision-making by finding similarities in large data sets and combine massive amounts of information from a large pool of patients. The Heavy Lifting Treatment Helper (HeaLTH) Algorithm proposed here aims to assist clinicians in clinical trial matching for cancer patients using the combination of logical brute-force approach and machine learning algorithms such as agglomerative clustering on clinical trial descriptions.

2   Related Works

The process of automatically identifying and clustering trials and eligibility features together based on similarity was performed in [4]. This was accomplished through the construction of a trial-feature matrix comprised of extracted semantic features from the text of the eligibility features for the clinical trials. Through the use of center-based clusters, pairwise similarities were calculated for each clinical trial based on the eligibility features. By using center-based clusters, a single trial was used as the center for each pairwise comparison, allowing for the identification of trials whose similarities to the center trial were no less than 0.9. The team performed their tests on 145,745 clinical trials and extracted a total of 5.5 million semantic features with 459,936 of those features being unique. 8806 center-based clusters were generated, and a sample of those clusters was evaluated using Amazon Mechanical Turk (MTurk) yielding a mean score of 4.331 (on a scale of 1–5).

The team of [5] sought to automate the processes of feature-based indexing, clustering and searching for clinical trials. Their approach was to decompose 80 randomly selected trials for Stage 3 Breast Cancer into a vector of eligibility features organized into a hierarchy. Trials were clustered based on the similarity of their eligibility features. To test their method, the team performed a simulated trial search process by manually selecting features to be used for generating eligibility questions for trial filtering. 1437 distinct eligibility features were extracted, and 80 trials were used. This resulted in 6 clusters which contained trials that took similar patient by patient features, 5 clusters based on disease features, and 2 clusters using mixed features. Additionally, the team demonstrated the utility of named entity recognition by mapping most features to one or more Unified Medical Language System Concepts.

Similarly, researchers [6] have used Natural language programming to increase clinicians' efficiency in selecting the right clinical trials for pediatric cancer patients. The selected narrative notes from 55 clinical trials from the clinicalTrials.gov and combined that with electronic health records from 215 oncology patients. With automation of the eligibility criteria, they were able to reduce the number of clinical trials matched and saved time for oncologists in choosing the right treatment plan.

3   Methodologies

3.1   Data

The data used in this project was provided as part of Oak Ridge National Lab, SMC conference data challenge 2020 which were originally derived from the United State government Clinical Trials website (ClinicalTrials.gov). It consists of 100 cancer patient records (SMC Dataset 2) containing information such as patients' age, gender, therapy history, Performance Status, as well as white blood cell (WBC) count, hemoglobin, platelets, and more (see Table 1 for a complete list of variables used in the study). Additionally, six eligibility criteria documents containing the subsets of the clinical trials (SMC Dataset 1) were provided. Each document lists clinical trials pertaining to particular variables seen in Table 1, with a total of 1005 trials across all datasets. The eligibility criteria documents contain six factors for clinical trial eligibility presented in Fig. 1, SMC Dataset 1. These factors are Hemoglobin count, WBC count, Platelets count, HIV, Performance Status, and Prior Therapy. For example, for the WBC factor, the clinical trials have inclusion and exclusion criteria related to a patient's white blood cell count. Additionally, each eligibility file contains seven columns, which can be seen in Table 2. Of note is the NCIT column in each eligibility file, which contains a logical statement using c-codes. C-codes are numerical codes that represent medical terminology, e.g., C25150 is age, C12767 is the pelvis. These codes represent human body parts, basic human information (age and gender), therapy trials, and more. Figure 1 shows the flowchart of data sources as well as the detailed steps we took to run our conditional logic and clustering analysis.

3.2   Logical Comparison

To assist in, and act as a baseline for, treatment matching, simple logical operations were performed on the c-codes for each trial in the different eligibility files. For example, in the WBC_Trials dataset, the NCIT column contains several logical statements per trial, such as $C51948>=4000$, which translates to white blood cell count greater than or equal to 4000 per milliliter of blood. The logical code takes the logical statements that accompany each trial in the eligibility file, finds the corresponding information that each c-code represents in a patient's

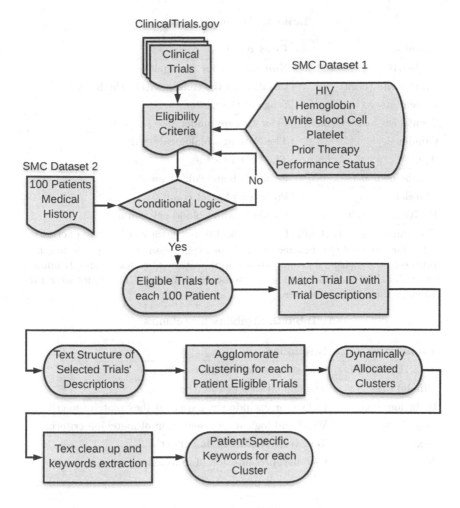

Fig. 1. Data processing framework

record, and calculates the logic. Any trial that returns a True statement is saved as a potential trial for that patient.

The first step necessary for logical comparison was the cleaning of the NCIT column values, as many entries had a mismatched number of parenthesis, missing c-codes, or blatant syntax errors. Once cleaned, each NCIT conditional statement was read in one at a time and broken into separate parts. For example, the statement $C51948>=4000$ was broken into three segments: *Code: C51948, CompOp: >=*, and *Value: 4000*. The code segment for each NCIT conditional was read in and the appropriate patient information was substituted in. So, for the code $C51948$, the patient's white blood cell count was placed in the code's place, and the three segments were combined to create a conditional statement. After the substitution, the statement $C51948>=4000$ becomes $X>=4000$, where X represents the current patient's white blood cell count.

Table 1. Patient information

Variable	Description
PatientID	Numerical value for a patient
Cancer site (bool)	Location of the cancer within the body
Cancer stage (bool)	Stage of the cancer
Treatment history (bool)	Prior therapy undergone by patient
Gender	The Patient's biological gender
Age	The Patient's age
Hemoglobin	Patient's hemoglobin count
Platelet	Patient's platelet count
White blood cell	Patient's white blood cell count
Performance status (bool)	Patient's ability to perform daily living activities

Note: for the variables marked with (bool), this means that variable had a c-code counterpart used for comparison simplification. C-codes are simply numerical codes that correspond to some medical terminology. The codes were provided by the SMC committee.

Table 2. Eligibility file columns

Variable	Description
NCI_ID/NCT_ID	Codes representing different trials
Official title	The official title of the trial
Inclusion indicator	include or exclude the patient if they match the criteria
Description	Word and logical representation of matching criteria
Text	Text version of matching criteria
NCIT	C-code representation of matching criteria

This process of patient data substitution was repeated for each portion of a conditional statement, as many trials had many conditional statements for inclusion or exclusion. The output of the logical statement returned a True or False for the whole trial in regards to whether or not the patient met the criteria for inclusion or exclusion.

3.3 Clustering

Preprocessing. The output of the logical comparison step is merged with the eligibility criteria dataset (e.g., hemoglobin trials, HIV trials, performance status trials, platelets trials, prior therapy trials, WBC trials). From the available columns of the merged dataset, the description, NCTid, and patientID columns are extracted and used for cluster assignment. The primary variable used for the creation of clusters is the "Description" column in the eligibility criteria datasets, while the other variables act as identification factors for the patient(s) and the clinical trials. Natural Language Processing (NLP) techniques were applied to the dataset to pre-process and clean up the text, extract keywords, apply term frequency-inverse document frequency (TFIDF) to get the frequency of those keywords. All the rows with NAN values were also removed from the dataset.

Jaccard Similarity. After the pre-processing step, the Jaccard similarity index is calculated to determine the similarities between the two sets of words. Jaccard only takes a unique set of words in each sentence, and the repetition of words does not reduce the similarity index. This is why it is preferred over other similarity measures such as cosine similarity, which takes the length of words of vectors [7]. We have applied lemmatization to reduce the words to the same root words and selected pairwise distance to compute the Jaccard similarity index. If the sets are similar, the similarity index will be equal to 1, otherwise, it will be equal to 0. Equation 1 shows how this similarity index is calculated.

$$J(A, B) = \frac{A \cap B}{A \cup B} \tag{1}$$

Agglomerative Clustering. Agglomerative clustering is a type of hierarchical clustering technique is that well-established in unsupervised machine learning [8]. In agglomerative clustering settings, the dataset is partitioned into singleton nodes and merged one by one with the current pair of mutually closest nodes into a new node until it is left with one last node, which makes up the whole dataset. This clustering method is different from other clustering methods in a way that it measures the inter-cluster dissimilarity and updates that after each step [8,9]. The clustering is applied to the trials which make it past the logical comparison filter. Once clustering is applied, there are N number of clusters that contain X number of possible trials. The number of clusters was selected dynamically depending on the size of trials for each patient. To find the optimal k number of clusters, we have computed the following equation:

$$k = floor(log_2(length(eligible\_trials))) \tag{2}$$

4   Results

The result of the logical comparison step is returned as a list of eligible clinical trials for each patient. The sample trials are presented in Table 3. Upon completion of the logical comparison step, the resulting list seen in Table 3 has clustering applied on a patient by patient case. Upon the completion of the logical comparison step, the average eligible trials across the 100 patients provided through the data challenge were 283 ± 69 from the total 1005 available trials across the six eligibility criteria files. The reduced number of trials for the first 10 patients in our dataset is presented in Fig. 2.

After cleaning these resulting trials for each patient by removing any empty descriptions of clinical trials and using the Eq. 2, we automatically selected the

Table 3. Sample trial match returns

NCI_ID	NCT_ID	Patient_ID
NCI-2009-00336	NCT00392327	1
NCI-2011-00878	NCT00956007	1
...	...	...
NCI-2016-00071	NCT03077451	100
NCI-2016-00787	NCT03030417	100

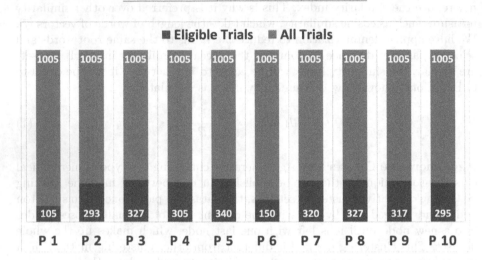

Fig. 2. Number of eligible trials outputted from the conditional logic algorithm for the first 10 patients (P1 to P10) reduced from the all available 1005 trials across all eligibility files

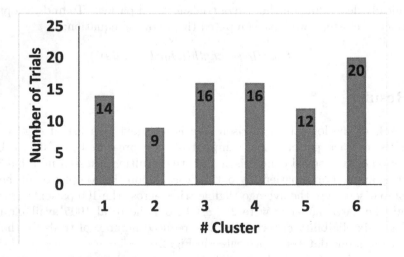

Fig. 3. Number of clinical trials in each 6 clusters of Patient 1

number of clusters for each of the 100 patients. This reduced the number of trials for Patient 1 to 83 trials and 6 clusters. Figure 3 shows the number of clusters for Patient 1, dynamically allocated using Eq. 2, along with how many trials each cluster contains. Once we have clusters for each patient, we took the top five most repeated words in each cluster. Figure 4 shows the most common words found in each of the corresponding clusters.

Figure 5, left, shows the overall clusters scatter plot for Patient 1 which is the result of agglomerative clustering. Principal Component Analysis (PCA) was used for visualization purposes to illustrate the distribution of each cluster in the first two principal components. Although we are only showing a 2D scatter plot here, there is a distinct separation between the clusters that are shown in Fig. 5 separated by different colors. Figure 5, right, shows the number of times the presented keywords repeated in the selected cluster after taking the three most common keywords in all clusters, e.g. "HIV", "Hemoglobin", and "Platelets" out of the accepted keywords in our algorithm.

5   Discussion

With the expansion of the number of available clinical trials available for clinicians and other health providers, it is almost impossible to choose the right treatment without spending hours to narrow down the choices. Machine learning techniques have begun to be used for optimizing this process. In our approach, there is a noticeable improvement when comparing the number of clinical trials that doctors have to go through before and after applying our algorithm. The results from the logical comparison presented here significantly narrows down the choices to about third on average for our pool of 100 patients. This was done by simply going through all the eligibility criteria and combine that with individual patient info to select the trials that the patient does not qualify for. This brute force approach alone yields valuable information and can increase efficiency by up to 300%. Alongside this method, the agglomerative clustering, which is a type of an unsupervised learning technique in machine learning, can further facilitate the clinical trial matching process by grouping the similar text derived from the trial descriptions.

The most frequently used words per cluster are provided to further inform doctors about each cluster so they can visually see the differences as well as use this type of categorization to make their decision and quickly gain insight into the types of trials being returned for the patient. As shown in Fig. 4, each cluster has common words embedded in them. Looking at the most frequently used words in trials for patient 1, all the words from the trials that are separated in each cluster are strongly related to HIV. For example, cluster 1 contains 54 occurrences of the word "HIV". Also, it has 13 occurrences of the word "cd4" which is also related to HIV. While all the clusters share some common words, there are other unique words that are not found in some clusters. The three keywords of HIV, Hemoglobin, and Platelets were commonly repeated across all the six clusters presented in Fig. 4 for the patient 1. That is mainly due

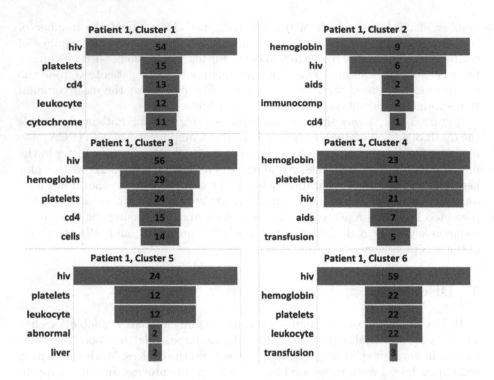

Fig. 4. Most frequent keywords in all six clusters of Patient 1

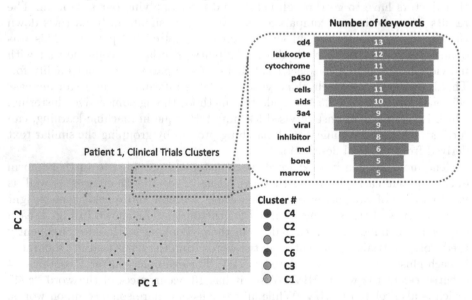

Fig. 5. Left: Scatter plot of all 6 clusters for Patient 1, cluster 1 is highlighted in the red-dashed box. Right: The number of times the most common keywords are repeated in cluster 1 after removing HIV, Hemoglobin, and Platelets from the keywords

to the fact that these keywords are parts of the eligibility criteria included in our analysis. Taking those keywords out can help with creating more distinct keywords among clusters, Fig. 5, right. There is also clearly a need for clinicians to review more than the top 5 keywords presented in Fig. 4. As also illustrated in Fig. 5, right, even the least frequent keywords, such as bone, marrow, and 3a4 can be very meaningful features of each cluster. In addition, by increasing the number of patients and the clinical trials, unsupervised learning is able to provide a better categorization of similarities in larger data sets which is required for future precision medicine applications. Ultimately, the HeaLTH algorithm provides a quick and easy approach to patient trial filtration and identification for clinicians and patients alike.

6   Conclusion

Utilizing a combination of brute-force logical comparison and machine learning clustering and classifying, our team has created an algorithm that significantly reduces the available trials for a patient-based on personal data matching, and uses hierarchical clustering to further simplify trial selection and examination. Doctors can use this algorithm to better identify the types of trials a particular patient is more likely to be assigned to, as well as filter out any trials that may or may not yield worthwhile results.

6.1   Limitations

The primary limitation of this project was the lack of additional patient data for testing. Furthermore, this algorithm is built around the way that the clinical trials were presented and may prove difficult to implement in a separate environment where clinical trials are presented in a different manner, e.g., if new clinical trials do not have specific inclusion/exclusion criteria presented in a conditional format.

6.2   Future Work

Future implementations of this project would be to further streamline the trial selection process for users. This can be accomplished by implementing a user interface with the algorithm that takes in the patient data and directly returns the clustered trials in an easy to read format. Additionally, the clustered patient trials can be directly compared to hand-picked trials for patients selected by clinicians to assist in further refinement and validation of trial selection for patients.

References

1. U.S. cancer statistics working group: U.S. Cancer statistics data visualizations tool, based on 2019 submission data (1999–2017): U.S. department of health and human services, centers for disease control and prevention and national cancer institute
2. Weir, H.K., et al.: The past, present, and future of cancer incidence in the United States: 1975 through 2020. Cancer **121**(11), 1827–1837 (2015)
3. Unger, J.M., et al.: The role of clinical trial participation in cancer research: barriers, evidence, and strategies. Am. Soc. Clin. Oncol. Educ. Book **36**, 185–198 (2016)
4. Hao, T., et al.: Clustering clinical trials with similar eligibility criteria features. J. Biomed. Inform. **52**, 112–120 (2014)
5. Boland, M.R., et al.: Feasibility of feature-based indexing, clustering, and search of clinical trials. Methods Inf. Med. **52**(05), 382–394 (2013)
6. Ni, Y., et al.: Increasing the efficiency of trial-patient matching: automated clinical trial eligibility pre-screening for pediatric oncology patients. BMC Med. Inform. Decis. Mak. **15**(1), 28 (2015). https://doi.org/10.1186/s12911-015-0149-3
7. Niwattanakul, S., et al.: Using of Jaccard coefficient for keywords similarity. In: Proceedings of the International Multiconference of Engineers and Computer Scientists, vol. 1. no. 6 (2013)
8. Müllner, D.: Modern hierarchical, agglomerative clustering algorithms. arXiv preprint arXiv:1109.2378 (2011)
9. Beeferman, D., Berger, A.: Agglomerative clustering of a search engine query log. In: Proceedings of the sixth ACM SIGKDD International Conference on Knowledge Discovery and Data Mining (2000)

Correction to: Performance Improvements on SNS and HFIR Instrument Data Reduction Workflows Using Mantid

William F. Godoy, Peter F. Peterson, Steven E. Hahn, John Hetrick, Mathieu Doucet, and Jay J. Billings

Correction to:
Chapter "Performance Improvements on SNS and HFIR Instrument Data Reduction Workflows Using Mantid" in: J. Nichols et al. (Eds.): *Driving Scientific and Engineering Discoveries Through the Convergence of HPC, Big Data and AI,* CCIS 1315, https://doi.org/10.1007/978-3-030-63393-6_12

In the originally published version of the chapter 12, the reference 21 contained a mistake in the name of the author. The author's name in the reference was changed to S. Hahn.

The updated version of this chapter can be found at
https://doi.org/10.1007/978-3-030-63393-6_12

Author Index

Printed in the United States
by Baker & Taylor Publisher Services